Gonzalo Fernández de Oviedo (Lucena),

the unknown son of the Ambassador Juan Ramírez de Lucena and

Author of La Celestina

Govert Westerveld
Volume I
2019

II

Gonzalo Fernández de Oviedo (Lucena),

the unknown son of the Ambassador Juan Ramírez de Lucena and

Author of La Celestina

Govert Westerveld
Volume I
2019

Gonzalo Fernández de Oviedo (Lucena), the unknown son of the Embassador Juan Ramírez de Lucena and author of La Celestina
© **Govert Westerveld**
Academia de Estudios Humanísticos de Blanca (Murcia) Spain

ISBN: 978-0-244-27298-2
Lulu Editors
© 2019 – 2020 Govert Westerveld
30540 Blanca (Murcia) Spain

IV

DEDICATION

To the great Celestina researcher
Ottavio di Camillo

I hope that this disturbing and intrustive book
gives him new ingenious ideas, such as the letter
«El autor a un su amigo» of La Celestina" which
we have seen in the past.

Preface

One thing should be clear to the readers: I was sure from the beginning that Lucena was the author of La Celestina. The challenge was to know the real name behind the pseudonym Lucena. In 2004 I thought that it was Juan del Encina. This was the result of intuition and much reading. Consequently when I stated that Juan del Encina was the writer of books such as La Celestina, Amadís, Carajicomedia, Sergan, etc., the reader should always bear in mind that at the first stage I reverted to Lucena and at the second stage to Juan del Encina.

I wrote this book in English, seeing the sarcastic comments I received in Salamanca and to which I will revert in this book, hoping that people in other countries will have a more open mind to innovation and new ideas. On the other hand, through English texts historians in my native country will also be aware of the importance of the Spanish literature around 1500, because till now they've stuck too much to French history.

With this book I intend to demonstrate to people in the university circles that researchers without many historical studies and without knowing much of history can play a very important role in the future, provided that they invest the necessary time in the investigation. About thirty years ago an important world historian of the game of draughts tried to stop me in my investigations, because according to him I was profane in the matter. Not having any degree in philology or history and not knowing anything about etymology made him decide not to take my research seriously, because I was "not qualified". It seems that without a university degree in philology and history one is automatically discarded as a researcher. A fact that I stubbornly oppose, because I have come to the conclusion that many great university historians also have big errors in their research. These errors can be due to lack of depth, time, budget, and other causes, hence being profane is no longer a definitely exclusive reason nor has any value if the profane investigator has enough time to investigate. The declaration or saying of the French professor Marc Bloch, so driven by the great medieval Murcian historian Professor Juan Torres Fontes, makes more and more sense:

Historians must be judged not by what they know, but by what they investigate.

Through trial and error it became clear about my first hypothesis in 2006 that I could not defend the position of Juan del Encina and that the pseudonym of Lucena was another author. Other ideas were the personas of Francesch Vicent and Dr. Luis de Lucena. I was still not happy with the findings on them in the research, hence decided to change my way of researching. I no longer believed in using solely the JGAAP program and looked for additional methods. I found them in using other software programs, CORDE, and the word studies of Rolf Eberenz. Thereafter the sun appeared through the clouds again and the results showed a continuous presence of Gonzalo Fernández de Oviedo in different books. However, I always bore in mind Josep Lluís Canet Vallés' hints to study more books and fit de periods of the different authors with those of La Celestina. The word studies of CORDE showed me more books and opened the way to thoroughly analyse them as Cannet Vallés suggested, and so I found additional books written by the Hellenist Fernández de Oviedo. Cannet Vallés' other suggestion to fit the periods was not a problem, since Fernández de Oviedo fully covered the failing parts of Lucena in 1497 and with those of his Italian movement around La Celestina.

José Antonio Garzón Roger, one of Spain's best chess researchers who helped me so much years ago, was of the opinion that the texts figuring in the draughts book of Timoneda published in 1635 in France could not have been Timoneda's. His studies in 2004 clearly gave an earlier period around 1518. Taking his study into account I made a word study of this draughts book and found the idiolect of Gonzalo Fernández de Oviedo again. The same happened with the chess book of 1497 written by Lucena.

Ottavio Di Camilo already informed us in 2001 that the letter in La Celestina contained rare words. An analysis of this text and of the foreword to La Celestina gave us not only the name of Juan del Encina, but also that of Gonzalo Fernández de Oviedo as the author. Now I am finishing the second volume in order to expose more information about other authors. At present I feel that the whole work of La Celestina was written by Fernández de Oviedo, but more research is needed.

Consequently, with this study I hope to have cleared up: 1. that the authentic name of Lucena is Gonzalo Fernández de Oviedo, one of the illegitimate sons of Juan Ramírez de Lucena, 2. that Fernández de Oviedo wrote Repetición de amores and Arte de Ajedrez, 3. that Fernández de Oviedo is the author of the foreword and the first act of La Celestina and was involved in other acts and the letter too, 4. that Fernández de Oviedo is the author of the ancient text of the draughts book Marro de Punta published by Juan de Timoneda in 1547, 5. that Fernández de Oviedo constantly used pseudonyms for most of his published books, most of which I try to reflect in the second volume.

My initial feeling that both Lozana Andaluza and Propalladia were written by Lucena was correct, because I find the linguistic style and words of Gonzalo Fernández de Oviedo. I could add to these findings the work of Thebayda. On the other hand it became clear to me that there was a lifelong friendship between Fernando de Rojas and Gonzalo Fernández de Oviedo.

I was puzzled by more than one book. I feel that the translation of the work El cortesano of Baltasar de Castiglione must have been done by Fernández de Oviedo. Many findings went in this direction, but there is the problem of the biography of Juan Boscan. I have found similar situations with the books of Juan and Alfonso de Valdés. The names of these persons were real and there are testaments of these two persons. Then we also have the difficult situation of Cristóbal de Villalon, but here I found that his books was connected to Gonzalo Fernández de Oviedo.

I wonder if Gonzalo Fernández de Oviedo really died in Santo Domingo, since I suspected that he could have died in Italy, but did not have enough time to investigate this.

Our Hellenist, unknown to many scholars, does not appear on Wikipedia's list of 18 Spanish Hellenists in the XVI century. It is clear that up to now historians and researchers believed what other scholars and historians had said about him and further research was therefore not necessary. Whatever might have been the reason for the silence in the literature about him, one thing is clear: our unknown Hellenist was an expert in languages, because he knew Valencian, Spanish, French, Italian, Portuguese, Greek, Latin, and probably also the language of his father, Hebrew.

He liked to speak in his literature about the university of Salamanca and Antonio de Nebrija, and maybe this was due to the fact that he started working as a translator and editor, while he kept a close contact with Antonio de Nebrija who worked on the Latin dictionary.

He was in charge of translating *Historia de duobus amantibus* (1444) by Eneas Silvio Piccolomini (Pope Pius II) in order to publish the *Estoria muy verdadera de dos amantes, Euríalo franco y Lucrecia senesa* in Salamanca in 1495. He could do so since his father was in the service of this Pope between 1560 and 1564 in Rome. His father's protector in those years was the cardinal Próspero Colonna (1426-1463), who opened the door to our Hellenist during his future book activities (*Tragicomedia, 1506*) with Gentile Montefeltro, her sister Agnesina Montefeltro (*Itinerario, 1508*), married to Fabricio Colonna (and Agnesina's daughter Vitoria Colonna (*La Propalladia, 1517*) who was married to the Marqies of Pescara, Fernando de Ávalos.

Our Hellenist was not just any character, because he was a descendent of an important family of which the members had royal occupations as courtiers. Thanks to his contacts with Nebrija he considers himself an expert in the Spanish language. This is reflected in his books when he (under pseudonyms) fiercely discusses printers who made mistakes and changed his text.

Already in his young years he had gained experience in France and Italy and probably due to the inquisitions he used pseudonyms, in all his books and manuscripts. At the beginning of the XVI century he decided to leave Spain and find his future in Italy. Thanks to his knowledge and the influence of his family it was not difficult for him to alternate with the characters at a high level. He could therefore establish early contact with Pietro Bembo, Federico Fregoso and Baldassarre Castiglione. His influence as Spanish courtier was so strong that various members of the humanistic circles of the court of Guidobaldo de Montefeltro started writing books. These humanistic circles would be a good springboard for our Hellenist in Italy, because he had contacts with Baltasar Castiglione, son of Luigia Gonzaga, César Gonzaga, Octavino Fregoso, and Pietro Bembo, brother-in-law of Cesar Gonzaga; also Julio de Medici and Federico Fregoso, son of Gentile Feltría.

Our Hellenist could have been for a short period the chess master of Lucrecia Borgia in Ferrara, because he also dedicated verses to her which were found in a version of one of his editions of Arnalte y Lucenda. There he had friendship with Jacopo Caviceo who wrote *Il Peregrino* in 1508 which was dedicated to Lucrecia Borgia. The influence of the work of Calisto and Melibea is noted throughout the work *Il Peregrino* and there is no doubt that Caviceo had contact with our Hellenist in Ferrara. It is logical to understand that the historians could never determine the biography of Hernán Díaz, the so-called translator of the Spanish work in 1516, known as *Libro de los honestos amores de Peregrino y Ginebra*, because it was a pseudonym of our Hellenist Fernández de Oviedo. Also in Ferrara our Hellenist could dispose of one of the many copies of Filippo Beroaldo's Latin work about *Asno de oro* and could have translated this work.

In those years our Hellenist was at the court of Vittoria Colonna, who was married to Fernando Francesco d'Ávalos, the 5th marquis of Pescara. Due to the fact that our Hellenist was rather active as writer and editor of many books he had very close contact with most Italian writers in Rome. He did not forget Spain and so we see his presence from time to time in Valencia and other places to publish his books under pseudonyms. Returning to Italy in later years he must have been in contact with the Viterbo group or other thinkers in Rome.

After having worked under the name Francisco Delicado in Rome and Venice for some time he was in France again and returned to Medina de Campo in Spain to arrange editing many books with helpers. Hence we see names such as Pedro de Mercado, Pedro de Castro, and Feliciano de Silva.

I have written 121 books including this one, but I must say that this one has been the most complicated one in my life, because for knowing the truth behind La Celestina one has to research in depth. This is of course something that I like doing because in my short carrier as professional draughts player I had to foresee many moves and was forced to think sometimes 40 minutes ahead before making a move. The same happened with this book. It took thousands of hours of thinking, because I always tried to put myself in the author's shoes.

Anyway, I hope you do not expect much from me, because I started in a company with new products and it went bankrupt after two years. On the other hand I had at least 90% failures in finding new products and applications. Only about 10% gave me success. I therefore consider myself a failure and never a winner. But I just love research and never give up.

Practically no one in Spain reads my books about La Celestina, because most of them know much more history than I do. Therefore I write this book in English, hoping that young students in other countries will study my disturbing and intrusive ideas with a more open mind.

Then they will fulfill my dream of being useful to the Historical Society.

Govert Westerveld

TABLE OF CONTENTS

XXII

1 The detractors

Researching is a very attractive job for me, because it means that I can put my intelligence in the face of constant challenges that involve asking questions about the world we live in. In the 40 years of international business I had to do a lot of research regarding innovation and new applications for existing products, and I wanted to continue on this path. I wanted to prove to myself again that a businessman can also be a good literary researcher. I loved the challenge of measuring my strength with the university researchers of *La Celestina* who couldn't find the name of the unknown author.

If we observe the newspapers and magazines, we will see that the current scientific activity in Spain happens in an environment unfavourable to the freedom and creativity necessary for quality science. Today Spanish universities do not seem to know what should be done to get out of the marasmus of scientific and intellectual mediocrity into which they have fallen. I have found many books in them that the students have not even read and of which the pages I had to open with a knife. On the other hand I was constantly missing books, since the University of Murcia did not have the books that I needed. I quickly came to the conclusion that I no longer needed the University of Murcia and it was better to investigate at home. Fortunately today we find many books from the fifteenth and sixteenth century on the Internet, so one can research with very little money.

Researching in Spain is currently difficult. The reasons are very diverse. People did not make my life easy and I do not want to waste time mentioning all the obstacles, but there were many. Then I had the impression that the research mentality is limited to a closed circuit. Thinking freely is not easy and there are always the evil ones who try to stop others, not realizing that intuition is a very powerful and necessary weapon in research. And if a digital newspaper has the courage to report something very different from the usual methods, there is no lack of detractors trying to crush your thousands of hours of work. In this sense

I thank the digital newspaper Salamanca24horas which dared to write about my findings about 11 years ago. My book now in your hands proves that my intuition did not misguide me about Lucena. Hereafter follows the texts of this newspaper in Spanish so that future generations can see what happened in this period to me.

http://www.salamanca24horas.com

Un historiador plantea que Fernando de Rojas no fue el verdadero autor de 'La Celestina'

Govert Westerveld, miembro de la Academia Alfonso X El Sabio, apunta a Juan del Enzina y Juan Ramírez de Lucena 28/07/2009

GOVERT WESTERVELD

Tras más de dos décadas de investigación sobre la historia de España durante el reinado de los Reyes Católicos, el historiador Govert Westerveld, holandés campeón de damas, cronista y miembro de la Academia Alfonso X El Sabio, plantea que Fernando de Rojas no fue el autor de 'La Celestina', pues la pista de los versos era un señuelo para despistar.

Asegura este investigador en el periódico 'La Opinión de Murcia' que Juan del Enzina y su protector, el protonotario y embajador de los Reyes Católicos, Juan Ramírez de Lucena, estaban implicados en esta obra. "El hombre que siempre usó muchos acrósticos en su 'Cancionero' de 1496 era el poeta Juan del Enzina, el cual se había comprometido con los duques de Alba a no escribir más teatro. Él y Fernando de Rojas deseaban entrar en el servicio del Príncipe, pero no quisieron usar sus nombres verdaderos y por eso 'El Arte de Ajedrez' (1497), dedicado al Príncipe, vino firmado con el nombre de Lucena", explica.

Continúa su tesis argumentando que el hombre que les protegió era Juan Ramírez de Lucena, a quien ellos llamaban 'padre'. "Otro hecho significativo es que el acróstico de 'La Celestina', tal como me indicó el historiador Garzón, es más bien un señuelo, pues en los versos finales de Proaza se descifra el acróstico, por lo que el mismo pierde su razón de ser. En suma, tomaron todas las medidas posibles para que el nombre de De Rojas llegara al lector, y desde luego que lo lograron", añade.

Govert Westerveld concluye que "lógicamente Juan del Enzina comenzó con los temas litúrgicos en Salamanca, igual como su rival Lucas Fernández, pero como Enzina era un constante innovador, también se dedicaba a escribir sobre el amor y su deidad, cambiando años más tarde su estilo y despistando a todo el mundo con el seudónimo de Bartolomé Torres Naharro y Francisco Delicado".

Comentarios: 5 comentarios

¿Cómo pueden hacerse eco como primera noticia de una chorrada de este calibre? Ni los argumentos, ni el sujeto tienen la mínima autoridad. Un poco de seriedad con las cosas de casa...
Autor: Rojas
Fecha: 28 de julio de 2009 - 09:12h
.

Sí, raro es... lo normal es que la primera noticia sea algo más importante y trascendetal tipo "Makulula perdió un taco en el entrenamiento", "tragedia: los jugadores de la unión no pudieron ducharse al no funcionar el calentador... la afición se manifiesta para pedir la dimisión del presidente" Éste es sólo un inutil, que como no sabía jugar al fútbol, estudio arquitectura, finanzas, historia... habla 4 idiomas, es un referente

en el mundo del ajedrez y durante muchos años ha sido el responsable de I+D, comercio internacional... en empresas de medio mundo. Menudo sujeto... seguro que no sabe que Stelea fue portero de la Unión
Autor: Rafita
Fecha: 28 de julio de 2009 - 10:56h

.

Y qué tiene que ver la Unión en todo esto? En cuanto a la noticia, a mi me gustaría saber qué piensa el gran profesor y estudioso de la Celestina Emilio de Miguel de todo esto.
Autor: PePe
Fecha: 28 de julio de 2009 - 12:18h

.

¿Qué pienso? Que Salamanca 24 horas es un gran periódico, inesperado en este páramo periodístico, el cual, eso sí, tiene que llenar sus páginas incluso en verano. Cuando la información que provoca esto termina recogiendo la teoría de ese ilustre desconocido, según la cual, Enzina terminó años más tarde cambiando su estilo y despistando a todo el mundo con el seudónimo de Bartolomé Torres Naharro y Francisco Delicado... Cuando leo eso, pienso que a ciertos extranjeros en ciertos congresos se les debería prohibir el acceso a la sangría. Saludos
Autor: Emilio de Miguel
Fecha: 28 de julio de 2009 - 13:31h

.

A mí me parece genial que el periódico te haga reír de vez en cuando. De hecho, habría que potenciarlo. Entre la noticia y los comentarios me lo he pasado a carcajada limpia.
Autor: Charrilandia
Fecha: 16 de agosto de 2009 - 04:11h

I have never understood this hostility to my new ideas. If we want to maximize our potential in business and move forward in history, it is important to have an open and flexible mind. I know from experience in business that it is necessary to make mistakes, because it brings much benefit and opens the way to become an expert on the matter.

2 JGAAP Program

JGAAP is quite an interesting program, but it is still not perfect. On the other hand we do not consider ourselves experts in using this program. Although our way of working has its doubts, some conclusions can be made with JGAAP used for identification of authorship. However, this program has its limitations and so we have to be careful in accepting what the program points at. It is necessary to find additional proofs to be sure of the findings of JGAAP.

2.1 JGAAP and Authorship Attribution

Authorship Attribution is a long-standing problem in text analysis, and indeed in the humanities in general. Law enforcement and forensic scientists are interested in these methods; Chaski reports on a court case where a body was discovered near a computer with an apparent suicide note typed into it. In case of a hand-written note, of course, handwriting specialists could be called in to verify that the note was in the handwriting of the deceased, but one flat-ASCII 'A' looks identical to any other. What was needed instead was an analysis based on writing style, and Chaski was able to prove that the deceased did not write the note, and a murder had been committed[1].

The JGAAP authorship identification tool can help us compare texts by writers known to us from the 15th-16th century with the texts that we possess by unknown authors. We have to rely on the well-tested assumption that people have a distinct way of writing. The characteristics manifest themselves in how writers use words, spell

---

[1] **JUOLA, Patrick** (2009) JGAAP: A System for Comparative Evaluation of Authorship Attribution. In: *JDHCS*, Volume 1, Number 1, pp. 1-5

certain words, structure sentences, and through many other individualities.

2.1.1 How to use JGAAP

Using JGAAP we formed a database of at least 50 authors known to us from the 15th-16th century. We used a text of about 5,000 words by each writer. With respect to the authors unknown to us we tried to use the text of an unknown author of a minimum of 500 words. However this is not always possible. We must also understand that the 5,000 words by an author could not always be 100% by the author. Authors in those times had the habit of copying texts of other writers and it will be clear to the lector that in such case the pattern is not 100% pure.

According to the user guide of JGAAP 5.1. one has to work in the following way:

Canonicizers:	Normalize Whitespace - Normalize ASCII
Event Drivers:	Character NGrams N: 4
	(others[2] use NGrams N: 2)
Event Cullers:	Most Common Events N: 50
Analysis method:	Nearest Neighbor Driver
	with metric Cosine Distance

2.1.2 The results with Arnalte y Lucenda

To test the efficiency of the JGAAP program we did a test of 473, 781, 1839, and 2687 words and another one of 3,470 words of the book *Arnalte y Lucenda*. Thanks to the test we can see the behaviour and results of the author Diego de San Pedro in the various tables. We can also find out whether *Arnalte y Lucenda* would indeed have the same linguistic characteristics as *Cárcel de amor*[3]. We applied the Character

---

[2] **GUPTA, Ravi & BROOKS, Hugh** (2013) *Using Social Media for Global Security.* John Wiley & Sons, Inc., Indianapolis, Indiana, p. 154.

[3] I have always suspected that both works had to do with the life of the protonotary Juan Ramírez de Lucena and that his son Lucena was involved in this, but this is not easy to prove. I consider Diego de San Pedro to be a pseudonym, not the real name of the author.

NGrams n:1, n:2, n:3, n:4, and n:5 in our five analyses and gave 5 points to number 1, 4 points to number 2, 3 points to number 3, 2 points to number 4, and 1 point to number 5. The results were the following:

Which authors of the text of 473 words are similar to the author of the book *Arnalte y Lucenda*?

Names	N:1	N:2	N:3	N:4	N:5	Total
Lucena	5	4	5	5	4	23
Juan de Flores	4	5	1		3	13
Juan del Encina		1		4	5	10
Hernán Díaz	1		3	3		7
Diego de San Pedro	3	2				5
Alonso de Proaza			4			4
Luis de Lucena			2			3
Alonso Núñez de Reinoso		3				3
Juan de Timoneda	2					2
Fernando de Rojas				2		2
Francisco Delicado					2	2
Hernando del Castillo				1		1
Carajicomedia Francisco Delicado					1	1

As we can see in the table of the various test methods with the Character NGrams n:1, n:2, n:3, n:4, and n:5, Diego de San Pedro comes in the fifth place, because the texts of 473 words have more linguistic characteristics of Lucena who occupies the first place. Therefore we did another test with 781 words.

Which authors of the text of 781 words are similar to the author of the book *Arnalte y Lucenda*?

Names	N:1	N:2	N:3	N:4	N:5	Total
Juan de Timoneda	4	5	4	3	3	19
Hernán Díaz		4	5	5	4	18
Lucena		2	3	4	5	14
Diego de San Pedro	5	3	1	2	1	12
Feliciano de Silva	2			1	2	5
Luis de Lucena		1	2			3
Diego Hurtado de Mendoza	3					3
Fco López de Villalobos	1					1

In this table we see that Diego de San Pedro now occupies the fourth place and the first place is occupied by Juan de Timoneda. More words are necessary to find out the real position of the book *Arnalte y Lucenda*.

Therefore we did a test with 1,839 words, which corresponds to about 11kb. We still do not see Diego de San Pedro in the first place in de table therafter. Lucena occupies it again and we observe Hernán Diaz in the second place. This gives us enough reasons to suspect that Lucena and Hernán Diaz are pseudonyms for an author who does not want to state his real name.

Which authors of the text of 1839 words (11kb) are similar to the author of *Arnalte y Lucenda*?

Names	N:1	N:2	N:3	N:4	N:5	Total
Lucena	3	3	4	4	5	19
Hernán Díaz		5	5	5	3	18
Diego de San Pedro	5	4	3			12
Feliciano de Silva		1	2	3	4	10
Juan de Timoneda	4	2		2		8
Diego Hurtado de Mendoza	2		1		1	4
Francisco López de Villalobos	1				2	3
Carajicomedia Fr. Delicado				1		1

Since we were still not satisfied with the obtained results we tested 2,687 words, which corresponds to 16kb.

Which authors of the text of 2687 words (16kb) are similar to the author of *Arnalte y Lucenda*?

Names	N:1	N:2	N:3	N:4	N:5	Total
Diego de San Pedro	5	5	4	3	5	22
Hernán Díaz		4	5	5	3	17
Lucena	4	3	3	1		11
Juan de Timoneda	3	2	1	2		8
Feliciano de Silva			2		4	6
Francisco Delicado	1			4		5
Francisco López de Villalobos	2				1	3
Alonso Núñez de Reinoso		1			2	3

Finally we see Diego de San Pedro in the first place and Hernán Díaz in the second one. We still do not consider the results satisfactory, because we wanted to see that Diego de San Pedro would appear in the first place in all the tests (n:1-n:5). Therefore we tested 3,470 words, which corresponds to 21kb.

Which authors of the text of 3470 words (21kb) are similar to the author of *Arnalte y Lucenda*?

Names	N:1	N:2	N:3	N:4	N:5	Total
Diego de San Pedro	5	5	5	5	5	25
Lucena	4	3	4	4	3	18
Hernán Díaz		4	3	2	1	10
Juan de Timoneda	3	2	1	1		7
Feliciano de Silva			2	3	2	7
Francisco López de Villalobos	2				4	6
Francisco Delicado	1					1
Alonso Núñez de Reinares		1				1

This time the results are satisfactory and we see that Diego de San Pedro occupies the first place in all the tests (n:1-n:5). Lucena, a pseudonym for an author, was probably also the author of *Arnalte y Lucenda* and *Cárcel de amor*.

This in accordance with Luis Miguel Vicente who saw Diego de San Pedro's work *Cárcel de amor have an influence* on *La Celestina*[4]. The same can be said about the study of José Luis Varela[5] who also observed the influence of *Cárcel de amor* on *La Celestina*. Even Marquez Villanueva[6] saw this influence, but his most important point is that he mentioned the name Juan Ramírez de Lucena.

---

[4] **VICENTE, Luis Miguel** (1988) El lamento de Pleberio: contraste y parecido con dos lamentos en Cárcel de Amor. In: *Celestinesca*, XII, pp. 35-43. Citation on p. 36
[5] **VARELA, José Luis** (1965) Revisión de la novela sentimental. In: *Revista de Filología Española,* 48, pp. 351-382. Citation on p. 367
[6] **MARQUEZ VILLANUEVA, Francisco** (1966) Cárcel de amor, novela política. In: *Revista de occidente*, 1966 – 4, pp. 185 - 200

Returning to our tables, for that reason we always apply 21kb of a work to a test with the JGAAP program if possible. Unfortunately this is not always possible and we sometimes have only short texts at our disposal. It is clear that the name of the author of a work should appear even in short tests. This can be in the text of the book or in the foreword. When the author does not appear in the text of the book with the n:1-n:5 analysis, it means that the author did not write the book, but is using the text of another author or translator. Normally in such case the author appears in the foreword.

An example of that is the work *La Vida y excelentes dichos de los mas Sabios Filosofos que uvo en este mundo* (1520) whose author is Hernán Díaz. We know that the work *Libro de los honestos amores de Peregrino y Ginebra* was written by Hernánd Díaz[7], but was he really the author of *La Vida y excelentes dichos de los mas Sabios Filosofos que uvo en este mundo?*

We only had 747 words at our disposal and as we have seen in the case of *Arnalte y Lucena* and its author Diego de San Pedro in the fifth place, something similar ought to occur now in this text. Thus in the short text of 747 words the name of Hernán Diaz has to appear as author, because the quantity of 747 words was sufficient for that purpose.

However, this is not the case and we cannot find any trace of Hernán Díaz in this work. The text of the book was not by Hernán Díaz, but he took it from somebody else. Was it Francisco López de Villalobos or Juan del Encina? The situation is different in the foreword of *La Vida y excelentes dichos de los mas Sabios Filosofos que uvo en este mundo.*

---

[7] **WESTERVELD, Govert** (2018). Draughts and La Celestina's creator Francesch Vicent (Lucena), author of: Peregrino y Ginebra, signed by Hernando Diaz. 412 pages. Lulu Editors. ISBN: 978-0-244-05324-6

Is Hernán Diaz the author of the 747 words of _La Vida y excelentes dichos de los mas Sabios Filosofos que uvo en este mundo?_

Names	N:1	N:2	N:3	N:4	N:5	Total
Francisco López de Villalobos	5	5	5		3	21
Juan del Encina	4	3	4	5	1	17
Alfonso de Valdes		4	2	1	5	12
Lucena	1	2		4	2	9
Diego Hurtado de Mendoza			1	3	4	8
Luis de Lucena			3	2		5
Alonso de Cardona	3					3
Juan de Flores	2					2
Alonso de Proaza		1				1

Is Hernán Diaz the author of the foreword of 473 words of _La Vida y excelentes dichos de los mas Sabios Filosofos que uvo en este mundo?_

Names	N:1	N:2	N:3	N:4	N:5	Total
Alonso de Proaza	3	4	5	3		15
Hernán Díaz	5		2	4		11
Feliciano de Silva				5	5	10
Juan de Flores		5	4			9
Lucena		2		1	4	7
Juan del Encina	4			2		6
Luis de Lucena			3		2	5
Francisco López de Villalobos	1	3				4
Francisco Delicado					3	3
Diego Hurtado de Mendoza	2					2
Alfonso de Valdes		1			1	2
Alonso Núñez de Reinoso			1			1

As we can observe from this short text, Hernán Díaz could perfectly have been the author of the foreword since he comes in the second place. Fortunately we have the full text of 1,164 words of the foreword at our disposal and the results are:

Is Hernán Diaz the author of the foreword of 1164 words of _La Vida y excelentes dichos de los mas Sabios Filosofos que uvo en este mundo?_

Names	N:1	N:2	N:3	N:4	N:5	Total
Alonso de Proaza	3	3	5	4		15
Hernán Díaz	5		4	5		14
Lucena	2	2		3	5	12
Juan del Encina	4		3	2		9
Juan de Flores	1	5	1			7
Feliciano de Silva				1	4	5
Francisco López de Villalobos		4			1	5
Luis de Lucena			2		2	4
Alfonso de Valdes		1			3	4

In this table we see that the positions of Hernán Díaz and Lucena become stronger. It is clear that Hernán Díaz (Lucena) was involved in the book.

Since we suspected that Diego de San Pedro is a pseudonym for Lucena and can say the same about some works of Cristóbal de Villalón which we deem to be another pseudonym of Lucena, we wanted to see the influence of the works of Cristóbal de Villalon on the poem _"las siete angustias de Nuestra Señora"_ from the work _Arnalte y Lucenda_. It appears that in another test, including the books of Cristóbal de Villalón as the possible author, there is indeed a relationship between these two pseudonyms. As we know Villalón wrote several books.

Who could be the author of the poem of 1128 words of _"las siete angustias de Nuestra Señora"_ of the work _Arnalte y Lucenda?_

Names	N:1	N:2	N:3	N:4	N:5	Total
Villalón - Mirrha	5	5	5	1	1	17
Alonso de Cardona	3	4	4	5		16
Villalón - Crotalon	2	2	3	2	5	14
Villalón - Provechoso	4	3	2		3	12
Diego de San Pedro			1	4	4	9
Alonso de Proaza	1	1		3		5
Lucena					2	2

We tested he same test, but now with a text of 3,470 words (21kb) that should give us the purest results:

Which authors of the text of 3470 words (21kb) are similar to the author of *Arnalte y Lucenda*?

Names	N:1	N:2	N:3	N:4	N:5	Total
Diego de San Pedro	5	5	5	5	5	25
Lucena	4	3	4	4	2	17
Hernán Díaz		4	3	1		8
Francisco López de Villalobos	3				4	7
Villalón - Crotalon			1	3	3	7
Juan de Flores	2			2		4
Alonso Núñez de Reinares	1	2				3
Villalón - Mirrha		1	2			3
Villalón - Turquía					1	1

Cristóbal de Villalón appears again, which is an indication that some of his books in fact could have been written by Lucena and that the name Cristóbal de Villalón could be a pseudonym. For that reason I have dedicated a chapter to Cristóbal de Villalón too.

2.2 Conclusion

If we suspect that an anonymous work could have been written by a certain author, then the JGAAP program is suitable for detecting the possible author if we include his suspected name in the study. Normally a test of 500 words, as described in this study, is sufficient to obtain an approximate access to the author.

As seen in this study, if we know the name of the author, then he must appear in the first five places of the ranking of the JGAAP analysis. If the author does not appear in a test of 500 words, then it is doubtful that the work was published by him.

In this study we observe that a text of 3,470 words (21kb) can disclose the author of the text who then comes in the first place, as well as the names of the other possible pseudonyms or candidates that will come in the 2nd to 5th place in the ranking.

I worked with JGAAP N:4 for this book.

3 Lucena's linguistic style

High performance liquid chromatography, or HPLC, is an analytical testing instrument used to separate components from a sample in an effort to identify and quantify the ingredients within a formulation. We always used it in the preparation of our pharmaceutical raw materials to identify all the active ingredients by a computer. For that reason I have a high expectation of the computer programs that analyse the linguistic style of unknown authors.

3.1 Rolf Eberenz

By somewhat studying the language Rolf Eberenz showed us that the examples of *tendr...* and *vendr...* in the literary texts are few[8], but Lucena, son of the protonotary Juan Ramírez de Lucena, is one of the few authors who uses them in *Repetición de amores*.

3.1.1 Words endings in: tendr.. and vendr..

Consequently the way of writing in this way will be an excellent additional tool to find out possible works of Lucena. And by applying this tool we saw a lot of our hypotheses confirmed in previous years.

We see the same thing appear in *El Peregrino:* vendr... (18 times) and tendre... (44 times).

---

[8] **EBERENZ, Rolf** (1998) La reproducción del discurso oral en las actas de la Inquisición (siglos XV y XVI). In: **OESTERREICHER, Wulf; STOLL, Eva; WESH, Andres** (1998) *Competencia escrita, tradiciones discursivas y variedades lingüísticas. Aspectos del español europeo y americano en los siglos XVI y XVII.* Gunter Narr Verlag, Tübinge, pp. 243-268. Citation on p. 254

Occurence of the endings of the words *tendr..* and *vendr..*

Year	Author	Title	tendr..	vendr..
1489	Anonym	*Linda Melosina*	1	
1491	Anonym	*Los siete sabios de Roma*	4	
1492	Diego de San Pedro	*Cárcel de amor*	7	0
1493	Gonzalo García de Santa María	*Evangelios e epistolas*		11
1495	Juan de Flores	*Grisel*	11	2
1496	Garci Rodriguez de Montalvo	*Amadis*	59	42
1496	Lucas Fernández	*Derreniego de amor*	1	
1497	Lucena	*Repetición de amores*	1	?
1500	Fernando de Rojas	*Tragicomedia de Calisto y Melibea*	18	16
1502	Anonym	*Leyes del estilo*	1	
1504	Anonym	*Thebayda*	21	13
1512	Anonym	*Cavallero cifar*	3	
1513	Diego López de Cortegana	*Asno de oro*	4	1
1514	Feliciano de Silva	*Lisuarte de Grecia*	1	3
1514	Jiménez de Urrea, Pedro Manuela	Penitencia de amor	3	
1516	Hernán Díaz	*El Peregrino*	44	18
1517	Anonym	*Arderique*	2	
1517	Bartolomé Torres Naharro	*Himenea*	1	
1521	Anonym	*Seraphina (Thebayda)*	9	1
1524	Bartolomé Torres Naharro	*Calamita*		1
1524?	Fernán Pérez de Oliva	*Amphitrion*	2	
1525?	Fernán Pérez de Oliva	*Historia de la invención de las Yndias*	1	
1526	Juan Díaz	*Lisuarte de Grecia*		3
1526	Fernando de Rojas	*Traso auto Celestina*	2	
1527	Alfonso de Valdés	*Diálogo de las cosas sucedidas en Roma*	7	1
1528	Juan Justiniano Traductor de Luis Vives	*Formación de mujer Tratado sobre la educación de la mujer cristiana*	9	
1529	Anonym Alfonso de Valdés	*Diálogo de Mercurio y Carón* - libro	4	8

16

1529	Anonym (Juan de Valdés)	*Doctrina cristiana libro*	10	3
1529	Fernán Pérez de Oliva	*Anfitrion*	2	
1530	Feliciano de Silva	*Amadís de Grecia*	34	14
1530	Francisco Delicado	*Lozana Andaluza Complete work*	13	32
1530	Francisco Delicado	*Lozana Argumento*		1
1530	Francisco Delicado	*Lozana epílogo*		1
1530	Francisco Delicado	*Lozana dedicatorio*		1
1534	Feliciano de Silva	*Segunda Celestina*	21	8
1535?	Anonym	*Manual de mugeres*	3	
1535?	Juan de Valdés	*Evangelio de San Mateo*	16	9
1536	Gaspar Gómez de Toledo	*Tercera parte de la Tragicomedia de Celestina*	16	4
1537	Alejo de Vanegas	*Agonia del transito de la muerte*	3	3
1537	Ludovico Scrivá	*Tribunal de Venus*	3	
1537	Juan de Valdés	*Alfabeto*	36	
1542	Sancho de Muñón	*Tercera Celestina Lysandro y Roselia*	6	6
1543	Juan de Boscán	*Las obras de Boscán con algunas de Garcilaso de la Vega*	1	
1545?	Diego Hurtado de Mendoza	*Arcadia*	2	
1546	Francisco Cervantes de Salazar	*Introducción para el camino de sabiduría*	2	
1547	Jerónimo Fernández	*Belianis de Grecia*	10	
1547	Sebastián Fernández	*Tragedia Policiana*	10	6
1547	Diego Hurtado de Mendoza	*Caronte*	1	
1548	Lope de Rueda	*Las aceitunas*	6	
1549	Martin Reyna	*El juego de ajedrez*	1	
1550	Pedro Lujan	*Coloquios matrimoniales*	3	
1551	Feliciano de Silva	*Florisel de Niqua-4 Libro XI Amadís*	1	0
1551	Juan de Luna	*Lazarillo segunda parte*		3
1552	Alonso Núñez de Reinoso	*Clareo y Florisea*	10	3
1552	Villalón	*Viaje a Turquía*	1	

17

1552	Francisco López de Gomara	*Historia General de las Indias*	18	
1552	Luis de Lucena	*Testamento*	1	
1552	Diego Núñez Alba	*Diálogos de la vida del soldado*	6	
1554	Alonso de Villega	*Comedia Selvagia*	36	10
1554	Juan Rodríguez Florián	*Florinea*	73	
1554	Alonso de Villega	*Selvagia*	37	
1556	Francisco de Enzinas	*El Testamento nuevo*	3	
1558	Bernardo de Quirós	*Viaje a Turquía*	1	
1560	Francisco Cervantes de Salazar	*Crónica de la nueva España*	15	
1560?	Sebastián de Horozco	*Cancionero*	9	
1579	Juan Huerte de San Juan	*Examen ingenios*	2	
1579	Jerónimo Fernández	*Hector*	17	
1580?	Sebastián de Horozco	*Entremeses*	1	
1780	Juan Gines de Sepulveda	*Historia de los españoles en el Nuevo Mundo y Mejico*	14	

3.1.2 Words endings in: *pondr..*

The example of *pondr* in the literary texts are few in the XV century, but Lucena, the son of the protonotary Juan Ramírez de Lucena, is one of the few authors who uses it in *Repetición de amores*.

Occurence of the endings of the word *pondr...* here *pondré*

Year	Author	Title	Total
1492	Diego de San Pedro	*Cárcel de amor*	1
1495	Piccolomini	*Traducción de Dos Amantes*	1
1496	Juan del Encina	*Églogas*	2
1496	Garci Rodríguez de Montalvo	*Amadía de Gaula*	5
1501	Anónimo	*Tristán de Leonís*	1
1506	Diego Álvarez Chanca	*Tratado nuevo no menos útil que necesario en que se declara de qué manera se ha de curar el mal de c..*	2
1511	Anónimo	*Traducción de Tirante el blanco de Joanot Martorell*	1
1511	Anónimo	*Palmerín de Olvia*	3
1512	Anónimo	*Primaleón*	6
1512	Juan de Ortega	*Composición del arte de la aritmética y geometría*	37
1514	Feliciano de Silva	*Lisuarte de Grecia*	1
1516	Hernán Diaz	*Peregrino*	
1517	Juan de Molina	*Libro del esforzado caballero Arderique*	2
1520?	Juan Agüero de Trasmiera	*Querella de judios*	1
1521	Anónimo	*Thebayda*	2
1525	Anónimo	*Manual de mujeres*	13
1527	Alonso de Chaves	*Quatri partitu en cosmografía práctica, y por otro nombre espejo de navegantes*	1
1528	Anonym	*Prólogo Formación mujer*	1
1528	Francisco Delicado	*La Lozana Andaluza*	1
1528	Juan Justiniano	*Instrucción de la mujer cristiana*	3
1529	Alfonso de Valdés	*Diálogo de Mercurio*	1

1530	Francisco Delicado	*Lozana Andaluza*	6
1534	Feliciano de Silva	*Segunda Celestina*	3
1536	Gaspar Gómez de Toledo	*Tercera parte de la Tragicomedia de Celestina*	10
1537	Juan de Valdés	*Alfabeto*	4
1537	Ludovico de Escriva	*Tribunal de venus*	1
1538	Pedro Ciruelo	*Reprobación de las supersticiones y hechicerías*	1
1540	Pedro Mejía	*Silva de varia lección*	2
1542	Sancho de Muñón	*Tercera Celestina Lysandro y Roselia*	2
1542	Sancho de Muñón	*Prólogo Tercera Celestina*	1
1543	Jorge de Montemayor	*Diálogo espiritual*	3
1547	Sebastián Fernández	*Tragedia Policiana*	1
1547	Jerónimo Fernández	*Belianís de Grecia*	7
1549	Jerónimo de Urrea	*Traducción de "Orlando furioso" de Ludovico Ariosto*	3
1550	Jerónimo de Urrea	*Clarisel de las flores*	1
1550	Martín de Santander	*Comedia Rosabella*	1
1550	Juan de Arce de Otárola	*Coloquios de Palatino y Pinciano*	3
1550	Pedro de Luján	*Coloquios matrimoniales*	1
1550	Anónimo	*Leyenda de Alejandro Magno*	1
1551	Martín Cortés Albacar	*Breve compendio de la esfera y de la arte de navegar*	1
1552	Francisco López de Gomara	*Historia General de las Indias*	3
1552	Pedro Hernández de Villaumbrales	*Peregrinación de la vida del hombre*	7
1552	Alonso Núñez de Reinoso	*Los amores de Clareo y Florisea*	1
1554	Alonso de Villega	*Selvagia*	1
1554	Juan Rodríguez Florián	*Comedia llamada Florinea*	4
1559	Jorge de Montemayor	*Los siete libros de La Diana*	1
1560	Francisco Cervantes Salazar	*Crónicas de Nueva España*	7

Occurence of the endings of the word *saldr...*   aqui saldré

Year	Author	Title	Total
1492	Diego de San Pedro	*Cárcel de amor*	1

Occurence of the endings of the word *saldr...*   aqui *saldría*

Year	Author	Title	Total
1492	Diego de San Pedro	*Cárcel de amor*	1

Occurence of the endings of the word *valdr...*   aqui *valdré*

Year	Author	Title	Total
1492	Diego de San Pedro	*Cárcel de amor*	1

3.1.3 The conjunction: Ya que

Studying the works of Rolf Eberenz we observed another linguistic proof that could say us much more about the way of writing of Lucena. It has to do with the conjunction of *ya que,* a form that was very little used and apparently the first author was Diego de San Pedro. This is of extremely importance, because if this conjunction is little used and Diego de San Pedro was the first author, then with some good luck this form of writing could be found in other books of Lucena. Here we partially mention the text of Eberenz[9]:

> **Ya que**
> This conjunction is from a relatively late date; in the temporal meaning of coincidence or posteriority it is found the first time in Diego de San Pedro. We think that the form *ya pues que,* documented in *El Cid* (v. 2.66r) and cited by Rivarola[10], should be interpreted rather as an expansion of the basic type *pues que,* that was very frequent at that time. The primitive meaning of *ya que* seems to have been precisely the temporary, from which would derive the causal - today the most common - and the concessive, of more sporadic use[11].
>
> "y *ya que* con mucho trabaio llegamos a lo alto della (s. de la sierra), acabó su respuesta" (San Pedro 118)[12].

In our database we have a lot of works that presumably could have been written by Lucena. In the following table we observe these works. Most of them are complete, but we also have books that are not complete which makes it more difficult to obtain a final opinion.

---

[9] **EBERENZ, Rolf** (1982). Las conjunciones temporales del español. Esbozo del sistema actual y de la trayectoria histórica en la norma peninsular. In: *Boletín de la Real Academia Española,* XVII, pp. 289-384. Citation on p. 372

[10] **RIVAROLA, J.L.** (1976). Las conjunciones concesivas en español medieval y clásico. In: *Beihefte der Zeitschrift für Romanische Philologie,* 154 (Tübingen). 76.149

[11] Rivarola 76.150

[12] **SAN PEDRO, Diego de** (1967). *Cárcel de amor.* In: Obras, "Clas. Castellanos" (Madrid, 1967), pp. 113-212.

Occurence of the conjunction *Ya que*

Year	Author	Title	Total
1482	Diego de San Pedro	*Arnalte y Lucenda*	1
1482	Juan Ramírez de Lucena	*Vita Beata*	3
1492	Diego de San Pedro	*Cárcel de amor*	3
1493	Anonym (Juan de Flores?)	*Crónica incompleta de los Reyes Católicos*	4
1494	Boccaccio	*De las mujeres illustres*	1
1495	Piccolomini	*Dos amantes*	1
1495	Juan de Flores	*Grisel*	5
1496	Garci Rodríguez de Montalvo	*Amadis de Gaula*	3
1499	Fernando de Rojas	*La Celestina*	0
1504	Anonym	*Theybayda*	9
1511	Francisco Vazquez	*Palmerín de Inglaterra*	2
1513	Diego López de Cortegana	*Asno de Oro*	5
1513	Anonym	*Trapesonda*	9
1514	Felician de Silva	*Lisuarte de Grecia*	13
1516	Hernando Díaz	*Peregrino y Ginebra*	4
1517	Anonym	*Arderique (Prólogo)*	1
1517 1521	Juan Acuario	*Renaldos de Montalbán – Balbo – 4 ° libro*	4
1517	Bartolomé Torres Naharro	*Propalladia (capítulos diversos)*	1
1517	Bartolomé Torres Naharro	*Propalladia: Diálogo de nacimiento*	1
1517	Bartolomé Torres Naharro	*Propalladia-Jacinta*	2
1519	Anonym	*Carajicomedia*	3
1519	González Fernández de Oviedo	*Claribalte*	5
1520	Cristóbal de Arcos	*Itinerario de Ludovico de Varthema*	3
1521	Anonym	*Thebayda Seraphina*	2
1524	Bartolomé Torres	*Propalladia-Calamita*	1
1524	Jeronimo López	*Clarian de Landanis Tercer primero*	1
1527	Gabriel Velazquez de Castillo	*Clarian de Landanis Libro primero*	1
1530	Feliciano de Silva	*Amadis de Grecia*	2
1530	Francisco Delicado	*Lozana Andalusa*	1

1530	Anonym (Alfonso de Valdés?)	*Diálogo de Roma*	5
1530	Anonym (Cristóbal de Villalón)	*Diálogo de las transformaciones de Pitágoras*	16
1532	Anonym (Alfonso de Valdés?)	*Mercurio y Carón*	5
1532	Feliciano de Silva	*Florisel 1-2*	4
1533	Anonym (Diego Hurtado de Mendoza?)	*Caronte*	3
1534	Feliciano de Silva	*Celestina*	29
1534	Francisco Vazquez	*Palmerín de Oliva (Prólogo)*	1
1535	Anonym (Juan de Valdés?)	*Diálogo de la lengua*	3
1535	Feliciano de Silva	*Florisel 3*	1
1536	Gaspar Gómez de Toledo	*Tercera parte de la Tragicomedia de Celestina*	10
1537	Ludovico Escriva	*Tribunal de Venus*	5
1538	Anonym (Cristóbal de Villalón)	*El Scholástico*	11
1538	Anonym (Cristóbal de Villalón)	*El Crotalón*	10
1540	Diego Hurtado de Mendoza	*Carta a Feliciano de Silva*	2
1540	Juan Sedeño	*Calisto y Melibea*	4
1542	Juan de Segura	*Cartas de amores*	5
1543	Sancho de Muñón	*Lisandro y Roselia*	1
1544	Alejo Venegas	*Agonia del transito de la muerte*	6
1544	Cristóbal de Castillejo (Venice)	*Diálogo de Mujeres*	4
1547	Jeronimo Fernández	*Belianis de Grecia*	2
1547	Sebastián Fernández	*Tragedia Policiana*	7
1548	Juan de Segura	*Queja y aviso contra el amor*	5
1550	Anonym	*Viaje a Turquia*	21
1551	Feliciano de Silva	*Florisel 4*	2
1552	Alonso Núñez de Reinoso	*Clareo y Florisea*	7
1552	Anonym	*Lazarilla*	8
1554	Alonso de Villega	*Comedia Selvagia*	7
1555	Anonym (Diego Hurtado de Mendoza?)	*Lazarilla, segunda parte*	9
1563	Juan de Timoneda	*Alivio de Caminantes*	7
1567	Juan de Timoneda	*Patrañuela*	1

24

In *Cárcel de amor* we observed the combination of *y ya que* early on.

Occurence of the three words *y ya que*

Year	Author	Title	Quantity
1482	Diego de San Pedro	*Arnalte y Lucenda*	1
1495	Juan de Flores	*Grimalte y Gradisa*	1
1496	Garci Rodríguez de Montalvo	*Amadís de Gaula*	1
1512	Anonym	*Primaleón*	3
1524	Gaspar Gómez de Toledo	*Tercera Celestina*	2
1526	Anonym	*Polindo*	1
1526	Anonym	*Chrónica rey Guillermo*	1
1527	Alonso de Chaves	*Quatri partitu cosmografía*	1
1528	Juan Justiniano	*Mujer cristiana*	2
1531	Antonio de Guevara	*Reloj de príncipes*	1
1534	Feliciano de Silva	*Segunda Celestina*	5
1534	Juan Boscán	*El Cortesano*	4
1539	Cristóbal de Villalón	*El Scholástico*	3
1542	Anonym	*Baldo*	1
1545	Anonym	*Sermón Aljubarrota*	1
1547	Jerónimo Fernández	*Belianís de Grecia*	1
1548	Juan de Segura	*Proceso de amor*	2
1550	Juan Arce de Otárola	*Coloquios Palatino*	4
1550	Pedro Luján	*Coloquios matrimoniales*	2
1551	Bernardino de Montaña de Monserrate	*Anothomía*	1
1552	Pedro Hernández de Villaumbrales	*Peregrinación de la vida del hombre*	1
1552	Diego Núñez Alba	*Diálogos vida soldado*	1
1555	Anonym	*Lazarillo Segunda parte*	1
1557	Bernardo Pérez de Chinchón	*La lengua de Erasmo*	3

3.1.4 The word: aqueste

According to Rolf Eberenz[13] the word *aqueste* figures in many works of the 15th century and among them *Repetición de amores* by Lucena. Due to the high quantity of works it is difficult to find out with which works Lucena continues this way of writing. Here I state some works:

Occurrence of the word *Aqueste* in some works

Year	Author	Title	Quantity
1483	Enrique de Villena	*Los doce trabajos de Hercules*	29
1495	Juan de Flores	*Triunfo de amor*	1
1497	Lucena	*Repetición de amores*	4
1511	Francisco Vázquez	*Palmerin de Olivia*	4
1511	Anonym	*Palmerín de olivia - Prólogo*	1
1516	Hernán Díaz	*El Peregrino y Ginebra*	186
1517	Bartolomé Torres Naharro	*Propalladia*	12
1519	González Fernandez de Oviedo	*Claribalte*	28
1527	Alonso Hernández Alemán	*Guarino mezquino*	4
1530	Francisco Delicado	*Lozana Andaluza*	2
1534	Feliciano de Silva	*Segunda Celestina*	1
1535	Anonym	*Diálogo de las transformaciones de Pitágoras*	2
1537	Anonym	*Lazarillo*	4
1539	Cristóbal de Villalón	*El Scholástico*	5
1552	Alonso Núñez de Reinoso	*Clareo y Florisa*	14

---

[13] **EBERENZ, Rolf** (2000). El español en el otoño de la Edad Media. Gredos, p. 250

3.1.5 The conjunction: pues que

Other words that we find in *Repetición de amores* and *La Celestina* are with the conjunction *pues que*.

Occurence of the conjunction *pues que*

Year	Author	Title	Total
1454	Pedro Tafur	*Andanzas y Viajes de Pedro Tafur*	5
1491	Diego de San Pedro	*Arnalte y Lucenda*	11
1496	Nicolás Núñez	*Continuación de Cárcel de Amor*	29
1497	Lucena	*Repetición de amores*	19
1499	Fernando de Rojas	*La Celestina*	9
1513	Anonym (Alfonso de Cardona?)	*Question de amor*	12
1519	González Fernandez de Oviedo	*Claribalte*	15
1530	Francisco de Osuna	*Segunda parte del Abecedario espiritual*	173
1534	Feliciano de Silva	*Segunda Celestina*	10
1535	Anonym (Juan de Valdés)	*Diálogo de la lengua*	10
1537	Ludovico Scrivá	*Tribunal de Venus*	11
1540	Francisco de Osuna	*Quinta parte del Abecedario espiritual*	160
1540	Francisco de Osuna	*Sexta parte del Abecedario espiritual*	116
1544	Feliciano de Silva	*Sueño de amor*	3
1544	Feliciano de Silva	*La muerte de Hector*	15
1552	Gonzalo Fernández de Oviedo	*Batallas y quinquagenas*	138
1557	Gonzalo Fernández de Oviedo	*Historia general y natural de las Indias*	395

3.1.6 The words: qualquiera and cualquiera

Another interesting word is *qualquiera* which according to Rolf Eberenz[14] figures in *Repetición de amores* 12 times.

The strange thing about this word is that it only occurs many times in *Cancionero, Repetición de amores,* and *La Celestina.* Most other authors published in those years all use them considerably less. Here are only some of them:

Occurence of the word *qualquiera*

Year	Author	Title	Total
1355	Boccaccio	*Laberinto de amor*	4
1454	Pedro Tafur	*Andanzas y Viajes de Pedro Tafur*	5
1494	Fray Vicente de Burgos	*Traduccion de Propietatibus Rerum*	19
1496	Juan del Encina	*Cancionero*	13
1496	Nicolás Núñez	*Tratado referente Cárcel de amor*	1
1497	Lucena	*Repetición de amores*	12
1499	Fernando de Rojas	*La Celestina*	10
1500	Anonym	*Cuatro Oraciones*	4
1511	Anonym	*Traducción de Tirante el Blanco*	40
1511	Anonym	*Palmerín de Olivia*	45
1512	Juan de Ortega	*Composición del arte de la aritmética y geometría*	215
1516	Fernando Díaz	*Vida y excelentes dichos (Prólogo)*	3
1526	Gonzalo Fernández de Oviedo	*Sumario de la natural y general historia de las Indias*	14
1535	Anonym (Juan de Valdés?)	*Diálogo de la lengua*	6
1535	Felicano de Silva	*Segunda Celestina*	3
1536	Gaspar Gómez de Toledo	*Tercera parte de la Tragicomedia de Celestina*	6

---

[14] **EBERENZ, Rolf** (2000). El español en el otoño de la Edad Media. Gredos, p. 409

1537	Ludovico Escrivà	*Veneris Tribunal*	1
1539	Anonym	*El Scholástico*	66
1540	Juan de Sedeño	*La Celestina – prosa*	8
1540	Juan de Sedeño	*Tragicomedia en verso*	13
1540	Hugo de Celso	*Repertorio universal*	44
1542	Ruy Díaz de Isla	*Fruto de todos los autos*	32
1546	Anony,	*Traducción del Laberinto de amor de Juan Boccaccio*	9
1547	Sebastián Fernández	*Tragedia Policiana*	1
1547	Jerónimo Fernández	*Belianis de Grecia*	71
1547	Alonso de Fuentes	*Suma de Filosofía natural*	17
1550	Pedro Mejía	*Silva de varia lección*	50
1552	Luis de Lucena	*Clausulas de su testamento*	2
1552	Antonio de Torquemada	*Manual de escribientes*	31
1554	Alonso de Villegas	*Comedia Selvagia*	1
1555	Diego Ortúñez de Calahora	*Espejo príncipes caballeros*	43

Occurence of the word *cualquiera*

Year	Author	Title	Total
1492	Garci Rodríguez de Montalvo	*Amadís de Gaula, libros I y II*	40
1503	Lucena	*Letter to king Ferdinand*	1
1512	Anonym	*Primaleón*	55
1516	Hernán Díaz	*El Peregrino*	78
1517	Bartolomé Torres Naharro	*Propalladia – algunos textos*	4
1517	Bartolomé Torres Naharro	*Propalladia Soldadesca*	1
1517	Bartolomé Torres Naharro	*Propalladia – Himenea*	3
1517	Bartolomé Torres Naharro	*Propalladia – Trofea*	2
1517	Bartolomé Torres Naharro	*Propalladia – Tinelaria*	1
1517	Bartolomé Torres Naharro	*Propalladia – Dialogo de nacimiento*	2
1517	Juan de Molina	*Libro del esforzado caballero Arderique*	19
1521	Anónimo	*Thebayda*	2

1527	Alonso de Chaves	*Quatri partitu en cosmografía práctica*	20
1527	Fray Bartolomé de las Casas	*Histoira de las Indias*	153
1535	Anonym	*Diálogo de las transformaciones de Pitágoras*	11
1542	Sancho de Muñón	*Tercera Celestina*	1
1542	Anonym	*Balbo*	26
1545	Diego Hermosilla	*Diálogo de los pajes*	20
1548	Jorge de Montemayor	*Diálogo espiritual*	18
1549	Jerónimo de Urrea	*Traducción de Orlando furioso*	32
1550	Juan de Arce de Otárola	*Coloquios de Palatino y Pinciano*	24
1550	Pedro de Luján	*Coloquios matrimoniales*	15
1550	Alonso de Santa Cruz	*Crónica del Emperador Carlos V*	123
1552	Fray Bartolomé de las Casas	*Tratado comprobatorio del Imperio Soberano*	49
1552	Fray Bartolomé de las Casas	*Entre los remedios para reformación de las Indias*	25
1555	Felipe de Meneses	*Luz del alma cristiana*	118
1556	Cristóbal de Villalón	*El Crótalon de Cristóforo Gnofoso*	46
1557	Gonzalo Fernández de Oviedo	*Historia general y natural de las Indias*	93

3.1.7 The word: veniendo

Carmen Quijada Van Den Berghe[15] let us know that Lucena still used the word *veniendo* instead of *viniendo*, as Rolf Eberenz[16] observed:

Occurence of the word *veniendo*

Year	Author	Title	Total
1490	Juan Ramirez de Lucena	*Gualardones*	6
1496	Garci Rodríguez de Montalvo	*Amadís de Gaula, libros 1 y 2*	16
1497	Lucena	*Repetición de amores*	2
1511	Anonym	*Traducción de Tirante el Blanco*	20
1511	Anonym	*Palmerín de Olivia*	12
1512	Anonym	*Primaleón*	10
1514	Feliciano de Silva	*Lisuarte de Grecia*	6
1516	Fernando Bernal	*Floriseo*	12
1520	Anonym	*Vida de Ysopo*	5
1528	Francisco Delicado	*Lozana Andaluza*	1
1534	Felicano de Silva	*Segunda Celestina*	2
1542	Sancho de Muñón	*Lisando y Roselia*	1

Other variants are *deziendo, contradeziendo, maldeziendo, feriendo, pediendo,* and *sentiendo*. A parallel phenomenon affects the "o" of the verbs dormir (to sleep) and morir (to die), viz. *dormiendo* instaed of *durmiendo* and *moriendo* instaed of *muriendo*.

---

[15] **QUIJADA VAN DEN BERGHE, Carmen** (2017). La parfacté méthode pour entrendre escrire, et parler la langue espagnole de charpentier (1596). Ediciones Universidad de Salamanca, p. 353

[16] **EBERENZ, Rolf** (2004). Cambios morfosintácticos en la Baja Edad Media. In: R. Cano (coord.): *Historia de la lengua española*. Barcelona: Ariel, pp. 613-641

3.1.8 The Word: vosotros

It is curious to observe that the word *vos* is not used in *La Celestina, Siervo libre de amor* and *Cárcel de amor*[17]. We encounter the use of the word *vosotros* in *Repetición de amores* as well as in *La Celestina*. Lucena liked to use this word more than other authors and this can give us an indication that he could have written the anonymous works. In this sense we refer to the anonymous authors of the manuscript *Diálogo de la lengua* which the experts think that was written by Juan de Valdés.

Occurence of the word *vosotros*

Year	Author	Title	Total
1490	Juan Ramirez de Lucena	*Gualardones*	6
1495	Juan de Flores	*Grisel*	12
1496	Garci Rodríguez de Montalvo	*Amadis de Gaula*	26
1497	Lucena	*Repetición de amores*	6
1499	Hernán Núñez	*Trescientas*	5
1500	Anonym Juan Ramírez de Lucena?	*Cuatro Oraciones*	3
1507	Fernando de Rojas	*La Celestina*	23
1514	Juan Diaz	*Lisuarte de Grecia*	7
1516	Hernando Díaz	*Peregrino*	38
1517	Bartolomé Torres	*Propalladia-Jacinta*	4
1517	Naharro	*Propalladia-Seraphina*	1
1517		*Propalladia-Soldadesca*	1
1524		*Propalladia-Calamita*	2
1519	Fernando de Oviedo	*Claribalte*	13
1521	Anonym Lucena?	*Theybada*	31
1529	Juan de Valdés	*Doctrina Cristiana*	8
1529	Anonym (Alfonso de Valdés?)	*Diálogo de mercurio y caron*	7
1530	Francisco Delicado	*Lozana Andaluza*	12

---

[17] **EBERENZ, Rolf** (2000). El español en el otoño de la Edad Media, p. 98. Cited by **ARIZA VIGUERA, Manuel & Others** (2005). Lengua Castellana y Literatura. Prueba Práctica...Editorial Mad, S.L., p. 36

1534	Feliciano de Silva	*La segunda Celestina*	23
1535	Juan de Valdés	*Diálogo de la lengua*	43
1536	Juan de Sedeño	*Coloquio de amores y buenaventurança*	2
1537	Ludovico Escriva	*Tribunal de venus (prólogo)*	2
1537	Anonym (Cristóbal de Villalón)	*Diálogo de las transformaciones de Pitágoras*	1
1538	Anonym Christóphoro Gnosopho	*Crótalon*	19
1538	Anonym (Cristóbal de Villalón)	*El Scholástico – volumen I*	14
1543	Sancho de Muñón	*La tercera Celestina Lysandro y Roselia*	8
1547	Sebastián Fernández	*Tragedia Policiana*	20
1551	Anonym	*Lazarillo second part*	3
1552	Anonym (Cristóbal de Villalón)	*Viaje de Turquía*	20
1552	Alonso Núñez de Reinoso	*Clareo y Florisea*	8
1554	Alonso de Villegas	*Comedia Selvagia*	17

In a very short text his father Juan Ramírez de Lucena used this word on 6 occasions. Consequently his son Lucena was used to this word.

3.1.9   The words: "y por tanto" or/and "por tanto"

"Por tanto" is a clear discursive used since as early as the fifteenth century, it is the least used in the Middle Ages compared to its current profusion[18]. We observe a general use in many works, but Juan del Encina did not use it. It is therefore characteristic of Lucena. Strangely it is not a word that occurs in Lozana Andaluza. Some books are:

Occurence of the words *y por tanto/ e, por tanto/y, por tanto*

Year	Author	Title	N°
1495	Piccolomini	*Dos amantes*	3
1497	Lucena	*Repetición de amores*	9
1498	Francisco López de Villalobos	*Costumbres humanas*	1
1499	Hernán Núñez	*Glosa a las Treszientas*	1
1499	Fernando de Rojas	*Comedia - Tragicomedia*	2
1511	Anonym	*Traducción Tirant el Blanco*	3
1512	Juan Argüero de Trasmiera	*Flores romanas*	1
1512	Juan de Ortega	*Aritmética y geometria*	68
1513	Alonso de Cardona	*Questión de amor*	3
1513	Hernán Díaz	*Peregrino*	1
1517	Bartolomé Torres Naharro	*Propaladia prólogo*	1
1517	Juan de Molina	*Arderique*	3
1520	Cristóbal de Arcos	*Itinerario de Ludovico de Varthema*	1
1520	Anonym	*Vida de Ysopo*	1
1521	Juan de Mandeville	*Maravillas del mundo 1521, 1524, 1541,1544 Valencia*	5
1527	Alonso de Chaves	*Espejo Navegantes*	3
1529	Juan de Valdés	*Doctrina cristiana*	1
1529	Alonso de Valdés	*Diálogo de Mercurio*	1
1530	Anonym	*Los siete sabios en Rome*	1
1533	Bernardo Pérez de Chinchón	*La lengua de Erasmo*	4
1534	Feliciano de Silva	*Celestina*	15

---

[18] **EBERENZ, Rolf** (2000). El español en el otoño de la Edad Media. Gredos, p. 123

1535	Juan de Valdés	*Diálogo de la lengua*	4
1536	Cristóbal de Villalón	*Tragedia de Mirrha*	1
1536	Gaspar Gómez de Toledo	*Tercera Celestina*	3
1537	Anonym	*Tratado arquitectura dedicado al Príncipe Felipe*	2
1539	Cristóbal de Villalón	*El Scholástico*	3
1540	Juan de Sedeño	*Celestina en prosa*	1
1540?	Cristóbal de Villalón	*El Crotalón*	2
1540	Pedro Mexía	*Silva de varia lección*	7
1541	Cristóbal de Villalón	*Provechoso tratado*	1
1542	Sancho de Muñón	*Tragicomedia de Lisandro y Roselia*	2
1542	Ruy Díaz de Isla	*Tratado mal serpetino*	11
1543	Luis de Alcalá	*Tratado materias préstamos*	1
1545	Anonym	*Sermón de Ajubarrota*	1
1546	Boccaccio, Giovanni Anonym translater	*Laberinto de amor*	1
1546	Anonym	*Astrología judiciaria*	5
1548?	Anonym	*Cosmografía Pedro Apiano*	2
1550	Juan Arce de Otárola	*Coloquios de Palatino*	3
1550	Pedro Luján	*Coloquios matrimoniales*	1
1551	Bernardino de Montaña de Monserrate	*Medicina*	1
1552	Alonso Núñez de Reinoso	*Clareo y Floriseo*	5
1552?	Anonym	*Lazarillo segunda parte*	1
1552	Pedro Hernández de Villaumbrales	*Peregrinación de la vida*	4
1554	Alonso de Villega	*Semblanza del autor de la Selvagia*	11
1554	Juan Rodríguez Florián	*Comedia llamada Florinea*	2
1554	Anonym	*Repertorio de los tiempos, el cual tura desde MDLIV*	2

3.2 Lola Pons Rodríguez

3.2.1 The Word ending in: ísimo

In *Repetición de amores* we find the superlative *ísimo* and this way of writing is rather rare at the end of the 15th century[19]. Apparently Lucena continues using it in his works under different pseudonyms.

Occurence of superlatives: "ísimo, ísimos, ísima and ísima

Year	Author	Title	Total
1496	Garci Rodríguez de Montalvo	*Amadis de Gaula*	1
1497	Lucena	*Repetición de amores*	1
1497	Lucena	*Arte de Ajedrez*	3
1499	Fernando de Rojas	*La Celestina* (Acts 1, 12, 14)	4
1504	Anonym	*Theybayda*	22
1513	Diego López de Cortegana	*Asno de Oro*	2
1517	Bartolomé Torres Naharro	*Propalladia*	6
1519	Anonym	*Carajicomedia*	1
1530	Francisco Delicado	*Lozana Andalusa*	13
1534	Feliciano de Silva	*Celestina*	4
1537	Ludovico Scrivà	*Veneris Tribunal*	57
1543	Sancho de Muñón	*Tragicomedia de Lisandro y Roselia*	11
1544	Alejo Venegas	*Agonia del transito de la muerte*	13
1552	Alonso Núñez de Reinoso	*Clareo y Florisea*	3
1552	Anonym	*Lazarillo*	16

---

[19] **PONS RODRÍGUEZ, Lola** (2012). La doble graduación *muy –ísimo* en la historia del español y su cambio variacional. In: Enrique Pato y Javier Rodríguez Molina (eds). *Estudios de filología y lingüística españolas. Nuevas voces en la disciplina,* Berna: Peter Lang, pp. 93-133

3.3 Ana Vian

3.3.1 The word: fue instead of fui

Since we suspected that some of the works of Cristóbal de Villalón could have a connection with Lucena because of so many coincidences with Italy, we carefully studied the comments of the various scholars who studied his works. One statement of Ana Vian captured our attention. She stated that[20]:

> El Diálogo de las Transformaciones employs, as El Crotalón and like all works of Villalón, the verbal form *fue* for the first person of the undefined verb *ser (fui)*, a rare form already in the prose of the mid sixteenth century despite still existing in the work *Guzmán de Alfarache*.

According to Ana Vian this is a significant feature even if it is not conclusive in itself, especially when in *El Diálogo de las Transformaciones* '*fue*' and *fui* alternate. Consequently it could be another proof in the case of *El Peregrino* and therefore we decided to make a simple proof with the words "yo fue" or "fue yo", hoping that *El Peregrino* would appear. This simple test proved that there was a link between *La Celestina, El Peregrino,* and the pseudonym Bachiller Villalón which is a pen name for Lucena.

3.3.2 The words: yo fue and fue yo

Occurrence of the words *yo fue*

Año	Author	Title	Total
1470	Anonym	*La demanda de Sanco Grial*	4

---

[20] **VIAN, Ana** (1984). El diálogo de las transformaciones y el enigma de su autoría. In: Dicenda. Cuadernos de Filología Hispánica, No. 3, pp. 117-140. Citation on p. 132

1490	Anonym	*Crónica Troyana*	2
1494	Boccaccio	*De las mujeres ilustres en romance*	1
1494	Garci Rodríguez de Montalvo	*Amadís de Gaula, libros I y II*	14
1498	Anonym	*El baladro del sabio Merlín con sus profecías*	3
1498	Anonym	*Historia de Enrique fijo de doña Oliva*	1
1501	Anonym	*Tristán de Leonis*	2
1504	Garci Rodríguez de Montalvo	*Las sergas del virtuoso caballero Esplandián*	5
1507	La Celestina	*Celestina complete work*	3
1511	Anonym	*Palmerín de Olivia*	7
1512	Anonym	*Primaleon*	10
1514	Feliciano de Silva	*Lisuarte de Grecia*	1
1516	Hernando Díaz	*El Peregrino*	1
1535?	Anonym	*Diálogo de las Transformaciones de Pitágoras*	2
1535?	Gonzalo Fernández de Oviedo	*Batallas y quinquagenas*	1
1536	Gaspar Gómez de Toledo	*Tercera Celestina*	4
1542	Anonym	*Baldo*	3
1552	Bartolomé de las Casas	*Brevísima relación de la destrucción de las Indias*	1
1553?	Cristóbal de Villalón	*El Crótalon de Cristóforo Gnofoso*	12

Occurence of the words *fue yo*

Year	Author	Title	Total
1490	Anonym	*Crónica Troyana*	2
1492	Garci Rodríguez de Montalvo	*Amadís de Gaula, libros I y II*	2
1494	Boccaccio	*Ilustres mujeres*	1
1495?	Juan de Flores	*Grimalte y Gradisa*	1
1498	Anonym	*El baladro del sabio Merlín con sus profecías*	1
1498	Anonym	*El baladro del sabio Merlín con sus profecías*	3

1507	La Celestina	*Celestina complete work*	1
1511	Anonym	*Palmerín de Olivia*	3
1512	Anonym	*Primaleón*	2
1512	Anonym	*Crónica popular del Cid*	1
1516	Hernando Díaz	*El Peregrino*	1
1535?	Anonym	*Diálogo de las transformaciones de Pitágoras*	1
1536	Gaspar Gómez de Toledo	*Tercera parte de la tragicomedia de Celestina*	10
1538	Anonym	*Crotalón*	2
1539	Cristóbal de Villalón	*El Scholástico*	1
1547	Jerónimo Fernández	*Belianís de Grecia*	1
1549	Jerónimo de Urrea	*Traducción de "Orlando furioso" de Ludovico Ariosto*	1
1553	Cristóbal de Villalón	*El Crótalon de Cristóforo Gnofoso*	2

3.3.3 The word: fueste

In line with the observation of Ana Vian we also analysed the word *fueste* instead of *fuiste* and again saw quite interesting figures. Surprisingly enough we found only a few works in our database of many authors from the XV and XVI century, in which the word *fueste* was found various times. The many authors from the XV and XVI century that are in CORDE[21] show more information about *fueste*. Although the word *fueste* was not detected in *Arte de Ajedrez con CL Juegos de Partido* and *Repetición de amores*, we know that *El Peregrino* was written by Lucena. (Hernán Díaz was a pseudonym for Lucena).

Occurence of the words *fueste*

Year	Author	Title	Total
1445	Juan de Mena	*Tratado de amor*	1
1470	Anonym	*La demanda del Sancto Grial*	3
1476	Lope García de Salazar	*Istoria de las bienandanzas e fortunas*	15
1480?	Fernández Madrigal, Alfonso de (El Tostado)	*Tratado que hizo el Tostado de cómo al ome es necesario amar*	1
1482	Anonym	*Esopete ystoriado*	1
1485	Fernando Mejía	*Libro intitulado nobiliario vero*	2
1485	Hernando del Pulgar	*Letras*	2
1487	Fray Hernando de Talaveera	*Católica impugnación del herético libelo madito y descomulgado*	1
1489	Anonym	*Historia de la linda Melosina*	1
1490	Anonym	*Crónica Troyana*	3
1492	Antonio de Nebrija	*Vocabulario español-latino*	1
1492	Antonio de Nebrija	*Gramática castellana*	1
1492	Anonym	*Documentos sobre judaizantes*	2

---

[21] **REAL ACADEMIA ESPAÑOLA:** Banco de datos (CORDE) [en línea]. *Corpus diacrónico del español.* <http://www.rae.es> [12.10.2018]

1494	Boccaccio	*De las mujeres ilustres en romance*	1
1495	Anonym	*Traducción de la Cirugía Mayor de Lanfranco*	11
1495?	Anonnym	*Piccolomini dos amantes*	1
1495?	Juan de Flores	*Grimalte y Gradisa*	3
1496	Juan del Encina	*Cancionero*	6
1498	Anonym	*El baladro de sabio Merlín con sus profecias*	1
1498	Martín Martínez de Amplés	*Traducción del Tratado de Roma*	1
1500	Fray Alonso de San Cristóbal	*Libro de Vegecio de la caballería*	1
1500	Martín Pérez	*Libro de las confesiones*	3
1501	Anonym	*Tristán de Leonis*	1
1502	Diego Enríquez del Castillo	*Crónica de Enrique IV*	8
1504	Garci Rodríguez de Montalvo	*Las sergas del virtuoso caballero Esplandían*	1
1507	La Celestina	*Celestina complete work (acts: 1, 6, 7 and 8)*	3
1509	Alonso de Proaza	*Romance [Primera parte de la Silva de varios romances]*	3
1511	Anonym	*Palmerín de Olivia*	2
1511	Anonym	*Romance [Primera parte de la Silva de varios romances]*	1
1512	Hernández Alemán, Alonso	*Guarino mezquino*	1
1512	Anonym	*Primaleón*	7
1512	Anonym	*Crónica popular del Cid*	1
1513	Juan del Encina	*Égloga de Plácida y Vitoriano*	1
1514	Feliciano de Silva	*Lisuarte de Grecia*	1
1516	Hernando Díaz	*El Peregrino*	17
1520	Anonym	*Vida de Ysopo*	3
1524	Bartolomé Torres Naharro	*Propalladia: Aquilana*	1
1527	Gabriel Velazquez de Castillo	*Clarian de Landanis*	1
1528	Francisco de Osuna	*Primera parte del Abecedario*	4
1529	Fray Antonio de Guevara	*Reloj de príncipes*	18
1530	Anonym (Cristóbal de Villalón)	*Diálogo de las transformaciones de Pitágoras*	12
1530	Francisco de Osuna	*Segunda parte del Abecedario espiritual*	1

1536	Bachiller Villalón Medina del Campo	*Tragedia de Mirrha* (Printer: Pedro Touraus)	3
1536	Gaspar Gómez de Toledo	*Tercera parte de la Tragicomedia de Celestina*	4
1538	Anonym (Cristóbal de Villalón)	*Crotalón* (Manuscript)	12
1539	Cristóbal de Villalón	*El Scholástico*	1
1540	Francisco de Osuna	*Quinta parte del Abecedaro espiritual*	2
1542	Sancho Muñón	*Cuarta Celestina – prólogo*	1
1550	Pedro Lujan	*Coloquios matrimoniales*	1
1552	Anonym	*Libro de las oracyones. Ferrara ladino siddur*	46
1553	Anonym	*Biblia de Ferrara*	65
1553	Juan de Dueñas	*Espejo del pecador*	1
1555	Diego Ortúñez de Calahorra	*Espejo de príncipes y caballeros.*	1

3.3.4 The Word: fueme

Another trial with the word *fueme* with our database and CORDE[22] also gives interesting results and the obtained works show possible authorship of Lucena. Although the word was not detected in *Arte de Ajedrez con CL Juegos de Partido* and *Repetición de amores,* we know that *El Peregrino* was written by Lucena. (Hernán Díaz was a pseudonym for Lucena).

Occurence of the words *fueme*

Year	Author	Title	Total
1470	Anonym	*La demanda del Sancto Grial*	2
1495?	Juan de Flores	*Grimalte y Gradisa*	4
1495	Anonym	*Traducción de la cirugía Mayor de Lanfranco*	1
1496	Nicolás Núñez	*Continuación de Cárcel de amor*	2
1496	Juan del Encina	*Cancionero*	3
1496	Garci Rodríguez de Montalvo	*Amadís de Gaula, libros I y II*	2
1498	Francisco López de Villalobos	*Sumario de la medicina con un compendio sobre las pestíferas bubas.*	1
1501	Anonym	*Tristán de Leonís*	1
1512	Anonym	*Primaleón*	1
1513	Diego López de Cortegana	*Asno de oro*	1
1516	Hernando Díaz	*El Peregrino*	6
1517 1542	Juan Acuario	*Renaldos de Montalbán – Balbo – 4 ° libro*	9
1520	Anonym	*Ysopo*	1
1526	Diego de Sagredo	*Medias del romano*	11
1528	Francisco Delicado	*Lozana Andaluza*	1
1534	Feliciano de Silva	*Segunda Celestina*	1

---

[22] **REAL ACADEMIA ESPAÑOLA:** Banco de datos (CORDE) [en línea]. *Corpus diacrónico del español.* <http://www.rae.es> [12.10.2018]

1535	Anonym	*Diálogo de las transformaciones de Pitágoras*	3
1540	Francisco de Osuna	*Quinta parte del Abecedario espiritual*	2
1544	Feliciano de Silva	*La muerte de Hector*	1
1549	Jerónimo de Urrea	*Traducción de "Orlando furioso" de* Ludovico Ariosto	1
1550	Anonym	*Lazarillo*	1
1553	Cristóbal de Villalón	*El Crótalon de Cristóforo Gnofoso*	3

3.3.5 The words: me fue

Even the words 'me fue' can give us more information about the writing style of certain authors. The following authors are highlighted: Fernando de Rojas (605kb – 6), Hernán Díaz (El Peregrino, 865kb – 38), and Cristóbal de Villalón (603kb – 14). Today we now that Lucena was involved in *La Celestina,* and that Hernán Díaz is a pseudonym for Lucena. So here we can probably trace the footsteps of Lucena. Was Cristóbal de Villalón another pseudonym for Lucena? All the other authors used the expression me fue much less in their works.

Occurence of the word *me fue*

Year	Author	Title	Total
1507	Fernando de Rojas	*La Celestina*	06
1516	Hernando Díaz	*El Peregrino*	38
1538	Anonym Cristóbal de Villalón	*Crotalón*	14

3.3.6 The word: fuemos

The trial with the word *fuemos* also gave interesting results and the obtained works show possible authorship of Lucena, although the word was not detected in *Arte de Ajedrez con CL Juegos de Partido* nor *Repetición de amores.*

Occurence of the words *fuemos*

Year	Author	Title	Total
1439	Pedro Tafur	*Andanzas y viajes de Pedro Tafur*	82
1492	Antonio de Nebrija	*Gramática castellana*	3
1492	Anonym	*Siddur Tefillot*	10
1493	Anonym	*Libro llamado Infancia Salvatoris*	1
1495	Giovanni Boccaccio	*Cayda Príncipe*	1
1495	Juan de Flores	*Grimalte y Gradisa*	2
1495	Antonio de Nebrija	*Vocabulario español-latino*	1
1496	Juan del Encina	*Églogas y otros textos*	1
1496	Garci Rodríguez de Montalvo	*Amadís de Gaula, libros I y II*	8
1498	Anonym	*El baladro del sabio Merlín con sus profecías*	1
1499	Anonym	*La historia de los nobles caballeros Oliveros de Castilla y Artús d'Algarbe*	2
1499	Rodrigo Fernández de Santaella	*Vocabulario eclesiástico*	1
1500	Anonym	*Coronación de la señora Gracísla – carta del amigo al autor*	1
1500	Vorágine, Jacobo de – traductor: Pedro de Vega	*Flos Sanctorum con sus ethimologias....*	1
1500	Anonym	*Historia de la reina Sebilla*	1
1500	Anonym	*Un sermonario castellano medieval*	9

1503	Rodrigo Fernández de Santaella	*Traducción del Libro de Marco Polo*	1
1504	Garci Rodríguez de Montalvo	*Las sergas del virtuoso caballero Esplandían*	11
1512	Anonym	*Primaleón*	4
1513	Anonym	*Questión de amor*	2
1514	Feliciano de Silva	*Lisuarte de Grecia*	4
1516	Hernán Díaz	*El Peregrino*	28
1519	Anonym	*Cancionero de obas de burlas provocantes a risa*	1
1520	Anonym	*Vida de Ysopo*	1
1526	Anonym	*Polindo*	1
1528	Francisco de Osuna	*Primera parte del Abecedario espiritual*	2
1531	Fray Antono de Guevara	*Reloj de príncipes*	10
1534	Feliciano de Silva	*Segunda Celestina*	1
1534	Feliciano de Silva	*Segunda Celestina*	1
1535	Anonym	*Diálogo de las transformaciones de Pitágoras*	3
1539	Cristóbal de Villalón	*El Scholástico*	1
1540	Francisco de Osuna	*Quinta parte del Abecedario espiritual*	1
1540	Francisco de Osuna	*Sexta parte del Abecedario espiritual*	1
1540	Micael de Carvajal	*Tragedia Josephina*	1
1542	Anonym	*Baldo renaldo- Trapesonda 4*	16
1544	Feliciano de Silva	*Hector*	1
1547	Portugal, Pedro de (Editado en Salamanca)	*I Libro del infante don Pedro de Portugal, el qual anduvo las cuatro partidas del mundo - obra*	52
1547	Alonso de Fuentes	*Suma de Filosofía natural*	1
1550	Anonym	*Leyenda de Alejandro Magno*	1
1552	Anonym	*Libro de las oracyones. Ferrara ladino siddur*	28
1553	Cristóbal de Villalón	*Crótalon*	30
1553	Antonio de Torquemada	*Coloqios satíricos*	2
1553	Anonym	*Biblia de Ferrara*	17

47

3.3.7 The words: fuenos

The latest table shows data on the word *fuenos* which gives only a few results and the obtained works show the possible authorship of Lucena, although the word was not detected in *Arte de Ajedrez con CL Juegos de Partido* and *Repetición de amores.*

Occurence of the words *fuenos*

Year	Author	Title	Total
1511	Dominguez, Luis? Anónimo?	*Trapesonda3 – Renaldos de Montalban*	1
1511	Anonym	*Palmerín de Olivia*	1
1526	Anonym	*Polindo*	1
1550	Cristóbol de Villalón	Viaje de Turquía	2
1550	Juan Arce de Otárola	*Coloquios de Palatino y Pinciano*	1
1550	Alonso de Santa Cruz	*Crónica del Emperador Carlos V*	1
1552	Diego Núñez Alba	*Diálogos de la vida del soldado*	1
1555	Anonym	*Segunda parte del Lazarillo de Tormes*	1

3.4 María Ángeles García Aranda

3.4.1 Possessive article structure

The structures with an article and possessive article decay at the end of the fifteenth century in the literary language, although specialized treatises or hagiographic writings such as those of Martín de Córdoba, Diego de Valera, Diego de Torres, Luis de Lucena, and Fernando del Pulgar still document some cases of the article before the possessive article[23].

3.4.1.1 The words: la mi

Occurence of the words *la mi*

Year	Author	Title	Total
1444	Alfonso Martínez de Toledo – Aripreste de Talavera	*Sanct Isidoro*	30
1483	Anonym	*Flos Sanctorum*	49
1495	Anonym	*Fabulas de Ysopo*	9
1496	Juan del Encina	*Cancionero*	6
1507	Fernando de Rojas	*La Celestina*	3
1512	Anonym	*Caballero cifar*	11
1516	Hernán Díaz	*Peregrino y Ginebra*	19
1520	Bartolomé Torres Naharro	*Propalladia -Aquilana*	1
1517	Bartolomé Torres Naharro	*Propalladia -Jacinta*	1
1517	Bartolomé Torres Naharro	*Propalladia -Ypolita*	3
1520	Bartolomé Torres Naharro	*Propalladia -Nacimiento*	1
1517	Bartolomé Torres Naharro	*Propalladia -Otros*	2
1519	Anonym	*Carajicomedia*	3
1521	Anonym	*Thebayda – Seraphina*	2

---

[23] **GARCÍA ARANDA, María Ángeles** (2013). Variación gramatical y géneros textuales en el manual de escribientes de Antonio de Torquemada (c. 1552). In: Anuario de Letras. Lingüística y Filología. Vol. 1, Núm. 1, pp. 71-119

1534	Feliciano de Silva	La Celestina	9
1538	Anonym	El Crotalón	9
1540	Juan de Sedeño	La Celestina prosa	18
1542	Sancho Muñón	La Celestina	3
1555	Anonym (Diego Hurtado de Mendoza?)	Lazarillo second part	6

There are many authors who still employ this way of writing in the 16th century. Here we give a list of some of the authors and as we will observe in the case of *la mi*, there is no mention of Lucena.

3.4.1.2 The words: el mi

Occurence of the words *el mi*

Year	Author	Title	Total
1444	Alfonso Martínez de Toledo – Aripreste de Talavera	Sanct Isidoro	9
1483	Anonym	Flos Sanctorum	27
1495	Anonym	Fabulas de Ysopo	2
1496	Juan del Encina	Cancionero	3
1497	Lucena	Repetición de amores	1
1500	Anonym	Historia reina Sebilla	3
1500	Anonym	Conde Partinuplés	3
1500	Martín Pérez	Libro confesiones	11
1501	Anonym	Tristán de Leonis	34
1504	García Rodríguez de Montalvo	Sergas Esplandián	9
1507	Alonso Fernández de Madrigal	Sobre los dioses de los gentiles	1
1511	Anonym	Tirante el Blanco	18
1511	Anonym	Palmerín de Olivia	15
1512	Anonym	Caballero cifar	8
1512	Anonym	Primaleón	59
1512	Anonym	Crónica popular Cid	15
1514	Feliciano de Silva	Lisuarte de Grecia	5
1516	Alonso de Santa Cruz	Crónica Reyes Católicos	1
1516	Hernán Díaz	Peregrino y Ginebra	15
1516	Fernando Bernal	Floriseo	1
1517	Bartolomé Torres Naharro	Propalladia - ypolita	1

1517	Anonym	*Abreviación del Halconero*	12
1517	Bartolomé Torres Naharro	*Soldadesca*	1
1517	Bartolomé Torres Naharro	*Diálogo del Nascimiento*	1
1519	Anonym	*Carajicomedia*	3
1520	Anonym	*Vida de Ysopo*	4
1521	Anonym	*Thebayda - Seraphina*	1
1521	Anonym	*Comedia Ypólito*	1
1528	Fray Antonio de Guevara	*Libro aureo de Marco Aurelio*	1
1530	Anonym	*Los siete sabios de Roma*	2
1534	Feliciano de Silva	*La Celestina*	2
1536	Gaspar Gómez de Toledo	*Tercera Celestina*	1
1536	Juan de Paris	*Égloga nuevamente compuesta*	1
1538	Anonym	*El Crotalón*	8
1539	Antonio de Guevara	*Menosprecios corte*	3
1540	Juan de Sedeño	*La Celestina prosa*	1
1540	Francisco de Osuna	*Abecedaro espiritual*	1
1541	Cristóbal de Villalón	*Provechoso*	1
1542	Sancho Muñón	*La Celestina*	4
1542	Ruy Díaz de Isla	*Tratado serpentino*	2
1543	Antonio de Guevara	*Epístolas familiares*	9
1545	Pedro de Medina	*Arte de navegar*	1
1547	Jerónimo Fernández	*Belianis de Grecia*	1
1549	Jerónimo de Urrea	*Orlando furioso – traducción*	1
1550	Francisco de las Natas	*Comedia Tidea*	1
1550	Juan Pastor	*Tragedia Lucrecia*	1
1552	Pedro Hernández de Villaumbrales	*Peregrinación*	1
1552	Antonio de Torquemada	*Manual de escribientes*	4
1552	Anonym	*Libro oracyones. Ferrara ladino siddur*	13
1553	Anonym	*Biblia de Ferrara*	12
1554	Juan Rodríguez Florián	*Florinea*	4
1554	Anonym	*Crónica del Rey Henrico Octavo*	2
1555	Anonym (Diego Hurtado de Mendoza?)	*Lazarillo segunda parte*	6

3.4.1.3 The words: el otro mi

Occurence of the words *el otro mi*

Year	Author	Title	Total
1496	Grarci Rodríguez de Montalvo	*Amadís de Gaula*	1
1526	Anonym	*Polindo*	1
1528	Francisco Delicado	*Lozana Andaluza*	1

3.4.1.4 The words: los otros mis

Occurence of the words *los otros mis*

Year	Author	Title	Total
1489 1517	Anonym	*Halconero*	1
1490	Anonym	*Crónica Troyana*	1
1507	Fernando de Rojas	*La Celestina*	1
1512	Anonym	*Crónica popular Cid*	1
1516	Hernán Díaz	*Peregrino y Ginebra*	1
1528	Pérez de Oliva, Fernando	*Agamenón*	1
1529	Alfonso de Valdés	*Diálogo de Mercurio*	1
1543	Guevara, Fray Antonio de	*Epístolas familiares*	1
1552	Torquemada, Antonio de	*Manual de escribientes*	4

3.4.1.5 The words: las otras mis

Occurence of the words *las otras mis*

Year	Author	Title	Total
1516	Hernán Díaz	*Peregrino y Ginebra*	1

3.5 Latinism

A Latinism can be considered when 'I' is used first and then another person[24]:

Yo y mi criado (In: *Lozana Andaluza*)

Occurrence of the words *Yo y mi / Yo y mis*

Year	Author	Book	Quantity
1496	Garci Rodriguez de Montalvo	*Amadis de Gaula, libro III*	1
1496	Garci Rodríguez de Montalvo	*Amadis de Gaula, libros I y II*	3
1500	Anonym	*Historia de la reina Sebilla*	1
1502	Diego Enríquez del Castillo	*Crónica de Enrique IV*	1
1503	Letter written by his son Lucena	*Letter of Juan Ramírez de Lucena to the king in 1503*	2
1504	Garci Rodríguez de Montalvo	*Las sergas del virtuoso caballero Esplandián*	2
1509	Anonym	*El Rey Canamor*	1
1511	Anonym	*Tirante el Blanco*	1
1512	Anonym	*Historia de Blanca flor*	1
1512	Anonym	*Primaleón*	1
1516	Fernando Bernal	*Floriseo*	1
1517	Bartolomé Torres Naharro	*Propalladia - Calamita*	1
1517	Bartolomé Torres Naharro	*Propalladia - Himenea*	1
1517	Juan de Molina	*Arderique*	1
1526	Anonym	*Polindo*	1
1530	Francisco Delicado	*Lozana Andaluza*	4
1531	Fernán Pérez de Oliva	*Hécuba triste*	1
1534	Feliciano de Silva	*Segunda Celestina*	1

---

[24] **CALERO, Francisco** (2017). Estudio de autoría de "Los Trabajos de Persiles y Sigismunda", «Philosophía antigua poética» y «Novelas ejemplares», p. 248

1535	Anonym	*Diálogo de las transformaciones de Pitágoras*	1
1542	Dominico de Robertis	*Baldo (IV Renaldos de Montalban)*	2
1545	Lope de Rueda	*Comedia "Los engañados"*	1
1550	Anonym	*Viaje a Turquía*	2
1550	Anonym	*Farsa Alarquina*	1
1550	Anonym	*Leyendo de Alejandro Magno*	2
1550	Alonso de Santa Cruz	*Crónica del Emperador Carlos V*	1
1552	Francisco López de Gomara	*Historia general de las Indias*	4
1552	Anonym	*Libro de las oracyones. Ferrara ladino siddur*	7
1552	Pedro Hernández de Villaumbrales	*Peregrinación de la vida del hombre*	1
1553	Anonym	*Biblia de Ferrara*	9
1554	Juan Rodríguez Florián	*Florinea*	1
1554	Alonso de Villega Selvago	*Comedia Selvagia*	1
1555	Anonym	*Lazarillo Segunda parte*	1
1555	Diego Ortúñez de Calahora	*Espejo de príncipes y caballeros*	4
1559	Jorge de Montemayor	*Los siete libros de la Diana*	1
1560	Francisco Cervantes de Salazar	*Crónica de la Nueva España*	1

4 Words in "Arte de ajedrez"

Several chess terms in Lucena's *Arte de Ajedrez* can reveal us through the CORDE database which authors made a special use of and this can direct us to the real author of the pseudonym Lucena.

Occurence of the words: *Axedrez / Axedres*

Year	Author	Book	Quantity
1481	Anonym	*Crónica de Enrique IV de Castilla 1454-1474*	2
1484	Hernando del Pulgar	*Crónica de los Reyes Católicos*	2
1491	Anonym	*Siete Partidas de Alfonso X*	1
1491	Anonym	*Cuentas de Gonzalo de Baeza, tesorero de Isabel la Católica*	3
1495	Antonio de Nebrija	*Vocabulario español-latino*	4
1498	Anonym	*Corónica del Cid Ruy Diaz*	2
1499	Rodrigo Fernández de Santaella	*Vicabulario eclesiástico*	1
1500	Anonym	*Libro del conde Partinuplés*	1
1501	Anonym	*Tristán de Leonis*	1
1511	Anonym	*Traducción de Tirante el Blanco*	4
1511	Anonym	*Romance (Primera parte de la Silva de varios romanes)*	1
1512	Juan de Ortega	*Composición del arte de la aritmética y geometria*	1
1512	Anonym	*Crónica popular del Cid*	1
1514	Feliciano de Silva	*Lisuarte de Grecia*	2
1514	Pedro Manuel de Urrea	*La penitencia de amor*	1
1516	Fernando Bernal	*Floriseo*	1
1516	Alonso de Santa Cruz	*Crónica de los Reyes Católicos*	2
1521	Fray Antonio de Guevara	*Epístolas familiars*	2
1527	Fray Bartolomé de las Casas	*Historia de las Indias*	1
1528	Fray Antonio de Guevara	*Libro áureo de Marco Aurelio*	1
1529	Fray Antonio de Guevara	*Reloj de príncipes*	2

1530	Francisco de Osuna	*Segunda parte del Abecedario spiritual*	1
1535	Gonzalo Fernández de Oviedo	*Batallas y quinquagenas*	2
1539	Cristóbal de Villalón	*El Scholástico*	5
1540	Hugo de Celso	*Repertorio universal de todas las leyes de estos reinos de Castilla*	2
1547	Gonzalo Fernández de Oviedo	*Libro de la Cámara real del Príncipe don Juan e oficios*	1
1548	Gaspar de Tejada	*Memorial de crianza y banquete virtuoso*	1
1549	Hernán Núñez	*Refranes o proverbios*	1
1551	Bernardino de Montaña de Monserrate	*Anothomía*	2
1551	Anonym	*Romance (Tercera parte de la Silva de varios romanes)*	1
1553	Antonio de Torquemada	*Coloquios satíricos*	1
1553	Cristóbal Méndez	*Libro del ejercicio coporal y de sus provechos,*	7

Occurence of the words: *Primer lance*

Year	Author	Book	Quantity
1528	Francisco Delicado	*La Lozana Andaluza*	1

Occurence of the words: *xaque, xaques, jaque, jaques*

Year	Author	Book	Quantity
1496	Juan del Encina	*Cancionero*	2
1499	Fernando de Rojas	*La Celestina*	2
1508	Francisco de Ávila	*La vida y la muerte o Vergel de discretos*	1
1511	Anonym	*Traducción de Tirante el Blanco*	1
1511	Anonym	*Primera parte de la Silva de varios romanes*	1
1517	Bartolomé Torres Naharro	*Diálogo del Nascimiento*	2
1520	Anonym	*Cancionero de Juan Fernández de Íxar*	1

1525	Francés de Zúñiga	*Crónica burlesca del emperador Carlos V*	4
1535	Anonym	*Auto de Clarindo*	1
1535	Gonzalo Fernández de Oviedo	*Historia General y natural de las Indias*	3
1542	Juan Boscán	*Poesías*	2
1549	Hernán Núñez	*Refranes o proverbios en romance*	1
1550	Fray Alonso de San Cristóbal	*Crónica burlesca del emperador Carlos V*	4
1550	Luis de Pinedo	*Libro de chistes*	1
1550	Juan Arce de Otárola	*Coloquios de Palatino y Pinciano*	1
1550	Alonso de Santa Cruz	*Crónica del Emperador Carlos V*	1
1552	Antonio de Torquemada	*Manual de escribientes*	1
1555	Anonym	*Segunda parte del Lazarillo de Tormes*	2

Occurrence of the words to prince Johan

Nº	Words	Author	Cases	Other authors
1.	Dotrinar	Gonzalo Fernánde de Oviedo	4	10
2.	Esclarecido	Jerónimo Fernández	2	52
3.	Heis	Gonzalo Fernández de Oviedo	7	37
4.	Livianamente	Gonzalo Fernández de Oviedo	2	37
5.	Preclarísimo	Fray Bartolomé de las Casas	1	2
6.	Rosario	Gonzalo Fernández de Oviedo	3	18
7.	Trasponer	Gonzalo Fernández de Oviedo	3	18
8.	Traspuesto	Gonzalo Fernández de Oviedo	4	29
9.	Xaque	Bartolomé Torres Naharro	2	9
10.	De enmedio	Gonzalo Fernández de Oviedo	4	12
11.	De noche con	Gonzalo Fernández de Oviedo	4	40

12.	De otra manera porque	Gonzalo Fernández de Oviedo	5	12
13.	De parte a parte	Gonzalo Fernández de Oviedo	17	46
14.	De qué suerte	Jerónimo Fernández	1	13
15.	Desseoso de server a	Traducción Tirante el Blanco	1	2
16.	Digno de pena	Oliveros de Castilla	1	6
17.	En aquesta manera	Traducción Tirante el Blanco	1	20
18.	Por cuya causa	Gonzalo Fernández de Oviedo	2	39
19.	Por mejor dezir	Feliciando de Silva = Gonzalo Fernández de Oviedo (Celestina)	3	40
20.	Porque cada vez	Lazarillo el Tormes	1	10
21.	Primer lance	Francisco Delicado	1	0
22.	Que de necesidad	Gonzalo Fernández de Oviedo	1	16
23.	Que muchas veces	Gonzalo Fernández de Oviedo	25	48
24.	Que perdido	Gonzalo Fernández de Oviedo	1	33
25.	Sabiendo como	Gonzalo Fernández de Oviedo	1	17
26.	Salvo si por	Gonzalo Fernández de Oviedo	1	13
27.	Señor del campo	Gonzalo Fernández de Oviedo	3	6
28.	Sus cenizas	Gonzalo Fernández de Oviedo	1	9
29.	Tablero de Axedrez	Gonzalo Fernández de Oviedo	1	0

We observe that the writer of *Arte de Axedrez* liked to use strange words. For example, the expression 'señor del campo' was used 3 times by Gonzalo Fernández de Oviedo, while there were only 6 more authors for this expression.

5 The kingdom of Castile

Nobody understands how it was possible that suddenly the influence of the kingdom of Castile was more important than the kingdom of Aragon. However, this was promoted by the same King John II of Aragon and his court. In the early fifteenth century the Castilian dynasty of Trastamara had begun with Ferdinand I of Trastamara in 1412 in the Crown of Aragon through which the Castilian language gradually became the language of the court, the Aragonian nobility, and the upper classes[25].

> Although we do not know the author of the *Triste deleytación,* its origin seems to be Catalan according to the researchers. The preference for the Castilian language - even when some authors cite other geographic origins - seems to attest to the existence of a shared linguistic paradigm, but ultimately it is a consequence of the expansion of Castile and its cultural prestige from the marriage of the Catholic Monarchs. In our view this is not enough to postulate the sentimental fiction as a genre, although it seems to be an attitude that shows that these writers felt immersed in the same cultural environment[26].

The fact that his successors, i.e. all the monarchs of the dynasty, married Castilian nobles strengthened the presence of the Castilian language. The new dynasty by origin would change the political orientation of Aragonian life. For the same formal reason, without diminishing its status, the Kingdom bowed before eastward will now after swinging go back to the west[27]. Thus we see that in 1430 the Truce of Majano (Soria),

---

[25] **COUTADO DOMÉNECH, Esperanza** (2008) La complejidad de las actitudes lingüísticas hacia las lenguas minoritarias. E caso del valle de Benasque. Tesis doctoral, Universidad de Zaragoza, p. 148.

[26] **GARCÍA RODRÍGUEZ, Rocío I.** (2012) La elipsis gramatical en la ficción sentimental. Tesis doctoral dirigida por la Dra. Dña. Inés Carrasco Cantos. Departamento de Filología Española I y Filología Románica. Universidad de Málaga, p. 61

[27] **GONZÁLEZ OLLÉ, Fernando** (2010) Actitudes lingüisticas de los Reyes de Aragón. In: Baxar para subir. Colectánea de estudios en memoria de Tomás Buesa Oliver, pp. 85-110

arranged by the kings of Aragon, Navarra and Castile consist written in Castilian[28].

Castilian was the usual language of Alfonso V (married to the Trastámara Queen Mary) and his Neapolitan court was mostly Castilian[29]. It is clear that the everyday family language among Aragonian Trastámaras was Castilian. The great power of Castile and the decline of the Crown of Aragon explain the markedly Castilian character of modern Spain. Both King Juan II and his son Prince Ferdinand II of Aragon spoke Castilian, since everyday family language among the Aragonian Trastamaras was Castilian[30]. The linguistic behavior of the sovereigns throughout the court circles would extend or increase. After the marriage of Isabella I of Castile to Ferdinand II of Aragon some of the Aragonian courtiers were immersed in the early acceptance of Castilian customs. This is something that we have to bear in mind.

An article in the newspaper *Levante-emv.com* broadly describes the change of the Valencian language to the Castilian one. The date was 1510. A Valencian writer explicitly abjures from Catalan, which he considers *"a barbaric language"*. The traitor is Narcis Vinyoles. However, as a good servant of King Fernando the traitor Narcis Vinyoles had long before accepted in Valencian language the superiority of Castile, which we see reflected, strange enough, on the chessboard with the introduction of the new powerful lady [dama]. Castile's superiority was in the atmosphere in the fifteenth century, even the King John II wanted to see his son Ferdinand I married to the future Queen of Castile.

[28] **GUAL CAMARENA, M.** (1951) Treguas de Majano entre Aragón, Navarra y Castilla. In: CHE, 16, pp. 78-109

[29] **CROCE, B.** (1968) La Spagna nella vita italiana durante la Rinascenza, Bari Laterza, p. 36.

[30] **GONZÁLEZ OLLÉ, Fernando** (2010) Actitudes lingüísticas de los Reyes de Aragón. In: Baxar para subir. Colectánea de estudios en memoria de Tomás Buesa Oliver, pp. 85-110

Narcis Vinyoles

The translation of the abbreviated *Levante-emv.com* newspaper story says[31]:

As argues the Professor of Catalan Philology of the University of Valencia and academician of the AVL Antoni Ferrando[32], "deep inferiority complex takes over the Catalan speakers against an imperial Castilian language, now considered an elegant and refined language par excellence". It is the time of change of language, the linguistic transvestism. The first verses in Castilian created in Valencia arrive in the last third of the fifteenth century timid and snobbish. But it is in 1510 when the turning point of sociolinguistics inversion occurs. And it comes from the hand of the Valencian poet Narcís Vinyoles. Firstly because Vinyoles chose translating the Latin work *Supplementum chronicarum*, a commission of Baron of Toga, Lluís Carròs, and Baron of

---

[31] 500 años de desprecio al valenciano. In: Levante-emv.com, 3 de agosto de 2010 http://www.levante-emv.com/comunitat-valenciana/2010/08/03/500-anos-desprecio-valenciano/728102.html

[32] **FERRANDO FRANCÉS, Antoni** (1985) Presente y futuro de la normalización lingüística en el País Valenciano. In: Revista de Filología Románica, vol. III-1985. Editorial de la Universidad Complutense de Madrid, pp. 35-45

61

Manises Pere Boïl into Castilian, not into Valencian as was the habit. Secondly and more importantly, by the justification Narcis Vinyoles gives in his prologue to the work. "More out of desire to serve and please many than out of presumptuous boldness I dared to lend my fearful hand - he says - to put this work into this clean, elegant, and graceful Castilian Spanish that may without lies and flattery among many barbars and savages from our Spain be called Latin, sonorous, and most elegant.

....

Who was this poet who for many has passed into history as the first traitor to the Valencian country and language? Besides being a poet Narcís Vinyoles was a five-times councilor of the city of Valencia, four times a jurat, and four times an administrator of the Llotja Nova. He was nominated twice for mostassa and twice for the post of civil justice. He reached the post of accountant of the Generalitat and was recommended by   Ferdinand II of Aragon for being elected as Criminal Justice of Valencia. He was loyal to King Ferdinand II of Aragon (Ferdinand the Catholic), collaborator of the court of the Inquisition in Valencia and, as Mary Carmen Romeo says, "faithful server to the royal policy of centralization". Therefore, and as some experts cite, the filocastellano speech of Vinyoles could be a tactic to ingratiate himself with the royal Spanish power. Antoni Ferrando, author of *Narcís Vinyoles i seva obra,* believes that the poet's words are "a great praise to the Castilian language, that's obvious, or even the expression of a complex or profound admiration, but no automatic hatred towards the language that he used after 1510 for writing some poems."

From this text and the texts of *Scachs d'amor* it becomes clear that the traitor Narcis Vinyoles was already a traitor in the early stages by fully accepting the Castilian manners and habits in the court of King Ferdinand II of Aragon, immediately after the marriage of King Ferdinand II of Aragon to Isabella I of Castile.

Once the Kingdom of Aragon merged with the Kingdom of Castile, King Ferdinand and Queen Isabella formally enjoined a single-minded effort to create a new unitary state in which linguistic and other differences would become undesirable.

6 Name and movement of "Dama"

The term "Dama" (French: Dame) was already used in Spain before 1255 and refers to an important woman, the mother of Jesus Christ. While human beings remain within the parameters of service to God and his mother, their salvations – entrance into the Kingdom of heaven – are assured: This is our Sire and that is our Dame (Esti es nuestro Sire e ésta Nuestra Dama)[33].

> Disso el omne bonno a los de la aljama:
> «Esti es nuestro Sire e ésta nuestra Dama;
> Siempre es bien apreso qui a ellos se clama
> Qui en ellos no cree bevrá fuego e flama».

This poem was written by Gonzalo de Berceo (ca. 1197 – before 1264). He was a Castilian poet born in the Riojan village of Berceo, close to the major Benedictine monastery of San Millán de la Cogolla. He is celebrated for his poems on religious subjects written in a style of verse which has been called Mester de Clerecía, shared with more secular productions such as *Libro de Alexandre*, or *Libro de Apolonio*. He is considered the first Castilian poet known by name.

---

[33] **BERCEO, Gonzalo de** (1255) Los milagros de nuestra señora

6.1 The King's Library MS

For the word dame in the sense of chess queen we have to go to France. We should not forget the MS King's, 13, A. XVIII (K), written in Anglo-French, which contains a number of treatises from the 13th and 14th centuries. Murray states:

Notre Dame dedicated to the Virgin Mary, Mother of God

The King's Library MS. is a quarto parchment MS. which contains a number of different treatises in different hands of the 13th and 14th centuries. The chess work follows a short treatise upon the game of tables (ff. 157 b-160a), and is entitled *Ici comencent les iupertiez des eschez*. It occupies ff. 161-73 (old foliation 166-9, 190-8, but there is nothing wanting). Both works are in the same hand, of the last quarter of the 13h century, as a short chronicle of England down to the reign of Henry III (1216-72). The chess work is written in Anglo-French (without trace of any English words), and forms a poem of 1,843 lines divided into an introduction and 55 sections, each numbered with an Arabic numeral.

6.2 Civis Bononiae

Civis Bononiae 249

In this MS there is a game of playing chess with dames that is called Le Guy de Dames[34]:

Le Guy de Dames (Civis Bononiae 249)

Apres les guys de chiualer. De guy de **dames** volie parler. E pur ceo ke ou dames est la medlé. Le guy de **dames** si est nomé. Tiel es de ceo guy le couenaunt. Ke .xvi. fierces auera le vn iuaunt. L'altre soun rey soulement auera. E en quel poynt qe ly plest si saudra. Si noun par force rolle luy seyt. E a dreyn par force mate sereyt. Primes deyt il soun rey asscer. La v il vaudra en le eschecker. E en la manere cum cy veyes. Les fierces si asseyeres. E à checun tret eschec dires. E à dreyn par force li materes. Par vn soul poynt ne remeyndra. V le rey reposa porra. Mes à primes del couenaunt fet soyt. Ke nul fierce pris iseyt (67-86).

White mates the solitary King (who can play to any square) by placing 16 fidated Qs on the board[35].

---

[34] **MURRAY, Harold James Ruthven** (1913) The History of Chess, Oxford, pp. 581-589

[35] **MURRAY, Harold James Ruthven** (1913). The History of Chess, Oxford, p. 674

6.3 Bonus Socios

There is a Latin work (collected in Lombardy in the medieval period) known as **Bonus Socius**. The handwriting dates from the 14th century and has a chess position with five black against four white queens (Bonus Socios 185). This manuscript should have reached early France already in the 14th century, because they know at least 7 handwritings of French origin. It may be concluded from the text that the word **dama** is used to signify an important woman. The same position occurs in the chess manuscript **Civis Bononiae** under number 247.

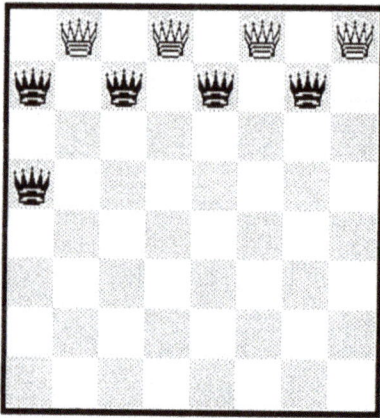

Bonus Socios 185

One of the French translations of the Bonus Socios is the MS. Nat. Lib. Paris, F. fr. 1173 of the 14th century with text in the Picard or Walloon dialect of French that consists of 216 folio leaves[36]. Antonius van der Linde[37] gives a text that figures on folio 3 of the manuscript with the word **dama**, but he erroneously considered the word **daiue** to be dama.

---

[36] **MURRAY, Harold James Ruthven** (1913) The History of Chess, Oxford, pp. 620, 621, 674 and 701

[37] **LINDE, Antonio van der** (1874) Geschichte und Literatur des Schachspiels. Zwei Bände in einem Band. Editions Olms of 1981, Zúrich, p. 286

This was rectified by the great Murray[38]. Nevertheless the same manuscript bears the word **dama**, but in the sense 'important woman':

Folio 2

On dist es prouerbes anciens ke mal est science emploiie en cuer auariscieus du monstrer. Car chascuns ki mix set se doit traueillier a chou ke il puist les autres enseignier. Et pour chou ke ie ne vauroie iestre repris de si vilain pechiet comme dauarise. Jou Nicholes de St. Nicholai clers a laude de chelui ki est fontaine de sapience vous. Vueu enseignier et demonstrer une partie du sentement de mon cuer et especiaument sor li gieu des eskies et premiers coument par cui ne en quel lieu il fu trouues premierement. En apres de la maniere du gieu et des assises et comment il puet iestre abregies par partures. Sachiez kil fu trouues an siege de troie la grant par .i. ch'r sage et hardi et par une **dame** la quele estoit sa chiere amee car li ch'rs et la **dame** se seoient en .i.vergi et dehors les murs de la cite et regardoient comment chil de dehors requeroient chiaus de dedans et comment cil de dedans les recheuoient et se deffendoient uiguereusement et comment il prendoient et desconfisoient li vn les autes et li plus grant les plus petis, et li plus fort les plus febles et comparerent leur gieu selonc lordenement ke il auoient veu es assaus et es batailles. Et apres che ke la cites fu destruite li ch'rs et la **dame** repairierent en lor paiis. Con apiele lombardie. Et fu li gieus espandus par tout le paiis de coi vous faites et veoir le poes aparetment ke lombart sont li plus sage et li plus soutil de cel gieu ki soient. Si ke por le souillece de cel gieu le doiuent desirer a sauoir toute gentil gent et doiuent metre diligaument lor estude et especiaument amant par amors car damour damant et **dame** vint il premierement. Mais pour chou ke li humaine conditions est oscurchie en l'offisse de le celle memoratiue par l'empeechement de nostre premier pere si ke le pert legierement chou ke le ne voit ou pense assidueument. Jou Nicholes deuant dis demourans en lombardie a le priere et a le requeste de mes compaignons ai compilet che liuret de partures ke iai escrito par men estude dou gieu des eschies et des taules et des merelles. Et por chou ke nule choes ne puet iestre parfaite je depri a mes segneurs mes amis et mes compaignons as quels chis presens liures sera parvenus sour imperfection de ceste oeure ke il le uueillent deboinairement rechevoir et corriger saucune chose iest trouuee ki ait mestier de correction.

[38] **MURRAY, Harold James Ruthven** (1913) The History of Chess, Oxford, p. 490

6.4 Sir Ferumbras

Murray erroneously states that the earliest mention of the draughts game (Jeu de dames) dates from the second half of the 14th century (Sir Ferumbras of c. 1380). Here is part of the poem of Sir Ferumbras[39]:

> "þe manere of hem," þan sayde he "is erly gon to cherche,
> & after-ward ech man on his degree after his stat þay werche.
> þo þat lordes buþ of þe lond in som tyme of the ȝere,
> þay takeþ hure facouns faire an hond & fareþ to ryuere;
> & Summe a deer honteþ of hem þar went & some to fox and hare;
> & to ioustes and tornyment wel mo þer wendeþ ofte þare.
> þo þat willieþ to leue at hame pleyeþ to þe eschekkere,
> & summe of hem to iew-de-**dame** & summe to tablere:
> Summe þay vseþ a maner of play to caste wel a spere;
> And somme for to sckyrme asay with swerd & bokelere.
> þys buþ þe games of my contre þat y þe telle here."

However, this is not a draughts game, but a game wherein several damas were used.

---

[39] **MURRAY, Harold James Ruthven** (1913) The History of Chess, Oxford, p. 429

6.5 Guillaume de Saint André (c. 1320 – c. 1390)

Murray states erroneously that there is a French manuscript of a metrical version of 1200 lines written by Guillaume de Saint André in the 15th century[40]. It talks about the chess game and the moves are described in 42 lines (139-180). The king's leap and the double step of the pawn are stated; the Queen is only given her Muslim move. The pieces are called *roy, roigne, or dame, daufflin, chevalier,* and *paonnet, pion, paont,* or *paon.* According to Murray the initial letters of the last 22 lines, when read in the reverse order, give the author's name.

However, Murray does not give the name of the French manuscript; it is known as *Le jeu des échecs moralisé*[41]. The apostolic notary Guillaume de Saint André was as secretary in service of Juan IV, the duke of Britanny. He wrote this chess poem between 1381 and 1385 and in this poem the word "dame" is used as chess queen. Consequently this poem is not from the 15th century as stated by Murray, but from the 14th century.

135 Or mettez doncq voustre pouair
    Savoir comment on doibt jouer
    -. Si feroy ge certainement,
    Car ge en ay moult grant tallant !
    -. Voyez cy doncq en l'eschiquier
140 Le tret du roy qui es moult fier
    Du premier point doux poins sauldra
    Mais que les poins ne soient gardez
    De mille gens, ne occupez;
145 Et que ce coup rien il ne prenge,
    Le sault en est moult bien estrange !
    La **dame** si en peult autant faire;
    Mais que la place ne soit contraire;
    Et si peult alller davant soy,
150 Ou de cornier, tresbien le scoy !

[40] **MURRAY, Harold James Ruthven** (1913) The History of Chess, Oxford, p. 546
[41] **CAUNEAU, Jean-Michel & PHILIPPE, Dominique** (1996) Le jeu des échecs moralisés de Guillaume de Saint-André. In: Annales de Bretagne et des pays de l'Ouest. Tome 103, number 1, pp. 7-65

Le roy peult bien partout aller,
En blanca, en noir, par le tablier,
Mes si la **dame** se siet en blanc,
Elle tendrá touz diz son ranc.
151 L'auffin qui est en noir assis
Au tiers point sauldra par avis.
Il n mura j asa color,
Non será le blanc par nul jour.
Ainczoys vont touz dous de corniere
160 Qui veult bien savoir la maniere.
Le chevalier change pour voir,
Quar moult bien sault du blanc en noir.
Ou tiers point touz dis s'asserra
Et, s'il vault, il retournera.
165 Les deux rocs si courent partout,
De long de travers et de bout,
Et, si vont de long et de lé,
Rien en leur voie n'est espargné.
Mes ils ne vont point de corniere,
170 Combien qu'ilz retornent arriere.
Au premier coup, le paonnet
Davont soy en un poins se vet;
Mais il ne prent fors de corniere,
Ne ne peut retourner arriere.
175 Tant qu'il ait au bout a esté
Lors est il en sa majesté;
Quar il a auxi grant noblesse
Comme la royne, par sa prouesse.
Et si peut aller et venir
180 Par l'eschiquier, a son plair.

The Spanish *alferza* was a feminine noun in chess and it was changed by the new powerful *dama* (chess queen) in Spain only in the 15th century, while the name of the weak *dame* (chess queen) in France was centuries earlier. I wrote in various magazins and books, as from 1990, that my hypothesis about the new powerful chess queen is based on Isabel la Catolica[42]. Finally José Antonio arzon Roger could confirm

[42] **WESTERVELD, Govert** (1987) Dutch draughts magazine *Het Nieuwe Damspel*, p. 71.
WESTERVELD, Govert (1988) Dutch draughts magazine *Het Nieuwe Damspel*, p. 29.

that with documents and with new documents concerning their love for the chess game[43].

It will be clear to the experts of the chess game that the piece with the word *dama* is coming from France and that this piece representing the chess queen suddenly gained more power changing to a new powerful dama or queen. Consequently we have to explain why people suddenly chose the name dama and why they increased the power of the piece. This I have explained in another book[44].

Now knowing about the life of protonotary Juan Ramírez de Lucena[45] it is clear that he was involved with the introduction of the new powerful dama in the chess game. Was it in the time that he was working with

WESTERVELD, Govert (1990). Las Damas: Ciencia sobre un tablero. Volume I.

WESTERVELD, GOVERT (1994) Homo Ludens, Der Spielende Mensch IV. Internationale Beiträge des Institutes für Spielforschung und Spielpädagogik an der Hochschule Mozarteum Salzburg, Salzburg. Page 104 says: Her movement, which until then was between adjacent squares spread over the entire board. This new capability or "power" of the queen appears to be linked, according to my studies, with the influence on all areas of social, cultural, and political-military at the time, held by the figure of Queen Isabella the Catholic.

[42] WESTERVELD, Govert (1997) De invloed van de Spaanse koningin Isabel la Católica op de nieuwe sterke dame in de oorsprong van het dam- en moderne schaakspel. Spaanse literatuur, jaren 1283-1700. (La influencia de la reina Isabel la Católica sobre la nueva dama poderosa en el origen del juego de las damas y el ajedrez modern. Literatura Española, años 1283-1700).

[43] WESTERVELD, Govert (2004) La reina Isabel la Católica: su reflejo en la dama poderosa de Valencia, cuna del ajedrez moderno y origen del juego de damas. In colaboración con José Antonio Garzón Roger. Generalidad Valenciana. Consellería de Cultura, Educació i Esport, Valencia, p. 401. ISBN: 84-482-3718-8

GARZÓN ROGER, José Antonio (2010). Nuevos documentos reativos a la afición de los Reyes Católicos al ajedrez. In: Luca D'Ambrosio et al. (Ed.). Publicación Jubilar en honor de Alessandro Sanvito. Contribuciones internacionales sobre Historia y Bibliografía del ajedrez. Vindobona, pp. 251-271. Separatum Number 6.

[44] WESTERVELD, Govert (2015). The Training of Isabella I of Castile as the Virgin Mary by Churchman Martin de Cordoba. 172 pages. Lulu Editors. ISBN: 978-1-326-40364-5

[45] WESTERVELD, Govert (2015) The Ambassador Juan Ramírez de Lucena, the father of the chessbook writer Lucena. 226 pages. Lulu Editors. ISBN: 978-1-326-37728-1

Prince Ferdinand in Valencia (1968-1970) or was it in the time when the protonotary was working as with Catholic Monarch (1970-1974)?

6.6 Conclusion

Cesolis' chess books inform us that the figures on the chess board are a mirror of the daily life[46]. Stanza 54 of *Scachs d'amor* states that the queen (dama) in the new game had received the sword, the scepter, and the throne. This only happened to Isabella I of Castile in Spain in the XV century. She became the new powerful queen on the chess board with a long move. Dr. Arie van der Stoep had proved with his doctoral dissertation that the Spanish word "dama" originally came from France, where the word is "dame". In France we only had a weak queen with a short move. Isabella I of Castile became the leading figure in Spain and Castilian habits and language were quickly accepted by the Aragonese courtiers who wanted to serve his King. Castile's superiority was in the atmosphere and according to Prof. Antoni Ferrando there was a deep inferiority complex of the Catalan speakers against the imperial Castilian language. As we know, Narcis Vinyoles was one of the three poets who wrote the poem *Scachs d'amor* in 1475. However, one of the first traitors to the Valencian region and language in 1510 was the poet Narcís Vinyoles. If this is true, then he also was one of the first traitors to the Valencian region in 1475 and was thus in line with his behavior.

---

[46] The symbolizing of the game of chess was intended to relate the nature and movement of its pieces with the different classes of society, their role and their duties.

7 The virgin Mary and Chess

Already in the seventies the future Queen Isabella I of Castile was an important figure in Spanish life. The church was involved around 1469 in persuading the princes that she had a divine mission to govern Castile. She became for the church as the Virgin Mary. Those years the church, through Pope Pius II, venerated in all places the Virgin Mary. The first book in the Valencian language in 1474 was a set of texts in praise of Virgin Mary. Since in chess, according to Cessolis, the order of the board pieces is the order of the world, shortly thereafter one sees a poem by three poets appear speaking about a new powerful queen on the chessboard. I want to prove in this article with additional proofs that the new powerful queen is Isabella I of Castile.

Valencia was the Spanish city where the art of printing was first exercised in 1474. The earliest work printed there was *Obres, o Trobes les quales tracten de las hors de la Sacratíssima Verge Maria*. This work was the result of a contest promoted by the viceroy of the Kingdom of Valencia, Luis Despuig. Bernard Fenollar, a priest of the Cathedral, acted as secretary of the jury and the organizer. At least thirty-eight poets participated in this contest, among them Bernard Fenollar, Narcis Vinyoles, and Francesc Castellví.

7.1 Juan Ramírez de Lucena

Now knowing about the life of protonotary Juan Ramírez de Lucena[47] it is clear that he was involved with the introduction of the new powerful dama in the chess game. Being involved as confessor of the catholic monarchs, queen's exalted messianic magnification was expressed by him on the chessboard.

The Dutch historian Dr. Arie van der Stoep[48] made his doctoral dissertation on the word *dame* and so we know that this word is of French origin. The son of Juan Ramírez de Lucena with the sole name of Lucena publised a chess book in 1497 in Salamanca. The embassador, prothonotary and confessor Juan Ramírez de Lucena was in the service of Prince Ferdinand II in 1968-1970 and from 1970 in the service of Queen Isabella I of Castile (Isabel la Católica) and King Ferdinand II of Aragon until his death around 1504. Between the years 1470 and 1474 he was in France to defend the interest of the future monarchs and there he could have obtained the necessary chess books with the weak *dame*.

---

[47] **WESTERVELD, Govert** (2015) The Ambassador Juan Ramírez de Lucena, the father of the chessbook writer Lucena. 226 pages. Lulu Editors. 978-1-326-37728-1
[48] **STOEP, Arie van der** (1997). Over de herkomst van het word damspel: een problem uit de geschiedenis van het bordspel en bordspelterminologie. Thesis. University of Leiden.

7.2 Joachim Petzold

Professor Petzold (1933-1999) has since 1981 represented the opinion that the term *dama* (lady) could be derived in chess from *Notre Dame*, the Mother of God[49]. He justified this assumption in more detail in his book *Kulturgeschichte des Schachspiels*[50]. In a letter to me on 11 August 1994 he asked:

> If Valencia were the birthplace of both the new chess and the draughts game, then I would take a look at the print shop owner Dr. Miguel Albert who competed in 1474 for the price of a hymn to the Virgin Mary[51], and perhaps even brought out the lost book of Vincent. Can something still be determined about him in the city archives?

In an article presented at the Vienna workshop from 3 to 5 November 1994 Professor Petzold showed an interesting study about Virgin Mary[52]. He explained that the English "Moralitas de scaccario" about the chess sermon of Jacobus de Cessolis until the editing by Konrad von Amme Hausen had the principle that "The order of the board pieces is the order of the world[53]." In the 15th century the artistically-minded

---

[49] Joachim Petzold: König und Dame. Figuren im Schach, in: Urania, 1981, Nr. 6. p. 3 ff.

[50] **PETZOLD, Joachim** (1986). Schach. Das Königliche Spiel. Eine Kulturgeschichte, Leipzig 1986, p. 151. Compare the recent keyword Dame in "Meyers Schachlexikon, herausgegeben und bearbeitet von Otto Borik ... in Zusammenarbeit mit ... Joachim Petzold u. a., Mannheim 1993, p. 59"

[51] **WESTERVELD, Govert** (2004) La reina Isabel la Católica: su reflejo en la dama poderosa de Valencia, cuna del ajedrez moderno y origen del juego de damas. In colaboración con José Antonio Garzón Roger. Generalidad Valenciana. Consellería de Cultura, Educació i Esport, Valencia, p. 401. ISBN: 84-482-3718-8

José Antonio Garzón Roger observes: "But we also perceive that this Queen's Chess is very new and it is being invented at the very moment. Was the new Chess created in Bernat Fenollar's literary circle soon after the 1474 literary competition in honour of the Virgin Mary? We must take into account the sequence of historical events surrounding the new monarchs in 1475-1476. The poets seemed to know about these events, as they show in their work. Was their proposal also a gift to this new monarchy whose very strong Queen had, in turn, inspired them?"

[52] **PETZOLD, Joachim** (1994) Wie erklärt sich der Name Dame im Schach? Beitrag zum Wiener Workshop vom 3. bis 5. November 1994 zum Thema von Wesir zur Dame.

[53] **BORST, Otto** (1983) Alltagsleben im Mittelalter, Frankfurt am Main, p. 59.

Pope Pius II (Enea Silvio Piccolomini) praised Germany for its many churches dedicated to Virgin Mary.

Prof. Joachim Petzold

In an article presented at the Vienna workshop from 3 to 5 November 1994 Professor Petzold showed an interesting study about Virgin Mary[54]. He explained that the English "Moralitas de scaccario" about the chess sermon of Jacobus de Cessolis until the editing by Konrad von Amme Hausen had the principle that "The order of the board pieces is the order of the world[55]." In the 15th century the artistically-minded Pope Pius II (Enea Silvio Piccolomini) praised Germany for its many churches dedicated to Virgin Mary.

As we know, Juan Ramírez de Lucena worked with the Pope Pius II for several years and perfectly knew the influence of Virgin Mary in many countries. Furthermore Petzold stated that probably around 1300 in England a collection of stories was compiled from the ancient Roman period under the name of "*Gesta Romanorum*" (Gestis Romanorum). It narrates the legends about the origins of the game of chess. The chapter "the chess game" reads that the powerful King on the 64 fields of the chessboard could be considered as "our Lord Jesus Christ who is the

---

[54] **PETZOLD, Joachim** (1994) Wie erklärt sich der Name Dame im Schach? Beitrag zum Wiener Workshop vom 3. bis 5. November 1994 zum Thema von Wesir zur Dame.

[55] **BORST, Otto** (1983) Alltagsleben im Mittelalter, Frankfurt am Main, p. 59.

King of all in heaven and on Earth". He could move to any place. "Finally he also takes with him the Queen, i.e. the religious mother of mercy, Virgin Maria[56]."

In the following picture we see a wall painting from the late 12th century AD. It is of a dead Nubian Queen being cradled by Virgin Mary who is also cradling Baby Jesus. It is very similar to the wall painting 'Christ Victor Trampling Evil Powers' made during the late 8th, early 9th century AD[57]. It probably still has nothing to do with the game of chess, but there was already an early connection between Virgin Mary and a Queen.

The Nubian Queen

---

[56] **TRILLITZCH, Winfried** (1973) Gesta Romanorum. Geschichten von den Römern. Ein Erzählbuch des Mittelalters. Erstmals in vollständiger Übersetzung herausgegeben von Winfried Trillitzsch, Leipzig. The Chapter about Chess is in p. 166.
[57] Drawing by Mohammed Awad.
http://www.britishmuseum.org/explore/young_explorers/childrens_online_tours/suda n_ancient_treasures/wall_painting_of_a_nubian_quee.aspx
By Saeed Abdel-Gadir, Mohammed Awad, Mohamed El-Mahadi, Yassin Abdelazim

7.3 The chess piece Dame in France

By the end of the 12th century the queen replaced the vizier throughout Europe (except in Spain). In the 12th and 13th centuries people developed an extraordinary veneration for Virgin Mary. She was the queen in heaven.

Gautier de Coincy's Les Miracles de Nostre Dame is an extraordinary 13th-century collection of songs, prayers, versed sermons, and stories that recount miracles associated with Virgin Mary translated from Latin sources, reset into French verse, and joined with various combinations of original music and trouvère love songs. Gautier de Coinci compares Virgin Mary to the Chess Queen. Unfortunately some authors see this Chess Queen with a powerful move. Yalom[58] refers to Steven M. Taylor[59]. However, we have to take into account the chess expert and historian Murray who only speaks about a weak chess queen[60].

> Gautier de Coinci (c. 1230) includes a long elaborate allegory of the spiritual life, imagined as a game of chess between God and the Devil, in his *Miracle de la Sainte Vierge* (ed. Paris, 1857, cols. 7-10, 128 lines in all). The Devil has driven man into an angle of the board and is one the points of mating him:

Tost nous aura en l'angle traiz; Nous serons pris et mat ce cuit.	

His strongest move had been the expulsion of Adam and Eve from the Garden of Eden. At this moment God comes to the rescue and makes a Fers which covers the check and finally mates the enemy:

Mez touz ces traiz fit il en vain, Quar Diex une tel fyerce fist Qui le mata et desconfit.	But he (Devil) made all these moves in vain, For God created a queen[61]

---

[58] **YALOM, Marilyn** (2009) Birth of the Chess Queen. London, HarperCollins ebooks, p. 100 and 217.

[59] **TAYLOR, Steven M.** (1990) God's Queen: Chess Imagery in the Poetry of Gautier de Coinci. In: Fifteenth Century Studies, 17, pp. 403-419.

[60] **MURRAY, H.J.R.** (1913) The History of Chess, p. 749.

[61] **HUNT, Tony** (2007) Miraculous Rhymes: The Writin of Gautier de Coinci, Cambridge, pp. 53-59.

Quant li doux Diex vit vers la fin	who checkmated and defeated him.
Que n'avait truie nes d'aufin	When gentle God saw towards the end
Et qu'anemis par son desroi	That he had no safeguard, not even a
Chevalier, Roc, fierce ne Roi,	bishop,
Nes ne poon ni voulait laissier	And that the Enemy in his excess would
Au jeu se daigna abaissier	Leave no knight, rook, queen, king,
Et fist un trait soutil et gent	Not even a pawn, he humbled himself
Par quoi rescout toute sa gent.	To play the game
C'est fierce traist par tel seus,	and made a subtle, noble move
Que l'anemie mate par tel sens.	by which he rescued his people.

The Fers that so happily turns the tables upon the Devil is Virgin Mary, and Gautier devotes many lines to the praise of this piece:

Ceste fierce n'est pas d'ivoire,	This queen is no ivory one,
Ainz es la fierce au roy de gloire	she belongs to the King of Glory
Qui rescout toute sa maisnée	who saved his people
Qu'avoit déables defrainée.	whom the Devil had claimed.
Ceste fierce le mate en roie,	This Queen checkmates him in a row,
Ceste fierce le mate en l'angle,	This Queen checkmates him in a
Ceste fierce li tolt la jangle,	corner,
Ceste fierce li tolt sa proie,	This Queen removes his ruse,
Ceste fierce touzjors l'asproie,	This Queen removes his prey,
Ceste fierce touzjourz le point,	This Queen constantly harries him
Ceste fierce de point en point	This Queen constantly presses him,
Par fine force le dechace	This Queen se déplace à travers les
	lignes horizontales ....

The poet is so delighted with his allegory that the returns to it again and again. The last extract from Gautier de Coinci shows conclusively that the Fers had only their weak Muslim move.

Etymologically[62] the process operated in the specific case of the *dame* was that the Firzan passed to alferza, a name given by King Alfonso the Wise in his famous chess manuscript. This name became fercia in Latin, being the key step for sexual metamorphosis, because the alferza of King Alfonso remained to be of a male character. The French used fierce and later vierge (virgin), associating it with Virgin Mary, through which

---

[62] The expert in Etymology of the word *dama* is Dr. Arie van der Stoep:
http://history.chess.free.fr/papers/van%20der%20Stoep%202002.pdf
http://www.draughtshistory.nl/origin13.htm

the piece changed into a female piece. The works in Latin baptized the piece in regina, partly because Virgin Mary is the Queen of Heaven, or Regina Coelis, and partly because in most medieval monarchies the Queen occupied an important place in human life.

7.4 The Gesta Romanorum

In the foreword of the first of the four books of the Amadis published in Venice in 1533, Lucena[63] through Francisco Delicado appears to know the *Gesta Romanorum*:

> Cuan marauillosamente este Autor uos pinto este cauallero Amadis de Gaula? Y hizolo por fazer la razon. Que los Pintores & Poetas y estoriadores como el. Tienen licencia de Pintar/y dezir lo que a ellos mejor les pareciere. Para fazer sus obras en todo & a todos hermosas. Diole a este cauallero Amadis de Gaula tres fortunas muy apropiadas. La primera echado en el arca cerrada por las aguas del mar y en esto se assemejo a aquel gran Profeta. Moyses y como cuenta el libro que ha nombre. (gesta Romanorun) de san Gregorio que fue / por el semejante lançado en el mar/ de su madre y hermana.

> **Translation:**

> How beautifully this author paints you this knight Amadis of Gaul? And he did it to be right. The Painters and Poets and historians like him have authorization to paint and to tell what seems better to them. To make his works complete and beautiful he gave this knight Amadis of Gaul three very appropriate fortunes. The first thrown into the closed ark by the seawaters and in this it is similar to the great Prophet Moyses, and as the book tells with the name (Gesta Romanorum) of St. Gregory that was by such thrown into the sea by his mother and sister.

As indicated before, Lucena knew the work of *Gesta Romanorum*[64] and there is no doubt that his father Juan Ramírez de Lucena also knew this work, because he had a good library[65].

---

[63] JGAAP shows Lucena.

[64] **WESTERVELD, Govert** (in press) The Wanderings of the Chess Book Writer Lucena

[65] **MIGUEL BRIONGOS, Jerónimo** (2014) Juan de Lucena. Diálogo sobre la vida feliz. Epístola exhortatoria a las letras. Real Academia Española, p. XCV

At that time I could not devote attention to the different ways of investigation that Dr. Petzold had suggested to me because of a lack of time, knowledge, and my other professional obligations. Now 21 years later the situation has changed. I have written many more books about the history of modern chess and the draughts game and even a book about the chess author Lucena[66] and another one about his father, the protonotary Juan Ramírez de Lucena. On the other hand I now have more time and the professional obligations are becoming fewer due to my retirement. So the time has come to pay more attention to the studies of the much too young departed Professor Petzold. In this respect I will discuss three points of his interesting study of 1994 presented in November to the Vienna Workshop. The first point refers to Pope Pius II and we know that the protonotary Juan Ramírez de Lucena was his dependant and maybe his dinner companion:

> The great Italian poet Dante is not afraid to compare in his "divine comedy" his earthly beloved with the heavenly Virgin Mary below and to worship both accordingly. Something similar is to be said of the last minstrel Heinrich von Meissen, who for that reason was given the honorary name "Frauenlob". Contemplating the late medieval images of Mary more closely it seems that they are thoroughly permeated by this spirit. Even the grieving Mother of God in Michelangelo's famous Pieta sculpture is according to age a virgin. They took no offense because the Queen of Heaven was also portrayed as the queen of the earthly in a very personal sense. The art wise Pius II (Enea Silvio Piccolomini) praised in the XV century Germany for his many churches consecrated to Virgin Mary[67].

---

[66] **VALLE DE RICOTE, Gofredo** (2008). Los tres autores de La Celestina: El judeoconverso Juan Ramírez de Lucena, sus hijos Fernando de Rojas (Lucena) y Juan del Encina (alias Bartolomé Torres Naharro y Francisco Delicado). Tomo II: bajo el seudónimo de Godofredo Valle de Ricote. El libro perdido de Lucena. "Tractado sobre la muerte de Don Diego de Azevedo". Blanca. ISBN – 10: 978-84-612-604-0-9

[67] **PETZOLD, Dr. Joachim** (1994) Wie erklart sich der Name Dame im Schach. Beitrag zum Wiener Workshop between 3 and 5th November, 1994, concerning Thema "Vom Wesir zur Dame", pp. 1-10 Cited, p. 5
Petzold mentions two important identifications of Virgin Mary with the Chess Queen:
- **TRILLITZSCH, W.** (1973) Gesta Romanorum, kap. 166, p. 179f.
- **SCHRÖDER, E.** (1882) Das *Goldene Spiel* Von *Meister* Ingold, P. 41

In 1994 Professor Petzold was not aware of the life of Juan Ramírez de Lucena, the father of Lucena, since his first biography[68] (In Spanish) was written in 2006. The presence of Juan Ramírez de Lucena in Rome is reflected in his *Epístola Exhortatoria*[69] and documents place him as a member of the entourage of the powerful Cardinal Prospero Colonna, cousin of Pope Martin (1417-1431). Some bulls of Pope Pius II (Enea Silvio Piccolomini) might tell us the movement of Juan Ramírez de Lucena. In the Bull Nº. 1173 Juan de Lucena is called "beloved filio" when in 1458 Pope Pius II gives Juan de Lucena one canonicato that has become vacant in Sevilla after the death of Gonzalo Sánchez de Córdoba[70].

Di Camillo says that Juan de Lucena was «familiari continuo commensali» of Cardinal Prospero Colonna (1426-1463) in 1458. On the other hand Lucena was bachelor in 1458 and was licensed in 1461, so Lucena studied for three years in Rome[71]. Medina also says that from a document we learn that Lucena was still "bachelor" and had also been «familiari continuo commensali» of Cardinal Prospero Colonna, head

---

[68] **VALLE DE RICOTE, Gofredo** (2006) Los tres autores de la Celestina: el judeoconverso Juan Ramírez de Lucena, sus hijos Fernando de Rojas (Lucena) y Juan del Encina (alias Bartolomé Torres Naharro y Francisco Delicado). Tomo I: Biografía, estudio y documentos del antiguo autor de la Celestina, el ajedrecista Juan Ramírez de Lucena. (Prólogo Prof. Dr. Ángel Alcalá). Blanca. ISBN 84-923151-4-8

[69] **LUCENA, JUAN DE** (1892) Epístola Exhortatoria a las letras (en A. Paz y Meliá (editor): Opúsculos literarios de los siglos XIX a XVI (Madrid: Sociedad de Bibliófilos Españoles, 1892), p. 215. Cited by **MEDINA BERMUDEZ, ALEJANDRO** (1998) El diálogo De Vita Beata, de Juan de Lucena: un rompecabezas histórico (II). Dicenda. Cuadernos de Filología Hispánica, No. 16, pp. 135-170, also p. 158. **RICO, Francisco** (1978, Nebrija frente a los bárbaros, p. 38) refers to p. 215 of the book of Paz y Meliá saying: «yo fui a Roma grandevo y mi gramática castellana troqué con los niños por la suya italiana», furthermore explaining «that the career and personality of Lucena will be cleared up definitively in the dissertation of Jerónimo Miguel Briongos».

[70] **BELTRÁN DE HEREDIA, VICENTE** (1967) Bulario de la Universidad de Salamanca (1219 – 1549), 3 vols. Bula 1173, p. 93. Cited by **MEDINA BERMUDEZ, ALEJANDRO** (1998) El diálogo De Vita Beata, de Juan de Lucena: un rompecabezas histórico (II). Dicenda. Cuadernos de Filología Hispánica, no. 16, pp. 135-170, pp. 153 y 160

[71] **DI CAMILLO, Ottavio** (1976) El humanismo castellano del siglo XV, New York, p. 247

of the Church of St. George in Velabro[72]. In the Bull 1201 dated November 3 1461 Lucena is called «Dilecto filio Joanni de Lucena…, vero familiari nostro continuo commensali…» and the Pope extended the privilege of *familiarity* for one more year, forcing Lucena to remain beside him in Rome for another year [73].

In other words the protonotary Juan Ramírez de Lucena as dependant and dinner companion of the Pope Pius II was aware that many churches in Germany were consecrated to Virgin Mary.

7.5 King Ferdinand

But which events bring our Juan Ramírez de Lucena to Valencia? This is a document made in Valladolid on 2 January 1970 in which Ferdinand, Principe of Castile, Leon, and Aragon, King of Sicilia, appointed doctor Juan Ramírez de Lucena as counsellor of the Kingdom of Castile stating in the document: *e los muchos, buenos e leales seruiçios que me avedes fecho e fasedes de cada día* (and the many good and loyal services you gave and give me every day). According to Miguel Briongos this is an unequivocal recognition that the protonotary had for some time been in the service of Prince Ferdinand of Aragon. It should be taken into account that appointment of any person to an important position such as that of a member of the Council was not performed without a good knowledge of the person's qualities, merits obtained, and above all, trust[74]. This means that Juan Ramírez de Lucena was before 1470 in the service of Prince Ferdinand and Miguel Briongos thinks that it might be in 1468 or 1469.

---

[72] **MEDINA BERMUDEZ, ALEJANDRO** (1998) El diálogo De Vita Beata, de Juan de Lucena: un rompecabezas histórico (II). Dicenda. Cuadernos de Filología Hispánica, no. 16, pp. 135-170, citation on p. 160
[73] **BELTRÁN DE HEREDIA, VICENTE** (1967) Bulario de la Universidad de Salamanca (1219 – 1549), 3 vols. Bula 1201, p. 117. Cited by **MEDINA BERMUDEZ, ALEJANDRO** (1998) El diálogo De Vita Beata, de Juan de Lucena: un rompecabezas histórico (II). Dicenda. Cuadernos de Filología Hispánica, no. 16, pp. 135-170, pp. 153 y 161
[74] **MIGUEL BRIONGOS, Jerónimo** (2014) Juan de Lucena. Diálogo sobe la vida feliz. Epístola exhortatoria a las letras. Real Academia Española, pp. 23-24

7.6 The Holy Virgin

The second point concerns Dr. Miguel Albert of Valencia to whom Professor Petzold refers when discussing the praise songs of 1474 and the book of Francesch Vicent:

> In Valencia, Spain lived Dr. Miguel Albert who not only participated in a hymns competition of 1474 to the Holy Virgin, but twenty years later as a print shop owner also edited with the German printers Peter Trincher and Lope de la Roca (Wolf of Stone) the unfortunately lost chess book of Vicent Francesch. We do not know whether this standing book already contained, on the threshold of transition of chess from old to new, the term Dama. That would have had importance[75] in this context for the very speculative assumption that the Madonna praising Albert had been involved in the transmission of religious interpretations of the term Dame in the game of chess.

The observations of Dr. Petzold are quite interesting with regards to the prevailing religious life in the XV century. He did not participate in the hymns competition of 1474, but on May 13 1475 he was appointed Judge of appeals for review of notaries and since then we know him as one of the main contributors to the definitive establishment of printing in Valencia. We know that the term *Dama* appears in the poem of *Scachs d'amor*, but we do not know whether Dr. Miguel Albert really had anything to do with that. However, the near connection of Dr. Miguel Albert with the Holy Virgin in 1474, his appointment as judge in 1475, the poem *Scachs d'amor* in 1475 by the three poets[76], and his connection with the writer Francesc Vicent in 1495 is very suspicious.

---

[75] The manuscript of Perugia is just text, with the exception of Per. 63. In the manuscript of Cesena there are multiple languages: Italian, Spanish, Valencian or Latin; plus the many abbreviations in these languages. Most of the time the piece of Dama is abbreviated to "D." or "d.", and as the text is written in a mixture of Spanish and Italian it is not easy to deduce what the abbreviation really means, although it can be "Dama", because normally the uses of technical terms are chosen by the graphs in Castilian: lance, take, etc., a fact that led Pratesi to think that the author was a Spaniard. Occasionally we see the whole word "Dama", and sometimes "Dona" in the manuscripts. (Personal communication from the chess historical expert José Antonio Garzón Roger, Valencia)

[76] **WESTERVELD, Govert** (2015). The Poem Scachs d'amor (1475). First Text of Modern Chess. 144 pages. Lulu Editors. ISBN: 978-1-326-37491-4

The poem *Scachs d'amor* was written by Bernard de Fenollar (a priest of the Cathedral), Narcís Vinyoles (lawyer and politician) and Francesc de Castelví. The *Scachs d'amor* or *Chess of Love*, is a poem based on a chess game between Francesc de Castellvi and Narcís Vinyoles, while Bernat Fenollar comments and establishes the rules. It is the first documented game played with the modern rules of chess. Dr. Petzold third and last point refers to the Spanish Queen Isabella I of Castile:

> In Lucenas chess-Dama the spirit does not embody the final minnesongs, but it is a new era that began to change in order to match the relationship between the sexes. Involuntarily one is reminded of the Spanish Queen Isabella I of Castile who united Spain by her marriage to Ferdinand of Aragon and made clear to Spain that in a royal ruling family the man did not have in any case the upper hand.

Dr. Joachim Petzold

It is quite clear that Petzold with his article[77] of late 1994 referred to the fact that Isabella I of Castile could have been the new powerful dama, but he still did not dare to give a firm hypothesis in this sense and gives various options in his study. He highlights the art-wise Pius II (Enea Silvio Piccolomini) who in the XV century praised Germany for its many churches consecrated to Virgin Mary. The protonotary Juan Ramirez de Lucena was dependant of the Pope Enea Silvio Piccolomini and Ambassador of the queen Isabella I of Castile. Dr. Petzold was on the right track without a doubt, but at that time little was known about Juan Ramírez de Lucena.

Researching Lucena was not easy. It took me several years and my friend Jerónimo Miguel Briongos from Barcelona took more than 36 years to write his doctoral thesis. I know him since 2004 when I was already for years involved in the study of the life of this protonotary, father of Lucena. He gave me several interesting hints for my book about Juan Ramírez de Lucena and he was one of the first people who obtained my book. All these years I encouraged him to finish his dissertation, because the world was waiting for it. It is quite interesting to see that he amply discussed my book about Juan de Lucena (Juan Ramírez de Lucena) in his doctoral thesis[78]. In 1975 Miguel Briongos wrote his first dissertation[79] about Juan de Lucena for obtaining his academic degree of the University of Barcelona.

But let us see what Juan Ramírez de Lucena was writing about Isabel I of Castile in his Epístola Exhortatoria a las letras. He compares the Queen with Diana, always as something very exceptional:

> Callemos de todos; todos callemos ante la muy resplandeciente Diana, Reina nuestra Isabel, casada, madre, reina, y tan grande, asentando nuestros reales,

---

[77] **PETZOLD, Dr. Joachim** (1994) Wie erklart sich der Name Dame im Schach. Beitrag zum Wiener Workshop between 3 and 5 November, 1994, concerning Thema "Vom Wesir zur Dame", pp. 1-10

[78] **MIGUEL BRIONGOS, Jerónimo** (2012). El De vita felici o diálogo sobre la vida feliz, de Juan de Lucena. Tesis doctoral. Universitat Autònoma de Barcelona.

[79] **MIGUEL BRIONGOS, Jerónimo** (1975) Juan de Lucena: breve estudio de conjunto en torno a su vida y producción literaria; bajo la dirección del Dr. Francisco Rico. Universitat autònoma de Barcelona.

ordenando nuestras batallas; nuestros cercos parando; oyendo nuestras querellas; nuestros juicios formando; inventando vestires; pompas hablando; escuchando músicos; toreas mirando; rodando sus reinos; andando, andando, y nunca parando; gramática oyendo, recrea. ¡O ingenio del cielo armado en la tierra! ¡O esfuerzo real, asentado en flaqueza! ¡O corazón de varon vestido de hembra, ejemplo de todas las reinas, de todas las mugeres dechado, y de todos los hombres materia de letras! ¿Quién tan torpe, tan rudo, que non las aprenda?

La muy clara ninfa Carmenta letras latinas nos dio; perdidas en nuestra Castilla, esta diua serena las anda buscando. Si al su resplandor miramos todos por ellas, non puede ser que non las hallemos. Si las manda su grandeza pregonar: Quien sabe de las letras latinas que perdió Castilla, véngalo á decir á su dueño, y habrá buen hallazgo; por cobdicia del premio, más presto se hallarán que se perdieron. Honor pare artes, y á todos enciende al estudio la gloria. ¿Non vedes cuántos comienzan á aprender admirando su Realeza? Lo que los reyes hacen, bueno ó malo, todos ensayamos de hacer. Si es bueno, por aplacer á nos mesmos; y si malo, por aplacer á ellos. Jugaba el Rey, éramos todos tahúres; studia la Reina, somos agora studiantes. Y si vos me confesáis lo cierto, es cierto que su studio es causa del vuestro; ó sea por agradarla, ó sea porque os agrada, ó por envidia de los que han comenzado á seguirla.

Translation

All shut up; all shut up at the very radiant Diana, our Queen Isabella, married, mother, queen, and so great, sprawling our actual ordering our battles; our fences stopping; hearing our complaints; our judgments forming; inventing vestires; talking bubbles; listening to musicians; looking at toreas; moving through her kingdoms; walking, walking, never stopping; listening grammar, recreating. What a genius of heaven, armed on earth! What a real effort seated in weakness! What a heart of man with female clothes, example of all queens, paragon of all wives, and all men, matter of letters! Who so clumsy, so rough do not learn? The very clear Carmenta nymph gave Latin letters; lost in our Castile, this serene diva is looking for it. If we look at their shining all for them, it may not be that we do not find them. If the commands proclaim his greatness: Who knows about the Latin letters that lost Castile, come to say it to his owner, and there will be a good find; by the covetousness prize, more quickly they are found than those who were lost. Honour stops arts, and all turn to study the glory. Do you not see how many started the study admiring the Royals? What kings do, good or bad, all rehearsed to do it. If it is good, it is delighting four ourselves, and if it is bad, it is delighting to them. If the King plays, we were all gamblers; if the Queen studies, we all are now students. And if you confess me right, it is true that here study is the cause of your study; or whether by pleasing her, or it is because you like it, or by envy of those who have begun to follow.

One thing is clear from that time: King John II of Aragon considered in 1475-1476 the protonotary Juan de Lucena a servant of the Cardinal and House of Mendoza[80].

The disguised complaint of the king [of Aragon]
The king confirmed that the Duke of Burgundy and the King of England had much disdain; and for this reason the protonotary Lucena was persuaded to broker the marriage of the princess and the Dauphin of France; and the King of Aragon came about this information having very little knowledge of the deal. And he said that without consultation with him about talks about marriage the deal should not go through; and although the fault was ascribed to Lucena as he was a servant of the Cardinal and the House of Mendoza, the king must have had sorrowful feelings regarding the Cardinal and the main advisors to the King and Queen and their children who ruled those negotiations.

---

[80] **ZURITA, Jerónimo** (1610) Anales de Aragón. Libro XIX, Cap. XXI. Cited by **MENÉNDEZ PIDAL, Ramon** (1969). Historia de España, dirigida por R. Menéndez Pidal. Tomo XVII, p. 118.

7.7 Isabella I of Castile

Concentrating now on Virgin Mary in relationship with Isabella I of Castile we observe that the Augustinian monastic Martin de Córdoba[81] with his work *El Jardin de las donzellas* of 1468 is the first writer who draws equivalencies between Isabella and Virgin Mary[82], which became one of her standard portrayals.

In one of her studies, Garretas Rivera says[83]:

> In the sacristy of the Toro's collegiate there is a painting[84] called Our Lady of the Fly (La virgen de la mosca) which depicts Mary of Nazareth with her son surrounded by Mary Magdalene and Catherine of Alexandria. Catalina's face is that of the young Isabel the Catholic (...) Isabel wears a crown and has an open book in her lap. Behind Isabel standing in the background an older man - perhaps a prophet or a humanist - looks at her with a book in his hand. Catalina / Isabel occupies the foreground of the picture. The altarpiece - of uncertain authorship - has been attributed to Hans Memling [deceased around 1494]. (....) What is it that Isabel says by the symbol of Catherine of Alexandria? Inspiration, intelligence, wisdom, beauty is what the figure represents; also the force, indicated by a sword half hidden at the foot of the holy queen. A combination of male and female attributes that the humanistic Isabel perhaps thinks were embodied in her being a woman in the new stage of the history of Castile. Maybe she imagines it and communicates it in this way.

---

[81] **CÓRDOBA, Martín Alonso de** (1468) El Jardin de las donzellas

[82] **SÁNCHEZ DUEÑAS, Blas** (2001) Una particular visión de la mujer en el siglo XV: Jardín de nobles doncellas de Fray Martín de Córdoba. In: Boletín de la Real Academia de Córdoba 141, pp. 291-299

VAL VALDIVIESO, María Isabel del (2006) Isabel la Católica y la educación. In: Aragón en la Edad Media, N° 19, pp. 555-562

[83] **RIVERA GARETTAS, María-Milagros** (1998). Catalina de Alejandría, representada en Isabel I de Castilla.In: (Ana Isabel Cerrada Jiménez y Josemi Lorenzo Arribas, eds.) *De los símbolos al orden simbólico femenino (ss. IV-XVII)*. Madrid, Al-Mudayna, 1998, pp. 137-143. Citations in pp. 137 and 142. Cited by **MÉRIDA JIMÉNEZ, Rafael M.** (2013). Transmisión y difusión de la literatura caballeresca. Doce estudios de recepción cultural hispánica (siglos XIII-XVII), pp. 83-84.

[84]

VIRGEN DE LA MOSCA
Anónimo flamenco. Varias atribuciones. En torno a 1520-1525
Sacristía-Museo de la Colegiata de Santa María la Mayor de Toro (Zamora)

The work *El Jardin de nobles doncellas* of Friar Martin de Cordoba, written in 1468, was printed in Valladolid by Juan de Burgos in 1500 and according to Ana Isabel Carrasco Manchado[85] no manuscript had

---

[85] **CARRASCO MANCHADO, Ana Isabel** (2005) La toma del poder de Isabel I de Castilla. Golpe a la legitimidad de Enrique IV. In:Coups d''État à la fin du Moyen Âge? Aux fondements du pouvoir politique en Europe occidentale. Casa de Velázquez, Madrid, p. 331-350. Citation in p. 336

been preserved. In the eyes of the Church, Isabel had to be the perfect woman equal to the Virgin herself?

Patricia Grieves informs that apparently since the beginning of her reign an observer warned that "many men believed that Isabella had been created miraculously to the redemption of the lost kingdoms"; in fact, the contemporary chronicles referred to the Queen as "the second Virgin Mary" and Cardinal Mendoza proclaimed that the union of Isabella and Fernando was the incarnation of a Christian national identity that would soon unite Spain[86].

The Church's expectations were very high for Isabella. Finaly Grieves remembers the Eulogy (poem) that Diego de San Pedro directs to Queen Isabella I of Castile in the *Tractado de amores de Arnalte y Lucenda*[87].

To emphasize the comparison between Isabella I and the Mother of Jesus, Diego de San Pedro 'framed' *Tratado de amores de Arnalte y Lucenda* between a poem in honor of the queen at the beginning of the work, and an extensive 'invocation of Our Lady at the end.

As a result of the succession to the throne in Segovia in December 1474 Isabella I of Castile quickly became the subject of political suspicion and apparent adulation by many poets and writers. Many of these were converted Jews and descendants of those who had converted from Judaism to Christianity in the course of the previous two generations. They often compared the queen directly with the Virgin and there was little difference between the two. Isabel was presented as the pure, perfect woman. 1474 becomes a key date and serves as a point of reference; before it there is chaos, anarchy, impotence; after it, as if by magic, everything becomes tidy: submitted noblemen; nobody bothers

---

[86] **RUBIN, N.** (1993) Isabel de Castilla. La primera reina del Renacimiento, Madrid, Apóstrofe, p. 220

[87] **SORIANO, Catherine** (1997) Conveniencia política y tópico literario en el *Jardín de nobles doncellas* (1468?) de Fray Martín Alonso de Córdoba. In: Actas del VI Congreso Internacional de la Asociación Hispánica de Literatura Medieval (Alcalá de Henares, 12-16 de septiembre de 1995). Servicio de Publicaciones Universidad de Alcalá. Tomo II, pp. 1457-1466

the travelers on the roads of Spain, and people can finally work in peace and know they can count on the Catholic Monarchs for justice.

The Franciscan poet friar Inigo de Mendoza composed a panegyric evidently written before 1479] where he put Isabella I of Castile in a place that the Church reserves for the Mother of God in the history of salvation:

Alta reyna esclarecida,
guarnecida
de grandezas muy reales,
a remediar nuestros males
desiguales,
por gracia de Dios venida;
como quando fue perdida
nuestra vida
por culpa de vna muger [Eva],
nos quiere Dios guarnecer
e rehacer
por aquel modo y medida
que lleuó nuestra caída.

Perhaps the most extravagant of the first part of of Isabella I of Castile's reign is in the *Canción en loor de la Reyna Doña Isabel I de Castilla* composed by the Cordovan poet Anton de Montoro. He was without a doubt a converted Jew and obviously finished his poem between 1474 and 1477. In the Cancionero de Pedro Guillén de Sevilla we observe that Montoro compares Isabella I of Castile with Virgin Mary:

Alta Reyna soberana
si fuerades antes vos
que la hija de Sant' Ana,
de vos el Hijo de dios
recibiera carne humana.
Que bella, santa, discreta,
Por espiriencia se prueve,
Aquélla Virgen perfeta,
La divinidad ecepta,
Esso le debéys que os deve.
Y pues que por vos se gana
La vida y gloria de nos,
si no pariera Sant' Ana

hasta ser nascida vos,
de vos el Hijo de Dios
rescibiera carne humana.

Diego de San Pedro in his *Tractado de amores de Arnalte a Luçenda* (Burgos, 1491) also refers to Virgin Mary by a verse dedicated to Isabella I of Castile and shows her as an image or representation of God.

La más alta maravilla
  de cuantas pensar podeis
  después de la sin mancilla (Virgin Mary)
es la reina de Castilla ...

Pedro de Cartagena (d. 1486) wrote couplets in honor of the Queen Isabella I of Castile which figure in the book *Cancionero General* by Hernando del Castillo. Here we also see the Queen as a divine being in heaven.

Coplas a la reina doña Isabel
Es que sois mujer entera /
  en la tierra la primera /
  y en el cielo la segunda

The couplets of Juan Alvarez Gato about Queen Isabella I of Castile are another example of the queen's divine attributes. The couplets were probably written at the end of the 1470s when the poet was in the court of Isabella and Ferdinand. Parts of the poem are reflected here:

De grandes loores digna
la sagrada mano diestra
os hizo muy más veçina
de su Magestad divina
que a la forma común nuestra;
que aunque lo callase yo,
vuestro gesto es buen testigo
de la graçia que vos dio,
y quánto se travaxó
para ygualaros consigo.

Esta sola diferençia
de Él a vos quiso que uviese,
por guardar su preheminençia
ynfinito se dixese.
Por ende vuestra morada
hizo en este mundo pobre,
do sois peor empleada
que rica perla engastada
en falsa chapa de cobre.

The historians and contemporary chroniclers refer to Isabella I of Castile as superior to women in general and comparable to Virgin Mary and Patricia E. Grieve gives us the best description for that[88] taking into account the *Jardin de nobles doncellas* by Friar Martin de Cordoba:

Martín de Córdoba employs the topos of Spain as a paradise and reinforces the fifteenth-century Spanish view that there were two thrones in the universe, God's celestial throne in the East and in the West "la silla del Rey de España" (the throne of the King of Spain), which. If politics played out the way the author hoped and expected, would be occupied not by a "Rey," but for the first time by a "Reina." To imply that the queen of Spain would, in effect, be the ruler of the world was not only bold, but prophetic, given her role as mother of an empire. By describing Mary's reversal of the sin of Eve—"E la Virgen Maria, Nuestra Señora nos paró la visión de Dios, la qual Eua nos quitó, ca por su glorioso parto fue fecho visible el que primero hera inuisible" (And Virgin Mary, Our Lady, gave birth to the sight of God, which Eve had taken from us, because by that glorious birth was made visible what was before invisible;)— Martín de Córdoba suggests that Isabel will do the same for Spain. Poetically, then, and in the national imaginary of Spain, she will be opposed to La Cava, the Eve of Spanish history. Martín de Córdoba further links Isabel to Virgin Mary by emphasizing that Mary herself was the daughter of kings: "[L]a señora Princesa, por que es de linaje real, como la Virgen que fue fija de reyes, e por que es doncella, como hera la Virgen cuando concibio al fijo de Dios, e por que espera de ser reyna, como la Virgen que es Reyna delos cielos, señora delos angeles, madre de los pecadores e manto de todos los fieles." (The Princess, being of royal lineage, just as the Virgin was the daughter of kings, and by being a maiden, as the Virgin was when she conceived the son of God, and because she expects to be Queen, as the Virgin is Queen of Heaven, Mistress

[88] **GRIEVE, Patricia E.** (2011) The Eve of Spain; Myths of Origins in the History of Christian, Muslim, and Jewish Conflict. The Johns Hopkins University Press, Baltimore, Maryland, pp. 85-86

of the Angels, mother of sinners, and protector of the faithful;). The author returns to this theme of shared qualities between Virgin Mary and the princess when he describes the expected comportment of women who would be rulers. Although all women should incline to piety, as one of their natural virtues, a noblewoman should be the most pious of all ("avn que todas las mugeres sean naturalmente piadosas, pero las grandes lo deuen ser mas que todas";).

Amy G. Remensnyder investigated martial aspects of Virgin Mary[89]. On the other hand Elizabeth Lehfeldt[90] made clear that Virgin Mary became a model for Isabella I as ruling queen:

One of Isabel's favorite poets, fray Iñigo de Mendoza wrote that she had come by the grace of God to rescue the people whose lives had been lost by the sin of "una muger," which is to say Eve. By the twelfth century theologians had drawn parallels between the Virgin and a woman prophesied in the Book of Genesis: "I will put enmities between thee and the woman, and thy seed and her seed: she shall crush thy head, and thou shalt lie in wait for her heel." This portrayal of the woman crushing the serpent's head was the promised redemption offered by Mary. Isabel's association with this image mitigated her sexuality and her bearing of Eve's punishment of the pains of childbirth. Yet childbirth could, properly modeled and fashioned, also be redemptive. Although she had already given birth to a daughter Juana in 1470, a greater outpouring of enthusiasm greeted the birth of Isabel's first son Juan in 1478. With this act Isabel, in the eyes of her chroniclers and contemporaries, delivered Spain into the long-promised Golden Age. She had provided a male heir to the throne. Here the parallels with the Virgin were obvious. Mary had offered the world the ultimate redemption: the son of God. Isabel offered a similar redemption. She gave Castile an indisputable male heir who stood in a direct line to the throne. Pulgar suggested that God had chosen Isabel especially, rather than seeking the succession of the throne in either the offspring of Enrique or Alfonso (Isabel's brother who had died in 1468). In this Isabel had redeemed the ultimate imperfection of her own ascendance to the throne: the lack of a male heir. Yet just as Mary's human role in Christ's birth raised questions for some about her sinful nature and cast doubt on her purity, so, too, Isabel's redemptive powers in bringing forth a human son who would act as Spain's savior, seemed potentially compromised. Mary, despite her

[89] REMENSNYDER, Amy G. (2000) The Colonization of Sacred Architecture: The Virgin Mary, Mosques, and Temples in Medieval Spain and Early Sixteenth-Century Mexico," in *Monks and Nuns, Saints and Outcasts: Religious Expression and Social Meaning in the Middle Ages*, ed. Sharon Farmer and Barbara Rosenwein (Ithaca, N.Y: Cornell University Press, 2000), pp. 189-219
[90] LEHFELDT, Elizabeth A. (2000) Ruling Sexuality: The Political Legitimacy of Isabel of Castile. In: Renaissance Quarterly 53, pp. 31-46

participation in the birth of the Savior, had been granted virginal status. Hers was a conception free from the sin of sexual intercourse. From the days of the early Church, however, debate surrounded Mary's concupiscence or participation in original sin. Mary needed to be preserved from all sin in order to be "the sole proper instrument by which God became man." Although a subject of controversy into the nineteenth century before it was resolved by the papal bull *Ineffabilis Deus,* the resolution was the doctrine of the Immaculate Conception, according to which Mary was free from the burden of sin and sinful desires." Spanish intellectuals would offer a similar solution for Isabel. Her redemptive role would be likened to Mary's and although Isabel of course remained fully human, parallels were drawn between her purity and the Immaculate Conception." Devotion to the doctrine of the Immaculate Conception was particularly enthusiastic in Spain in the late Middle Ages and Renaissance. It seems to have been cultivated most prodigiously first in Aragon and Barcelona, owing largely to its championing by the famous mystic Ramón Lull."

As a member of the intellectually active court of Bishop Alonso de Cartagena, Juan Ramirez de Lucena had likely developed curiosity for anything new early in his life, which was further stimulated when his protector sent him to Italy to enter the service of the humanist Pope, Pius II (1458).

Alonso de Cartagena (1384-1456), the distinguished Bishop, diplomat, historian, courtier, and precursor of Spanish humanism was one of the major figures among these *Converso* theologians. Alonso de Cartagena (1384-1456) continued his father's path as Bishop of Burgos and also elaborated on the idea that Santa Maria family were scions of both the tribe of Levi and of Virgin Mary.

So the adoration to Virgin Mary was not new to the converted Juan Ramirez de Lucena who wrote *Vita Beata,* a fictitious dialogue between Juan de Mena, Alonso de Cartagena, and the marqués de Santillana.

According to the historian Palencia from 1475 the king was dominated by "mad love" for his wife (coactus insano erga amore uxoris) while Isabella was becoming a dubious person with unwillingness both in the domestic and public sphere". In 1479 Palencia summarizes the situation in this way: "The Queen had for a long time been preparing something

96

that according to the judgment of a prudent man is not suitable for future succession of these kingdoms: reducing the influence of her husband, just in case by her death there was any contingency in the regular course of heredity if she died earlier than her husband[91]."

The chronicler seems to allude to the determination of Isabella I of Castile that her first daughter, also named Isabella, would succeed her if necessary to the Castilian throne. Both her husband and his supporters naturally felt that he should be the heir, something that Isabella did not agree to even in his will and codicil of October and November 1504.

Madonna of the Catholic Monarchs (Fernando Gallego, 1490-1495)

---

[91] **PALENCIA, Alfonso de** (ed. 1970-1974): *Cuarta Década, estudio, texto latino y traducción castellana*, ed. de J. López de Toro, Madrid, Real Academia de la Historia, 2 vols., pp. 2, 38, 48, 164, 192. Cited by **EDWARDS, John** (2004). Isabel la Católica: poder y fama, p. 71.

In any event, Alfonso de Palencia[92] described Isabella as a "master of disguises and deceptions" as a direct result of his criticism of the queen and defending his professional integrity in Toledo in 1480[93].

Was it the intentional campaign of propaganda used by Isabella to raise herself as an equally pure woman as the Virgin?

Lucio Marineo Sículo[94] said that Isabella had "desires of high praises and clear fame". Isabella, now with the help of Pedro González de Mendoza, knew how to use the church for her cause. Castilla would be a valuable ally for the papacy, and the Pope could use this alliance to weaken either Aragon or France, the two main external threats in Italian politics. The great power of Castile and decline of the Crown of Aragon markedly towards Castilian habits explain the character of modern Spain. Bernat Fenollar, the poet who made the new rules in *Scachs d'amor,* already felt the changes in an early stage.

Le Roman de la Rose, started by Guillaume de Lorris ca. 1230 with 4000 verses and completed in a different style in ca. 1270-80 by Jean de Meun with 1800 verses. This time with chess allegories made under Jacobus de Cessolis's book. *De moribus hominum et de officiis nobilium super ludo scaccorum* was written between 1300 and 1330 by Jacobus de Cessolis, was a very popular chess book in the Middle Ages because it talks about morality and good government. Evrart de Conty had his inspiration from *Roman de la Rose* and the work of Jacques de Cessolis, writing a chess work in verse called *Les eschéz d'amour* (*Eschés amoureux)* around 1375. In 1405 we see appear his work *Le livre des*

---

[92] **SANTA MARIA, Luys** (1958). Isabel la Católica, pp. 15-58 and 61-71. Cited by **EDWARDS, John** (2004). Isabel la Católica: poder y fama, p. 71.

[93] **TATE, Robert Brian.** (1994). Políticas sexuales: de Enrique el Impotente a Isabel, maestra de engaños. In: **HITCHCOCK, Richard & PENNY, Ralph,** eds., *Actas del Primer Congreso Anglo-Hispano, III: Historia. In memoriam Derek Lomax,* Madrid, pp. 165-176. Cited by **EDWARDS, John** (2004). Isabel la Católica: poder y fama, p. 71.

[94] **FERNÁNDEZ DE CÓRDOVA MIRALLES, Álvaro** (2005) Imagen de los Reyes Católicos en la Roma pontificia. In: En la España Medieval, 28, pp. 259-354. Citation in p. 263.

eschéz amoureux moralisés that was written in prose. The manuscript *Scachs d'amor* was under French influence and for the first time in Spain we see the word "dama" appear. Maybe it also had to do with the *Le Champion des dames*, a work written by Martin Le Franc between 1442 and 1443 and dedicated to Philip the Good of Burgundy[95].

Strangely enough the poem of *Scachs d'amor* was never published in any work, although the changes of the queen and bishop[96] were new and rather important. Until now nobody could give an explanation for the new increasing move of the bishop, precisely at the time of the new queen Isabella I of Castile. This was also silenced in literature. Could the poets not publish this poem due to possible problems with the justice or King Ferdinand II? Why could they not change the name of the alfil to that of the Bishop in the poem? Was any or everyone afraid to give too much power to Pedro Gonzalez de Mendoza?

[95] **LHÔTE, Jean-Marie** (2002) Martin Le Franc et la dame enragée. In: Board Game Studies, 5, pp. 105-110
[96] **WESTERVELD, Govert** (2015). The Birth of a new Bishop in Chess. 172 pages. Lulu Editors. ISBN: 978-1-326-37044-2

7.8 The Satiric School in Valencia

Bernard Fenollar formed part of the Satiric School in Valencia and was known for his satiric compositions. Rafael Alemany[97] let us know that if the crown is gradually deselecting the direction of cultural life and the religious establishment restricts the social dimension of its influence, it is clear that the stimulus that allows the 14th-century literary splendor comes from other classes. As for Valencia in particular, these are the local gentry and urban patriciate. Both will become the real drivers of the letters of the fifteenth century who benefit from the great possibilities that gave the printing houses in this city. In this context occurs one of the most significant cultural developments: the emergence of new platforms such as the literary circles on the one hand and poetry contests on the other hand. An example of the literary circles is Bernat Fenollar's poetic circle where Jaume Gassull, Narcis Vinyoles, Francesc de Castellví, Joan Moreno, et al are integrated. All these writers are characterized by cultivating poetry, especially but not exclusively satirical, in which the burlesque treatment of erotic and sexual material acquires a notable role, as well as the fact of producing their work collaboratively: indeed, the great constants of this literary circle are works written by more than one author, debates, questions, and answers.

Jaume Roig (ca. 1400-1478), author of *Espill* or *Llibre de les dones*, started with the Valencian satiric school. One can say that the author of *Espill* did not hate women insofar as can be seen in the work, but his misogyny was rather moralistic burlesque, in line with the Valencian Satirical School. *Espill* would be a book destined for reading by men of that time and the fact that Roig presented an exaggerated misogyny would provoke ridicule and laughter in the reader. With all this one cannot deny the misogynist nature of this work. *Espill* incorporates all antifeminist stereotypes of the Middle Ages because all the evils, all the vileness and possible crimes are attributed to women, and they have

---

[97] **ALEMANY FERRER, Rafael** (2000) Ausiàs March y las letras valencianas del s. XV: vasos comunicantes. In: Altra ed.: Lourdes Sánchez Rodrigo i Enrique J. Nogueras Valdivieso (eds.), Ausiàs March y las literaturas de su época, Granada, Universidad de Granada, 2000, pp. 111-131.

been the cause of all the ills of humanity. Only two are the exception: the Virgin Mary and Isabel Pellisser.

Was the poem intended as politic propaganda for Isabel I of Castile who had the same characteristics as the Virgin Mary or wanted the poets to mock the queen? Maybe Prof. Alcalá[98] is right when he states:

> Yo creo ver en todo esto de que la reina del ajedrez personifique a Isabel más que un elogio una especie de ironía, de tomadura de pelo por parte, precisamente, de tratadistas (Lucena, los valencianos) que o no están a su servicio, sino de Fernando, o no son ni siquiera castellanos[99], por lo cual tenían que alimentar cierto resentimiento contra una mujer que había haciendo desde el primer momento de su coronación y seguía haciendo todo lo posible para mangonear y mandar más que su marido, contra lo que tradicionalmente había pasado siempre. Me puedo imaginar a los tahures, al mover la nueva reina mandona, diciendo en las tabernas y las casas de juego: "Aí va, la mandona, la mujerona, la virago!!!"

Translation:

> I believe in all this that the chess queen does not personify Isabel I of Castile with eulogy, but rather a kind of irony, teasing by precisely from writers (Lucena, Valencian poets) who are not in her service, but in the service of Fernando. They are not even Castilians, so they had to feed resentment against a woman who since the first moment of her coronation was making every effort to bully and command more than her husband, contrary to what traditionally had always been the habit. I can imagine the gamblers moving the bossy new queen, saying in taverns and gambling dens: 'Here is the bossy big woman, the virago[100]!!!'

Interesting to see is the signification of virago in relationship with the term dama:

> A virago is a woman who demonstrates exemplary and heroic qualities. The word comes from the Latin word *vir* meaning 'man' to which the suffix -ago is added, a suffix that ...

---

[98] Personal communication
[99] With exemption of Juan Ramírez de Lucena
[100] A virago is a woman who demonstrates exemplary and heroic qualities. The word comes from the Latin word *vir* meaning 'man' to which the suffix -ago is added.

In the Spanish draughts game we know the term virol[101] that also has to do with the term dama:

Virol se entiende cuando se tiene encerrada en una calle por donde corre á una dama enemiga sin poder salir de ella.

Translation:

Virol means a position when you have locked in a line the enemy lady (dama), making it impossible for her to leave.

Whatever will be the reason of the sudden change of weak chess queen in powerful chess queen in Valencia, one thing is clear with respect to her name abroad. There the powerful was received in a mocky way:

échecs de la dame *enragée*"	- France
"alla rabiosa"	- Italy
"Welsches-*Schachspiel*	- *Germany*
"Mad Queen Chess"	- *Great Britain*

The control that the Church exercised was felt throughout the peninsula in those years. The Virgin Mary was adored by the whole population. That was the reason, that we see appear in Valencia many books about the Virgin Mary. Worth mentioning is the fact that in the book *Homelia sobre lo psalm "De profundis"*, printed in the printing house of Lambert Palmart, readers see a splendid image of the Virgin Mary[102].

---

[101] **PIFERRER, Juan Francisco** (1839) Juego de las damas, Barcelona, p. 3
GARCÍA CANALEJAS, Juan (1650) Libro del juego de las damas dividido en tres tratados, Zaragoza, p. 95
[102] **FUSTER, Jeronim** (1490). Homelia sobre lo psalm "De profundis".

Date	Author	Work
1487.04.14	DIEZ, Fernando	Obra de la sacratissima concepció de la Verge Maria. Valencia: Lambert Palmart, 14 Apr. 1487
1493.01.11	FENOLLAR, Bernat MARTINEZ, Pere	Història de la passió de N.S. Jesu Christi en cobles. Add: Johan Scrivá: Contemplaciò a Jesus crucificat. Joan Roiç de Corella: Oració a la S. Verge Maria tenint son fill Jesus deuallat de la creu. Valencia: [Peter Hagembach and Leonardus Hutz], for Jacobus de Villa.
1494.07.25	PEREZ, Miguel	Vida de la Verge Maria. Valencia: Nicolaus Spindeler.
1495.02.16	SAXONIA, Ludolphus de	Vita Christi [Catalan] Lo quart del Cartoxá (Tr: Joan Roiç de Corella). Add: Joan Roiç de Corella: Oració a la S. Verge Maria tenint son fill Jesus deuallat de la creu. Valencia: [Peter Hagembach and Leonardus Hutz].
1495.11.06	SAXONIA, Ludolphus de	Vita Christi [Catalan] Lo quart del Cartoxá (Tr: Joan Roiç de Corella). Add: Joan Roiç de Corella: Oració a la S. Verge Maria tenint son fill Jesus deuallat de la creu. Valencia: [Lope de la Roca, for Miquel Albert].

Draw of the Virgin Mary in the book *Homelia sobre lo psalm "De profundis"*

7.9 The unfortunate Maria de Castilla

Outside Castile the wife of Alfonso V of Aragon (Alfonso the Magnanimou) and daughter of Henry III occupied an important place in history. Her name was Maria de Castilla and she excelled in the chronicle as a positive model for the Queen. She was the aunt of Isabel I of Castile and highlighted the key benchmark of claiming politic leadership by Isabel. This Maria de Castilla:

> Governó los reynos de Aragón por espacio de treynta años seyendo absente su marido ocupado en la guerra de Napol con tanta prudencia e justicia que los tobo este tiempo en tanta paz e concordia como nunca antes ni después estuvieron, e bivió en tanta honestad que por todos fue llamada espeio de limpieza e de toda bondad e no menos a toda virtud se dio[103].

Translation:

> Governed the kingdoms of Aragón for thirty years while her husband was absent due to being occupied in the war of Naples. She did it with so much prudence and justice in those years that peace and harmony were obtained as never before and neither thereafter. This queen lived in such way of honesty that she was called mirror of cleanness and all goodness and not least of all virtue.

Agusti Mezquida, a filmmaker, considers that the appearance of the dama (lady) in *Scachs d'amor* (1475) could be more related to Maria of Castile (1401-1458), the consort of Alfonso the Magnanimous (1396-1458). However, this unfortunate queen was disowned by her husband for thirty years and she never was more important than Alfonso the Magnanimous. On the contrary the king did not mention her in his testament and had children by Lucrecia de Alagno (ca. 1430-1479) whom he could not marry. Although the king requested to marry Lucrecia, Pope Calixto III did not agree to repudiate his wife Maria de Castile.

---

[103] **VALERA, Diego de** (1959) *Tratado de las epístolas*, Biblioteca de Autores Españoles, vol. CXVI, Madrid, 1959, fol. 153v.

Quite different was the situation for Isabella I of Castile who had preeminence over Ferdinand who was an instrument of blind obedience to Isabel. Apart from that there is a problem of time; Maria de Castile died about twenty years earlier than the date of the poem *Scachs d'amor*. Isabella did not want to live like her aunt and had taken the necessary steps to avoid that. With regards to the preeminence Alfonso de Palencia said[104]:

> The new queen is preceded by Gutierrez de Cardenas who takes a naked sword caught by the tip, the handle up, in the Spanish style, so that, seen by all, even the most distant approaching knew that she would punish the guilty with real authority. This was not a custom of queens. Ferdinand did not please it. This lust for power by the queen would be a cause of constant friction. It was a clear and evident sign of her preeminence over Fernando.

---

[104] **PALENCIA, Alonso.** (1904-1914) *Crónica de Enrique IV escrita en latín por Alfonso de Palencia*. Traducida y prologada por Antonio Paz y Melia. Madrid, Década II, libro II, p. 155ª. Década III, libro III, p. 46ª y Década III, libro II p. 292ª: *"Castellani autem regem suum incusabant quod neglexisset opem fere suis et opes multas hosti dimisisset in opprobrium clademque suorum atque hostium sublimationem"*.

King Alfonso the Magnanimous in his chamber of the royal palace,
accompanied by his confessor Fray Joan of Casanova.

Maria de Castilla represented in the book of privilegis i ordinacions dels
Hortolans de Sant Antoni de Barcelona (ordinances and privileges of the Sant
Antoni's Gardeners of Barcelona)
(Historical Archives of the City of Barcelona,
Fund guild 2-1 XV-century).

The use of the sword could not cause astonishment to the three poets of *Scachs d'amor* in the kingdom of Aragon, contrary to the assertions of Palencia. Although women of royal blood were displaced from the ownership of the throne, they had an important and effective role as governors or lieutenants of the king in this kingdom when the king was not personally there to exercise power or justice. In the minds of many it would not be possible to erase the image of Mary of Castile, wife of Alfonso the Magnanimous who met other representatives of the kingdom in councils, courts, and assemblies. The figure of Maria of Castile has been immortalized precisely in a legislative assembly before Barcelona's councilors, sitting on her throne with crown and sword in hand, symbolizing justice as shown in the illustration on the cover of the gloss of the *Comentaris dels Usatges* of Barcelona, dedicated to the very queen by the author James Marquilles[105].

**Folio of the *Commentaria super Usaticis Barchinonensis* (Comentaris dels Usatges de Barcelona).
Legal work of James Marquilles (1448-1450)**

---

[105] **CARRASCO MANCHADO, Ana Isabel** (2006) Isabel I de Castilla y la sombra de la ilegitimidad: propaganda y representación en el conflicto sucesorio (1474-1482). Madrid, p. 30

7.10 Conclusion:

The introduction of a new powerful chess queen (Dama) took place in Spain. According to Cessolis, the order of the board pieces of Chess is the order of the world. Martín de Córdoba, in 1468, linked Isabel I of Castile to Virgin Mary. This new game had to do with the term Virgin Mary when the three poets participated in a hymn competition of 1474 to the Holy Virgin. We see one year later, in 1475, the activity of Dr. Miguel Albert as protector of the printing houses and a poem by the three poets about this new powerful chess queen. Twenty years later, in 1495, as a print shop owner Dr. Miguel Albert also edited with the German printers Peter Trincher and Lope de la Roca (Wolf of Stone) the unfortunately lost chess book of Vicent Francesch. It is known that the protonotary Juan Ramirez de Lucena was already in the Aragonese court around 1468 and that he was one of the advisers of the young prince Ferdinand II, the future husband of queen Isabella I of Castile. Virgin Mary's influence was great in those years and the church extended it in Valencia to the chessboard. The man who had influence in the court to change the rules of the chess game was the protonotary Juan Ramírez de Lucena, follower of the pope Pius II. He was a great admirer of Isabella I of Castile and his protector was the archbishop of Seville and great cardinal of Spain, Pedro Gonzalez de Mendoza. Due to his travelling abroad he was aware of the necessary chess manuscripts and chess positions that later resulted in a chess book printed by his son Lucena in 1495. The manuscript of "Scachs d'amor" was written in 1475, precisely in the year of pestilence in Valencia and when the influence of Queen Isabella I of Castile reached the peak of her power against her husband Ferdinand II of Aragon. And so we see appear Isabella I of Castile, as the Virgin Mary, on the chessboard.

8 The mysterious Lucena

We are still to find out who is behind the pseudonym Lucena. In the meantime I have discarded the figure of Juan del Encina and we have the figure of Francesch Vicent, which according to Garzón has nothing to do with Lucena. In this great puzzle we cannot forget that the protonotary had two children (hijos). Maybe he referred to his son and daughter. However, the Spanish word *hijos* does not make it clear in his letter to Rey Ferdinand in 1503, hence I hypothetically take the two sons, seeing Lucena's great activities with books in Spain and Italy. In other words, Lucena was had helpers. That is, if we find the name of a son, we probably still have to find the other. Two of the helpers could have been Fernando de Rojas and Juan del Encina. Fernando de Rojas, because many of the books in his possession had to do with Lucena's writing activities. On the other hand Juan del Encina was always travelling and could have been occupied with printing activities in Italy and Spain.

8.1 Lucena's Repetición de amores

The language of Lucena's *Repetición de amores* (1497) is somewhat archaic, so that one automatically speculates on the father's Autorship. By somewhat studying the language Rolf Eberenz showed us that the examples of tendr... and vendr... in the literary texts are few[106], but Lucena, son of the protonotary Juan Ramírez de Lucena, is one of the few Autors who uses them in *Repetición de amores*. Consequently the way of writing in this way will be an excellent additional tool to find out possible works of Lucena. And by applying this tool we saw a lot of our hypotheses confirmed in previous years. After many trials and studies I

---

[106] **EBERENZ, Rolf** (1998) La reproducción del discurso oral en las actas de la Inquisición (siglos XV y XVI). In: **OESTERREICHER, Wulf; STOLL, Eva; WESH, Andres** (1998) Competencia escrita, tradiciones discursivas y variedades lingüísticas. Aspectos del español europeo y americano en los siglos XVI y XVII. Gunter Narr Verlag, Tübinge, pp. 243-268. Citation on p. 254

consider that Lucena could have been involved with some of the following books:

Occurence of the endings of the words *tendr..* and *vendr..*

Year	Author	Book	tendr	vendr	pondr
1482	Anonym	*Esopete ystoriado*	1		
1489	Anonym	*Linda Melosina*	5		
1490	Anonym	*Crónica Troyana*	1		
1491	Anonym	*Los siete sabios de Roma*	4		
1491	Alonso de Santa Cruz	*Crónica de los Reyes Católicos*	4		
1492	Diego de San Pedro	*Cárcel de amor*	7	0	1
1492	Anonym	*La corónica de Adramón*	33		
1493	Gonzalo García de Santa María	*Evangelios e epistolas*		11	
1493	Anonym	*Traducción del Tratado de cirugía de Guido de Cauliaca*	2		
1494	Fray Vicente de Burgos	*Traducción de El libro de Propietatibus Rerum de Bartolomé Anglicus*	3		
1494	Anonym	*Traducción del Tratado Phisonomía en breue summa contenida..*	1		
1495	Juan de Flores	*Grisel*	11	2	
1495	Francisco de Prato	*Primera respuesta informe de Francisco de Prato*	2		
1496	Garci Rodriguez de Montalvo	*Amadis*	59	42	5
1496	Lucas Fernández	*Derreniego de amor*	1		
1497	Lucena	*Repetición de amores*	1	?	
1498	Francisco López de Villalobos	*Sumario de la medicina con un compendio sobre las pestíferas*	1		
1500	Fernando de Rojas	*Tragicomedia de Calisto y Melibea*	18	16	
1500	Anonym	*Tratado medico*	1		

1500	Anonym	Libro de recetas. Salamanca, Universitaria	1		
1501	Anonym	Tristán de Leonís	3		1
1502	Anonym	Leyes del estilo	1		
1504	Anonym	Thebayda	21	13	
1506	Diego Álvarez Chanca	Tratado nuevo no menos útil que necesario en que se declara....	1		2
1509	Anonym	Traducción del Tratado de cirugía de Tedrico	1		
1511	Anonym	Traducción de Tirante de Blanco	7		1
1511	Anonym	Palmerín de Olivia	32		3
1512	Anonym	Primaleón	68		6
1512	Anonym	Crónica popular del Cid	2		
1512	Juan de Ortega	Composición del arte de la aritmética y geometría	131		37
1512	Anonym	Cavallero cifar	3		
1513	Diego López de Cortegana	Asno de oro	4	1	
1513	Gabriel Alonso de Herrera	Obra agricultura	1		
1514	Feliciano de Silva	Lisuarte de Grecia	16	3	1
1514	Jiménez de Urrea, Pedro Manuela	Penitencia de amor	3		
1516	Hernán Díaz	El Peregrino	44	18	
1517	Juan de Molina	Libro del esforzado caballero Arderique	5		2
1517	Bartolomé Torres Naharro	Himenea	1		
1521	Anonym	Seraphina (Thebayda)	9	1	
1524	Bartolomé Torres Naharro	Calamita		1	
1524?	Fernán Pérez de Oliva	Amphitrion	2		
1524	Fernán Pérez de Oliva	Razonamiento sobre la navegación del Guadalquivir	1		

Year	Author	Work			
1524	Juan de Molina	*Traducción de la Crónica de Aragón*	1		
1525?	Fernán Pérez de Oliva	*Historia de la invención de las Yndias*	1		
1525	Anonym	*Manual de mugeres en el qual se contienen muchas y diversas reçeutas muy buenas*	2		13
1526	Juan Díaz	*Lisuarte de Grecia*		3	
1526	Anonym	*Polindo*	10		
1526	Fernando de Rojas	*Traso auto Celestina*	2		
1527	Fray Bartolomé de las Casas	*Historia de las Indias*	1		
1527	Alfonso de Valdés	*Diálogo de las cosas sucedidas en Roma*	2	1	
1528	Juan Justiniano Traductor de Luis Vives	*Formación de mujer Tratado sobre la educación de la mujer cristiana*	50		3
1529	Fray Antonio de Guevara	*Reloj de príncipes*	2		
1529	Anonym Alfonso de Valdés	*Diálogo de Mercurio y Carón* - libro	4	8	1
1529	Anonym (Juan de Valdés)	*Doctrina cristiana* libro	10	3	
1529	Fernán Pérez de Oliva	*Anfitrion*	2		
1530	Feliciano de Silva	*Amadís de Grecia*	34	14	
1530	Francisco Delicado	*Lozana Andaluza* Complete work	13	32	6
1530	Francisco Delicado	*Lozana Argumento*		1	
1530	Francisco Delicado	*Lozana epílogo*		1	
1530	Francisco Delicado	*Lozana dedicatorio*		1	
1532	Alonso de Virués	*Colloquio de Erasmo*	2		
1534	Feliciano de Silva	*Segunda Celestina*	21	8	3
1535?	Anonym	*Manual de mugeres*	3		

114

1535?	Juan de Valdés	*Evangelio de San Mateo*	16	9	
1535	Gonzalo Fernández de Oviedo	*Historia general y natural de las Indias*	3		
1525	Gonzalo Fernández de Oviedo	*Batallas y quinquagenas*	2		
1536	Gaspar Gómez de Toledo	*Tercera parte de la Tragicomedia de Celestina*	43	4	10
1536	Diego de Salazar	*Tratado de Re Militari*	2		
1537	Alejo de Vanegas	*Agonia del transito de la muerte*	3	3	
1537	Ludovico Scrivá Luis Escrivá	*Tribunal de Venus Veneris tribunal*	3		1
1537	Anonym	*Tratado anónimo de arquitectura*	2		
1537	Juan de Valdés	*Alfabeto*	36		4
1538	Pedro Ciruelo	*Reprobación de las supersticiones y hechicerías*	4		1
1539	Fray Antonio de Guevara	*Arte de marear*	1		
1540	Pedro Mejía	*Silva de varia lección*	6		2
1540	Hugo de Celso	*Repertorio universal de todas las leyes de estos reinos de Castilla*	8		
1541	Anonym	*Relación de las cerimonias y rictos y población....*	10		
1542	Sancho de Muñón	*Tercera Celestina Lysandro y Roselia*	6	6	2
1542	Anonym	*Baldo*	1		
1542	Diego del Castillo	*Tratado de cuentas*	2		
1543	Jorge de Montemayor	*Diálogo spiritual*	38		3
1543	Juan de Boscán	*Las obras de Boscán con algunas de Garcilaso de la Vega*	1		
1543	Fray Domingo de Soto	*Deliberación en la causa de los pobres*	2		

1545?	Diego Hurtado de Mendoza	*Arcadia*	2		
1545	Diego Hurtado de Mendoza	*Traducción de la Mechánica de Aristóteles*	1		
1545?	Anonym	*Sermón de Aljubarrota con las glosas de Diego Hurtado de Mendoza*	5		
1545	Diego Hermosilla	*Diálogo de los pajes en que se trata de la vida que a mediados del siglo XVI llevaban en los palacio*	16		
1546	Francisco Cervantes de Salazar	*Introducción para el camino de sabiduría*	2		
1547	Jerónimo Fernández	*Belianis de Grecia*	61		7
1547	Sebastián Fernández	*Tragedia Policiana*	10	6	1
1547	Diego Hurtado de Mendoza	*Caronte*	1		
1548	Lope de Rueda	*Las aceitunas*	6		
1548	Anonym	*Traducción de la Cosmografía de Pedro Apiano*	1		
1549	Martin Reyna	*El juego de ajedrez*	1		
1549	Francisco Sánchez de las Brozas	*Traducción de la Declaración y uso del relox español....*	6		
1549	Jerónimo de Urrea	*Traducción de "Orlando furioso" de Ludovico Ariosto*	75		3
1549	Anonymn	*Crónica del Rey Henrico Octavo de Inglaterra*	11		
1550	Pedro Lujan	*Coloquios matrimoniales*	14		1
1550	Juan Pastor	*Tragedia de la castidad de Lucrecia*	2		
1550	Juan de Arce de Otárola	*Coloquios de Palatino y Pinciano*	12		3
1550	Luis de PLinedo	*Libro de chistes*	1		

1550	Diego Hurtado de Mendoza	*Carta del Bachiller de Arcadia al capitán Salazar*	2		
1550	Alonso de Santa Cruz	*Crónica del Emperador Carlos V*	121		
1551	Feliciano de Silva	*Florisel de Niqua-4 Libro XI Amadís*	1	0	
1551	Juan de Betanzos	*Suma y narración de los incas*	2		
1551	Juan de Luna	*Lazarillo segunda parte*		3	
1551	Martín Cortés Albacar	*Breve compendio de la esfera y de la arte de navegar*	3		1
1552	Alonso Núñez de Reinoso	*Clareo y Florisea*	16	3	1
1552	Antonio de Torquemada	*Manual de escribientes*	24		
1552	Villalón	*Viaje a Turquía*	1		
1552	Francisco López de Gomara	*Historia General de las Indias*	18		
1552	Luis de Lucena	*Testamento*	1		
1552	Diego Núñez Alba	*Diálogos de la vida del soldado*	12		
1552	Pedro Hernández de Villaumbrales	*Peregrinación de la vida del hombre*	11		1
1552	Fray Bartolomé de las Casas	*Brevísima relación de la destrucción de las Indias*	1		
1553	Diego Núñez Alba	*Dedicatoria al señor don Fernandálvarez de Toledo*	2		
1553	Antonio de Torquemada	*Coloquios satíricos*	30		
1553	Perálvarez de Ayllón	*Comedia tibalda*	2		
1554	Alonso de Villega	*Comedia Selvagia*	36	10	1
1554	Juan Rodríguez Florián	*Florinea*	73		4
1554	Anonym	*Repertorio de los tiempos, el cual tura desde el año MDLIV hasta el año MDCII*	1		

1555	Anonym	*Segunda parte del Lazarillo de Tormes*	4		
1555	Diego Ortúñez de Calahorra	*Espejo de príncipes y caballeros*	100		
1556	Francisco de Enzinas	*El Testamento nuevo*	3		
1556	Francisco de Sosa	*Endecálogo contra "Antoniana Margarita"*	2		
1557	Juan de Valdés	*Comentario o declaración familiar y compendiosa sobre..*	15		
1558	Bernardo de Quirós	*Viaje a Turquía*	1		
1560	Francisco Cervantes de Salazar	*Crónica de la nueva España*	15		7
1560?	Sebastián de Horozco	*Cancionero*	9		
1579	Juan Huerte de San Juan	*Examen ingenios*	2		
1579	Jerónimo Fernández	*Hector*	17		

I already published some studies where I observed that Juan de Flores, Diego de San Pedro, Hernán Díaz, and other anonymous authors were none other than Lucena[107].

Taking the different linguistic analysis of Rolf Eberenz into account we observe that Lucena's linguistic style, that is to say the endings of the

---

[107] **WESTERVELD, Govert** (2018). Draughts and La Celestina's Creator Francesch Vicent (Lucena), Author of: Peregrino y Ginebra, signed by Hernando Diaz. 412 pages. Lulu Editors. 978-0-244-05324-6

WESTERVELD, Govert (2018). Diego de San Pedro and Juan de Flores: the Pseudonyms of Lucena, the Son of Doctor Juan Ramírez de Lucena. Lulu Editors. 428 pages. Lulu Editors. ISBN: 978-0-244-72298-2

WESTERVELD, Govert (2018). Doubt About the Authorship of Asno de oro Published in Seville around 1513. 225 pages. KDP Amazon Editors. ISBN: 978-1-792-03946-1

WESTERVELD, Govert (2019). *El Lazarillo,* initiated by Lucena and finished by Bernardo de Quirós. 282 pages. KDP Amazon Editors. 978-1-793-28591-1

words in tendr/vendr/pondr, is still manifested in the works after the death of Juan del Encina and Fernando de Rojas.

I already observed this linguistic style of Lucena in the work of Sancho de Muñón who was referring to a forthcoming book of Héctor. Sancho de Muñón who appears to be Lucena according to my analysis, used the pseudonym Jerónimo Fernández in 1547 to publish the book *Belianis de Grecia*.

Occurrence of the endings of the words *tendr..*, *vendr..* and *pondr..*

Year	Author	Book	tendr..	vendr..	Pondr..
1542	Sancho de Muñón	*Tercera Celestina Lysandro y Roselia Prólogo*	6	6	2 1
1543	Juan de Boscán	*Las obras de Boscán con algunas de Garcilaso de la Vega*	1		
1543	Jorge de Montemayor	*Diálogo espiritual*			3
1545	Lope de Rueda	*Comedia llamada de "Los engañados"*	1		
1545?	Diego Hurtado de Mendoza	*Arcadia*	2		
1546	Francisco Cervantes de Salazar	*Introducción para el camino de sabiduría*	2		
1546	Gonzalo Fernández de Oviedo	*Laberinto*		2	1
1547	Jerónimo Fernández	*Belianis de Grecia*	10		7
1547	Sebastián Fernández	*Tragedia Policiana*	10	6	1
1547	Diego Hurtado de Mendoza	*Caronte*	1		
1548	Lope de Rueda	*Las aceitunas*	6		
1549	Martin Reyna	*El juego de ajedrez*	1		
1549	Jerónimo de Urrea	*Traducción de "Orlando furioso" de Ludovico Ariosto*			3

1550	Jerónimo de Urrea	*Clarisel de las flores*			1
1550	Martín de Santander	*Comedia Rosabella*			1
1550	Pedro Lujan	*Coloquios matrimoniales*	3		1
1550	Juan de Arce de Otárola	*Coloquios de Palatino y Pinciano*			3
1550	Anónimo	*Leyenda de Alejandro Magno*			1
1551	Feliciano de Silva	*Florisel de Niqua-4 Libro XI Amadís*	1	0	
1551	Juan de Luna	*Lazarillo segunda parte*		3	
1551	Martín Cortés Albacar	*Breve compendio de la esfera y de la arte de navegar*			1
1552	Alonso Núñez de Reinoso	*Clareo y Florisea*	10	3	1
1552	Bernardo de Quirós	*Viaje a Turquía*	1		8
1552	Francisco López de Gomara	*Historia General de las Indias*	18		3
1552	Luis de Lucena	*Testamento*	1		
1552	Diego Núñez Alba	*Diálogos de la vida del soldado*	6		
1552	Fray Bartolomé de las Casas	*Tratado sobre los indios que han sido hechos esclavos*	1		
1552	Pedro Hernández de Villaumbrales	*Peregrinación de la vida del hombre*			7
1554	Alonso de Villega	*Comedia Selvagia*	36	10	1
1554	Juan Rodríguez Florián	*Florinea*	74		4
1554	Alonso de Villega	*Selvagia*	37		
1555	Anonym	*El Lazarillo Segunda parte*			1

These occurrences open a door of hope for the search for Lucena's real name. It is necessary to find the author who could have written *La Repetición de amores* and *La Celestina*, which originate before the year 1480 and still live at least until 1554.

8.1.1 Revealing the pseudonym Lucena

We have developed a list of authors from the fifteenth and sixteenth centuries (Appendix 15.1.1.) and finally come to a list of 5 people. Which of them is the mysterious Lucena? And is his possible brother among them?

Possible authors of the pseudonym of Lucena

N°	Birth	Death	Author
1	1478	1553	Núñez de Toledo, Hernán
2	1480?	1554	Rodríguez Florián, Juan
3	1486?	1554	Silva, Feliciano de
4	1478	1557	Fernández de Oviedo, Gonzalo
5	1480?	1558	Montaña de Monserrate, Bernardino de

9 Lucena and draughts

As we can read in Appendix II of one of my books[108] in 1997 I held the opinion that the majority of texts figuring in the book of Timoneda printed in 1635 belonged to the work of Antonio de Torquemada[109] printed in 1547. In 2004 I stated in another book[110] that I could not believe that Torquemada could have written a draughts book and that I believed more in Juan de Timoneda[111] around 1547. This hypothesis was confirmed by the research and book of José Antonio Garzón Roger[112]. As we know, Juan de Timoneda was a plagiarist of many books, and that is why we have to think of another author of the texts figuring in the book of 1635[113].

---

[108] **WESTERVELD, Govert** (2015) El Ingenio ó Juego de Marro, de Punta ó Damas de Antonio de Torquemada (1547), pp. 102-111. ISBN: 978-1-326-40451-2

[109] **WESTERVELD, Govert** (1997) De invloed van de Spaanse koningin Isabel la Catolica op de nieuwe sterke dame in de oorsprong van het dam- en modern schaakspel. (The influence of the queen Isabel la Catolica on the new powerful dama in the origin of the draughts and modern chess game), Beniel, Chapter 12, pp. 227-236. ISBN: 84-605-6372-3

[110] **WESTERVELD, Govert** (2004) La reina Isabel la Católica, su reflejo en la dama poderosa de Valencia, cuna de ajedrez moderno y origen del juego de damas. In collaboration with José Antonio Garzón Roger, Valencia. Generalidad Valenciana, Secretaria Autonómica de Cultura, pp. 313-323. ISBN: 84-482-3718-8

[111] **WESTERVELD, Govert** (2004) La reina Isabel la Católica: See chapter 4 of this book

[112] **GARZON ROGER, José Antonio** (2010) "Luces sobre el Ingenio, el pionero libro del juego llamado marro de punta, de Juan Timonedo". Centro Francisco Tomás y Valencia, UNED Alzira-Valencia

[113] **TIMONEDA, Juan** (1635) Libro llamado Ingenio, el cual trata del Juego del Marro de punta", hecho por Juan de Timoneda, Dedicado al Mvy magnifico Señnor don Ynnigo de Losca Capitan en las Galeras de España. Al qual se han annadido ocho trechas de mucho primor, por Antonio Miron y del Castillo, Tolosa

9.1 Timoneda and Antonio de Torquemada

Since 2009 Garzon and I decided to write together a historical book about Juan de Timoneda, because we are both convinced about the idea that there never existed a book about Antonio de Torquemada. However, due to serious health problems and lack of time, I suggested that Garzón write the work alone, to which he initially did not agree. After much insistence from me he fortunately decided to do the work alone and again it was Garzón who with documents confirmed my hypothesis on Torquemada and Timoneda.

José Antonio Garzón Roger
Photo: Kindness of www.chessbase.com

José Antonio Garzón Roger (Chelva, 1963) is a real specialist in chess history. He belongs to the Comission of the Chess History of the Spanish Chess Federation. Apart from that he was the man in the field of chess history responsible for the Valencian Chess Federation. He also belongs to the Ken Whyld Association in Amsterdam and the Paluzie Circle. He is a good professional journalist, writer, and marketing man. In 2009 he helped organize the International Symposium of the chess history "Valencia, Birthplace of modern chess" with great success in Valencia between 21 and 25 September, in which participated outstanding personalities, among them various chess and boardgame historians, such as Dr. Ulrich Schädler, Prof. Antoni Ferrando, Joseph Alio, José Antonio Garzón, Alessandro Sanvito, Yuri Averbakh, J.M. Fraguela, José María Gutiérrez, Lothar Schmid, Rafael Solaz, Rafael Ferrando, Thomas Thomsen, ex-world draughts champion Harm Wiersma, and Govert Westerveld.

V A L E N C I A
Cuna del Ajedrez Moderno

The symposium was held precisely during the match between Kasparov and Karpov in honor of the queen as a chess piece, which emerged from the region of Valencia in the XV century, thus setting the beginning of the modern chess rules. The organizer of the match was Don Basilio Lopez, who had received the full support of the Chess Federation of Valencia.

Yet the time had come to communicate on international level the development of the latest chess research in Spain with regards to the town of Valencia: the Jewish chess author Francesch Vicent, Queen Isabelle of Castile and Juan de Timoneda. In such case nothing is better than a symposium and so the commission organized inviting leading researchers in connection with chess and board games to the Palace of Arts in Valencia. They also remembered to invite one of the world champions of draughts, my childhood friend Harm Wiersma.

Garzon is an author of various books and articles about chess history[114]. He was granted in 2008 the journalism award Capea (Premio Capea de Periodismo).

---

[114] **GARZON ROGER, José Antonio** (2001) En pos del incunable perdido. Francesch Vicent: Llibre dels jochs partitis dels schachs, Valencia, 1495. (Prólogo Dr. Ricardo Calvo). Biblioteca Valenciana.

Consequently Garzon started with new research and was able to find the necessary proofs that the work of Torquemada about the draughts game never existed.

José Antonio Garzón Roger

The book was edited by the UNED of Valencia and Garzon presented his book on 22 June, 2010 in "Ambito Cultural" on the 6th floor of El

WESTERVELD, Govert (2004) La reina Isabel la Católica, su reflejo en la dama poderosa de Valencia, cuna de ajedrez moderno y origen del juego de damas. En colaboración con José Antonio Garzón Roger, Valencia. (Prólogo de Prof. Dr. Juan Torres Fontes). Generalidad Valenciana, Secretaria Automòmica de Cultura. ISBN: 84-482-3718-8

GARZON ROGER, José Antonio (2005) The Return of Francesch Vicent: the history of the birth and expansion of modern chess; translated by Manuel Pérez Carballo. (Foreword Anatali Karpov). Generalitat Valenciana, Consellería de Cultura, Educació i Esport: Fundación Jaume II el Just, Valencia.

GARZON ROGER, José Antonio (2007) Estudio del tratado ajedrecístico de Luca Pacioli. Valencia.

GARZON ROGER, José Antonio (2010) "Luces sobre el Ingenio, el pionero libro del juego llamado marro de punta, de Juan Timonedo". Centro Francisco Tomás y Valencia, UNED Alzira-Valencia.

Corte Ingles of Valencia, an event directed by the director of the UNED Javier Paniagua.

Ámbito Cultural de El Corte Inglés
tiene el placer de invitarle a la conferencia con
José A. Garzón
en torno a su obra
Luces sobre *ingenio*, el pionero libro sobre el juego
llamado *marro de punta*, de Juan Timoneda
El acto se celebrará el martes 22 de junio de 2010 a las 19 h.
en Ámbito Cultural de El Corte Inglés de Colón, 27 (6ª Planta).

Intervendrá:
Javier Paniagua
Director de la UNED Alzira-Valencia
Editor del libro

AJUNTAMENT DE VALÈNCIA **UNED** ·ÁMBITO **cultural**

It was a nice gesture of Garzon's to dedicate the work to me. The foreword was written by Rafael Solaz, a famous bibliophile from Valencia and expert in ancient books. Among the many points that led the research evidence surprisingly appeared the connection between the game of chess and draughts, and that the first generation of draughts players used a chess language taking it as their own language for the nascent draughts game. It seems unlikely that in such a condensed book so much evidence would be concentrated, some strong, all designed to demonstrate conclusively that Juan Timoneda published the first book in the world of the draughts game in Valencia in 1547.

Garzón has a duality that makes this type of research work much easier for him: the constancy of a historian and chess expert with extensive knowledge of technique. This faculty is not reachable by other researchers who want to delve into this type of study.

9.1.1 The definitive proof

Thanks to Garzon's research we now know that the work of Antonio de Torquemada never existed. Garzon's book is written in Spanish and in one of my books I discussed several points of his research[115].

9.2 El Juego de Marro, de Punta

Til now researchers and historians could not trace the draughts book of Antonio de Torquemada, known as the first printed draughts book in the world in Valencia in 1547. In the draughts game[116] (Spanish: Juego de damas) we have the same mystery as in the chess game. What in the chess game is the lost work of Francesch Vicent (1495), according to the historians in the draughts world we have the lost book of Antonio de Torquemada. Thus in this respect we have similar cases in the Spanish chess and draughts history. After 30 years of research, the origin of the title of the draughts book of Antonio de Torquemada (Valencia, 1547) has now finally been traced. This latest research is of great value, because there is a relationship between the texts and diagrams of the first draughts book and the texts and diagrams of the chess books of Francesch Vicent, Lucena, and Damiano.

---

[115] **WESTERVELD, Govert** (2015). El Ingenio ó Juego de Marro, de Punta ó Damas de Antonio de Torquemada. 228 pages. Lulu Editors. ISBN 978-1-326-40451-2

[116] **WESTERVELD, Govert** (2016) *The Origin of the Checkers and Modern Chess.* Volume I. Academia de Estudios Humanísticos de Blanca. Lulu editors. ISBN: 978-1-326-60212-3 - 316 pages

WESTERVELD, Govert (2017) *The Origin of the Checkers and Modern Chess.* Volume II. Academia de Estudios Humanísticos de Blanca. Lulu editors. ISBN: 978-0-244-04257-8 - 300 pages

WESTERVELD, Govert (2015) *The Origin of the Checkers and Modern Chess.* Volume III. Academia de Estudios Humanísticos de Blanca. Lulu editors. ISBN: 978-1-326-60244-4 - 312 pages

The text of the first draughts book uses Spanish from at least the mid 16th century, but what is more revealing is that it uses certain technical terms and expressions which unexpectedly situate us in the period when modern chess was introduced (together with draughts), more specifically in the last two decades where old Arab-medieval chess and modern chess coexisted in the literature: 1495-1512 (1520 at the latest)[117].

The first chess books and manuscripts are collections of problems, surprisingly like the first draughts book - the only one in the draughts bibliography. The chessbook by Ruy López of 1561 inaugurates a new phase, showing a preference for treatises on openings to the detriment of problems, which is consistent with the development of modern chess. We see the same thing happen in draughts, the books of Pedro Ruiz Montero (1591) and Lorenzo Valls (1597) were opening treatises.

Interestingly the design of the pieces used in the first draughts book is more similar to the second edition of Damiano's (1518) which is less elaborate than the 1512 edition. In the post-1524 Damiano editions the diagrams did not have any decorations. On the other hand, the decorations of the diagrams in the first draughts book look more like those in Lucena's chess book of 1497.

Garzón, in a splendid study, presented at least 14 strong points[118] to prove that the draughts book of Timoneda printed in 1635 has much to do with Lucena and Damiano.

---

[117] **GARZON ROGER, José Antonio** (2004). In: **WESTERVELD, Govert** (2004) La reina Isabel la Católica, su reflejo en la dama poderosa de Valencia, cuna de ajedrez moderno y origen del juego de damas. In collaboration with José Antonio Garzón Roger, Valencia. Generalidad Valenciana, Secretaria Autonómica de Cultura, pp. 313-323. ISBN: 84-482-3718-8

[118] **GARZON ROGER, José Antonio** (2004). In: **WESTERVELD, Govert** (2004) La reina Isabel la Católica, su reflejo en la dama poderosa de Valencia, cuna de ajedrez moderno y origen del juego de damas. In collaboration with José Antonio Garzón Roger, Valencia. Generalidad Valenciana, Secretaria Autonómica de Cultura, pp. 313-323. ISBN: 84-482-3718-8
One strong point is:

In my book about Lucena[119] I have taken as hypothesis - based on the JGAAP authorship program - that Damiano is also Lucena. The time has now come to indicate that JGAAP gave us some interesting results with regards to the book of Juan Timoneda about el *Juego de Marro* printed in 1635 in Tolosa. I found that the *Introduction* (Appendix 15.2.1) and *Epistle* (Appendix 15.2.2) were written by Gonzalo Fernández de Oviedo according to JGAAP. Anyway, we have to take into account that Professor Fuster, during my visit to him, could not believe that the poem was written by Timoneda.

The text by Timoneda uses Spanish from at least the mid 16th century, but even more revealing is that it uses certain technical terms and expressions which unexpectedly situate us in the period when modern chess was introduced (together with draughts), more specifically in the last two decades where old Arab-medieval chess and modern chess coexisted in the literature: 1495-1512 (1520 at the latest). For this reason we have analysed the Timoneda book, comparing it with the following works and printed documents on modern chess:
  - Llibre dels jochs partitis dels Schachs. Francesch Vicent, Valencia, 1495. We now know many things about this book, especially as a result of my research. The book had diagrams and contained 100 problems which were organised according to the number of plays required to solve the problems. Lucena's book had a similar structure in the form and subject matter.
- Arte de Ajedrez, Lucena, printed in Salamanca in 1497
- The MS. from El Escorial from the beginning of the 16th century
- The MS. of the Casanatense Library of Rome, dated 1511
- The book by Damiano of which the first edition is from 1512 and the second from 1518.
[119] **WESTERVELD, Govert** (in Press) *The Wanderings of the Chess Book Writer Lucena.*

9.2.1 Epistle in the draughts book

Analysing the words and expressions I found in the *Epistle* we come again to the writer Gonzalo Fernández de Oviedo.

In this book of Timoneda we observe an *Epistle* directed to Yñigo de Losca which follows:

> Epistola **endereçada** al muy magnifico señor don Yñigo de Losca Capitan en las galerias de Espanna.
> Mvy noble y magnifico señor desseando muchos dias ha, como criado menor de vuestra merced hazelie algun seruicio, y como nunca hallasse oportunidad conueniente hasta agora **en que poder** en alguna manera **cumplir mi desseo**, y ha sido que como me acordasse que entrando yo muchas vezes en las galerias a besar las manos de vuestra merced, vn criado suyo llamado Diego de Sosa, y yo començamos a iugar al **marro** que llaman de punta, acaso estauanos mirando vuestra merced y a mi parescerse fue acepto: y no me marauillo **porque en verdad** fue iestriste vida la de la galera los juegos **passatempos** de aca en alguna manera podriaser tenidos por virtud: y assi **he procurado con la maior diligencia** que me hasido possible el colegir algunas **trechas**, o **por mejor dezir** partidas del dicho juego, en las quales se hallaran muchos primores, y de todas hazer vn librillo, y como a persona a quien mas que a otra alguna desseo seruir lo he querido dedicar a vuestra merced; y aunque es **la menor cosa** que a su seruicio se puede ofrescer, recibalo v.m. con aquella benignidad que acostubre recebir los seruicios de sus seruidores. Si algunas faltas o correctiones en el vuiere saliendo la emienda de su plano tenerlas he por acertamientos pues un remedio esperauan. Y assi quedo rogando a nuestro sennor le de largos annos de vida, con **acrecentamiento de estado**: y le de gracia de hazer cosas dignas de su noble animo.

Although JGAAP states that the text of the *Epistle* is by Fernández de Oviedo, this cannot be said about the first top word that should be "que" for him.

Frequency and top words :

Word	Occurrences	Frequency
de	17	6.5%
y	12	4.6%
a	9	3.4%
en	8	3%
que	8	3%
la	5	1.9%
las	4	1.5%
como	4	1.5%
vuestra	4	1.5%
merced	4	1.5%

The frequency top word "de" was used by Juan del Encina. However, CORDE also goes in the direction of Fernández de Oviedo.

Strange words used in the epistle to Yñigo de Losca

N°	Words	Author	Cases	Other authors
1.	Endereçada(s) o(s) Enderezada(s) o(s)	Gonzalo Fernández de Oviedo	2	+50
2.	marro	Gonzalo Fernández de Oviedo	1	3
3.	Trechas	Feliciando de Silva = Gonzalo Fernández de Oviedo (Celestina)	3	10
4.	Acrecentamiento	Gonzalo Fernández de Oviedo	2	+50
5.	Pasatiempos	Diego de San Pedro	2	+50
6.	Porque en verdad	Gonzalo Fernández de Oviedo	4	22
7.	En que poder	Gonzalo Fernández de Oviedo	1	7

8.	Cumplir mi deseo	Jerónimo Fernández	1	7
9.	Por mejor dezir	Feliciando de Silva = Gonzalo Fernández de Oviedo (Celestina)	3	40
10.	He procurado con	Gonzalo Fernández de Oviedo	1	0
11.	La menor cosa	Gonzalo Fernández de Oviedo	1	17
12.	Con la mayor diligencia	Gonzalo Fernández de Oviedo	3	8

The analysis of the words made by Corpus Diacrónico del Español (CORDE) between the years 1480 and 1560 gave me the expected results since the JGAAP analysis already showed me that this text of the *Epistle* was by Gonzalo Fernández de Oviedo (Appendix 15.2.2). The words 'muy magnífico señor', 'Acrecentimiento de Estado' were used by secretaries in important documents. On the other hand I observed that the words 'cumplir mi des(s)eo' were used not only by Jerónimo Fernández, but also by the anonymous author of *El Lazarillo,* Alonso Núñez de Reinosa, and the anonymous author of *Baldo.* The expression "he procurado con" was used only by Gonzalo Fernández de Oviedo in the literature (Appendix 15.2.3).

9.2.2 Introduction in the draughts book

JGAAP states that the text of the *Introduction* of the draughts book is by Fernández de Oviedo. (Appendix 15.2.1). The same can be said about his first top word 'que'.

Frequency and top words :

Word	Occurrences	Frequency
que	27	5.6%
de	25	5.2%
y	22	4.6%
en	18	3.7%
el	16	3.3%
la	13	2.7%
las	10	2.1%
se	9	1.9%
para	8	1.7%
ha	8	1.7%

The beginning (Introduction) of the book of Timoneda states the following rules of the game of draughts:

Declaracion de la presente tabla para saber de que manera se ha de regir en iugar las siguientes trechas.

Ha de saber señor que la presente tabla que ve figurada es para iugar el juego del marro de punta, y porque mejor lo entienda assi vuestra merced, como quienlo quisiere iugar es necessario que sepa que ay en la siguiente tabla treintay dos casas blancas las quales siruen para el juego del marro de punta: y el regimiento que se ha de lleuar en la presente tabla, es por a.b.c. según se ve aquí figurado començando de la primera casa blanca en A. y en b. y en c. discurriendo hasta la vltima casa que acaba en '. Assi que quando en alguna trecha le due que juegue de peon o de dama en A. o en b. & c. ha de mirar la letra que yo señalare, y desta suerte no podra errar en ninguna manera: como largamente lo podra muy bien ver por la experiencia y pratica.

Declaracion del modo que seha detener en jugar las siguientes trechas.

Ha de saber vuestra merced que para iugarse bien las trechas del siguiente libro, es menester que quando tenga que comer, assi el blanco como el negro que ha de comer por força, y quien no comiere que pierda el juego. Y si por ventura el vno puede comer dos pieças y de otra parte vna, y come aquella y dexa de comer las dos, que pierda tambien el negro: y assi han de comer sempre las mas, porque de otra suerte no le podran jugar las siguientes trechas sino se guarda la regla presente.

Declaracion de los dos renglones questan puestos vno a cada parte del tablero.

Mas se ha de notar que se dize la parte del juego del blanco por ser su jugar aquel y el negro para hazer dama, ha de entrar en aquella parte: y assi mismo el blanco en la parte del negro.

A los que menos saben.

Ben soy cierto que algunos diran. Dexaos daquesse libro ques todo ayre y prolixidad: digo señor que los tales no entienden ninguna cosa, y el no entender ciega y priua el juyzio de la razon, porque si miran bien en el veran para lo questa aparejado: assi para saber de juego jugado, como para quando esta el juego en primor que se puede perder o ganar en vna trecha. Y mas que por marauilla acontesce jugar este iuego que no acontezca venir alguna trecha de las questan aquí puestas, y assi el que entendera este tratado vera lo que digo ser verdad, y podra dezir ser libro de mucho passatienpo y sin ofensa de la policia humana: porque teniendo vn tablero y escriuiendo en las casas blancas el A.b.c.como aquí se hos figura podra armar todas las trechas que aquí se muestra con mucho plazer.

Analysing the words and expressions that I found at the beginning of the book, which I refer to as *Introduction,* we see the pen of the writer Gonzalo Fernández de Oviedo again.

134

10 Francesch Vicent and chess

The first mention of a new powerful dama appears in chess, where the manuscript[120] Scachs d'amor of 1475 describes the new powerful dama by means of the verses of a long poem. The second mention appears in the Latin dictionary of Antonio de Nebrija[121]. The third mention appears in the first printed chess book in the world by Francesch Vicent[122], and the fourth mention in the second printed chess book in the world by Lucena[123], son of Juan Ramírez de Lucena, and ambassador of the Catholic Monarchs. The latest book of Lucena was bound with the work *Repeticion de amores*. Around this time Lucena wrote another work[124] that was lost.

The situation of Francesch Vicent is not much better than that of Lucena. After publishing his chess book in 1495 we can probably only trace the name of Francesch Vicent once.   It was that time when the chess historian Alessandro Sanvito[125] discovered that a certain Spaniard by the name of Francesco served as chessmaster of Lucrezia Borgia in March 1506. Chess historians agree that this name can refer to the chessmaster Francesch Vicent. Today we know that Lucena (Gonzalo Fernández de Oviedo) used many pseudonyms for his work. Was

---

[120] **RIBELLES COMIN, José** (1915) Bibliografia de la lengua Valenciana. "Scachs d'amor, feta per Don Françi de Castelui e Narçis Vinyoles e Mossen Fenolar, Madrid.
[121] **NEBRIJA, Antonio de** (1495) Dictionarium hispano-latinum, Salamanca. (reprint in 1951 by the Real Academia Española -Diccionario Romance (Spanish) in Latin
[122] **VICENT, Francesch** (1495) Libre dels joch partitis del Scachs en nombre de 100 ordenat e compost per mi Francesh Vicent, nat en la ciutat de Segorbe, criat e vehí de la insigne e valeroso ciutat de Valencia. Y acaba: A loor e gloria de nostre Redemtor Jesu Christ fou acabat lo dit libre dels jochs partitis dels scachs en la sinsigne ciutat de Valencia e estampat per mans de Lope de Roca Alemany e Pere Trinchet librere á XV días de Maig del any MCCCCLXXXXV
[123] **LUCENA** (1497) Repetición de amores e arte de Axedres con CL Juegos de Partido. Salamanca
[124] **LUCENA** (1497?) Tractado sobre la muerte de don Diego de Azevedo, compuesto por Lucena.
[125] **SANVITO, Alessandro (1999)** Il maestro di scacchi spagnola di Lucecia Borgia. In: L'Italia Scacchistica, issue 1131, December 1999, pp. 392 and 393

Francesch Vicent another one? The fact that there was a Spanish chessmaster by the name of Francesco is a great obstacle to fully discarding Francesch Vicent. On the other hand it is difficult to believe that Fernández de Oviedo was in Ferrara in 1506.

Consequently both Lucena and Francesch Vicent do not use their names in social life anymore either. The reason was unknown till now. We know that the father of Lucena had big problems with the Inquisition[126] and similar problems occurred in Valencia. Just in January of 1500 the famous Valencian synagogue was discovered that had been run secretly by the Vives family. Precisely in 1501 the tribunal decided to arrest those suspected of attending services and therefore many Jews tried to escape or hid[127]. There was persecution against the Jews again and it was better for them to seek safer places.

Was this also the reason for Francesch Vicent to leave Valencia or for Lucena to use the name of Francesch Vicent for his activities in Valencia?

10.1 Writings relating to Francesch Vicent

However, writers cannot suddenly disappear, because they like writing and so we have to trace the whereabouts of Lucena and Francesch Vicent, probably under other names and activities. Chess historians studied various chess manuscripts in Italy. Their findings clearly show that Francesch Vicent continued to be active not only in Ferrara, but also in Cesena, Perugia, and Rome.

---

[126] **ORTIZ, Alonso** (1493) Los tratados del doctor Alonso Ortiz. Tratado de la herida del rey. Tratado consolatorio a la princesa de Portugal. Item vna oración a los reyes en latín y en romance. Item dos cartas mensajeras a los reyes, vna que embió la cibdad, la otra el cabildo de la yglesia de Toledo. Tratado contra la carta del prothonotario de Lucena. – Sevilla, por tres Alemanes compañeros, 1493

[127] AHN, Inquisition, March 29, 1553, lib. 960, ffs. 6-6v. Cited by **HALICZER, Stephen** (1990) Inquisition and Society in the Kingdom of Valencia, 1478-1834, p. 197

10.1.1 1502-1512 MS Cesena

One anonymous chess manuscript was discovered by Dr. Franco Pratesi[128] in the Malatestiana Library (Biblioteca Malatestiana) in Cesena. This was the first European civic library and it dates back to 1452. The manuscript of Cesena of 356 pages has a lot of similarities with the Perugia Manuscript. The Codex in the register of the library is recorded as Ludi varii, idest Ludus rebellionis. Ludus subtilitatis primorum. Partiti de 2 tracti. Ludus ad capiendum ovines. The content of Francesch Vicent's chess book in the MS. 166.74 of the Malatestiana Library of Cesena was studied by José Antonio Garzón Roger[129].

10.1.2 1502-1506 MS Perugia

Another anonymous chess manuscript is the one from Perugia. Today this manuscript of 196 pages is preserved in the Augusta Library of Perugia[130] under the signature MS 775 (L.27). This manuscript, in relationship with Francesch Vicent, is not complete and was studied by Antonio Garzón Roger[131].

---

[128] **PRATESI, Franco** (1996) Il manoscritto scacchistico di Cesena. Venezia
PRATESI, Franco (1996) Il Manoscritto Scacchistico di Cesena. In: Scacchi e Scienze Aplicate. Supplement to issue 2, fascicle 16, 16 pages, Venice.
PRATESI, F. (1996).Misterioso, ma oggi un po' meno. In: Informazione Scacchi, 4. Bergamo, pp. 163-166
PRATESI, Franco (1996) Damasport, Number 3, p. 14
[129] **GARZÓN ROGER, José Antonio** (2005) *The Return of Francesch Vicent. The History of the Birth and Expansion of Modern Chess.* (Foreword Anatoli Karpov). Generalitat Valenciana, Conselleria de Cultura, Educació i Esport: Fundació Jaume II el Just, Valencia, pp. 398 and 440
[130] **SANVITO, Alessandro** (2002) Das Rätsel des Kelten-Spiels. In: Board Game Studies, Number 5, pp. 9-24. Citation on p. 19
[131] **GARZÓN ROGER, José Antonio** (2005) *The Return of Francesch Vicent. The History of the Birth and Expansion of Modern Chess.* (Foreword Anatoli Karpov). Generalitat Valenciana, Conselleria de Cultura, Educació i Esport: Fundació Jaume II el Just, Valencia, p. 398

10.1.2.1 Ludus Dominarum

In the manuscripts of Cesena (1502) as well as in the Manuscript of Perugia[132] (1503 - 1506) there is a draughts diagram under the name of Ludus dominarum and three diagrams of Ludus rebellionis. Thanks to these positions Francesch Vicent emerged to be a real innovator of new games. The Ludus dominarum is called Marro de Punta in the world's first printed book about draughts printed in Valencia[133] in 1547.

Ludus Dominarum D.

---

[132] More information about the manuscript of Perugia can be obtained from the following authors:

RONCETTI, M. (1977) Scacchi storici. Il "códice erugino". In: La Nazione, ediz. Dell'Umbria, 13-7-1977. Perugia

RONCETTI, M. (1977) Scacchi storici. Il "códice erugino". In: La Nazione, ediz. Dell'Umbria, 2-8-1977. Perugia

CHICO, A. (1984) I Misteri del Codice perugino. In: Contromossa, March 1984.

PRATESI, F. (1996) Misterioso, ma oggi un po' meno. In: Informazione Scacchi, 4. Bergamo, pp. 163-166

SANVITO, A. (1996) Il manoscritto progresista di Perugia. In: L'Italia Scacchistica. Milano

[133] **TORQUEMADA, Antonio de** (1547) El Ingenio o juego de marro de punta o damas, Valencia

There is every reason to believe that this diagram appears in the book of Francesch Vicent from 1495, because practically all the chess diagrams of the Manuscript of Cesena and Perugia appear in the lost book of Vicent too.

According to Friar Benito Ribas[134] the book of Vicent is nothing else than the "juego de las damas o ajedrez" (game of the damas or chess). This striking phrase of Ribas is confusing draughts with chess. Joseph Vargas Ponce[135] (1760-1821), a known scholar, paid a visit to the Monastery of Montserrat in 1799, an event that was recorded by Alexandre Oliver[136] too. Vargas Ponce described various works, among them the book of Francesh Vicent:

> Vicente Francisco, sobre el Juego de damas, en Valencia, 1 tomo, 4º, por Antonio López de la Roca.

Translation:

> Vicente Francisco, about the draughts (chess?) game, at Valencia, 1 Volume, 4º, by Antonio López de la Roca.

Due to the short time available and as the work is written in Valencia, Varga may have been confusing things. The fact that he mentions that the book discusses the game of draughts could have been motivated by a hurry, as he had to quickly page through the books and probably saw several times the term "de la dama" and thereafter a draughts diagram at the beginning or end of this book, such as appearing the manuscript of Cesena and Perugia. In the manuscript of Cesena the draughts diagram adjoins the first chess technical position and in the one of

[134] **DIOSDADO CABALLERO, Raymundo.** (1793) De Prima Typographiae Hispaniae. Roma, pp. 93-94.

[135] **BARAUT, Cebrià** (1968) Viatge de Joseph Vargas Ponce a Montserrat l'any 1799. In. :Miscellania Barcinonensia 7, number XVIII, 1968, pp. 7-37.

[136] **OLIVER, Alexandre** (1990) Els incunables conservats a la Biblioteca de Montserrat, Publicaciones de l'Abadia de Montserra, Barcelona.

Perugia it is destined to close the chess session[137]. It could also be possible that he was still thinking in chess with the term "juego de damas".

10.1.3 1511 Giovanni Chachi's manuscript

The Dominican Library „Regia Biblioteca Casanatense" in Rome houses an Italian chess manuscript (Cod. E. VI. 3. 4°) of Joannes Chachi from 1511. Apparently he came from Terni in Umbria[138]. The manuscript of 158 problems was bundled together with a Latin treatise about Rythomachy written by an Englishman at the instance of George Neville, Archbishop of York (1465-1476). Each problem occupies a page in the manuscript as should have ocurred in the book of Francesch Vicent (1495). According to the researches of Garzón in 2001 the author of the MS., Joannes Chachi, took the book of Vicent (1495) as base and not that one of Lucena (1497), although it was extremely related to the book of Lucena. Garzon observes[139]:

> And the MS in the Casanatense Library of Rome has 12 modern sets and 146 old ones. This last manuscript, closely related to the book of Lucena, allows us to develop our hypothesis.

> There are actually 144 problems of the old ones, for one, 92 is a fictitious problem, the famous problem in which the knight without stepping on the same square twice runs through the board, in this case half of it, both in 31 different jumps. This problem had always interested inventors and mathematicians. In the eighteenth century the subject had such illustrious passionate mathematicians as Euler and De Moivre. Euler in 1759 gave some solutions of great interest for the polygraphy forming the knight's movement. One is in the book written by Borao (Zaragoza, 1858). Interestingly, he proposed some in which it moved through half the board, and then the other half forming a closed and symmetrical polygraphy. Surprisingly the problem is presented on half board in the MS of Chachi, already in 1511.

---

[137] **GARZÓN ROGER, José Antonio** (2005) The return of Franchesch Vicent. The history of the Birth and Expansion of Modern Chess, p. 171

[138] **MURRAY, Harold J.R.** (1913). A History of Chess, pp. 727-733.

[139] **GARZON ROGER, JOSÉ ANTONIO** (2001). En Pos del Incunable perdido Francesh Vicent: Llibre dels jochs partitis dels schachs, Valencia, p. 121.

This type of springing using the horse brings us back to the father of Lucena, the prothonotary Juan Ramirez de Lucena[140], who was an expert in encrypted language or cryptographer[141]. Murray gives full details of this manuscript from 1511 and among many observations states[142]:

> This MS. has a special interest as dating for the transition period when the old and the modern game were co-existent; Chachi must have known both varieties of chess, for he has not added any note as to the difences between the two games or their respective rules. Either does he give any indication as to which game was the more popular with players or problem-lovers.

10.1.4 1512 The chess book of Damiano

The chess book of Damiano was printed in Rome in 1512 by Stephen Guillireti and Herenles Nani. The work by means of a foreword was dedicated to Sr. Joangeorgio Caesarino Romano. The book (Appendix 15.4.3) and foreword (Appendix 15.4.4) were written by Lucena according to JGAAP[143].

By 2004 it was clear to me that this personage whose name was Damiano was a pseudonym[144] for our Francesch Vicent, in service of

---

[140] **WESTERVELD, Govert** (2015) *The Ambassador Juan Ramirez de Lucena, the Father of the Chess Book Writer Lucena.* 226 pages. Lulu Editrs. ISBN: 978-1-326-37728-1

[141] **PAZ Y MELIA, A.** (1892) (editor): *Opúsculos literarios de los siglos XIX a XVI* (Madrid: Sociedad de Bibliófilos Españoles, Vita Beata, p. 200

[142] **MURRAY, H. J. R.** (1913) *A History of Chess.* Oxford University Press, pp. 727-733

[143] The Java Graphical Authorship Attribution Program

[144] Garzón has found an encrypted message on the (3) covers of the 2nd edition of Damian (1518). In one of them they are marked in black letters V, E, T, of the word "QUESTO". These letters make up the name of the author of *Segorbe* = VicEnT. But there are more encrypted messages clarified by Garzón. A mystery clarified five centuries later. Cf. **GARZÓN ROGER, José Antonio** (2005) *Vicent y Damiano. La expansión del ajedrez moderno en Italia. El misterio del tratado de 1512,* In: *El regreso de Francesch Vicent. La historia del nacimiento y expansión del ajedrez*

141

Lucrecia Borgia as a master of chess who did not want his name to appear anywhere because of possible problems with the Holy Inquisition. But this dared thought was nothing new. The Portuguese Dagoberto Markl had arrived at the same conclusion by 2001. Dagoberto Markl did not believe in the author Damiano, but rather in the Hebrew doctor Judah Abrabanel (c.1465-1523) whose work *Dialoghi d'Amore With the Pseudonymous Leo the Hebrew* is known from 1535. On the other hand it is believed that the author of the work had passed away in 1524[145]. That suggests that converted Jews probably used pseudonyms to distance themselves with more freedom.

Consequently, Damiano wrote a chess book in Rome in 1512 that appears to be a pseudonym for Francesch Vicent (Lucena?). This is followed by the editions of Damiano in Rome in 1518, 1524 and 1535. Antonio Blado printed the chess book of Damiano in 1524 and was involved in the tricky printing of *La Celestina* in 1520, which bears the year 1502 and was destined for Antonio de Salamanca who was an editor in Rome.

10.1.5 1525 Liber Scacchorum

Marco Gerolamo Vida was a major Italian poet and scholar who allegedly began to write a Latin manuscript with the poem of *Scacchia Ludus* or *De ludo scaccorum* in 1507, which ended in 1510. The poem was instructed by Federico Fregoso, son of Gentile Feltria de Montefeltro. Murray[146] tells us that in 1525 a work was published with

---

moderno, Generalidad Valenciana, Fundación Jaime II el Just, pp. 458-478. Citation on pp. 465-468

[145] **ALLIEVI, Roberto** (2004) *Il libro di Damiano da Odemira*, In: *L'Italia scacchistica*, N° 1168, May 2004, pp. 164-171

MARKL, Dagoberto (s.a.), *Damiano portogese dito Damiao de Odemira*, Alguns esclarecimientos. (www.al-shatrandj.com). Cited by **GARZÓN ROGER, José Antonio** (2005) *Vicent y Damiano, La expansión del ajedrez moderno en Italia. El misterio del tratado de 1512.* In: *El regreso de Francesch Vicent, La historia del nacimiento y expansión del ajedrez moderno,* Generalidad Valenciana. Fundación Jaime II el Just, pp. 458-478.

[146] **MURRAY, H. J. R.** (1913) *A History of Chess.* Oxford University Press, p. 790

a poem of 742 lines under the title *Liber Scacchorum* without the permission of author, who then made a publication in 1527.

10.1.6 1527 Liber Scacchorum
The papal scribe Ludovicum Vicentinum, known in Rome by the nickname of "Il Vicentino", printed in May of 1527 the *Liber Scacchorum* as his latest book printed in Rome[147].

10.1.7 JGAAP analysis
This program shows that the book of Damiano was written by Lucena. On the other hand the program reveals that the texts were similar to the MS 1520 of La Celestina (second place) and that the texts had a connection to Gonzalo Fernández de Oviedo (third place). I do not understand how this program could analyse the Italian texts of Damiano so well that it refers to these three names.

10.1.8 Valencia has the best courtesan model
For Gonzalo Fernández de Oviedo the best courtesan town in Spain was Valencia[148]:

> El mejor castellano no sería, para nuestro autor, el de Salamanca y su universidad, sino el más «conversable» que utilizaban los cortesanos para comunicarse entre sí y con su señor. Del mismo modo, la ciudad de Valencia merecía ser distinguida entre todas las de España como «arrabal», o lugar más próximo al modelo cortesano, por el cultivo de los modos caballerescos y de la conversación humana y afable entre sus habitantes.

---

[147] **GIROLAMO VIDA, Marco** (1527) *Marci Hieronymi Vidae Cremonensis de arte poetica lib. III. Eiusdem de bombyce lib. II. Eiusdem de ludo scacchorum lib. I. Eiusdem Hymni. Eiusdem Bucolica.* [Romae, apud Ludouicum Vicentinum, 1527 mense Maio]

[148] *Batallas,* batalla I, quinquágena II, diálogo XXXVIII, Biblioteca del Palacio Real, ms. II-2604, fol. 38. Cited by **CARRILLO CASTILLO, Jesús** (1998-1999). Cultura cortesana e imperio: el *Libro del blasón,* de Gonzalo Fernández de Oviedo. In: LOCVS AMOENVS 4, pp. 137-154

10.2 Conclusion:

It is dangerous to accept any name that figures in the book of the 16th century as the real author. I say this, because Garzón had shown through technical data and deep analysis that Francesch Vicent could have been the author of the content of the chess manuscript *Cesena* and one of the authors of the book known as '*The Book of Damiano* edited in 1512. The supposed Portuguese author Peter Damiano, who was the apothecary of Odemira[149], was dismissed.

On the other hand we observe that Dr. Ricardo Calvo did not believe in the name of Joannes Chachi[150]: "No sé si pensar que en vez de un nombre se trate de un pseudónimo, puesto que su pronunciación en alta voz dice: *Yoan escaqui* o *jugando al ajedrez*" (Yoan escaqui or playing chess). Chachi is not a surname in Italy.

After 1497 we do not see the name Lucena appear in Spain nor Italy. The situation is different for a chess manuscript in France. The name Lucena was implied in some chess manuscripts in France without stating his full name. Was it really Francesch Vicent who was involved in the chess manuscript of Giovanni Chachi and Damiano? In this respect we may observe that the JGAAP nullifies my hypothesis of Ludovico Vicentino (= Francesch Vicent?)[151] and that Gonzalo Fernández de Oviedo always used pseudonyms for the books he wrote. In other words Francesch Vicent could have been another pseudonym of Fernández de Oviedo.

---

[149] Cited by **GARZÓN ROGER, José Antonio** (2005) El regreso de Francesch Vicent. La historia del nacimiento y expansión del ajedrez moderno. Generalidad Valenciana. Fundación Jaime II el Just
[150] **CALVO, Ricardo** (1999) *Lucena: La evasión en ajedrez del converso Calisto.* Perea Ediciones, p. 126
[151] **WESTERVELD, Govert** (2015) The life of Ludovico Vicentino degli Arrighi between 1504 and 1534. 264 pages. Lulu Editors. ISBN: 978-1-326-81393-2

We must admit that books of another genre written and published by Fernández de Oviedo never will show his real name, only pseudonyms.

This means that there could be a lot of books in Spain with authors' names fabricated by Lucena (Gonzalo Fernández de Oviedo) as Francesch Vicent, Hernán Díaz[152] (El Peregrino), Feliciano de Silva[153] (only in the case of the Segunda Celestina), Francisco Delicado, Bartolomé Torres Naharro, and many others.

Consequently it is worthwhile to put a big question mark over the names of writers who appear as authors only in the titles of certain books from the 15th and 16th century.

At the moment I hypothesise that Francesch Vicent was a pseudonym of Lucena (Gonzalo Fernández de Oviedo). Writing a chess book with nice diagrams is a very costly matter. However, if a member of the royal family is involved, then of course money is always available. Lucena was the page of prince Juan and had his opportunities at the court. We should not forget that Lucena was a great innovator and we find his new ideas in chess, draughts, and his books. On the other hand I have already expressed in my other books about him that Lucena constantly used pseudonyms for his books. So why not also use the pseudonym Francesch Vicent?

---

[152] **WESTERVELD, Govert** (2016) Research on the Mysterious Aragonese Author of La Celestina. Academia de Estudios Humanísticos de Blanca. 288 pages. Lulu Editors. ISBN: 978-1-326-81331-4
[153] **WESTERVELD, Govert** (in press) The Wanderings of the Chess Book Writer Lucena

11 Lucena and Chess

Francesch Vicent wrote a now lost chess book about modern chess in Valencia in 1495. Thereafter we see the oldest book of modern chess still in existence. It was published by Lucena, son of the prothonotary and ambassador Juan Ramírez de Lucena in 1497. This book was printed in Salamanca by the printers Leonardo Hutz and Sanz with the title *Arte de axedres con CL juegos de partido.*

Lucena has two other names in the Spanish literature: Luis de Lucena and Luis Ramírez de Lucena. However, the chess book of 1497 clearly states only the name of Lucena, never Luis de Lucena. Lucena completely disappeared from the scene in 1497 and we find his name again in two foreign chess manuscripts in France, one from around 1515 and the other from around 1530 where anonymous writers mention the name Lucena. The name Ludovico Lucena appears in a French medical book from 1523 and as from 1540 we see this name appear in Rome.

In this paragraph I will try to find out who could possibly have written *Arte de Ajedrez* from 1497. I never doubted the fact that Lucena was a son of the prothonotary. However, I tried to find the son's real name, as I suspected from the beginning that his surname was not Lucena. I suspected that the son had another surname. The first attempt of Juan del Encina did not give the expected result. The second attempt of Francesch Vincent also had problems. Here I tried again to find the real name of the author of this chess book who called himself Lucena. I used text from the introduction to this book directed to prince Johan and looked for strange words and different word combinations to find out the author with the help of CORDE. I used the text of the introduction to find the possible author with JGAAP.

11.1 Text of the Introduction

Arte breve e introducción muy necesaria para saber jugar al axedres, con ciento y cincuenta juegos de partido; intitulada al serenísimo y muy **esclarecido** don Johan el tercero, príncipe de las Spañas. Por Lucena, hijo del muy sapientísimo doctor y reverendo prothonotario don Johan Ramírez de Lucena, embaxador y del consejo de los Reyes nuestros señores, studiando en el **preclarísimo** studio de la muy noble cibdad de Salamanca.

En que todos los hombres por la mayor parte cristianissimo príncipe y muy poderoso señor trabajé hazer **sus cenizas** immortales: y esto por diversas operaciones cada qual porlo que que mas se ha exercitado, no tanto yo movido or la semejante ambicion quanto **desseoso de servir a** vuestra serenissima alteza: tuve mas cuydado screvir en que tretraydo de sus nobles pensamientos: y fcas operaciones pudiesse recreando se aliviar la fatiga por ello: que querer dexar gloria delo que por no saber hazer seria antes **digno de pena.** Quien empero no perdera el temor donde ay tanta clemencia: y la murmuracion del que mal le paresciere: si su amparo le favoresce., pues en bondad: justicia: liberalidad: mansedumbre: facilidad: prudencia: consejo: magnanimidad: y potencia: tiene a todos los sacros principes monarchia. Loaron los antiguos a Elristides: a Gefilao: a Trajano: por justos, y quien mas que vuestra esclarecida potencia pudo remover las injurias: quitar las discordias: refrenar los delictos: y los buenos remunderar: y si en arte de cavalleria a Publio cornelio Scipion el affricano segundo: y de paciencia a Mucio Sceuvola: y de constancia a Fulvio flaco: y de contiencia a Edruos: y de liberalidad a Quinto fabio mario: y de humildad a Siphar Rey de nuicia.

Al Serenisimo y muy Sclarecido Don Johan el tercero. Príncipe de las Spañas.

Entre el ajedrez viejo que antes se usaba y el juego que agora jugamos que se dice de la dama. Poco tiempo y la apuesta sea tan poca que perdida no le pese. Que yo he podido por mi mesmo alcanzar. Y esto no se hace por otra cosa salvo por desbaratar sus peones y que no se pueda **trasponer**. Mirad cómo le tenéis más suiecto que él a vos, sabiendo guiar el juego, Jugad el caballo de la dama sobre su dama y hála perdido a cualquiera casa que vaya, o con jaque del un caballo o con descubierta del otro. Y en esta manera quedará el juego vuestro, que todas las piezas tienen lugar por do salir y bien asentarlas. Y si tiempo os da que podáis jugar todos los cuatro peones **de enmedio** a una regla, no lo dejéis. Y después las cuatro piezas detrás de ellos. Y **en aquesta manera** seréis **señor del campo.** Jugareis el peón de la dama a cuatro casas porqué tengíais tan buen juego como él. Y aquesto porqué jugéis de los alfiles: el de rey a tres casas de la dama y el de la dama a tres casas del rey.

Y asi siguiendo el juego lo llevas mejor, puesto que no él. Las blancas juegan y dan mate en cinco jugadas.

[...]po de la mayor necesidad: porque a las veces y por la mayor parte **descubriendo** vuestro rey podéis perder el juego, y así teniendo vuestro rey en salvo podéis sin miedo con la otra gente darle guerra, **que de necesidad** no se puede hacer sino defenderse, quedando vos **señor del campo** para lo cual, **de qué suerte** se ha de platicar, entiendo escribir todos los mejores juegos que yo en Roma e por toda Italia y Francia y España he visto jugar a jugadores y yo he podido por mi mesmo alcanzar. La segunda regla es jugar del peón de rey a cuatro casas, que se entiende contando de donde está el rey. E si el que jugare con vos jugare el mesmo peón a otras cuatro, jugaredes del caballo del rey a tres casas del alfil del rey, e si guarda su peón con el peón del alfil del rey, darle **heis** el caballo por el peón que está a cuatro casas de su rey.

Siguen se las reglas.

A primera regla es a **dotrinar** a los que no saben nada en este juego: por que no caresca mi obra de principio. en lo qual **sabiendo como**
juega cada pieza se conoscera la differencia que es entre el juego que agora jugamos que se dize dela dama: y el viejo que antes se jugava: la qual declararacion aprovechara assi mesmo para entender la diversidad delos juegos de partido que son ciento y ciencuenta como **rosario** complido: el qual bien sabido aprovechara para saber mucho jugar de peones: los quales puestos todos arreo en la segunda barra del tablero teniendo casa a blanca a mano derecha assentareys los roques en las ultimas casas de cada parte en la barra primera: y cabe ellos los cauallos: luego los arfiles: despues su rey blanco en casa negra: y rey negro en casa blanca: y junto con ellos las damas: y assi bien entablado vuestro juego conuiene sepays como se muda y prende cada pieza. Los peones primeramente pueden el **primer lance** jugar a vna casa o a dos despues a vna siempre y por barra prenden por esquina: y pueden passar batalla que quiere dezir que estando el peon del otro en contrario podeys passar vuestro peon otra casa mas adelante de la casa del encuentro quedando enla eleccion del otro dexar lo passar o prenderlo. Item que allegado a la barra del rey de su contrario tiene fuerza de dama y da **xaque** sin trasponer: y no solo como dama pero si vuestras mercedes quisieren al juego que po vso que por aquella vez que entra dama y el primer lance que della iugare que prenda y de xaque como dama y cauallo por lo mucho que alas mugeres se les deue: y de alli adelante por barra: o por esquina solamente al juego viejo el primer lance que iuega puede saltar tres casas por barra o por esquina: mas no puede prender: y puede saltar sobre otra pieza qualquiera que sea de aqui adelante de casa en casa y por esquina el rey assi mesmo el primer lance puede saltar a tercera casa como quisiere salvo con **xaque** sino fuere de cauallo por euuitar el mate de los desperados que llaman: mas queno trasponga sobre xaque no que no pueda trasponer si le han

dado xaque que bien puede si no se ha mudado mas que no falte sobre la barra enla qual si quisiesse entrar no pudiesse por xaque. Los arfiles van por esquina **de parte a parte** salvo que al iuego vicio siempre van de tres en tres casas y tan bien por esquina: y puede saltar y tomar sobre otra pieza si quiere: los cauallos iuegan de tercera en tercera casa no iugando por esquina: ni por barra. Los roques siempre por barra y no por esquina ni como cauallos. Resta agora declarar algunas dubdas **que muchas veces** entre los que poco saben comunmente acaescen: y es que si digo daros he mate de peon que se entiende con peon y no xaque de vno y mate de otro si no lo especifican. Item que si digo: yos dare mate con este peon señalando lo que si lo hazeys dama y le days mate con ella vale. Item que mate ahogado es mate no para ganar doblado como dando xaque y mate el qual me paresce buen iuego: y no se deue vsar **de otra manera porque** os despierta y haze alcanzar muchos lanzes assi mesmo acaesce que el otro os da xaque y calla lo y vos no viendo lo jugayas otra cosa que si el otro despues de hauer vos jugado antes que toca pieza dize sallid de xaque que se tome lo que jugastes y salgays de xaque en otra manera a viendo vos jugado y el tocado pieza que no salgays **porque cada vez** se lo harie quienquiera porque podrie hombre jugar de vn cauallo: o de otra pieza sobre vuestra dama: o sobre otra qualquier pieza y dezir sallid de xaque: y despues lleuaros la **por cuya causa** no solamente no haueys de sallir de xaque pero si con otra pieza os diesse xaque podeys entrar enla mesma barra del xaque callado: saluo si conla mesma pieza no os diesse otra vez xaque. Assi mesmo aprouecha mucho vsar jugar siempre con vnos juegos special con los negros: y quando assi los tuuiessedes en vso y el otro no quisiesse jugar si no con ellos boluelde el tablero: y assi es todo vna cosa porque siempre os viene el rey a mano ysquierda. Si jugaredes **de noche con** una sola candela haced si pudieredes que esté siempre a mano izquierda porque no turba tanto la vista, y si jugaredes de dia que agays assentar el otro en derecho de la luz que es una gran ventaja: quiere tambien este juego tomar al otro sobre haber bien comido y bevido: aunque para haber de jugar mucho tiempo aprovecha haber comido algo **liuianamente** porque no se desvanesca la cabeza, el beber sea agua y no vino en ninguna manera: y el que fuere estudiante creame porque sé que es que si quiere que la aproveche, assi para el ingenio como para la memoria aque juegue poco tiempo y el precio sea tan poco **que perdido** no le pese: porque desta manera alteraria el ingenio y turbaria la memoria. Item si vos me days el rey **traspuesto** se entiende que vos no podeys trasponer **saluo si por** pacto no lo sacassedes. Item que quien da el peon del arfil del rey no se traspone si no lo saca assi mesmo por partido. Item que aunque no se ponga jugando precio en tocando pieza ha de jugar della saluo si fuere dela encubierta que entonces ha de iugar del rey. Item que aunque tocada la pieza haya de iugar della que no por esso aunque toque casa la de assentar enella por euitar bozes. Finalmente conuiene ordenar bien vuestro juego enlo qual consiste la perfecion de esta sciencia: y despues saber a cometer quanto es tiempo y quando no estar quedo. y la manera del romper es siempre por la parte de la dama: y no por la parte del rey: haziendos alli fuerte hasta el tiempo dela mayor necessidad: porque a las veces y por la mayor parte descubriendo vuestro rey podéis perder el juego, y así teniendo vuestro rey en salvo podéis sin miedo con la otra gente darle guerra, que de necesidad no se puede hacer sino defenderse, quedando vos señor del campo para lo cual, de qué suerte se ha de platicar, entiendo escribir todos los mejores juegos que yo en Roma e por toda Italia y Francia y España he visto jugar a jugadores y yo he podido por mi mesmo alcanzar.

11.2 Words used in the Introduction

Strange words used in the "Introduction" to *Arte de Ajedrez* to prince Johan

Nº	Words	Author	Cases	Other authors
30.	Dotrinar	Gonzalo Fernánde de Oviedo	4	10
31.	Esclarecido	Jerónimo Fernández	2	52
32.	Heis	Gonzalo Fernández de Oviedo	7	37
33.	Livianamente	Gonzalo Fernández de Oviedo	2	37
34.	Preclarísimo	Fray Bartolomé de las Casas	1	2
35.	Rosario	Gonzalo Fernández de Oviedo	3	18
36.	Trasponer	Gonzalo Fernández de Oviedo	3	18
37.	Traspuesto	Gonzalo Fernández de Oviedo	4	29
38.	Xaque	Bartolomé Torres Naharro	2	9
39.	De enmedio	Gonzalo Fernández de Oviedo	4	12
40.	De noche con	Gonzalo Fernández de Oviedo	4	40
41.	De otra manera porque	Gonzalo Fernández de Oviedo	5	12
42.	De parte a parte	Gonzalo Fernández de Oviedo	17	46
43.	De qué suerte	Jerónimo Fernández	1	13
44.	Desseoso de server a	Traducción Tirante el Blanco	1	2
45.	Digno de pena	Oliveros de Castilla	1	6
46.	En aquesta manera	Traducción Tirante el Blanco	1	20

47.	Por cuya causa	Gonzalo Fernández de Oviedo	2	39
48.	Por mejor dezir	Feliciando de Silva = Gonzalo Fernández de Oviedo (Celestina)	3	40
49.	Porque cada vez	Lazarillo el Tormes	1	10
50.	Primer lance	Francisco Delicado	1	0
51.	Que de necesidad	Gonzalo Fernández de Oviedo	1	16
52.	Que muchas veces	Gonzalo Fernández de Oviedo	25	48
53.	Que perdido	Gonzalo Fernández de Oviedo	1	33
54.	Sabiendo como	Gonzalo Fernández de Oviedo	1	17
55.	Salvo si por	Gonzalo Fernández de Oviedo	1	13
56.	Señor del campo	Gonzalo Fernández de Oviedo	3	6
57.	Sus cenizas	Gonzalo Fernández de Oviedo	1	9
58.	Tablero de Axedrez	Gonzalo Fernández de Oviedo	1	0

We observe that the writer of *Arte de Axedrez* liked to use strange words in his text. For example, the phrase 'señor del campo' was used 3 times by Gonzalo Fernández de Oviedo, while there were only 6 more authors for this word combination.

11.2.1 JGAAP analysis

We will observe in the JGAAP analysis (Appendix 15.3.1) that the linguistic analysis of Lucena corresponds to different authors, among them Juan de Sedeño, Ludovico Escriva, Jerónimo Fernandez, and Gonzalo Fernández de Oviedo. I think that the first three authors mentioned here correspond to pseudonyms and the only real name is Gonzalo Fernández de Oviedo.

11.3 Chess manuscripts relating to Lucena

As we have pointed out before, writers cannot disappear suddenly, because they like writing, and so we have to trace the whereabouts of Lucena after 1497. Lucena continued to be active in France. However, in this case I prefer to think of the activities of Dr. Luis de Lucena in France, but this is something that certainly needs more research.

11.3.1 1505-1515 the Göttingen

1)   The *Göttingen manuscript is* one of the earliest known works devoted entirely to modern chess that is preserved in the Georg-August-Universität Göttingen (Germany), Sign. MS. Philos. 85. It is a Latin text of 33 leaves that contains twelve opening games and thirty problems with exclusively modern rules. It is held at the University of Göttingen. The authorship and exact date of the manuscript are unknown. Similarities to Lucena's *Repeticion de Amores e Arte de Axedres con CL iuegos de partido* (c. 1497) has led some scholars to surmise that it was written by Lucena or that it was one of Lucena's sources.

2)   Although the manuscript is generally assumed to be older than Lucena's work, this is not established, because Murray thought that the chess problems of this manuscript are of a more advanced stage than the problems of Lucena's book of 1497[154]. Maybe the idea that this manuscript was older than Lucena (1497) was due to the fact that Dr. Fritz Clemens Görschen (1911–1981) wrote in Schach Echo (1975) that King Alfonso V of Portugal had the manuscript when he visited France in the winter of 1474–5 and that it had been written in 1471[155]. However, one should take into account that Richard Eales sees this as simple speculation[156].

---

[154] **MURRAY, H. J. R.** (1913) *A History of Chess,* Oxford University Press, pp. 782–784.
[155] **HOOPER, David; WHYLD, Kenneth** (1996) *The Göttingen Manuscript.* The Oxford Companion to Chess (2 ed.), Oxford University, p. 156.
[156] **EALES, Richard** (1985) *Chess, The History of a Game,* B.T. Batsford, p. 74.

11.3.2   1515-1520 MS. F. allem. 107

This manuscript is written in German and contains 89 leaves with 14 rules and opening games. The nationality of the author is unknown. It does not contain the new rules of the MS Paris/DeLucia. The manuscript is preserved in the National Library of France.

11.3.3   1530 Chess Manuscript Paris/DeLucia

The confusion about Lucena's authorship and even the dating of the Göttingen manuscript (early 16th century) and the Paris/Place manuscript is now considered obsolete. A well-documented work on the matter, which clears any doubts, was done by Joaquín Pérez de Arriaga[157]. Hoping to bring an end to this issue, which incomprehensibly still comes up from time to time in scholarly circles[158], Garzón studied this matter carefully[159]. Since 1991 the Paris/Place[160] manuscript has been in the possession of the New Yorker bibliophile David DeLucia[161] and NEBEA[162] thinks that the date of the

---

[157] **PEREZ DE ARRIAGA, Joaquín** (1997) El incunable de Lucena. Primer Arte de Ajedrez Moderno.(Ediciones Polifemo. Madrid

[158] Ricardo Calvo told Garzón that in the Conference of Historians in Amsterdam (2002) a colleague of his still suggested that the Lucena manuscripts were written before Arte de Ajedrez and that this idea was not poorly received. As Garzón told Ricardo, there is no longer room for such thinking if a serious study, such as the one Garzón was presenting, is conducted about the manuscripts and Lucena's treatise, in connection with his era and the work of Damiano, etc.

[159] **GARZÓN ROGER, José Antonio**, *The Definitive Proof of the Valencian Origins of Modern Chess*. In: **WESTERVELD, Govert** (2015) *The Origin of the Checkers and Modern Chess Game*. Volume III, 312 pages. Lulu Editors, pp. 127-128. ISBN: 978-1-326-60244-4

[160] **PLACE, Victor** (1922) Lucena, D'après un ancien manuscrit inédit. In: La Stratégie, Paris, Year 56: N° 1, January, 1922, pp. 1-8. See also: N° 2, February, 1922, pp. 29-35; N° 3, March 1922 pp. 53-61; N° 4, April, 1922, pp. 77-84

[161] **GARZÓN ROGER, José Antonio** (2005) *The return of Francesch Vicent*. The History of the Birth and Expansion of Modern Chess. (Foreword Anatoli Karpov). Generalitat Valenciana, Conselleria de Cultura, Educació i Esport: Fundació Jaume II el Just, Valencia, p. 16.

[162] **GARZON ROGER, José Antonio; ALIÓ, Josep; ARTIGAS, Miquel** (2012) Nuevo Ensayo de Bibliografía Español de Ajedrez (NEBEA) 1238 – 1938. Rom Editors

manuscript was around 1530. The manuscript contains 42 leaves and 84 pages. The book has 20 rules and 28 opening games.

11.4 Pierpont Morgan Library

The old Spanish chess books of the XV-century continues to be interested books for the chess historians[163]. Chess scholars found an old chess book of Lucena in the Pierpont Morgan Library in New York[164].

It was a surprise to see in this book handwritten notes at the end of many problems, because they are written in Valencian by a chess player at the end of the XV-century or at most in the early sixteenth century. Thanks to the work and analysis of Garzón it was possible to obtain sufficient handwritten text.

The JGAAP analysis (Appendix 15.3.2) shows that the handwritten text was most likely written by Gonzalo Fernández de Oviedo, since we can discard Baltasar del Río and Juan de Valdés.

[163] **D'ELIA, Diego** (2006). Sulla più testimonianza di un testo scacchistico a stampa: le bozze di stampa dell'incunabolo "Arte de Axeddrez" di Luis Ramírez de Lucena". *Culture del testo del documento,* 19, pp. 81-98.
[164] **GARZÓN ROGER, José Antonio** (2014). La búsqueda del Santo Grial del Ajedrez. Versión provisional para web. In: Pasiones bibliográficas. Trabajos conmemorativos del XX Aniversario de la Societat Bibliogràfica Valenciana Jerònima Galés, pp. 1-19.

12 Lucena and La Celestina

As we know Lucena was the author of *Repetición de amores* and *arte de ajedrez, con CL juegos de partido*. Luis Rubio García of the University of Murcia was in his time a good connoisseur of *Repetición de amores* and his comments cleary showed that Lucena could have been the author of the first six acts of La Celestina[165].

However, Rubio García was not the first with this idea. Antonio Carballo[166]. also saw similiarity between *Repetición de amores* and *La Celestina*. Parilla[167] observed that the first act of *La Celestina* is similar to the *Historia de duobus amantibus* a manuscript that the father of Lucena must have had in his big library, because he had worked as scribe of Pope Pio II (Eneas Silvio Piccolomini) in Rome. Pedro Catédra[168] saw similarity between the first act of *La Celestina, the Repeticion de amores* of Lucena and the *Tratado de cómo al hombre es necesario amar*. Antonio Cortijo[169] also thought that the first act of *La Celestina* had to do with Lucena who wrote the *Repetición de amores*. Bienvenido Morros[170] also saw similarity between the work *Repetición de amores* and the first text of the ancient author of *La Celestina*. Lucena was in charge of the editions of 1499 (Burgos), 1500 (Toledo), 1501

---

[165] **RUBIO GARCÍA, Luis** (1985). Estudios sobre La Celestina, pp. 247-248

[166] **CARBALLO PICAZO, Antonio** (1956). Res. De Repetición de amores, ed. Jaco Ornstein. Revista de Filologia Española, N° 40, (pp. 299 – 303), citation on p. 302.

[167] **PARRILLA, Carmen** (1985). "El Tratado de amores: nuevo relato sentimental del siglo XV". El Crotalón: Anuario de Filología Española 2: (pp. 473-496), citation on p. 476.

[168] **CÁTEDRA, Pedro. M.** (1989). Amor y pedagogía en la Edad Media. Salamanca: Universidad. pp. 114 - 141

[169] **CORTIJO OCAÑA, Antonio** (1999). An Inane Hypothesis: Torroella, Flores, Lucena, and Celestina?. In: Research Series/Number 103. Multicultural Iberia: Language, Literature, and music. Dru Dougherty and Milton M. Azevedo, Editors. University of California at Berkeley. (pp. 40 – 56).

[170] **MORROS, Bienvenido** (2004). Una nueva fuente de Luis de Lucena. In: Bulletin of Spanish Studies, Volume LXXXI, Number 1, (pp. 1-14), citation on p. 14

(Seville) and 1507 (Zaragoza) and was heavily involved with the Italian editions of *La Celestina*.

12.1 Proofs

Here we try to prove that Lucena was indeed the main author of *La Celestina*. Lucena, a writer and editor who used many pseudonyms, always wanted to have very nice books with images and few linguistic mistakes.

12.1.1 The word alahé

Analyzing the *La Celestina* I found the word *alahé* 7 times[171], viz: 4 times in the act 1; once in act 3, once in act 7 and once in act 11. Thereafter I have tried to find this word in other books of the 15th and 16th century. Strangely enough, I only found it in Juan Ramírez de Lucena's *Vita Beata* and in the *Libro de Buen Amor*. Consequently it is clear that Lucena borrowed it word from his father's book[172] and so he was one of the authors of *La Celestina* and probably the ancient author.

Appearance of the word: alahé

Year	Author	Book	Quantity
1440	Juan Ruiz	*Libro de Buen Amor*	2
1482	Juan Ramirez de Lucena	*Vita Beata*	1
1499	Lucena	*La Celestina (Act 1)*	4
1499	Lucena	*La Celestina (Act 3)*	1
1499	Lucena	*La Celestina (Act 7)*	1
1499	Lucena	*La Celestina (Act 11)*	1
1514	Lucas Fernández	*Auto of Farsa Nascimiento*	1

---

[171] **CATOIRA, Loreto** (2012). Valores semánticos de *alahé* en las traducciones inglesas de *La Celestina*. In: Lemir 16, pp. 283-300.
[172] **FOTHERGILL-PAYNE, Louise** (1988). Seneca and Celestina. Cambridge University Press, New York, p.65

12.2 Renaissance Dialogues

Lucena borrowed writing in dialogues from his father. Juan Ramírez de Lucena wrote *Vita Beata* around 1482 in dialogue. We see that La Celestina was also written in dialogue. Juan de Lucena imitated or translated Bartolomé Fazio, but with complete freedom of style. We will also observe this freedom of style in the translations of Gonzalo Fernández de Oviedo.

12.2.1 The word lozano

Lucena could have had Piccolomini's manuscripts at his disposal and translated this work, because his father was at the Papal court around 1460.

To prove this we have to revert to the Dissertation of Blanca Garrido Martín who shows that the term *Lozano* is found in *Repetición de amores* and our analysis of other works showed that this is also the case in other works very few times, among them the translation of *Duobus amantibus*[173].

---

[173] **GARRIDO MARTÍN, Blanca** (2016). La *Atalaya de las Corónicas* (1443) de Alfonso Martínez de Toledo: Edición crítica y estudio lingüístico. Tesis Doctoral, Volume II, Departamento de Lengua Española, Lingüística y Teoría de la Literatura. Sevilla, p. 713

Occurence of the word *Lozano*

Year	Author	Book	Total
1495	Piccolomini	*duobus amantibus*	1
1496	Garci Rodriguez de Montalvo	*Amadis*	5
1496	Lucas Fernández	*Dereniego del amor*	1
1497	Lucena	*Repetición de amores*	2
1511	Anónimo	*Palmerín de Olivia*	1
1520	Bartolomé Torres Naharro	*Propalladia - Calamita*	1
1525	Gil Vicente	*Tragicomedia de don Duardos*	1
1528	Juan Justiniano	*Instrucción de la mujer cristiana*	1
1530	Francisco Delicado	*Lozana Andaluza*	1
1534	Juan Boscán	*Traducción de El cortesano de Baltasar de Castiglione*	1
1540	Juan de Sedeño	*Celestina en versos*	1
1549	Jerónimo de Urrea	*Traducción de "Orlando furioso" de Ludovico Ariosto*	2
1550	Juan de Arce de Otárola	*Coloquios de Palatino y Pinciano*	2
1550	Jerónimo de Urrea	*Clarisel de las flores*	1
1552	Alonso Núñez de Reinoso	*Clareo y Florisea*	2

Occurence of the word *Lozana*

Year	Author	Book	Total
1490	Anónimo	*Crónica Troyana*	1
1494	Juan del Encina	*Égloga representada en requesta de unos amores*	1
1517	Bartolomé Torres Naharro	*Propalladia Comedia Jacinta*	3
1517	Bartolomé Torres Naharro	*Propalladia Seraphina*	1
1520	Bartolomé Torres Naharro	*Propalladia - Calamita*	1

158

1528	Juan Justiniano	_Instrucción de la mujer cristiana_	1
1530	Francisco Delicado	_Lozana Andaluza_	55
1534	Juan Boscán	_Traducción de El cortesano de Baltasar de Castiglione_	2
1540	López de Gomara	_Historia General de las Indias_	1
1544	Cristóbal de Castillejo	_Diálogo de mujeres_	1
1547	Juan de Segura	_Queja y aviso contra el amor_	1
1549	Jerónimo de Urrea	_Traducción de "Orlando furioso" de Ludovico Ariosto_	2
1553	Alonso Núñez de Reinoso	_Clareo y Florisea_	2
1564	Anónimo	_Polidoro y Casandría_	4

12.2.2 Similar texts in books

Another proof that _La Celestina_ was written by Lucena as continuation of the work _Repetición de amores_ is the fact that we see similar texts in both works:

Repetición de amores:

Es otrosí la muger **principio de pecado, arma del diablo**[174], **expulsión del parayso,** vivera de delictos, transgressión de la ley, doctrina de perdición, dessuelo muy sabido, amiga de discordia, confusión del hombre, pena que

---

[174] Cardinal Albornoz founded the school of San Clemente of the Spaniards of Bologna thanks to a bull of Pope Urban V of September 25, 1369. The clause of the statutes by which the cardinal prohibited the entry of women into his school says: "La mujer es cabeza del pecado, arma del diablo, expulsión del paraíso y corrupción de la ley antigua, por lo que toda conversación con ella ha de ser evitada: prohíbo que nadie se atreva a introducir en el colegio mujer alguna, aun cuando fuera honrada". Cfr. Los estatutos de "El Real Colegio San Clemente de los Españoles de Bolonia".
In La Celestina we find:
Por ellas es dicho: arma del diablo, cabeça de pecado, destruyción de parayso. ¿No has rezado en la festiuidad de Sant Juan, do dize: Las mugeres e el vino hazen los hombres renegar; do dize: "Esta es la muger, antigua malicia que a Adán echó de los deleytes de parayso; esta el linaje humano metió en el infierno; a esta menospreció Helías propheta &c.?"

desechar no se puede, notorio mal, continua tentación, mal de todos deseado, pelea que nunca cessa, daño continuo, casa de tempestad, impedimento solícito, desvío de castidad, puerta de la muerte, sendero herrado, llaga de scorpión, camino para el fuego, universal temptación, mal incomportable, compañía peligrosa, destrucción de la gracia, de salud enemiga, de méritos disminución, de virtud siniestro desagradescimiento de servicios, enfermedad incurable, de ánimas ratonera, de la vida ladrón, muerte suave, herida sin sentimiento, delicada destrución, rosa que hiede, lisonja crecida, pestilencia que manzilla al ánima, diminución de las fuerzas y disformación, y destrución con que Dios se dessirve y el ánima se pierde, y el próximo se offende, por quien cuerpo y ánima *reciben aposentamiento en el infierno; porque ella ciega el sentido y aparta el pensamiento de Dios y nos haze inconstante y caher de cabeça, y por quien somos de Dios aborrecidos y a este siglo aficionados y del cielo enagenados.

Primer acto de la Comedia Calisto y Melibea:

SEMPRONIO.- ¿Escociote? Lee los ystoriales, estudia los filósofos, mira los poetas. Llenos están los libros de sus viles e malos exemplos e de las caydas que leuaron los que en algo, como tú, las reputaron. Oye a Salomón do dize que las mugeres e el vino hazen a los hombres renegar. Conséjate con Séneca e verás en qué las tiene. Escucha al Aristóteles, mira a Bernardo. Gentiles, judíos, cristianos e moros, todos en esta concordia están. Pero lo dicho e lo que dellas dixere no te contezca error de tomarlo en común. Que muchas houo e ay sanctas e virtuosas e notables, cuya resplandesciente corona quita el general vituperio. Pero destas otras, ¿quién te contaría sus mentiras, sus tráfagos, sus cambios, su liuiandad, sus lagrimillas, sus alteraciones, sus osadías? Que todo lo que piensan, osan sin deliberar. ¿Sus disimulaciones, su lengua, su engaño, su oluido, su desamor, su ingratitud, su inconstancia, su testimoniar, su negar, su reboluer, su presunción, su vanagloria, su abatimiento, su locura, su desdén, su soberuia, su subjeción, su parlería, su golosina, su luxuria e suziedad, su miedo, su atreuemiento, sus hechizerías, sus embaymientos, sus escarnios, su deslenguamiento, su desvergüença, su alcahuetería? Considera, ¡qué sesito está debaxo de aquellas grandes e delgadas tocas! ¡Qué pensamientos so aquellas gorgueras, so aquel fausto, so aquellas largas e autorizantes ropas! ¡Qué imperfición, qué aluañares debaxo de templos pintados! Por ellas es dicho: **arma del diablo, cabeça de pecado, destruyción de parayso.** ¿No has rezado en la festiuidad de Sant Juan, do dize: Las mugeres e el vino hazen los hombres renegar; do dize: Esta es la muger, antigua malicia que a Adán echó de los deleytes de parayso; esta el linaje humano metió en el infierno; a esta menospreció Helías propheta &c.?

12.2.3 The acrostics

Dr. Ricardo Calvo[175] found an acrostic in *Repetición de amores,* where the book is completed with a hyperbolic commendation from the Villoslada bachelor, through a poem that carries some acrostic verses, and putting together the first letter of each one reads "A Villoslada".

Here is the poem which, according to the chess historian José Antonio Garzón Roger,[176] the bachelor Villoslada did not write, but Lucena himself.

A quien siempre, por serviros
nunca bive sin dolor,
no le negéys el favor.

Bive siempre padeciendo
de no veros, con temor;
está en pena aunque biviendo,
pues os llama ya muriendo;
no le negéys el favor.

Jamás cessan sus sospiros
que le causa vuestro amor;
por quereros y seguiros
nunca cessa de pediros;
no le negéys el favor.

La menor de sus pasiones
le pone tanto pavor,
que le causa mil prisiones;
y pues ay diez mil razones,
no le negéys el favor.

---

[175] **CALVO, Ricardo** (1997). Lucena. La evasión en ajedrez del converso Calisto. Perea Ediciones. Pedro Muñoz (Ciudad Real), p. 20
[176] The acrostic is "Abjlloslada", Lucena indicates that it is dedicated to A. Villoslada. Personal communication in 2006. With thanks to José Antonio Garzón Roger.

La menor de sus pasiones
le pone tanto pavor,
que le causa mil prisiones;
y pues ay diez mil razones,
no le negéys el favor.

La tristeza de sus males
no sabe pena mayor;
que sus angustias finales
os supplican ya mortales;
no le negéys el favor.

Otro bien si a vos no tiene,
soys su luz y su claror;
pues quien tanta se sostiene
y es contento, aunque más pene;
no le negéys el favor.

Solo fué causa escribir
publicar vuestro loor;
pues que no basta sofrir;
Assin vos poder vivir
no le negéys el favor.

La virtud y la nobleza
nunca muestra desamor,
pues porque mostráys crueza
a tan crescida proheza;
no le negéys el favor.

A la fe de bien serviros,
que jamás suffrió herror,
ya no basta consetiros
mas supplicar y deziros;
no le negéys el favor.

Después que por fuerte ser

y no oystes el su amor
distes causa a padescer;
y, no queriendo valer,
le neguastes el favor.

Ansí que pues hizo veros
fuesse vuestro servidor;
pues es siervo por quereros,
déle vida conosceros;
no le negéys el favor.

In other words, Fernando de Rojas was not the first author who used an acrostic in 1500, because before him we see Lucena and the poet Juan del Encina.

It is very likely that Juan Ramírez de Lucena had met Leon Battista Alberti who was once a famous architect and writer. Battista was aware of the great work of Marco Vitruvio Polión, *Los diez libros de Arquitectura*. On the other hand Battista was the secretary to Pope Eugene in 1432 and five more popes. He wrote the comedy Philodoxeos that circulated anonymously (1424-1426). Alberti also invented the first polyalphabetical cryptographic system. Juan Ramírez de Lucena was a keen expert in encryption and in the court of Pope Pio III he already worked with various alphabetical codes. Protonotary Lucena was aware of Philodoxeos and the secret alphabetical codes of Alberti and his son Lucena was not going to be any less.

Another acrostic is in the *Tragicomedia of Lisandro y Roselia*. Some authors call it the third Celestina and others the fourth Celestina. This book was printed in 1542 and the acrostic shows the name Sancho de Muñón. However, this is another joke of Lucena who does not reveal his name and prefers to mislead readers. He has done this in more than one case. For example, the work Asno de oro was translated by Lucena, but the acrostic in a Latin verse shows the name Cortegana. This was reason enough for the scholars to baptize the name of Diego López de Cortegana, but with this idea we have Lucena as a dark horse in the background.

12.2.4 Great organizer

Luis Rubio García was of the opinion that the first six acts were from Lucena and the remainder acts from Fernando de Rojas:

> ...Dada la prioridad de Lucena, la cuestión a plantear sería ¿quién copió a quién? Se podría pensar si en sus encuentros o en las aulas discutieron sobre esta temática. O bien se encontraron ya escrito un modelo común, pero en tal caso no debía limitarse a un acto, sino a los seis primeros de *La Celestina*, que son en esquema los que recoge Lucena. Me inclino que el argumento sería conocido no sólo por la tradición clásica que imperaba en las aulas salmantinas, sino como ya hemos apuntado que se hagan eco de algún suceso notario o conocida tradición de Salamanca, aunque luego el tratamiento como hemos visto seguiría caminos distintos, y Lucena no se aproximaría a la genialidad de Rojas.

Translation:
Given the priority of Lucena, the question to ask would be who copied who? You could think if in their meetings or in the classrooms they discussed this topic. Or there was already written a common model, but in such a case it should not be limited to one act, but the first six of La Celestina, which are in outline those collected by Lucena. I am inclined that the argument would be known not only for the classical tradition that prevailed in the Salamanca classrooms, but as we have already pointed out that they echo some notary event or well-known tradition of Salamanca, although later the treatment as we have seen would follow different paths, and Lucena would not approach the genius style of Rojas.

Apparently *La Celestina* had helpers: Lucena as the main author, then Encina helped him in Spain and Italy, and Fernando de Rojas could have worked with some small additional work, but he is not detected in the JGAAP analysis. The main organizer of this work is Lucena. Rolf Eberenz[177] noted that the editions of Burgos (1499-1502), Toledo (1500), Sevilla (1501), and Zaragoza (1507) showed the form *leístas,* while the other editions contain *lo.* This could be an indication that these

---

[177] **EBERENZ, Rolf** (2000). El español en el otoño de la Edad Media, Gredos, Madrid, pp. 232 and 236

164

first four editions had to do with Lucena. Lucena was probably in charge of the various editions in those years.

12.2.5 Translation of Duobus amantibus

Parilla[178] observed that the first act of *La Celestina* is similar to the *Historia de duobus amantibus*. Juan Ramirez de Lucena, the father of Lucena, must have had in his big library a manuscript of this work, because he had worked as scribe for Pope Pio II (Eneas Silvio Piccolomini) in Rome between 1460 and 1464.

We see in the *Historia de duobus amantibus Eurialo et Lucretia*, written in 1444 by the humanist Aeneas Silvo Piccolomini, later known as Pope Pius II, the first use of the epistolary form in the novel. Juan Ramírez de Lucena knew this manuscript and that one of *Remedium amoris,* written in 1446. He had many books and ofcourse his son Lucena must have been aware of this Latin manuscript.

The possible translator of this Latin work apparently is Lucena. It is quite well possible that he translated and printed this work and *Remedium amoris* in Salamanca around 1496. However, this matter needs much more study, since scholars believe that the translator was Diego López de Cortegana[179] to which I cannot agree.

Apart from the edition in Salamanca in 1496 other editions were printed by the Crombergers in Seville in 1512, 1524 and 1530. Appearantly there was also an edition published in Toledo in 1538, but copies of this

---

[178] **PARRILLA, Carmen** (1985). "El Tratado de amores: nuevo relato sentimental del siglo XV". El Crotalón: Anuario de Filología Española 2: (pp. 473-496), citation on p. 476.

[179] **ESCOBAR BORREGO, Francisco J.; DÍEZ REBOSO, Samuel; RIVERO GARCÍA, Luis** (2012). La *Metamorfosis* de un Inquisidor: El humanista Diego López de Cortegana (1455-1524), Universidad de Huelva, p. 161.

latest edition were not found[180]. But I continue with Cortijo, because his research is truly brilliant and shed unexpected light on Lucena[181]:

> Moreover, the initial episode of the *Repetición* also includes an *ad pedem litterae* translation of the beginning of the *Historia de duobus amantibus* (1444). No one has suggested the possibility that Juan de Lucena—Juan II's ambassador to Rome and to the family of Eneas Silvio Picolomini—might very well have been responsible for introducing the *Historia* in the Iberian Peninsula since he is one of the most plausible candidates. It would not be surprising then that his successor, Luis de Lucena[182], given that he was acquainted with Picolomini's text, might have decided to incorporate a burlesque paraphrase of the *Historia* within his university parody, the *Repetición*.

Lucena knew Hebrew, Latin, Greek, French, Italian, and Spanish. He made a translation of the *Historia de duobus amantibus* and we can find his linguistic style in the JGAAP analysis of this work (Appendix 15.4.1).

Printing house of Lopez Sanz in Salamanca

Fecha:	Author	Título:
1494	Rodrigo Basurto	Tractatus de natura loci et temporis
1494	Sedulius	Paschale
1495	Leo Servita	Sacerdotum servitus
1495	Rodrigo Basurto	Additamentum ad calendarium Joannis de Monteregio
1495	Diego de San Pedro	La Pasión trobada
1495	(Sedulio)	Passio domini nostri Jesus Christi
End 1495		Aristóteles, De secreta secretorum
		As from 08.01.1496 Lope Sanz working now with Leonardo Hutz

---

[180] **PÉREZ FERNÁNDEZ, José María & WILSON-LEE, Edward** (2014). Translation and the Book Trade in Early Modern Europe, p. 49.

[181] **CORTIJO OCAÑA, Antonio** (1999). An Inane Hypothesis: Torroella, Flores, Lucena, and Celestina?. In: Research Series/Number 103. Multicultural Iberia: Language, Literature, and music. Dru Dougherty and Milton M. Azevedo, Editors. University of California at Berkeley. (pp. 40 – 56), p. 47.

[182] This is a mistake of Cortijo. The name is Lucena in the book of 1497 and never Luis de Lucena.

08.01.1496	Gonzalo de Villadiego	Grundisalvi de Villadiego Sacri Palatii Apostolici Auditoris Tractatus contra hereticam pravitatem (Dedicado a la Reyna Doña Isabel) & de regularitate...
26.02.1496	S. Thomas	Super Aristotelis de generatione.
1496		Textus abbreviatus logicem Aristoteles
1496	Eneas Silvio Piccolomini	Estoria muy verdadera de dos amantes Spanish translation of: *Historia de duobus amantibus* (1444)
1496	Eneas Silvio Piccolomini	Tratado muy provechoso de remedios contra el amor. Spanish translation of: *Remedium amoris* (1446)
10.02.1497		Leyes del estilo o Declaraciones sobre las Leyes del Fuero.
1497	Basurto, Rodrigo	Additamentum ad calendarium Johannis de Monteregio
01.11.1497	Lucena	Repetición de amores y arte de ajedrez (Dedicated to Prince John)

12.2.6 Lucena's manuscripts

The work and influence on literature get even clearer if we look at several manuscripts in relation to possible works by Lucena. In this respect we should take into account that he was at the Royal Court and had a very good reputation like his father.

12.2.6.1 Ms II-1520
There was a famous manuscript of Palacio MS II-1520. This manuscript was already studied in 1972 by Professor Angel Alcala[183] without

---

[183] On April 21, 1972, from New York, Alcalá directed a letter with his questions on the codex II - 1520 that contains the beginning of *La Celestina* and *Vita Beata*, to the then director of the Biblioteca de Palacio, Consolación Morales, daughter from his old teacher Mr. Luis Morales Oliver. His letter was answered by her on June 28, 1972. Later, even in the same year, Alcalá visited the Biblioteca de Palacio to see the manuscript. He did not break the news to the world, since he was preparing a book about the protonotario Juan Ramírez de Lucena. Unfortunately this book was never finished by Professor Alcalá. (Private communication, with thanks to Professor Alcalá).

paying more attention to it. Years later Faulhaber[184] rediscovered in 1989 the manuscript bearing the following text[185]:

The manuscript MS II-1520 showed us again the relationship with the Lucena clan and the work *La Celestina:*

> **Biblioteca de Palacio de Madrid, MS II-1520**
>
> 1) *Diálogo De Vita Beata,* by Juan de Lucena; fols. 1r-92v, CNUM 4304.
> 2) *Glosa al romance 'Rey que no hace justicia,'* anonymous?; fol. 93r, CNUM 5590.
> 3) *Comedia de Calisto y Melibea,* auto I, Cota?, Juan de Mena?, Luis de Lucena?, anonymous?; fols. 93v-100v, CNUM 5591.
> 4) *Sermón en alabanza de los Reyes Católicos por la conquista de Granada,* anonymous?; fols. 101r-106r, CNUM 5592.18

Apparently in the ninetees of the fifteenth century there was a development of the gender pre-Celestina. The issue now becomes very interesting when one considers what Cortijo is saying[186]:

See also: **ALCALÁ GALVÉ, Ángel** (1995). Tres cuestiones en busca de respuesta: Invalidez del bautismo "forzado", "conversión" de judíos, trato "cristiano" al converso. In: Judíos. Sefarditas. Conversos. La expulsión de 1492 y sus consecuencias, pp. 523-541. Citation on p. 541 nota 25. y pp. 529-530.

[184] **FAULHABER, Charles** (1990). Celestina de Palacio: Madrid, Biblioteca de Palacio, Ms 1520. In: Celestinesca, nov. 14-2, pp. 3-40.

[185] **FAULHABER, Charles B.** (1990). "*Celestina* de Palacio: Madrid, Biblioteca de Palacio, MS 1520". *Celestinesca* 14: 3-9. Cited by **CORTIJO OCAÑA, Antonio** (1999). An Inane Hypothesis: Torroella, Flores, Lucena, and Celestina?. In: Research Series/Number 103. Multicultural Iberia: Language, Literature, and music. Dru Dougherty and Milton M. Azevedo, Editors. University of California at Berkeley. (pp. 40 – 56), p.48.

FAULHABER, Charles B. (1991). Celestina de Palacio: Madrid, Biblioteca de Palacio, Ms 1520. In: Celestinesca, 1991, 15 – 1. pp. 3-52

FAULHABER, Charles B. (1993). MS 1520 de la Biblioteca de Palacio. De los 'papeles del antiguo auctor' a la *Comedia de Calisto y Melibea*: Fernando de Rojas trabaja su fuente. In: Literatura Medieval. Actas do IV Congresso da Associação Hispânica de Literatura Medieval (Lisboa, 1-5 Outubro 1991), Lisboa, Edições Cosmos, II, pp. 283-287.

[186] **CORTIJO OCAÑA, Antonio** (1999). An Inane Hypothesis: Torroella, Flores, Lucena, and Celestina?. In: Research Series/Number 103. Multicultural Iberia: Language, Literature, and music. Dru Dougherty and Milton M. Azevedo, Editors. University of California at Berkeley. (pp. 40 – 56), pp. 48 y 49.

168

"Scholars have not questioned why Lucena's work and the first act of the Celestina are copied together in the same manuscript. But according to facts previously explained, it is likely that their co-appearancein MS II-1520 is not coincidental. Otherwise, how could we explain the presence of this third manuscript (the first being MS 22018-21 at the Biblioteca Nacional, and the second being MS 5-3-20 at the Colombina) containing both sentimental works and Lucena's compositions? At this point, it is helpful to recall a study by Serrano y Sanz which linked Fernando de Rojas to a "Juan de Lucena," a printer in the Puebla de Montalbán. Although the article by Serrano y Sanz concluded that this Juan de Lucena, a printer, was not our Juan de Lucena, translator of Fazio's dialogue, this scholar proved that both Lucenas were blood relatives. Now our suspicions (again, just suspicions) are even greater: **both Lucenas, Picolomini, Puebla de Montalbán, Salamanca, students in Salamanca around 1490–95, the first act of the Celestina, and Fernando de Rojas?"

12.2.6.2 Ms 5-3-20

Lucena, heavily involved in translation and printing activities, used the pseudonym Diego de San Pedro at the beginning of the nineties, and changed his pseudonym to Juan de Flores when he worked in Salamanca.

Ms. 5-3-20 of the Library Colombina in Seville

The work *Grisel y Mirabella* appears in a Ms. 5-3-20 of the Library Colombina in Seville, having the following works[187]:

Biblioteca Colombina of Seville, MS 5-3-20
1) *Cuatro oraciones a la República,* by Stephano Porcari, anonymous translator?; fols. 1r-16r CNUM 2315, 7119, 7120, 7121 (Parrilla 1986).14
2) *Fragmento del Tratado de amores,* anonymous?; fols. 17r-22r, CNUM 2316 (Parrilla 1985).15

---

[187] **FAULHABER, Charles B. et all.** (1992). *BETA* : Bibliografía Española de Textos Antiguos. Madrid: Mirconet. Cited by **CORTIJO OCAÑA, Antonio** (1999). An Inane Hypothesis: Torroella, Flores, Lucena, and Celestina?. In: Research Series/Number 103. Multicultural Iberia: Language, Literature, and music. Dru Dougherty and Milton M. Azevedo, Editors. University of California at Berkeley. (pp. 40 – 56), p. 45.

3) *Epístola exortatoria a las letras,* by Juan de Lucena to Fernando Alvarez Zapata; fols. 22v-26r, CNUM 2317.

4) *Triunfo de Amor,* by Juan de Flores; fols. 27r-68r, CNUM 2318 (Fernández Jiménez).

5) *Fragmento de la Historia de Torrellas y Brianda,* fragment of *Grisel y Mirabella,* by Juan de Flores; fols. 69r-86r, CNUM 2319.

6) *Carta de buena nota,* Gómez Manrique addressee, anonymous?; fols. 86v-87r, CNUM 2320.

7) *Respuesta de Gómez Manrique [a la Carta de buena nota];* fols. 87r-89r, CNUM 2321.

8) *Cartas de Grimalte y Fiometa,* fragment of *Grimalte y Gradissa,* by Juan de Flores; fols. 90r-101v, 2322.

In manuscript 5-3-20, compiled according to the apistolary criterion, we also see that Juan Ramirez de Lucena and Juan de Flores are the authors of most of the works. According to Antonio Cortijo some anonymous works can therefore be attributed to Juan [Ramirez] de Lucena and Juan de Flores. Cortijo refers primarily to the work *Tratado de amores* incorporating an episode similar to Celestina, based on the *Historia de Duobus amantibus*[188] of Piccolomini (similar to *Repetición de amores?*). The history of *Duobus amantibus* could be inspired by *Amadis de Gaula,* as pointed by Amador Rios[189].

JGAAP detected Diego de San Pedro as the anonymous writer of the *Tratado de amores.* On the other hand somebody with the linguistic style of Hernán Díaz, the autor of *El Peregrino,* could have been the translater of the anonymous[190] *Cuatro oraciones a la República.* Probably the manuscript Ms. 5-3-20 of the Library Colombina in Seville belonged in the past to Lucena, son of Juan Ramírez de Lucena.

---

[188] Impreso en Salamanca, el 18 de octubre de 1496 en una imprenta desconocida.

[189] **RIOS, Amador de los** (1865). Historia crítica de la literatura española, Madrid. T. VI, p. 364. Cited by **DURÁN, Armando** (1973). Estructura y técnicas de la novela sentimental y caballeresca, p. 20.

[190] **PARRILLA, Carmen** (1995). Una traducción anónima de cuatro oraciones a la república de Florencia en la biblioteca Colombina. In: Revista de Literatura Medieval, VII, pp. 9-38 (full text).

As already observed, Lucena was heavily involved with translation and printing activities. He used the pseudonym Diego de San Pedro in the beginning of the ninetees, changing his name to another pseudonym Juan de Flores when he worked in Salamanca. There is another manuscript that must have belong to him:

12.2.6.3 Mss 22018-21
Set of manuscripts in the National Library of Madrid
In the National Library of Madrid there is a set of manuscripts that carry different numbers and whose content is as follows[191]:

National Library of Madrid, MSS 22018-21
1) *Grimalte y Gradissa,* by Juan de Flores; MS 22018, CNUM 2144.
2) *Triunfo de Amor,* by Juan de Flores; MS 22019, CNUM 2145 (Fernández Jiménez 1986).
3) *La coronación de la señora Gracisla,* anonymous?; MS 22020, CNUM 2146.11
4) *Carta consolatoria que enbió el prothonotario de Lucena a Gómeç Manrique quando murió su hija doña Kathalina, muger de Diego García de Toledo;* MS 22021, fols. 1r-2v, CNUM 2147.
5) *Respuesta de Gómeç Manrique al prothonotario de Lucena;* MS 22021, fols. 3r-8r, CNUM 2148.12
6) *Carta enviada por Hiseo la Brunda a Tristán de Leonís quexándosedel porqué la dexó presa a su causa y se casó con Hiseo de las Blancas Manos,* anonymous?; MS 22021, fols. 8v-10r, CNUM 2149.
7) *Respuesta de Tristán desculpándose de la innocente culpa que le encargan,* anonymous?; MS 22021, fols. 10v-12v, CNUM 2150.13

---

[191] **FAULHABER, Charles B. et all.** (1992). *BETA* : Bibliografía Española de Textos Antiguos. Madrid: Mirconet. Cited by **CORTIJO OCAÑA, Antonio** (1999). An Inane Hypothesis: Torroella, Flores, Lucena, and Celestina?. In: Research Series/Number 103. Multicultural Iberia: Language, Literature, and music. Dru Dougherty and Milton M. Azevedo, Editors. University of California at Berkeley. (pp. 40 – 56), p. 44

8) *Arnalte y Lucenda,* by Diego de San Pedro; MS 22021, fols. 13r-63r, CNUM 2151.

Some of these texts were studied by Fernando Gómez Redondo[192] who informs that J. L. Gili said that the work originated around 1500. Not all texts were collected on continuing basis, as various kinds of paper were used (without watermark). Traces of the Aragonese language are being present throughout the codex, not only in spelling and in phonological and morphological features, but also in the interpretive senses derived from some of the works. Given these data K. Whinnom[193] concludes: "facts known lead us to imagine that a certain Aragonese, fond of letters, in the early sixteenth century, did transcribe various manuscripts that he possessed or that he borrowed from the owners".

The fact that there are traces of the Aragonese language in the manuscript is according to my research due to the fact that Lucena was in the service of Aragonese patrons in his youth.

JGAAP let us know that *La coronación de la señora Gracisla* probably was written by Juan de Flores (Lucena). With respect to the *Carta enviada por Hiseo la Brunda a Tristán de Leonís* this letter seems to have been written by Nicolás Núñez (Lucena), and the *Respuesta de Tristán* probably by Diego de San Pedro (Lucena).

12.2.7 The chess writer Francesch Vicent

Francesch Vicent was the author of a chess book in Valencia in 1495. The chess historian José Antonio Garzón Roger has written awesome books about him[194].

---

[192] **GÓMEZ REDONDO, Fernando** (2000). Carta de Iseo y respuesta de Tristán. In: DICENDA. Cuadernos de Filología Hispánica, N°. 7, pp. 327-356.

[193] **WHINNOM, Keith** (1979). Dos opúsculos isabelinos. "La coronación ..." y Nicolás Núñez "Cárcel de Amor". Exeter: University Hispanic Texts,

[194] **GARZÓN ROGER, José Antonio** (2001). "En pos del incunable perdido. Francesch Vicent: Llibre dels jochs partitis dels schachs, Valencia, 1495". (Prólogo Dr. Ricardo Calvo). Biblioteca Valenciana.

An author who did not like to say his name and used the pseudonym of Lucena was author of a chess book printed in Salamanca in 1497. In Ferrara we observe that a servant with the name of Francesco was the chess teacher of Lucrecia Borgia in 1505. Chess researchers think that this person was Francesch Vicent[195].

There is all reason to believe that this chess teacher or in an earlier stage, Gonzalo Fernández de Oviedo, had a good friendship with Ludovico Ariosto in Ferrara. The latest had the idea to write about the courtiers. And so we saw appear years later   *Il Cortegiano* by Baldassare Castiglione that was dedicated to Ludovico Ariosto.

It was, Mrs. Gentile Feltria de Campo Fregoso, the bastard sister of Guidobaldo de Montefeltro, who financed the work *Tragicomedia* of *Celestina y Melibea*, which was published in January 1506 by the printer Eucharius Silber in Rome. The work was translated into Italian[196] in 1505 by Alonso Ordóñez, a messmate of the Pope. Ordóñez came originally from the town Segorbe like Francesch Vicent. We see this Ordóñez years later in 1517 next to or displacing Alonso de Proaza at the University of Valencia[197] or was this another person with the same name?

Marco Gerolamo Vida was a major Italian poet and scholar, who apparently began to write a Latin manuscript of *Scacchia Ludus* or *De ludo scaccorum* in 1507, which ended in 1510. The poem was instructed by Federico Fregoso, the son of Gentile Feltria de Montefeltro.

GARZÓN ROGER, José Antonio (2005). "El regreso de Francesch Vicent: la historia del nacimiento y expansión del ajedrez moderno". (Prólogo Anatali Karpov). Generalitat Valenciana, Conselleria de Cultura, Educació i Esport: Fundació Jaume II el Just, Valencia.

[195] L'italia scacchistica, diciembre de 1999.

[196] **SCOLAS, Emma** (1961). Note sulla prima traduzione italiana della Celestina. In: Studi Romanzi XXXIII, pp. 153-217

[197] **FEBRER ROMAGUERA, Manuel** (2003). Ortodoxia y humanismo: el estudio general de Valencia durante el rectorado de Joan de Salaya (1525-1558). Universidad de Valencia, p. 244

Murray[198] tells us that in 1525 a work was published with a poem of 742 lines under the title *Liber Scacchorum* without the permission of the author, who then made a publication in 1527 through Ludovico Vicentino.

Murray also observed that the poem of *Scachs d'amor* has some striking resemblances to Vida's Scaccha Ludus[199]. This betrays the fact that Francesch Vicent was aware of this manuscript of *Scachs d'amor* and had informed Federico Fregoso about it.

Gonzalo Fernández de Oviedo (Lucena) was in Italy for some years between 1497 and 1502 and had contact with the main Italian courts. He probably had the necessary contacts with Pietro Bembo and other eminent humanists (Gerolamo Fracastoro) and all these contacts were on the highest level. We see years thereafter that his books were printed in Venice and I revert to *La Celestina*, *Amadís*, *Cárcel de amor*, *Primaleón*, and *Palmerín de Olivia* between 1533 and 1534 under pseudonyms. In this case Francisco Delicado was the corrector of the books. However, in 1534 we also see a translated book of Gonzalo Fernández de Oviedo with the title *Libro secondo delle Indie Occidentale*. Was Fernández de Oviedo in Venice in those years?

Was the name Francesch Vicent another joke of Gonzalo Fernández de Oviedo? We do not know, but it is very strange to observe that the only reference to Vicent is a chess master by the name of Francesco in March 1506. Was Fernández de Oviedo in Ferrara in that year? Thereafter we no longer observe the name Francesco (Francesch Vicent?). In 1511 and 1512 we see chess books, but without the name Francesch Vicent.

What we observe from the short Valencian text of Francesch Vicent's book (the book had been lost) is that the JGAAP analysis refers to Fernando de Rojas and Gonzalo Fernández de Oviedo (Appendix 15.4.2). This is a rather strange matter, because one can ask how is it possible that JGAAP refers to these two possible authors despite as many as 80 options. The text to which I refer is:

---

[198] **MURRAY, H. J. R.** (1913) *A History of Chess*. Oxford University Press, p. 790
[199] **MURRAY, H. J. R.** (1913) *A History of Chess*, p. 781

"Libre dels jochs partits dels schacs en nombre de 100, ordenat e compost per mi Francesch Vicent nat en la ciutat de Segorb e criat e vehi de la insigne e valerosa ciutat de Valencia".

"A loor e gloria de nostre Redemtor Jesu Christ fonc acabat lo dit libre que ha nom libre dels jochs partits dels schachs en la insigne ciutat de Valencia e estampat per mans de Lope de Roca Alemany e Pere Trinchet librere a XV dies de Mag del any MCCCCLXXXXV".

I also made a JGAAP analysis of a part of the Italian texts in the chess book by Damiano (Appendix 15.4.3). Strangely enough, JGAAP detected the name of Lucena, La Celestina MS 1520, and Gonzalo Fernández de Oviedo. With respect to the Italian foreword of this book we observe Fernando de Rojas, La Celestina MS 1520, and Gonzalo Fernández de Oviedo as authors (Appendix 15.4.4).

The role of Fernando de Rojas is disturbing, but I cannot explain why he figures earlier in the list than the other authors. What we know is that Gonzalo Fernández de Oviedo had some time to spend in Rome in 1511 and 1512. Maybe his friend Juan del Encina was also involved in the printing of Damiano. Or was it Francesch Vicent?

Since the text in this study of Francesch Vicent are not in Spanish but in Valencian and Italian, I'm not inclined to assign them much value. However, I wanted to show them because of the strange results through JGAAP that lead to Gonzalo Fernández de Oviedo.

12.2.8 The court of Lucrecia Borgia

Keith Whinnom made a careful study of Diego de San Pedro and Queen Isabel[200] with respect to the dates of the book *Arnalte y Lucenda*. Another investigation of Whinnom's book Arnalte and Lucenda could betray a very suspicious connection with Francesch Vicent, who at that

---

[200] **WHINNOM, Keith** (1960). The religious poems of Diego de San Pedro: their relationship and dating. E: Hispanic Review. 1960 – XXVIII, pp. 1-15. Cita en pp. 13-14

time was under the orders of Lucrecia Borgia, trying to teach her the game of chess.

The year 1500 was precisely when Gonzalo Fernández de Oviedo was in those Italian circles and the date of 1505 corresponds more or less with Francesch Vicent's stay in Ferrara and in Italy. On the other hand the Italian version of La Celestina was printed in 1505.

Whinnom[201] observes the following in relation to Lucrecia Borgia in Ferrara:

> Además, hubo otra edición de la novela anterior a la de 1522, según se puede demostrar por una poesía manuscrita, escrita hacia 1505, en loor de Lucrecia Borgia; copiada de la poesía de (Diego de) San Pedro en loor de Isabel la Católica y adaptada sólo en lo esencial ("Ferrara" por "Castilla", etcétera), la poesía a Lucrecia exhibe variantes que coinciden con las de la versión del panegírico en el *Arnalte* de 1522 y contrastan con las lecturas del de 1491, de manera que hay que pensar en una edición impresa hacia 1500 (?)....

Translation:

> In addition, there was another edition of the novel prior to that of 1522, as can be demonstrated by a handwritten poetry, written around 1505, copied from the poetry of (Diego de) San Pedro in honour of Isabel la Católica and adapted only in the essential ("Ferrara" by "Castilla", etc.), that the poetry to Lucrecia exhibits variants that coincide with those of the panegyric version in the Arnalte book of 1522 and contrast with the readings of the 1491 book. Consequently one has to think of a print edition towards 1500 (?).

> *Muy alta Yl^{ma} ex^a*
>
> *Los que merescieron en las tales causas escrevir de quatro virtudes deven ser guarnecidos: de discricion y gracia, autoridad y favor; y como todas estas de mi estan muy desviadas, los, que esta obra veran, con justa razon dino de reprehension pueden hazerme; y aunque este conocimiento no me falta, tomando por fundamento aquella palabra de Orfeo quando al ynfierno entrar determino de su querida Euredize sacar, pensando en los peligrosas afanes que de pasar avia, dixo: el deseo haze olvidar el temor, y con este todo inconviniente posoponiendo, con solo acordarme a V.E. servir, determine est pobre tratado*

---

[201] **WHINNON, Keith** (1985). Diego de San Pedro. Obras Completas, I. Tractado de amores de Arnalte y Lucenda. Sermón. Clásicos Castalia, Madrid. pp. 44 y 45

hazer mas de palabras verdaderas escrito que de dulces razones senbrado, en que mui ciertos loores de vuestra excelencia se veran y de vuestras donzallas conoscida alabança.

Comiençan las alabaças de V.E.

Poema dedicada a Lucrecia Borgia	Poema dedicada a Isabel la Católica
Soys, duquesa, tan real en Ferara tan querida, qu'el bueno i el comunal, de todos en general, soys amada, soys temida. Soys plaziente a los ajenos soy atajo d'entrevalos, soys anparo de los menos, sois amiga de los buenos y enemiga de los malos.	Es nuestra Reina real en su España assi tenido que del bueno y comunal, de todos en general es amada y es temida; es plaziente a los ajenos, es atajo de entrevalos, es amparo de los menos, es gozo para los buenos, es pena para los malos.
Anima que nunca yerra, soys un lauro divinal; soys la gloria desta tierra, sois la paz de nuestra g(u)erra. sois el bien de nuestro mal. sois ygual de todas suertes, sois plaziente a los estraños, sois el yugo de los fuertes, remedio de muchas muertes, sois consuelo de mil daños.	Es reina que nunca yerra es freno del desigual, es gloria para la tierra, es la paz de nuestra guerra, es el bien de nuestro mal; es igual a todas suertes de gentes para sus quiebras, es yugo para los fuertes, es vida de nuestras muertes, es luz de nuestras tiniebras.
Si vuestro ser sojuzgase todo quanto dios a hecho, si el mundo no s'alargase o vuestro valer menguase, no teneis vuestro derecho, sois quien no deviera ser del metal que somos nos, mas quisolo dios hazer por darnos a conoscer quien es el, pues hizo a vos.	Es tal que, aunque sojuzgase todo cuanto Dios ha fecho, si el mundo se ensanchasse o su valer se estrechasse, no ternía, su derecho; es tal que no havía de ser humandad puesta en ella, mas guísola Dios fazer por darnos a conoscer quién es El, pues fizo a ella.
Si vuestra magnificencia no diese arriba consuelo vuestra sin para ixcelencia pornia (a) gran diferencia entre la terra y el cielo. y por vuestro meresçer	Es tal que si su conciencia no diesse arriba consuelo, de envidia de su exelencia havría gran diferencia entre la tierra ye el cielo; es tal que por causa d[e] ella

177

dios os quiere aca dexar vuestros dias floreçer, escusando alla el plazer por no dar aca pesar.	havría, aunque oviesse batalla, siempre cizaña y centella en la tierra por tenella y en el cielo por llevalla.
De los vicios soys ajena, de las virtudes escala, de la cor dura cadena, nunca errando cosa buena, nunca hazeis cosa mala. sois entera providencia, aboresceis la malicia; guarnecida de prudencia, perdonando con clemencia, castigais con la justicia.	Es de los vicios ajena, es de virtudes escala, con gran cordura condena, nunca yerra cosa buena, nunca haza cosa mala; teme a Dios y a su sentencia, aborresce la malicia, abráçase con prudencia, perdona con la clemencia, castiga con la justicia.
Con fuerça de fe i firmeza, teneis cierta ell esperança; animais con la franqueza, sojusgais con fortaleza, ordenais con temperança. guarneceis con caridad las obras de devocion, ganais con la voluntad, conservais con la verdad, governais con la rrazón.	Con cuerdas de fee y firmeza tiene atada la esperança, anima con la franqueza, sojuzga con fortaleza, aplace con la templança; guarnesce con caridad las obras de devoción, gana con la voluntad, conserva con la verdad, govierna con la razón.
Allegrais los virtuosos, quitais los malos de vos, despedis los maliciosos, desdeñais a los viciosos, sobre todo amais a dios. Estimais los verdaderos, no os engañan los que engañan, aborreceis los groseros, desamais los ligongeros, no escuchais los que cizañan.	Allega los virtuosos, quita daños de entre nos, estraña los maliciosos, reprehende los viciosos, ama a los que aman a Dios; quiere bien los verdaderos, no la engañan los que engañan, aborresce los groseros, desama los lisonjeros, no escucha los que cizañan.
Pues ¿quién osara tocar en vuestra gran hermosura? que quien mas pienza hablar en ella avra de quedar ofendido de locura. Es publicar mi defeto en ponerme en esta cosa, pues no basto a dalle efeto sino fuese mas discreto, siendo vos menos hermosa.	Pues ¿quién osara tocar en su grande hermosura? pues quien más piensa hablar en ella havrá de quedar ofendido de locura; es publicar mi defecto en ponerme en la tal cosa, pues no puede haver efecto, si no fuese más discreto o ella menos hermosa.

Mas aun que lo diga mal, digo que son las hermosas ante vos, sol divinal, que es el pobre metal con ricas piedras preciosas. Son con vuestra perfigcion qual la noche con el dia, qual con descanso prision, qual el viernes de pasion con la pascua d'alegria.	Mas aunque lo diga mal, digo que son las hermosas ante su cara real cual es el pobre metal con ricas piedras preciosas; son con su gran perfección cual la noche con el día, cual con descanso prisión, cual el viernes de Pasión con la Pascua de alegría.
Teniendo tan alto ser, siempre aveis representado en las obras el valer, en la rrazon el saber, en la presencia ell estado; y la gran bondad d'aquel que tal gracia puso en vos, os midio con tal nivel por que alabemos de el quando vieremos a vos.	E esta que tal pudo ser ha siempre representado en las obras el valer y en la razón el saber, y en la prresencia el estado, y la gran bondad de Aquel que tal gracia puso en ella, la midió por su nivel, porque demos gloria a El cuando miramos a ella.
La debida presuncion, la mesura mas presciada, las obras del galardon en vuestra gran condicion tienen tomada posada. Soys y fuestes siempre una en los contrastes y pena; resistiendo a la fortuna, no teneis falta ninguna, no teneis cosa no buena.	La devida presunción, la mesura más preciada, las obras del galardón, en su real condición tienen tomada posada; es y ha sido siempre una en dar por el vicio pena, supo vencer la Fortuna no tiene falta ninguna, no tiene cosa no buena.
Pues ¿quién podra recontar, por mas que se padezir, vuestro discreto hablar, vuestro gracioso mirar, vuestro galante vestir? Un poner de tal manera, de tal forma y de tal suerte, que anque la gala muriera, en vuestro dechado oviera la vida para su muerte.	Pues ¿quién podrá recontar, por más que sepa dezir, la gracia de su mirar, el primor de su hablar, la gala de su vestir? su valer es en manera y en tal forma y de tal suerte, que aunque la gala muriera, en sus dechados hoviera la vida para su muerte.
Si las famosas pasadas agora fueran presentes, no fueran ellas nonbradas, por que en vos son demostradas virtudes mas excelentes.	

En la tierra vos soys una en medio vuestras donzellas mas luziente que ninguna, como en el cielo la luna entre las claras estrellas.	
O quantas vezes contenplo, con gran dulces melodias yreis all eterno templo segud muestra vuestro enexmplo ya despues de largos dias; pues poniendo ya cilencio acuerdo, pues mal alabo, con rrazon de quien me venço de quedar en el començo pues no se llegar al cabo.	¡Oh, cuántas vezes contemplo con qué dulces melodías ha de ir al eterno templo! según nos dize su enxiemplo ya después de largos días; y después que así la elijo, pienso con alma elevada en el gozo sin letijo que havrán la Madre y el Hijo con la huéspeda llegada.
Fyn, mas no de serviros	

A JGAAP analysis of the poem to Lucrecia Borgia (Appendix 15.4.5) shows the idiolect of the foreword to *La Celestina*. As I already observed in this book, the foreword to *La Celestina* corresponds to Gonzalo Fernández de Oviedo. However, before discovering Fernández de Oviedo the JGAAP analysis would have appointed to Juan del Encina as the author of the poem (Appendix 15.4.6).

12.2.9 The court of Urbino

After the death of Prince Johan, Fernández de Oviedo (Lucena) departed to Italy with a chess book under his arm and was with the painters Leonardo da Vinci, Ticiano, and Michelangelo; the poets Serafino dell'Aquila, Jacopo Sannazaro, and Urbino. There he studied the Tuscan language[202].

The question is when did Lucena go to Italy. His father Juan Ramírez de Lucena's Vita Beata was printed on 8 August, 1499 and again on 8

---

[202] **FERNÁNDEZ DE OVIEDO, Gonzalo** (1535). La Historia General y Natural de Indias. Edición de José Amador de los Ríos, Parte I, Madrid, 1851, p. XVII y XVIII

October, 1502, and logically speaking Lucena was involved in it (Appendix), since I found his idiolect through a JGAAP analysis. So he could have been in Italy the whole of 1498 and 7 months of 1499. Or did he go to Italy with his friend Juan del Encina? Did Lucena have a twin brother or was Fernando de Rojas in charge of the printing of Vita Beata? I think it is much more reasonable to think that Fernando de Rojas was a brother of Fernández de Oviedo, but it is clear that much more research is needed.

Anyway, this matter needs a special research when we take into account that *Vita Beata* was bound together with *Los doce trabajos de Hercules* of Enrique de Villena. The work of Villena has the idiolect (Appendix 15.4.7) of Juan de Sedeño (=Gonzalo Fernández de Oviedo), the proem by Juan del Encina (Appendix 15.4.8) and the foreword were written by Juan Ramírez de Lucena. This could mean Juan del Encina was in charge of the publication of this work, not Gonzalo Fernández de Oviedo. In other words, Fernández de Oviedo could have gone to Italy already at the end of 1497. However, it is necessary to study more books, because Fernández de Oviedo was involved in more books.

According to my research I once thought that Lucena was a pseudonym of Francesch Vicent who worked at the court of Lucrecia Borgia in Ferrara as her chess master under the name of Francesco. In 1507 Lucena went to Zaragoza, probably with Juan del Encina, to print the Tragicomedia. Then I thought that in 1508 Lucena worked in Rome under the name Ludovico Vicentino degli Arrighi[203] until 1527. Thereafter he was in Venice for some years using the pseudonym Francisco Delicado[204]. However, I had to rectify many of these theories.

I already stated in this book that Murray also observed that the poem of *Scachs d'amor* has some striking resemblances to Vida's Scaccha

---

[203] **WESTERVELD, Govert** (2016). Research of the Mysterious Aragonese Author of La Celestina, 288 pages. Editor: Lulu Press, Inc. ISBN: 978-1-326-81331-4
[204] **WESTERVELD, Govert** (2016). The Life of Francisco Delicado in Rome: 1508-1527, 264 pages. Editor: Lulu Press, Inc. ISBN: 978-1-326-81393-2

Ludus[205]. Lucena (Gonzalo Fernández de Oviedo), aware of the manuscript *Scachs d'amor* had informed Federico Fregoso about it.

Again we see the influence of Lucena. Federico Fregoso was a friend of Castiglione and Bembo[206]. Bembo[207] was between 1502 and 1503 in the service of Lucrecia Borgia and between 1506-1512 he was with Guidobaldo de Montefeltro and his wife Elisabetta Gonzaga, that is, in the Court of Urbino. On the other hand Baldassarre Castiglione lived in the court of Urbino with Duke Guidobaldo di Montefeltro and his wife Elisabetta Gonzaga between the years 1504 and 1506[208]. In 1506 he was traveling in England, to receive from the hands of Henry VII the order of the Garter for Duke Guidobaldo and in 1507 was as Ambassador of Guidobaldo in Milan near the French King Louis XII.

Studying Castiglione's book I have always had the idea that this author to write his book had noticed the authors of the Lucena clan. Lucena spent some time on the Urbino court and spoke ofcourse about chess. It was said in the book of Il Cortegiano by Baldassare Castiglione: "Guardate i Spagnoli, i quali par che siano maestri della Cortegiania?". Castiglione says the following about chess[209]:

> "And what," replied my lord Gaspar, "do you say of the game of chess?" "It is certainly a pleasant and ingenious amusement" said messer Frederico. "But I think there is one defect in it. And that is, there is too much to know, so that whoever would excell in the game of chess must spend much time on it, methinks, and give it as much study as if he would learn some noble science or

[205] **MURRAY, H. J. R.** (1913). A History of Chess, p. 781

[206] **OSBORNE, June & CORNISH, Joe** (2003). Urbino: The Story of a Renaissance City, p. 157
CASTIGLIONE, Baldassarre & BAUDI DI VESME, Carlo (1854). Il Cortegiano. Firenze. Felice Le Monnier. Tomo I, p. 322

[207] Mas sobre Bembo in: **CLOUGH, Cecil H.** (1965). Pietro Bembo's Library Represented in the British Museum. In: The Britisch Museum Quarterly, Vol. 30, No. 1 / 2 (Autumn, 1965), pp. 3-17

[208] **RODRÍGUEZ VALENCIA, Vicente** (1970). Isabel la Católica en la opinión de españoles y extranjeros. Siglos XV al XX. Instituto Isabel la Católica de Historia Eclesiástica. Valladolid, p. 216

[209] Strangely enough the chess issue was not indicated in the book of Boscan.
BOSCÁN, Juan (1873) Los cuatro libros del Cortesano. Edición dirigida por D. Antonio María Fabié, Madrid

do anything else of imortance you please; and yet in the end with all his pains he has learned nothing but a game. Therefore I think a ver unusual thing is true of it, namely that mediocrity is more praiseworthy than excellence."

My lord Gaspar replied:
" Many Spaniards excel in this and divers other games, yet without giving them much study or neglecting other things."

" Believe me," replied messer Federico, " they do give much study thereto, although covertly. But those other games you speak of, besides chess, are perhaps like many I have seen played (although of little moment), which serve only to make the vulgar marvel; wherefore methinks they deserve no other praise or reward than that which Alexander the Great gave the fellow who at a good distance impaled chick-peas on the point of a needle.'"

The chess issue was not indicated in the book of Juan Boscan in 1534 and this is quite suspicious, hence this translation of the Italian book needs much more study.

Without Lucena, Castiglione could never have written his book. The book of The Courtesan was dedicated to Alfonso Ariosto (1475-1525) of Ferrara, a cousin of Ludovico Ariosto, since he had given the idea to Castiglione. Logically speaking, it was Alfonso Ariosto who was in contact with Lucena in Ferrara, because he served the Eastern family in Ferrara in the same place where a chess teacher with the name Francesco was around 1506.

Ludovico Ariosto (1474-1533) also learned from the courtier Lucena, since in 1508 he presented his first comedy, the Cassaria, in Ferrara, and today Ludovico Ariosto is considered one of the patriarchs of comedy[210].

A proof in this sense is the influence of Amadís de Gaule on Ludovico Ariosto[211]. This Italian author, in his *Orlando furioso*, written in 1516, speaks of Reinaldo de Montalbán, another book of Lucena. The work was written in Ferrarese, the dialect used in Ferrara. It is possible that

---

[210] **VECCHIO, Laura M. del** (2002). Archetypal female figures in the works of Bartolomé de Torres Naharro and other renaissance spanish and italian dramatists. Tesis doctoral, State university of New York at Buffalo,m p. 66
[211] **RAJNA, Pio** (1876). Le fonti dell' Orlando Furioso.

this Italian poet saw the work Reinaldos de Montalbán, by the efforts of Lucena. Apart from the influence of Amadís de Gaula another work of the Lucena[212] also influenced on the work of Ludovico Ariosto, in this case the book by *Grisel y Mirabella*[213] and again we see the hand of Lucena.

Was there already in the duchy of Urbino a contact between Castiglione, Bembo, and Lucena? It is almost certain and Castiglione noticed Lucena and other Spaniards as good courtiers and chess players. Castiglione was aware of the works of Lucena the fact that the *Cárcel de amor* had already been translated into Italian implied that Castiglione used this book in later years[214].

12.2.10　　The authors of La Celestina

Apparently *La Celestina* had three authors: Lucena as the ancient author, then Gil Vicente or Encina helped him in Spain and in Italy and Fernando de Rojas could have worked with some small additional work, but he is not detected in the JGAAP analysis. The great organizator of this work is Lucena. Rolf Eberenz[215] noted that the editions of Burgos (1499-1502), Toledo (1500), Sevilla (1501) and Zaragoza (1507) showed the form „*leístas*", while the other editions contains *lo*. This could be an indication that these first four editons had to do with Lucena. Probably Lucena's helpers were in charge of the various editions in the years 1499-1507.

Did the expulsion of the Jews and the inquisitional proceedings with his family have something to do with his pessimism and tragic view of life?

---

[212] It is advisable that philologists analyze the similarity between the texts of *Repeticiónb de amores* (Lucena, 1497) and the work of *Grisel y Mirabella.*
[213] **MATULKA, Barbara** (1974). The novels of Juan de Flores and their european difusión. Slatkin Reprints, Genève, p. 189.
[214] **GIANNINI, A.** (1919). La Cárcel de amor y el Cortegiano de B. Castiglione. In: Revue Hispanique, XLVI, pp. 547-568
[215] **EBERENZ, Rolf** (2000). El español en el otoño de la Edad Media, Gredos, Madrid, pp. 232 and 236.

Lucena probably wanted to express his feelings about the human conflicts and discoveries in his books for future generations.

12.2.11   La Celestina and Chess

A discovery by Calvo[216] judges Calisto to be a literary reincarnation of Lucena in his book. Dr. Ricardo Calvo was right when he predicted in 1999 that Calisto was Lucena[217].

Juan Ramírez de Lucena, his son Lucena, and the courtier Juan del Encina were all chess players. We also see it in this act where they speak of the chess term "arm mates[218]". According to Calvo the most important and decisive fact is that Calisto in the comedy of Calisto and Melibea is a chess player. "Not only a player, but a lover of chess problems, like Lucena's 150 games. Sempronio in Act II recommends the following distractions to his master"[219]:

SEMPRONIO
Donde, si perseveras, o de muerto o loco no podrás escapar, si siempre no te acompaña quien te allegue plazeres, diga donayres, tenga canciones alegres, cante romaneces, cuente ystorias, pinte motes, finja cuentos, juegue a naypes, **arme mates**[220].

---

[216] **CALVO, Ricardo** (1997). Lucena. La evasión en ajedrez del converso Calisto. Ciudad Real: Perea Ediciones, p. 55

[217] **CALVO, Ricardo** (1997). Lucena. La evasión en ajedrez del converso Calisto. Ciudad Real: Perea Ediciones, p. 55

[218] Cfr. **CAPPELLI, Guido M. & VALLÍN, Gema** (1999). Fernando de Rojas. La Celestina. Edición de Guido M. Cappelli y Gema Vallín. Circulo de Lectores. Barcelona, p. 129

[219] **CALVO, Ricardo** (1997). Lucena. La evasión en ajedrez del converso Calisto. Ciudad Real: Perea Ediciones, pp. 56-57

Calvo says: "Prof. Peter Russell of Oxford informed me when I presented my draft with this idea in 1984 that in the first Italian edition of La Celestina, "arm mates" had been translated, less exactly, as "giocare agli scacchi" or playing chess games".

[220] armar mates: preparing checkmates in the chess game.

Scene 4

The chess theme is visible again in the words "al tablero" of *La Celestina's* procuress[221]:

> CELESTINA
>
> Pues amargas cient monedas serían éstas. ¡Ay cuitada de mí! ¡En qué lazo me he metido! Que por me mostrar solícita y esforzada pongo mi persona **al tablero.**

> CELESTINA
>
> ¿qué dirá, qué hará, qué pensará, sino que hay nuevo engaño en mis pisadas, y que yo he descubierto la **celada** por haber más provecho desta otra parte, como sofística prevaricadora?

Scene 7

We found a chess term "jaques" in the seventh scene of *La Celestina*[222]

> CELESTINA
>
> Si te lo prometí, no lo he olvidado, ni creas que he perdido con los años la memoria. Que más de tres **jaques** ha recibido de mí sobre ello en tu ausencia.

Again the chess term "mate". This time with a double meaning[223].

> CELESTINA
>
> ...Ya creo que estará bien madura. Vamos de camino por casa, que no se podrá **escapar de mate.** Que esto es lo menos que yo por ti tengo de hacer.

---

[221] 'arriesgo la vida', metaphor taken from the game. Cfr. **CAPPELLI, Guido M. & VALLÍN, Gema** (1999). Fernando de Rojas. La Celestina. Edición de Guido M. Cappelli y Gema Vallín. Circulo de Lectores. Barcelona, p. 146

[222] *jagues*. 'acometidas, asaltos', in the language of chess. Cfr. **CAPPELLI, Guido M. & VALLÍN, Gema** (1999). Fernando de Rojas. La Celestina. Edición de Guido M. Cappelli y Gema Vallín. Circulo de Lectores. Barcelona, pp. 199-200

[223] He continues with the metaphor of the game, quite common in the lyric of love; Here it can have a second sexual sense. Cfr. **CAPPELLI, Guido M. & VALLÍN, Gema** (1999). Fernando de Rojas. La Celestina. Edición de Guido M. Cappelli y Gema Vallín. Circulo de Lectores. Barcelona, p. 200

Scene 21

We also find the chess term "celada" in the twenty-first scene of *La Celestina*:

PLEBERIO
Corremos por los prados de tus viciosos vicios muy descuidados, a rienda suelta; descúbresnos la **celada** cuando ya no hay lugar de Volver.

12.2.12   Magnifying his merits

One of the curious aspects of Gonzalo Fernández de Oviedo's personality is that he always seeks to magnify himself in his writings and highlights his relationships with important characters. The proclivity of Oviedo to the vainglory is always present. We observe the same attitude in him when he wrote a book under the pseudonym Lucena. This, of course, is a quite interesting aspect, because his expressions "todo lo que yo" could have been used in some of his books.

In *Repetition de amores* we find a text where the author says that the work was written by Lucena, son of the "muy sapientísimo" (very sapient) doctor and reverend protonotary Don Juan Ramírez de Lucena, ambassador and from the Council of the Kings. Here we see that he liked to magnify his persona.

Although he does not like to say in his writings who exactly he is, we can observe in his writings (with pseudonymous names) a lot of his personal life and experiences.

12.2.13   References to his father

We find two references to a father in the Comedy Calisto and Melibea. Sempronio, now in the words of Juan del Encina, says addressing Calisto in act II:

> " Y, por tanto, no te estimes en la claridad de tu padre, que tan magnífico fue, sino en la tuya;
> Translation:
> "And therefore, do not estimate yourself in the clarity of your father, how magnificent he was, but in yours;

and Calisto refers to his father in the monologue of Act XIV:

> ¡O cruel juez!, ¡e qué mal pago me has dado del pan, que de mi padre comiste!
> Translation:
> O cruel judge! And what a bad payment you have given me in bread which you ate from my father!

In this case Calisto is Lucena, which implies that Lucena was involved both in *Repetición de amores* and in the *Comedia de Calisto y Melibea*. Fernando de Rojas probably participated very little, since he was still studying. For this reason the one who wrote most of the *Comedia de Calisto y Melibea* was Lucena.

The biography of Gonzalo Fernández de Oviedo remains a mystery in relation to his father. Mariano Cuesta Domingo describes it this way:

> Recuerda de su progenitor que «con gran curiosidad notó y escribió algunas cosas notables que en su tiempo acaecieron», cuando se hallaba en negociaciones entre los Reyes Católicos y Alfonso V de Portugal. Así pues, ha sorprendido el hecho de que, a pesar del demostrado interés genealógico, Fernández de Oviedo no mencionó expresamente a su padre y, sin embargo, por el contrario, fueron frecuentes los recuerdos que plasmó sobre Juana de Oviedo, su madre. Alguna disquisición ha llegado a la deducción de un origen ilegítimo.
>
> **Translation:**

He remembers that his father "with great curiosity he noticed and wrote some notable things that happened in his time" when he was in negotiations between the Catholic monarchs and Alfonso V of Portugal. Thus he was surprised by the fact that despite the demonstrated genealogical interest Fernández de Oviedo did not expressly mention his father and, on the contrary, the memories he expressed about his mother Juana de Oviedo were frequent. Some disquisition has reached the deduction of an illegitimate origin.

If we study the works of Gonzalo Fernández de Oviedo, we will also find that this author refers to his father several times. We learn from one of his books that his father was related to the court of Henry IV of Castile[224]. In this respect we cannot forget that Juan Ramírez de Lucena's manuscript *Vita Beata* was dedicated exactly to this king[225] in 1463.

Oviedo recounts that as a young man at the court his father acquired the habit of jotting down notes about the notable events of his days and that he, the *cronista*, had preserved some of these notes until his old age. Gonzalo followed his father's example of recording his own observations of life at the court and the accounts which he took *via voce* from the actors in the great events of his days[226].

12.2.13.1   The monologue of Calisto

A JGAAP analysis of Calisto's monologues between the 5th and 14th act pointed at the linguistic style of Sancho de Muñón. According to our study Sancho the Muñón is a pseudonym for Gonzalo Fernández de Oviedo (Lucena). The text relating to this cruel judge in act 14 is as follows:

---

[224] **FERNÁNDEZ DE OVIEDO, Gonzalo** (1535). La Historia General y Natural de Indias. Edición de José Amador de los Ríos, Parte I, Madrid, 1851, p. XIII

[225] **MEDINA BERMUDEZ, ALEJANDRO** (1997). El diálogo De Vita Beata, de Juan de Lucena: un rompecabezas histórico (I). Dicenda. Cuadernos de Filología Hispánica, no. 15, pp. 251-269, citation on p. 263

[226] **TURNER, Daymond** (1963). Biblioteca Ovetense: A Speculative Reconstruction of the Library of the First Chronicler of the Indies. In: The Papers of the Bibliographical Society of America. Vol. 57, N°. 2 (Second Quarter), pp. 157-183. Citation on p. 180

¡Oh mezquino yo!, cuánto me es agradable de mi natural la solicitud y silencio y oscuridad. No sé si lo causa que me vino a la memoria la traición que hice en partir de aquella señora, que tanto amo, hasta que más fuera de día, o el dolor de mi deshonra. ¡Ay, ay!, que esto es. Esta herida es la que siento ahora, que se ha resfriado. Ahora que está helada la sangre, que ayer hervía; ahora que veo la mengua de mi casa, la falta de mi servicio, la perdición de mi patrimonio, la infamia que tiene mi persona de la muerte, que de mis criados se ha seguido. ¿Qué hice? ¿En qué me detuve? ¿Cómo me puedo sufrir, que no me mostré luego presente, como hombre injuriado, vengador, soberbio y acelerado de la manifiesta injusticia que me fue hecha?

¡Oh mísera suavidad de esta brevísima vida! ¿Quién es de ti tan codicioso que no quiera más morir luego que gozar un año de vida denostado y prorrogarle con deshonra, corrompiendo la buena fama de los pasados? Mayormente que no hay hora cierta ni limitada ni a un solo momento. Deudores somos sin tiempo, continuo estamos obligados a pagar luego. ¿Por qué no salí a inquirir siquiera la verdad de la secreta causa de mi manifiesta perdición? ¡Oh breve deleite mundano! ¡Cómo duran poco y cuestan mucho tus dulzores! No se compra tan caro el arrepentir.

¡Oh triste yo! ¿Cuándo se restaurará tan grande pérdida? ¿Qué haré? ¿Qué consejo tomaré? ¿A quién descubriré mi mengua? ¿Por qué lo celo a los otros mis servidores y parientes? Trasquílanme en concejo y no lo saben en mi casa. Salir quiero; pero, si salgo para decir que he estado presente, es tarde; si ausente, es temprano. Y para proveer amigos y criados antiguos, parientes y allegados, es menester tiempo, y para buscar armas y otros aparejos de venganza. ¡Oh cruel juez!, ¡y qué mal pago me has dado del pan que de mi padre comiste! Yo pensaba que pudiera con tu favor matar mil hombres sin temor de castigo, inicuo falsario, perseguidor de verdad, hombre de bajo suelo. Bien dirán de ti que te hizo alcalde mengua de hombres buenos.

Miraras que tú y los que mataste en servir a mis pasados y a mí érades compañeros; mas, cuando el vil está rico, no tiene pariente ni amigo. ¿Quién pensara que tú me habías de destruir? No hay, cierto, cosa más empecible que el incogitado enemigo. ¿Por qué quisiste que dijesen: del monte sale con que se arde y que crié cuervo que me sacase el ojo? Tú eres público delincuente y mataste a los que son privados. Y pues sabe que menor delito es el privado que el público, menor su utilidad, según las leyes de Atenas disponen. Las cuales no son escritas con sangre; antes muestran que es menor yerro no condenar los malhechores, que punir los inocentes. ¡Oh cuán peligroso es seguir justa causa delante de injusto juez!

12.2.14   Nobleman and noble

Francisco Delicado let us know that he was noble: "digo que mi oficio me hizo noble" (I say that my profession made me noble).

The destiny of Gonzalo Fernández de Oviedo as a chamber waiter was considered a position of distinction, since it required belonging to the nobility.

As we know, his father Juan Ramírez de Lucena belonged to the nobility of his town of Soria.

12.2.15   Glorification of the Spanish Empire

The life of the protonotary Juan Ramírez de Lucena[227] could perfectly have been connected to the introduction of the new powerful dama in chess. Was it at the time when he was working with Prince Ferdinand in Valencia (1968-1970) or was it at the time when the protonotary was working with the Catholic monarch (1970-1974)? The new word 'dama' for the chess queen in Spain was already in use in France and it was exactly Juan Ramírez de Lucena who was a long time ambassador for the Catholic monarchs in France during the years 1970-1974.

His son Lucena (Gonzalo Fernández de Oviedo) defended the glory of the new chess queen in Spain through his chess book in 1497.

Gonzalo Fernández de Oviedo (Lucena) continued his work by means of writing the history of the Castilian monarchy as another expression of the glory of the Castilian Empire.

---

[227] **WESTERVELD, Govert** (2015) The Ambassador Juan Ramírez de Lucena, the Father of the Chessbook Writer Lucena. 226 pages. Lulu Editors. ISBN: 978-1-326-37728-1

12.2.16   Amadís books in possession of his protector

When studying the books that his protector Fernando de Aragón, Duke of Calabria had in his library, we observe that he had all the books of *Amadís*. I think that most of them had a connection to Gonzalo Fernández de Oviedo, plus the fourth book of *Reynaldo, Trapisonda, Palmerín de Olivia,* and others. In this case I can highlight the book of *Los tratados de Alonso Ortiz* (1493), because one of the treatises fully discusses the letter of the prothonotary Lucena, Gonzalo Fernández de Oviedo's father[228].

12.2.17   Prolific writer

Lucena was a prolific writer and I will revert to that again in detail in the last chapter. The testament of Rojas states that Rojas had a chess book. It must be Lucena's *Arte de Ajedrez* from 1497. He also had the *libro de Calisto,* which should probably refer to the first book of 1499? in Burgos, where we find the word Calisto in the Argument of the first act of this comedy, since this book did not have a cover. He also had *Margarita poética* written by Albert von Eyb, published in Rome in 1480. This work includes fragments of the Philodoxus, a comedy that Lucena and his father the protonotary Juan Ramírez de Lucena knew from their stays in Italy. These three books are sufficient to indicate that Lucena was actually related to the University of Salamanca and involved in some translations and works, among them *Repetición de amores* and *Arte de Ajedrez* (1497) as well as in the *Comedia de Calisto y Melibea* edited in Burgos around 1500. His father Juan Ramírez de Lucena's *Vita Beata* was also published in Burgos in 1499 and 1502, and it is assumed that Lucena was in charge of these two editions, as well as the editions of *La Celestina* in the years 1499, 1500, 1501, and 1507, probably with helpers.

---

[228] **SUCESORES DE RIVADENEYRA** (1875). Inventario de los libros de Don Fernando de Aragón, duque de Calabria.

12.2.18   Chess and Prince Johan

In 1496 in Almazán the Catholic monarchs decided to give their son his own house experienced noblemen. Prince Johan signed a title given to Gonzalo Fernández de Oviedo in relation to custody and keys to the prince's chamber[229].

The chess book[230] of 1497, cited Lucena as the writer of this book, in spite of the fact that more than one author has called him Luis. Bartolomé José Gallardo called him Luis de Lucena in 1888 and since that date everybody copied him[231], but this is a mistake.

Lucena quickly prepared two works, *Repetición de amores* and *Arte de Ajedrez (*Repetition of loves and The art of chess), of which the latter was dedicated to Prince Johan, as the Prince was a big chess fan and player, just like his father, king Ferdinand. Lucena wanted to have his own place in the court of Prince Johan. A year earlier, in 1496, Juan del Encina had dedicated his *Cancionero* (songbook) to Prince Johan and secured a position at his court.

Lucena's new chess book is proof that he had visited Italy – or better said Ferrera - because Lucena used the Civis Bononiae of the Estense library of Modena. The fact that the Modena chess manuscript is in the Estense Library of Modena does not necessarily imply that the manuscript originates in Modena. People also performed for Andrea Gualengo and Orsina d'Este on the occasion of their wedding in 1469 the Bible of Borso d'Este in Ferrara under the direction of Taddeo Crivelli and Franco de Russi, probably between 1455 and 1461, and now the manuscript is in the Estense Library of Modena. So here it is quite

---

[229] **FERNÁNDEZ DE OVIEDO, Gonzalo** (1535). La Historia General y Natural de Indias. Edición de José Amador de los Ríos, Parte I, Madrid, 1851, p. XVI
[230] **LUCENA** (1497) Repetición de amores y Arte de ajedrez.
[231]   **GALLARDO, Bartolomé José** (1888). Ensayo de una biblioteca española de libros raros y curiosos, formada con los apuntamientos de B.J. Gallardo, coordinados y aumentados por M.R. Zarco del Valle y J. Sancho Rayón, Madrid: Imprenta y fundición de Manuel Tello, - 4 Volumes, Dict. Volume 3, col. 546-548, N° 2829, 2830 and 2831.

possible that this chess manuscript (*Tractatus partitorum Schachorum Tabularum et Merelorum Scriptus anno 1454*), which is now in Modena, came from the court of Ferrara.

The question now is whether this manuscript was actually written in Italy or whether it was a Spanish manuscript brought by a Spanish chess player to Ferrara or Modena. Pérez de Arriaga[232] makes an interesting comment concerning this manuscript:

> El manuscrito de la familia Civis Bononiae que se conserva en la Biblioteca Estense de Módena, fechado en el año 1454, es sin duda el modelo de la colección de juegos de partido que manejó Lucena. Así nos lo confirma la procedencia de la mayoría de los juegos de partido, de cuya literal reproducción acabamos de ver un ejemplo. Además de eso existen algunos casos singulares que así nos lo confirman. El juego de partido Luc 6 había sido hasta ahora causa de una cierta perplejidad. Por una parte su arcaica forma procedente del ajedrez árabe y por otra su original solución hacían dudar para atribuirlo a Lucena. La consideración del manuscrito de Módena nos permite aclarar que Lucena copió literalmente del juego Mod 487, que allí puede verse. Este juego de partido y su solución no se encuentra en ningún otro manuscrito conocido. Este sólo caso bastaría para poder aseverar que Lucena dispuso de un manuscrito semejante al de Módena. Otro caso clarísimo es el juego Luc 12. Hasta ahora venía considerándose su origen el juego Picc 20, pero también se encuentra en el manuscrito de Módena, Mod 374, de donde pudo ser copiado por Lucena, ya que no está en ningún otro manuscrito de la familia Civis Bononiae.

Translation:

The manuscript of the Civis Bononiae family that is conserved in the Biblioteca Estense Modena, dated in 1454, is certainly a model from the collection of party games that Lucena managed. The origin of most party games, whose literal reproduction we just saw an example of, confirms this to us. Besides that, there are some unique cases confirming us the same. The party game Luc 6 had been until now the cause of certain perplexity. On one hand its archaic form from the Arabic chess and on the other hand its original solution cast doubt attributing it to Lucena. Consideration of the Modena manuscript allows us to clarify that Lucena literally copied the game Mod 487, that there is to be seen. This party game and its solution is not found in any other known manuscript. This case alone would be sufficient to assert that Lucena disposed of a manuscript similar to Modena. Another clear case is the game Luc 12. So far

---

[232] **PÉREZ DE ARRIAGA, JOAQUIN** (1997). El incunable de Lucena. Primer arte de ajedrez modern, p. 177

194

researchers considered its origin in the game Picc 20, but it is also found in the manuscript of Modena, Mod 374 of which it could have been copied by Lucena since it is not in any other manuscript of the Civis Bononiae family.

12.2.19   Disrespectful treatment to the prince

Gonzalo Fernández de Oviedo was the confidant and friend of prince Johan and this is reflected in the chess texts where he takes excessive confidence in dealing with the prince. Arriaga says in this respect[233]:

> Lucena deja escapar en numerosas ocasiones un irrespetuoso "tú" y enseña pequeñas trapacerías para ganar lo apostado, indignas del Príncipe al que se dirige el libro. Si el *Arte de ajedrez* hubiera sido redactado como obra dedicada al principe Juan, cuesta mucho admitir el desenfado y confianzudo tratamiento que aparece en sus páginas hacia el lector. Más bien parece que se dirige a compañeros suyos de estudios y que, como demuestra en la Primera regla, era el tipo de lector que estaba en su mente cuando dice "el que fuere estudiante".

Translation:

> Lucena lets out on many occasions a disrespectful "you" and teaches small traps to win the bet, unworthy of the Prince to whom the book is directed. If the *Arte de ajedrez* had been written as a work dedicated to Prince Johan, it is very difficult to admit the carefree and confident treatment that appears in its pages to the reader. Rather it seems that he addresses his fellow students and that, as he demonstrates in the First Rule, he was the type of reader who was in his mind when he says "he who was a student".

12.2.20   The death of Prince Johan

The chess book of Lucena was dedicated to prince Johan, but since he died on 4 October 1497 it was clear that Lucena could not have worked at the court of prince Johan. We know that after printing his chess book in 1497 there was a hurry to close the printing house of Lopez Sanz in Salamanca and that Leonardo Hutz rushed to Zaragoza to start working

---

[233] **PEREZ DE ARRIAGA, Joaquín** (1997) El incunable de Lucena. Primer Arte de Ajedrez Moderno.(Ediciones Polifemo). Madrid, p. 48

in the printing house of Jorge Coci. Gonzalo Fernández de Oviedo (Lucena) then probably travelled to Italy in November or December 1497 with a chess book under his arm and was with the painters Leonardo da Vinci, Ticiano, and Michelangelo, the poets Serafino dell'Aquila, Jacopo Sannazaro, and Urbino. There he studied the Tuscan lenguage[234]. His stay with Leonardo da Vinci had the necessary effects on *La Celestina,* as observed by Di Camilo[235]:

> Toward the end of the fourth scene, Calisto gives a description of Melibea's body concluding with an intriguing remark: "Aquella proporción que veer yo no pude, sin duda por el bulto de fuera, juzgo incomparablemente ser mejor que la que Paris juzgó entre las tres deesas" (247). The divine *proporción* Calisto alludes to is unmistakably the naked body of Melibea, a sight which would confirm the perfect proportionality of her anatomical beauty. Given the novelty of this concept of human physical proportion, the question arises as to when this classical idea of beauty enters the lexicon of Renaissance humanists. Though the question of proportionality had been the object of discussion among Italian artists and architects during the second half of the fifteenth century, it was Leonardo da Vinci who around 1490 synthesized through a simple design the famous 'Vitruvian man' representing the human body according to the measures set by Vitruvius within the square and the circle. As Leonardo explains in his drawing, only these two geometrical forms, believed to be perfect by Plato, can appropriately frame the mathematical proportions nature has given to the human body; it is an accurate rendition of the harmony that governs the universe from the human microcosm to the macrocosm. Until a similar expression as that articulated by Calisto is found in any other Castilian text, literary or non-literary, we have to assume that the reference to the golden proportion of physical beauty must have been conceived within an Italian cultural ambient. If this were the case, and no new evidence to the contrary comes to light, the year of Leonardo's drawing could even be used as a *terminus a quo* for dating the first Act of *La Celestina.*

[234] **FERNÁNDEZ DE OVIEDO, Gonzalo** (1535). La Historia General y Natural de Indias. Edición de José Amador de los Ríos, Parte I, Madrid, 1851, p. XVII y XVIII
[235] **DI CAMILLO, Ottavio** (2010). When and Where Was the First Act of La Celestina Composed? A Reconsideration. In: "De ninguna cosa es alegre posesión sin compañía". Estudios celestinescos y medievales en honor del profesor Joseph Thomas Snow. New York, pp. 91-152. Citation on p. 115

As we will observe hereafter, Gonzalo Fernández de Oviedo (Lucena) was in Milan and this we also observed in his letter, as part of *La Celestina,* directed to Prince Johan as posthum work:

> pero avn en particular vuestra misma persona, cuya juuentud de amor ser presa se me representa auer visto y dél cruelmente lastimada, a causa de le faltar las defensiuas armas para resistir sus fuegos, las quales hallé esculpidas en estos papeles, [armas] no fabricadas en las grandes herrerías de **Milán,**

12.2.21   Lucena in Milan

Apparently Gonzalo Fernández de Oviedo was in the service of the Duke of Milan and then in the palace of Marquis Francisco de Gonzaga. In Rome he met Antonio de Acuña, who then served in the chamber of Pope Alexander VI. He also witnessed the disagreements and bloody clashes between the Swiss soldiers of Duke Valentin and the Spanish soldiers who militated in the Pope's guard. He attended the famous duel of Ferrer de Lorca and the Castilian of Arche, where one of those challenges was faithfully reproduced, frequently narrated in the books of the Amadis and Esplandians[236].

Fernández de Oviedo (Lucena) explains his circumstances in *Soldadesca* of the Propalladia. I never believed in the author Bartolomé Torres Naharro, who for me was a pseudonym of Lucena[237]. I erroneously considered that Lucena was the pseudonym of Juan del Encina. JGAAP showed that Juan de Flores is the author of *Soldadesca.* (Appendix 15.4.10).

With regards to Amadís the Gaula and Sergas de Esplandián I believed years ago that these works were also written by Lucena[238] and that

---

[236] **FERNÁNDEZ DE OVIEDO, Gonzalo** (1535). La Historia General y Natural de Indias. Edición de José Amador de los Ríos, Parte I, Madrid, 1851, p. XVIII

[237] **WESTERVELD, Govert** (2013). Juan del Encina (alias Bartolomé Torres Naharro). Propalladia. 128 pages. Lulu Editors. ISBN: 978-1-291-63527-0

[238] **WESTERVELD, Govert** (2013). Amadis de Gaula. Juan del Encina y Alonso de Cardona. 84 pages. Lulu Editors. ISBN: 978-1-291-63990-2

Lucena was the pseudonym of Juan del Encina. I erroneously considered that Lucena was the pseudonym of Juan del Encina. Today I consider that the author was Gonzalo Fernández de Oviedo (Lucena) and the JGAAP analysis goes in this direction.

Gonzalo Fernández de Oviedo (Lucena's) stay in Milan can probably explain the presence of Lucena's works and Spanish manuscripts in this place. The manuscript 990 of the Trivulziana Library (Milan, Italy) transmits prose works of Juan de Flores (la Novela de Grisel y Mirabella) and Diego de San Pedro (el Tractado de amores de Arnalte y Lucenda), apart from the poetic texts of the Marquis of Santillana, Diego de Burgos and Costana. On the other hand the manuscript S.P. II. 100 of the Ambrosian Library in Milan has various anonymous couplets or couplets of authors such as Juan Álvarez Gato and Alfonso de Cartagena. These couplets were recollected by Pietro Bembo to please Lucrecia Borgia[239].

WESTERVELD, Govert (2013). Sergas de Esplandián y Juan del Encina. 82 pages. Lulu Editors. ISBN: 978-1-291-64130-1

[239] MAZZOCCHI, Giuseppe (1988). Un manoscritto milanese (Biblioteca Ambrosiana S.P.II.100) e l'ispanismo del Bembo. In: Cancioneros spagnoli a Milano, Firenze, La Nuova Italia, 1, pp. 67-101

MANERA, Anna (1988). I testi spagnoli nel codice 1001 della Biblioteca Trivulziana di Milano. In: Cancioneros spagnoli a Milano, Firenze, La Nuova Itaia, 1, pp. 101-232

MORELLI, Gabriele (2005). Esperienze e relazioni letterarie di Alfonso d'Ávalos, governatore di Milano, pp. 233-260

DANZI, Massimo (2005). La biblioteca del Cardenal Pietro Bembo, Genéve, Librairie Droz.

BALDISSERA, Andrea & MAZZOCCHI, Giuseppe (2005). I Canzoniere di Lucrezia, Padova, Unpress.

Works cited by ZINATO, Andrea (2014). Del cancionero de corte al canionero burgués: El caso de Nápoles, Milán y Venecia. In: Revista de poética medieval, 28, pp. 393-412. Citation on p. 400

According to the JGAAP analyses the works of Juan de Flores and Diego de San Pedro correspond to Lucena. I already wrote a book about these analyses[240].

We can now explain how it was possible that Pacioli could write a manuscript with the new chess rules. He obtained everything from Leonardo da Vinci, who had been in contact with Fernández de Oviedo. In this respect one should know that the manuscript of the famous Italian mathematician Luca Pacioli (c.1445-c.1517), which was believed to have been lost, has recently been discovered (announced Dec. 2006) by the Fondazione Palazzo Coronini Cronberg of Gorizia. This manuscript was dedicated to the marquise of Mantova, Isabella d'Este. The 48 papers of the Coronini Manuscript containing numerous practical demonstrations of the game of chess with the solution keys are perfectly kept and the chess pieces are finely drawn and coloured in black and red, so finely as to make the discoverer cautiously suspect that they might be done by the hand of another artist, maybe Leonardo da Vinci as they worked together around the year 1500. This manuscript has raised a lot of interest in the world of chess as it contains games from both the mediaeval rules and the new (*a la rabiosa*, "mad" queen) rules which were introduced at the end of the previous century.

12.2.22   Indirectly revealing his works and life

As we know, Francisco Delicado wrote the book *Lozana Andaluza*. In a fragment of this book we learn that Lozano has "las coplas de Fajardo" in his home. She then said to Silvano, referring to three works: "Quiero que me leáis, vos que tenéis gracia, las *coplas de Fajardo* y la comedia *Tinelaria* y a *Celestina,* que huelgo de oír leer estas cosas muncho".

---

[240] **WESTERVELD, Govert** (2018). Diego de San Pedro and Juan de Flores: the pseudonyms of Lucena, the son of doctor Juan Ramírez de Lucena, 428 pages. Lulu Editors. ISBN: 978-0-244-72298-2

Francisco Delicado is the pseudonym of Gonzalo Fernández de Oviedo and in reality Delicado is indirectly referring to three of his works. Fernández de Oviedo had a false modest style to express his opinions in many forewords to his books. In the foreword to *Propalladia* it becomes clear that Fernández de Oviedo is an explorer by ship of far foreign countries.

12.2.23   El juego de marro (damas)

With the introduction of the powerful new queen of chess the way chess was played drastically changed, and so did today's draughts which came about due to a radical modification of the game of andarraya. Today instead of playing with the pawns over lines the pawns of andarraya are placed on the chessboard, and the piece of the new powerful queen is introduced[241]. Nebrija[242] clearly said in his 1495 dictionary that andarraya was "novum", meanwhile the Spanish inventors of this new powerful queen were the cause of what would become a worldwide revolution regarding chess and draughts.

The King Alfonso X the wise

---

[241] The historian Kruijswijk also believes it to be likely that the introduction of the new powerful lady in checkers was originally from Spain.
[242] **NEBRIJA, ANTONIO DE** (1495) Dictionarium hispano-latinum, Salamanca. (reimpreso en 1951 por la Real Academia Española - Diccionario Romance (español) en latin. These editions of this book are known: 1494? Evora, 1503 Sevilla, 1506 Paris, and 1513 Madrid.

In the 16th century Castile we see the term andarraya replaced with "juego de damas" for the new game, as proven by the inventor's list Juan de Junta[243] de Burgos in 1556. Apparently the game of andarraya was sometimes played in the 16th century and both the game and the name are confused with the anterior game of alquerque.

We see an indication of this in the 1611 encyclopedia by Covarrubias[244] where they talked about the game of alquerque[245], but where the rules of playing reference the game of andarraya, because you can capture three pieces. In the case of "juego de marro" or draughts with the crown of Aragon it is still called the same (juego de marro, juego marro de punta) and only at the end of the 16th century is the term "juego de las damas" (draughts/checkers) introduced and it is Pedro Ruiz Monterro who states that Juego de las damas used to be vulgarly called "el marro", while Lorenzo Valls in 1597 is more exact with the title of his book "libro del juego de las damas[246] por otro nombre marro de punta" which

---

[243] **PETTAS, WILLIAM** (1995) A sixteenth-century Spanish bookstore: The inventory of Juan de Junta, American Philosophical Society, Independence Square, Philadelphia

[244] **COVARRUBIAS, SEBASTIAN DE** (1611) Tesoro de la lengua castellana o española. Madrid, 1611. Edición de Martín de Riquer de la Real Academia Española, Editorial Alta Fulla, Barcelona, 1987

WESTERVELD, Govert (2016) *The History of Alquerque-12. Spain and France.* Volume I. Academia de Estudios Humanísticos de Blanca. Lulu editors. ISBN: 978-1-291-66267-2 - 400 pages

WESTERVELD, Govert (2016) *The History of Alquerque-12. Remaining Countries.* Volume II. Academia de Estudios Humanísticos de Blanca. Lulu editors. ISBN: 978-1-326-17935-9 - 436 pages

[245] **WESTERVELD, Govert** (2018) *The History of Alquerque-12. Texts of the Game* - Volume III. 516 pages. Lulu Editors. ISBN: 978-0-244-07274-2

[246] We think that due to playing with ladies in the game of marro de punta people initially started calling it "el juego de las damas" (the game of the ladies), which was later abbreviated to "el juego de damas" or simply "damas". This term presumably made an entrance into the kingdom of Castile and over time was accepted into the kingdom of Aragon. So in the introduction of his book to the reader Pedro Ruiz Montero speaks of "el juego de las damas (the game of the ladies) and in the title of his 1591 book we see "el juego de damas" (the game of ladies), while Lorenzo Valls in the title of his 1597 book speaks of (juego de las damas" (game of ladies).

translates as Book of the Game of Draughts, known by another name of alquerque.

12.2.24 Valencianism

Due to Lucena's education he was well aware of the Valencian and Castillian languages, hence he was able to make good translations of Valencian books. It is therefore not easy to find valencianisms in *La Celestina*. There must be certain habits and words that can be considered to be valencianisms, but this is more the work of an expert. I have tried to find some of them.

12.2.24.1 The word: arrollada

We observe a valencianism in the 12th act of *La Celestina*:

> *A medio lado, abiertas las piernas, el pie izquierdo adelante, puesto en huida, las faldas en la cinta, la adarga arrollada, y so el sobaco, por que no me empache. ¡Que, por Dios, que creo huyese como un gamo, según el temor que tengo de estar aquí!*

The right way in Spanish is to use the verb *envolver* for *arrollar*

The word: arrollar

Year	Author	Book	Quantity
1499	Fernando de Rojas	*Comedia de Calisto y Melibea – Act 12*	1
1499	Rodrigo Fernández de Santaella	*Vocabulalrio eclesiástico*	1
1500	Fray Hernando de Talavera	*Instrucción para el regimen interior de su palacio*	1
1521	Fray Antonio de Guevara	*Epístolas familiars*	2

1527	Fray Bertolomé de las Casas	*Historia de las Indias*	1
1532	Anónimo	*Colloquio Traducción de los coloquios de Erasmo*	1
1532	Gonzalo Fernández de Oviedo	*Catálogo real*	1
1535	Gonzalo Fernández de Oviedo	*Historial general y natural de las Indias*	6
1539	Cristóbal de Villalón	*El Scholástico*	1
1549	Hernán Núñez	*Refranes o proverbios en romance*	1
1549	Jerónimo de Urrea	*Traducción de "Orlando furioso" de Ludovico Ariosto*	1
1553	Francisco López de Gómara	*Segunda parte de la Crónica general de las Indias*	3
1560	Francisco Cervantes de Salazar	*Crónica de la Nueva España*	1

12.2.24.2   The word: pobreto

The word: pobreto(s), pobreta(s)

Year	Author	Book	Quantity
1500	Cristóbal de Castillejo	*Reprensión contra los poetas españoles que escriben en italiano*	2
1517	Bartolomé Torres Naharro	*Concilio de los galanes y cortesanas de Roma*	1
1517	Bartolomé Torres Naharro	*Comedia Tinellaria (Propaladia)*	1
1517	Bartolomé Torres Naharro	*Comedia Soldadesca (Propaladia)*	2
1517	Bartolomé Torres Naharro	*Comedia Seraplhina (Propaladia)*	1
1517	Bartolomé Torres Naharro	*Comedia Jacinta (Propaladia)*	1
1520	Bartolomé Torres Naharro	*Comedia Calamita (Propaladia)*	1
1525	Francés de Zúñiga	*Crónica burlesca del emperador Carlos V*	3
1528	Francisco Delicado	*La Lozana Andaluza*	2
1528	Jaime de Huete	*Comedia Tesorina*	1
1536	Gaspar Gómez de Toledo	*Tercera parte de la Tragicomedia de Celestina*	1

1544	Cristóbal de Castillejo	*Diálogo de Mujeres*	4
1545	Lope de Rueda	*Pasos*	3
1545	Lope de Rueda	*Comedia llamada de "Los engañados"*	1
1545	Cristóbal de Castillejo	*Diálogo entre Adulación y Verdad*	1
1547	Cristóbal de Castillejo	*Aula de cortesanos*	2
1550	Juan de Arce de Otárola	*Coloquios de Palatino y Pinciano*	7
1550	Diego Hurtado de Mendoza	*Cartas del Bachiller de Arcadia al Capitán Salazar*	1
1554	Anónimo	*Lazarillo de Tormes*	1

12.2.24.3   The word: tastar

There is a valencianism in *Seraphina* by Bartolomé Torres Naharro

The word: tastar

Year	Author	Book	Total
1490	Alfonso de Palencia	*Universal vocabulario en latín y en romance*	5
1493	Anónimo	*Traducción del Tratado de cirugía de Cauliaco*	8
1494	Fray Vicente de Burgos	*Traducción de El Libro de Propietatibus Rerum de Bartolomé Anglicus*	1
1498	Boron, Robert de	*Baladro del sabio Merlín. Autor traducción desconocido*	1
1499	Ávila, Juan de	*Historia de los nobles, y caballeros Oliveros de Castilla...*	1
1511	Anónimo	*Traducción de Tirante el Blanco de Joanot Martorell*	1
1521	Anonym	*Thebayda: Seraphina*	1
1553	Anónimo	*Biblia de Ferrara*	1
1559	Juan de Timoneda	*La comedia de los Menemnos. Traducción de Plauto*	1
1559	Juan de Timoneda	*Comedia llamada Cornelia*	1

12.2.24.4   The words: en paciencia

Use of the preposition "en" instead of "con" (con paciencia)

The words: en paciencia

Year	Author	Book	Quantity
1535	Fernández de Oviedo	*Historia general y natural de las Indias*	6

12.2.24.5   The words: en el sudor

Use of the preposition "en" instead of "con" (con el sudor)

The words: en el sudor

Year	Author	Book	Quantity
1512	Antonio de Obregón	*Los seis triunfos de Petrarca*	1

12.2.24.6   The words: todos tres

The words: todos tres

Year	Author	Book	Quantity
1526	Fernández de Oviedo	*Sumario de la natural y general historia de las Indias*	3
1535	Fernández de Oviedo	*Historia general y natural de las Indias*	39
1535	Fernández de Oviedo	*Batallas y quinquagenas*	13

12.2.24.7 The words: todos cinco

The words: todos cinco

Year	Author	Book	Quantity
1501	Anonym	*Tristán de Leonis*	1
1511	Anonym	*Traducción de Tirante el Blanco de Joanot Martorell*	1
1529	Antonio de Guevara	*Reloj de príncipes*	3
1526	Anonym	*Polindo*	5

13 1496 Juan del Encina

If we are to believe Miguel Briongos[247], then the protonotary Juan Ramírez de Lucena had a son from a relationship with his servant Mari Diez. It seems that the child died shortly after birth. Miguel Briongos could obtain these dates from a lawsuit filed by Pedro de Carra on 16 December 1511 against the nephew and heir of the protonotary Juan Ramírez de Lucena. Pedro de Carra was also a servant of the protonotary, and the lawsuit was filed by him because the protonotary had promised him a certain quantity of maravedies provided he would marry Mari Diez. It becomes clear from the whole process that this is a clear case of cohabitation, and the marriage of two servants was but a cover to conceal the relationship and its fruit: the birth of one child. As it is clear from this document, most of it must have occurred around 1477. On 23 August of that year the protonotary extended a deed for which, by reason of the marriage of both servants, he undertook to give them fifty thousand maravedíes. The content of the process does not doubt the protonotary's generosity. It is evident that he always paid the servants in advance and helped them when necessary. He even took over the home education of Anne de la Carra, daughter of Pedro de la Carra and his wife Mari Diez. That he did until the child was twelve or thirteen years old. Thereafter he placed her with his brother the Commander Lucena, Diego Ramírez de Lucena, in Toledo and arranged to pay for her clothes and food.

---

[247] **MIGUEL BRIONGOS, Jerónimo** (2012) De Vita Felici o Diálogo sobre la Vida Feliz, de Juan de Lucena: Edición crítica. Tesis doctoral, Volume I, Departamento de Filología Española. Universidad autónoma de Barcelona, pp. XCVII-XCVIII

13.1 The children of Juan Ramírez de Lucena

We can learn from a chapter mentioned earlier that the protonotary had children whom he later protected. Such events could also have taken place with Gonzalo Fernández de Oviedo. The protonotary had children who later adopted the name of the mother or another father. Knowing this, it will be much easier to understand that Juan del Encina could have been a child of the ambassador Juan Ramírez de Lucena. Consequently one will also better understand my initial hypothesis of:

> **VALLE DE RICOTE, Gofredo** (2006-2009). Los tres autores de La Celestina: El judeoconverso Juan Ramírez de Lucena, sus hijos Fernando de Rojas (Lucena) y Juan del Encina (alias Bartolomé Torres Naharro y Francisco Delicado). Four volumes.

This hypothesis was based on reading many books and on the idiolect of Juan del Encina.

13.2 The idiolect of Juan del Encina

Hernando del Castillo says that he wrote another *cancionero*, but since I do not see any other song book with his name I guess that he must have worked under another name. The idiolect of Hernando del Castillo shows Juan del Encina, but study of the words of the *Cancionero general* published by Hernando del Castillo shows that they could be Gonzalo Fernández de Oviedo's. One of the big problems I encountered was that the idiolect of Juan del Encina is very similar to that of Gonzalo Fernández de Oviedo.

13.3 Juan del Encina

Another test that can give us more information about the idiolect of Juan del Encina is the frequency of certain words. With the webpage Textalyser.net it became clear that Gonzalo Fernández de Oviedo used more the word "que", while Juan del Encina used the word "de".

Wordfrecuency in percentages of various books of Fernández de Oviedo

Words	Claribalte Work	Sumario Dedicatory	India T 1 Proem	Catálogo Proem
Que	5.4	5.5	5.7	4.7
De	4.9	6.7	4.9	4.3
Y	4.1	5.9	3.7	-
La	2.9	2.1	3.2	1.9
En	2.9	4.0	4.6	3.6
Lo	-	2.4	-	1.6

Wordfrecuency in percentages of texts of Juan del Encina

Words	Bubólica Foreword to Monarch	Bubólica Foreword to Prince	Cancionero Alba's child Foreword	Cancionero Alba - Duke Foreword
Que	3.8	2.9	5.7	3.7
De	5.8	6.1	4.9	5.9
Y	-	-	3.7	5.0
La	2.3	2.1	3.2	3.6
En	3.1	2.9	4.6	2.2
Lo	-	-	-	-
e	3.1	6.0	-	-

Wordfrecuency in percentages of texts of Juan del Encina

Words	Cancionero Prínce Proem	Cancionero Monarchs Proem	Book 1521	Bubólica Argument
Que	4.5	3.4	4.3	3.9
De	5.8	5.7	3.2	5.1
Y	4.3	6.2	6.3	-
La	2.5	2.9	2.0	1.7
En	2.8	2.6	3.1	3.4
Lo	-	-	-	-
e	3.1	-	-	4.5

13.3.1 The Bucólica in the Cancionero of 1496

Did Juan del Encina really translate the *Bucólica*? I mention this fact because a JGAAP analysis shows the idiolect of Gonzalez Fernández de Oviedo near Juan del Encina (Appendix 15.5.1 and 15.5.2). Maybe they did it together, who knows? The proem directed at the monarch shows the idiolect (15.5.3) of Juan Ramírez de Lucena. (My intuition expected a much more prominent role for Juan Ramírez de Lucena with regards to the writing of books, but apart from *Vita Beata* I could not find them till now). The other proem directed at the prince also shows the idiolect of Juan del Encina (15.5.4), and the same can be said about the foreword to the Duke of Alba (15.5.5). Strangely enough the foreword to the *Cancionero* directed at the child of Alba has nothing to do with Juan del Encina (15.5.6). Hereafter follows a table with these findings, as well as some forewords and proems.

JGAAP analysis of the forewords and proem, Cancionero general 1496

001	Foreword to Bubólica for Monarchs	1-Juan del Encina 2-Gonzalo Fernández de Oviedo 3-Duobus amantibus
002	Foreword to Bubólica for Prince	1-Juan del Encina 2-Gonzalo Fernández de Oviedo 3-Gonzalo de Ayora
003	Proem to Cancionero for Monarchs	1-Juan Ramírez de Lucena 2-Juan Ramírez de Lucena 3-Juan de Flores
004	Proem to Cancionero for Prince	1-Juan del Encina 1-Alfonso el Sabio (=Juan del Encina) 2-Alonso Fernández de Madrid
005	Foreword to Cancionero for Alba	1-Juan del Encina 2-Garci Rodríguez de Montalvo 3-Gonzalo de ayora
006	Foreword to Cancionero for Child of Alba	1-Martín Martínez de Ampies 2.-Pedro Carillo de Huete 3-Gonzalo de Ayora

13.3.2 Foreword to Bucólica for the Monarchs

Comiença el prólogo de la translación de las «Bucólicas» de Virgilio por Juan del Enzina.

La grandeza de **vuestras hazañas**, dignas de **inmortalidad**, muy altos e muy poderosos reyes, despierta las lenguas de los dormidos coraçones e no dexa tener sufrimiento para que puedan callar avn los que hablar no saben; mas ¿quién será tan digno, por mucho saber que alcance, que deue tener confianza en su ingenio para dignamente llegar á contar el menor quilate de las excelencias de vuestra real majestad? Quanto más yo, que aun agora soy nueuo en las armas é muy flaco para nauegar por el gran mar de vuestras alabanzas? ¡O inuitíssimos príncipes! ¿quién supiese recontar las vitorias e triunfos que en los reynos, por vuestra mano conquistados, hauéys recebido; (fue no solamente el reino de Granada, más avn, el vuestro de Castilla, casi todo ganastes **con fuerza de armas,** queriendo Dios ayudaros? e avnque aquesto agora nos parece mucho, es cierto después nos parecerá casi nada **en comparación de** las victorias que os están guardadas. ¿Pues qué diré de vuestra poderosa justicia, e con quánta paz e sosiego **vuestros reynos** son regidos, hallando como los hallastes tan **estragados**, que, según el gran daño que en ellos estaua, no se esperaua remedio, e, sobre todo nuestra fe, que ya estaua puesta en despeñadero donde muchos deslizauan. Vosotros, cristianísimos reyes, la restaurastes y esclarecistes, que quiso Dios escogeros para remedio de tantos males. Vosotros sois la cumbre de todos los príncipes é reyes á donde la fe e la justicia se conoce bien quien son, á donde la munificencia tiene sus fuerzas enteras, soys la mesma libertad en las cosas que **lícitamente** podéis usar della; no sé para qué me pongo en alabaros, pues entrar por este camino es querer agotar el mar, ni mi saber da lugar para ello. Mas como el desseo de seruir á vuestra alteza sea mayor que el temor de descubrir **mis defetos**, avnque grandes, no quiero escusarme de salir á barrera y ensayarme primero en algún baxo estillo, más alto si en ello mostráis seruiros. **E porque mi** desseo consiga effeto más concertado, acordé dedicaros las *Bucólicas* de Virgilio, que es la primera de sus obras, adonde habla de pastores, siguiendo, como dize el Donato, la orden de los mortales, cuyo exercicio primeramente fué guardar ganados, manteniéndose de frutas siluestres; é después siguióle la agricultura, é andando más el tiempo nacieron batallas. Y en esta manera el estilo del gran Homero mantuano en sus tres obras principales procedió. De las quales, por agora, para entrada y preludio de mi propósito, estas *Bucólicas* quise trasladar, trobadas en estilo pastoril, aplicándolas á los muy loable fechos de vuestro reynar, según parece en el argumenta de cada vna. E dexadas otras muchas razones que á ella me mouieron, parecióme ser deuda muy conocida á tales príncipes é reyes, que tan gran primado y excelencia tienen sobre todos los otros, se ouiesse de consagrar é dirigir obra de tan gran poeta, á quien el nuestro Quintiliana da la palma entre los latinos, y esso mesmo Macrobio e Seruio e todos los que se pusieren á cotejar los estilos poéticos. E assí coma haziendo mención de poeta sin añadir otro nombre, entendemos de Virgilio por excelencia, assí es mucha razón que haziendo mención de reyes, por excelencia entendamos de vuestra real corona. ¿Quién ouo que tan gran magestad de palabras alcançasse como Virgilio? ¿Qué sentencia ó que seta de fílósofos ouo que él no comprendiesse? No sin mérito, dize Cicerón auerle llamado segunda esperanza de Roma cuando en su mocedad pronunciaua ciertos versos en el teatro romano. No tengáis por mal, magnánimos príncipes, en dedicaros obras de pastores, pues que no ay nombre más conuenible al estado-real, del qual nuestro Redentor, que es el verdadero rey de los reyes, se precia mucho, según parece en muchos lugares de la Sagrada Escritura. E las alabanças de la vida pastoril, no sólo Virgilio é otros poetas, más avn Plinio, grauíssimo autor, las pone en el décimo otauo libro de la natural hystoria, hablando muy largamente de la vida rústica e no menos de agricultura; e testigo es Catón el mayor en el libro De *rebus rusticis*, adonde dize que cuando antiguamente alabauan algún hombre, llamáuanle buen laborador. E avn los poetas é hombres doctos desseauan lugares apartados, assí como bosques e montes e otras siluas'e arboledas, e con este desseo dezía Virgilio: *O quime sistat in vallibus Hemi.* Mas tornando en mí quiero saber quién me traxo en tan gran cuydado, que á reyes tan excelentes mi pluma osasse llenar nueuas de mi desseo; que no soy digno para ponerme en aplicar esta obra á

vuestros tan altos primores. ¡O, quántas vezes me paro á pensar, desconfíando de mi ingenio, quién me puso en este trabajo, auiendo otros muchos que muy mejor que yo lo pudieran tomar! Mas consuéleme con aquello que dize Tulío en el libro *De perfecto oratore* á Marco Bruto, diciendo que ninguno deue desesperar de trabajar en las letras, e si no pudiere llegar al más alto escalón, llegará al segundo ó tercero ó quarto; que en tiempo de Homero fueron otros, avnque no tan notables, y esso mesmo quando Archiloco e Sófocles e Píndaro florescieron, no faltaron otros que escriuiessen, avnque no pudieron bolar tan alto, que ni el gran estilo de Platón espantó á Aristóteles, ni el mesmo Aristóteles e otros muchos sin cuento, ni Demóstenes, que fué el más excellente orador de Grecia, espantó á otros algunos de su tiempo, e no solamente fué esto en las artes excelentes, más avn entre los maestros de otras obras, según parece en los pintores que avn no pudieron imitar la hermosura de vna ymagen que estaua en Rodas, ni la de Venus que estaua en la insola Coo, ni la de Júpiter Olímpico, no por esso dexaron de pintar. É assí yo, aunque mi obra no merezca ser muy alabada en perfección, á lo menos no dexaré de tentar vados para ver si podré alcanzar algún poco de loor con esfuerço de aquellas palabras que Virgilio dice: *Tentanda via est qua me quoque possim tollere humo, victorque virum volitare per ora.* E muchas dificultades hallo en la tradución de aquesta obra por el gran defeta de vocablos que ay en la lengua castellana en comparación de la latina, de donde se causa en muchos lugares no poderles dar la propia significación, quanto más que por razón del metro e consonantes será forjado algunas vezes de impropiar las palabras e acrecentar ó menguar, según fiziere á mi caso, e avn muchas razones aura que no se puedan traer al propósito; mas aquellas tales, según dice Seruio, auémoslas de tomar como razones pastoriles, assí simplemente dichas; e si fuese necesario vsar de aquello que vsan los eclesiásticos, diziendo vn psalmo por
vn solo verso que haze al caso de la fiesta. Mas en quanta yo pudiere e mi saber alcanzare, siempre procuraré seguir la letra, aplicándola á vuestras más que reales personas y enderezando parte dello al nuestro muy esclarecido príncipe D. Juan, vuestro bienauenturado hijo. E atribuyendo cada cosa al que mejor se pudiere atribuyr. E avnque en los más de los lugares no hable sino de vno, será por más verdaderamente seguir al poeta, e porque son vuestras virtudes y excelencias tan pareadas e puestas en vnidad, que no se pueden tocar las del vno sin que

suenen las del otro. E pues el grandíssimo desseo de seruir á vuestra alteza me puso en este cuydado, con aquella humildad e acatamiento que deuo, suplico á vuestra real magestad quiera recibir este pequeño presente de su sieruo con aquellas manos triunphales e bulto sereno con que yllustra toda la monarchía de España e modera e rige la occidental región, e con que combida á su amistad, no solamente á los príncipes de la religión cristiana, mas avn á gran parte de la barbárica gente.

Words and expressions used in the foreword of Bubólica to the Monarchs

Nº	Words en Bubólica de Juan del Encina	Words en Gonzalo Fernández de Oviedo	Cases	Other authors
1.	Inmortalidad	Historia general y natural de las Indias	6	38
2.	Estragados	Tirante el Blanco	1	13
3.	Lícitamente	Lucena Repetición de amores	1	33
4.	Vuestras hazañas	Belianis de Grecia Jerónimo Fernández	5	9
5.	En comparación de	Historia general y natural de las Indias	12	52
6.	Con fuerza de armas	Historia general y natural de las Indias	1	1
7.	Vuestros reynos	Sumario	1	17
8.	Mis defetos	Historia general y natural de las Indias	1	2
9.	E porque mi	Tirante el Blanco	1	2
10.	Me puso en	Historia general y natural de las Indias	3	27

13.3.2.1 Foreword to Bubólica for Prince John

Al muy **esclarecido y bienauenturado príncipe** don Juan
Comiença el prólogo en la traslación de las *Bucolicas* de Virgillio por Juan del Enzina

Suelen aquellos que dan obra a las letras, príncipe muy excelente, esperimentar sus ingenios en trasladar libros y autores griegos en lengua latina, y assí mesmo los hombres de nuestra nación procuran tomar experimento de su estudio bolviendo libros de latín **en nuestra lengua castellana**, y no solamente los hombres de mediano saber, mas aun entre otros varones muy dotos no rehusó aquel ejercicio Tulio, puesto en la cumbre de **todos los ingenios**, que volvió a la lengua latina muchas obras griegas ya perdidas por negligencia de nuestros antecesores, principalmente aquellas muy altas "Oraciones" de Esquines e Demóstenes, cuyo argumento parece, las cuales nuevamente trasladó Leonardo Aretino poco tiempo há; e la "Etica" de Aristóteles, que agora se lee, e otros libros de Platon. E áun entre los santos doctores no dió pequeña gloria a Sant Hierónimo la interpretación e traducción de la "Biblia"; y en este trabajo se ocuparon Aquila é Symaco, Teodoción, Orígenes y Eusebio. E de los modernos, no solamente Leonardo e Filelpho se pusieron á trasladar de vna lengua en otra, mas también otros muchos gastaron parte de su tiempo en semejantes exercicios, dedicando sus obras á quien su desseo les aconsejaua. E como quiera que yo sea tan desseoso del servicio de vuestra alteza como el que más, con aquella fee que á vuestros claríssimos padres, procurando mostrar algo de mi desseo, en las *Bucólicas* de Virgilio metí la pluma, temblando, con mucha razón, viendo el valer de vuestro gran merecimiento, e amonestado por Orado en el arte de poesía, donde dize los escriptores hauer de elegir materias yguales á las fuerças de sus ingenios.

O **bienauenturado príncipe**; esperanza de las Españas; espejo e claridad de tantos reynos e de otros muchos más merecedor, e quién será tan fuera de sentido, que quanto más piense que sabe, tanto más no tema de escriuir obra de vuestro nombre? No con poco temor mili vezes boluiera las riendas si no me atajara Marcial, que en sus epigramas e título de baxas obras y entre sus procaces é desuergonzadas palabras entretexiera el nombre de Domiciano, el más soberuio e vanaglorioso de todos los emperadores romanos. El qual pestífero vicio está muy alongado de la real magestad de vuestros padres e vuestra.

Asi que con este esfuerzo mi verdadero deseo e vuestras muy claras virtudes me dieron atrevimiento para dirigir e consagrar estas *Bubólicas* a nuestros muy poderosos reyes, e aplicaros parte dellas, porque creo que en vuestra tierna edad os habréis ejercitado en las obras de aqueste poeta; e porque favoreceis tanto la sciencia andando acompañado de tantos e tan doctíssimos varones, que no menos dejaréis **perdurable memoria** de haber alargado e extendido los límites e términos de la sciencia, que los del ingenio; mas por no engendrar fastidio a los lectores desta obra, acordé de la trobar en diversos géneros de metro y en estilo rústico, por consonar con el poeta, que introduce personas pastoriles. Aunque debaxo de aquella corteza e rústica simplicidad puso sentencias muy altas e alegóricos sentidos, y en esta obra se mostró no menos gracioso que docto en la *Geórgica* e graue en la *Eneyda*. E no en poca estimación era tenida la vida rústica antiguamente, que de allí nacían e se engendrauan los varones e capitanes fortíssimos, según dize Catón el Censorio en su libro de agricultura; e aquesta fué la que dio nombre á las familias de los sabios Pisones, Cicerones e Léntulos, y en este exercicio estaua ocupado Cincinato quando lo denunciaron de parte del Senado romano ser criado dictador; e aquesta agricultura sustentaua á Marco Régulo, cuyo mayordomo muerto quiso dexar la capitanía e hueste que en África gobernaua para venir á labrar sus tierras; mas el Senado e pueblo romano no ouo vergüenza de ser su mayordomo e labrarle las tierras. ¿Pues qué diré de aquel primer justo Abel, que guardando estaua ganado quando su hermano le mató? E Noé labrador era; e Abrahan e Isaac e Jacob con sus doce hijos pastores fueron; e Moysés en su vida pastoril estaua metido quando vio aquella visión de la çarça; e Dauid, siendo pastor e andando con sus ganados, exercitaua las fuerças matando ossos e leones e otros fieros animales, e de allí fué vngido por rey, del qual dixo Dios *Inueni virum secundum cor meum.* Y todos los más de los patriarcas e profetas beuieron en semejantes vidas. Ni tuuieron por mal muchos grandes filósofos oradores e poetas escriuir de pastores e ornamento del campo; mas dexados agora todos los otros, assí griegos como latinos, que en esta facultad escriuierón libros que á nuestras manos no han venido, yo hallo aquel Marco Varrón, á quien Sancto Agustino, en el tercero de La *Cibdad de Dios* llama el más ensoñado de los romanos, auer escrito d'aqueste rústico exercicio, siendo de ochenta años, assí como él confíessa en el prohemio de vna obra que compuso, enseñando á su muger cómo labrasse vna heredad que auía mercado, e también Tulio en el *De Senactute* faze mención de las alabanças de la rústica vida, e no menos Paladio ocupó su pluma en semejante estilo; e assí mismo Plinio e Columela escriuieron largamente de agricultura, e, según ellos dizen, mochos culpan agora á la tierra,

216

porque no dé tanto fruto como en otro tiempo, e dize que la causa estar ya cansada de engendrar; mas estos dos **claros varones** dañan la tal opinión, e afirman ser la causa porque agora las heredades e tierras son labradas por manos de sieruos e hombres viles e de baxa suerte, e no dan tanto fruto como cuando las labraban aquellas manos que regían las riendas de los carros triunphales; porque entonces, con aquel cuydado e diligencia que tratauan las guerras, con aquel labrauan el campo, e de aquí dauan las coronas cínicas murales e obsidionales gran ornamento de la milicia, e aquí mandauan las leyes de Licurgo que se criasen los hijos de los espartanos fasta que fuessen para tomar las armas. E pues tan excelentes cosas se siguieron del campo e tan grandes hombres amaron la agricultura e vida rústica y escriuieron de ella, no deue ser despreciada mi obra por ser escrita en estilo pastoril, e no dudo que mi trabajo sea iré prehendido de muchos por auerme puesto á trasladar con mi poco saber obra de tan gran poeta, mayormente atreuiéndome á dedicarlo á los más altos principes del mundo; mas los que maliciosos no fueren, no la obra, sino la voluntad e desseo deue juzgar, e consuéleme con esto que avn á Sant Hierónymo, en quien ninguna causa de reprehensión auía, **no faltaron maldizientes** y embidíosos que le reprendiessen, según él se quexa en diversos lugares; ni menos careció Virgilio de quien le motejasse, e avn, según dize Quintiliano, no se pudo defender Cicerón, en cuyo ingenio las virtudes oratorias e retóricas se encerraron sin que detratores le tocassen. Mas si vuestra alteza mi baxo seruicio manda recibir por suyo, lo cual le suplico con el temor e vergüenza que á príncipe tan esclarecido se deue, podrán muy poco dañarme quantos maldizientes biuen.

Words and expressions used in the foreword to Bubólica for prince John

Nº	Words en Bubólica de Juan del Encina	Words en Gonzalo Fernández de Oviedo	Cases	Other authors
1.	Bienaventurado príncipe	Catálogo	1	0
2.	Poderosos príncipes	Belianis de Grecia 1579 Jerónimo Fernández	1	0

3.	En nuestra lengua castellana	1.- Historia general y natural de las Indias	1	12
		2.- Batallas y quinquagenas	1	
4.	Esclarecido príncipe	Belianis de Grecia 1547 Jerónimo Fernández	1	4
5.	Cristianísimo Rey	Historia general y natural de las Indias	2	5
6.	Todos los ingenios	Belianis de Grecia 1547 Jerónimo Fernández	1	6
7.	Perdurable memoria	El Peregrino Hernán Díaz	1	5
8.	Claros varones	Batallas y quinquagenas	2	15
9.	No faltaron maldizientes	Catálogo real	1	0
10	Griegos como latinos	Lozana Andalusa	1	8

We observe in this text by Juan del Encina the typical linguistic style of Gonzalo Fernández de Oviedo: He speaks about himself (yo, mi, acordé) and indicates his knowledge of Greek and its authors. He indicates the great importance of the Spanish prince, monarchs, etc. in nice words (bienaventurado, poderoso, esclarecido, claro). On the other hand he always wants to serve the prince and kings and glorify the importance of Spain and its language as well as the important people in this country (ingenioso). He likes to use a false modest style in order to ask for favours. In many cases we observe that Fernández de Oviedo is afraid of the detractors.

13.4 The cancionero of 1496

13.4.1 Proem to the Cancionero for the Monarchs

A los muy poderosos y cristianísimos príncipes don Hernando y doña Isabel. Comienza el prohemio por Juan del Encina en la copilación de sus obras.

Si **el mucho temor** y turbación que la grandeza de vuestra real magestad pone a los más **altos ingenios** y más fortalecidos de saber, no cobrasse algún esfuerço y aliento en la fuente de vuestra virtud, ¿quién osaría mover la pluma para escrevir vuestro nombre?, y yo, lo con este esfuerço muertas obras, atrevíme a dirigir y aplicar la copilación dellas a vuestra gran ecelencia. Dizen los antiguos y fabulosos poetas que Prometeo, hijo de Japeto, acostumbrado a fabricar cuerpos umanos de barro, subió al cielo con ayuda y favor de Minerva y traxo de una rueda del sol un poco de fuego con que después introduzía vida y ánima en aquellos cuerpos. **Y assí yo**, desta manera, viéndome con favor del duque y duquesa de Alva, mis señores, subí a la gran altura de la contemplación de vuestras ecelencias por alcançar siquiera una centella de su resplandor, para poder, en mi muerta lavor y de barro, introduzir **espíritus vitales**. Y **por mandado de** estos mis señores que no solamente ellos, mas aun **el menor de sus** siervos quieren que enderece sus pensamientos y desseos **en el servicio de vuestra** alteza, hallándome muy dichoso en averme recebido por suyo, **he copilado** las obras que en este cancionero se contienen, adonde principalmente van algunas que no con poco temor avía dedicado a vuestra real señoría. Y, porque lo que es de César se dé a César, quise primero darles la obediencia de este mi trabajo con la umildad y acatamiento que devo, suplicándoles, si algo bueno huviere, estimando cada cosa en su estado, lo manden favorecer, y lo malo corregir, pues a los príncipes y emperadores conviene tener debaxo de su imperio assí malos como buenos, los malos para en ellos ejecutar la justicia y disposición de sus leyes, y los buenos para favorecerlos y gratificarlos y en ellos estender la manificencia de sus mercedes, que si malos no huviesse, no serían estimados los buenos, porque por los unos venimos en conocimiento de los otros. Y bien creo en esta mi copilación avrá tanto de malo que lo bueno no se parezca, mas esfuerço con esto que todas son obras hechas desde los catorze años hasta los veynte y cinco, adonde para lo que en mi favor no hiziere me podré bien llamar a menor de hedad. Pues, invitíssimos y siempre vitoriosos príncipes, no neguéys vuestro favor a **mis continuas** vigilias porque enmudezcan todos los detratores y maldizientes. No ay cosa de tanta magnificencia ni que tan bien parezca a los príncipes como favorecer a los umildes, ayudar a los afligidos, y assí defender a los menores que no sean opressos ni de los mayores maltratados. Vosotros levantáys los caýdos, esentáys los apremiados y redemís los cativos, y vivificáys a los que ya están sin esperança de vida. De tal manera Naturaleza, por la Providencia Divina, de don especial os adornó, que todas quantas virtudes pudo en vosotros aposentó, y aposentadas las esperimentó, y esperimentadas están puestas en vosotros para que a todos los otros príncipes seáys enxemplo y dechado. Regís todos vuestros reynos y señoríos con tanta prudencia, con tanta fortaleza, con tanta justicia y temperança, que todos los que retamente dessean regir, os tienen siempre por espejo remirándose en vosotros para imitaros y seguiros, y para tomar reglas y preceptos de reynar. Todas quantas cosas ay escritas de buen regimiento de príncipes, de tal manera las guardáys, que no ay cosa buena que los escritores ayan instituydo, que vosotros no la pongáys en obra, y no obráys cosa que no esté instituyda por muy buena; y aunque las tales instituciones no so huviera, de vuestras obras mesmas se pudieran muy bien colegir y sacar trasunto de vida perfeta. Si os queremos comparar a algunos príncipes passados, hallaremos que las ecelencias que cada uno dellos con gran dificultad y en diversas edades alcançó, en vosotros cada día muy perfeta y abundosamente se ven. Leemos de Arístides, Agesilao y Trajano aver sido justos, de vosotros sabémoslo y cada día lo vemos por esperiencia. De la gran clemencia de Julio César la antigüedad nos da testimonio, mas de la vuestra, que no es menor, nosotros podemos dar fe, pues continuamente gozamos della. Muy gran ygualdad dizen ser la de Pompeo, mas mucho mayor se halla en vosotros y assí lo sienten todos los pueblos. Alabaron los antiguos la piedad de Metelo, mas mucho más deve ser alabada la vuestra que cara a cara la contemplamos. Ensalçó la antigüedad el gran ánimo de Alexánder, mas mucho más nuestros siglos con perpetuas alabanças engrandecen el vuestro. Las estorias antiguas gran testimonio dan de la disciplina militar de los emperadores griegos y romanos, mas no menos en vosotros toda España la ha esperimentado. La prudencia de Temístocles, la constancia de Fabio, la continencia de Cipión, las memorias antiguas la celebraron; mas en vosotros todas estas gracias y virtudes, no solamente las oýmos y vemos escritas, mas aun siempre con biva boz las cantamos. Por mucho que todo el mundo cante y pregone de vuestros loores y alabanças, no lo toméys por lisonja que no es sino la verdad que da testimonio de sí mesma. Por de sí mesma. Por todo el mundo se celebra la claridad de vuestro nombre, y no solamente mandáys en vuestros señoríos y reynos, mas aun en los

220

agenos disponéys y cumplís vuestros desseos, en vuestra mano está cerrar y abrir las puertas de Jallo y de Mars. ¡O, cuántos y cuán grandes movimientos y discordias de guerra en los años passados avéys amansado en España, y de cuán gran incendio librada, la avéys buelto a verdadera paz y tranquilidad!, y no solamente avéys sido autores de paz, mas aun conservadores. En vosotros ambos maravillosamente florece todo lo que fortuna, naturaleza, o umana diligencia tiene por principal. Alcançastes lo que todos los mortales han por muy grave de alcançar. Alcançastes mucha gracia con mucha gloria, y lo que más es y quasi increýble, que avéys sobrepujado y vencido las embidias con vuestra firme virtud. Estas cosas todas y otras muchas infinitas que a todo el mundo son muy notorias, seguramente las puedo contar, aunque, cierto, de mi mano muy más pobladas yrán de fe que de eloqüencia; y perdone vuestra real magestad, pues donde las fuerças del sentido desfallecen, la fe basta para suplir los defetos.

Words and expressions used in the foreword to Cancionero for the Monarchs

Nº	Words en Bubólica de Juan del Encina	Words en Gonzalo Fernández de Oviedo	Cases	Other authors
1.	El mucho temor	Historia general y natural de las Indias	1	1
2.	Altos ingenios	Historia general y natural de las Indias	1	1
3.	Y as(s) yo	1.- Juan de Flores (Triunfo de amor) 2.- Fernández de Oviedo (Silva-TresRomances	1	3
4.	Espíritus vitales	Jerónimo Fernández Belianis de Grecia (1547)	1	12
5.	Por mandato de	Batallas y quinquagenas	1	8
6.	El menor de sus	Oliveros de Castilla Anonym	1	7
7.	En el servicio de vuestra	Traducción Tirante el Blanco - Anonym	1	3

8.	He copilado	Historia general y natural de las Indias	1	1
9.	En vuestra mano está	Traducción Tirante el Blanco - Anonym	1	5
10	Mis continuas	Batallas y quinquagenas	1	7

The following text also belongs to the Proem to the Cancionero for the monarchs, but I did not study the words with CORDE. What I observed is that Gonzalo Fernández de Oviedo used a lot of strange words. When reading proses of Juan del Encina (and there are not many) I always have the feeling that I am reading Fernández de Oviedo's texts. One should take special care to separate them.

Capítulo I.

Al muy esclarecido y bienaventurado príncipe don Juan. Comiença el prohemio en una Arte de Poesía castellana compuesta por Juan del Enzina.

Cuán ligero y penetrable fuesse el ingenio de los antiguos Y cuán enemigos de la ociosidad, muy esclarecido príncipe, notorio es a vuestra alteza, como cuenta Cicerón de Africano el mayor, que dezía nunca estar menos ocioso que quando estava ocioso ni menos solo que quando solo, dando a entender que nunca holgava su juyzio. Y según sentencia de aquel Catón censorino, no solamente son obligados los hombres que biven según razón a dar cuenta de sus negocios, mas aun tan negocios, mas aun tan bien del tiempo de su ocio, quanto mas los que fuemos dichosos de alcançar a ser súditos y bivir debaxo de tan poderosos y cristianíssimos príncipes, que assí artes bélicas como de paz están ya tan puestas en perfeción en estos reynos por su buena governación, que, quien piensa las cosas que por armas se han acabado, no parece aver quedado tiempo de pacificarlas como oy están. Ya no nos falta de buscar sino escoger en qué gastemos el tiempo, pues lo tenemos qual lo desseamos, que puede ser en el ocio más alegre y más proprio de umanidad, como Tulio dize, que sermón gracioso y polido; y pues entre las otras cosas en que ecedemos a los animales brutos es una de las principales, que hablando podemos espremir lo que sentimos, ¿quién no trabajará por eceder a otro en aquello que los hombres eceden a los animales? Bien parece vuestra real ecelencia aver leýdo aquello que Ciro usava dezir: «Cosa torpe es imperar el que no ecede a sus súditos en todo género de virtud»; y vuestra muy alta señoría que tiene tal dechado de que sacar mirando a las ecelencias y virtudes de sus claríssimos padres, bien lo pone por la obra, pues dexados los primeros rudimentos y cunábulos, entre sus claras vitorias se ha criado en el gremio de la dulce filosofía, favoreciendo los ingenios de sus súditos, incitándolos a la ciencia con enxemplo de sí mesmo. Assí que, mirando todas estas cosas, acordé de hazer un Arte de poesía castellana, por donde se pueda mejor sentir lo bien o mal trobado, y para enseñar a trobar en nuestra lengua, si enseñar se puede, porque es muy gentil exercicio en el tiempo de ociosidad. Y confiando en la virtud de vuestra real magestad,de vuestra real magestad, atrevíme a dedicar esta obra a su ecelente ingenio, donde ya florecen los remos de la sabiduría, para si fuere servido, estando desocupado de sus arduos negocios, exercitarse en cosas poéticas y trobadas en nuestro castellano estilo, porque lo que ya su bivo juyzio por natural razón conoce, lo pueda ver puesto en arte, según lo que mi flaco saber alcança; no porque crea que los poetas y trobadores se ayan de regir por ella, siendo yo el menor dellos, mas por no ser ingratoso a esta facultad si algún nombre me ha dado, o si merezco tener siquiera el más baxo lugar entre los poetas de nuestra nación. Y assí mesmo porque según dize el dotíssimo maestro Antonio de Lebrixa, aquél que desterró de nuestra España los barbarismos que en la lengua latina se avían criado, una de las que le movieron a hazer Arte de romance fue que creýa nuestra lengua estar agora más empinada y polida que jamás estuvo, de donde más se podía temer el descendimiento que la subida. Y assí yo, por esta mesma razón, creyendo nunca aver estado tan puesta en la cumbre nuestra poesía y manera de trobar, parecióme ser cosa muy provechosa ponerla en arte y encerrarla debaxo de ciertas leyes y reglas, porque ninguna antigüedad de tiempos le pueda traer olvido. Y digo estar agora puesta en la cumbre, a lo menos quanto a las observaciones, que no dudo nuestros antecesores aver escrito cosas más dinas de memoria, porque allende de tener más bivos ingenios, llegaron primero y aposentáronse en las mejores razones y sentencias; y si algo de bueno nosotros dezimos, dellos lo tomamos, que quando más procuramos huyr de lo que ellos dixeron, entonces vamos a caer en ello, por lo quel será forçado cerrar quel será forçado cerrar la boca o hablar por boca de otro, que según dize un común proverbio: «No ay cosa que no estén dicha», y bien creo aver otros que primero que yo tomassen este trabajo y más copiosamente, mas es cierto que a mí noticia no ha llegado, salvo aquello que el notable maestro de Lebrixa en su Arte de romance acerca desta facultad muy perfetamente puso. Mas yo no entiendo entrar en tan estrecha cuenta, lo uno por la falta de mi saber, y lo otro porque no quiero tocar más de lo que a nuestra lengua satisfaze, y algo de lo que toca a la dinidad de la poesía, que no en poca estima y veneración era tenida entre los antiguos, pues el esordio y invención della fue referido a sus dioses, assí como Apolo, Mercurio y Baco, y a las musas, según parece por las invocaciones de los antiguos poetas, de donde nosotros las tomamos, no porque creamos como ellos ni los tengamos por dioses invocándolos, que sería grandíssimo error y eregía, mas por seguir su gala y orden poética, que es aver de proponer, invocar y narrar o contar en las ficiones graves y arduas, de tal manera que siendo ficción la obra, es mucha razón que no menos sea fingida y no verdadera la invocación della. Mas quando hazemos alguna obra principal de devoción o que toque a nuestra fe, invocamos al que es la mesma verdad o a su Madre preciosa o a algunos santos que sean intercessores y medianeros para alcançarnos la gracia. Hallamos esso mesmo acerca de los antiguos, que sus oráculos y vaticinaciones se davan en versos, y de aquí vino los poetas llamarse vates, assí como hombres que cantan las cosas divinas, y no solamente la poesía tuvo solamente la poesía tuvo esta preminencia en la vana gentilidad, mas aun muchos libros del Testamento Viejo, según da testimonio San Gerónimo, fueron escritos en metro en aquella lengua hebrayca, la qual, según nuestros dotores, fue más antigua que la de los griegos, porque no se hallará escritura griega tan antigua como los cinco libros de Moysén; y no menos en Grecia que fue la madre de las liberales artes, podemos creer la poesía ser más antigua que la oratoria. Quanto al efeto de la poesía, quiéromе contentar con dos enxemplos que escrive Justino en su Epitoma, porque si oviesse de contar todas las alabanças y efetos della, por larga que fuesse la vida antes faltaría el tiempo que la materia; y es el primero enxemplo que como entre los atenienses y megarenses se recibiessen grandes daños de una parte a la otra, sobre la possessión de la isla Salamina, fatigados ambos pueblos de las continuas muertes, començaron assí, los unos como los otros, a poner pena capital entre sí a qualquiera que hiziesse mención de tal demanda. Solón, legislador de Atenas, viendo el daño de su república, simulándose loco salió delante todo el pueblo y amonestándolo en versos le movió de tal manera que no se dilató más la guerra, de la qual consiguieron vitoria. El segundo enxemplo es que teniendo los lacedemonios guerra con los messenios fueles dicho por sus oráculos que no podían vencer sin capitán ateniense, y los atenienses, en menosprecio, embiáronles un poeta coxo, llamado Tirteo, para que lo tomassen por capitán. Los lacedemonios muy fatigados con los daños recebidos, se bolvían a su tierra, más con mengua que con onrra, a los quales el poeta Tirteo, con la fuerça de sus versos de tal manera inflamó, que olvidados de sus proprias vidas mudaron el proprias vidas mudaron el propósito y, bolviendo, quedaron vitoriosos. Y no en vano cantaron los poetas que Orfeo ablandava las piedras con sus dulces versos, pues que la suavidad de la poesía enternecía los duros coraçones de los tiranos, como parece por una epístola de Falaris, tirano famoso en crueldad, que no por otra cosa otorgó la vida a Estesícoro, poeta, salvo porque hazía graciosos versos, y Pisístrato, tirano de Atenas, no halló otro camino para echar de sí el odio de la tiranía y gratificarse con el pueblo, salvo mandando buscar los versos de Homero, propuesto premio a quien los pusiesse por orden. Pues ¿qué diré en nuestra religión cristiana quánto conmueven a devoción los devotos y dulces ynos, cuyos autores fueron Ylario, Ambrosio y otros muy prudentes y santíssimos varones?; y santo Agustino escrivió seys libros desta facultad intitulados Música, para descanso de otros más graves estudios, en los quales seys libros trata de los géneros de versos y de quántos pies consta cada verso, y cada pie de quántas sílabas. Suficientemente creo aver provado la autoridad y antigüedad de la poesía y en quánta estima fue tenida acerca de los antiguos y de los nuestros, aunque algunos ay que, queriendo parecer graves y severos, malinamente la destierran de entre los umanos como ciencia ociosa, bolviendo a la facultad la culpa de aquellos que mal usan della, a los quales devía bastar, para convencer su error, la multitud de poetas que florecieron en Grecia y en Roma, que, cierto, si no fuera facultad onesta, no creo que Sófocles alcançara magistrados, preturas y capitanías en Atenas, madre de las ciencias de umanidad. Mas dexados éstos con su livor y malicia, bienaventurado príncipe, suplico a vuestra real señoría para en tiempo de ocio reciba este pequeño servicio por muestra de servicio por muestra de mi desseo. Sentencia es muy averiguada entre los poetas latinos ser por vicio reputado el acabar de los versos en consonantes y en semejança de palabras, aunque algunas vezes hallamos los poetas de mucha autoridad, con el atrevimiento de su saber, aver usado y puesto por gala aquello que a otros fuera condenación de su fama, como parece por Virgilio en el epigrama que dize «Sic vos non vobis», etc. Mas los santos y prudentes varones que compusieron los ynos en nuestra cristiana religión, escogieron por bueno lo que acerca de los poetas era tenido por malo, que gran parte de los ynos van compuestos por consonantes y encerrados debaxo de cierto número de sílabas; y no sin causa estos sabios y dotíssimos varones en este exercicio se ocuparon, porque bien mirado, estando el sentido repartido entre la letra y el canto, muy mejor puede sentir y acordarse de lo que va cantando por consonantes que en otra manera, porque no ay cosa que más a la memoria nos traya lo passado que la semejança dello. De aquí creo aver venido nuestra manera de trobar, aunque no dudo que en Ytalia floreciesse primero que en nuestra España y de allí decendiesse a nosotros; porque si bien queremos considerar, según sentencia de Virgilio, allí fue el solar del linage latino, y quando Roma se enseñoreó de aquesta tierra, no solamente recebimos sus leyes y constituciones, mas aun el romance, según su nombre da testimonio, que no es otra cosa nuestra lengua sino latín corrompido. Pues, ¿por qué no confessaremos aquello que del latín deciende, averlo recebido de quien la lengua latina y el romance recebimos?, quanto más que claramente parece, en la lengua ytaliana aver avido muy más antiguos poetas que en la nuestra, assí como el nuestra, assí como el Dante y Francisco Petrarca y otros notables varones que fueron antes y después, de donde muchos de los nuestros hurtaron gran copia de singulares sentencias, el qual hurto, como dize Virgilio, no deve ser vituperado, mas dino de mucho loor, quando de una lengua en otra se sabe galanamente cometer. Y si queremos arguyr de la etimología del vocablo, si bien miramos, trobar, vocablo ytaliano es, que no quiere dezir otra cosa trobar, en lengua ytaliana, sino hallar; pues, ¿qué cosa es trobar, en nuestra lengua, sino hallar sentencias y razones y consonantes y pies de cierta medida adonde las incluyr y encerrar? Assí que, concluyamos luego el trobar aver cobrado sus fuerças en Ytalia, y de allí esparzídolas por nuestra España, adonde creo que ya florece más que en otra ninguna parte.

Capítulo II.
De cómo consiste en arte la poesía y el trobar.

Aunque otra cosa no respondiéssemos para provar que la poesía consiste
en arte, bastava el juyzio de los claríssimos autores que intitularon de
arte poética los libros que desta facultad escrivieron, y ¿quién será tan
fuera de razón, que llamándose arte el oficio de texer o herrería, o hazer
vasijas de barro o cosas semejantes, piense la poesía y el trobar aver
venido sin arte en tanta dinidad? Bien sé que muchos contenderán para
en esta facultad ninguna otra cosa requerirse, salvo el buen natural, y
concedo ser esto lo principal y el fundamento; mas tan bien afirmo
polirse y alindarse mucho con las osservaciones del arte, que si al buen
ingenio no se juntasse el arte, sería como una tierra frutífera y no
labrada. Conviene luego confessar desta facultad lo que Cicerón en el
De perfeto oratore, y lo que los profesiones de gramática suelen hazer
en la en la difinición della, y lo que creo ser de todas las otras artes, que
no son sino osservaciones sacadas de la flor del uso de varones
dotíssimos, y reduzidas en reglas y precetos, porque según dizen los que
hablaron del arte, todas las artes conviene que tengan cierta materia, y
algunos afirman la oratoria no tener cierta materia, a los quales
convence Quintiliano diziendo que el fin del orador o retórico es dezir
cosas, aunque algunas vezes no verdaderas, pero verisímiles, y lo último
es persuadir y demulcir el oýdo. Y si esto es común a la poesía con la
oratoria o retórica, queda lo principal, conviene a saber, yr incluydo en
números ciertos, para lo qual el que no discutiere los autores y precetos,
es impossible que no le engañe el oýdo, porque según dotrina de Boecio
en el libro de música, muchas vezes nos engañan los sentidos; por tanto,
devemos dar mayor crédito a la razón. Comoquiera que, según nos
demuestra Tulio y Quintiliano, números ay que deve seguir el orador, y
huyr otros, mas esto ha de ser más dissimuladamente y no tiene de yr
astrito a ellos como el poeta que no es éste su fin.

Capítulo III.
De la diferencia que hay entre poeta y trobador.

Según es común uso de hablar en nuestra lengua, al trobador llaman
poeta y al poeta trobador, ora guarde la ley de los metros ora no; mas a

mí me parece que quanta diferencia ay entre músico y cantor, entre geómetra y pedrero, tanta deve aver entre poeta y trobador. Quanta diferencia aya del músico al cantor y del geómetra al pedrero, Boecio nos lo enseña, que el músico contempla en la especulación de la música, y el cantor es oficial della. Esto mesmo es entre el geómetradifinición della, es entre el geómetra y pedrero y poeta y trobador, porque el poeta contempla en los géneros de los versos, y de quántos pies consta cada verso, y el pie de quántas sílabas, y aún no se contenta con esto, sin examinar la quantidad dellas. Contempla, esso mesmo, qué cosa sea consonante s y assonante, y quando passa una sílaba por dos, y dos sílabas por una, y otras muchas cosas de las quales en su lugar adelante trataremos. Assí que, quánta diferencia ay de señor a esclavo, de capitán a hombre de armas sugeto a su capitanía, tanta a mi ver ay de trobador a poeta; mas pues estos dos nombres sin ninguna diferencia entre los de nuestra nación confundimos, mucha razón es que quien quisiere gozar del nombre de poeta o trobador, aya de tener todas estas cosas. ¡O, quántos vemos en nuestra España estar en reputación de trobadores, que no se les da más por echar una sílaba y dos demasiadas que de menos, ni se curan que sea buen consonante que malo!; y pues se ponen a hazer en metro, deven mirar y saber que metro no quiere dezir otra cosa sino mensura, de manera que lo que no lleva cierta mensura y medida, no devemos dezir que va en metro, ni el que lo haze deve gozar de nombre de poeta ni trobador.

Capítulo IV.
De lo principal que se requiere para aprender a trobar.

En lo primero amonestamos a los que carecen de ingenio y son más aptos para otros estudios y exercicios, que no gasten su tiempo en vano leyendo nuestros precetos, podiéndolo emplear en otra cosa que les sea más natural, y tomen por sí aquel dicho de Quintiliano, en el primero de sus Instituciones, que ninguna cosa aprovechan las artes y aprovechan las artes y precetos, adonde fallece natura, que a quien ingenio falta, no le aprovecha más esta arte que precetos de agricultura a tierras estériles. De aqueste género de hombres avrá muchos que reprehenderán esta obra, unos que no la entenderán, otros que no sabrán usar della, a los quales respondo con un dicho de Santo Agustino, en el primero de

Dotrina cristiana, diziendo que si yo con mi dedo mostrasse a uno alguna estrella, y él tuviesse tan debilitados los ojos que ni viesse el dedo ni la estrella, no por esso me devía culpar, y esso mesmo si viesse el dedo y no la estrella, devía culpar el defeto de su vista y no a mí. Assí que, aqueste nuestro poeta que establecemos instituyr, en lo primero venga dotado de buen ingenio; y porque creo que para los medianamente enseñados está la verdad más clara que la luz, si oviere algunos tan bárbaros que persistan en su pertinacia, dexados como incurables, nuestra exortación se enderece a los mancebos estudiosos, cuyas orejas las dulces musas tienen conciliadas. Es menester, allende desto, que el tal poeta no menosprecie la elocución, que consiste en hablar puramente, elegante y alto quando fuere menester, según la materia lo requiere, los quales precetos porque son comunes a los oradores y poetas, no los esperen de mí, que no es mi intención hablar, salvo de sólo aquello que es proprio del poeta. Mas, para quanto a la elocución, mucho aprovecha, según es dotrina de Quintiliano, criarse desde la tierna niñez adonde hablen muy bien, porque como nos enseña Oracio, qualquiera vasija de barro guarda para siempre aquel olor que recibió quando nueva. Y después desto deve exercitarse en leer no solamente poetas y estorias en nuestra lengua, mas tan bien en lengua latina; y en lengua latina; y no solamente leerlos como dize Quintiliano, mas discutirlos en los estilos y sentencias y en las licencias, que no leerá cosa el poeta en ninguna facultad de que no se aproveche para la copia que le es muy necessaria, principalmente en obra larga.

Capítulo V.
De la mensura y esaminación de los pies y de las maneras de trobar.

Toda la fuerça del trobar está en saber hazer y conocer los pies, porque dellos se hazen las coplas y por ellos se miden; y pues assí es, sepamos qué cosa es pie. Pie no es otra cosa en el trobar sino un ayuntamiento de cierto número de sílabas, y llámasse pie porque por él se mide todo lo que trobamos y sobre los tales pies corre y roda el sonido de la copla. Mas para que mejor vengamos en el verdadero conocimiento, devemos considerar que los latinos llaman verso a lo que nosotros llamamos pie, y nosotros podremos llamar verso adondequiera que ay ayuntamiento de pies que comúnmente llamamos copla, que quiere decir cópula o ayuntamiento. Y bien podemos dezir que en una copla aya dos versos, assí como si es de ocho pies y va de cuatro en cuatro son dos versos, o si es de nueve, el un verso es de cinco y el otro de cuatro, y si es de diez puede ser el un verso de cinco y el otro de otros cinco, y assí por esta manera podemos poner otros enxemplos infinitos. Ay en nuestro vulgar castellano dos géneros de versos o coplas, el uno quando el pie consta de ocho sílabas o su equivalencia, que se llama arte real, y el otro se compone de doze o su equivalencia, que se llama arte mayor, digo su equivalencia porque bien puede equivalencia porque bien puede ser que tenga más o menos en cantidad, mas en valor es impossible para ser el pie perfeto. Y bien parece nosotros aver tomado del latín el trobar, pues en él se hallan estos dos géneros antiguamente, de ocho sílabas assí como «Jam lucis orto sidere», de doze assí como «Mecenas atavis edite regibus», assí que quando el pie no tuviere más de ocho sílabas llamarle hemos de arte real, como lo que dixo Juan de Mena: «Después quel pintor del mundo», y si fuere de doze ya sabremos ques de arte mayor, assí como el mesmo Juan de Mena en las Trezientas: «Al muy prepotente don Juan el segundo». Dixe que podían, a las vezes, llevar más o menos sílabas los pies, entiéndese aquello en cantidad o contando cada una por sí, mas en el valor o pronunciación ni son más ni menos. Pueden ser más en cantidad quando una dición acaba en vocal y la otra que se sigue tan bien en el mesmo pie comiença en vocal, que, aunque son dos sílabas, no valen sino por una, ni tardamos más tiempo en pronunciar ambas que una, assí como dize Juan de Mena: «Paró nuestra vida ufana». Avemos tan bien de mirar que quando entre la una vocal y la otra estuviere la h, que es aspiración, entonces, a las vezes acontece que passan por dos y a las vezes por una, y juzgarlo hemos según el común uso de hablar o según viéremos que el pie lo requiere, y esto tan bien avrá lugar en las dos vocales sin aspiración. Tan bien pueden ser más quando las dos sílabas postreras del pie son ambas breves, que entonces no valen ambas sino por una; mas es en tanto grado nuestro común acentuar en la común acentuar en la penúltima sílaba, que muchas vezes quando aquellas dos sílabas del cabo vienen breves, hazemos luenga la que está antes de la postrera, assí como en otro pie dize: «De la biuda Penelópe». Puede tan bien, al contrario, ser menos de ocho y den doze quando la última es luenga, que entonces vale por dos y tanto tardamos en pronunciar aquella sílaba como dos, de manera que passarán siete por ocho, como dixo frey Ýñigo: «Aclara sol divinal». Mas, porque en el arte mayor los pies son intercisos, que se pueden partir por medio, no solamente puede passar una sílaba por dos quando la postrera es luenga, mas tan bien, si la primera o la postrera fuera luenga, assí del un medio pie como del otro, que cada una valdrá por dos. Ay otro género de trobar que resulta de los sobredichos que se llama pie quebrado, que es medio pie, assí de arte real como de mayor; del arte real son cuatro sílabas o su equivalencia y éste suélese trobar, el pie quebrado mezclado con los enteros, y a las vezes passan cinco sílabas por medio pie y entonces dezimos que va la una perdida, assí como dixo don Jorge: «como devemos». En el arte mayor, quando se parten los pies y van quebrados, nunca suelen mezclarse con los enteros, mas antes todos son quebrados, según parece por muchos villancicos que ay de aquesta arte trobados.

Capítulo VI.
De los consonantes y assonantes y de la esaminación dellos.

Después de aver visto y conocido la mensura y esaminación de los pies, resta conocer los consonantes y assonantes, los quales siempre se aposentan y assinan en el cabo de cada pie y son principales miembros y partes del mesmo pie; y porque el proprio acento de nuestra proprio acento de nuestra lengua comúnmente es en la penúltima sílaba, allí devemos buscar y esaminar los consonantes y assonantes. Consonante se llama todas aquellas letras o sílabas que se ponen desde donde está el postrer acento agudo o alto hasta el fin del pie, assí como si el un pie acabasse en esta dición: «vida», y el otro acabasse en otra dición que dixesse: «despedida», entonces diremos que desde la «i», donde está el acento largo, hasta el cabo es consonante, y por esso se llama consonante, porque ha de consonar el un pie con el otro con las mesmas letras desde aquel acento agudo o alto que es aquella «i». Mas quando el pie acaba en una sílaba luenga que vale por dos, entonces contamos aquella sola por última y penúltima y desde aquella vocal donde está el postrer acento largo, desde allí ha de consonar un pie con otro con las mesmas letras, assí como si el un pie acaba en «coraçón», y el otro en «passión», desde aquel «ón», que vale por dos sílabas, dezimos que es el consonante. Y si acabasse el pie en dos sílabas breves y estuviesse el acento agudo en la antepenúltima, entonces diremos que el consonante es desde aquella antepenúltima, porque las dos postreras, que son breves, no valen sino por una, de manera que todo se sale a un cuento, assí como si el pie acabasse en «quiéreme», y el otro en «hiéreme», entonces desde la «e» primera adonde está el acento alto es consonante que ha de consonar con las mesmas letras. Ay tan bien otros que se llaman assonantes, y cuéntanse por los mesmos acentos de los consonantes, mas difiere el un assonante del otro en alguna letra de las consonantes, que no de las vocales; y llámasse .las vocales; y llámasse assonante porque es a semejança del consonante, aunque no con todas las mesmas letras, assí como Juan de Mena dixo en la Coronación, que acabó un pie en «proverbios», y otro en «sobervios», adonde passa una v por una b, y esto suélese hazer en defeto de consonante, aunque b por v, y v por b muy usado está, porque tienen gran hermandad entre sí, assí como si dezimos biva y reciba, y otros muchos enxemplos pudiéramos traer, mas dexémoslos por evitar prolixidad. Y allende desto, avémosnos de guardar que no pongamos un consonante dos vezes en una copla, y aun si ser pudiere no lo devemos repetir hasta que passen veynte coplas, salvo si fuere obra larga, que entonces podrémoslo tornar a repetir a tercera copla o dende adelante aviendo necessidad; y qualquiera copla se ha de hazer de diversos consonantes, dando a cada pie compañero o compañeros, porque si fuessen todos los pies de unos consonantes parecería muy mal. Y avemos de notar que sílabas breves en el romance llamamos todas las que tienen el acento baxo, y luengas o agudas se dizen las que tienen alto el acento, aunque en el latín no vayan por esta cuenta.

Capítulo VII.
De los versos y coplas y de su diversidad.

Según ya deximos arriba, devemos mirar que de los pies se hazen los versos y coplas; mas porque algunos querrán saber de quántos pies han de ser, digamos algo dello brevemente. Muchas vezes vemos que algunos hazen sólo un pie y aquél ni es verso ni copla porque avían de ser pies y no sólo un pie, ni ay allí consonante, pues que no tiene compañero, y aquel tal suélese llamar mote; y si tiene dos pies llamámosle tan bien mote o villancico, o letra o villancico, o letra de alguna invención por la mayor parte; si tiene tres pies enteros o el uno quebrado tan bien será villancico o letra de invención, y entonces el un pie ha de quedar sin consonante, según más común uso; y algunos ay del tiempo antiguo de dos pies y de tres que no van en consonante, porque entonces no guardavan tan estrechamente las osservaciones del trobar. Y si es de cuatro pies puede ser canción y ya se puede llamar copla, y aun los romances suelen yr de cuatro en cuatro pies, aunque no van en consonante sino el segundo y el cuarto pie y aun los del tiempo viejo no van por verdaderos consonantes. Y todas estas cosas suelen ser de arte real, que el arte mayor es más propria para cosas graves y arduas; y de cinco pies tan bien ay canciones y de seys; y puédense llamar versos y coplas y hazer tantas diversidades cuantas maneras huviere de trocarse los pies; mas desde seys pies arriba por la mayor parte suelen tornar a hazer otro ayuntamiento de pies, de manera que serán dos versos en una copla, y comúnmente no sube ninguna copla de doze pies arriba porque parecería desvariada cosa, salvo los romances, que no tienen número cierto.

Capítulo IX y final.
De cómo se deven escrevir y leer las coplas.

Dévense escrevir las coplas de manera que cada pie vaya en su renglón, ora sea de arte real ora de arte mayor, ora sea de pie quebrado ora de entero, y si en la copla huviere dos usos, assí como si es de siete y los cuatro pies son un uso y los tres otro, o si es de ocho y los cuatro son un uso y los otros cuatro otro, o si es de nueve y los cinco son un verso y los cuatro otro, etc.,siempre entre uso y uso se ponga coma: que son dos puntos uno sobre otro, y en fin de la copia hase de poner colum que es un punto solo, y en los nombres proprios que no son muy conocidos o en las palabras que pueden tener dos acentos, devemos poner sobre la vocal poner sobre la vocal adonde se haze el acento luengo un ápice, que es un rasguito como el de la «i», assí como en ámo quando yo ámo, y amó quando otro amó, y hanse de leer de manera que entre pie y pie se pare un poquito sin cobrar aliento, y entre verso y verso parar un poquito más, y entre copla y copla un poco más para tomar aliento.

14 1511 Hernando del Castillo

The case of Hernando del Castillo is a difficult one. The JGAAP analysis shows that the author could be Alfonso el Sabio, Garcí Rodríguez de Montalvo, Juan del Encina or Francisco López de Villalobos (Appendix 15.6.1). However, the idiolect of the unknown author of *Siete partidas de Alfonso X el Sabio* (1491) clearly shows the idiolect of Juan del Encina (Appendix 15.6.2). We know that for 20 years Hernando del Castillo was compiling poetry, which is equal to the year 1490. This is exactly when Gonzalo Fernández de Oviedo started writing.

We do not know too much about Juan del Encina during 1508 and 1509, and it is possible that he was at the court of the Count of Oliva Serafín de Centelles y Urrea for some of this time to prepare his manuscript of the General Songbook under the pseudonym Hernando del Castillo. This manuscript would probably be completed at the end of 1509, since we know that Hernando del Castillo formed a partnership with Cristóbal Cofman and Lorenzo Ganoto on December 22, 1509 to print a thousand volumes of the General Songbook[248]. On January 15, 1511 the printing of the General Songbook was finished. This book was published in Spain several times, namely:

Cancionero general. Valencia, 1511
Cancionero general. Valencia, 1514
Cancionero general. Toledo, 1517
Cancionero general. Toledo, 1520
Cancionero general. Toledo, 1527.
Cancionero general. Sevilla, 1535

---

[248] **SERRANO Y MORALES, José Enrique** (1898-1899). Reseña histórica en forma de diccionario de las imprentas que han existido en Valencia. Valencia, pp. 78-79. Document of the Archivo del Real Colegio Seminario del Corpus Christi de Valencia, Protocolos J. Casanova (sign. 6104). Cited by **CASTILLO, Hernando de** (2004). Cancionero General. 5 tomos. Tomo V. Edición de Joaquín González Cuenca. Editorial Castalia, pp. 549-550

Perea Rodríguez does not want to exclude that the unknown Hernando de Castillo was a Jewish convert. Whatever he was, the documentary inquiries about the origin of this editor were totally contradictory and insufficient[249]. Perea Rodríguez indicates that some time ago Castillo's wife Joana Diez died and Hernando del Castillo paid his son Pedro del Castillo an amount of the maternal dowry[250] on November 23, 1518. On January 7, 1519 Hernando del Castillo teamed up with two other well known Valencian booksellers Gaspar Trincher and Joan Uguet to edit books of a religious, missal, and brevian nature[251]. This is the latest news about Hernando del Castillo in Valencia. As we know Juan del Encina went to Jerusalem, where he sang his first mass. He also wrote about the events during his pilgrimage to Jerusalem in *Tribagia o Via Sacra de Hierusalem*. Perea Rodríguez does not forget to wonder if perhaps Fernando del Castillo is behind the *Paraiso del amor en coplas*[252], printed in Naples in 1526, a book registered by Hernando Colón in his *Abecedarium*[253].

---

[249] **PEREA RODRÍGUEZ, Óscar** (2007). Estudio biográfico sobre los poetas del Cancionero General. Consejo Superior de Investigaciones Científicas, Madrid, pp. 49-51

[250] Archivo de Protocolos del Colegio del Corpus Christi, Valencia, Protocolos de Jerónimo Carbonell, 23 de noviembre, sig. 712. The document was published by **BERGER, Philippe** (1987). Libro y lectura en la Valencia del renacimiento (2). Edicions Alfons el Magnànim Institució Valenciana d'Estudes i Investigació, p. 525

[251] Archivo de Protocolos del Colegio del Corpus Christi, Valencia, Protocolos de Jerónimo Carbonell, 7 de enero de 1519, sig. 712. The document was published by **BERGER, Philippe** (1987). Libro y lectura en la Valencia del renacimiento (2). Edicions Alfons el Magnànim Institució Valenciana d'Estudes i Investigació, pp. 474-476. Cited by **PEREA RODRÍGUEZ, Óscar** (2007). Estudio biográfico sobre los poetas del Cancionero General. Consejo Superior de Investigaciones Científicas, Madrid, p. 49

[252] **RODRÍGUEZ-MOÑINO, Antonio** (1968). Poesía y cancioneros (siglo XVI), Madrid. Pg. 67. Cited by **PEREA RODRÍGUEZ, Óscar** (2007). Estudio biográfico sobre los poetas del Cancionero General. Consejo Superior de Investigaciones Científicas, Madrid, p. 51

[253] **RODRÍGUEZ-MOÑINO, Antonio** (1997). Nuevo diccionario bibliográfico de pliegos sueltos poéticos (siglo XVI), eds. Arthur L.-F Askins y Victor Infantes, Madrid, Castalia. Pg. 207. Cited by **PEREA RODRÍGUEZ, Óscar** (2007). Estudio biográfico sobre los poetas del Cancionero General. Consejo Superior de Investigaciones Científicas, Madrid, p. 51

14.1 Reinaldos de Montalbán

The work *Renaldos de Montabán* belongs to the group of novels of chivalry based on a translation of an anonymous cantare in ottava rima, the Innamoramento di Carlo Magno (1481-91). This work was printed by Jorge Costilla in Valencia in 1511. On August 11, 1511 Hernando del Castillo required by notary Jorge Costilla and Juan Uguet denouncing the irregularities committed by its members to add *Lo enamorament del rey Carlo* to the edition of Reinaldo de Montalbán without his consent.

Two years later and in different editions (1513, 1533) we see that Hernando del Castillo was involved in the third book of *Reinaldo de Montalbán* called *Trapesonda*[254]. His right-hand man to finance the printing of the work was the Italian Lorenzo Ganoto and Castillo used to work against a commission of 25% of the benefits of the printing cost.

Here we know that the idiolect of *Renaldos de Montalbán* (books I and II) is similar to the unknown author of *Oliveros de Castilla* (Appendix 15.6.3) according to JGAAP. *Oliveros de Castilla* belongs to Fernández de Oviedo (Appendix 15.6.4) according to JGAAP. However, the author was Juan de Ávila. The idiolect of Trapesonda (1513, 1533) is similar to the author of *El Cortesano* (Appendix 15.6.5), probably a pseudonym of Gonzalo Fernández de Oviedo (Appendix), and the same can be said about *Baldo* (1542), the fourth book of *Renaldos de Montalbán* (15.6.6). So we can see that Hernando de Castillo had to do with Juan del Encina and Gonzalo Fernández de Oviedo.

We observe the same tendency in the foreword to *Cancionero general*, because many words used in it go in the direction to Juan del Encina and Fernández de Oviedo. Both authors liked to use words such as: ingenio, doctos varones, esclarecido, etc.

---

[254] **CAMPS I PERARNAU, Susana** (2008). Diego de Gumiel, impressor del *Tirant lo blanch* (1497) I del *Tirante el Blanco* (1511). Universitat Autónoma de Barcelona. Tesis doctoral, p. 270

236

14.2 Juan del Encina

An analysis of the foreword to *Cancionero general* with Textalyser shows that the first word in the rank is "Y", the second word is "que", and the third word is "de". Even with this analysis it is difficult to confirm that Juan del Encina is the real author of the pseudonym Hernando del Castillo.

Frequency of words in the foreword to Cancionero general

Word	Occurrences	Frequency	Rank
y	48	5.1%	1
que	47	5%	2
de	45	4.8%	3
en	29	3.1%	4
las	24	2.6%	5
la	23	2.4%	6
los	20	2.1%	7
por	18	1.9%	8
no	14	1.5%	9
el	14	1.5%	9

14.3 Foreword to Cancionero general.

The foreword to the Cancionero general shows many words that were used by Gonzalo Fernández de Oviedo. However, this analysis is not enough seeing that JGAAP showed the idiolect of Juan del Encina. So other texts are necessary. What we have learned from this chapter is that Juan del Encina and Gonzalo Fernández de Oviedo probably worked together. In other words, I see Juan del Encina as Fernández de Oviedo's helper to publish his books in Spain and Italy.

Todos los **ingenios** qu' el vniuersal formador de las cosas crió, muy espectable y manífico Señor, vemos ser inclinados naturalmente á diuersos exercicios, como en el género de las letras á diuersos estudios. En ellas, vnos á latin, otros á romance, vnos á prosa, otros á uerso. El mió, Señor muy espectable, tal qual él aya sydo, fué siempre tan afectado á las cosas del metro, en qualquier lengua que sea, mayormente en la castellana, maternal y propia mia, que, de veynte años á esta parte, esta natural inclinación me hizo inuestigar, auer y recolegir de diuersas partes y diuersos auctores, con la más diligencia que pude, todas las obras que de Juan de Mena acá se escriuieron, ó á mi noticia pudieron venir, de los auctores que en este género de escreuir auctoridad tienen en nuestro tienpo. Donde **copilé** vn Cancionero, al parescer mió, assí en generalidad de obras, como en precio dellas, si no muy excelente, á lo menos no malo. E por auer sydo de ingenios muy loados **que en mi poder** le vieron, loado por bueno, y porque la cosa más propia y essencial de lo bueno es ser comunicado, paresciome ser género de auaricia no comunicar y **sacar á luz** lo que á muchos juzgaua ser vtil y agradable; v que injuriaua á los auctores de las mismas obras que, por ser muy buenas, dessean con ellas perpetuar sus nonbres, y que sean vistas y leydas de todos; y no menos agrauiaua á los claros entendimientos y afectados á la galanía de semejante escreuir, **encelándoles** el tesoro que más que otra cosa posseer dessean. Acordé, pues, por las razones ya dichas, **sacar en limpio** el Cancionero ya nonbrado, ó la mayor parte d' él, y dar manera cómo fuese comunicado á todos. Y assí ordenado y corregido por la mejor manera y diligencia que pude, trabajé ponerlo en impression para comun vtilidad ó passa tienpo, mayormente de aquellos á quien semejante escriptura más que otra aplaze. E porque lleuasse el título y amparo que todas las obras que no quieren tener aduersarios ni lenguas venenosas procuran y suelen leuar, dediquélo tanbien al nonbre y protección de vuestra gran Señoría. No porque claramente no conozca ser temerario atreuimiento osar yo consagrar tan baxos trabajos á tan alto lugar, y á quien Titu Liuio apenas osara dedicar sus Crónicas, ni Plinio su Universal Hystoria, según los claros ornamentos, assí morales como del entendimiento que en vuestra Señoría más que en otro resplandescen; mas porque me páresela cometer crimen de ingratitud, si obra alguna de mis manos saliesse, que soy obra y hechura de las de vuestra Señoría, que á aquel no fuesse

238

intitulada, á cuyo seruicio yo después que soy en este reyno estoy dedicado y ofrescido. A qual, pues, suplico que, quando la **especulación** de cosas más altas y graues le dieren lugar, como á horas hurtadas, passe los ojos por esta lectura, y mande corregir y enmendar en ella **lo que yo por** ventura en prejuyzio de alguno, ó no pude ó no supe corregir ni mejor ordenar. E si alguna cosa el más **claro ingenio** de vuestra Señoría ó de los otros lectores hallaren mal puesta ó mudada de aquel tenpre que sacó de la primera fragua de sus auctores, ó variación en los títulos de aquellos, suplico á vuestra Señoría y ruego á todos **me perdonen** y enmienden lo que bien no les parescerá. E el que hallare agena marca en sus obras, que la raya y ponga la propia, y haga lo mismo el que la suya sin ninguna hallare. E si alguna culpa en esto se me atribuyere, asuéluame la buena intención y fin mió, que fué á mi pensamiento aprouechar, y conplazer á muchos y seruir á todos. E escúseme tanbien la manera que tuue en la recolection destas obras, que con toda la diligencia que puse, aunque no pequeña, no fué en mi mano auer todas las obras que aquí van de los verdaderos originales, ó de cierta relación de los auctores que las hizieron, por ser cosa casi impossible, según la variación de los tienpos y distancia de los lugares en que las dichas obras se conpusieron. E porque **todos los ingenios** de los ombres naturalmente mucho aman la orden, y ni á todos aplazen vnas materias, ni á todos **desagradan,** ordené y distinguí la presente obra por partes y distinciones de materias, en el modo que se sigue. Que luego en el principio puse las cosas de devoción y moralidad; continué á éstas las **cosas de amores**, diferenciando las vnas y las otras por los títulos y nonbres de sus auctores. Y tanbien puse juntas á vna parte todas las Canciones; los Romances assímismo á otra; las Invenciones y Letras de **justadores** en otro capítulo, y tras éstas las Glosas de motes, y luego los Villancicos, y después las Preguntas. É por quitar el **fastío** á los lectores que por ventura las muchas obras granes arriba leydas les causaron, puse á la fin las cosas de *Burlas prouocantes á risa*, con que concluye la obra, porque coja cada vno por orden lo que más agrada á su apetito. E por quitar ó aliuiar tanbien con **este trabajo mió** el enojo que se suele causar en buscar las materias por la obra derramadas que á cada vno más plazen, hize tabla y, si no **m'engaño**, pro suficiente sobre todo el libro; por donde en modo tan cierto como breue, con poco trabajo se hallarán las materias generales y particulares que por toda la obra son difusas. **Suplico, pues,** á vuestra Señoría que, por interese á lo menos de los

altos ingenios que en esta lectura se desuelaron, reciba la dicha recopilación ó Cancionero, porque las claras centellas de vuestra Señoría hagan resplandecer en ella lo que mis baxos trabajos y poco saber escurescieron, y deste Castillo que vuestra Señoría de los primeros cimientos obró, sienpre se acuerde.

Words and expressions used in the foreword to Hernando de Castillo

Nº	Words	Author	Cases	Other authors
1.	Galandía	Juan del Encina	5	4
2.	Encelar	La Celestina	1	3
3.	Especulación	Gonzalo Fernández de Oviedo	1	13
4.	Fastío	Gonzalo Fernández de Oviedo	1	15
5.	Justadores	Gonzalo Fernández de Oviedo	3	14
6.	Desagradan	Gonzalo Fernández de Oviedo	1	12
7.	Ordené	Diego de San Pedro	1	18
8.	Altos ingenios	Gonzalo Fernández de Oviedo	2	3
9.	Sacar en limpio	Gonzalo Fernández de Oviedo	9	7
10.	Me engañó	Gonzalo Fernández de Oviedo	1	16
11.	Cosas de amores	Gonzalo Fernández de Oviedo	1	12
12.	Claro ingenio	Gonzalo Fernández de Oviedo	1	10
13.	Me ponen	Diego de San Pedro	2	31
14.	Que en mi poder	Jerónimo Fernández	1	3
15.	Sacar a luz	Gonzalo Fernández de Oviedo	2	9
16.	Lo que yo por	Gonzalo Fernández de Oviedo	1	13
17.	Todos los ingenios	Jerónimo Fernández	1	7
18.	Este trabajo mío	Gonzalo Fernández de Oviedo	1	0
19.	Suplico pues	Jerónimo Fernández	1	12
20.	Tan alto lugar	Hernán Díaz	1	16

15 Appendixes

15.1 Chapter 8

15.1.1 Authors: XV- XVI centuries

We observe that we have the following authors to analyze in the XV and XVI century:

N°	Birth	Death	Author
1.	1480?		Acuario, Juan
2.	1493		Agüero de Trasmiera, Juan
3.	1515?	1562?	Arce de Otálora, Juan
4.	1480?		Arcos, Cristóbal de
5.	1490?	1542?	Boscán, Juan
6.	1520	1593	Calvete de Estrella, Juan Cristóbal
7.	1480?		Cardona, Alonso de
8.	1484	1566	Casas, Bartolomé de las
9.	1490	1550	Castillejo, Cristóbal de
10.	1480?		Castillo, Hernando del
11.	1513?	1575	Cervantes de Salazar, Francisco
12.	1470	1548	Ciruelo, Pedro
13.	1491	1552	Delicado, Francisco
14.	1480?		Díaz, Hernán
15.	1468	1535	Encinas, Juan del
16.	1500		Escriva, Ludovico
17.	1478	1557	Fernández de Oviedo, Gonzalo
18.	1500		Fernández, Jerónimo
19.	1474	1542	Fernández, Lucas
20.	1480?		Fernández, Sebastián
21.	1455?	1525?	Flores, Juan de
22.	1500		Gómez de Toledo, Gaspar
23.	1480	1545	Guevara, Antonio de
24.	1480?		Hernández Alemán, Alonso
25.	1510?		Hernández de Villaumbrales, Pedro
26.	1510	1579	Horozco, Sebastián de
27.	1529	1588	Huerte de San Juan, Juan
28.	1503?	1575	Hurtado de Mendoza, Diego

29.	1523	1590	Hurtado de Toledo, Luis
30.	1510	1573	Jiménez de Urrea, Jerónimo
31.	1480?		Justiniano, Juan
32.	1455	1524	López de Cortegana, Diego
33.	1511	1566	López de Gomara Francisco
34.	1473	1549	López de Villalobos, Francisco
35.	1500?		López, Jerónimo
36.	1470?	1530?	Lucena
37.	1493	1552	Lucena, Luis de
38.	1520?		Luján, Pedro
39.	1497	1551	Mejía, Pedro
40.	1485?	1552?	Molina, Juan de
41.	1480?	1558	Montaña de Monserrate, Bernardino de
42.	1480?		Muñón, Sancho de
43.	1520?		Natas, Francisco de las
44.	1500	1553?	Núñez Alba, Diego
45.	1480?		Núñez de Reinosa, Alonso
46.	1478	1553	Núñez de Toledo, Hernán
47.	1480?		Núñez, Nicolás de
48.	1510	1570	Paez de Castro, Juan
49.	1510?	1560?	Pastor, Juan
50.	1480	1548	Pérez de Chinchón, Bernardo
51.	1492	1533	Pérez de Oliva, Fernando
52.	1480?		Petras, Ramón de
53.	1445	1519	Proaza, Alonso de
54.	1480?		Quirós, Bernardo de
55.	1530	1504	Ramírez de Lucena, Juan
56.	1450		Rodríguez de Montalvo, Garcí
57.	1480?	1554	Rodríguez Florián, Juan
58.	1475	1541	Rojas, Fernando de
59.	1505?	1565	Rueda, Lope de
60.	1510	1576	Salazar, Pedro de
61.	1480?		San Pedro, Diego de
62.	1480?		Sedeño, Juan
63.	1525?	1575?	Segura, Juan de
64.	1490	1573	Sepulveda, Juan Ginés de
65.	1486?	1554	Silva, Feliciano de
66.	1405?	1480?	Tafur, Pedro
67.	1520		Timoneda, Juan de
68.	1485?	1530?	Torres Naharro, Bartolomé
69.	1490	1532	Valdés, Alfonso de
70.	1509	1541	Valdés, Juan de
71.	1480?		Vazquez, Francisco

72.	1480?		Velazquez de Castillo, Gabriel
73.	1497?	1562	Venegas, Alejo
74.	1465	1536?	Vicente, Gil
75.	1480?		Villalón, Cristóbal de
76.	1533	1603	Villegas Selvago, Alonso de
77.	1492	1540	Vives, Juan Luis

15.2 Chapter 9

15.2.1 1547 Marro 1635 - Introducción

timoneda damboekintroduction3kb.txt C:\Users\Govert\Desktop\Signatura comienzo 19.11.2019\timoneda damboekintroduction3kb.txt
Canonicizers:
    Normalize Whitespace
EventDrivers:
    Character NGrams n : 4
        EventCullers:
            Most Common Events numevents : 50
Analysis:
    Nearest Neighbor Driver with metric Cosine Distance
1. Gonzalo Fernández de Oviedo -C:\Users\Govert\Desktop\Signatura comienzo 19.11.2019\FernandezOviedoClaribalte21kb.txt 0.057071992067315946
2. Juan de Valdés -C:\Users\Govert\Desktop\Signatura comienzo 19.11.2019\ValdesJuanCartas1-3-completo114kb.txt 0.06878939567490816
3. Juan Huarte de San Juan -C:\Users\Govert\Desktop\Signatura comienzo 19.11.2019\HuarteExamen Ingenios21kb.txt 0.07362871979504071
4. Lope de Rueda -C:\Users\Govert\Desktop\Signatura comienzo 19.11.2019\LopedeRuedaEufemia37kb.txt 0.07573039573054352
5. Diego de San Pedro -C:\Users\Govert\Desktop\Signatura comienzo 19.11.2019\carceldeamor21kb.txt 0.0758905013543616
6. Luis de Lucena -C:\Users\Govert\Desktop\Signatura comienzo 19.11.2019\LuisdeLucenaParteTestamento14kb.txt 0.07654379414002721
7. Bernardo de Quirós -C:\Users\Govert\Desktop\Signatura comienzo 19.11.2019\VillalonViajeTurquiaVillalon109kb.txt 0.0769563698742145
8. Lope de Rueda -C:\Users\Govert\Desktop\Signatura comienzo 19.11.2019\lopederuedaAceitunas42kb.txt 0.07703877343641363

9. Juan de Timoneda -C:\Users\Govert\Desktop\Signatura comienzo 19.11.2019\TimonedaCaminantes21kb.txt 0.08055374397723891

10. El cortesano -C:\Users\Govert\Desktop\Signatura comienzo 19.11.2019\BoscanElCortesano47kb.txt 0.08121068084966121

11. Cristóbal Castillejo -C:\Users\Govert\Desktop\Signatura comienzo 19.11.2019\CristobalCastillejoDialogodeMujeres21kb.txt 0.08327520459240556

12. Lucena -C:\Users\Govert\Desktop\Signatura comienzo 19.11.2019\repeticionamores114kb.txt 0.08460085348061408

13. Thebayda anónym -C:\Users\Govert\Desktop\Signatura comienzo 19.11.2019\thebaida incompleta21kb.txt 0.08469242616847428

14. Juan Paez de Castro -C:\Users\Govert\Desktop\Signatura comienzo 19.11.2019\juanpaezdecastroCartas23kb.txt 0.08519191220415889

15. Juan de Flores -C:\Users\Govert\Desktop\Signatura comienzo 19.11.2019\griselobra89kb.txt 0.08675870183857515

16. Alfonso de Valdés -C:\Users\Govert\Desktop\Signatura comienzo 19.11.2019\valdesAlfonsoCartas34kb.txt 0.08774325782231263

17. Gonzalo Fernández de Oviedo -C:\Users\Govert\Desktop\Signatura comienzo 19.11.2019\fernandezoviedobatalla90-130tiene34kb.txt 0.08865637005094928

18. Juan Ramírez de Lucena -C:\Users\Govert\Desktop\Signatura comienzo 19.11.2019\Ramirez Lucena exhortatoria.txt 0.08971370926829159

19. Diego de San Pedro -C:\Users\Govert\Desktop\Signatura comienzo 19.11.2019\arnalte incompleta21kb.txt 0.08979543646241717

20. Juan Ramírez de Lucena -C:\Users\Govert\Desktop\Signatura comienzo 19.11.2019\RamirezLucena a Zapata.txt 0.09006971194310376

21. Juan del Encina -C:\Users\Govert\Desktop\Signatura comienzo 19.11.2019\encina textos al rey75kb.txt 0.09036309221649905

22. Francisco Delicado -C:\Users\Govert\Desktop\Signatura comienzo 19.11.2019\legno2 8kb.txt 0.0908265926000279

23. Jerónimo Fernández -C:\Users\Govert\Desktop\Signatura comienzo 19.11.2019\jeronimofernandez3año1579-113kb.txt 0.09328291884882411

24. Feliciano de Silva -C:\Users\Govert\Desktop\Signatura comienzo 19.11.2019\Silva amadis de grecia20kb.txt 0.09438135594349062

25. Baltasar del Rio -C:\Users\Govert\Desktop\Signatura comienzo 19.11.2019\baltasardelrio1504Tratado22kb.txt 0.0953268613370436

26. Francisco Cervantes de Salazar -C:\Users\Govert\Desktop\Signatura comienzo 19.11.2019\CervantesSalazarCronicaNuevEspaña21kb.txt 0.09604119703948077

27. Francisco Delicado -C:\Users\Govert\Desktop\Signatura comienzo 19.11.2019\lozanaapologia6kb.txt 0.09615518938032619

28. Gonzalo Fernández de Oviedo -C:\Users\Govert\Desktop\Signatura comienzo 19.11.2019\FernandezOviedoSumarioIndias21kb.txt 0.09668628065608531

29. Gonzalo Fernández de Oviedo -C:\Users\Govert\Desktop\Signatura comienzo 19.11.2019\fernandezOviedo-indias 21kb.txt 0.0975224808004651

30. Cristóbal Castillejo -C:\Users\Govert\Desktop\Signatura comienzo 19.11.2019\CristobalCastellejoAulaCortesano21kb.txt 0.09860167469217795

31. Juan de Valdés -C:\Users\Govert\Desktop\Signatura comienzo 19.11.2019\ValdesJuan doctrinacristiana75kb.txt 0.09895358128110088

32. Hernando del Castillo -C:\Users\Govert\Desktop\Signatura comienzo 19.11.2019\hernando de castillo prologo6kb.txt 0.09895382954912169

33. Juan Justiniano -C:\Users\Govert\Desktop\Signatura comienzo 19.11.2019\luisvivesformacionmujer84kb.txt 0.09964659433854195

34. Gil Vicente -C:\Users\Govert\Desktop\Signatura comienzo 19.11.2019\GilVicente AutoPastoril1502 16kb.txt 0.1003347227032213

35. Hernán Pérez de Olivia -C:\Users\Govert\Desktop\Signatura comienzo 19.11.2019\perezolivaRioGuadalquivirRazonamiento23kb.txt 0.10108916338772811

36. Francisco López de Villalobos -C:\Users\Govert\Desktop\Signatura comienzo 19.11.2019\villalobos obra completa costumbres humanas141kb.txt 0.10168405469716468

37. Jerónimo Fernández -C:\Users\Govert\Desktop\Signatura comienzo 19.11.2019\jeronimofernandezhector1547-5-17kb.txt 0.10176947095043254

38. Cristóbal Castillejo -C:\Users\Govert\Desktop\Signatura comienzo 19.11.2019\CristobalCastillejoDialogoSobreMujeres21kb.txt 0.10213421754708774

39. Alonso Núñez de Reinoso -C:\Users\Govert\Desktop\Signatura comienzo 19.11.2019\clareoyfloriseaReinoso132kb.txt 0.1022147041007847

40. Sancho Muñón -C:\Users\Govert\Desktop\Signatura comienzo 19.11.2019\Acevedo Celestina151kb.txt 0.10241303611470298

41. Gil Vicente -C:\Users\Govert\Desktop\Signatura comienzo 19.11.2019\GilVicenteSibila31kb.txt 0.10270317026010523

42. Hernán Pérez de Olivia -C:\Users\Govert\Desktop\Signatura comienzo 19.11.2019\perezolivaSalamanca Razonamiento24 kb.txt 0.1032996175794989

43. Sebastián de Horozco -C:\Users\Govert\Desktop\Signatura comienzo 19.11.2019\HorozcoHistoriaEvangelica.txt 0.1040369645551148

44. Ludovico Escriva -C:\Users\Govert\Desktop\Signatura comienzo 19.11.2019\EscrivaLudovico1537y21kb.txt 0.10410689563530173

45. Gáspar Gómez de Toledo -C:\Users\Govert\Desktop\Signatura comienzo 19.11.2019\gaspargomezdeToledoObra23kb.txt 0.10686998503269685

46. Francisco Delicado -C:\Users\Govert\Desktop\Signatura comienzo 19.11.2019\lozano54kb.txt 0.1079893625752415

47. Sebastián de Horozco -C:\Users\Govert\Desktop\Signatura comienzo 19.11.2019\HorozcoEntremeses.txt 0.10803771119030847

48. Ramón de Petras -C:\Users\Govert\Desktop\Signatura comienzo 19.11.2019\traso auto11kb.txt 0.10859291467860988

49. Feliciano de Silva -C:\Users\Govert\Desktop\Signatura comienzo 19.11.2019\Silva Celestina Segunda Parcial177kb.txt 0.1114216130894865

50. Fray Antonio de Guevara -C:\Users\Govert\Desktop\Signatura comienzo 19.11.2019\guevaraEpistolasfamiliares21kb.txt 0.11245029390226802

51. Alonso de Cardona -C:\Users\Govert\Desktop\Signatura comienzo 19.11.2019\alonsodecardona22kb.txt 0.11254001705575478

52. Juan de Segura -C:\Users\Govert\Desktop\Signatura comienzo 19.11.2019\JuandeSeguraQuejayAvisoContraElAmor21kb.txt 0.11316708738631776

53. Gonzalo García de Santa María -C:\Users\Govert\Desktop\Signatura comienzo 19.11.2019\GarciaSantaMariaCoronicaAragonObra27kb.txt 0.11418267371404478

54. Juan de Sedeño -C:\Users\Govert\Desktop\Signatura comienzo 19.11.2019\sedeño summaaobra21kb.txt 0.11588354623448938

55. Gil Vicente -C:\Users\Govert\Desktop\Signatura comienzo 19.11.2019\GilVicente Don Duardos65kb.txt 0.11596441290400561

56. Hernán Núñez -C:\Users\Govert\Desktop\Signatura comienzo 19.11.2019\hernannuñez Trescientas120kb.txt 0.11942348754185883

57. Juan de Flores -C:\Users\Govert\Desktop\Signatura comienzo 19.11.2019\grimalteobra21kb.txt 0.11957664510218113

58. Sebastián de Horozco -C:\Users\Govert\Desktop\Signatura comienzo 19.11.2019\HorozcoRuth.txt 0.12157791758978398

59. Hernán Díaz -C:\Users\Govert\Desktop\Signatura comienzo 19.11.2019\peregrino obra135kb.txt 0.12218483163418004

60. Juan de Sedeño -C:\Users\Govert\Desktop\Signatura comienzo 19.11.2019\sedeñocalisto111kb.txt 0.12280016338357314

61. Juan de Sedeño -C:\Users\Govert\Desktop\Signatura comienzo 19.11.2019\sedeñoAmores Buenaventurança26kb.txt 0.12349330619809629

62. Lucena -C:\Users\Govert\Desktop\Signatura comienzo 19.11.2019\repeticionamores ajedrez4kb.txt 0.1253424351386827

63. Alonso de Proaza -C:\Users\Govert\Desktop\Signatura comienzo 19.11.2019\alonsodeproazaProsa no Celestina-12kb.txt 0.12564810418648598

64. Gil Vicente -C:\Users\Govert\Desktop\Signatura comienzo 19.11.2019\GilVicenteComediaViudo20kb.txt 0.12623263047818112

65. Nicolás Núñez -C:\Users\Govert\Desktop\Signatura comienzo 19.11.2019\NicolasNuñezTractado32kb.txt 0.128037549978834

66. Francisco Delicado -C:\Users\Govert\Desktop\Signatura comienzo 19.11.2019\lozanaepilogo5kb.txt 0.12839479601690806

67. Juan del Encina -C:\Users\Govert\Desktop\Signatura comienzo 19.11.2019\Encina eglogasantes1509 num3-40kb.txt 0.1287286526504099

68. Juan de Sedeño -C:\Users\Govert\Desktop\Signatura comienzo 19.11.2019\sedeño summaPrologo y Epistola19kb.txt 0.13684814016325453

69. Lucas Fernández -C:\Users\Govert\Desktop\Signatura comienzo 19.11.2019\lucasfernandez dereniego del amor169kb.txt 0.1403838063742372

70. Gil Vicente -C:\Users\Govert\Desktop\Signatura comienzo 19.11.2019\GilVicenteCuatroTiempos21kb.txt 0.14653310040416523

71. Diego Hurtado de Mendoza -C:\Users\Govert\Desktop\Signatura comienzo 19.11.2019\diegohurtadodemendoza granada171kb.txt 0.14814146827565355

72. La Celestina -C:\Users\Govert\Desktop\Signatura comienzo 19.11.2019\CelestinaComedia-1.txt 0.14869342500744376

73. Juan de Sedeño -C:\Users\Govert\Desktop\Signatura comienzo 19.11.2019\sedeño summaEpistolaobra54kb.txt 0.15140707707167766

74. Fray Antonio de Guevara -C:\Users\Govert\Desktop\Signatura comienzo 19.11.2019\GuevaraMarcoAurelioObra22kb.txt 0.15470884921402017

75. Francisco Delicado -C:\Users\Govert\Desktop\Signatura comienzo 19.11.2019\lozanaepistola3kb.txt 0.1594127890399677

76. Juan Ramírez de Lucena -C:\Users\Govert\Desktop\Signatura comienzo 19.11.2019\vita beata13 1kb.txt 0.16440009204600048

77. Juan Agüero de Trasmiera -C:\Users\Govert\Desktop\Signatura comienzo 19.11.2019\trasmiera salamanca21kb.txt 0.2007107973672012

78. Juan Ramírez de Lucena -C:\Users\Govert\Desktop\Signatura comienzo 19.11.2019\RamirezLucena a galardones.txt 0.23389933817953845

79. Juan de Timoneda -C:\Users\Govert\Desktop\Signatura comienzo 19.11.2019\timoneda damboek.txt 0.2423314591653707

80. Fernando de Rojas -C:\Users\Govert\Desktop\Signatura comienzo 19.11.2019\fernando de rojas14kb test2.txt 0.24800743149347593

81. La Celestina -C:\Users\Govert\Desktop\Signatura comienzo 19.11.2019\CelestinaMs1520TextoCorrecto27kb.txt 0.27750022002386343

15.2.2 1547 Juego de Marro 1635 - Epístola

Timoneda epistoladamas2kb.txt C:\Users\Govert\Desktop\Signatura comienzo 19.11.2019\Timoneda epistoladamas2kb.txt
Canonicizers:
    Normalize Whitespace
EventDrivers:
    Character NGrams n : 4
        EventCullers:
            Most Common Events numevents : 50
Analysis:
    Nearest Neighbor Driver with metric Cosine Distance
1. Gonzalo Fernández de Oviedo -C:\Users\Govert\Desktop\Signatura comienzo 19.11.2019\fernandezOviedo-indias 21kb.txt 0.09457068399288093
2. Feliciano de Silva -C:\Users\Govert\Desktop\Signatura comienzo 19.11.2019\Silva amadis de grecia20kb.txt 0.09790114862059374
3. Luis de Lucena -C:\Users\Govert\Desktop\Signatura comienzo 19.11.2019\LuisdeLucenaParteTestamento14kb.txt 0.0988223361433328
4. Gonzalo Fernández de Oviedo -C:\Users\Govert\Desktop\Signatura comienzo 19.11.2019\FernandezOviedoClaribalte21kb.txt 0.10070073018081593
5. Cristóbal Castillejo -C:\Users\Govert\Desktop\Signatura comienzo 19.11.2019\CristobalCastellejoAulaCortesano21kb.txt 0.1020217933023364

6. Jerónimo Fernández -C:\Users\Govert\Desktop\Signatura comienzo 19.11.2019\jeronimofernandezhector1547-5-17kb.txt 0.10219823190181898

7. Hernán Díaz -C:\Users\Govert\Desktop\Signatura comienzo 19.11.2019\peregrino obra135kb.txt 0.10321088944288204

8. Bernardo de Quirós -C:\Users\Govert\Desktop\Signatura comienzo 19.11.2019\VillalonViajeTurquiaVillalon109kb.txt 0.10421893886421385

9. Juan del Encina -C:\Users\Govert\Desktop\Signatura comienzo 19.11.2019\encina textos al rey75kb.txt 0.1044832179833366

10. Thebayda anónym -C:\Users\Govert\Desktop\Signatura comienzo 19.11.2019\thebaida incompleta21kb.txt 0.10474705479228741

11. Lucas Fernández -C:\Users\Govert\Desktop\Signatura comienzo 19.11.2019\lucasfernandez dereniego del amor169kb.txt 0.10582675569804023

12. Juan Ramírez de Lucena -C:\Users\Govert\Desktop\Signatura comienzo 19.11.2019\Ramirez Lucena exhortatoria.txt 0.10585284488716706

13. Juan Ramírez de Lucena -C:\Users\Govert\Desktop\Signatura comienzo 19.11.2019\RamirezLucena a Zapata.txt 0.10592624345416723

14. Juan de Sedeño -C:\Users\Govert\Desktop\Signatura comienzo 19.11.2019\sedeño summaPrologo y Epistola19kb.txt 0.10593265574769739

15. Juan de Sedeño -C:\Users\Govert\Desktop\Signatura comienzo 19.11.2019\sedeño summaaobra21kb.txt 0.10784921498352207

16. Diego Hurtado de Mendoza -C:\Users\Govert\Desktop\Signatura comienzo 19.11.2019\diegohurtadodemendoza granada171kb.txt 0.10802775915839291

17. Juan de Sedeño -C:\Users\Govert\Desktop\Signatura comienzo 19.11.2019\sedeño summaEpistolaobra54kb.txt 0.10866038378979048

18. Diego de San Pedro -C:\Users\Govert\Desktop\Signatura comienzo 19.11 2019\arnalte incompleta21kb.txt 0.10883572027884658

19. Alonso de Proaza -C:\Users\Govert\Desktop\Signatura comienzo 19.11.2019\alonsodeproazaProsa no Celestina-12kb.txt 0.1088690544743518

20. Hernán Núñez -C:\Users\Govert\Desktop\Signatura comienzo 19.11.2019\hernannuñez Trescientas120kb.txt 0.1131268647827468

21. Hernán Pérez de Olivia -C:\Users\Govert\Desktop\Signatura comienzo 19.11.2019\perezolivaRioGuadalquivirRazonamiento23kb.txt 0.11352291855148133

22. Juan Paez de Castro -C:\Users\Govert\Desktop\Signatura comienzo 19.11.2019\juanpaezdecastroCartas23kb.txt 0.11375520223153857

23. Cristóbal Castillejo -C:\Users\Govert\Desktop\Signatura comienzo 19.11.2019\CristobalCastillejoDialogoSobreMujeres21kb.txt 0.11436250531951964

24. Diego de San Pedro -C:\Users\Govert\Desktop\Signatura comienzo 19.11.2019\carceldeamor21kb.txt 0.11495505473042678

25. Sancho Muñón -C:\Users\Govert\Desktop\Signatura comienzo 19.11.2019\Acevedo Celestina151kb.txt 0.11521472949689349

26. Hernando del Castillo -C:\Users\Govert\Desktop\Signatura comienzo 19.11.2019\hernando de castillo prologo6kb.txt 0.11595368714927279

27. Lope de Rueda -C:\Users\Govert\Desktop\Signatura comienzo 19.11.2019\lopederuedaAceitunas42kb.txt 0.11601334955820564

28. Lope de Rueda -C:\Users\Govert\Desktop\Signatura comienzo 19.11.2019\LopedeRuedaEufemia37kb.txt 0.11610509928564183

29. Lucena -C:\Users\Govert\Desktop\Signatura comienzo 19.11.2019\repeticionamores114kb.txt 0.11686091374052587

30. Gonzalo Fernández de Oviedo -C:\Users\Govert\Desktop\Signatura comienzo 19.11.2019\FernandezOviedoSumarioIndias21kb.txt 0.11744799805614081

31. Alonso Núñez de Reinoso -C:\Users\Govert\Desktop\Signatura comienzo 19.11.2019\clareoyfloriseaReinoso132kb.txt 0.11817355943202879

32. Juan Justiniano -C:\Users\Govert\Desktop\Signatura comienzo 19.11.2019\luisvivesformacionmujer84kb.txt 0.11899071329500854

33. Francisco Delicado -C:\Users\Govert\Desktop\Signatura comienzo 19.11.2019\legno2 8kb.txt 0.11976849009428969

34. Hernán Pérez de Olivia -C:\Users\Govert\Desktop\Signatura comienzo 19.11.2019\perezolivaSalamanca Razonamiento24 kb.txt 0.12025690899078367

35. Jerónimo Fernández -C:\Users\Govert\Desktop\Signatura comienzo 19.11.2019\jeronimofernandez3año1579-113kb.txt 0.12040849680330579

36. Juan de Flores -C:\Users\Govert\Desktop\Signatura comienzo 19.11.2019\griselobra89kb.txt 0.12048295881878279

37. El cortesano -C:\Users\Govert\Desktop\Signatura comienzo 19.11.2019\BoscanElCortesano47kb.txt 0.12245253575223836

38. Gil Vicente -C:\Users\Govert\Desktop\Signatura comienzo 19.11.2019\GilVicenteComediaViudo20kb.txt 0.1251099386357727

39. Francisco Cervantes de Salazar -C:\Users\Govert\Desktop\Signatura comienzo 19.11.2019\CervantesSalazarCronicaNuevEspaña21kb.txt 0.12523804565561392

40. Juan de Sedeño -C:\Users\Govert\Desktop\Signatura comienzo 19.11.2019\sedeñoAmores Buenaventurança26kb.txt 0.12763787964591444

41. Juan de Timoneda -C:\Users\Govert\Desktop\Signatura comienzo 19.11.2019\TimonedaCaminantes21kb.txt 0.12802412312676348

42. La Celestina -C:\Users\Govert\Desktop\Signatura comienzo 19.11.2019\CelestinaComedia-1.txt 0.1284392431658793

43. Gil Vicente -C:\Users\Govert\Desktop\Signatura comienzo 19.11.2019\GilVicenteSibila31kb.txt 0.13319354056626143

44. Juan de Valdés -C:\Users\Govert\Desktop\Signatura comienzo 19.11.2019\ValdesJuanCartas1-3-completo114kb.txt 0.13486746285429174

45. Cristóbal Castillejo -C:\Users\Govert\Desktop\Signatura comienzo 19.11.2019\CristobalCastillejoDialogodeMujeres21kb.txt 0.1352743851056425

46. Baltasar del Rio -C:\Users\Govert\Desktop\Signatura comienzo 19.11.2019\baltasardelrio1504Tratado22kb.txt 0.13625377539134198

47. Gonzalo Fernández de Oviedo -C:\Users\Govert\Desktop\Signatura comienzo 19.11.2019\fernandezoviedobatalla90-130tiene34kb.txt 0.13643632603890166

48. Juan Ramírez de Lucena -C:\Users\Govert\Desktop\Signatura comienzo 19.11.2019\vita beata131kb.txt 0.1383829256751945

49. Juan de Flores -C:\Users\Govert\Desktop\Signatura comienzo 19.11.2019\grimalteobra21kb.txt 0.13932834393266125

50. Francisco López de Villalobos -C:\Users\Govert\Desktop\Signatura comienzo 19.11.2019\villalobos obra completa costumbres humanas141kb.txt 0.141337209106715

51. Ramón de Petras -C:\Users\Govert\Desktop\Signatura comienzo 19.11.2019\traso auto11kb.txt 0.14153606487601067

52. Gil Vicente -C:\Users\Govert\Desktop\Signatura comienzo 19.11.2019\GilVicenteCuatroTiempos21kb.txt 0.14185946364150404

53. Gonzalo García de Santa María -C:\Users\Govert\Desktop\Signatura comienzo 19.11.2019\GarciaSantaMariaCoronicaAragonObra27kb.txt 0.14570319717559677

54. Gil Vicente -C:\Users\Govert\Desktop\Signatura comienzo 19.11.2019\GilVicente Don Duardos65kb.txt 0.14575546471541556

55. Juan Huarte de San Juan -C:\Users\Govert\Desktop\Signatura comienzo 19.11.2019\HuarteExamen Ingenios21kb.txt 0.14580393602454422

56. Fray Antonio de Guevara -C:\Users\Govert\Desktop\Signatura comienzo 19.11.2019\GuevaraMarcoAurelioObra22kb.txt 0.14778115660237

57. Francisco Delicado -C:\Users\Govert\Desktop\Signatura comienzo 19.11.2019\lozano54kb.txt 0.15207504064433608

58. Ludovico Escriva -C:\Users\Govert\Desktop\Signatura comienzo 19.11.2019\EscrivaLudovico1537y21kb.txt 0.1535092468392616

59. Sebastián de Horozco -C:\Users\Govert\Desktop\Signatura comienzo 19.11.2019\HorozcoEntremeses.txt 0.15410782857647354

60. Alfonso de Valdés -C:\Users\Govert\Desktop\Signatura comienzo 19.11.2019\valdesAlfonsoCartas34kb.txt 0.15676832826232467

61. Juan del Encina -C:\Users\Govert\Desktop\Signatura comienzo 19.11.2019\Encina eglogasantes1509 num3-40kb.txt 0.1577754315663249

62. Gil Vicente -C:\Users\Govert\Desktop\Signatura comienzo 19.11.2019\GilVicente AutoPastoril1502 16kb.txt 0.15796120424316018

63. Fray Antonio de Guevara -C:\Users\Govert\Desktop\Signatura comienzo 19.11.2019\guevaraEpistolasfamiliares21kb.txt 0.15801470647489058

64. Fernando de Rojas -C:\Users\Govert\Desktop\Signatura comienzo 19.11.2019\fernando de rojas14kb test2.txt 0.15810590443623906

65. Juan Agüero de Trasmiera -C:\Users\Govert\Desktop\Signatura comienzo 19.11.2019\trasmiera salamanca21kb.txt 0.15836525448951533

66. Juan de Valdés -C:\Users\Govert\Desktop\Signatura comienzo 19.11.2019\ValdesJuan doctrinacristiana75kb.txt 0.16202391022336582

67. Alonso de Cardona -C:\Users\Govert\Desktop\Signatura comienzo 19.11.2019\alonsodecardona22kb.txt 0.1633772888636017

68. Sebastián de Horozco -C:\Users\Govert\Desktop\Signatura comienzo 19.11.2019\HorozcoHistoriaEvangelica.txt 0.1659108384351481

69. Lucena -C:\Users\Govert\Desktop\Signatura comienzo 19.11.2019\repeticionamores ajedrez4kb.txt 0.1675003127084962

70. Gáspar Gómez de Toledo -C:\Users\Govert\Desktop\Signatura comienzo 19.11.2019\gaspargomezdeToledoObra23kb.txt 0.16975753530485027

71. Juan de Sedeño -C:\Users\Govert\Desktop\Signatura comienzo 19.11.2019\sedeñocalisto111kb.txt 0.1796800215158728

72. Sebastián de Horozco -C:\Users\Govert\Desktop\Signatura comienzo 19.11.2019\HorozcoRuth.txt 0.1828276552497181

73. Feliciano de Silva -C:\Users\Govert\Desktop\Signatura comienzo 19.11.2019\Silva Celestina Segunda Parcial177kb.txt 0.1941909023999977

74. La Celestina -C:\Users\Govert\Desktop\Signatura comienzo 19.11.2019\CelestinaMs1520TextoCorrecto27kb.txt 0.1943049732815615

75. Juan de Segura -C:\Users\Govert\Desktop\Signatura comienzo 19.11.2019\JuandeSeguraQuejayAvisoContraElAmor21kb.txt 0.19466996763612854

76. Nicolás Núñez -C:\Users\Govert\Desktop\Signatura comienzo 19.11.2019\NicolasNuñezTractado32kb.txt 0.1969499269344973

77. Francisco Delicado -C:\Users\Govert\Desktop\Signatura comienzo 19.11.2019\lozanaapologia6kb.txt 0.19729646082726593

78. Francisco Delicado -C:\Users\Govert\Desktop\Signatura comienzo 19.11.2019\lozanaepilogo5kb.txt 0.19974321103936354

79. Juan Ramírez de Lucena -C:\Users\Govert\Desktop\Signatura comienzo 19.11.2019\RamirezLucena a galardones.txt 0.2073476125079441

80. Francisco Delicado -C:\Users\Govert\Desktop\Signatura comienzo 19.11.2019\lozanaepistola3kb.txt 0.22845009481022738

81. Juan de Timoneda -C:\Users\Govert\Desktop\Signatura comienzo 19.11.2019\timoneda damboek.txt 0.31881267768287247

15.2.3 Strange words in Epistle

15.2.3.1 The word: Endereçada

Occurrence of the word "Endereç(z)ada(s) o(s)

Year	Author	Book	Cases
1535	Gonzalo Fernández de Oviedo	*Historial general y natural de las Indias*	2

Too many cases. Not applicable.

15.2.3.2 The word: Marro

Occurrence of the word "Marro"

Year	Author	Book	Cases
1535	**Gonzalo Fernández de Oviedo**	*Batallas y quinquagenas*	**2**
1550	Martin de Santander	*Comedia Rosabella*	1
1532	Gonzalo Fernández de Oviedo	*Catálogo Real de Castilla*	1
1513	Anonym	*Question de amor*	1

15.2.3.3 The word: Trechas

Occurrence of the word "Trecha(s)"

Year	Author	Book	Cases
1508	Francisco de Ávila	*La vida y la muerte o Vergel de discretos*	1
1513	Anonym	*Question de amor*	1
1514	Juan Boscán	*Poesías*	2
1525	Gil Vicente	*Tragicomedia de don Duardos*	1
1527	Fray Bartolomé de las Casas	*Apòlogética historia sumaria*	2
1534	**Feliciano de Silva = Gonzalo Fernández de Ovido**	*Segunda Celestina*	**3**
1540	Macael de Carvajal	*Tragedia Josephina*	5
1540	Anonym	*Cancionero de Velázquez de Ávila*	1
1545	Lope de Rueda	*Pasos*	1
1547	Cristóbal de Castillejo	*Aula de cortesanos*	1
1549	Hernán Núñez	*Refranes o proverbios en romance*	1

15.2.3.4 The word: Acrecentamiento

Occurrence of the word "Acrecentamiento"

Year	Author	Book	Cases
1535	Gonzalo Fernández de Oviedo	*Historial general y natural de las Indias*	2

Too many cases.

15.2.3.5 The word: Pasatiempos

Occurrence of the word "Pas(s)atiempo(s)"

Year	Author	Book	Cases
1526	Gonzalo Fernández de Oviedo	*Sumario de la natural y general historia de las Indias*	1
1535	Gonzalo Fernández de Oviedo	*Batallas y quinquagenas*	5
1535	Gonzalo Fernández de Oviedo	*Historia general y natural de las Indias*	15
1547	Gonzalo Fernández de Oviedo	*Libro de la Cámara real del Príncipe don Juan e oficios de su casa e servicio ordinario*	1

Too many authors.

15.2.3.6 The expression: Porque en verdad

Occurrence of the expression "Porque en verdad"

Year	Author	Book	Cases
1470	Hernando del Pulgar	*Letras*	1
1511	Anonym	*Traducción del Tirante el Blanco*	3
1516	Fernando Bernal	*Floriseo*	3
1521	Fray Antonio de Guervara	*Epístolas familiars*	1
1525	Francés de Zúñiga	*Crónica burlesca del emperador Carlos V*	1
1526	**Gonzalo Fernández de Oviedo**	***Sumario de la natural y general historia de las Indias***	**1**
1527	Bartolomé de las Casas	*Historia de las Indias*	1
1530	Francisco de Osuna	*Segunda parte del Abecedario spiritual*	1
1532	Anonym	*Traducción de los coloquios de Erasmo*	2
1533	Bernardo Pérez de Chinchón	*La lengua de Erasmo nuevamente romançada por muy elegante estilo*	1
1534	Juan Boscán	*Traducción de El Cortesano de Baltasar de Castiglione*	6
1535	Gonzalo Fernández de Oviedo	*Historia general y natural de las Indias*	2
1535	Gonzalo Fernández de Oviedo	*Batallas y quinquagenas*	1
1538	Fray Luis de Granada	*Epistolario*	1
1540	Francisco de Osuna	*Quinta parte del Abecedario spiritual*	2
1541	Cristóbal de Villalón	*Provechoso tratado de cambios y contrataciones de mercaderes y reprobación de usura*	1
1542	Anonym	*Baldo*	3
1542	Diego del Castillo	*Tratado de cuentas*	1
1549	Anonym	*Crónica del Rey Henrico Octavo de Inglaterra*	1
1550	Pedro de Luján	*Coloquios matrimoniales*	1

254

1550	Alonso de Santa Cruz	*Crónica del Emperador Carlos V*	3
1552	Pedro Hernández de Villaumbrales	*Peregrinación de la vida del hombre*	2
1552	Alonso Núñez de Reinoso	*Los amores de Clareo y Florisea*	2
1552	Fray Bartolomé de las Casas	*Brevísima relación de la destrucción de las Indias*	1

15.2.3.7 The expression: En que poder

Occurrence of the expression "En que poder"

Year	Author	Book	Cases
1513	Anonym	*Question de amor*	1
1535	**Gonzalo Fernández de Oviedo**	***Historia general y natural de las Indias***	1
1552	Antonio de Torquemada	*Manual de escribientes*	2
1553	Antonio de Torquemada	*Coloquios satíricos*	1
1554	Fray Luis de Granada	*Libro de la oración y meditación*	2
1555	Diego Ortúñez de Calahora	*Espejo de príncipes y caballeros*	1
1560	Francisco Cervantes de Salazar	*Crónica de la Nueva España*	1

15.2.3.8 The expression: Cumplir mi deseo

Occurrence of the expression "Cumplir mi deseo"

Year	Author	Book	Cases
1511	Anonym	*Traducción de tirante el Blanco*	4
1555	Diego Ortúñez de Calahorra	*Espejo de príncipes y caballeros*	1
1547	**Jerónimo Fernández = Gonzalo Fernández de Oviedo**	***Belianis de Grecia***	**2**

255

1542	Anonym	*Baldo*	1
1511	Anonym	*Palmerín de Olivia*	1
1554	Anonym	*Lazarillo de Tormes*	1
1552	Alonso Núñez de Reinoso	*Los amores de Clareo y Florisea*	1
1528	Fernán Pérez de Olivia	*La venganza de Agamenón*	1
1525	Diego Sánchez de Badajoz	*Farsa racional del libre albedrío*	1
1547	Cristóbal de Castillejo	*Aula de cortesanos*	1

15.2.3.9 The expression: Por mejor dec(z)ir

Occurrence of the expression "Por mejor dezir"

Year	Author	Book	Cases
1498	Martín Martínez de Ampiés	*Traducción del Tratado de Roma*	1
1513	Alonso de Herrera Gabriel	*Obra agricultura*	1
1521	Fray Antonio de Guevara	*Epístolas familiars*	14
1527	Anonym	*Diálogo de las cosas acaecidas en Roma*	2
1527	Fray Bartolomé de las Casas	*Historia de las Indias*	30
1527	Fray Bartolomé de las Casas	*Apologética histoia sumaria*	20
1528	Juan Justiniano	*Instrucción de la mujer Cristiana*	3
1528	Fray Antonio de Guevara	*Libro áureo de Marco Aurelio*	2
1528	Francisco de Osuna	*Primera parte del Abecedario espiritual*	5
1529	Fray Antonio de Guevara	*Reloj de príncipes*	12
1529	Alfonso de Valdés	*Diálogo de Mercurio y Carón*	2
1530	Francisco de Osuna	*Segunda parte del Abecedario spiritual*	4
1532	Anonym	*Origen de los mexianos*	1

1533	Bernardo Pérez de Chinchón	*La lengua de Erasmo*	2
1533	Garcilaso de la Vega	*Epistolario*	2
1534	Juan Boscán	*Traducción de El Cortesano*	2
1534	Feliciano de Silva	*Segunda Celestina*	3
1535	**Gonzalo Fernández de Oviedo**	***Historia general y natural de las Indias***	**2**
1535	Juan de Valdés	*Diálogo de la lengua*	8
1536	Motolinía Fray Toribio de Benavanente	*Historia de los Indios de la Nueva España*	2
1536	Gaspar Gómez de Toledo	*Tercera parte de la tragicomedia de Celestina*	1
1537	Luis Escrivá	*Veneris tribunal*	4
1539	Fray Antonio de Guevara	*Menosprecio de corte y alabanza de aldea*	3
1540	Pedro Mejía	*Silva de varia lección*	3
1540	Francisco de Osuna	*Quinta parte del Abecedario spiritual*	5
1540	Micael de Carvajal	*Tragedia Josephina*	1
1541	Damián Carbón	*Libro del arte de las comadres*	1
1542	Anonym	*Baldo*	1
1543	Jorge de Montemayor	*Diálogo spiritual*	3
1544	Luis Seravia de la Calle	*Instrucción de merecaderes*	1
1545	Anonym	*Sermón de Aljubarrota, con las glosas de Diego Hurtado*	1
1545	Lope de Rueda	*Pasos*	2
1547	Alonso de Fuentes	*Suma de Filosofía natural*	1
1548	San Francisco de Borja	*Seis tratados muy devotos y útiles para cualquier fiel Cristiano*	1
1549	Pedro Gutiérrez de Santa Clara	*Quinquenarios o Historia de las guerras civiles del Perú*	14
1550	Pedro de Luján	*Coloquios matrimoniales*	7
1550	Alonso de Santa Cruz	*Crónica del Emperador Carlos V*	12
1550	Fray Luis de León	*Traducciones sacras*	1
1551	Bernardino de Montaña de Monserrate	*Anothomía*	1
1551	Martin Cortés Albacar	*Breve compendio de la esfera y de la arte de navegar*	2
1552	Pedro Hernández de Villaumbrales	*Peregrinación de la vida del hombre*	3
1552	Diego Núñez Alba	*Diálogos de la vida del soldado*	1

1552	Fray Bartolomé de las Casas	*Tratado comprobatorio del Imperio Soberano*	1
1552	Fray Bartolomé de las Casas	*Avisos para confesores*	1
1552	Fray Bartolomé de las Casas	*Entre los remedios para reformación de las Indias*	1
1552	Fray Bartolomé de las Casas	*Tratado sobre los indios que han sido hechos esclavos*	3
1552	Fray Bartolomé de las Casas	*Brevísima relación de la destrucción de las Indias*	2
1552	Diego Núñez Alba	*Diálogos de la vida del soldado*	2
1552	Luis Mejía	*Traducción de los coloquios de Erasmo*	1
1552	Antonio de Torquemada	*Manual de escribientes*	5
1553	Pedro Cieza de León	*Las guerras civiles peruanas*	3
1553	Cristóbal de Villalón	*El Crótalon*	3
1553	Antonio de Torquemada	*Coloquios satíricos*	5
1553	Diego Núñez Alba	*Dedicatoria al señor don Fernand Álvarez de Toledo*	1
1553	Juan de Dueñas	*Espejo del picador*	3
1553	Francisco López de Gómara	*Segunda parte de la Crónica general de las Indias*	2
1554	Anonym	*Lazarillo de Tormes*	5
1554	Fray Luis de Granada	*Libro de la oración y meditación*	2
1554	Juan Rodríguez Florián	*Comedia llamada Florinea*	2
1554	Francisco López de Gómara	*La primera parte de la Historia natural de las Indias*	2
1555	Anonym	*Segunda parte del Lazarillo de Tormes*	3
1555	Felipe de Meneses	*Luz del alma Cristiana*	9
1555	Diego Ortúñez de Calahorra	*Espejo de príncipes y caballeros*	1
1559	Jorge de Montemayor	*Los siete libros de la Diana*	2
1559	Fray Luis de Granada	*Manual de diversas oraciones*	1
1560	Francisco Cervantes de Salazar	*Crónica de la Nueva España*	10
1560	Juan Pérez	*Breve tratado de doctrina*	1

15.2.3.10   The expression: He procurado con

Occurrence of the expression "He procurado con"

Year	Author	Book	Cases
1535	Gonzalo Fernández de Oviedo	*Historia general y natural de las Indias*	1

15.2.3.11   The expression: La menor cosa

Occurrence of the expression "La menor cosa"

Year	Author	Book	Cases
1492	Garci Rodríguez de Montalvo	*Amadís de Gaula, libros I y II*	2
1492	Anonym	*La corónica de Adramón*	1
1504	Garci Rodríguez de Montalvo	*Las sergas del virtuoso caballero Esplandián*	1
1511	Anonym	*Palmerín de Olivia*	1
1512	Anonym	*Primaleón*	1
1512	Anonym	*Crónica popular del Cid*	1
1519	Hernán Cortés	*Cartas de relación*	1
1535	**Gonzalo Fernández de Oviedo**	***Historia general y natural de las Indias***	1
1538	Pedro Ciruelo	*Reprobación de las supersticiones y hechicerías*	1
1540	Bartolomé Torres Naharro	*Romance – Primera parte de la Silva de varios romances*	1
1540	Sebastián de Horozco	*Cancionero*	1
1549	Anonym	*Crónica del Rey Henrico Octavo de Inglaterra*	1
1550	Pedro Luján	*Coloquios matrimoniales*	1
1552	Fray Bartolomé de las Casas	*Brevísima relación de la destrucción de las Indias*	1
1555	Felipe de Meneses	*Luz del alma Cristiana*	2
1559	Jorge de Montemayor	*Los siete libros de La Diana*	1

15.2.3.12   Expr.: Con la mayor diligencia

Occurrence of the expression "Con la mayor diligencia"

Year	Author	Book	Cases
1527	Alfonso de Valdés	*Diálogo de las cosas acaecidas en Roma*	1
1495	Juan de Flores	*Grimalte y Gradisa*	1
1517	Juan de Molina	*Libro del esforzado caballero Arderique*	1
1540	Pedro Mejía	*Silva de varia lección*	1
1535	Gonzalo Fernández de Oviedo	*Historia general y natural de las Indias*	3
1506	Diego Álvarez Chanca	*Tratado nuevo no menos útil que necesario en que se declara de qué manera se ha de cural el mal*	1
1550	Alonso de Santa Cruz	*Crónica del Emperador Carlos V*	3
1560	Francisco Cervantes de Salazar	*Crónica de la Nueva España*	1
1550	Pedro de Valdivia	*A sus apoderados en la Corte*	1

15.3 Chapter 11

15.3.1 Arte de Ajedrez – introduction

repeticionamores ajedrez4kb.txt C:\Users\Govert\Desktop\Signatura comienzo 19.11.2019\repeticionamores ajedrez4kb.txt
Canonicizers:
   Normalize Whitespace
EventDrivers:
   Character NGrams n : 4
      EventCullers:
         Most Common Events numevents : 50
Analysis:
   Nearest Neighbor Driver with metric Cosine Distance
1.   Lucena   -C:\Users\Govert\Desktop\Signatura   comienzo 19.11.2019\repeticionamores ajedrez4kb.txt 0.0
2. Juan de Sedeño -C:\Users\Govert\Desktop\Signatura comienzo 19.11.2019\sedeño summaaobra21kb.txt 0.056265164904751086
3. Gonzalo García Santa Maria -C:\Users\Govert\Desktop\Signatura comienzo 19.11.2019\GarciaSantaMariaCoronicaAragonObra27kb.txt 0.05936962105063037
4.   Ludovico   Escriva   -C:\Users\Govert\Desktop\Signatura   comienzo 19.11.2019\EscrivaLudovico1537y21kb.txt 0.0608243299913658604
5.   Jerónimo   Fernández   -C:\Users\Govert\Desktop\Signatura   comienzo 19.11.2019\jeronimofernandezhector1547-5-17kb.txt 0.062267168795330674
6. Gonzalo Fernández de Oviedo -C:\Users\Govert\Desktop\Signatura comienzo 19.11.2019\fernandezOviedo-indias 21kb.txt 0.06842334892252844
7. Gonzalo Fernández de Oviedo -C:\Users\Govert\Desktop\Signatura comienzo 19.11.2019\fernandezOviedo1532catálogo21kb.txt 0.07051046849366716
8. Lucena -C:\Users\Govert\Desktop\Signatura comienzo 19.11.2019\repamores mitad libro51kb.txt 0.07428319758835233
9.   Jerónimo   Fernández   -C:\Users\Govert\Desktop\Signatura   comienzo 19.11.2019\jeronimofernandez3año1579-113kb.txt 0.07577122334419162
10.   Hernán   Núñez   -C:\Users\Govert\Desktop\Signatura   comienzo 19.11.2019\hernannuñez Trescientas21.txt 0.07979981993860563
11. Juan de Sedeño -C:\Users\Govert\Desktop\Signatura comienzo 19.11.2019\sedeño summaEpistolaobra54kb.txt 0.08000569361597287
12. Diego Hurtado de Mendoza -C:\Users\Govert\Desktop\Signatura comienzo 19.11.2019\diegohurtadodemendoza granada171kb.txt 0.08098650436298305
13. Hernán Diaz -C:\Users\Govert\Desktop\Signatura comienzo 19.11.2019\peregrino obra135kb.txt 0.08138002900302732
14. Francisco Cervantes de Salazar -C:\Users\Govert\Desktop\Signatura comienzo 19.11.2019\CervantesSalazarCronicaNuevEspaña21kb.txt 0.08148198073756807

15. Juan del Encina -C:\Users\Govert\Desktop\Signatura comienzo 19.11.2019\encina textos al rey75kb.txt 0.0816496054676148

16. Juan de Sedeño -C:\Users\Govert\Desktop\Signatura comienzo 19.11.2019\sedeño summaPrologo y Epistola19kb.txt 0.08254157371507187

17. Alonso de Proaza -C:\Users\Govert\Desktop\Signatura comienzo 19.11.2019\alonsodeproazaProsa no Celestina-12kb.txt 0.08307744010984675

18. Luis de Lucena -C:\Users\Govert\Desktop\Signatura comienzo 19.11.2019\LuisdeLucenaParteTestamento14kb.txt 0.08325077775616962

19. Gonzalo Fernández de Oviedo -C:\Users\Govert\Desktop\Signatura comienzo 19.11.2019\FernandezOviedoSumarioIndias27kb.txt 0.08384013342942132

20. Sancho de Muñón -C:\Users\Govert\Desktop\Signatura comienzo 19.11.2019\Acevedo Celestina corto21kb.txt 0.08630039843623138

21. Francisco López de Villalobos -C:\Users\Govert\Desktop\Signatura comienzo 19.11.2019\villaloboscostumbres humanas21kb.txt 0.08753710846883134

22. Gonzalo Fernández de Oviedo -C:\Users\Govert\Desktop\Signatura comienzo 19.11.2019\fernandezoviedobatalla90-130tiene34kb.txt 0.0888420672597533

23. Juan de Boscan -C:\Users\Govert\Desktop\Signatura comienzo 19.11.2019\BoscanElCortesano47kb.txt 0.09060497050567817

24. Juan de Sedeño -C:\Users\Govert\Desktop\Signatura comienzo 19.11.2019\sedeñoAmores Buenaventurança26kb.txt 0.09223719262910057

25. Feliciano de Silva -C:\Users\Govert\Desktop\Signatura comienzo 19.11.2019\Silva amadis de grecia20kb.txt 0.09468604638971512

26. Cristóbal de Castellejo -C:\Users\Govert\Desktop\Signatura comienzo 19.11.2019\CristobalCastellejoAulaCortesano21kb.txt 0.09901686546191568

27. Hernán Pérez de Olivia -C:\Users\Govert\Desktop\Signatura comienzo 19.11.2019\perezolivaRioGuadalquivirRazonamiento23kb.txt 0.10018942896452321

28. Juan Ramírez de Lucena -C:\Users\Govert\Desktop\Signatura comienzo 19.11.2019\vita beata21kb.txt 0.10055629030453272

29. Diego de San Pedro -C:\Users\Govert\Desktop\Signatura comienzo 19.11.2019\arnalte incompleta21kb.txt 0.10106089881573332

30. Baltasar del Rio -C:\Users\Govert\Desktop\Signatura comienzo 19.11.2019\baltasardelrio1504Tratado22kb.txt 0.10116171897553383

31. Juan Ramírez de Lucena -C:\Users\Govert\Desktop\Signatura comienzo 19.11.2019\Ramirez Lucena exhortatoria.txt 0.10161741389714873

32. Juan Ramírez de Lucena -C:\Users\Govert\Desktop\Signatura comienzo 19.11.2019\RamirezLucena a Zapata.txt 0.10169221325224498

33. Juan Justaniano -C:\Users\Govert\Desktop\Signatura comienzo 19.11.2019\luisvives formacion21kb.txt 0.10423610710658338

34. La Celestina -C:\Users\Govert\Desktop\Signatura comienzo 19.11.2019\CelestinaComedia-1.txt 0.10428913146453078

35. Francisco Delicado -C:\Users\Govert\Desktop\Signatura comienzo 19.11.2019\legno2 8kb.txt 0.10466281427135804

36. Cristóbal de Castellejo -C:\Users\Govert\Desktop\Signatura comienzo 19.11.2019\CristobalCastillejoDialogodeMujeres21kb.txt 0.10627574432611409

37. Francisco Delicado -C:\Users\Govert\Desktop\Signatura comienzo 19.11.2019\lozanaepilogo5kb.txt 0.10649313981054809

38. Fray Antonio de Guevara -C:\Users\Govert\Desktop\Signatura comienzo 19.11.2019\guevaraEpistolasfamiliares21kb.txt 0.10674454981682968

39. Juan de Flores -C:\Users\Govert\Desktop\Signatura comienzo 19.11.2019\griselobra21kb.txt 0.10815257126327127

40. Gil Vicente -C:\Users\Govert\Desktop\Signatura comienzo 19.11.2019\GilVicenteCuatroTiempos21kb.txt 0.10829349564037927

41. Bernardo de Quirós -C:\Users\Govert\Desktop\Signatura comienzo 19.11.2019\VillalonViajeTurquiaVillalon109kb.txt 0.10875393242815579

42. Gonzalo Fernández de Oviedo -C:\Users\Govert\Desktop\Signatura comienzo 19.11.2019\FernandezOviedoClaribalte21kb.txt 0.10968255037161645

43. Cristóbal de Castellejo -C:\Users\Govert\Desktop\Signatura comienzo 19.11.2019\CristobalCastillejoDialogoSobreMujeres21kb.txt 0.111054977341148

44. Juan de Valdés -C:\Users\Govert\Desktop\Signatura comienzo 19.11.2019\ValdesJuanCartas1-3-completo114kb.txt 0.11299256703498806

45. Lope de Rueda -C:\Users\Govert\Desktop\Signatura comienzo 19.11.2019\lopederuedaAceitunas42kb.txt 0.11374303121117324

46. Alonso Núñez de Reinoso -C:\Users\Govert\Desktop\Signatura comienzo 19.11.2019\clareoyfloriseaCorto21kb.txt 0.11428811260432048

47. Diego de San Pedro -C:\Users\Govert\Desktop\Signatura comienzo 19.11.2019\carceldeamor21kb.txt 0.11453689434684233

48. Fray Antonio de Guevara -C:\Users\Govert\Desktop\Signatura comienzo 19.11.2019\GuevaraMarcoAurelioObra22kb.txt 0.11490630667182211

49. Juan de Timoneda -C:\Users\Govert\Desktop\Signatura comienzo 19.11.2019\TimonedaCaminantes21kb.txt 0.1165806307685292

50. Thebayda -C:\Users\Govert\Desktop\Signatura comienzo 19.11.2019\thebaida incompleta21kb.txt 0.11722231870632238

51. Hernando del Castillo -C:\Users\Govert\Desktop\Signatura comienzo 19.11.2019\hernando de castillo prologo6kb.txt 0.12212486293585445

52. Lope de Rueda -C:\Users\Govert\Desktop\Signatura comienzo 19.11.2019\LopedeRuedaEufemia37kb.txt 0.12213124637171469

53. Ramón de Petras -C:\Users\Govert\Desktop\Signatura comienzo 19.11.2019\traso auto11kb.txt 0.12542581588279178

54. Alonso de Cardona -C:\Users\Govert\Desktop\Signatura comienzo 19.11.2019\alonsodecardona22kb.txt 0.1256478526985908

55. Gil Vicente -C:\Users\Govert\Desktop\Signatura comienzo 19.11.2019\GilVicenteComediaViudo20kb.txt 0.1256909916351736

56. Gil Vicente -C:\Users\Govert\Desktop\Signatura comienzo 19.11.2019\GilVicenteSibila31kb.txt 0.12649000022158075

57. Bartolomé de las Casas -C:\Users\Govert\Desktop\Signatura comienzo 19.11.2019\BartolomeDeLasCasasBrevisimak34b.txt 0.126805257783422

58. Juan Paez de Castro -C:\Users\Govert\Desktop\Signatura comienzo 19.11.2019\juanpaezdecastroCartas23kb.txt 0.1275744123368846

59. Alfonso de Valdés -C:\Users\Govert\Desktop\Signatura comienzo 19.11.2019\valdesAlfonsoCartas34kb.txt 0.13042871725569694

60. Juan del Encina -C:\Users\Govert\Desktop\Signatura comienzo 19.11.2019\Encina eglogasantes1509 num3-40kb.txt 0.1312988123830755

61. Centurio 1507 -C:\Users\Govert\Desktop\Signatura comienzo 19.11.2019\Celestina viejos archivos\celestina cap15-19 Centurio.txt 0.13238507335864025

62. Gil Vicente -C:\Users\Govert\Desktop\Signatura comienzo 19.11.2019\GilVicente AutoPastoril1502 16kb.txt 0.1325038220213901

63. Gil Vicente -C:\Users\Govert\Desktop\Signatura comienzo 19.11.2019\GilVicente Don Duardos65kb.txt 0.13338124765326365

64. Francisco Delicado -C:\Users\Govert\Desktop\Signatura comienzo 19.11.2019\lozanaepistola3kb.txt 0.14056937965402083

65. Francisco Delicado -C:\Users\Govert\Desktop\Signatura comienzo 19.11.2019\lozanaapologia6kb.txt 0.14278596638205598

66. Sebastián de Horozco -C:\Users\Govert\Desktop\Signatura comienzo 19.11.2019\HorozcoEntremeses.txt 0.1439428855239565

67. Juan Ramírez de Lucena -C:\Users\Govert\Desktop\Signatura comienzo 19.11.2019\RamirezLucena a galardones.txt 0.14442094194145527

68. Juan de Valdés -C:\Users\Govert\Desktop\Signatura comienzo 19.11.2019\ValdesJuan doctrinacristiana75kb.txt 0.14540020850700763

69. Juan Agüero de Trasmiera -C:\Users\Govert\Desktop\Signatura comienzo 19.11.2019\trasmiera salamanca21kb.txt 0.14644240826721422

70. Juan de Flores -C:\Users\Govert\Desktop\Signatura comienzo 19.11.2019\grimalteobra21kb.txt 0.14699958342078023

71. Hernán Pérez de Olivia -C:\Users\Govert\Desktop\Signatura comienzo 19.11.2019\perezolivaSalamanca Razonamiento24 kb.txt 0.14772927728577478

72. Sebastián de Horozco -C:\Users\Govert\Desktop\Signatura comienzo 19.11.2019\HorozcoHistoriaEvangelica.txt 0.15022717696081478

73. Feliciano de Silva -C:\Users\Govert\Desktop\Signatura comienzo 19.11.2019\silva Celestina39kb.txt 0.15516882185449132

74. Juan de Sedeño -C:\Users\Govert\Desktop\Signatura comienzo 19.11.2019\sedeñocalisto111kb.txt 0.15830844820791423

75. Juan de Segura -C:\Users\Govert\Desktop\Signatura comienzo 19.11.2019\JuandeSeguraQuejayAvisoContraElAmor21kb.txt 0.15938692388465314

76. Fernando de Rojas -C:\Users\Govert\Desktop\Signatura comienzo 19.11.2019\fernando de rojas14kb test2.txt 0.16198650146211813

77. Sebastián de Horozco -C:\Users\Govert\Desktop\Signatura comienzo 19.11.2019\HorozcoRuth.txt 0.16601463485867474

78. Gáspar de Gómez -C:\Users\Govert\Desktop\Signatura comienzo 19.11.2019\gaspargomezdeToledoObra23kb.txt 0.1683127895181683

79. Lucas Fernández -C:\Users\Govert\Desktop\Signatura comienzo 19.11.2019\lucasfernandez dereniego del amor21kb.txt 0.16983966314510412

80. Nicolás Núñez -C:\Users\Govert\Desktop\Signatura comienzo 19.11.2019\NicolasNuñezTractado32kb.txt 0.17289521919227413
81. La Celestina -C:\Users\Govert\Desktop\Signatura comienzo 19.11.2019\CelestinaMs1520TextoCorrecto27kb.txt 0.1802780010088929
82. Francisco Delicado -C:\Users\Govert\Desktop\Signatura comienzo 19.11.2019\lozano54kb.txt 0.18284733579644008
83. manual de mujeres -C:\Users\Govert\Desktop\Signatura comienzo 19.11.2019\manualdemujeres21kb.txt 0.2500926348541527

15.3.2 1497 Annotations Lucena's book

vicent2015-2 Lucena New York.txt C:\Users\Govert\Desktop\Signatura comienzo 19.11.2019\vicent2015-2 Lucena New York.txt
Canonicizers:
    Normalize Whitespace
EventDrivers:
    Character NGrams n : 4
        EventCullers:
        Most Common Events numevents : 50
Analysis:
    Nearest Neighbor Driver with metric Cosine Distance
1. Baltasar del Rio -C:\Users\Govert\Desktop\Signatura comienzo 19.11.2019\baltasardelrio1504Tratado22kb.txt 0.1788171326000294
2. Juan de Valdés -C:\Users\Govert\Desktop\Signatura comienzo 19.11.2019\ValdesJuanCartas1-3-completo114kb.txt 0.1932678054547815
3. Gonzalo Fernández de Oviedo -C:\Users\Govert\Desktop\Signatura comienzo 19.11.2019\fernandezoviedobatalla90-130tiene34kb.txt 0.19448160250407986
4. Lope de Rueda -C:\Users\Govert\Desktop\Signatura comienzo 19.11.2019\lopederuedaAceitunas42kb.txt 0.19783180191494587
5. Gonzalo Fernández de Oviedo -C:\Users\Govert\Desktop\Signatura comienzo 19.11.2019\fernandezOviedo1532catálogo21kb.txt 0.19989426007815103
6. Gonzalo Fernández de Oviedo -C:\Users\Govert\Desktop\Signatura comienzo 19.11.2019\FernandezOviedoClaribalte21kb.txt 0.20400357280073944
7. Juan Paez de Castro -C:\Users\Govert\Desktop\Signatura comienzo 19.11.2019\juanpaezdecastroCartas23kb.txt 0.20646554068472234
8. Diego de San Pedro -C:\Users\Govert\Desktop\Signatura comienzo 19.11.2019\carceldeamor21kb.txt 0.20668335485365086
9. Cristóbal de Castellejo -C:\Users\Govert\Desktop\Signatura comienzo 19.11.2019\CristobalCastellejoAulaCortesano21kb.txt 0.20673881759461
10. Gonzalo Fernández de Oviedo -C:\Users\Govert\Desktop\Signatura comienzo 19.11.2019\fernandezOviedo-indias 21kb.txt 0.20720826554025473

11. Ludovico Escriva -C:\Users\Govert\Desktop\Signatura comienzo 19.11.2019\EscrivaLudovico1537y21kb.txt 0.20741153072335483

12. Lope de Rueda -C:\Users\Govert\Desktop\Signatura comienzo 19.11.2019\LopedeRuedaEufemia37kb.txt 0.20752694201772548

13. Thebayda -C:\Users\Govert\Desktop\Signatura comienzo 19.11.2019\thebaida incompleta21kb.txt 0.20837676621202028

14. Sancho de Muñón -C:\Users\Govert\Desktop\Signatura comienzo 19.11.2019\Acevedo Celestina corto21kb.txt 0.20966147435095717

15. Bernardo de Quirós -C:\Users\Govert\Desktop\Signatura comienzo 19.11.2019\VillalonViajeTurquiaVillalon109kb.txt 0.21316552843240344

16. Lucena -C:\Users\Govert\Desktop\Signatura comienzo 19.11.2019\repamores mitad libro51kb.txt 0.2134317527223274

17. Ramón de Petras -C:\Users\Govert\Desktop\Signatura comienzo 19.11.2019\traso auto11kb.txt 0.21389954922785093

18. Hernán Pérez de Olivia -C:\Users\Govert\Desktop\Signatura comienzo 19.11.2019\perezolivaRioGuadalquivirRazonamiento23kb.txt 0.21650470050558224

19. Francisco Cervantes de Salazar -C:\Users\Govert\Desktop\Signatura comienzo 19.11.2019\CervantesSalazarCronicaNuevEspaña21kb.txt 0.21651947165526064

20. Juan del Encina -C:\Users\Govert\Desktop\Signatura comienzo 19.11.2019\encina textos al rey75kb.txt 0.2198637653199993

21. Feliciano de Silva -C:\Users\Govert\Desktop\Signatura comienzo 19.11.2019\Silva amadis de grecia20kb.txt 0.22025108671622806

22. Juan de Valdés -C:\Users\Govert\Desktop\Signatura comienzo 19.11.2019\ValdesJuan doctrinacristiana75kb.txt 0.22048829592263341

23. Juan de Boscan -C:\Users\Govert\Desktop\Signatura comienzo 19.11.2019\BoscanElCortesano47kb.txt 0.22220734951080257

24. Juan de Flores -C:\Users\Govert\Desktop\Signatura comienzo 19.11.2019\griselobra21kb.txt 0.22236016946604387

25. Jerónimo Fernández -C:\Users\Govert\Desktop\Signatura comienzo 19.11.2019\jeronimofernandezhector1547-5-17kb.txt 0.2228727308688947

26. Gonzalo Fernández de Oviedo -C:\Users\Govert\Desktop\Signatura comienzo 19.11.2019\FernandezOviedoSumarioIndias27kb.txt 0.2244355116245249

27. Cristóbal de Castellejo -C:\Users\Govert\Desktop\Signatura comienzo 19.11.2019\CristobalCastillejoDialogodeMujeres21kb.txt 0.2245261113938325

28. Luis de Lucena -C:\Users\Govert\Desktop\Signatura comienzo 19.11.2019\LuisdeLucenaParteTestamento14kb.txt 0.2247208511900488

29. Nicolás Núñez -C:\Users\Govert\Desktop\Signatura comienzo 19.11.2019\NicolasNuñezTractado32kb.txt 0.22523808470223117

30. Alfonso de Valdés -C:\Users\Govert\Desktop\Signatura comienzo 19.11.2019\valdesAlfonsoCartas34kb.txt 0.22685941124595232

31. Diego de San Pedro -C:\Users\Govert\Desktop\Signatura comienzo 19.11.2019\arnalte incompleta21kb.txt 0.22714179339352203

32. Francisco López de Villalobos -C:\Users\Govert\Desktop\Signatura comienzo 19.11.2019\villaloboscostumbres humanas21kb.txt 0.22752855936189453

33. Hernán Núñez -C:\Users\Govert\Desktop\Signatura comienzo 19.11.2019\hernannuñez Trescientas21.txt 0.23177895039786844

34. Juan del Encina -C:\Users\Govert\Desktop\Signatura comienzo 19.11.2019\Encina eglogasantes1509 num3-40kb.txt 0.23274089782557283

35. Hernán Diaz -C:\Users\Govert\Desktop\Signatura comienzo 19.11.2019\peregrino obra135kb.txt 0.23301003046408597

36. Hernán Pérez de Olivia -C:\Users\Govert\Desktop\Signatura comienzo 19.11.2019\perezolivaSalamanca Razonamiento24 kb.txt 0.23632061249314917

37. Francisco Delicado -C:\Users\Govert\Desktop\Signatura comienzo 19.11.2019\legno2 8kb.txt 0.2378071342587328

38. Alonso de Proaza -C:\Users\Govert\Desktop\Signatura comienzo 19.11.2019\alonsodeproazaProsa no Celestina-12kb.txt 0.23803067621050555

39. La Celestina -C:\Users\Govert\Desktop\Signatura comienzo 19.11.2019\CelestinaComedia-1.txt 0.23930366996232322

40. Cristóbal de Castellejo -C:\Users\Govert\Desktop\Signatura comienzo 19.11.2019\CristobalCastillejoDialogoSobreMujeres21kb.txt 0.24017522323913643

41. Juan de Timoneda -C:\Users\Govert\Desktop\Signatura comienzo 19.11.2019\TimonedaCaminantes21kb.txt 0.24031330202503365

42. Alonso Núñez de Reinoso -C:\Users\Govert\Desktop\Signatura comienzo 19.11.2019\clareoyfloriseaCorto21kb.txt 0.2413341478372667

43. Jerónimo Fernández -C:\Users\Govert\Desktop\Signatura comienzo 19.11.2019\jeronimofernandez3año1579-113kb.txt 0.24138581519302393

44. Fray Antonio de Guevara -C:\Users\Govert\Desktop\Signatura comienzo 19.11.2019\guevaraEpistolasfamiliares21kb.txt 0.24263546100803468

45. Gil Vicente -C:\Users\Govert\Desktop\Signatura comienzo 19.11.2019\GilVicenteComediaViudo20kb.txt 0.24295534020362386

46. Gil Vicente -C:\Users\Govert\Desktop\Signatura comienzo 19.11.2019\GilVicente Don Duardos65kb.txt 0.24377050870306527

47. Hernando del Castillo -C:\Users\Govert\Desktop\Signatura comienzo 19.11.2019\hernando de castillo prologo6kb.txt 0.24381738204310655

48. Juan de Sedeño -C:\Users\Govert\Desktop\Signatura comienzo 19.11.2019\sedeño summaaobra21kb.txt 0.24470136774982276

49. Gil Vicente -C:\Users\Govert\Desktop\Signatura comienzo 19.11.2019\GilVicenteSibila31kb.txt 0.24508843937644176

50. Centurio 1507 -C:\Users\Govert\Desktop\Signatura comienzo 19.11.2019\Celestina viejos archivos\celestina cap15-19 Centurio.txt 0.2475585253216661

51. Juan Ramírez de Lucena -C:\Users\Govert\Desktop\Signatura comienzo 19.11.2019\vita beata21kb.txt 0.24822935522941747

52. Juan de Sedeño -C:\Users\Govert\Desktop\Signatura comienzo 19.11.2019\sedeño summaPrologo y Epistola19kb.txt 0.24835108122794658

53. Gáspar de Gómez -C:\Users\Govert\Desktop\Signatura comienzo 19.11.2019\gaspargomezdeToledoObra23kb.txt 0.24886228101990793

54. Lucena -C:\Users\Govert\Desktop\Signatura comienzo 19.11.2019\repeticionamores ajedrez4kb.txt 0.2490589725947161

55. Sebastián de Horozco -C:\Users\Govert\Desktop\Signatura comienzo 19.11.2019\HorozcoHistoriaEvangelica.txt 0.24993328103079748

56. Juan de Sedeño -C:\Users\Govert\Desktop\Signatura comienzo 19.11.2019\sedeñoAmores Buenaventurança26kb.txt 0.25240427627814166

57. Juan Justaniano -C:\Users\Govert\Desktop\Signatura comienzo 19.11.2019\luisvives formacion21kb.txt 0.25336865799117014

58. Juan de Sedeño -C:\Users\Govert\Desktop\Signatura comienzo 19.11.2019\sedeñocalisto111kb.txt 0.25494710721400804

59. Gonzalo García Santa Maria -C:\Users\Govert\Desktop\Signatura comienzo 19.11.2019\GarciaSantaMariaCoronicaAragonObra27kb.txt 0.2555760017922559

60. Francisco Delicado -C:\Users\Govert\Desktop\Signatura comienzo 19.11.2019\lozano54kb.txt 0.25644680173630674

61. Sebastián de Horozco -C:\Users\Govert\Desktop\Signatura comienzo 19.11.2019\HorozcoEntremeses.txt 0.25686153042737503

62. Feliciano de Silva -C:\Users\Govert\Desktop\Signatura comienzo 19.11.2019\silva Celestina39kb.txt 0.2579013243825792

63. Alonso de Cardona -C:\Users\Govert\Desktop\Signatura comienzo 19.11.2019\alonsodecardona22kb.txt 0.25960610534247996

64. Juan de Flores -C:\Users\Govert\Desktop\Signatura comienzo 19.11.2019\grimalteobra21kb.txt 0.2626320061316161

65. Diego Hurtado de Mendoza -C:\Users\Govert\Desktop\Signatura comienzo 19.11.2019\diegohurtadodemendoza granada171kb.txt 0.2646085513885841

66. Juan Ramírez de Lucena -C:\Users\Govert\Desktop\Signatura comienzo 19.11.2019\Ramirez Lucena exhortatoria.txt 0.26928171871131557

67. Francisco Delicado -C:\Users\Govert\Desktop\Signatura comienzo 19.11.2019\lozanaapologia6kb.txt 0.2694371166892374

68. Juan de Sedeño -C:\Users\Govert\Desktop\Signatura comienzo 19.11.2019\sedeño summaEpistolaobra54kb.txt 0.269473090512268

69. Juan Ramírez de Lucena -C:\Users\Govert\Desktop\Signatura comienzo 19.11.2019\RamirezLucena a Zapata.txt 0.26982208674467734

70. Fray Antonio de Guevara -C:\Users\Govert\Desktop\Signatura comienzo 19.11.2019\GuevaraMarcoAurelioObra22kb.txt 0.27110190684660296

71. Sebastián de Horozco -C:\Users\Govert\Desktop\Signatura comienzo 19.11.2019\HorozcoRuth.txt 0.2713306800758345

72. Gil Vicente -C:\Users\Govert\Desktop\Signatura comienzo 19.11.2019\GilVicente AutoPastoril1502 16kb.txt 0.2749279515929607

73. Bartolomé de las Casas -C:\Users\Govert\Desktop\Signatura comienzo 19.11.2019\BartolomeDeLasCasasBrevisimak34b.txt 0.28027329520466593

74. Juan de Segura -C:\Users\Govert\Desktop\Signatura comienzo 19.11.2019\JuandeSeguraQuejayAvisoContraElAmor21kb.txt 0.2841847403865754

75. Lucas Fernández -C:\Users\Govert\Desktop\Signatura comienzo 19.11.2019\lucasfernandez dereniego del amor21kb.txt 0.2868095238593209

76. Francisco Delicado -C:\Users\Govert\Desktop\Signatura comienzo 19.11.2019\lozanaepilogo5kb.txt 0.28724056773264306

77. Francisco Delicado -C:\Users\Govert\Desktop\Signatura comienzo 19.11.2019\lozanaepistola3kb.txt 0.29548265993256617

78. Juan Agüero de Trasmiera -C:\Users\Govert\Desktop\Signatura comienzo 19.11.2019\trasmiera salamanca21kb.txt 0.2975244132280833

79. Gil Vicente -C:\Users\Govert\Desktop\Signatura comienzo 19.11.2019\GilVicenteCuatroTiempos21kb.txt 0.3139608580393942

80. Fernando de Rojas -C:\Users\Govert\Desktop\Signatura comienzo 19.11.2019\fernando de rojas14kb test2.txt 0.31919871927106735

81. La Celestina -C:\Users\Govert\Desktop\Signatura comienzo 19.11.2019\CelestinaMs1520TextoCorrecto27kb.txt 0.35222485577771667

82. Juan Ramírez de Lucena -C:\Users\Govert\Desktop\Signatura comienzo 19.11.2019\RamirezLucena a galardones.txt 0.35683991274165083

83. manual de mujeres -C:\Users\Govert\Desktop\Signatura comienzo 19.11.2019\manualdemujeres21kb.txt 0.39928931361523345

15.4 Chapter 12

15.4.1 JGaap analysis of "duobus amantibus"

piccolomini pp31-58.txt C:\Users\Govert\Desktop\Signatura comienzo 19.11.2019\piccolomini pp31-58.txt
Canonicizers:
    Normalize Whitespace
EventDrivers:
    Character NGrams n : 4
        EventCullers:
            Most Common Events numevents : 50
Analysis:
    Nearest Neighbor Driver with metric Cosine Distance
1.   Lucena   -C:\Users\Govert\Desktop\Signatura   comienzo 19.11.2019\repeticionamores114kb.txt 0.021335511387817307
2.   Jerónimo   Fernández   -C:\Users\Govert\Desktop\Signatura   comienzo 19.11.2019\jeronimofernandez3año1579-113kb.txt 0.023465542002435003
3. Juan del Encina -C:\Users\Govert\Desktop\Signatura comienzo 19.11.2019\encina textos al rey75kb.txt 0.024893953535265356
4.   Juan   Justiniano   -C:\Users\Govert\Desktop\Signatura   comienzo 19.11.2019\luisvivesformacionmujer84kb.txt 0.02771610503570221
5.   Lucas   Fernández   -C:\Users\Govert\Desktop\Signatura   comienzo 19.11.2019\lucasfernandez dereniego del amor169kb.txt 0.02816782553350705
6.   Sancho   Muñón   -C:\Users\Govert\Desktop\Signatura   comienzo 19.11.2019\Acevedo Celestina151kb.txt 0.0287704029670639
7.   Bernardo   de   Quirós   -C:\Users\Govert\Desktop\Signatura   comienzo 19.11.2019\VillalonViajeTurquiaVillalon109kb.txt 0.030141285140624974
8. Hernán Díaz -C:\Users\Govert\Desktop\Signatura comienzo 19.11.2019\peregrino obra135kb.txt 0.03070604465044524
9.   Gil   Vicente   -C:\Users\Govert\Desktop\Signatura   comienzo 19.11.2019\GilVicenteSibila31kb.txt 0.030963462172321488
10.   Diego   de   San   Pedro   -C:\Users\Govert\Desktop\Signatura   comienzo 19.11.2019\arnalte obra completa120kb.txt 0.03225239843106531
11.   Ludovico   Escriva   -C:\Users\Govert\Desktop\Signatura   comienzo 19.11.2019\EscrivaLudovico1537y21kb.txt 0.03238156519627411
12. Gonzalo Fernández de Oviedo -C:\Users\Govert\Desktop\Signatura comienzo 19.11.2019\fernandezoviedobatalla90-130tiene34kb.txt 0.03251247409999691
13.   Feliciano   de   Silva   -C:\Users\Govert\Desktop\Signatura   comienzo 19.11.2019\Silva amadis de grecia20kb.txt 0.03445508142251008

14. Francisco López de Villalobos -C:\Users\Govert\Desktop\Signatura comienzo 19.11.2019\villalobos obra completa costumbres humanas141kb.txt 0.03491993334400656

15. Juan de Flores -C:\Users\Govert\Desktop\Signatura comienzo 19.11.2019\griselobra89kb.txt 0.03757368913410086

16. Lope de Rueda -C:\Users\Govert\Desktop\Signatura comienzo 19.11.2019\lopederuedaAceitunas42kb.txt 0.03867606412290525

17. Thebayda anónym -C:\Users\Govert\Desktop\Signatura comienzo 19.11.2019\thebaida incompleta 92kb.txt 0.03984512861831724

18. La Celestina -C:\Users\Govert\Desktop\Signatura comienzo 19.11.2019\CelestinaComedia-1.txt 0.04131333388524716

19. Diego de San Pedro -C:\Users\Govert\Desktop\Signatura comienzo 19.11.2019\carceldeamor obra completa134kb.txt 0.0415962247069257

20. Juan de Timoneda -C:\Users\Govert\Desktop\Signatura comienzo 19.11.2019\Timoneda Patrañuela30kb.txt 0.04162192728886949

21. Gil Vicente -C:\Users\Govert\Desktop\Signatura comienzo 19.11.2019\GilVicenteComediaViudo20kb.txt 0.041701265569419

22. Gonzalo Fernández de Oviedo -C:\Users\Govert\Desktop\Signatura comienzo 19.11.2019\FernandezOviedoSumarioIndias21kb.txt 0.0419470303639925

23. Juan Paez de Castro -C:\Users\Govert\Desktop\Signatura comienzo 19.11.2019\juanpaezdecastroCartas23kb.txt 0.04237496161263765

24. Hernán Núñez -C:\Users\Govert\Desktop\Signatura comienzo 19.11.2019\hernannuñez Trescientas120kb.txt 0.042713688334580446

25. Ramón de Petras -C:\Users\Govert\Desktop\Signatura comienzo 19.11.2019\traso auto11kb.txt 0.04290449233099636

26. Gil Vicente -C:\Users\Govert\Desktop\Signatura comienzo 19.11.2019\GilVicente Don Duardos65kb.txt 0.044152935500379464

27. Juan Huarte de San Juan -C:\Users\Govert\Desktop\Signatura comienzo 19.11.2019\HuarteExamen Ingenios21kb.txt 0.0442412061101487

28. Lope de Rueda -C:\Users\Govert\Desktop\Signatura comienzo 19.11.2019\LopedeRuedaEufemia37kb.txt 0.04570267137566997

29. Gil Vicente -C:\Users\Govert\Desktop\Signatura comienzo 19.11.2019\GilVicenteCuatroTiempos21kb.txt 0.04592205634226143

30. Luis de Lucena -C:\Users\Govert\Desktop\Signatura comienzo 19.11.2019\LuisdeLucenaParteTestamento14kb.txt 0.04723083912629278

31. Hernán Pérez de Olivia -C:\Users\Govert\Desktop\Signatura comienzo 19.11.2019\perezolivaRioGuadalquivirRazonamiento23kb.txt 0.04874844057590055

32. Hernán Pérez de Olivia -C:\Users\Govert\Desktop\Signatura comienzo 19.11.2019\perezolivaSalamanca Razonamiento24 kb.txt 0.04929823666914168

33. Francisco Delicado -C:\Users\Govert\Desktop\Signatura comienzo 19.11.2019\legno2 8kb.txt 0.04970231960028359.5

34. Juan de Sedeño -C:\Users\Govert\Desktop\Signatura comienzo 19.11.2019\sedeñoAmores Buenaventurança26kb.txt 0.049713834360568754

35. Juan de Timoneda -C:\Users\Govert\Desktop\Signatura comienzo 19.11.2019\TimonedaCaminantes21kb.txt 0.050408648446540694

36. Gonzalo Fernández de Oviedo -C:\Users\Govert\Desktop\Signatura comienzo 19.11.2019\FernandezOviedoClaribalte21kb.txt 0.050721302707421145

37. Francisco Delicado -C:\Users\Govert\Desktop\Signatura comienzo 19.11.2019\lozanaepilogo5kb.txt 0.05091973061181598

38. Juan Ramírez de Lucena -C:\Users\Govert\Desktop\Signatura comienzo 19.11.2019\vita beata131kb.txt 0.051188746754971315

39. Jerónimo Fernández -C:\Users\Govert\Desktop\Signatura comienzo 19.11.2019\jeronimofernandezhector1547-5-17kb.txt 0.052606832117179536

40. Alfonso de Valdés -C:\Users\Govert\Desktop\Signatura comienzo 19.11.2019\valdesAlfonsoCartas34kb.txt 0.05314625881252766

41. Juan de Valdés -C:\Users\Govert\Desktop\Signatura comienzo 19.11.2019\ValdesJuanCartas1-3-completo114kb.txt 0.05416266035121842

42. Gil Vicente -C:\Users\Govert\Desktop\Signatura comienzo 19.11.2019\GilVicente AutoPastoril1502 16kb.txt 0.0543331262226132844

43. Francisco Cervantes de Salazar -C:\Users\Govert\Desktop\Signatura comienzo 19.11.2019\CervantesSalazarCronicaNuevEspaña21kb.txt 0.0552475494823923

44. Alonso de Cardona -C:\Users\Govert\Desktop\Signatura comienzo 19.11.2019\alonsodecardona22kb.txt 0.05783595302094624

45. Alonso Núñez de Reinoso -C:\Users\Govert\Desktop\Signatura comienzo 19.11.2019\clareoyfloriseaReinoso132kb.txt 0.05944966512980221

46. Juan de Sedeño -C:\Users\Govert\Desktop\Signatura comienzo 19.11.2019\sedeño summaPrologo y Epistola19kb.txt 0.060320765387839925

47. Juan del Encina -C:\Users\Govert\Desktop\Signatura comienzo 19.11.2019\Encina eglogasantes1509 num3-40kb.txt 0.06098771446025775

48. Sebastián de Horozco -C:\Users\Govert\Desktop\Signatura comienzo 19.11.2019\HorozcoEntremeses.txt 0.061048450735282866

49. Diego Hurtado de Mendoza -C:\Users\Govert\Desktop\Signatura comienzo 19.11.2019\diegohurtadodemendoza granada171kb.txt 0.061267436081961724

50. Gonzalo Fernández de Oviedo -C:\Users\Govert\Desktop\Signatura comienzo 19.11.2019\fernandezOviedo-indias 21kb.txt 0.06234750509152609

51. Juan de Sedeño -C:\Users\Govert\Desktop\Signatura comienzo 19.11.2019\sedeño summaaobra21kb.txt 0.06399218997002054

52. Juan de Sedeño -C:\Users\Govert\Desktop\Signatura comienzo 19.11.2019\sedeñocalisto111kb.txt 0.06419539914663719

53. Juan de Valdés -C:\Users\Govert\Desktop\Signatura comienzo 19.11.2019\ValdesJuan doctrinacristiana75kb.txt 0.06436263794992414

54. Hernando de Castillo -C:\Users\Govert\Desktop\Signatura comienzo 19.11.2019\hernando de castillo prologo6kb.txt 0.0663489055648141

55. Juan de Flores -C:\Users\Govert\Desktop\Signatura comienzo 19.11.2019\grimalteobra21kb.txt 0.0680678177407058

56. Gonzalo García de Santa María -C:\Users\Govert\Desktop\Signatura comienzo 19.11.2019\GarciaSantaMariaCoronicaAragonObra27kb.txt 0.07153793631821925

57. Alonso de Proaza -C:\Users\Govert\Desktop\Signatura comienzo 19.11.2019\alonsodeproazaProsa no Celestina-12kb.txt 0.07157457349653273

58. Francisco Delicado -C:\Users\Govert\Desktop\Signatura comienzo 19.11.2019\lozanaapologia6kb.txt 0.07165055809414778

59. Sebastián de Horozco -C:\Users\Govert\Desktop\Signatura comienzo 19.11.2019\HorozcoHistoriaEvangelica.txt 0.07305267067638743

60. Gáspar Gómez de Toledo -C:\Users\Govert\Desktop\Signatura comienzo 19.11.2019\gaspargomezdeToledoObra23kb.txt 0.07398052541468336

61. Sebastián de Horozco -C:\Users\Govert\Desktop\Signatura comienzo 19.11.2019\HorozcoRuth.txt 0.07441122756394358

62. Juan Ramírez de Lucena -C:\Users\Govert\Desktop\Signatura comienzo 19.11.2019\Ramirez Lucena a Jorge Manrique.txt 0.07668367350730154

63. Juan Ramírez de Lucena -C:\Users\Govert\Desktop\Signatura comienzo 19.11.2019\Ramirez Lucena exhortatoria.txt 0.07987189054629618

64. Juan Ramírez de Lucena -C:\Users\Govert\Desktop\Signatura comienzo 19.11.2019\RamirezLucena a Zapata.txt 0.08022161070235778

65. Feliciano de Silva -C:\Users\Govert\Desktop\Signatura comienzo 19.11.2019\Silva Celestina Segunda Parcial177kb.txt 0.08043827614755739

66. Juan de Sedeño -C:\Users\Govert\Desktop\Signatura comienzo 19.11.2019\sedeño summaEpistolaobra54kb.txt 0.08116841951100984

67. Francisco Delicado -C:\Users\Govert\Desktop\Signatura comienzo 19.11.2019\lozano54kb.txt 0.082550732264557

68. Lucena -C:\Users\Govert\Desktop\Signatura comienzo 19.11.2019\repeticionamores ajedrez4kb.txt 0.0836559870254755

69. Nicolás Núñez -C:\Users\Govert\Desktop\Signatura comienzo 19.11.2019\NicolasNuñezTractado32kb.txt 0.08697002336935022

70. Juan Agüero de Trasmiera -C:\Users\Govert\Desktop\Signatura comienzo 19.11.2019\trasmiera salamanca21kb.txt 0.11525987673404725

71. Juan Ramírez de Lucena -C:\Users\Govert\Desktop\Signatura comienzo 19.11.2019\RamirezLucena a galardones.txt 0.11702835629295893

72. Francisco Delicado -C:\Users\Govert\Desktop\Signatura comienzo 19.11.2019\lozanadedicatoria2kb.txt 0.1172498697083213

73. Juan de Segura -C:\Users\Govert\Desktop\Signatura comienzo 19.11.2019\JuandeSeguraQuejayAvisoContraElAmor21kb.txt 0.1177656824673925

74. Francisco Delicado -C:\Users\Govert\Desktop\Signatura comienzo 19.11.2019\lozanaepistola3kb.txt 0.12310723114004485

75. La Celestina -C:\Users\Govert\Desktop\Signatura comienzo 19.11.2019\CelestinaMs1520TextoCorrecto27kb.txt 0.13859610481772022

76. Juan de Timoneda -C:\Users\Govert\Desktop\Signatura comienzo 19.11.2019\Timoneda Disculpa7kb.txt 0.15823596342913004

77. Francisco Delicado -C:\Users\Govert\Desktop\Signatura comienzo 19.11.2019\lozanaargumento3kb.txt 0.1611007401020057

78. Fernando de Rojas -C:\Users\Govert\Desktop\Signatura comienzo 19.11.2019\fernando de rojas14kb test2.txt 0.17920773605728768

79. Juan de Timoneda -C:\Users\Govert\Desktop\Signatura comienzo 19.11.2019\timonedalibrodamas21kb.txt 0.32610608224813253

80. Juan Ramírez de Lucena -C:\Users\Govert\Desktop\Signatura comienzo 19.11.2019\ramirezlucenaJuanOratioEmbajadores1472.txt 0.417581902229897

15.4.2 1495 Francesch Vicent, chessbook title

vicent1495.txt   C:\Users\Govert\Desktop\Signatura   comienzo 19.11.2019\vicent1495.txt
Canonicizers:
    Normalize Whitespace
EventDrivers:
    Character NGrams n : 4
        EventCullers:
            Most Common Events numevents : 50
Analysis:
    Nearest Neighbor Driver with metric Cosine Distance
1. Fernando de Rojas -C:\Users\Govert\Desktop\Signatura comienzo 19.11.2019\fernando de rojas14kb test2.txt 0.24991417302107233
2. Gonzalo Fernández de Oviedo -C:\Users\Govert\Desktop\Signatura comienzo 19.11.2019\fernandezOviedo-indias 21kb.txt 0.27619085370649354
3. La Celestina -C:\Users\Govert\Desktop\Signatura comienzo 19.11.2019\CelestinaMs1520TextoCorrecto27kb.txt 0.2782552913769014
4. Jerónimo Fernández -C:\Users\Govert\Desktop\Signatura comienzo 19.11.2019\jeronimofernandezhector1547-5-17kb.txt 0.2949103512929997
5. Juan de Sedeño -C:\Users\Govert\Desktop\Signatura comienzo 19.11.2019\sedeño summaEpistolaobra54kb.txt 0.2973480242555929
6. Juan de Sedeño -C:\Users\Govert\Desktop\Signatura comienzo 19.11.2019\sedeño summaaobra21kb.txt 0.3105734806471929
7. Diego Hurtado de Mendoza -C:\Users\Govert\Desktop\Signatura comienzo 19.11.2019\diegohurtadodemendoza granada171kb.txt 0.31613123437889623
8. Juan de Timoneda -C:\Users\Govert\Desktop\Signatura comienzo 19.11.2019\Timoneda Disculpa7kb.txt 0.3271527034984948
9. Hernán Díaz -C:\Users\Govert\Desktop\Signatura comienzo 19.11.2019\peregrino obra135kb.txt 0.3376190685849906
10. Juan Agüero de Trasmiera -C:\Users\Govert\Desktop\Signatura comienzo 19.11.2019\trasmiera salamanca21kb.txt 0.3409768892874184
11. Luis de Lucena -C:\Users\Govert\Desktop\Signatura comienzo 19.11.2019\LuisdeLucenaParteTestamento14kb.txt 0.3476454013296285
12. La Celestina -C:\Users\Govert\Desktop\Signatura comienzo 19.11.2019\CelestinaComedia-1.txt 0.34837770268671797
13. Hernán Núñez -C:\Users\Govert\Desktop\Signatura comienzo 19.11.2019\hernannuñez Trescientas120kb.txt 0.34991793386415315

14. Juan de Sedeño -C:\Users\Govert\Desktop\Signatura comienzo 19.11.2019\sedeño summaPrologo y Epistola19kb.txt 0.3598202895548607

15. Lucena -C:\Users\Govert\Desktop\Signatura comienzo 19.11.2019\repeticionamores ajedrez4kb.txt 0.36534775279077625

16. Francisco Cervantes de Salazar -C:\Users\Govert\Desktop\Signatura comienzo 19.11.2019\CervantesSalazarCronicaNuevEspaña21kb.txt 0.3715690333962106

17. Lucas Fernández -C:\Users\Govert\Desktop\Signatura comienzo 19.11.2019\lucasfernandez dereniego del amor169kb.txt 0.3723035750382595

18. Hernán Pérez de Olivia -C:\Users\Govert\Desktop\Signatura comienzo 19.11.2019\perezolivaRioGuadalquivirRazonamiento23kb.txt 0.3770656447961208

19. Gonzalo García de Santa María -C:\Users\Govert\Desktop\Signatura comienzo 19.11.2019\GarciaSantaMariaCoronicaAragonObra27kb.txt 0.3911900168282474

20. Juan Justiniano -C:\Users\Govert\Desktop\Signatura comienzo 19.11.2019\luisvivesformacionmujer84kb.txt 0.39475251663726474

21. Alonso de Proaza -C:\Users\Govert\Desktop\Signatura comienzo 19.11.2019\alonsodeproazaProsa no Celestina-12kb.txt 0.3962397256238218

22. Juan del Encina -C:\Users\Govert\Desktop\Signatura comienzo 19.11.2019\encina textos al rey75kb.txt 0.39643018440978917

23. Lope de Rueda -C:\Users\Govert\Desktop\Signatura comienzo 19.11.2019\lopederuedaAceitunas42kb.txt 0.3996512042172764

24. Francisco Delicado -C:\Users\Govert\Desktop\Signatura comienzo 19.11.2019\legno2 8kb.txt 0.4016919363768251

25. Feliciano de Silva -C:\Users\Govert\Desktop\Signatura comienzo 19.11.2019\Silva amadis de grecia20kb.txt 0.40214651039640503

26. Juan Ramírez de Lucena -C:\Users\Govert\Desktop\Signatura comienzo 19.11.2019\vita beata131kb.txt 0.40256955682175855

27. Juan de Timoneda -C:\Users\Govert\Desktop\Signatura comienzo 19.11.2019\Timoneda Patrañuela30kb.txt 0.40696442490678986

28. Gonzalo Fernández de Oviedo -C:\Users\Govert\Desktop\Signatura comienzo 19.11.2019\FernandezOviedoClaribalte21kb.txt 0.410106064316605

29. Gil Vicente -C:\Users\Govert\Desktop\Signatura comienzo 19.11.2019\GilVicenteComediaViudo20kb.txt 0.41050073199943027

30. Lucena -C:\Users\Govert\Desktop\Signatura comienzo 19.11.2019\repeticionamores114kb.txt 0.4110767862200856

31. Juan de Sedeño -C:\Users\Govert\Desktop\Signatura comienzo 19.11.2019\sedeñoAmores Buenaventurança26kb.txt 0.4123450056554988

32. Lope de Rueda -C:\Users\Govert\Desktop\Signatura comienzo 19.11.2019\LopedeRuedaEufemia37kb.txt 0.4169696079733599

33. Thebayda anónym -C:\Users\Govert\Desktop\Signatura comienzo 19.11.2019\thebaida incompleta 92kb.txt 0.4184610361307576

34. Gonzalo Fernández de Oviedo -C:\Users\Govert\Desktop\Signatura comienzo 19.11.2019\fernandezoviedobatalla90-130tiene34kb.txt 0.4237404515960833

35. Gonzalo Fernández de Oviedo -C:\Users\Govert\Desktop\Signatura comienzo 19.11.2019\FernandezOviedoSumarioIndias21kb.txt 0.42383698240798184

36. Bernardo de Quirós -C:\Users\Govert\Desktop\Signatura comienzo 19.11.2019\VillalonViajeTurquiaVillalon109kb.txt 0.4246397552951421

37. Sancho Muñón -C:\Users\Govert\Desktop\Signatura comienzo 19.11.2019\Acevedo Celestina151kb.txt 0.4270083893856351

38. Gil Vicente -C:\Users\Govert\Desktop\Signatura comienzo 19.11.2019\GilVicenteCuatroTiempos21kb.txt 0.4288404893870744

39. Juan Paez de Castro -C:\Users\Govert\Desktop\Signatura comienzo 19.11.2019\juanpaezdecastroCartas23kb.txt 0.43198890440427695

40. Juan de Valdés -C:\Users\Govert\Desktop\Signatura comienzo 19.11.2019\ValdesJuanCartas1-3-completo114kb.txt 0.4321366927542716

41. Diego de San Pedro -C:\Users\Govert\Desktop\Signatura comienzo 19.11.2019\arnalte obra completa120kb.txt 0.4326847149404901

42. Ludovico Escriva -C:\Users\Govert\Desktop\Signatura comienzo 19.11.2019\EscrivaLudovico1537y21kb.txt 0.435118981442291

43. Jerónimo Fernández -C:\Users\Govert\Desktop\Signatura comienzo 19.11.2019\jeronimofernandez3año1579-113kb.txt 0.4387793147471921

44. Hernán Pérez de Olivia -C:\Users\Govert\Desktop\Signatura comienzo 19.11.2019\perezolivaSalamanca Razonamiento24 kb.txt 0.4396602212901761

45. Hernando de Castillo -C:\Users\Govert\Desktop\Signatura comienzo 19.11.2019\hernando de castillo prologo6kb.txt 0.44509565763520187

46. Diego de San Pedro -C:\Users\Govert\Desktop\Signatura comienzo 19.11.2019\carceldeamor obra completa134kb.txt 0.45142921095163446

47. Juan Ramírez de Lucena -C:\Users\Govert\Desktop\Signatura comienzo 19.11.2019\RamirezLucena a galardones.txt 0.45160051076373053

48. Juan del Encina -C:\Users\Govert\Desktop\Signatura comienzo 19.11.2019\Encina eglogasantes1509 num3-40kb.txt 0.4565701522348219

49. Francisco López de Villalobos -C:\Users\Govert\Desktop\Signatura comienzo 19.11.2019\villalobos obra completa costumbres humanas141kb.txt 0.4595802062359401

50. Juan de Flores -C:\Users\Govert\Desktop\Signatura comienzo 19.11.2019\griselobra89kb.txt 0.4615576393979899

51. Gil Vicente -C:\Users\Govert\Desktop\Signatura comienzo 19.11.2019\GilVicenteSibila31kb.txt 0.463263613272341

52. Ramón de Petras -C:\Users\Govert\Desktop\Signatura comienzo 19.11.2019\traso auto11kb.txt 0.46442005022053245

53. Juan de Timoneda -C:\Users\Govert\Desktop\Signatura comienzo 19.11.2019\timonedalibrodamas21kb.txt 0.46666056572679104

54. Juan Ramírez de Lucena -C:\Users\Govert\Desktop\Signatura comienzo 19.11.2019\Ramirez Lucena exhortatoria.txt 0.4684741974065567

55. Juan Ramírez de Lucena -C:\Users\Govert\Desktop\Signatura comienzo 19.11.2019\RamirezLucena a Zapata.txt 0.46886825533971443

56. Alonso de Cardona -C:\Users\Govert\Desktop\Signatura comienzo 19.11.2019\alonsodecardona22kb.txt 0.4699481012396032

57. Gil Vicente -C:\Users\Govert\Desktop\Signatura comienzo 19.11.2019\GilVicente Don Duardos65kb.txt 0.47261503037830244

58. Juan de Timoneda -C:\Users\Govert\Desktop\Signatura comienzo 19.11.2019\TimonedaCaminantes21kb.txt 0.4737618425203207

59. Sebastián de Horozco -C:\Users\Govert\Desktop\Signatura comienzo 19.11.2019\HorozcoEntremeses.txt 0.47923833579302944

60. Juan Ramírez de Lucena -C:\Users\Govert\Desktop\Signatura comienzo 19.11.2019\Ramirez Lucena a Jorge Manrique.txt 0.4798180575948452

61. Alonso Núñez de Reinoso -C:\Users\Govert\Desktop\Signatura comienzo 19.11.2019\clareoyfloriseaReinoso132kb.txt 0.4809209609471572

62. Juan Huarte de San Juan -C:\Users\Govert\Desktop\Signatura comienzo 19.11.2019\HuarteExamen Ingenios21kb.txt 0.48345506387453197

63. Gil Vicente -C:\Users\Govert\Desktop\Signatura comienzo 19.11.2019\GilVicente AutoPastoril1502 16kb.txt 0.49011699040987755

64. Francisco Delicado -C:\Users\Govert\Desktop\Signatura comienzo 19.11.2019\lozano54kb.txt 0.49662936806291036

65. Nicolás Núñez -C:\Users\Govert\Desktop\Signatura comienzo 19.11.2019\NicolasNuñezTractado32kb.txt 0.5016119626749018

66. Juan de Valdés -C:\Users\Govert\Desktop\Signatura comienzo 19.11.2019\ValdesJuan doctrinacristiana75kb.txt 0.5016765027646206

67. Alfonso de Valdés -C:\Users\Govert\Desktop\Signatura comienzo 19.11.2019\valdesAlfonsoCartas34kb.txt 0.5018080258932482

68. Francisco Delicado -C:\Users\Govert\Desktop\Signatura comienzo 19.11.2019\lozanaepilogo5kb.txt 0.5076731170690675

69. Sebastián de Horozco -C:\Users\Govert\Desktop\Signatura comienzo 19.11.2019\HorozcoHistoriaEvangelica.txt 0.5079944427795712

70. Juan de Flores -C:\Users\Govert\Desktop\Signatura comienzo 19.11.2019\grimalteobra21kb.txt 0.5102408723094998

71. Gáspar Gómez de Toledo -C:\Users\Govert\Desktop\Signatura comienzo 19.11.2019\gaspargomezdeToledoObra23kb.txt 0.5226242426540337

72. Feliciano de Silva -C:\Users\Govert\Desktop\Signatura comienzo 19.11.2019\Silva Celestina Segunda Parcial177kb.txt 0.5263801681704914

73. Juan de Sedeño -C:\Users\Govert\Desktop\Signatura comienzo 19.11.2019\sedeñocalisto111kb.txt 0.5294017032587868

74. Sebastián de Horozco -C:\Users\Govert\Desktop\Signatura comienzo 19.11.2019\HorozcoRuth.txt 0.5348802117330697

75. Juan de Segura -C:\Users\Govert\Desktop\Signatura comienzo 19.11.2019\JuandeSeguraQuejayAvisoContraElAmor21kb.txt 0.5366916983954283

76. Francisco Delicado -C:\Users\Govert\Desktop\Signatura comienzo 19.11.2019\lozanaepistola3kb.txt 0.5678706333132985

77. Francisco Delicado -C:\Users\Govert\Desktop\Signatura comienzo 19.11.2019\lozanaapologia6kb.txt 0.5722809907087778

78. Francisco Delicado -C:\Users\Govert\Desktop\Signatura comienzo 19.11.2019\lozanadedicatoria2kb.txt 0.5732834106350027

79. Francisco Delicado -C:\Users\Govert\Desktop\Signatura comienzo 19.11.2019\lozanaargumento3kb.txt 0.64855007996236

80. Juan Ramírez de Lucena -C:\Users\Govert\Desktop\Signatura comienzo 19.11.2019\ramirezlucenaJuanOratioEmbajadores1472.txt 0.7501583447852302

15.4.3 1512 Damiano's book

damianolibro1.txt   C:\Users\Govert\Desktop\Signatura   comienzo 19.11.2019\damianolibro1.txt
Canonicizers:
    Normalize Whitespace
EventDrivers:
    Character NGrams n : 4
        EventCullers:
            Most Common Events numevents : 50
Analysis:
    Nearest Neighbor Driver with metric Cosine Distance
1.   Lucena   -C:\Users\Govert\Desktop\Signatura   comienzo 19.11.2019\repeticionamores ajedrez4kb.txt 0.33888630992372193
2.   La   Celestina   -C:\Users\Govert\Desktop\Signatura   comienzo 19.11.2019\CelestinaMs1520TextoCorrecto27kb.txt 0.36970649463673244
3. Gonzalo Fernández de Oviedo -C:\Users\Govert\Desktop\Signatura comienzo 19.11.2019\fernandezOviedo-indias 21kb.txt 0.3784762883081775
4. Jerónimo   Fernández   -C:\Users\Govert\Desktop\Signatura   comienzo 19.11.2019\jeronimofernandezhector1547-5-17kb.txt 0.3841125124838174
5.   Juan   de   Timoneda   -C:\Users\Govert\Desktop\Signatura   comienzo 19.11.2019\Timoneda Disculpa7kb.txt 0.39152304028123586
6.   Alonso   de   Proaza   -C:\Users\Govert\Desktop\Signatura   comienzo 19.11.2019\alonsodeproazaProsa no Celestina-12kb.txt 0.3953328666081294
7. Juan de Sedeño -C:\Users\Govert\Desktop\Signatura comienzo 19.11.2019\sedeño summaaobra21kb.txt 0.4088435739091637
8.   Juan   de   Sedeño   -C:\Users\Govert\Desktop\Signatura   comienzo 19.11.2019\sedeñoAmores Buenaventurança26kb.txt 0.414460180065674
9. Gonzalo García de Santa María -C:\Users\Govert\Desktop\Signatura comienzo 19.11.2019\GarciaSantaMariaCoronicaAragonObra27kb.txt 0.4163325540376972
10.   La   Celestina   -C:\Users\Govert\Desktop\Signatura   comienzo 19.11.2019\CelestinaComedia-1.txt 0.4202239607624806
11. Hernán Díaz -C:\Users\Govert\Desktop\Signatura comienzo 19.11.2019\peregrino obra135kb.txt 0.4229212510389513
12.   Ludovico   Escriva   -C:\Users\Govert\Desktop\Signatura   comienzo 19.11.2019\EscrivaLudovico1537y21kb.txt 0.42805546149807594
13.   Luis   de   Lucena   -C:\Users\Govert\Desktop\Signatura   comienzo 19.11.2019\LuisdeLucenaParteTestamento14kb.txt 0.4375288026182492

14. Diego Hurtado de Mendoza -C:\Users\Govert\Desktop\Signatura comienzo 19.11.2019\diegohurtadodemendoza granada171kb.txt 0.4382116613334095

15. Juan de Sedeño -C:\Users\Govert\Desktop\Signatura comienzo 19.11.2019\sedeño summaEpistolaobra54kb.txt 0.4386014566180053

16. Lucena -C:\Users\Govert\Desktop\Signatura comienzo 19.11.2019\repeticionamores114kb.txt 0.44322001538262723

17. Francisco Cervantes de Salazar -C:\Users\Govert\Desktop\Signatura comienzo 19.11.2019\CervantesSalazarCronicaNuevEspaña21kb.txt 0.4458477149466945

18. Hernán Núñez -C:\Users\Govert\Desktop\Signatura comienzo 19.11.2019\hernannuñez Trescientas120kb.txt 0.4462147038072072

19. Juan Ramírez de Lucena -C:\Users\Govert\Desktop\Signatura comienzo 19.11.2019\vita beata131kb.txt 0.4487088118420526

20. Lucas Fernández -C:\Users\Govert\Desktop\Signatura comienzo 19.11.2019\lucasfernandez dereniego del amor169kb.txt 0.4531582688954007

21. Fernando de Rojas -C:\Users\Govert\Desktop\Signatura comienzo 19.11.2019\fernando de rojas14kb test2.txt 0.4542454091715462

22. Juan Agüero de Trasmiera -C:\Users\Govert\Desktop\Signatura comienzo 19.11.2019\trasmiera salamanca21kb.txt 0.4544605946253095

23. Jerónimo Fernández -C:\Users\Govert\Desktop\Signatura comienzo 19.11.2019\jeronimofernandez3año1579-113kb.txt 0.46210389143433506

24. Gonzalo Fernández de Oviedo -C:\Users\Govert\Desktop\Signatura comienzo 19.11.2019\FernandezOviedoSumarioIndias21kb.txt 0.4659359925339701

25. Gil Vicente -C:\Users\Govert\Desktop\Signatura comienzo 19.11.2019\GilVicenteComediaViudo20kb.txt 0.46812874062182075

26. Juan Justiniano -C:\Users\Govert\Desktop\Signatura comienzo 19.11.2019\luisvivesformacionmujer84kb.txt 0.4699104575691122

27. Francisco Delicado -C:\Users\Govert\Desktop\Signatura comienzo 19.11.2019\lozanaepilogo5kb.txt 0.47139200531794667

28. Juan de Timoneda -C:\Users\Govert\Desktop\Signatura comienzo 19.11.2019\Timoneda Patrañuela30kb.txt 0.4757223941695716

29. Gonzalo Fernández de Oviedo -C:\Users\Govert\Desktop\Signatura comienzo 19.11.2019\fernandezoviedobatalla90-130tiene34kb.txt 0.47620520328749283

30. Juan de Sedeño -C:\Users\Govert\Desktop\Signatura comienzo 19.11.2019\sedeño summaPrologo y Epistola19kb.txt 0.4807534639520654

31. Juan Ramírez de Lucena -C:\Users\Govert\Desktop\Signatura comienzo 19.11.2019\Ramirez Lucena a Jorge Manrique.txt 0.4884031113097381

32. Alonso de Cardona -C:\Users\Govert\Desktop\Signatura comienzo 19.11.2019\alonsodecardona22kb.txt 0.49039461162727094

33. Francisco Delicado -C:\Users\Govert\Desktop\Signatura comienzo 19.11.2019\legno2 8kb.txt 0.49061288839337325

34. Feliciano de Silva -C:\Users\Govert\Desktop\Signatura comienzo 19.11.2019\Silva amadis de grecia20kb.txt 0.5013015832861514

35. Lope de Rueda -C:\Users\Govert\Desktop\Signatura comienzo 19.11.2019\lopederuedaAceitunas42kb.txt 0.5069808563783215

36. Diego de San Pedro -C:\Users\Govert\Desktop\Signatura comienzo 19.11.2019\arnalte obra completa120kb.txt 0.5072459552002399

37. Juan de Valdés -C:\Users\Govert\Desktop\Signatura comienzo 19.11.2019\ValdesJuanCartas1-3-completo114kb.txt 0.5079691100822483

38. Thebayda anónym -C:\Users\Govert\Desktop\Signatura comienzo 19.11.2019\thebaida incompleta 92kb.txt 0.5080112741521793

39. Francisco López de Villalobos -C:\Users\Govert\Desktop\Signatura comienzo 19.11.2019\villalobos obra completa costumbres humanas141kb.txt 0.5085328295063826

40. Juan del Encina -C:\Users\Govert\Desktop\Signatura comienzo 19.11.2019\encina textos al rey75kb.txt 0.5125825978336356

41. Gil Vicente -C:\Users\Govert\Desktop\Signatura comienzo 19.11.2019\GilVicente AutoPastoril1502 16kb.txt 0.516552615321921

42. Gonzalo Fernández de Oviedo -C:\Users\Govert\Desktop\Signatura comienzo 19.11.2019\FernandezOviedoClaribalte21kb.txt 0.5171009865196801

43. Alfonso de Valdés -C:\Users\Govert\Desktop\Signatura comienzo 19.11.2019\valdesAlfonsoCartas34kb.txt 0.5195071401800944

44. Francisco Delicado -C:\Users\Govert\Desktop\Signatura comienzo 19.11.2019\lozanaapologia6kb.txt 0.519955679689984

45. Juan de Timoneda -C:\Users\Govert\Desktop\Signatura comienzo 19.11.2019\TimonedaCaminantes21kb.txt 0.5214197136296431

46. Sancho Muñón -C:\Users\Govert\Desktop\Signatura comienzo 19.11.2019\Acevedo Celestina151kb.txt 0.526390793647054

47. Hernán Pérez de Olivia -C:\Users\Govert\Desktop\Signatura comienzo 19.11.2019\perezolivaRioGuadalquivirRazonamiento23kb.txt 0.5268595739630422

48. Gil Vicente -C:\Users\Govert\Desktop\Signatura comienzo 19.11.2019\GilVicenteCuatroTiempos21kb.txt 0.5271225028460371

49. Nicolás Núñez -C:\Users\Govert\Desktop\Signatura comienzo 19.11.2019\NicolasNuñezTractado32kb.txt 0.5275427358859021

50. Juan Huarte de San Juan -C:\Users\Govert\Desktop\Signatura comienzo 19.11.2019\HuarteExamen Ingenios21kb.txt 0.5289459295645542

51. Juan Paez de Castro -C:\Users\Govert\Desktop\Signatura comienzo 19.11.2019\juanpaezdecastroCartas23kb.txt 0.5305802786815266

52. Diego de San Pedro -C:\Users\Govert\Desktop\Signatura comienzo 19.11.2019\carceldeamor obra completa134kb.txt 0.5314740362471243

53. Juan del Encina -C:\Users\Govert\Desktop\Signatura comienzo 19.11.2019\Encina eglogasantes1509 num3-40kb.txt 0.5332699178231338

54. Lope de Rueda -C:\Users\Govert\Desktop\Signatura comienzo 19.11.2019\LopedeRuedaEufemia37kb.txt 0.5361729999624287

55. Juan Ramírez de Lucena -C:\Users\Govert\Desktop\Signatura comienzo 19.11.2019\RamirezLucena a galardones.txt 0.538660777571675

56. Bernardo de Quirós -C:\Users\Govert\Desktop\Signatura comienzo 19.11.2019\VillalonViajeTurquiaVillalon109kb.txt 0.5397419096910401

57. Gil Vicente -C:\Users\Govert\Desktop\Signatura comienzo 19.11.2019\GilVicenteSibila31kb.txt 0.5409087449463815

58. Juan Ramírez de Lucena -C:\Users\Govert\Desktop\Signatura comienzo 19.11.2019\RamirezLucena a Zapata.txt 0.5410832164145156

59. Juan Ramírez de Lucena -C:\Users\Govert\Desktop\Signatura comienzo 19.11.2019\Ramirez Lucena exhortatoria.txt 0.5411016712424923

60. Alonso Núñez de Reinoso -C:\Users\Govert\Desktop\Signatura comienzo 19.11.2019\clareoyfloriseaReinoso132kb.txt 0.5433817329091546

61. Juan de Flores -C:\Users\Govert\Desktop\Signatura comienzo 19.11.2019\griselobra89kb.txt 0.5440703955296726

62. Ramón de Petras -C:\Users\Govert\Desktop\Signatura comienzo 19.11.2019\traso auto11kb.txt 0.5483693452707781

63. Gil Vicente -C:\Users\Govert\Desktop\Signatura comienzo 19.11.2019\GilVicente Don Duardos65kb.txt 0.5537000064609792

64. Juan de Timoneda -C:\Users\Govert\Desktop\Signatura comienzo 19.11.2019\timonedalibrodamas21kb.txt 0.5646197178967154

65. Juan de Flores -C:\Users\Govert\Desktop\Signatura comienzo 19.11.2019\grimalteobra21kb.txt 0.5650117132890646

66. Sebastián de Horozco -C:\Users\Govert\Desktop\Signatura comienzo 19.11.2019\HorozcoRuth.txt 0.5651717901743865

67. Gáspar Gómez de Toledo -C:\Users\Govert\Desktop\Signatura comienzo 19.11.2019\gaspargomezdeToledoObra23kb.txt 0.5713577633919051

68. Sebastián de Horozco -C:\Users\Govert\Desktop\Signatura comienzo 19.11.2019\HorozcoEntremeses.txt 0.5731878907100085

69. Juan de Valdés -C:\Users\Govert\Desktop\Signatura comienzo 19.11.2019\ValdesJuan doctrinacristiana75kb.txt 0.5765157760383287

70. Sebastián de Horozco -C:\Users\Govert\Desktop\Signatura comienzo 19.11.2019\HorozcoHistoriaEvangelica.txt 0.5776899161343528

71. Feliciano de Silva -C:\Users\Govert\Desktop\Signatura comienzo 19.11.2019\Silva Celestina Segunda Parcial177kb.txt 0.5792598834787367

72. Francisco Delicado -C:\Users\Govert\Desktop\Signatura comienzo 19.11.2019\lozanaepistola3kb.txt 0.5872419780562781

73. Juan de Sedeño -C:\Users\Govert\Desktop\Signatura comienzo 19.11.2019\sedeñocalisto111kb.txt 0.5875206561094511

74. Hernando de Castillo -C:\Users\Govert\Desktop\Signatura comienzo 19.11.2019\hernando de castillo prologo6kb.txt 0.5943464039112674

75. Juan de Segura -C:\Users\Govert\Desktop\Signatura comienzo 19.11.2019\JuandeSeguraQuejayAvisoContraElAmor21kb.txt 0.598318988476441

76. Francisco Delicado -C:\Users\Govert\Desktop\Signatura comienzo 19.11.2019\lozanadedicatoria2kb.txt 0.6044020512338653

77. Hernán Pérez de Olivia -C:\Users\Govert\Desktop\Signatura comienzo 19.11.2019\perezolivaSalamanca Razonamiento24 kb.txt 0.6055079950942351

78. Francisco Delicado -C:\Users\Govert\Desktop\Signatura comienzo 19.11.2019\lozano54kb.txt 0.6150610405570045

79. Francisco Delicado -C:\Users\Govert\Desktop\Signatura comienzo 19.11.2019\lozanaargumento3kb.txt 0.6592269088218838

80. Juan Ramírez de Lucena -C:\Users\Govert\Desktop\Signatura comienzo 19.11.2019\ramirezlucenaJuanOratioEmbajadores1472.txt 0.8167762907494955

15.4.4 1512 Damiano, foreword in book

damianoforeword1.txt   C:\Users\Govert\Desktop\Signatura   comienzo 19.11.2019\damianoforeword1.txt
Canonicizers:
    Normalize Whitespace
EventDrivers:
    Character NGrams n : 4
        EventCullers:
            Most Common Events numevents : 50
Analysis:
    Nearest Neighbor Driver with metric Cosine Distance
1.   Fernando   de   Rojas   -C:\Users\Govert\Desktop\Signatura   comienzo 19.11.2019\fernando de rojas14kb test2.txt 0.2586989689310163
2. Hernán Díaz -C:\Users\Govert\Desktop\Signatura comienzo 19.11.2019\peregrino obra135kb.txt 0.2606640615314201
3.   La   Celestina   -C:\Users\Govert\Desktop\Signatura   comienzo 19.11.2019\CelestinaMs1520TextoCorrecto27kb.txt 0.26070913309176436
4. Gonzalo Fernández de Oviedo -C:\Users\Govert\Desktop\Signatura comienzo 19.11.2019\fernandezOviedo-indias 21kb.txt 0.27525297709119025
5. Juan de Sedeño -C:\Users\Govert\Desktop\Signatura comienzo 19.11.2019\sedeño summaEpistolaobra54kb.txt 0.2883364562818139
6.   Jerónimo   Fernández   -C:\Users\Govert\Desktop\Signatura   comienzo 19.11.2019\jeronimofernandezhector1547-5-17kb.txt 0.291757129486764
7. Juan de Sedeño -C:\Users\Govert\Desktop\Signatura comienzo 19.11.2019\sedeño summaaobra21kb.txt 0.29974148465925654
8. Diego Hurtado de Mendoza -C:\Users\Govert\Desktop\Signatura comienzo 19.11.2019\diegohurtadodemendoza granada171kb.txt 0.29979570364760433
9.   Alonso   de   Proaza   -C:\Users\Govert\Desktop\Signatura   comienzo 19.11.2019\alonsodeproazaProsa no Celestina-12kb.txt 0.3097351458565023
10. Francisco Cervantes de Salazar -C:\Users\Govert\Desktop\Signatura comienzo 19.11.2019\CervantesSalazarCronicaNuevEspaña21kb.txt 0.319912982133695
11. Juan Agüero de Trasmiera -C:\Users\Govert\Desktop\Signatura comienzo 19.11.2019\trasmiera salamanca21kb.txt 0.3223969736924962
12.   Luis   de   Lucena   -C:\Users\Govert\Desktop\Signatura   comienzo 19.11.2019\LuisdeLucenaParteTestamento14kb.txt 0.3289513804577041
13.   Lucas   Fernández   -C:\Users\Govert\Desktop\Signatura   comienzo 19.11.2019\lucasfernandez dereniego del amor169kb.txt 0.3356695858272126

14. Hernán Núñez -C:\Users\Govert\Desktop\Signatura comienzo 19.11.2019\hernannuñez Trescientas120kb.txt 0.33651014415687286

15. Juan de Sedeño -C:\Users\Govert\Desktop\Signatura comienzo 19.11.2019\sedeñoAmores Buenaventurança26kb.txt 0.3371292758977912

16. Juan de Timoneda -C:\Users\Govert\Desktop\Signatura comienzo 19.11.2019\Timoneda Patrañuela30kb.txt 0.3399787307183919

17. Juan de Sedeño -C:\Users\Govert\Desktop\Signatura comienzo 19.11.2019\sedeño summaPrologo y Epistola19kb.txt 0.34403886461083477

18. Juan Justiniano -C:\Users\Govert\Desktop\Signatura comienzo 19.11.2019\luisvivesformacionmujer84kb.txt 0.3441269529886217

19. Jerónimo Fernández -C:\Users\Govert\Desktop\Signatura comienzo 19.11.2019\jeronimofernandez3año1579-113kb.txt 0.3607868369211392

20. Lucena -C:\Users\Govert\Desktop\Signatura comienzo 19.11.2019\repeticionamores114kb.txt 0.3609444196423043

21. Gonzalo García de Santa María -C:\Users\Govert\Desktop\Signatura comienzo 19.11.2019\GarciaSantaMariaCoronicaAragonObra27kb.txt 0.36795871350328946

22. Gil Vicente -C:\Users\Govert\Desktop\Signatura comienzo 19.11.2019\GilVicenteComediaViudo20kb.txt 0.3701349117618824

23. Alonso de Cardona -C:\Users\Govert\Desktop\Signatura comienzo 19.11.2019\alonsodecardona22kb.txt 0.37302669183077986

24. Lucena -C:\Users\Govert\Desktop\Signatura comienzo 19.11.2019\repeticionamores ajedrez4kb.txt 0.3763653115804183

25. La Celestina -C:\Users\Govert\Desktop\Signatura comienzo 19.11.2019\CelestinaComedia-1.txt 0.38098795185359025

26. Gonzalo Fernández de Oviedo -C:\Users\Govert\Desktop\Signatura comienzo 19.11.2019\FernandezOviedoSumarioIndias21kb.txt 0.3824877048913704

27. Lope de Rueda -C:\Users\Govert\Desktop\Signatura comienzo 19.11.2019\lopederuedaAceitunas42kb.txt 0.38353636670999935

28. Thebayda anónym -C:\Users\Govert\Desktop\Signatura comienzo 19.11.2019\thebaida incompleta 92kb.txt 0.38848642598151695

29. Hernán Pérez de Olivia -C:\Users\Govert\Desktop\Signatura comienzo 19.11.2019\perezolivaRioGuadalquivirRazonamiento23kb.txt 0.39113824323199353

30. Feliciano de Silva -C:\Users\Govert\Desktop\Signatura comienzo 19.11.2019\Silva amadis de grecia20kb.txt 0.3929374589072103

31. Juan del Encina -C:\Users\Govert\Desktop\Signatura comienzo 19.11.2019\encina textos al rey75kb.txt 0.39316460435595424

32. Juan Ramírez de Lucena -C:\Users\Govert\Desktop\Signatura comienzo 19.11.2019\vita beata131kb.txt 0.39438631199250396

33. Francisco Delicado -C:\Users\Govert\Desktop\Signatura comienzo 19.11.2019\legno2 8kb.txt 0.4007328341769736

34. Lope de Rueda -C:\Users\Govert\Desktop\Signatura comienzo 19.11.2019\LopedeRuedaEufemia37kb.txt 0.4026248752314301

35. Diego de San Pedro -C:\Users\Govert\Desktop\Signatura comienzo 19.11.2019\arnalte obra completa120kb.txt 0.4030159577951744

36. Gonzalo Fernández de Oviedo -C:\Users\Govert\Desktop\Signatura comienzo 19.11.2019\FernandezOviedoClaribalte21kb.txt 0.40654361011551854

37. Juan Ramírez de Lucena -C:\Users\Govert\Desktop\Signatura comienzo 19.11.2019\Ramirez Lucena a Jorge Manrique.txt 0.40939966700718144

38. Alonso Núñez de Reinoso -C:\Users\Govert\Desktop\Signatura comienzo 19.11.2019\clareoyfloriseaReinoso132kb.txt 0.4097819508026739

39. Juan Paez de Castro -C:\Users\Govert\Desktop\Signatura comienzo 19.11.2019\juanpaezdecastroCartas23kb.txt 0.41055127357386567

40. Juan Huarte de San Juan -C:\Users\Govert\Desktop\Signatura comienzo 19.11.2019\HuarteExamen Ingenios21kb.txt 0.41374782190534587

41. Juan de Valdés -C:\Users\Govert\Desktop\Signatura comienzo 19.11.2019\ValdesJuanCartas1-3-completo114kb.txt 0.41391438242033796

42. Gonzalo Fernández de Oviedo -C:\Users\Govert\Desktop\Signatura comienzo 19.11.2019\fernandezoviedobatalla90-130tiene34kb.txt 0.41472081964040175

43. Juan de Timoneda -C:\Users\Govert\Desktop\Signatura comienzo 19.11.2019\TimonedaCaminantes21kb.txt 0.4150417577507731

44. Sancho Muñón -C:\Users\Govert\Desktop\Signatura comienzo 19.11.2019\Acevedo Celestina151kb.txt 0.4152774911402676

45. Juan de Timoneda -C:\Users\Govert\Desktop\Signatura comienzo 19.11.2019\Timoneda Disculpa7kb.txt 0.4184626048529757

46. Bernardo de Quirós -C:\Users\Govert\Desktop\Signatura comienzo 19.11.2019\VillalonViajeTurquiaVillalon109kb.txt 0.41998221795182844

47. Ludovico Escriva -C:\Users\Govert\Desktop\Signatura comienzo 19.11.2019\EscrivaLudovico1537y21kb.txt 0.4216206528650207

48. Gil Vicente -C:\Users\Govert\Desktop\Signatura comienzo 19.11.2019\GilVicenteSibila31kb.txt 0.4233915058583778

49. Diego de San Pedro -C:\Users\Govert\Desktop\Signatura comienzo 19.11.2019\carceldeamor obra completa134kb.txt 0.4248981963004901

50. Francisco Delicado -C:\Users\Govert\Desktop\Signatura comienzo 19.11.2019\lozanaepilogo5kb.txt 0.4272482511641271

51. Gil Vicente -C:\Users\Govert\Desktop\Signatura comienzo 19.11.2019\GilVicenteCuatroTiempos21kb.txt 0.4364177288263513

52. Francisco López de Villalobos -C:\Users\Govert\Desktop\Signatura comienzo 19.11.2019\villalobos obra completa costumbres humanas141kb.txt 0.43667119731284365

53. Alfonso de Valdés -C:\Users\Govert\Desktop\Signatura comienzo 19.11.2019\valdesAlfonsoCartas34kb.txt 0.43798162311624667

54. Juan de Flores -C:\Users\Govert\Desktop\Signatura comienzo 19.11.2019\griselobra89kb.txt 0.4385915767192996

55. Ramón de Petras -C:\Users\Govert\Desktop\Signatura comienzo 19.11.2019\traso auto11kb.txt 0.43944003938238774

56. Juan Ramírez de Lucena -C:\Users\Govert\Desktop\Signatura comienzo 19.11.2019\RamirezLucena a Zapata.txt 0.4494938239903603

57. Juan Ramírez de Lucena -C:\Users\Govert\Desktop\Signatura comienzo 19.11.2019\Ramirez Lucena exhortatoria.txt 0.4502375310539103

284

58. Hernán Pérez de Olivia -C:\Users\Govert\Desktop\Signatura comienzo 19.11.2019\perezolivaSalamanca Razonamiento24 kb.txt 0.45230231438241975

59. Gil Vicente -C:\Users\Govert\Desktop\Signatura comienzo 19.11.2019\GilVicente Don Duardos65kb.txt 0.4565739737754586

60. Sebastián de Horozco -C:\Users\Govert\Desktop\Signatura comienzo 19.11.2019\HorozcoRuth.txt 0.45678629687936734

61. Nicolás Núñez -C:\Users\Govert\Desktop\Signatura comienzo 19.11.2019\NicolasNuñezTractado32kb.txt 0.45679812890507754

62. Juan de Flores -C:\Users\Govert\Desktop\Signatura comienzo 19.11.2019\grimalteobra21kb.txt 0.4615990171746709

63. Gil Vicente -C:\Users\Govert\Desktop\Signatura comienzo 19.11.2019\GilVicente AutoPastoril1502 16kb.txt 0.4627220286311635

64. Hernando de Castillo -C:\Users\Govert\Desktop\Signatura comienzo 19.11.2019\hernando de castillo prologo6kb.txt 0.46669840973976673

65. Juan del Encina -C:\Users\Govert\Desktop\Signatura comienzo 19.11.2019\Encina eglogasantes1509 num3-40kb.txt 0.46683565320850506

66. Juan Ramírez de Lucena -C:\Users\Govert\Desktop\Signatura comienzo 19.11.2019\RamirezLucena a galardones.txt 0.4720572528791269

67. Gáspar Gómez de Toledo -C:\Users\Govert\Desktop\Signatura comienzo 19.11.2019\gaspargomezdeToledoObra23kb.txt 0.4746566695622394

68. Sebastián de Horozco -C:\Users\Govert\Desktop\Signatura comienzo 19.11.2019\HorozcoEntremeses.txt 0.4776809908514521

69. Juan de Valdés -C:\Users\Govert\Desktop\Signatura comienzo 19.11.2019\ValdesJuan doctrinacristiana75kb.txt 0.4838346218790829

70. Juan de Segura -C:\Users\Govert\Desktop\Signatura comienzo 19.11.2019\JuandeSeguraQuejayAvisoContraElAmor21kb.txt 0.49166320261361884

71. Juan de Sedeño -C:\Users\Govert\Desktop\Signatura comienzo 19.11.2019\sedeñocalisto111kb.txt 0.49394183297458893

72. Feliciano de Silva -C:\Users\Govert\Desktop\Signatura comienzo 19.11.2019\Silva Celestina Segunda Parcial177kb.txt 0.4976844568542631

73. Francisco Delicado -C:\Users\Govert\Desktop\Signatura comienzo 19.11.2019\lozano54kb.txt 0.49948889761952053

74. Sebastián de Horozco -C:\Users\Govert\Desktop\Signatura comienzo 19.11.2019\HorozcoHistoriaEvangelica.txt 0.5071781831549504

75. Francisco Delicado -C:\Users\Govert\Desktop\Signatura comienzo 19.11.2019\lozanadedicatoria2kb.txt 0.5109674935842439

76. Francisco Delicado -C:\Users\Govert\Desktop\Signatura comienzo 19.11.2019\lozanaepistola3kb.txt 0.5145451509197912

77. Francisco Delicado -C:\Users\Govert\Desktop\Signatura comienzo 19.11.2019\lozanaapologia6kb.txt 0.5277992043401212

78. Juan de Timoneda -C:\Users\Govert\Desktop\Signatura comienzo 19.11.2019\timonedalibrodamas21kb.txt 0.5624878251053402

79. Francisco Delicado -C:\Users\Govert\Desktop\Signatura comienzo 19.11.2019\lozanaargumento3kb.txt 0.6021851019851523

80. Juan Ramírez de Lucena -C:\Users\Govert\Desktop\Signatura comienzo 19.11.2019\ramirezlucenaJuanOratioEmbajadores1472.txt 0.6664355863385085

15.4.5 Poem addressed to Lucrecia Borgia

Arnalte lucrecia 1521.txt C:\Users\Govert\Desktop\Signatura comienzo 19.11.2019\Arnalte lucrecia 1521.txt
Canonicizers:
    Normalize Whitespace
EventDrivers:
    Character NGrams n : 4
        EventCullers:
            Most Common Events numevents : 50
Analysis:
    Nearest Neighbor Driver with metric Cosine Distance
1. La Celestina -C:\Users\Govert\Desktop\Signatura comienzo 19.11.2019\CelestinaPrologo9kb.txt 0.07832556978233507
2. Juan del Encina -C:\Users\Govert\Desktop\Signatura comienzo 19.11.2019\EncinaCancioneroReyesProhemio7kb.txt 0.08530213170144452
3. Diego Hurtado de Mendoza -C:\Users\Govert\Desktop\Signatura comienzo 19.11.2019\diegohurtadodemendoza granada47kb.txt 0.09011655900782356
4. Juan Justaniano -C:\Users\Govert\Desktop\Signatura comienzo 19.11.2019\luisvives formacion21kb.txt 0.09714091738631991
5. Hernán Núñez -C:\Users\Govert\Desktop\Signatura comienzo 19.11.2019\hernannuñez Trescientas21.txt 0.09944188395710407
6. Juan de Sedeño -C:\Users\Govert\Desktop\Signatura comienzo 19.11.2019\sedeño summaPrologo y Epistola19kb.txt 0.10655312342249601
7. Juan de Sedeño -C:\Users\Govert\Desktop\Signatura comienzo 19.11.2019\sedeño summaEpistolaobra54kb.txt 0.1102814383884616
8. Juan Ramírez de Lucena -C:\Users\Govert\Desktop\Signatura comienzo 19.11.2019\vita beata21kb.txt 0.11176080659837928
9. Prologos Fernández de Oviedo -C:\Users\Govert\Desktop\Signatura comienzo 19.11.2019\PrologosFernandezOviedo2-93kb.txt 0.11361957064538308
10. Ludovico Escriva -C:\Users\Govert\Desktop\Signatura comienzo 19.11.2019\EscrivaLudovico1537y21kb.txt 0.1136606676409827
11. Fray Antonio de Guevara -C:\Users\Govert\Desktop\Signatura comienzo 19.11.2019\GuevaraMarcoAurelioObra22kb.txt 0.11393222982776452
12. Jerónimo Fernández -C:\Users\Govert\Desktop\Signatura comienzo 19.11.2019\jeronimofernandez3año1579-113kb.txt 0.1167682117466099
13. Juan del Encina -C:\Users\Govert\Desktop\Signatura comienzo 19.11.2019\EncinaBubolicaPrincipePrologo8kb.txt 0.1206774419106561

14. Juan del Encina -C:\Users\Govert\Desktop\Signatura comienzo 19.11.2019\EncinaBubolicaReyesPrologo8kb.txt 0.12167148245515469

15. Juan del Encina -C:\Users\Govert\Desktop\Signatura comienzo 19.11.2019\EncinaCancioneroPrincipeProhemio29kb.txt 0.1221043083801826

16. Hernán Diaz -C:\Users\Govert\Desktop\Signatura comienzo 19.11.2019\peregrino obra135kb.txt 0.12237378149729317

17. Lucena -C:\Users\Govert\Desktop\Signatura comienzo 19.11.2019\repamores mitad libro51kb.txt 0.12285790863187773

18. Gonzalo Fernández de Oviedo -C:\Users\Govert\Desktop\Signatura comienzo 19.11.2019\FernandezOviedoSumarioIndias27kb.txt 0.12337930650428897

19. Juan Ramírez de Lucena -C:\Users\Govert\Desktop\Signatura comienzo 19.11.2019\RamirezLucena a galardones.txt 0.12389428514304879

20. Diego de San Pedro -C:\Users\Govert\Desktop\Signatura comienzo 19.11.2019\arnalte incompleta21kb.txt 0.130457992233592

21. Francisco Delicado -C:\Users\Govert\Desktop\Signatura comienzo 19.11.2019\lozanaepilogo5kb.txt 0.13209635931895625

22. Hernán Pérez de Olivia -C:\Users\Govert\Desktop\Signatura comienzo 19.11.2019\perezolivaRioGuadalquivirRazonamiento23kb.txt 0.13271241775338938

23. Feliciano de Silva -C:\Users\Govert\Desktop\Signatura comienzo 19.11.2019\Silva amadis de grecia20kb.txt 0.13297435379887967

24. Francisco de Osuna -C:\Users\Govert\Desktop\Signatura comienzo 19.11.2019\OsunaTerceraParteAbecedario64kb.txt 0.1356465817050012

25. Jerónimo de Urrea -C:\Users\Govert\Desktop\Signatura comienzo 19.11.2019\UrreaJeronimoOrlandoFuriosoTraduccion22kb.txt 0.13698470128818185

26. Juan del Encina -C:\Users\Govert\Desktop\Signatura comienzo 19.11.2019\EncinaCancioneroAlbaPrologo6kb.txt 0.1381686356586712

27. Jerónimo de Urrea -C:\Users\Govert\Desktop\Signatura comienzo 19.11.2019\UrreaJeronimoClarisel42kb.txt 0.14045359860200268

28. Francisco de Osuna -C:\Users\Govert\Desktop\Signatura comienzo 19.11.2019\OsunaTerceraParteAbecedarioPrologo13kb.txt 0.1424579808200338

29. Gil Vicente -C:\Users\Govert\Desktop\Signatura comienzo 19.11.2019\GilVicenteCuatroTiempos21kb.txt 0.14259121510707606

30. Francisco López de Villalobos -C:\Users\Govert\Desktop\Signatura comienzo 19.11.2019\villaloboscostumbres humanas21kb.txt 0.14268436945826102

31. Gonzalo de Ayora -C:\Users\Govert\Desktop\Signatura comienzo 19.11.2019\gonzaloayoraAvila67kb.txt 0.14496169223092614

32. Jerónimo Fernández -C:\Users\Govert\Desktop\Signatura comienzo 19.11.2019\jeronimofernandezhector1547-5-17kb.txt 0.14518642680166027

33. Francisco Delicado -C:\Users\Govert\Desktop\Signatura comienzo 19.11.2019\legno2 8kb.txt 0.14551336674271875

34. Cristóbal de Castellejo -C:\Users\Govert\Desktop\Signatura comienzo 19.11.2019\CristobalCastellejoAulaCortesano21kb.txt 0.14727902998513975

35. Juan Agüero de Trasmiera -C:\Users\Govert\Desktop\Signatura comienzo 19.11.2019\trasmiera salamanca21kb.txt 0.14731329485087574

36. Cristóbal de Castellejo -C:\Users\Govert\Desktop\Signatura comienzo 19.11.2019\CristobalCastillejoDialogoSobreMujeres21kb.txt 0.14895377104205676

37. Sancho de Muñón -C:\Users\Govert\Desktop\Signatura comienzo 19.11.2019\Acevedo Celestina corto21kb.txt 0.1490875214446269

38. Bartolomé de las Casas -C:\Users\Govert\Desktop\Signatura comienzo 19.11.2019\BartolomeDeLasCasasBrevisimak34b.txt 0.15067695101835687

39. Juan del Encina -C:\Users\Govert\Desktop\Signatura comienzo 19.11.2019\encina eglogas antes 1509-287kb.txt 0.15402043073704452

40. Baltasar del Rio -C:\Users\Govert\Desktop\Signatura comienzo 19.11.2019\baltasardelrio1504Tratado22kb.txt 0.15570846664130789

41. La Celestina -C:\Users\Govert\Desktop\Signatura comienzo 19.11.2019\CelestinaComedia-1.txt 0.15762438391416622

42. Francisco Cervantes de Salazar -C:\Users\Govert\Desktop\Signatura comienzo 19.11.2019\CervantesSalazarCronicaNuevEspaña21kb.txt 0.15789411913913842

43. Cristóbal de Castellejo -C:\Users\Govert\Desktop\Signatura comienzo 19.11.2019\CristobalCastillejoDialogodeMujeres21kb.txt 0.1586074503433944

44. Juan del Encina -C:\Users\Govert\Desktop\Signatura comienzo 19.11.2019\encina1521-8kb.txt 0.1602262274071894

45. Juan de Boscan -C:\Users\Govert\Desktop\Signatura comienzo 19.11.2019\BoscanElCortesano47kb.txt 0.16033003907163523

46. Gonzalo Fernández de Oviedo -C:\Users\Govert\Desktop\Signatura comienzo 19.11.2019\fernandezoviedobatalla90-130tiene34kb.txt 0.16203723006924908

47. Hernando del Castillo -C:\Users\Govert\Desktop\Signatura comienzo 19.11.2019\hernando de castillo prologo6kb.txt 0.16315030575793066

48. Alonso de Proaza -C:\Users\Govert\Desktop\Signatura comienzo 19.11.2019\alonsodeproazaProsa no Celestina-12kb.txt 0.16317759068278792

49. Juan de Flores -C:\Users\Govert\Desktop\Signatura comienzo 19.11.2019\griselobra21kb.txt 0.16595348709661895

50. Gonzalo Fernández de Oviedo -C:\Users\Govert\Desktop\Signatura comienzo 19.11.2019\fernandezOviedo1532catálogo21kb.txt 0.16630244694968677

51. Francisco López de Villalobos -C:\Users\Govert\Desktop\Signatura comienzo 19.11.2019\VillalobosAnfitrionTextosProsa38kb.txt 0.1680915564429728

52. Gil Vicente -C:\Users\Govert\Desktop\Signatura comienzo 19.11.2019\GilVicenteComediaViudo20kb.txt 0.1704606136712956

53. Fray Antonio de Guevara -C:\Users\Govert\Desktop\Signatura comienzo 19.11.2019\guevaraEpistolasfamiliares21kb.txt 0.1722716956338337

54. Alonso Núñez de Reinoso -C:\Users\Govert\Desktop\Signatura comienzo 19.11.2019\clareoyfloriseaCorto21kb.txt 0.17336685271983598

55. Bernardo de Quirós -C:\Users\Govert\Desktop\Signatura comienzo 19.11.2019\VillalonViajeTurquiaVillalon109kb.txt 0.17656996279517279

56. Juan Ramírez de Lucena -C:\Users\Govert\Desktop\Signatura comienzo 19.11.2019\Ramirez Lucena exhortatoria.txt 0.18019258363807955

57. Juan Ramírez de Lucena -C:\Users\Govert\Desktop\Signatura comienzo 19.11.2019\RamirezLucena a Zapata.txt 0.1802192886245385

58. Francisco López de Villalobos -C:\Users\Govert\Desktop\Signatura comienzo 19.11.2019\VillalobosTresGrandesObra35kb.txt 0.18034374177805712

59. Hernando del Castillo -C:\Users\Govert\Desktop\Signatura comienzo 19.11.2019\Hernando de CastilloSantoDomingoObra5kb.txt 0.18041659394010578

60. Francisco López de Villalobos -C:\Users\Govert\Desktop\Signatura comienzo 19.11.2019\VillalobosTresGrandesObra21kb.txt 0.18102199462064572

61. Thebayda -C:\Users\Govert\Desktop\Signatura comienzo 19.11.2019\thebaida incompleta21kb.txt 0.18119890480383039

62. La Celestina -C:\Users\Govert\Desktop\Signatura comienzo 19.11.2019\carta celestina1501-3kb.txt 0.1823423763595453

63. Lucena -C:\Users\Govert\Desktop\Signatura comienzo 19.11.2019\repeticionamores ajedrez4kb.txt 0.18297277599399042

64. Gonzalo Fernández de Oviedo -C:\Users\Govert\Desktop\Signatura comienzo 19.11.2019\fernandezOviedo-indias 21kb.txt 0.18301761178490084

65. Juan de Sedeño -C:\Users\Govert\Desktop\Signatura comienzo 19.11.2019\sedeñoAmores Buenaventurança26kb.txt 0.1841604929371392

66. Gil Vicente -C:\Users\Govert\Desktop\Signatura comienzo 19.11.2019\GilVicenteSibila31kb.txt 0.18452937962063498

67. Hernán Pérez de Olivia -C:\Users\Govert\Desktop\Signatura comienzo 19.11.2019\perezolivaSalamanca Razonamiento24 kb.txt 0.18589186801657287

68. Lope de Rueda -C:\Users\Govert\Desktop\Signatura comienzo 19.11.2019\lopederuedaAceitunas42kb.txt 0.18605441788234034

69. Luis de Lucena -C:\Users\Govert\Desktop\Signatura comienzo 19.11.2019\LuisdeLucenaParteTestamento14kb.txt 0.18721094432815488

70. Juan Paez de Castro -C:\Users\Govert\Desktop\Signatura comienzo 19.11.2019\juanpaezdecastroCartas23kb.txt 0.1945115011814924

71. Gil Vicente -C:\Users\Govert\Desktop\Signatura comienzo 19.11.2019\GilVicente Don Duardos65kb.txt 0.19561703292276633

72. Gonzalo de Ayora -C:\Users\Govert\Desktop\Signatura comienzo 19.11.2019\GonzaloAyoraA MiguelPerezAlmazan15kb.txt 0.19640356986521024

73. Diego de San Pedro -C:\Users\Govert\Desktop\Signatura comienzo 19.11.2019\carceldeamor21kb.txt 0.19677077901765605

74. Gonzalo García Santa Maria -C:\Users\Govert\Desktop\Signatura comienzo 19.11.2019\GarciaSantaMariaCoronicaAragonObra27kb.txt 0.1996407522495457

75. Ramón de Petras -C:\Users\Govert\Desktop\Signatura comienzo 19.11.2019\traso auto11kb.txt 0.20484108575632287

76. La Celestina -C:\Users\Govert\Desktop\Signatura comienzo 19.11.2019\CelestinaMs1520TextoCorrecto27kb.txt 0.20809734639072752

77. Jorge de Montemayor -C:\Users\Govert\Desktop\Signatura comienzo 19.11.2019\MontemayorDianaObra73kb.txt 0.20821315391045092

78. Juan de Flores -C:\Users\Govert\Desktop\Signatura comienzo 19.11.2019\grimalteobra21kb.txt 0.20827780963092613

79. Juan del Encina -C:\Users\Govert\Desktop\Signatura comienzo 19.11.2019\EncinaCancioneroAlbaHijoPrologo4kb.txt 0.20838312140814874

80. Gil Vicente -C:\Users\Govert\Desktop\Signatura comienzo 19.11.2019\GilVicente AutoPastoril1502 16kb.txt 0.209152086849141

81. Centurio 1507 -C:\Users\Govert\Desktop\Signatura comienzo 19.11.2019\Celestina viejos archivos\celestina cap15-19 Centurio.txt 0.21091572722520802

82. Gonzalo Fernández de Oviedo -C:\Users\Govert\Desktop\Signatura comienzo 19.11.2019\FernandezOviedoClaribalte21kb.txt 0.21108127776164853

83. Juan de Timoneda -C:\Users\Govert\Desktop\Signatura comienzo 19.11.2019\TimonedaCaminantes21kb.txt 0.2111964007372802

84. Gonzalo de Ayora -C:\Users\Govert\Desktop\Signatura comienzo 19.11.2019\GonzaloAyora79kb.txt 0.21184108273829938

85. Lucas Fernández -C:\Users\Govert\Desktop\Signatura comienzo 19.11.2019\lucasfernandez dereniego del amor21kb.txt 0.21373799717029873

86. Juan de Valdés -C:\Users\Govert\Desktop\Signatura comienzo 19.11.2019\ValdesJuan doctrinacristiana75kb.txt 0.21416356562909666

87. Juan Manuel Calvete de Estrella -C:\Users\Govert\Desktop\Signatura comienzo 19.11.2019\CalveteEstrellaViajeDonFelipe53kb.txt 0.21470725602014562

88. Lope de Rueda -C:\Users\Govert\Desktop\Signatura comienzo 19.11.2019\LopedeRuedaEufemia37kb.txt 0.21494093392961833

89. Hernando del Castillo -C:\Users\Govert\Desktop\Signatura comienzo 19.11.2019\Hernando de CastilloSantoDomingoLector9kb.txt 0.21640615175383782

90. Alfonso de Valdés -C:\Users\Govert\Desktop\Signatura comienzo 19.11.2019\valdesAlfonsoCartas34kb.txt 0.21871369124315077

91. Francisco Delicado -C:\Users\Govert\Desktop\Signatura comienzo 19.11.2019\lozanaapologia6kb.txt 0.22375450451532863

92. Alonso de Cardona -C:\Users\Govert\Desktop\Signatura comienzo 19.11.2019\alonsodecardona22kb.txt 0.22609117557459002

93. Juan de Sedeño -C:\Users\Govert\Desktop\Signatura comienzo 19.11.2019\sedeñocalisto111kb.txt 0.2271010025425314

94. manual de mujeres -C:\Users\Govert\Desktop\Signatura comienzo 19.11.2019\manualdemujeres21kb.txt 0.23110079965475272

95. Juan de Valdés -C:\Users\Govert\Desktop\Signatura comienzo 19.11.2019\ValdesJuanCartas1-3-completo114kb.txt 0.23615832383560809

96. Sebastián de Horozco -C:\Users\Govert\Desktop\Signatura comienzo 19.11.2019\HorozcoEntremeses.txt 0.23706382382379465

97. Feliciano de Silva -C:\Users\Govert\Desktop\Signatura comienzo 19.11.2019\silva Celestina39kb.txt 0.24060074214952065

98. Sebastián de Horozco -C:\Users\Govert\Desktop\Signatura comienzo 19.11.2019\HorozcoRuth.txt 0.2419062210404237

99. Hernando del Castillo -C:\Users\Govert\Desktop\Signatura comienzo 19.11.2019\hernando de castillo1527 prologo5kb.txt 0.24598101536450867

100. Fernando de Rojas -C:\Users\Govert\Desktop\Signatura comienzo 19.11.2019\fernando de rojas14kb test2.txt 0.25048177327971044

101. Nicolás Núñez -C:\Users\Govert\Desktop\Signatura comienzo 19.11.2019\NicolasNuñezTractado32kb.txt 0.25155737255366006

102.   Francisco   Delicado   -C:\Users\Govert\Desktop\Signatura   comienzo 19.11.2019\lozanaepistola3kb.txt 0.2530349685437435
103.   Gáspar   de   Gómez   -C:\Users\Govert\Desktop\Signatura   comienzo 19.11.2019\gaspargomezdeToledoObra23kb.txt 0.2617833789164281
104.   Francisco   Delicado   -C:\Users\Govert\Desktop\Signatura   comienzo 19.11.2019\lozano54kb.txt 0.2627046090485986
105.   Sebastián   de   Horozco   -C:\Users\Govert\Desktop\Signatura   comienzo 19.11.2019\HorozcoHistoriaEvangelica.txt 0.26285090784123244
106.   Juan   de   Segura   -C:\Users\Govert\Desktop\Signatura   comienzo 19.11.2019\JuandeSeguraQuejayAvisoContraElAmor21kb.txt 0.29204673344023435

15.4.6 Poem to Lucrecia second analysis

Arnalte   lucrecia   1521.txt   C:\Users\Govert\Desktop\Signatura   comienzo 19.11.2019\Arnalte lucrecia 1521.txt
Canonicizers:
    Normalize Whitespace
EventDrivers:
    Character NGrams n : 4
        EventCullers:
            Most Common Events numevents : 50
Analysis:
    Nearest Neighbor Driver with metric Cosine Distance
1.   Juan   del   Encina   -C:\Users\Govert\Desktop\Signatura   comienzo 19.11.2019\EncinaCancioneroReyesProhemio7kb.txt 0.08605092528757474
2.   Juan   de   Flores   -C:\Users\Govert\Desktop\Signatura   comienzo 19.11.2019\triunfodeamor7kb.txt 0.10782178277868115
3.   La   Celestina   -C:\Users\Govert\Desktop\Signatura   comienzo 19.11.2019\CelestinaPrologo9kb.txt 0.11074236932639048
4.   Juan   del   Encina   -C:\Users\Govert\Desktop\Signatura   comienzo 19.11.2019\EncinaBubolicaPrincipePrologo8kb.txt 0.11150738900477641
5.   Juan   del   Encina   -C:\Users\Govert\Desktop\Signatura   comienzo 19.11.2019\EncinaBubolicaReyesPrologo8kb.txt 0.11506913203578473
6.   Juan   del   Encina   -C:\Users\Govert\Desktop\Signatura   comienzo 19.11.2019\EncinaCancioneroAlbaPrologo6kb.txt 0.11928096523618748
7.   Juan   de   Capua   -C:\Users\Govert\Desktop\Signatura   comienzo 19.11.2019\engañosypeligrosObra25kb.txt 0.12098643642150486
8.   Juan   Ramírez   de   Lucena   -C:\Users\Govert\Desktop\Signatura   comienzo 19.11.2019\vita beata21kb.txt 0.12108950371914062
9.   Boccaccio   -C:\Users\Govert\Desktop\Signatura   comienzo 19.11.2019\BoccaccioIlustresmujeresobra21kb.txt 0.12119891799050198

10. Hernán Núñez -C:\Users\Govert\Desktop\Signatura comienzo 19.11.2019\hernannuñez Trescientas21.txt 0.12130902597944704

11. Prologos Fernández de Oviedo -C:\Users\Govert\Desktop\Signatura comienzo 19.11.2019\PrologosFernandezOviedo2-93kb.txt 0.12377457488513699

12. Juan del Encina -C:\Users\Govert\Desktop\Signatura comienzo 19.11.2019\encinabubolicaArgumentos5kb.txt 0.12501500814153577

13. Pedro de Portugal -C:\Users\Govert\Desktop\Signatura comienzo 19.11.2019\condestablePortugalSatira90kb.txt 0.12692154518737886

14. Duobus amantibus -C:\Users\Govert\Desktop\Signatura comienzo 19.11.2019\piccolomini pp20 hasta30-21kb.txt 0.1348710193430427

15. Juan del Encina -C:\Users\Govert\Desktop\Signatura comienzo 19.11.2019\EncinaCancioneroPrincipeProhemio29kb.txt 0.13500092055691282

16. Juan Ramírez de Lucena -C:\Users\Govert\Desktop\Signatura comienzo 19.11.2019\RamirezLucena a galardones.txt 0.13637740150884559

17. Jacobo de la Voragine -C:\Users\Govert\Desktop\Signatura comienzo 19.11.2019\flos sanctorum21kb.txt 0.138532539630688

18. Juan de Padilla -C:\Users\Govert\Desktop\Signatura comienzo 19.11.2019\retablo cartujo14kb.txt 0.138838381850391

19. Gonzalo Fernández de Oviedo -C:\Users\Govert\Desktop\Signatura comienzo 19.11.2019\FernandezOviedoSumarioIndias27kb.txt 0.14105005368501788

20. Gordonio Niños -C:\Users\Govert\Desktop\Signatura comienzo 19.11.2019\GordonioNiños32kb.txt 0.14163776199173927

21. Boccaccio -C:\Users\Govert\Desktop\Signatura comienzo 19.11.2019\BoccaccioIlustresmujeresprologo9kb.txt 0.1444117501961626

22. Martin de Cordoba Jardin doncellas -C:\Users\Govert\Desktop\Signatura comienzo 19.11.2019\martindecordobaprohemio2kb.txt 0.14545422631821736

23. Lucena -C:\Users\Govert\Desktop\Signatura comienzo 19.11.2019\repamores mitad libro51kb.txt 0.147082117555434

24. Tratado de Fisonomía -C:\Users\Govert\Desktop\Signatura comienzo 19.11.2019\tratadofisonomiaIntroduccion3kb.txt 0.15007369891916134

25. Juan de Flores -C:\Users\Govert\Desktop\Signatura comienzo 19.11.2019\grimalte prologo3kb.txt 0.15075583840603335

26. Diego de San Pedro -C:\Users\Govert\Desktop\Signatura comienzo 19.11.2019\arnalte incompleta21kb.txt 0.15113480956254444

27. Cronica anónima Reyes Católicos -C:\Users\Govert\Desktop\Signatura comienzo 19.11.2019\cronicalucena21kb.txt 0.15210706264144813

28. Ysopo -C:\Users\Govert\Desktop\Signatura comienzo 19.11.2019\ysope primer libro1495.txt 0.15472803693995585

29. Juan de Flores -C:\Users\Govert\Desktop\Signatura comienzo 19.11.2019\triunfodeamorprologo4kb.txt 0.15560890831069674

30. Juan del Encina -C:\Users\Govert\Desktop\Signatura comienzo 19.11.2019\encina eglogas antes 1509-287kb.txt 0.15980243947080286

31. Gil Vicente -C:\Users\Govert\Desktop\Signatura comienzo 19.11.2019\GilVicenteCuatroTiempos21kb.txt 0.1606957408371631

32. Alonso de Proaza -C:\Users\Govert\Desktop\Signatura comienzo 19.11.2019\alonsodeproazaProsa no Celestina-12kb.txt 0.16380992129388172

33. Francisco López de Villalobos -C:\Users\Govert\Desktop\Signatura comienzo 19.11.2019\villaloboscostumbres humanas21kb.txt 0.1643817969191962

34. Martin de Cordoba Jardin doncellas -C:\Users\Govert\Desktop\Signatura comienzo 19.11.2019\martindecordoba12kb.txt 0.16575815071496813

35. Vidal de Noya -C:\Users\Govert\Desktop\Signatura comienzo 19.11.2019\vidal de noyaJugurthaguerra28kb.txt 0.16674668604254206

36. Gil Vicente -C:\Users\Govert\Desktop\Signatura comienzo 19.11.2019\GilVicenteComediaViudo20kb.txt 0.16754399835321243

37. Hernando del Castillo -C:\Users\Govert\Desktop\Signatura comienzo 19.11.2019\hernando de castillo prologo6kb.txt 0.16767830000734263

38. Tratado de Fisonomía -C:\Users\Govert\Desktop\Signatura comienzo 19.11.2019\tratadofisonomiaProemio8kb.txt 0.16812867233285378

39. Gonzalo de Ayora -C:\Users\Govert\Desktop\Signatura comienzo 19.11.2019\gonzaloayoraAvila67kb.txt 0.168953928500729

40. Juan de Ávila - Oliveros -C:\Users\Govert\Desktop\Signatura comienzo 19.11.2019\oliveros de castilla obra21kb.txt 0.16958086589230148

41. Flor de virtudes -C:\Users\Govert\Desktop\Signatura comienzo 19.11.2019\flordevirtudesobra22kb.txt 0.17383362519498746

42. Lucena -C:\Users\Govert\Desktop\Signatura comienzo 19.11.2019\repeticionamores ajedrez4kb.txt 0.17412910604023923

43. Garci Rodríguez de Montalvo -C:\Users\Govert\Desktop\Signatura comienzo 19.11.2019\amadisdegaula1496 prologo8kb.txt 0.17413956356869564

44. Juan de Flores -C:\Users\Govert\Desktop\Signatura comienzo 19.11.2019\griselobra21kb.txt 0.1749426198148123

45. Gonzalo Fernández de Oviedo -C:\Users\Govert\Desktop\Signatura comienzo 19.11.2019\fernandezOviedo1532catálogo21kb.txt 0.1776138597609208

46. Garci Rodríguez de Montalvo -C:\Users\Govert\Desktop\Signatura comienzo 19.11.2019\AmadisUno21kb.txt 0.17779693371620808

47. Gonzalo Fernández de Oviedo -C:\Users\Govert\Desktop\Signatura comienzo 19.11.2019\fernandezoviedobatalla90-130tiene34kb.txt 0.1782196110289146

48. Garci Rodríguez de Montalvo -C:\Users\Govert\Desktop\Signatura comienzo 19.11.2019\AmadisDos21kb.txt 0.1783277960266415

49. Corónica Adramon -C:\Users\Govert\Desktop\Signatura comienzo 19.11.2019\adramonObra30kb.txt 0.17834285018267104

50. Juan del Encina - Alonso el Sabio -C:\Users\Govert\Desktop\Signatura comienzo 19.11.2019\sietepartidas24kb.txt 0.1785906135652333

51. Juan del Encina -C:\Users\Govert\Desktop\Signatura comienzo 19.11.2019\encina1521-8kb.txt 0.18193274320779573

52. Andrés de Li -C:\Users\Govert\Desktop\Signatura comienzo 19.11.2019\SumaDePaciencia1493Prologo6kb.txt 0.18254333938193446

52. Andrés de Li -C:\Users\Govert\Desktop\Signatura comienzo 19.11.2019\SumaDePaciencia1493Prologo6kb.txt 0.18254333938193446

54. Garci Rodríguez de Montalvo -C:\Users\Govert\Desktop\Signatura comienzo 19.11.2019\AmadisCuatro21kb.txt 0.18589608487140485

55. Juan del Encina -C:\Users\Govert\Desktop\Signatura comienzo 19.11.2019\encinacoplas1521.txt 0.1860062805705961

56. Juan Ramírez de Lucena -C:\Users\Govert\Desktop\Signatura comienzo 19.11.2019\Ramirez Lucena exhortatoria.txt 0.18716976890488157

57. Juan Ramírez de Lucena -C:\Users\Govert\Desktop\Signatura comienzo 19.11.2019\RamirezLucena a Zapata.txt 0.18719965893989643

58. Tercer Viaje de Colon -C:\Users\Govert\Desktop\Signatura comienzo 19.11.2019\TercerViajeColon24kb.txt 0.18860171460267106

59. Carta Hiseo respuesta Tristan -C:\Users\Govert\Desktop\Signatura comienzo 19.11.2019\respuestadetristan.txt 0.18896537760395615

60. Juan del Encina - Linda Melosina -C:\Users\Govert\Desktop\Signatura comienzo 19.11.2019\lindamelosina21kb.txt 0.18937786703563297

61. Pedro Carrillo de Huete -C:\Users\Govert\Desktop\Signatura comienzo 19.11.2019\halconero1489year32kb.txt 0.19074060219313194

62. Infancia Salvatoris -C:\Users\Govert\Desktop\Signatura comienzo 19.11.2019\InfanciaSalvatoris36kb.txt 0.19225232688021288

63. Lucas Fernández -C:\Users\Govert\Desktop\Signatura comienzo 19.11.2019\lucasfernandez dereniego del amor21kb.txt 0.19472253819652985

64. Gil Vicente -C:\Users\Govert\Desktop\Signatura comienzo 19.11.2019\GilVicenteSibila31kb.txt 0.19500713996782082

65. Gonzalo de Ayora -C:\Users\Govert\Desktop\Signatura comienzo 19.11.2019\GonzaloAyoraA MiguelPerezAlmazan15kb.txt 0.19771184673786502

66. Tratado generación criatura -C:\Users\Govert\Desktop\Signatura comienzo 19.11.2019\TratadoGeneracionCriaturaObra24kb.txt 0.19937101848246963

67. Gonzalo Fernández de Oviedo -C:\Users\Govert\Desktop\Signatura comienzo 19.11.2019\fernandezOviedo-indias 21kb.txt 0.20159428425256443

68. Thebayda -C:\Users\Govert\Desktop\Signatura comienzo 19.11.2019\thebaida incompleta21kb.txt 0.20442105669077726

69. Gonzalo García Santa Maria -C:\Users\Govert\Desktop\Signatura comienzo 19.11.2019\evangeliosepistolas1485-64kb.txt 0.20486050922134158

70. Tratado de Fisonomía -C:\Users\Govert\Desktop\Signatura comienzo 19.11.2019\tratadofisonomiaObra22kb.txt 0.2101354406936916

71. Balado Merlin anonimo -C:\Users\Govert\Desktop\Signatura comienzo 19.11.2019\baladroprologo1498-7kb.txt 0.21065545091767213

72. Gil Vicente -C:\Users\Govert\Desktop\Signatura comienzo 19.11.2019\GilVicente Don Duardos65kb.txt 0.2114869337358508

73. Juan de Flores -C:\Users\Govert\Desktop\Signatura comienzo 19.11.2019\griselprologo2kb.txt 0.21218249150427704

74. Gonzalo García Santa Maria -C:\Users\Govert\Desktop\Signatura comienzo 19.11.2019\GarciaSantaMariaCoronicaAragonObra27kb.txt 0.21233843920566475

75. Garci Rodríguez de Montalvo -C:\Users\Govert\Desktop\Signatura comienzo 19.11.2019\AmadisTres21kb.txt 0.21359705051211075

76. Diego de San Pedro -C:\Users\Govert\Desktop\Signatura comienzo 19.11.2019\carceldeamor21kb.txt 0.21394659167637098

77. Juan de Flores -C:\Users\Govert\Desktop\Signatura comienzo 19.11.2019\grimalteobra21kb.txt 0.21495663431501966

78. Juan Paez de Castro -C:\Users\Govert\Desktop\Signatura comienzo 19.11.2019\juanpaezdecastroCartas23kb.txt 0.21638175737632692

79. Tratado de amores -C:\Users\Govert\Desktop\Signatura comienzo 19.11.2019\tratadodeamores15kb.txt 0.21928475497252897

80. Enrique fi de Oliva -C:\Users\Govert\Desktop\Signatura comienzo 19.11.2019\enrique fi de oliva21kb.txt 0.22133296076524323

81. Gonzalo Fernández de Oviedo -C:\Users\Govert\Desktop\Signatura comienzo 19.11.2019\FernandezOviedoClaribalte21kb.txt 0.22141661417329916

82. Juan del Encina -C:\Users\Govert\Desktop\Signatura comienzo 19.11.2019\EncinaCancioneroAlbaHijoPrologo4kb.txt 0.22177353723976023

83. Gonzalo de Ayora -C:\Users\Govert\Desktop\Signatura comienzo 19.11.2019\GonzaloAyora79kb.txt 0.22443314700699202

84. Gil Vicente -C:\Users\Govert\Desktop\Signatura comienzo 19.11.2019\GilVicente AutoPastoril1502 16kb.txt 0.22512616145956077

85. Alonso de Cardona -C:\Users\Govert\Desktop\Signatura comienzo 19.11.2019\alonsodecardona22kb.txt 0.22635939468839605

86. Balado Merlin anonimo -C:\Users\Govert\Desktop\Signatura comienzo 19.11.2019\baladromerlin21kb.txt 0.22643373016347934

87. Juan de Ávila - Oliveros -C:\Users\Govert\Desktop\Signatura comienzo 19.11.2019\oliverosdecastilla introduccion.txt 0.2283385992593311

88. Juan de Ávila - Oliveros -C:\Users\Govert\Desktop\Signatura comienzo 19.11.2019\olveros de castilla prologo1498and1499.txt 0.23009260180412727

89. Cronica Troyana -C:\Users\Govert\Desktop\Signatura comienzo 19.11.2019\cronica troyana obra21kb.txt 0.24099557059197485

90. Andrés de Li -C:\Users\Govert\Desktop\Signatura comienzo 19.11.2019\SumadePaciencia32kb.txt 0.24345382686009254

91. Juan de Ávila - Oliveros -C:\Users\Govert\Desktop\Signatura comienzo 19.11.2019\olveros de castilla epílogo.txt 0.24504155878295208

92. Carta Hiseo respuesta Tristan -C:\Users\Govert\Desktop\Signatura comienzo 19.11.2019\cartahiseolabrunda.txt 0.2517683578676576

93. Boccaccio -C:\Users\Govert\Desktop\Signatura comienzo 19.11.2019\BoccaccioCaydaPrincipe.txt 0.2518923812243332

94. Fernando de Rojas -C:\Users\Govert\Desktop\Signatura comienzo 19.11.2019\fernando de rojas14kb test2.txt 0.2542382971733853

95. Juan de Flores -C:\Users\Govert\Desktop\Signatura comienzo 19.11.2019\grisel introduccion2kb.txt 0.2614587127268999

96. Nicolás Núñez -C:\Users\Govert\Desktop\Signatura comienzo 19.11.2019\NicolasNuñezTractado32kb.txt 0.2672059258491455

97. Libro hebreo oraciones -C:\Users\Govert\Desktop\Signatura comienzo 19.11.2019\siddurtefillot21kb.txt 0.2832638405100766

98. Compendio de Salud humana -C:\Users\Govert\Desktop\Signatura comienzo 19.11.2019\compendioSaludHumana25kb.txt 0.3268768963175337
99. Compendio de Salud humana -C:\Users\Govert\Desktop\Signatura comienzo 19.11.2019\CompendioSaludhumanaprologo13kb.txt 0.3993464056957955

15.4.7 1499 Los doce trabajos de Hércules

villenaobracompleta1499-21kb.txt   C:\Users\Govert\Desktop\Signatura   comienzo 19.11.2019\villenaobracompleta1499-21kb.txt
Canonicizers:
    Normalize Whitespace
EventDrivers:
    Character NGrams n : 4
        EventCullers:
            Most Common Events numevents : 50
Analysis:
    Nearest Neighbor Driver with metric Cosine Distance
1.   Juan   de   Flores   -C:\Users\Govert\Desktop\Signatura   comienzo 19.11.2019\triunfodeamor7kb.txt 0.03734482829703889
2.   Juan   de   Capua   -C:\Users\Govert\Desktop\Signatura   comienzo 19.11.2019\engañosypeligrosObra25kb.txt 0.04299545373356517
3.   Boccaccio   -C:\Users\Govert\Desktop\Signatura   comienzo 19.11.2019\BoccaccioIlustresmujeresobra21kb.txt 0.04820065670590945
4. Cronica anónima Reyes Católicos -C:\Users\Govert\Desktop\Signatura comienzo 19.11.2019\cronicalucena21kb.txt 0.05439156086963892
5   Hernán   Núñez   -C:\Users\Govert\Desktop\Signatura   comienzo 19.11.2019\hernannuñez Trescientas21.txt 0.05625066383202792
6.   Gonzalo   de   Ayora   -C:\Users\Govert\Desktop\Signatura   comienzo 19.11.2019\gonzaloayoraAvila67kb.txt 0.05655369545271971
7. Prologos Fernández de Oviedo -C:\Users\Govert\Desktop\Signatura comienzo 19.11.2019\PrologosFernandezOviedo2-93kb.txt 0.056897646084258624
8.   La   Celestina   -C:\Users\Govert\Desktop\Signatura   comienzo 19.11.2019\CelestinaPrologo9kb.txt 0.05891101318047953
9.   Pedro   de   Portugal   -C:\Users\Govert\Desktop\Signatura   comienzo 19.11.2019\condestablePortugalSatira90kb.txt 0.059219554352301085
10.   Gordonio   Niños   -C:\Users\Govert\Desktop\Signatura   comienzo 19.11.2019\GordonioNiños32kb.txt 0.05975119716395805
11.   Jacobo   de   la   Voragine   -C:\Users\Govert\Desktop\Signatura   comienzo 19.11.2019\flos sanctorum21kb.txt 0.0603446426732811
12.   Juan   del   Encina   -C:\Users\Govert\Desktop\Signatura   comienzo 19.11.2019\EncinaBubolicaPrincipePrologo8kb.txt 0.06086802374669409
13.   Tratado   de   Fisonomía   -C:\Users\Govert\Desktop\Signatura   comienzo 19.11.2019\tratadofisonomiaProemio8kb.txt 0.06258953497171582

14. Juan del Encina -C:\Users\Govert\Desktop\Signatura comienzo 19.11.2019\EncinaCancioneroReyesProhemio7kb.txt 0.06347387278912964

15. Gil Vicente -C:\Users\Govert\Desktop\Signatura comienzo 19.11.2019\GilVicenteCuatroTiempos21kb.txt 0.06432939646005109

16. Juan de Padilla -C:\Users\Govert\Desktop\Signatura comienzo 19.11.2019\retablo cartujo14kb.txt 0.06861586735419734

17. Juan del Encina -C:\Users\Govert\Desktop\Signatura comienzo 19.11.2019\EncinaCancioneroPrincipeProhemio29kb.txt 0.07007728680871983

18. Lucena -C:\Users\Govert\Desktop\Signatura comienzo 19.11.2019\repamores mitad libro51kb.txt 0.07033104759481335

19. Juan Ramírez de Lucena -C:\Users\Govert\Desktop\Signatura comienzo 19.11.2019\vita beata21kb.txt 0.07318707310966821

20. Juan del Encina -C:\Users\Govert\Desktop\Signatura comienzo 19.11.2019\EncinaCancioneroAlbaPrologo6kb.txt 0.07357945628730411

21. Juan del Encina - Alonso el Sabio -C:\Users\Govert\Desktop\Signatura comienzo 19.11.2019\sietepartidas24kb.txt 0.07400164874548709

22. Duobus amantibus -C:\Users\Govert\Desktop\Signatura comienzo 19.11.2019\piccolomini pp20 hasta30-21kb.txt 0.07737019260474987

23. Francisco López de Villalobos -C:\Users\Govert\Desktop\Signatura comienzo 19.11.2019\villaloboscostumbres humanas21kb.txt 0.07854950351912893

24. Juan del Encina -C:\Users\Govert\Desktop\Signatura comienzo 19.11.2019\EncinaBubolicaReyesPrologo8kb.txt 0.07953423053095898

25. Ysopo -C:\Users\Govert\Desktop\Signatura comienzo 19.11.2019\ysope primer libro1495.txt 0.08035348895216365

26. Juan Ramírez de Lucena -C:\Users\Govert\Desktop\Signatura comienzo 19.11.2019\RamirezLucena a galardones.txt 0.08262636068989415

27. Gonzalo Fernández de Oviedo -C:\Users\Govert\Desktop\Signatura comienzo 19.11.2019\FernandezOviedoSumarioIndias27kb.txt 0.0829542259441911

28. Garci Rodríguez de Montalvo -C:\Users\Govert\Desktop\Signatura comienzo 19.11.2019\AmadisDos21kb.txt 0.08459119354504885

29. Gil Vicente -C:\Users\Govert\Desktop\Signatura comienzo 19.11.2019\GilVicenteComediaViudo20kb.txt 0.08729281732502592

30. Gonzalo Fernández de Oviedo -C:\Users\Govert\Desktop\Signatura comienzo 19.11.2019\fernandezOviedo-indias 21kb.txt 0.08730682853829608

31. Martin de Cordoba Jardin doncellas -C:\Users\Govert\Desktop\Signatura comienzo 19.11.2019\martindecordoba12kb.txt 0.08790930830865884

32. Boccaccio -C:\Users\Govert\Desktop\Signatura comienzo 19.11.2019\BoccaccioIlustresmujeresprologo9kb.txt 0.08830455962206618

33. Juan del Encina -C:\Users\Govert\Desktop\Signatura comienzo 19.11.2019\encinabubolicaArgumentos5kb.txt 0.08999709382666188

34. Hernando del Castillo -C:\Users\Govert\Desktop\Signatura comienzo 19.11.2019\hernando de castillo prologo6kb.txt 0.09197890888998994

35. Juan de Flores -C:\Users\Govert\Desktop\Signatura comienzo 19.11.2019\grimalte prologo3kb.txt 0.09257317347308502

36. Tercer Viaje de Colon -C:\Users\Govert\Desktop\Signatura comienzo 19.11.2019\TercerViajeColon24kb.txt 0.09514629051134904

37. Juan de Ávila - Oliveros -C:\Users\Govert\Desktop\Signatura comienzo 19.11.2019\oliveros de castilla obra21kb.txt 0.09550312107911008

38. Garci Rodríguez de Montalvo -C:\Users\Govert\Desktop\Signatura comienzo 19.11.2019\amadisdegaula1496 prologo8kb.txt 0.09578698220206994

39. Flor de virtudes -C:\Users\Govert\Desktop\Signatura comienzo 19.11.2019\flordevirtudesobra22kb.txt 0.09666032189820262

40. Vidal de Noya -C:\Users\Govert\Desktop\Signatura comienzo 19.11.2019\vidal de noyaJugurthaguerra28kb.txt 0.09717894610920741

41. Martin de Cordoba Jardin doncellas -C:\Users\Govert\Desktop\Signatura comienzo 19.11.2019\martindecordobaprohemio2kb.txt 0.09762887065245518

42. Tratado generación criatura -C:\Users\Govert\Desktop\Signatura comienzo 19.11.2019\TratadoGeneracionCriaturaObra24kb.txt 0.0982624573539782

43. Tratado de Fisonomía -C:\Users\Govert\Desktop\Signatura comienzo 19.11.2019\tratadofisonomiaIntroduccion3kb.txt 0.0993335244472563

44. Gonzalo García Santa Maria -C:\Users\Govert\Desktop\Signatura comienzo 19.11.2019\evangeliosepistolas1485-64kb.txt 0.1009739155496816

45. Garci Rodríguez de Montalvo -C:\Users\Govert\Desktop\Signatura comienzo 19.11.2019\AmadisCuatro21kb.txt 0.10235307667718141

46. Gonzalo Fernández de Oviedo -C:\Users\Govert\Desktop\Signatura comienzo 19.11.2019\fernandezOviedo1532catálogo21kb.txt 0.10236756956372828

47. Alonso de Proaza -C:\Users\Govert\Desktop\Signatura comienzo 19.11.2019\alonsodeproazaProsa no Celestina-12kb.txt 0.10314610934308444

48. Juan Ramírez de Lucena -C:\Users\Govert\Desktop\Signatura comienzo 19.11.2019\RamirezLucena a Zapata.txt 0.10350725391570337

49. Juan Ramírez de Lucena -C:\Users\Govert\Desktop\Signatura comienzo 19.11.2019\Ramirez Lucena exhortatoria.txt 0.10362641891007807

50. Garci Rodríguez de Montalvo -C:\Users\Govert\Desktop\Signatura comienzo 19.11.2019\AmadisUno21kb.txt 0.10377746697532131

51. Lucena -C:\Users\Govert\Desktop\Signatura 19.11.2019\repeticionamores ajedrez4kb.txt 0.10433328626484228

52. Gonzalo Fernández de Oviedo -C:\Users\Govert\Desktop\Signatura comienzo 19.11.2019\fernandezoviedobatalla90-130tiene34kb.txt 0.1049047017525696

53. Juan de Ávila - Oliveros -C:\Users\Govert\Desktop\Signatura comienzo 19.11.2019\olveros de castilla epílogo.txt 0.10519135023904536

54. Juan del Encina -C:\Users\Govert\Desktop\Signatura comienzo 19.11.2019\encina eglogas antes 1509-287kb.txt 0.10584619338189127

55. Diego de San Pedro -C:\Users\Govert\Desktop\Signatura comienzo 19.11.2019\arnalte incompleta21kb.txt 0.10599008571819124

56. Juan de Flores -C:\Users\Govert\Desktop\Signatura comienzo 19.11.2019\triunfodeamorprologo4kb.txt 0.10641390513036486

57. Corónica Adramon -C:\Users\Govert\Desktop\Signatura comienzo 19.11.2019\adramonObra30kb.txt 0.10642054690940383

58. Infancia Salvatoris -C:\Users\Govert\Desktop\Signatura comienzo 19.11.2019\InfanciaSalvatoris36kb.txt 0.11046473523567424

59. Pedro Carrillo de Huete -C:\Users\Govert\Desktop\Signatura comienzo 19.11.2019\halconero1489year32kb.txt 0.11508783479346363

60. Andrés de Li -C:\Users\Govert\Desktop\Signatura comienzo 19.11.2019\SumaDePaciencia1493Prologo6kb.txt 0.11802512858091685

60. Andrés de Li -C:\Users\Govert\Desktop\Signatura comienzo 19.11.2019\SumaDePaciencia1493Prologo6kb.txt 0.11802512858091685

62. Gonzalo García Santa Maria -C:\Users\Govert\Desktop\Signatura comienzo 19.11.2019\GarciaSantaMariaCoronicaAragonObra27kb.txt 0.11844806754513415

63. Juan de Flores -C:\Users\Govert\Desktop\Signatura comienzo 19.11.2019\griselobra21kb.txt 0.11955564858940826

64. Lucas Fernández -C:\Users\Govert\Desktop\Signatura comienzo 19.11.2019\lucasfernandez dereniego del amor21kb.txt 0.11990840828783911

65. Cronica Troyana -C:\Users\Govert\Desktop\Signatura comienzo 19.11.2019\cronica troyana obra21kb.txt 0.12037730474933306

66. Juan de Ávila - Oliveros -C:\Users\Govert\Desktop\Signatura comienzo 19.11.2019\oliverosdecastilla introduccion.txt 0.1206441220473794

67. Juan de Ávila - Oliveros -C:\Users\Govert\Desktop\Signatura comienzo 19.11.2019\olveros de castilla prologo1498and1499.txt 0.12156218230766724

68. Juan del Encina - Linda Melosina -C:\Users\Govert\Desktop\Signatura comienzo 19.11.2019\lindamelosina21kb.txt 0.12495201539579703

69. Andrés de Li -C:\Users\Govert\Desktop\Signatura comienzo 19.11.2019\SumadePaciencia32kb.txt 0.1252418900808835

70. Gil Vicente -C:\Users\Govert\Desktop\Signatura comienzo 19.11.2019\GilVicenteSibila31kb.txt 0.12800139946924283

71. Diego de San Pedro -C:\Users\Govert\Desktop\Signatura comienzo 19.11.2019\carceldeamor21kb.txt 0.13022354968303906

72. Juan del Encina -C:\Users\Govert\Desktop\Signatura comienzo 19.11.2019\EncinaCancioneroAlbaHijoPrologo4kb.txt 0.13078321915410063

73. Balado Merlin anonimo -C:\Users\Govert\Desktop\Signatura comienzo 19.11.2019\baladroprologo1498-7kb.txt 0.13195790961714404

74. Tratado de Fisonomía -C:\Users\Govert\Desktop\Signatura comienzo 19.11.2019\tratadofisonomiaObra22kb.txt 0.13326567729919914

75. Gonzalo Fernández de Oviedo -C:\Users\Govert\Desktop\Signatura comienzo 19.11.2019\FernandezOviedoClaribalte21kb.txt 0.13370907658252495

76. Gonzalo de Ayora -C:\Users\Govert\Desktop\Signatura comienzo 19.11.2019\GonzaloAyoraA MiguelPerezAlmazan15kb.txt 0.13390540860707079

77. Thebayda -C:\Users\Govert\Desktop\Signatura comienzo 19.11.2019\thebaida incompleta21kb.txt 0.13553900696178067

78. Gonzalo de Ayora -C:\Users\Govert\Desktop\Signatura comienzo 19.11.2019\GonzaloAyora79kb.txt 0.13715760057877824

79. Carta Hiseo respuesta Tristan -C:\Users\Govert\Desktop\Signatura comienzo 19.11.2019\respuestadetristan.txt 0.13857205525379013

80. Juan del Encina -C:\Users\Govert\Desktop\Signatura comienzo 19.11.2019\encina1521-8kb.txt 0.13963785002283957

81. Gil Vicente -C:\Users\Govert\Desktop\Signatura comienzo 19.11.2019\GilVicente AutoPastoril1502 16kb.txt 0.14076633347879053

82. Garci Rodríguez de Montalvo -C:\Users\Govert\Desktop\Signatura comienzo 19.11.2019\AmadisTres21kb.txt 0.14143100123749763

83. Juan Paez de Castro -C:\Users\Govert\Desktop\Signatura comienzo 19.11.2019\juanpaezdecastroCartas23kb.txt 0.1416320793754936

84. Juan del Encina -C:\Users\Govert\Desktop\Signatura comienzo 19.11.2019\encinacoplas1521.txt 0.14233471491964478

85. Boccaccio -C:\Users\Govert\Desktop\Signatura comienzo 19.11.2019\BoccaccioCaydaPrincipe.txt 0.14438964634680718

86. Balado Merlin anonimo -C:\Users\Govert\Desktop\Signatura comienzo 19.11.2019\baladromerlin21kb.txt 0.14907710416323072

87. Gil Vicente -C:\Users\Govert\Desktop\Signatura comienzo 19.11.2019\GilVicente Don Duardos65kb.txt 0.1501830048081444

88. Tratado de amores -C:\Users\Govert\Desktop\Signatura comienzo 19.11.2019\tratadodeamores15kb.txt 0.1553396279393806

89. Juan de Flores -C:\Users\Govert\Desktop\Signatura comienzo 19.11.2019\grimalteobra21kb.txt 0.16091262779027338

90. Alonso de Cardona -C:\Users\Govert\Desktop\Signatura comienzo 19.11.2019\alonsodecardona22kb.txt 0.16742707828427583

91. Enrique fi de Oliva -C:\Users\Govert\Desktop\Signatura comienzo 19.11.2019\enrique fi de oliva21kb.txt 0.1686478655915098

92. Fernando de Rojas -C:\Users\Govert\Desktop\Signatura comienzo 19.11.2019\fernando de rojas14kb test2.txt 0.1960005593158074

93. Juan de Flores -C:\Users\Govert\Desktop\Signatura comienzo 19.11.2019\griselprologo2kb.txt 0.19807465939499347

94. Libro hebreo oraciones -C:\Users\Govert\Desktop\Signatura comienzo 19.11.2019\siddurtefillot21kb.txt 0.21190510951895103

95. Compendio de Salud humana -C:\Users\Govert\Desktop\Signatura comienzo 19.11.2019\compendioSaludHumana25kb.txt 0.21323347534380444

96. Carta Hiseo respuesta Tristan -C:\Users\Govert\Desktop\Signatura comienzo 19.11.2019\cartahiseolabrunda.txt 0.21341328900500434

97. Nicolás Núñez -C:\Users\Govert\Desktop\Signatura comienzo 19.11.2019\NicolasNuñezTractado32kb.txt 0.22381531307523816

98. Juan de Flores -C:\Users\Govert\Desktop\Signatura comienzo 19.11.2019\grisel introduccion2kb.txt 0.24819918492241366

99. Compendio de Salud humana -C:\Users\Govert\Desktop\Signatura comienzo 19.11.2019\CompendioSaludhumanaprologo13kb.txt 0.2918194643466421

15.4.8 1499 Hércules Proem

villenaproemio1499 - 8 kb.txt C:\Users\Govert\Desktop\Signatura comienzo 19.11.2019\villenaproemio1499 - 8 kb.txt
Canonicizers:
  Normalize Whitespace
EventDrivers:
  Character NGrams n : 4
    EventCullers:
      Most Common Events numevents : 50
Analysis:
  Nearest Neighbor Driver with metric Cosine Distance
1. Juan del Encina -C:\Users\Govert\Desktop\Signatura comienzo 19.11.2019\EncinaCancioneroReyesProhemio7kb.txt 0.11837715378497371
2. Gil Vicente -C:\Users\Govert\Desktop\Signatura comienzo 19.11.2019\GilVicenteCuatroTiempos21kb.txt 0.12248898752719062
3. Juan del Encina -C:\Users\Govert\Desktop\Signatura comienzo 19.11.2019\EncinaBubolicaPrincipePrologo8kb.txt 0.12280511382346238
4. Gonzalo de Ayora -C:\Users\Govert\Desktop\Signatura comienzo 19.11.2019\gonzaloayoraAvila67kb.txt 0.12975846557944837
5. Juan de Flores -C:\Users\Govert\Desktop\Signatura comienzo 19.11.2019\triunfodeamor7kb.txt 0.13428486152897656
6. Juan Ramírez de Lucena -C:\Users\Govert\Desktop\Signatura comienzo 19.11.2019\RamirezLucena a galardones.txt 0.1345085799715704
7. Juan de Padilla -C:\Users\Govert\Desktop\Signatura comienzo 19.11.2019\retablo cartujo14kb.txt 0.14154998431873123
8. Cronica anónima Reyes Católicos -C:\Users\Govert\Desktop\Signatura comienzo 19.11.2019\cronicalucena21kb.txt 0.14270919589164643
9. Juan Ramírez de Lucena -C:\Users\Govert\Desktop\Signatura comienzo 19.11.2019\vita beata21kb.txt 0.14288621258355738
10. Hernán Núñez -C:\Users\Govert\Desktop\Signatura comienzo 19.11.2019\hernannuñez Trescientas21.txt 0.145305736040641
11. Juan del Encina -C:\Users\Govert\Desktop\Signatura comienzo 19.11.2019\EncinaCancioneroAlbaPrologo6kb.txt 0.1569468813017224
12. Juan del Encina -C:\Users\Govert\Desktop\Signatura comienzo 19.11.2019\EncinaCancioneroPrincipeProhemio29kb.txt 0.15772717811103742
13. Juan del Encina -C:\Users\Govert\Desktop\Signatura comienzo 19.11.2019\EncinaBubolicaReyesPrologo8kb.txt 0.16678855967481554
14. Boccaccio -C:\Users\Govert\Desktop\Signatura comienzo 19.11.2019\BoccaccioIlustresmujeresobra21kb.txt 0.16906721053527074
15. Garci Rodríguez de Montalvo -C:\Users\Govert\Desktop\Signatura comienzo 19.11.2019\amadisdegaula1496 prologo8kb.txt 0.17105223289272686
16. Gonzalo Fernández de Oviedo -C:\Users\Govert\Desktop\Signatura comienzo 19.11.2019\fernandezOviedo-indias 21kb.txt 0.17330920096406854

17. Garci Rodríguez de Montalvo -C:\Users\Govert\Desktop\Signatura comienzo 19.11.2019\AmadisDos21kb.txt 0.1734415088122796

18. Juan del Encina -C:\Users\Govert\Desktop\Signatura comienzo 19.11.2019\EncinaCancioneroAlbaHijoPrologo4kb.txt 0.17996159076121876

19. Juan del Encina -C:\Users\Govert\Desktop\Signatura comienzo 19.11.2019\encinabubolicaArgumentos5kb.txt 0.18019360689371988

20. Gonzalo Fernández de Oviedo -C:\Users\Govert\Desktop\Signatura comienzo 19.11.2019\FernandezOviedoSumarioIndias27kb.txt 0.18137161429566084

21. Juan de Flores -C:\Users\Govert\Desktop\Signatura comienzo 19.11.2019\triunfodeamorprologo4kb.txt 0.18138816557230297

22. Prologos Fernández de Oviedo -C:\Users\Govert\Desktop\Signatura comienzo 19.11.2019\PrologosFernandezOviedo2-93kb.txt 0.18234508511205483

23. Francisco López de Villalobos -C:\Users\Govert\Desktop\Signatura comienzo 19.11.2019\villaloboscostumbres humanas21kb.txt 0.18611516564687614

24. Juan de Capua -C:\Users\Govert\Desktop\Signatura comienzo 19.11.2019\engañosypeligrosObra25kb.txt 0.18635406099067675

25. Andrés de Li -C:\Users\Govert\Desktop\Signatura comienzo 19.11.2019\SumaDePaciencia1493Prologo6kb.txt 0.1869966250419801

25. Andrés de Li -C:\Users\Govert\Desktop\Signatura comienzo 19.11.2019\SumaDePaciencia1493Prologo6kb.txt 0.1869966250419801

27. Lucas Fernández -C:\Users\Govert\Desktop\Signatura comienzo 19.11.2019\lucasfernandez dereniego del amor21kb.txt 0.1895690390227195

28. Jacobo de la Voragine -C:\Users\Govert\Desktop\Signatura comienzo 19.11.2019\flos sanctorum21kb.txt 0.1897819566276342

29. Juan del Encina - Alonso el Sabio -C:\Users\Govert\Desktop\Signatura comienzo 19.11.2019\sietepartidas24kb.txt 0.19164774103018967

30. La Celestina -C:\Users\Govert\Desktop\Signatura comienzo 19.11.2019\CelestinaPrologo9kb.txt 0.193846089627968

31. Tratado de Fisonomía -C:\Users\Govert\Desktop\Signatura comienzo 19.11.2019\tratadofisonomiaProemio8kb.txt 0.19553438645188193

32. Tercer Viaje de Colon -C:\Users\Govert\Desktop\Signatura comienzo 19.11.2019\TercerViajeColon24kb.txt 0.1985699896425437

33. Gonzalo García Santa Maria -C:\Users\Govert\Desktop\Signatura comienzo 19.11.2019\evangeliosepistolas1485-64kb.txt 0.19868958689812788

34. Hernando del Castillo -C:\Users\Govert\Desktop\Signatura comienzo 19.11.2019\hernando de castillo prologo6kb.txt 0.19940463691443222

35. Pedro Carrillo de Huete -C:\Users\Govert\Desktop\Signatura comienzo 19.11.2019\halconero1489year32kb.txt 0.20210482482393033

36. Andrés de Li -C:\Users\Govert\Desktop\Signatura comienzo 19.11.2019\SumadePaciencia32kb.txt 0.20322420092643556

37. Juan de Ávila - Oliveros -C:\Users\Govert\Desktop\Signatura comienzo 19.11.2019\olveros de castilla prologo1498and1499.txt 0.20575716648484343

38. Juan de Ávila - Oliveros -C:\Users\Govert\Desktop\Signatura comienzo 19.11.2019\oliverosdecastilla introduccion.txt 0.20663328171194129

39. Lucena -C:\Users\Govert\Desktop\Signatura comienzo 19.11.2019\repamores mitad libro51kb.txt 0.20711139840912252

40. Juan del Encina -C:\Users\Govert\Desktop\Signatura comienzo 19.11.2019\encina eglogas antes 1509-287kb.txt 0.20859606654089102

41. Balado Merlin anonimo -C:\Users\Govert\Desktop\Signatura comienzo 19.11.2019\baladromerlin21kb.txt 0.20938511588145814

42. Ysopo -C:\Users\Govert\Desktop\Signatura comienzo 19.11.2019\ysope primer libro1495.txt 0.20959167706964155

43. Gordonio Niños -C:\Users\Govert\Desktop\Signatura comienzo 19.11.2019\GordonioNiños32kb.txt 0.21087892350294424

44. Duobus amantibus -C:\Users\Govert\Desktop\Signatura comienzo 19.11.2019\piccolomini pp20 hasta30-21kb.txt 0.21219188949255463

45. Juan Ramírez de Lucena -C:\Users\Govert\Desktop\Signatura comienzo 19.11.2019\RamirezLucena a Zapata.txt 0.21273757482412814

46. Juan Ramírez de Lucena -C:\Users\Govert\Desktop\Signatura comienzo 19.11.2019\Ramirez Lucena exhortatoria.txt 0.21284786363860186

47. Gonzalo de Ayora -C:\Users\Govert\Desktop\Signatura comienzo 19.11.2019\GonzaloAyoraA MiguelPerezAlmazan15kb.txt 0.21357743574153631

48. Vidal de Noya -C:\Users\Govert\Desktop\Signatura comienzo 19.11.2019\vidal de noyaJugurthaguerra28kb.txt 0.21499904683523985

49. Martin de Cordoba Jardin doncellas -C:\Users\Govert\Desktop\Signatura comienzo 19.11.2019\martindecordoba12kb.txt 0.21995457484396475

50. Gonzalo Fernández de Oviedo -C:\Users\Govert\Desktop\Signatura comienzo 19.11.2019\fernandezoviedobatalla90-130tiene34kb.txt 0.22007700540965003

51. Pedro de Portugal -C:\Users\Govert\Desktop\Signatura comienzo 19.11.2019\condestablePortugalSatira90kb.txt 0.2210945293489298

52. Corónica Adramon -C:\Users\Govert\Desktop\Signatura comienzo 19.11.2019\adramonObra30kb.txt 0.22481883204978703

53. Juan de Ávila - Oliveros -C:\Users\Govert\Desktop\Signatura comienzo 19.11.2019\oliveros de castilla obra21kb.txt 0.2252403755187301

54. Martin de Cordoba Jardin doncellas -C:\Users\Govert\Desktop\Signatura comienzo 19.11.2019\martindecordobaprohemio2kb.txt 0.22551433161914936

55. Gonzalo de Ayora -C:\Users\Govert\Desktop\Signatura comienzo 19.11.2019\GonzaloAyora79kb.txt 0.225748023030381

56. Alonso de Proaza -C:\Users\Govert\Desktop\Signatura comienzo 19.11.2019\alonsodeproazaProsa no Celestina-12kb.txt 0.22684697658325315

57. Tratado de Fisonomía -C:\Users\Govert\Desktop\Signatura comienzo 19.11.2019\tratadofisonomiaIntroduccion3kb.txt 0.2272337691897558

58. Boccaccio -C:\Users\Govert\Desktop\Signatura comienzo 19.11.2019\BoccaccioIlustresmujeresprologo9kb.txt 0.22745810337263883

59. Gil Vicente -C:\Users\Govert\Desktop\Signatura comienzo 19.11.2019\GilVicenteComediaViudo20kb.txt 0.2274835144084697

60. Garci Rodríguez de Montalvo -C:\Users\Govert\Desktop\Signatura comienzo 19.11.2019\AmadisCuatro21kb.txt 0.22846261363978826

61.	Lucena	-C:\Users\Govert\Desktop\Signatura	comienzo 19.11.2019\repeticionamores ajedrez4kb.txt 0.23068977533896717

62.	Tratado de Fisonomía	-C:\Users\Govert\Desktop\Signatura	comienzo 19.11.2019\tratadofisonomiaObra22kb.txt 0.23304017008309008

63.	Gonzalo García Santa Maria	-C:\Users\Govert\Desktop\Signatura comienzo 19.11.2019\GarciaSantaMariaCoronicaAragonObra27kb.txt 0.23621667185720696

64.	Gonzalo Fernández de Oviedo	-C:\Users\Govert\Desktop\Signatura comienzo 19.11.2019\fernandezOviedo1532catálogo21kb.txt 0.2367179226425553

65.	Garci Rodríguez de Montalvo	-C:\Users\Govert\Desktop\Signatura comienzo 19.11.2019\AmadisTres21kb.txt 0.23929505090441905

66.	Infancia Salvatoris	-C:\Users\Govert\Desktop\Signatura	comienzo 19.11.2019\InfanciaSalvatoris36kb.txt 0.24050899968037798

67.	Gil Vicente	-C:\Users\Govert\Desktop\Signatura	comienzo 19.11.2019\GilVicenteSibila31kb.txt 0.24097326293769583

68.	Libro hebreo oraciones	-C:\Users\Govert\Desktop\Signatura	comienzo 19.11.2019\siddurtefillot21kb.txt 0.241010857224204

69.	Juan Paez de Castro	-C:\Users\Govert\Desktop\Signatura	comienzo 19.11.2019\juanpaezdecastroCartas23kb.txt 0.24178197103235088

70.	Gonzalo Fernández de Oviedo	-C:\Users\Govert\Desktop\Signatura	comienzo 19.11.2019\FernandezOviedoClaribalte21kb.txt 0.24610047342719454

71.	Cronica Troyana	-C:\Users\Govert\Desktop\Signatura	comienzo 19.11.2019\cronica troyana obra21kb.txt 0.24615000770453122

72.	Juan del Encina	-C:\Users\Govert\Desktop\Signatura	comienzo 19.11.2019\encina1521-8kb.txt 0.246791951345241

73.	Garci Rodríguez de Montalvo	-C:\Users\Govert\Desktop\Signatura comienzo 19.11.2019\AmadisUno21kb.txt 0.24693674071830718

74.	Juan de Ávila - Oliveros	-C:\Users\Govert\Desktop\Signatura comienzo 19.11.2019\olveros de castilla epílogo.txt 0.2483649633840418

75.	Tratado generación criatura	-C:\Users\Govert\Desktop\Signatura comienzo 19.11.2019\TratadoGeneracionCriaturaObra24kb.txt 0.2497323219865314

76.	Thebayda -C:\Users\Govert\Desktop\Signatura comienzo 19.11.2019\thebaida incompleta21kb.txt 0.2509877261352361

77.	Juan del Encina	-C:\Users\Govert\Desktop\Signatura	comienzo 19.11.2019\encinacoplas1521.txt 0.25334441624989923

78.	Balado Merlin anonimo	-C:\Users\Govert\Desktop\Signatura	comienzo 19.11.2019\baladroprologo1498-7kb.txt 0.25714765950792307

79.	Gil Vicente	-C:\Users\Govert\Desktop\Signatura	comienzo 19.11.2019\GilVicente AutoPastoril1502 16kb.txt 0.2601222986498266

80.	Tratado de amores	-C:\Users\Govert\Desktop\Signatura	comienzo 19.11.2019\tratadodeamores15kb.txt 0.26195108677835577

81.	Diego de San Pedro	-C:\Users\Govert\Desktop\Signatura	comienzo 19.11.2019\arnalte incompleta21kb.txt 0.2624306407392615

82.	Juan de Flores	-C:\Users\Govert\Desktop\Signatura	comienzo 19.11.2019\griselobra21kb.txt 0.2650371017496309

83. Juan del Encina - Linda Melosina -C:\Users\Govert\Desktop\Signatura comienzo 19.11.2019\lindamelosina21kb.txt 0.26834229556533984

84.   Boccaccio   -C:\Users\Govert\Desktop\Signatura   comienzo 19.11.2019\BoccaccioCaydaPrincipe.txt 0.27346504250060455

85.   Flor   de   virtudes   -C:\Users\Govert\Desktop\Signatura   comienzo 19.11.2019\flordevirtudesobra22kb.txt 0.2774402402080046

86.   Gil   Vicente   -C:\Users\Govert\Desktop\Signatura   comienzo 19.11.2019\GilVicente Don Duardos65kb.txt 0.28331941277448736

87.   Diego   de   San   Pedro   -C:\Users\Govert\Desktop\Signatura   comienzo 19.11.2019\carceldeamor21kb.txt 0.28346372790070307

88.   Juan   de   Flores   -C:\Users\Govert\Desktop\Signatura   comienzo 19.11.2019\grimalte prologo3kb.txt 0.28370783447276016

89.   Fernando   de   Rojas   -C:\Users\Govert\Desktop\Signatura   comienzo 19.11.2019\fernando de rojas14kb test2.txt 0.29041854806380774

90. Carta Hiseo respuesta Tristan -C:\Users\Govert\Desktop\Signatura comienzo 19.11.2019\respuestadetristan.txt 0.2972866306301084

91.   Juan   de   Flores   -C:\Users\Govert\Desktop\Signatura   comienzo 19.11.2019\grimalteobra21kb.txt 0.3052648616473874

92.   Juan   de   Flores   -C:\Users\Govert\Desktop\Signatura   comienzo 19.11.2019\griselprologo2kb.txt 0.3087559510732413

93.   Alonso   de   Cardona   -C:\Users\Govert\Desktop\Signatura   comienzo 19.11.2019\alonsodecardona22kb.txt 0.32094320743964777

94.   Enrique   fi   de   Oliva   -C:\Users\Govert\Desktop\Signatura   comienzo 19.11.2019\enrique fi de oliva21kb.txt 0.32928707969069126

95. Compendio de Salud humana -C:\Users\Govert\Desktop\Signatura comienzo 19.11.2019\compendioSaludHumana25kb.txt 0.34901182123993457

96. Juan de Flores -C:\Users\Govert\Desktop\Signatura comienzo 19.11.2019\grisel introduccion2kb.txt 0.3601623299129777

97. Carta Hiseo respuesta Tristan -C:\Users\Govert\Desktop\Signatura comienzo 19.11.2019\cartahiseolabrunda.txt 0.3925768423015312

98.   Nicolás   Núñez   -C:\Users\Govert\Desktop\Signatura   comienzo 19.11.2019\NicolasNuñezTractado32kb.txt 0.3952726452524761

99. Compendio de Salud humana -C:\Users\Govert\Desktop\Signatura comienzo 19.11.2019\CompendioSaludhumanaprologo13kb.txt 0.48732648457955285

15.4.9 1499 Hércules Foreword

villenaprologo1499   -4kb.txt   C:\Users\Govert\Desktop\Signatura   comienzo 19.11.2019\villenaprologo1499 -4kb.txt
Canonicizers:
    Normalize Whitespace
EventDrivers:
    Character NGrams n : 4

EventCullers:

Most Common Events numevents : 50

Analysis:

Nearest Neighbor Driver with metric Cosine Distance

1. Juan Ramírez de Lucena -C:\Users\Govert\Desktop\Signatura comienzo 19.11.2019\RamirezLucena a galardones.txt 0.08285593912002454

2. Juan del Encina -C:\Users\Govert\Desktop\Signatura comienzo 19.11.2019\EncinaCancioneroReyesProhemio7kb.txt 0.08819748926136017

3. Juan Ramírez de Lucena -C:\Users\Govert\Desktop\Signatura comienzo 19.11.2019\vita beata21kb.txt 0.09190385257592726

4. Gonzalo de Ayora -C:\Users\Govert\Desktop\Signatura comienzo 19.11.2019\gonzaloayoraAvila67kb.txt 0.09207435497122163

5. Cronica anónima Reyes Católicos -C:\Users\Govert\Desktop\Signatura comienzo 19.11.2019\cronicalucena21kb.txt 0.09761707489812943

6. Juan de Capua -C:\Users\Govert\Desktop\Signatura comienzo 19.11.2019\engañosypeligrosObra25kb.txt 0.09810324535785442

7. Tratado de Fisonomía -C:\Users\Govert\Desktop\Signatura comienzo 19.11.2019\tratadofisonomiaProemio8kb.txt 0.10053737494303383

8. Juan del Encina -C:\Users\Govert\Desktop\Signatura comienzo 19.11.2019\EncinaBubolicaPrincipePrologo8kb.txt 0.10159986942526611

9. Juan de Flores -C:\Users\Govert\Desktop\Signatura comienzo 19.11.2019\triunfodeamor7kb.txt 0.10247024966460228

10. Juan del Encina -C:\Users\Govert\Desktop\Signatura comienzo 19.11.2019\EncinaCancioneroPrincipeProhemio29kb.txt 0.10307390203407862

11. Juan de Ávila - Oliveros -C:\Users\Govert\Desktop\Signatura comienzo 19.11.2019\olveros de castilla prologo1498and1499.txt 0.10536362720504511

12. Boccaccio -C:\Users\Govert\Desktop\Signatura comienzo 19.11.2019\BoccaccioIlustresmujeresobra21kb.txt 0.10676989687866867

13. Juan de Ávila - Oliveros -C:\Users\Govert\Desktop\Signatura comienzo 19.11.2019\oliverosdecastilla introduccion.txt 0.10823173344144865

14. Martin de Cordoba Jardin doncellas -C:\Users\Govert\Desktop\Signatura comienzo 19.11.2019\martindecordobaprohemio2kb.txt 0.10904726526781605

15. Hernando del Castillo -C:\Users\Govert\Desktop\Signatura comienzo 19.11.2019\hernando de castillo prologo6kb.txt 0.10916636596850526

16. Hernán Núñez -C:\Users\Govert\Desktop\Signatura comienzo 19.11.2019\hernannuñez Trescientas21.txt 0.10967151515191653

17. Juan de Padilla -C:\Users\Govert\Desktop\Signatura comienzo 19.11.2019\retablo cartujo14kb.txt 0.1103738747770645

18. Gil Vicente -C:\Users\Govert\Desktop\Signatura comienzo 19.11.2019\GilVicenteCuatroTiempos21kb.txt 0.11131917062599195

19. Jacobo de la Voragine -C:\Users\Govert\Desktop\Signatura comienzo 19.11.2019\flos sanctorum21kb.txt 0.11457705538388818

20. Prologos Fernández de Oviedo -C:\Users\Govert\Desktop\Signatura comienzo 19.11.2019\PrologosFernandezOviedo2-93kb.txt 0.11931395709154713

21. Garci Rodríguez de Montalvo -C:\Users\Govert\Desktop\Signatura comienzo 19.11.2019\amadisdegaula1496 prologo8kb.txt 0.12024889560758367

22. Juan del Encina -C:\Users\Govert\Desktop\Signatura comienzo 19.11.2019\EncinaBubolicaReyesPrologo8kb.txt 0.12256193083407407

23. Juan del Encina -C:\Users\Govert\Desktop\Signatura comienzo 19.11.2019\EncinaCancioneroAlbaPrologo6kb.txt 0.1239613714783665

24. Pedro de Portugal -C:\Users\Govert\Desktop\Signatura comienzo 19.11.2019\condestablePortugalSatira90kb.txt 0.12920295179272

25. Juan del Encina - Alonso el Sabio -C:\Users\Govert\Desktop\Signatura comienzo 19.11.2019\sietepartidas24kb.txt 0.13093525729487276

26. Francisco López de Villalobos -C:\Users\Govert\Desktop\Signatura comienzo 19.11.2019\villaloboscostumbres humanas21kb.txt 0.13135566057474435

27. Boccaccio -C:\Users\Govert\Desktop\Signatura comienzo 19.11.2019\BoccaccioIlustresmujeresprologo9kb.txt 0.13685619308057995

28. Juan Ramírez de Lucena -C:\Users\Govert\Desktop\Signatura comienzo 19.11.2019\RamirezLucena a Zapata.txt 0.137267394657278

29. Juan Ramírez de Lucena -C:\Users\Govert\Desktop\Signatura comienzo 19.11.2019\Ramirez Lucena exhortatoria.txt 0.13732240837859

30. Gonzalo Fernández de Oviedo -C:\Users\Govert\Desktop\Signatura comienzo 19.11.2019\FernandezOviedoSumarioIndias27kb.txt 0.13821168706742293

31. Lucena -C:\Users\Govert\Desktop\Signatura comienzo 19.11.2019\repamores mitad libro51kb.txt 0.13826141598909925

32. Tratado de Fisonomía -C:\Users\Govert\Desktop\Signatura comienzo 19.11.2019\tratadofisonomiaObra22kb.txt 0.14180625802569446

33. Juan de Flores -C:\Users\Govert\Desktop\Signatura comienzo 19.11.2019\triunfodeamorprologo4kb.txt 0.1423770855337052

34. Gonzalo Fernández de Oviedo -C:\Users\Govert\Desktop\Signatura comienzo 19.11.2019\fernandezOviedo-indias 21kb.txt 0.14359417324259027

35. Garci Rodríguez de Montalvo -C:\Users\Govert\Desktop\Signatura comienzo 19.11.2019\AmadisDos21kb.txt 0.14674242957761996

36. Andrés de Li -C:\Users\Govert\Desktop\Signatura comienzo 19.11.2019\SumaDePaciencia1493Prologo6kb.txt 0.14690409625247014

36. Andrés de Li -C:\Users\Govert\Desktop\Signatura comienzo 19.11.2019\SumaDePaciencia1493Prologo6kb.txt 0.14690409625247014

38. Juan del Encina -C:\Users\Govert\Desktop\Signatura comienzo 19.11.2019\encinabubolicaArgumentos5kb.txt 0.14742045627998723

39. Gordonio Niños -C:\Users\Govert\Desktop\Signatura comienzo 19.11.2019\GordonioNiños32kb.txt 0.14802297697277922

40. Gonzalo García Santa Maria -C:\Users\Govert\Desktop\Signatura comienzo 19.11.2019\evangeliosepistolas1485-64kb.txt 0.14926560850296466

41. Duobus amantibus -C:\Users\Govert\Desktop\Signatura comienzo 19.11.2019\piccolomini pp20 hasta30-21kb.txt 0.15021189184332573

42. Ysopo -C:\Users\Govert\Desktop\Signatura comienzo 19.11.2019\ysope primer libro1495.txt 0.1509509368934554

43. Vidal de Noya -C:\Users\Govert\Desktop\Signatura comienzo 19.11.2019\vidal de noyaJugurthaguerra28kb.txt 0.15186859910041017

44. La Celestina -C:\Users\Govert\Desktop\Signatura comienzo 19.11.2019\CelestinaPrologo9kb.txt 0.15213284479726685

45. Andrés de Li -C:\Users\Govert\Desktop\Signatura comienzo 19.11.2019\SumadePaciencia32kb.txt 0.15291206437055294

46. Juan del Encina -C:\Users\Govert\Desktop\Signatura comienzo 19.11.2019\encina eglogas antes 1509-287kb.txt 0.15398697377651094

47. Juan del Encina -C:\Users\Govert\Desktop\Signatura comienzo 19.11.2019\EncinaCancioneroAlbaHijoPrologo4kb.txt 0.1546173867611439

48. Juan de Ávila - Oliveros -C:\Users\Govert\Desktop\Signatura comienzo 19.11.2019\oliveros de castilla obra21kb.txt 0.15464693912928795

49. Martin de Cordoba Jardin doncellas -C:\Users\Govert\Desktop\Signatura comienzo 19.11.2019\martindecordoba12kb.txt 0.15977587802721738

50. Lucena -C:\Users\Govert\Desktop\Signatura comienzo 19.11.2019\repeticionamores ajedrez4kb.txt 0.15985152037535422

51. Gonzalo Fernández de Oviedo -C:\Users\Govert\Desktop\Signatura comienzo 19.11.2019\fernandezoviedobatalla90-130tiene34kb.txt 0.16360845516997746

52. Tratado de Fisonomía -C:\Users\Govert\Desktop\Signatura comienzo 19.11.2019\tratadofisonomiaIntroduccion3kb.txt 0.16508061838510035

53. Juan del Encina - Linda Melosina -C:\Users\Govert\Desktop\Signatura comienzo 19.11.2019\lindamelosina21kb.txt 0.165370804996529

54. Corónica Adramon -C:\Users\Govert\Desktop\Signatura comienzo 19.11.2019\adramonObra30kb.txt 0.1683568057291166

55. Juan del Encina -C:\Users\Govert\Desktop\Signatura comienzo 19.11.2019\encina1521-8kb.txt 0.1697390445186553

56. Juan del Encina -C:\Users\Govert\Desktop\Signatura comienzo 19.11.2019\encinacoplas1521.txt 0.17112097862385234

57. Juan de Ávila - Oliveros -C:\Users\Govert\Desktop\Signatura comienzo 19.11.2019\olveros de castilla epílogo.txt 0.17159733473398353

58. Tratado generación criatura -C:\Users\Govert\Desktop\Signatura comienzo 19.11.2019\TratadoGeneracionCriaturaObra24kb.txt 0.17451815984852714

59. Gonzalo García Santa Maria -C:\Users\Govert\Desktop\Signatura comienzo 19.11.2019\GarciaSantaMariaCoronicaAragonObra27kb.txt 0.1760278124398137

60. Tercer Viaje de Colon -C:\Users\Govert\Desktop\Signatura comienzo 19.11.2019\TercerViajeColon24kb.txt 0.17654101500032604

61. Alonso de Proaza -C:\Users\Govert\Desktop\Signatura comienzo 19.11.2019\alonsodeproazaProsa no Celestina-12kb.txt 0.1787835095755541

62. Juan de Flores -C:\Users\Govert\Desktop\Signatura comienzo 19.11.2019\griselobra21kb.txt 0.17879793657478793

63. Gonzalo de Ayora -C:\Users\Govert\Desktop\Signatura comienzo 19.11.2019\GonzaloAyoraA MiguelPerezAlmazan15kb.txt 0.17992364456404797

64. Diego de San Pedro -C:\Users\Govert\Desktop\Signatura comienzo 19.11.2019\arnalte incompleta21kb.txt 0.1816540600425055

65. Gil Vicente -C:\Users\Govert\Desktop\Signatura comienzo 19.11.2019\GilVicenteComediaViudo20kb.txt 0.18268392453061655

66. Pedro Carrillo de Huete -C:\Users\Govert\Desktop\Signatura comienzo 19.11.2019\halconero1489year32kb.txt 0.18306241178021476

67. Flor de virtudes -C:\Users\Govert\Desktop\Signatura comienzo 19.11.2019\flordevirtudesobra22kb.txt 0.1843671859343451

68. Garci Rodríguez de Montalvo -C:\Users\Govert\Desktop\Signatura comienzo 19.11.2019\AmadisCuatro21kb.txt 0.18531335550725658

69. Garci Rodríguez de Montalvo -C:\Users\Govert\Desktop\Signatura comienzo 19.11.2019\AmadisUno21kb.txt 0.1868419882493595

70. Balado Merlin anonimo -C:\Users\Govert\Desktop\Signatura comienzo 19.11.2019\baladromerlin21kb.txt 0.18870457687211528

71. Gonzalo de Ayora -C:\Users\Govert\Desktop\Signatura comienzo 19.11.2019\GonzaloAyora79kb.txt 0.18955245391953757

72. Juan de Flores -C:\Users\Govert\Desktop\Signatura comienzo 19.11.2019\grimalte prologo3kb.txt 0.1902525480906121

73. Infancia Salvatoris -C:\Users\Govert\Desktop\Signatura comienzo 19.11.2019\InfanciaSalvatoris36kb.txt 0.19034499087390744

74. Gonzalo Fernández de Oviedo -C:\Users\Govert\Desktop\Signatura comienzo 19.11.2019\FernandezOviedoClaribalte21kb.txt 0.19050192361142093

75. Boccaccio -C:\Users\Govert\Desktop\Signatura comienzo 19.11.2019\BoccaccioCaydaPrincipe.txt 0.19085862586596003

76. Balado Merlin anonimo -C:\Users\Govert\Desktop\Signatura comienzo 19.11.2019\baladroprologo1498-7kb.txt 0.19296279976534447

77. Garci Rodríguez de Montalvo -C:\Users\Govert\Desktop\Signatura comienzo 19.11.2019\AmadisTres21kb.txt 0.1935015217262961

78. Cronica Troyana -C:\Users\Govert\Desktop\Signatura comienzo 19.11.2019\cronica troyana obra21kb.txt 0.1952384623556248

79. Gil Vicente -C:\Users\Govert\Desktop\Signatura comienzo 19.11.2019\GilVicenteSibila31kb.txt 0.19797626424048365

80. Lucas Fernández -C:\Users\Govert\Desktop\Signatura comienzo 19.11.2019\lucasfernandez dereniego del amor21kb.txt 0.20582504221866582

81. Gonzalo Fernández de Oviedo -C:\Users\Govert\Desktop\Signatura comienzo 19.11.2019\fernandezOviedo1532catálogo21kb.txt 0.20597905500935187

82. Carta Hiseo respuesta Tristan -C:\Users\Govert\Desktop\Signatura comienzo 19.11.2019\respuestadetristan.txt 0.20916038036829632

83. Juan Paez de Castro -C:\Users\Govert\Desktop\Signatura comienzo 19.11.2019\juanpaezdecastroCartas23kb.txt 0.21423842494823164

84. Thebayda -C:\Users\Govert\Desktop\Signatura comienzo 19.11.2019\thebaida incompleta21kb.txt 0.21635448248460776

85. Juan de Flores -C:\Users\Govert\Desktop\Signatura comienzo 19.11.2019\grimalteobra21kb.txt 0.2197774902273345

86. Diego de San Pedro -C:\Users\Govert\Desktop\Signatura comienzo 19.11.2019\carceldeamor21kb.txt 0.22124171811241722

87. Tratado de amores -C:\Users\Govert\Desktop\Signatura comienzo 19.11.2019\tratadodeamores15kb.txt 0.22303659029151934

88. Gil Vicente -C:\Users\Govert\Desktop\Signatura comienzo 19.11.2019\GilVicente Don Duardos65kb.txt 0.23110378879668636

89. Juan de Flores -C:\Users\Govert\Desktop\Signatura comienzo 19.11.2019\griselprologo2kb.txt 0.23612943309254253

90. Gil Vicente -C:\Users\Govert\Desktop\Signatura comienzo 19.11.2019\GilVicente AutoPastoril1502 16kb.txt 0.2388911825168425

91. Enrique fi de Oliva -C:\Users\Govert\Desktop\Signatura comienzo 19.11.2019\enrique fi de oliva21kb.txt 0.2543361865424607

92. Alonso de Cardona -C:\Users\Govert\Desktop\Signatura comienzo 19.11.2019\alonsodecardona22kb.txt 0.255564814822859

93. Libro hebreo oraciones -C:\Users\Govert\Desktop\Signatura comienzo 19.11.2019\siddurtefillot21kb.txt 0.265509425086349

94. Fernando de Rojas -C:\Users\Govert\Desktop\Signatura comienzo 19.11.2019\fernando de rojas14kb test2.txt 0.2873579870009293

95. Juan de Flores -C:\Users\Govert\Desktop\Signatura comienzo 19.11.2019\grisel introduccion2kb.txt 0.2898964171034766

96. Carta Hiseo respuesta Tristan -C:\Users\Govert\Desktop\Signatura comienzo 19.11.2019\cartahiseolabrunda.txt 0.299876949913801

97. Nicolás Núñez -C:\Users\Govert\Desktop\Signatura comienzo 19.11.2019\NicolasNuñezTractado32kb.txt 0.3152620447220038

98. Compendio de Salud humana -C:\Users\Govert\Desktop\Signatura comienzo 19.11.2019\compendioSaludHumana25kb.txt 0.33528796881341094

99. Compendio de Salud humana -C:\Users\Govert\Desktop\Signatura comienzo 19.11.2019\CompendioSaludhumanaprologo13kb.txt 0.38049034470915644

15.4.10 JGaap analysis of "Soldadesca"

propaladiasoldadesca21kbCorto.txt C:\Users\Govert\Desktop\Signatura comienzo 19.11.2019\propaladiasoldadesca21kbCorto.txt
Canonicizers:
  Normalize Whitespace
EventDrivers:
  Character NGrams n : 4
    EventCullers:
      Most Common Events numevents : 50
Analysis:
  Nearest Neighbor Driver with metric Cosine Distance
1. Bernardo de Quirós -C:\Users\Govert\Desktop\Signatura comienzo 19.11.2019\VillalonViajeTurquiaVillalon109kb.txt 0.02682119384909687

2. Juan de Flores -C:\Users\Govert\Desktop\Signatura comienzo 19.11.2019\griselobra89kb.txt 0.031573120606455896

3. Francisco López de Villalobos -C:\Users\Govert\Desktop\Signatura comienzo 19.11.2019\villalobos obra completa costumbres humanas141kb.txt 0.03228401858156815

4. Gil Vicente -C:\Users\Govert\Desktop\Signatura comienzo 19.11.2019\GilVicenteSibila31kb.txt 0.03310472899550554

5. Juan de Valdés -C:\Users\Govert\Desktop\Signatura comienzo 19.11.2019\ValdesJuan doctrinacristiana75kb.txt 0.03328510688588615

6. Gil Vicente -C:\Users\Govert\Desktop\Signatura comienzo 19.11.2019\GilVicente Don Duardos65kb.txt 0.03626059497642076

7. Sebastián de Horozco -C:\Users\Govert\Desktop\Signatura comienzo 19.11.2019\HorozcoHistoriaEvangelica.txt 0.03626818687229183

8. Alfonso de Valdés -C:\Users\Govert\Desktop\Signatura comienzo 19.11.2019\valdesAlfonsoCartas34kb.txt 0.03782051983057533

9. Juan de Sedeño -C:\Users\Govert\Desktop\Signatura comienzo 19.11.2019\sedeñocalisto111kb.txt 0.03796284218051715

10. Juan de Timoneda -C:\Users\Govert\Desktop\Signatura comienzo 19.11.2019\TimonedaCaminantes21kb.txt 0.038889685902793736

11. Juan del Encina -C:\Users\Govert\Desktop\Signatura comienzo 19.11.2019\Encina eglogasantes1509 num3-40kb.txt 0.03944875646826407

12. Sancho Muñón -C:\Users\Govert\Desktop\Signatura comienzo 19.11.2019\Acevedo Celestina151kb.txt 0.039567612224722715

13. Sebastián de Horozco -C:\Users\Govert\Desktop\Signatura comienzo 19.11.2019\HorozcoEntremeses.txt 0.03986874638345317

14. Alonso Núñez de Reinoso -C:\Users\Govert\Desktop\Signatura comienzo 19.11.2019\clareoyfloriseaReinoso132kb.txt 0.04283588080829248

15. Diego de San Pedro -C:\Users\Govert\Desktop\Signatura comienzo 19.11.2019\carceldeamor obra completa134kb.txt 0.0436343551915126

16. Diego de San Pedro -C:\Users\Govert\Desktop\Signatura comienzo 19.11.2019\arnalte obra completa120kb.txt 0.0445599975044636

17. Gonzalo Fernández de Oviedo -C:\Users\Govert\Desktop\Signatura comienzo 19.11.2019\fernandezoviedobatalla90-130tiene34kb.txt 0.04628401868610044

18. Juan del Encina -C:\Users\Govert\Desktop\Signatura comienzo 19.11.2019\encina textos al rey75kb.txt 0.046822984598746675

19. Lope de Rueda -C:\Users\Govert\Desktop\Signatura comienzo 19.11.2019\LopedeRuedaEufemia37kb.txt 0.047095236668811324

20. Hernán Pérez de Olivia -C:\Users\Govert\Desktop\Signatura comienzo 19.11.2019\perezolivaSalamanca Razonamiento24 kb.txt 0.04718297515690428

21. Ludovico Escriva -C:\Users\Govert\Desktop\Signatura comienzo 19.11.2019\EscrivaLudovico1537y21kb.txt 0.04975838667780286

22. Juan Paez de Castro -C:\Users\Govert\Desktop\Signatura comienzo 19.11.2019\juanpaezdecastroCartas23kb.txt 0.05023497405428501

23. Ramón de Petras -C:\Users\Govert\Desktop\Signatura comienzo 19.11.2019\traso auto11kb.txt 0.05024735013020565

24. Jerónimo Fernández -C:\Users\Govert\Desktop\Signatura comienzo 19.11.2019\jeronimofernandez3año1579-113kb.txt 0.05033082763236485

25. Gonzalo Fernández de Oviedo -C:\Users\Govert\Desktop\Signatura comienzo 19.11.2019\FernandezOviedoSumarioIndias21kb.txt 0.05056619006170415

26. Feliciano de Silva -C:\Users\Govert\Desktop\Signatura comienzo 19.11.2019\Silva amadis de grecia20kb.txt 0.05143550611978598

27. Thebayda anónym -C:\Users\Govert\Desktop\Signatura comienzo 19.11.2019\thebaida incompleta 92kb.txt 0.05166586749185342

28. Francisco Delicado -C:\Users\Govert\Desktop\Signatura comienzo 19.11.2019\lozanaepilogo5kb.txt 0.05175594893232538

29. Juan de Flores -C:\Users\Govert\Desktop\Signatura comienzo 19.11.2019\grimalteobra21kb.txt 0.05223545243621208

30. Francisco Delicado -C:\Users\Govert\Desktop\Signatura comienzo 19.11.2019\lozano54kb.txt 0.052370005712332746

31. Gáspar Gómez de Toledo -C:\Users\Govert\Desktop\Signatura comienzo 19.11.2019\gaspargomezdeToledoObra23kb.txt 0.05418986507693935

32. Feliciano de Silva -C:\Users\Govert\Desktop\Signatura comienzo 19.11.2019\Silva Celestina Segunda Parcial177kb.txt 0.0544277460267103

33. Francisco Delicado -C:\Users\Govert\Desktop\Signatura comienzo 19.11.2019\lozanaapologia6kb.txt 0.055280341137647904

34. Juan de Valdés -C:\Users\Govert\Desktop\Signatura comienzo 19.11.2019\ValdesJuanCartas1-3-completo114kb.txt 0.055588400406000105

35. Lucena -C:\Users\Govert\Desktop\Signatura comienzo 19.11.2019\repeticionamores114kb.txt 0.056294334835407356

36. Gonzalo Fernández de Oviedo -C:\Users\Govert\Desktop\Signatura comienzo 19.11.2019\FernandezOviedoClaribalte21kb.txt 0.05703279203127698

37. Sebastián de Horozco -C:\Users\Govert\Desktop\Signatura comienzo 19.11.2019\HorozcoRuth.txt 0.058611033273134105

38. Juan Huarte de San Juan -C:\Users\Govert\Desktop\Signatura comienzo 19.11.2019\HuarteExamen Ingenios21kb.txt 0.05884449561256133

39. Lope de Rueda -C:\Users\Govert\Desktop\Signatura comienzo 19.11.2019\lopederuedaAceitunas42kb.txt 0.05906617010322346

40. Gil Vicente -C:\Users\Govert\Desktop\Signatura comienzo 19.11.2019\GilVicenteCuatroTiempos21kb.txt 0.06226832790351622

41. Gil Vicente -C:\Users\Govert\Desktop\Signatura comienzo 19.11.2019\GilVicente AutoPastoril1502 16kb.txt 0.06415994927399771

42. Juan Ramírez de Lucena -C:\Users\Govert\Desktop\Signatura comienzo 19.11.2019\Ramirez Lucena exhortatoria.txt 0.06504357762271973

43. Juan Ramírez de Lucena -C:\Users\Govert\Desktop\Signatura comienzo 19.11.2019\RamirezLucena a Zapata.txt 0.06535953381156856

44. Juan Ramírez de Lucena -C:\Users\Govert\Desktop\Signatura comienzo 19.11.2019\vita beata131kb.txt 0.06737330055089497

45. Juan de Timoneda -C:\Users\Govert\Desktop\Signatura comienzo 19.11.2019\Timoneda Patrañuela30kb.txt 0.06763092502296186

46. Juan Justiniano -C:\Users\Govert\Desktop\Signatura comienzo 19.11.2019\luisvivesformacionmujer84kb.txt 0.07280254154245946

47. Juan de Segura -C:\Users\Govert\Desktop\Signatura comienzo 19.11.2019\JuandeSeguraQuejayAvisoContraElAmor21kb.txt 0.07452043883154069

48. Nicolás Núñez -C:\Users\Govert\Desktop\Signatura comienzo 19.11.2019\NicolasNuñezTractado32kb.txt 0.07469592607161502

49. Alonso de Cardona -C:\Users\Govert\Desktop\Signatura comienzo 19.11.2019\alonsodecardona22kb.txt 0.08043630128908141

50. Francisco Delicado -C:\Users\Govert\Desktop\Signatura comienzo 19.11.2019\lozanadedicatoria2kb.txt 0.08161793966665065

51. Hernán Pérez de Olivia -C:\Users\Govert\Desktop\Signatura comienzo 19.11.2019\perezolivaRioGuadalquivirRazonamiento23kb.txt 0.08240967512068287

52. Hernando de Castillo -C:\Users\Govert\Desktop\Signatura comienzo 19.11.2019\hernando de castillo prologo6kb.txt 0.08334927154162652

53. Juan Ramírez de Lucena -C:\Users\Govert\Desktop\Signatura comienzo 19.11.2019\Ramirez Lucena a Jorge Manrique.txt 0.08383422865767354

54. Juan de Sedeño -C:\Users\Govert\Desktop\Signatura comienzo 19.11.2019\sedeñoAmores Buenaventurança26kb.txt 0.08684304817919208

55. Francisco Delicado -C:\Users\Govert\Desktop\Signatura comienzo 19.11.2019\lozanaepistola3kb.txt 0.08989209665161002

56. Lucas Fernández -C:\Users\Govert\Desktop\Signatura comienzo 19.11.2019\lucasfernandez dereniego del amor169kb.txt 0.08993144536989006

57. Luis de Lucena -C:\Users\Govert\Desktop\Signatura comienzo 19.11.2019\LuisdeLucenaParteTestamento14kb.txt 0.09064365887155545

58. Hernán Díaz -C:\Users\Govert\Desktop\Signatura comienzo 19.11.2019\peregrino obra135kb.txt 0.09326011258428668

59. Gonzalo García de Santa María -C:\Users\Govert\Desktop\Signatura comienzo 19.11.2019\GarciaSantaMariaCoronicaAragonObra27kb.txt 0.09532083001701486

60. Francisco Delicado -C:\Users\Govert\Desktop\Signatura comienzo 19.11.2019\lozanaargumento3kb.txt 0.09567931550201814

61. Hernán Núñez -C:\Users\Govert\Desktop\Signatura comienzo 19.11.2019\hernannuñez Trescientas120kb.txt 0.10088958724293506

62. Francisco Delicado -C:\Users\Govert\Desktop\Signatura comienzo 19.11.2019\legno2 8kb.txt 0.10127807286477686

63. Alonso de Proaza -C:\Users\Govert\Desktop\Signatura comienzo 19.11.2019\alonsodeproazaProsa no Celestina-12kb.txt 0.10218931274927856

64. Gil Vicente -C:\Users\Govert\Desktop\Signatura comienzo 19.11.2019\GilVicenteComediaViudo20kb.txt 0.1046994743712466

65. Juan Ramírez de Lucena -C:\Users\Govert\Desktop\Signatura comienzo 19.11.2019\RamirezLucena a galardones.txt 0.10586742226191537

66. Francisco Cervantes de Salazar -C:\Users\Govert\Desktop\Signatura comienzo 19.11.2019\CervantesSalazarCronicaNuevEspaña21kb.txt 0.1059033497375631

67. La Celestina -C:\Users\Govert\Desktop\Signatura comienzo 19.11.2019\CelestinaComedia-1.txt 0.10845972325354569

68. Diego Hurtado de Mendoza -C:\Users\Govert\Desktop\Signatura comienzo 19.11.2019\diegohurtadodemendoza granada171kb.txt 0.11825165766404733

69. Juan de Sedeño -C:\Users\Govert\Desktop\Signatura comienzo 19.11.2019\sedeño summaPrologo y Epistola19kb.txt 0.12626383183048195

70. Juan de Sedeño -C:\Users\Govert\Desktop\Signatura comienzo 19.11.2019\sedeño summaaobra21kb.txt 0.12688878320151298

71. Gonzalo Fernández de Oviedo -C:\Users\Govert\Desktop\Signatura comienzo 19.11.2019\fernandezOviedo-indias 21kb.txt 0.13520182415477255

72. Lucena -C:\Users\Govert\Desktop\Signatura comienzo 19.11.2019\repeticionamores ajedrez4kb.txt 0.13623249893255818

73. Jerónimo Fernández -C:\Users\Govert\Desktop\Signatura comienzo 19.11.2019\jeronimofernandezhector1547-5-17kb.txt 0.14062479810392647

74. Juan de Sedeño -C:\Users\Govert\Desktop\Signatura comienzo 19.11.2019\sedeño summaEpistolaobra54kb.txt 0.1431905718710048

75. Juan Agüero de Trasmiera -C:\Users\Govert\Desktop\Signatura comienzo 19.11.2019\trasmiera salamanca21kb.txt 0.21592265040916003

76. Fernando de Rojas -C:\Users\Govert\Desktop\Signatura comienzo 19.11.2019\fernando de rojas14kb test2.txt 0.2530999066581947

77. La Celestina -C:\Users\Govert\Desktop\Signatura comienzo 19.11.2019\CelestinaMs1520TextoCorrecto27kb.txt 0.27726729310988496

78. Juan de Timoneda -C:\Users\Govert\Desktop\Signatura comienzo 19.11.2019\Timoneda Disculpa7kb.txt 0.27882914426800165

79. Juan Ramírez de Lucena -C:\Users\Govert\Desktop\Signatura comienzo 19.11.2019\ramirezlucenaJuanOratioEmbajadores1472.txt 0.3786852041095853

80. Juan de Timoneda -C:\Users\Govert\Desktop\Signatura comienzo 19.11.2019\timonedalibrodamas21kb.txt 0.4454661515415341

15.5 Chapter 13

15.5.1 1496 Bucolica to the Monarchs

EncinaBubolicaReyesPrologo8kb.txt C:\Users\Govert\Desktop\Signatura comienzo 19.11.2019\EncinaBubolicaReyesPrologo8kb.txt
Canonicizers:
    Normalize Whitespace
EventDrivers:
    Character NGrams n : 4
        EventCullers:
            Most Common Events numevents : 50
Analysis:
    Nearest Neighbor Driver with metric Cosine Distance
1. Juan del Encina -C:\Users\Govert\Desktop\Signatura comienzo 19.11.2019\EncinaBubolicaReyesPrologo8kb.txt 0.0
2. Juan del Encina -C:\Users\Govert\Desktop\Signatura comienzo 19.11.2019\encina al principe 28kb.txt 0.03425284761000047
3. Prologos Fernández de Oviedo -C:\Users\Govert\Desktop\Signatura comienzo 19.11.2019\PrologosFernandezOviedo1-96kb.txt 0.03555165989363851
4. Duobus amantibus -C:\Users\Govert\Desktop\Signatura comienzo 19.11.2019\piccolomini pp20 hasta30-21kb.txt 0.04684510862811175
5. Gonzalo Fernández de Oviedo -C:\Users\Govert\Desktop\Signatura comienzo 19.11.2019\FernandezOviedoSumarioIndias27kb.txt 0.04932046528305356
6. Pedro de Portugal -C:\Users\Govert\Desktop\Signatura comienzo 19.11.2019\condestablePortugalSatira90kb.txt 0.05237949760979388
7. Garci Rodríguez de Montalvo -C:\Users\Govert\Desktop\Signatura comienzo 19.11.2019\AmadisDos21kb.txt 0.05396065214809036
8. Tercer Viaje de Colon -C:\Users\Govert\Desktop\Signatura comienzo 19.11.2019\TercerViajeColon24kb.txt 0.05457951267968186
9. Alonso Fernández de Madrid -C:\Users\Govert\Desktop\Signatura comienzo 19.11.2019\fernandezdeMadridHernanTalavObra91kb.txt 0.057321943934312336
10. Alfonso el Sabio -C:\Users\Govert\Desktop\Signatura comienzo 19.11.2019\sietepartidas24kb.txt 0.057357207728396364
11. Linda Melosina -C:\Users\Govert\Desktop\Signatura comienzo 19.11.2019\lindamelosina21kb.txt 0.05815189598005732
12. Hernando del Castillo -C:\Users\Govert\Desktop\Signatura comienzo 19.11.2019\hernando de castillo prologo6kb.txt 0.059906231129332355
13. Gonzalo Fernández de Oviedo -C:\Users\Govert\Desktop\Signatura comienzo 19.11.2019\fernandezoviedobatalla90-130tiene34kb.txt 0.059982776462598086

14. Hernán Núñez -C:\Users\Govert\Desktop\Signatura comienzo 19.11.2019\hernannuñez Trescientas21.txt 0.060355554594407224

15. Lucas Fernández -C:\Users\Govert\Desktop\Signatura comienzo 19.11.2019\lucasfernandez dereniego del amor21kb.txt 0.0604012997898965

16. Juan de Flores -C:\Users\Govert\Desktop\Signatura comienzo 19.11.2019\triunfodeamorprologo4kb.txt 0.062262392620706764

17. Lucena -C:\Users\Govert\Desktop\Signatura comienzo 19.11.2019\repamores mitad libro51kb.txt 0.06324625708588172

18. Balado Merlin anonimo -C:\Users\Govert\Desktop\Signatura comienzo 19.11.2019\baladroprologo1498-7kb.txt 0.06347365626168622

19. Gonzalo de Ayora -C:\Users\Govert\Desktop\Signatura comienzo 19.11.2019\gonzaloayoraAvila67kb.txt 0.06357540025871244

20. Gil Vicente -C:\Users\Govert\Desktop\Signatura comienzo 19.11.2019\GilVicenteComediaViudo20kb.txt 0.06404561173590873

21. Juan de Flores -C:\Users\Govert\Desktop\Signatura comienzo 19.11.2019\griselobra21kb.txt 0.06651870657176007

22. Jacobo de la Voragine -C:\Users\Govert\Desktop\Signatura comienzo 19.11.2019\flos sanctorum21kb.txt 0.06653953498664256

23. Gil Vicente -C:\Users\Govert\Desktop\Signatura comienzo 19.11.2019\GilVicenteSibila31kb.txt 0.06722568697079634

24. Francisco López de Villalobos -C:\Users\Govert\Desktop\Signatura comienzo 19.11.2019\villaloboscostumbres humanas21kb.txt 0.06799717062768329

25. Gil Vicente -C:\Users\Govert\Desktop\Signatura comienzo 19.11.2019\GilVicenteCuatroTiempos21kb.txt 0.06838584597265052

26. Garci Rodríguez de Montalvo -C:\Users\Govert\Desktop\Signatura comienzo 19.11.2019\AmadisUno21kb.txt 0.06922892299758332

27. Cronica anónima Reyes Católicos -C:\Users\Govert\Desktop\Signatura comienzo 19.11.2019\cronicalucena21kb.txt 0.06981715188466564

28. Gonzalo Fernández de Oviedo -C:\Users\Govert\Desktop\Signatura comienzo 19.11.2019\FernandezOviedoClaribalte21kb.txt 0.07029293232472522

29. Juan de Ávila - Oliveros -C:\Users\Govert\Desktop\Signatura comienzo 19.11.2019\oliveros de castilla obra21kb.txt 0.07033254269138145

30. Juan del Encina -C:\Users\Govert\Desktop\Signatura comienzo 19.11.2019\EncinaCancioneroReyesProhemio7kb.txt 0.07039365653849394

31. Diego de San Pedro -C:\Users\Govert\Desktop\Signatura comienzo 19.11.2019\arnalte incompleta21kb.txt 0.07111866572518544

32. Gonzalo Fernández de Oviedo -C:\Users\Govert\Desktop\Signatura comienzo 19.11.2019\fernandezOviedo-indias 21kb.txt 0.07118122182052078

33. Thebayda -C:\Users\Govert\Desktop\Signatura comienzo 19.11.2019\thebaida incompleta21kb.txt 0.07138485474230061

34. Juan de Capua -C:\Users\Govert\Desktop\Signatura comienzo 19.11.2019\engañosypeligrosObra25kb.txt 0.07163499212401037

35. Gonzalo Fernández de Oviedo -C:\Users\Govert\Desktop\Signatura comienzo 19.11.2019\fernandezOviedo1532catálogo21kb.txt 0.07310196228012422

36. Boccaccio -C:\Users\Govert\Desktop\Signatura comienzo 19.11.2019\BoccaccioIlustresmujeresprologo9kb.txt 0.07354044938006266

37. Juan Ramírez de Lucena -C:\Users\Govert\Desktop\Signatura comienzo 19.11.2019\vita beata21kb.txt 0.07381278840781058

38. Gonzalo de Ayora -C:\Users\Govert\Desktop\Signatura comienzo 19.11.2019\GonzaloAyora79kb.txt 0.07498454973007795

39. Boccaccio -C:\Users\Govert\Desktop\Signatura comienzo 19.11.2019\BoccaccioIlustresmujeresobra21kb.txt 0.07528304008849307

40. Juan de Flores -C:\Users\Govert\Desktop\Signatura comienzo 19.11.2019\triunfodeamor7kb.txt 0.07565536108330517

41. Corónica Adramon -C:\Users\Govert\Desktop\Signatura comienzo 19.11.2019\adramonObra30kb.txt 0.07581021143562161

42. Garci Rodríguez de Montalvo -C:\Users\Govert\Desktop\Signatura comienzo 19.11.2019\AmadisCuatro21kb.txt 0.07611874900688331

43. Ysopo -C:\Users\Govert\Desktop\Signatura comienzo 19.11.2019\ysope primer libro1495.txt 0.07635989455789183

44. Juan Paez de Castro -C:\Users\Govert\Desktop\Signatura comienzo 19.11.2019\juanpaezdecastroCartas23kb.txt 0.07741889685138292

45. Martin de Cordoba Jardin doncellas -C:\Users\Govert\Desktop\Signatura comienzo 19.11.2019\martindecordoba12kb.txt 0.07770865656539805

46. Flor de virtudes -C:\Users\Govert\Desktop\Signatura comienzo 19.11.2019\flordevirtudesobra22kb.txt 0.07832441905590715

47. Diego de San Pedro -C:\Users\Govert\Desktop\Signatura comienzo 19.11.2019\carceldeamor21kb.txt 0.07890465658935031

48. Gonzalo de Ayora -C:\Users\Govert\Desktop\Signatura comienzo 19.11.2019\GonzaloAyoraA MiguelPerezAlmazan15kb.txt 0.07957232510421275

49. Tratado de amores -C:\Users\Govert\Desktop\Signatura comienzo 19.11.2019\tratadodeamores15kb.txt 0.08169763147286246

50. Pedro Carrillo de Huete -C:\Users\Govert\Desktop\Signatura comienzo 19.11.2019\halconero1489year32kb.txt 0.08237888566204943

51. Juan del Encina -C:\Users\Govert\Desktop\Signatura comienzo 19.11.2019\Encina eglogasantes1509 num3-40kb.txt 0.08278475805848418

52. Garci Rodríguez de Montalvo -C:\Users\Govert\Desktop\Signatura comienzo 19.11.2019\amadisdegaula1496 prologo8kb.txt 0.0838182350834713

53. Juan de Flores -C:\Users\Govert\Desktop\Signatura comienzo 19.11.2019\griselprologo2kb.txt 0.0839311905251493

54. Juan Ramírez de Lucena -C:\Users\Govert\Desktop\Signatura comienzo 19.11.2019\Ramirez Lucena exhortatoria.txt 0.08576430035304328

55. Juan Ramírez de Lucena -C:\Users\Govert\Desktop\Signatura comienzo 19.11.2019\RamirezLucena a Zapata.txt 0.08593565472454867

56. Gil Vicente -C:\Users\Govert\Desktop\Signatura comienzo 19.11.2019\GilVicente Don Duardos65kb.txt 0.08868786273113816

57. Lucena -C:\Users\Govert\Desktop\Signatura comienzo 19.11.2019\repeticionamores ajedrez4kb.txt 0.09088240885449805

58. Tratado generación criatura -C:\Users\Govert\Desktop\Signatura comienzo 19.11.2019\TratadoGeneracionCriaturaObra24kb.txt 0.09152118927403419

59. Gil Vicente -C:\Users\Govert\Desktop\Signatura comienzo 19.11.2019\GilVicente AutoPastoril1502 16kb.txt 0.09301738167974094

60. Carta Hiseo respuesta Tristan -C:\Users\Govert\Desktop\Signatura comienzo 19.11.2019\respuestadetristan.txt 0.09432414060989514

61. Gonzalo García Santa Maria -C:\Users\Govert\Desktop\Signatura comienzo 19.11.2019\GarciaSantaMariaCoronicaAragonObra27kb.txt 0.09462010247791253

62. Gordonio Niños -C:\Users\Govert\Desktop\Signatura comienzo 19.11.2019\GordonioNiños32kb.txt 0.09579147880757966

63. Juan de Flores -C:\Users\Govert\Desktop\Signatura comienzo 19.11.2019\grimalte prologo3kb.txt 0.0970335283735847

64. Garci Rodríguez de Montalvo -C:\Users\Govert\Desktop\Signatura comienzo 19.11.2019\AmadisTres21kb.txt 0.09749451909167584

65. Alonso de Proaza -C:\Users\Govert\Desktop\Signatura comienzo 19.11.2019\alonsodeproazaProsa no Celestina-12kb.txt 0.10192355705944511

66. Enrique fi de Oliva -C:\Users\Govert\Desktop\Signatura comienzo 19.11.2019\enrique fi de oliva21kb.txt 0.10291538227230201

67. Vidal de Noya -C:\Users\Govert\Desktop\Signatura comienzo 19.11.2019\vidal de noyaJugurthaguerra28kb.txt 0.10435988663728846

68. Alonso de Cardona -C:\Users\Govert\Desktop\Signatura comienzo 19.11.2019\alonsodecardona22kb.txt 0.10618676588088305

69. Juan de Flores -C:\Users\Govert\Desktop\Signatura comienzo 19.11.2019\grimalteobra21kb.txt 0.10793782579603028

70. Boccaccio -C:\Users\Govert\Desktop\Signatura comienzo 19.11.2019\BoccaccioCaydaPrincipe.txt 0.11089588976612563

71. Gonzalo García Santa Maria -C:\Users\Govert\Desktop\Signatura comienzo 19.11.2019\evangeliosepistolas1485-64kb.txt 0.11318808194685193

72. Juan de Flores -C:\Users\Govert\Desktop\Signatura comienzo 19.11.2019\grisel introduccion2kb.txt 0.1137815563711988

73. Cronica Troyana -C:\Users\Govert\Desktop\Signatura comienzo 19.11.2019\cronica troyana obra21kb.txt 0.11893118029989147

74. Juan de Ávila - Oliveros -C:\Users\Govert\Desktop\Signatura comienzo 19.11.2019\olveros de castilla epílogo.txt 0.11988187906747139

75. Martín Martínez de Ampiés -C:\Users\Govert\Desktop\Signatura comienzo 19.11.2019\BreidenbachTierraSantaRomaTratado8kb.txt 0.12328012432222968

76. Juan Ramírez de Lucena -C:\Users\Govert\Desktop\Signatura comienzo 19.11.2019\RamirezLucena a galardones.txt 0.1279359026561483

77. Infancia Salvatoris -C:\Users\Govert\Desktop\Signatura comienzo 19.11.2019\InfanciaSalvatoris36kb.txt 0.1314348774266404

78. Tratado de Fisonomía -C:\Users\Govert\Desktop\Signatura comienzo 19.11.2019\tratadofisonomiaProemio8kb.txt 0.13166496452616805

79. Juan de Padilla -C:\Users\Govert\Desktop\Signatura comienzo 19.11.2019\retablo cartujo14kb.txt 0.13655551067540594

80. Andrés de Li -C:\Users\Govert\Desktop\Signatura comienzo 19.11.2019\SumaDePaciencia1493Prologo6kb.txt 0.14061806966959522
80. Andrés de Li -C:\Users\Govert\Desktop\Signatura comienzo 19.11.2019\SumaDePaciencia1493Prologo6kb.txt 0.14061806966959522
82. Nicolás Núñez -C:\Users\Govert\Desktop\Signatura comienzo 19.11.2019\NicolasNuñezTractado32kb.txt 0.14083483604536873
83. Carta Hiseo respuesta Tristan -C:\Users\Govert\Desktop\Signatura comienzo 19.11.2019\cartahiseolabrunda.txt 0.14296514529468718
84. Juan de Ávila - Oliveros -C:\Users\Govert\Desktop\Signatura comienzo 19.11.2019\oliverosdecastilla introduccion.txt 0.16153160786063003
85. Fernando de Rojas -C:\Users\Govert\Desktop\Signatura comienzo 19.11.2019\fernando de rojas14kb test2.txt 0.16538692795891918
86. Balado Merlin anonimo -C:\Users\Govert\Desktop\Signatura comienzo 19.11.2019\baladromerlin21kb.txt 0.17003753550918554
87. Juan de Ávila - Oliveros -C:\Users\Govert\Desktop\Signatura comienzo 19.11.2019\olveros de castilla prologo1498and1499.txt 0.17022330676943798
88. Martin de Cordoba Jardin doncellas -C:\Users\Govert\Desktop\Signatura comienzo 19.11.2019\martindecordobaprohemio2kb.txt 0.17456566433015597
89. Nicolás Núñez -C:\Users\Govert\Desktop\Signatura comienzo 19.11.2019\NicolasNuñezTractadoprologo2kb.txt 0.1769810902058434
90. Tratado de Fisonomía -C:\Users\Govert\Desktop\Signatura comienzo 19.11.2019\tratadofisonomiaIntroduccion3kb.txt 0.1816073154871073
91. Libro hebreo oraciones -C:\Users\Govert\Desktop\Signatura comienzo 19.11.2019\siddurtefillot21kb.txt 0.19748805911537826
92. Tratado de Fisonomía -C:\Users\Govert\Desktop\Signatura comienzo 19.11.2019\tratadofisonomiaObra22kb.txt 0.19871483071303508
93. Andrés de Li -C:\Users\Govert\Desktop\Signatura comienzo 19.11.2019\SumadePaciencia32kb.txt 0.23287177698275185
94. Compendio de Salud humana -C:\Users\Govert\Desktop\Signatura comienzo 19.11.2019\compendioSaludHumana25kb.txt 0.2763841734343605
95. Compendio de Salud humana -C:\Users\Govert\Desktop\Signatura comienzo 19.11.2019\CompendioSaludhumanaprologo13kb.txt 0.3876199562437508

15.5.2 1496 Cancionero Bubólica to the prince

EncinaBubolicaPrincipePrologo8kb.txt C:\Users\Govert\Desktop\Signatura comienzo 19.11.2019\EncinaBubolicaPrincipePrologo8kb.txt
Canonicizers:
    Normalize Whitespace
EventDrivers:
    Character NGrams n : 4
        EventCullers:
            Most Common Events numevents : 50
Analysis:

Nearest Neighbor Driver with metric Cosine Distance

1. Juan del Encina -C:\Users\Govert\Desktop\Signatura comienzo 19.11.2019\EncinaBubolicaReyesPrologo8kb.txt 0.028476153737403975

2. Prologos Fernández de Oviedo -C:\Users\Govert\Desktop\Signatura comienzo 19.11.2019\PrologosFernandezOviedo1-96kb.txt 0.05289922805822178

3. Gonzalo de Ayora -C:\Users\Govert\Desktop\Signatura comienzo 19.11.2019\gonzaloayoraAvila67kb.txt 0.05534342693189376

4. Hernán Núñez -C:\Users\Govert\Desktop\Signatura comienzo 19.11.2019\hernannuñez Trescientas21.txt 0.058334950634155724

5. Juan de Flores -C:\Users\Govert\Desktop\Signatura comienzo 19.11.2019\triunfodeamorprologo4kb.txt 0.06031468264917894

6. Juan del Encina -C:\Users\Govert\Desktop\Signatura comienzo 19.11.2019\encina al principe 28kb.txt 0.06056610537201601

7. Juan del Encina -C:\Users\Govert\Desktop\Signatura comienzo 19.11.2019\EncinaCancioneroReyesProhemio7kb.txt 0.06637629438157056

8. Juan de Flores -C:\Users\Govert\Desktop\Signatura comienzo 19.11.2019\triunfodeamor7kb.txt 0.06638653910311809

9. Boccaccio -C:\Users\Govert\Desktop\Signatura comienzo 19.11.2019\BoccaccioIlustresmujeresobra21kb.txt 0.06644472375599453

10. Cronica anónima Reyes Católicos -C:\Users\Govert\Desktop\Signatura comienzo 19.11.2019\cronicalucena21kb.txt 0.06645235698917351

11. Duobus amantibus -C:\Users\Govert\Desktop\Signatura comienzo 19.11.2019\piccolomini pp20 hasta30-21kb.txt 0.06780030565690809

12. Pedro de Portugal -C:\Users\Govert\Desktop\Signatura comienzo 19.11.2019\condestablePortugalSatira90kb.txt 0.06822704229069654

13. Juan de Capua -C:\Users\Govert\Desktop\Signatura comienzo 19.11.2019\engañosypeligrosObra25kb.txt 0.06965029450636029

14. Alonso Fernández de Madrid -C:\Users\Govert\Desktop\Signatura comienzo 19.11.2019\fernandezdeMadridHernanTalavObra91kb.txt 0.06981858495061621

15. Gonzalo Fernández de Oviedo -C:\Users\Govert\Desktop\Signatura comienzo 19.11.2019\FernandezOviedoSumarioIndias27kb.txt 0.07088966738957747

16. Juan Ramírez de Lucena -C:\Users\Govert\Desktop\Signatura comienzo 19.11.2019\vita beata21kb.txt 0.07138002637448693

17. Garci Rodríguez de Montalvo -C:\Users\Govert\Desktop\Signatura comienzo 19.11.2019\AmadisDos21kb.txt 0.07233658469035797

18. Gonzalo Fernández de Oviedo -C:\Users\Govert\Desktop\Signatura comienzo 19.11.2019\fernandezOviedo-indias 21kb.txt 0.07408973754168868

19. Gil Vicente -C:\Users\Govert\Desktop\Signatura comienzo 19.11.2019\GilVicenteCuatroTiempos21kb.txt 0.07414439599710276

20. Boccaccio -C:\Users\Govert\Desktop\Signatura comienzo 19.11.2019\BoccaccioIlustresmujeresprologo9kb.txt 0.07510220317213423

21. Hernando del Castillo -C:\Users\Govert\Desktop\Signatura comienzo 19.11.2019\hernando de castillo prologo6kb.txt 0.07848273087397384

22. Tercer Viaje de Colon -C:\Users\Govert\Desktop\Signatura comienzo 19.11.2019\TercerViajeColon24kb.txt 0.07959107690918321

23. Gonzalo Fernández de Oviedo -C:\Users\Govert\Desktop\Signatura comienzo 19.11.2019\fernandezOviedo1532catálogo21kb.txt 0.08053982138367688

24. Gil Vicente -C:\Users\Govert\Desktop\Signatura comienzo 19.11.2019\GilVicenteComediaViudo20kb.txt 0.08166668271920396

25. Alfonso el Sabio -C:\Users\Govert\Desktop\Signatura comienzo 19.11.2019\sietepartidas24kb.txt 0.08267010599369884

26. Jacobo de la Voragine -C:\Users\Govert\Desktop\Signatura comienzo 19.11.2019\flos sanctorum21kb.txt 0.08303463784262011

27. Lucena -C:\Users\Govert\Desktop\Signatura comienzo 19.11.2019\repamores mitad libro51kb.txt 0.08562411413944304

28. Pedro Carrillo de Huete -C:\Users\Govert\Desktop\Signatura comienzo 19.11.2019\halconero1489year32kb.txt 0.0859735972763106

29. Lucas Fernández -C:\Users\Govert\Desktop\Signatura comienzo 19.11.2019\lucasfernandez dereniego del amor21kb.txt 0.08612946576545844

30. Francisco López de Villalobos -C:\Users\Govert\Desktop\Signatura comienzo 19.11.2019\villaloboscostumbres humanas21kb.txt 0.08973418284227652

31. Gordonio Niños -C:\Users\Govert\Desktop\Signatura comienzo 19.11.2019\GordonioNiños32kb.txt 0.09216756623215971

32. Garci Rodríguez de Montalvo -C:\Users\Govert\Desktop\Signatura comienzo 19.11.2019\AmadisUno21kb.txt 0.09505436419090818

33. Lucena -C:\Users\Govert\Desktop\Signatura comienzo 19.11.2019\repeticionamores ajedrez4kb.txt 0.0955589967188234

34. Diego de San Pedro -C:\Users\Govert\Desktop\Signatura comienzo 19.11.2019\arnalte incompleta21kb.txt 0.09581022223715496

35. Garci Rodríguez de Montalvo -C:\Users\Govert\Desktop\Signatura comienzo 19.11.2019\AmadisCuatro21kb.txt 0.09690375265320195

36. Gonzalo Fernández de Oviedo -C:\Users\Govert\Desktop\Signatura comienzo 19.11.2019\fernandezoviedobatalla90-130tiene34kb.txt 0.09711097140232572

37. Garci Rodríguez de Montalvo -C:\Users\Govert\Desktop\Signatura comienzo 19.11.2019\amadisdegaula1496 prologo8kb.txt 0.09761452290902939

38. Balado Merlin anonimo -C:\Users\Govert\Desktop\Signatura comienzo 19.11.2019\baladroprologo1498-7kb.txt 0.0977735312962128

39. Juan de Ávila - Oliveros -C:\Users\Govert\Desktop\Signatura comienzo 19.11.2019\oliveros de castilla obra21kb.txt 0.09890946010943735

40. Martín Martínez de Ampiés -C:\Users\Govert\Desktop\Signatura comienzo 19.11.2019\BreidenbachTierraSantaRomaTratado8kb.txt 0.10219225093803208

41. Juan Ramírez de Lucena -C:\Users\Govert\Desktop\Signatura comienzo 19.11.2019\Ramirez Lucena exhortatoria.txt 0.10423616904584909

42. Juan Ramírez de Lucena -C:\Users\Govert\Desktop\Signatura comienzo 19.11.2019\RamirezLucena a Zapata.txt 0.10438039105993424

43. Juan de Flores -C:\Users\Govert\Desktop\Signatura comienzo 19.11.2019\griselobra21kb.txt 0.10439702488655722

44. Juan de Padilla -C:\Users\Govert\Desktop\Signatura comienzo 19.11.2019\retablo cartujo14kb.txt 0.1044153561016179

45. Linda Melosina -C:\Users\Govert\Desktop\Signatura comienzo 19.11.2019\lindamelosina21kb.txt 0.10479046969870753

46. Ysopo -C:\Users\Govert\Desktop\Signatura comienzo 19.11.2019\ysope primer libro1495.txt 0.10574922520820196

47. Gonzalo Fernández de Oviedo -C:\Users\Govert\Desktop\Signatura comienzo 19.11.2019\FernandezOviedoClaribalte21kb.txt 0.1064792193293509

48. Martin de Cordoba Jardin doncellas -C:\Users\Govert\Desktop\Signatura comienzo 19.11.2019\martindecordoba12kb.txt 0.10650902013628039

49. Flor de virtudes -C:\Users\Govert\Desktop\Signatura comienzo 19.11.2019\flordevirtudesobra22kb.txt 0.10755243771476863

50. Thebayda -C:\Users\Govert\Desktop\Signatura comienzo 19.11.2019\thebaida incompleta21kb.txt 0.10761977368870712

51. Juan de Flores -C:\Users\Govert\Desktop\Signatura comienzo 19.11.2019\grimalte prologo3kb.txt 0.10789356941510397

52. Alonso de Proaza -C:\Users\Govert\Desktop\Signatura comienzo 19.11.2019\alonsodeproazaProsa no Celestina-12kb.txt 0.10846836349601618

53. Gonzalo de Ayora -C:\Users\Govert\Desktop\Signatura comienzo 19.11.2019\GonzaloAyora79kb.txt 0.1089845221201784

54. Gil Vicente -C:\Users\Govert\Desktop\Signatura comienzo 19.11.2019\GilVicenteSibila31kb.txt 0.11127842621001749

55. Juan de Ávila - Oliveros -C:\Users\Govert\Desktop\Signatura comienzo 19.11.2019\oliverosdecastilla introduccion.txt 0.11147572115431892

56. Vidal de Noya -C:\Users\Govert\Desktop\Signatura comienzo 19.11.2019\vidal de noyaJugurthaguerra28kb.txt 0.11285741133054283

57. Juan Paez de Castro -C:\Users\Govert\Desktop\Signatura comienzo 19.11.2019\juanpaezdecastroCartas23kb.txt 0.11324160443322329

58. Corónica Adramon -C:\Users\Govert\Desktop\Signatura comienzo 19.11.2019\adramonObra30kb.txt 0.1143278340860201

59. Tratado de amores -C:\Users\Govert\Desktop\Signatura comienzo 19.11.2019\tratadodeamores15kb.txt 0.11689372556742794

60. Gonzalo García Santa Maria -C:\Users\Govert\Desktop\Signatura comienzo 19.11.2019\GarciaSantaMariaCoronicaAragonObra27kb.txt 0.1173055120462716

61. Juan de Ávila - Oliveros -C:\Users\Govert\Desktop\Signatura comienzo 19.11.2019\olveros de castilla prologo1498and1499.txt 0.11766218249307958

62. Diego de San Pedro -C:\Users\Govert\Desktop\Signatura comienzo 19.11.2019\carceldeamor21kb.txt 0.11903097473439672

63. Juan de Flores -C:\Users\Govert\Desktop\Signatura comienzo 19.11.2019\griselprologo2kb.txt 0.12033161696881634

64. Gonzalo de Ayora -C:\Users\Govert\Desktop\Signatura comienzo 19.11.2019\GonzaloAyoraA MiguelPerezAlmazan15kb.txt 0.12040448749730293

65. Tratado generación criatura -C:\Users\Govert\Desktop\Signatura comienzo 19.11.2019\TratadoGeneracionCriaturaObra24kb.txt 0.12142042502497774

66. Tratado de Fisonomía -C:\Users\Govert\Desktop\Signatura comienzo 19.11.2019\tratadofisonomiaProemio8kb.txt 0.12197058904348212

67. Gonzalo García Santa Maria -C:\Users\Govert\Desktop\Signatura comienzo 19.11.2019\evangeliosepistolas1485-64kb.txt 0.12477660709258986

68. Juan del Encina -C:\Users\Govert\Desktop\Signatura comienzo 19.11.2019\Encina eglogasantes1509 num3-40kb.txt 0.12554438610056817

69. Juan Ramírez de Lucena -C:\Users\Govert\Desktop\Signatura comienzo 19.11.2019\RamirezLucena a galardones.txt 0.12773612706207826

70. Juan de Ávila - Oliveros -C:\Users\Govert\Desktop\Signatura comienzo 19.11.2019\olveros de castilla epílogo.txt 0.12838772483141547

71. Andrés de Li -C:\Users\Govert\Desktop\Signatura comienzo 19.11.2019\SumaDePaciencia1493Prologo6kb.txt 0.12871521740573655

71. Andrés de Li -C:\Users\Govert\Desktop\Signatura comienzo 19.11.2019\SumaDePaciencia1493Prologo6kb.txt 0.12871521740573655

73. Garci Rodríguez de Montalvo -C:\Users\Govert\Desktop\Signatura comienzo 19.11.2019\AmadisTres21kb.txt 0.13200660157854993

74. Carta Hiseo respuesta Tristan -C:\Users\Govert\Desktop\Signatura comienzo 19.11.2019\respuestadetristan.txt 0.1352524369806356

75. Boccaccio -C:\Users\Govert\Desktop\Signatura comienzo 19.11.2019\BoccaccioCaydaPrincipe.txt 0.1377239658231023

76. Tratado de Fisonomía -C:\Users\Govert\Desktop\Signatura comienzo 19.11.2019\tratadofisonomiaIntroduccion3kb.txt 0.13801317011375602

77. Cronica Troyana -C:\Users\Govert\Desktop\Signatura comienzo 19.11.2019\cronica troyana obra21kb.txt 0.13848164459290635

78. Gil Vicente -C:\Users\Govert\Desktop\Signatura comienzo 19.11.2019\GilVicente Don Duardos65kb.txt 0.13883686676389428

79. Balado Merlin anonimo -C:\Users\Govert\Desktop\Signatura comienzo 19.11.2019\baladromerlin21kb.txt 0.1405321540423713

80. Fernando de Rojas -C:\Users\Govert\Desktop\Signatura comienzo 19.11.2019\fernando de rojas14kb test2.txt 0.14978423426656373

81. Gil Vicente -C:\Users\Govert\Desktop\Signatura comienzo 19.11.2019\GilVicente AutoPastoril1502 16kb.txt 0.14990035862670115

82. Juan de Flores -C:\Users\Govert\Desktop\Signatura comienzo 19.11.2019\grimalteobra21kb.txt 0.1504640758066249

83. Alonso de Cardona -C:\Users\Govert\Desktop\Signatura comienzo 19.11.2019\alonsodecardona22kb.txt 0.1542611482289129

84. Enrique fi de Oliva -C:\Users\Govert\Desktop\Signatura comienzo 19.11.2019\enrique fi de oliva21kb.txt 0.1553569268915438

85. Juan de Flores -C:\Users\Govert\Desktop\Signatura comienzo 19.11.2019\grisel introduccion2kb.txt 0.1650534015038979

86. Martin de Cordoba Jardin doncellas -C:\Users\Govert\Desktop\Signatura comienzo 19.11.2019\martindecordobaprohemio2kb.txt 0.16566065404833796

87. Infancia Salvatoris -C:\Users\Govert\Desktop\Signatura comienzo 19.11.2019\InfanciaSalvatoris36kb.txt 0.16766131800355055

88. Libro hebreo oraciones -C:\Users\Govert\Desktop\Signatura comienzo 19.11.2019\siddurtefillot21kb.txt 0.16852683946548408

89. Tratado de Fisonomía -C:\Users\Govert\Desktop\Signatura comienzo 19.11.2019\tratadofisonomiaObra22kb.txt 0.18892705686355782

90. Andrés de Li -C:\Users\Govert\Desktop\Signatura comienzo 19.11.2019\SumadePaciencia32kb.txt 0.19189566108353417

91. Nicolás Núñez -C:\Users\Govert\Desktop\Signatura comienzo 19.11.2019\NicolasNuñezTractado32kb.txt 0.1985342920165123

92. Carta Hiseo respuesta Tristan -C:\Users\Govert\Desktop\Signatura comienzo 19.11.2019\cartahiseolabrunda.txt 0.20559174517547574

93. Nicolás Núñez -C:\Users\Govert\Desktop\Signatura comienzo 19.11.2019\NicolasNuñezTractadoprologo2kb.txt 0.22520351531639227

94. Compendio de Salud humana -C:\Users\Govert\Desktop\Signatura comienzo 19.11.2019\compendioSaludHumana25kb.txt 0.25556723368180745

95. Compendio de Salud humana -C:\Users\Govert\Desktop\Signatura comienzo 19.11.2019\CompendioSaludhumanaprologo13kb.txt 0.3541659454202969

15.5.3 1496 Cancionero Proem to Monarchs

EncinaCancioneroReyesProhemio7kb.txt   C:\Users\Govert\Desktop\Signatura comienzo 19.11.2019\EncinaCancioneroReyesProhemio7kb.txt
Canonicizers:
    Normalize Whitespace
EventDrivers:
    Character NGrams n : 4
        EventCullers:
            Most Common Events numevents : 50
Analysis:
    Nearest Neighbor Driver with metric Cosine Distance
1. Juan del Encina -C:\Users\Govert\Desktop\Signatura comienzo 19.11.2019\EncinaCancioneroReyesProhemio7kb.txt 0.0

2. Juan Ramírez de Lucena -C:\Users\Govert\Desktop\Signatura comienzo 19.11.2019\vita beata21kb.txt 0.04768439921403955

3. Juan Ramírez de Lucena -C:\Users\Govert\Desktop\Signatura comienzo 19.11.2019\RamirezLucena a galardones.txt 0.05138940779821699

4. Juan de Flores -C:\Users\Govert\Desktop\Signatura comienzo 19.11.2019\triunfodeamor7kb.txt 0.053804758240032946

5. Juan del Encina -C:\Users\Govert\Desktop\Signatura comienzo 19.11.2019\encina al principe 28kb.txt 0.056826348634721136

6. Francisco López de Villalobos -C:\Users\Govert\Desktop\Signatura comienzo 19.11.2019\villaloboscostumbres humanas21kb.txt 0.061876180377307244

7. Gonzalo de Ayora -C:\Users\Govert\Desktop\Signatura comienzo 19.11.2019\gonzaloayoraAvila67kb.txt 0.0631179752580091

8. Prologos Fernández de Oviedo -C:\Users\Govert\Desktop\Signatura comienzo 19.11.2019\PrologosFernandezOviedo1-96kb.txt 0.06496152381556364

9. Gil Vicente -C:\Users\Govert\Desktop\Signatura comienzo 19.11.2019\GilVicenteCuatroTiempos21kb.txt 0.06591123587177128

10. Alonso Fernández de Madrid -C:\Users\Govert\Desktop\Signatura comienzo 19.11.2019\fernandezdeMadridHernanTalavObra91kb.txt 0.06755372414839744

11. Boccaccio -C:\Users\Govert\Desktop\Signatura comienzo 19.11.2019\BoccaccioIlustresmujeresobra21kb.txt 0.06935465826164056

12. Cronica anónima Reyes Católicos -C:\Users\Govert\Desktop\Signatura comienzo 19.11.2019\cronicalucena21kb.txt 0.06978818660252106

13. Juan del Encina -C:\Users\Govert\Desktop\Signatura comienzo 19.11.2019\EncinaBubolicaReyesPrologo8kb.txt 0.07039365653849416

14. Hernando del Castillo -C:\Users\Govert\Desktop\Signatura comienzo 19.11.2019\hernando de castillo prologo6kb.txt 0.07111967041323697

15. Garci Rodríguez de Montalvo -C:\Users\Govert\Desktop\Signatura comienzo 19.11.2019\amadisdegaula1496 prologo8kb.txt 0.07327002052167009

16. Gonzalo Fernández de Oviedo -C:\Users\Govert\Desktop\Signatura comienzo 19.11.2019\FernandezOviedoSumarioIndias27kb.txt 0.07592385719628869

17. Pedro de Portugal -C:\Users\Govert\Desktop\Signatura comienzo 19.11.2019\condestablePortugalSatira90kb.txt 0.08058751697891087

18. Duobus amantibus -C:\Users\Govert\Desktop\Signatura comienzo 19.11.2019\piccolomini pp20 hasta30-21kb.txt 0.08145599914192303

19. Garci Rodríguez de Montalvo -C:\Users\Govert\Desktop\Signatura comienzo 19.11.2019\AmadisDos21kb.txt 0.08335249041631954

20. Lucena -C:\Users\Govert\Desktop\Signatura comienzo 19.11.2019\repamores mitad libro51kb.txt 0.08556927208413789

21. Alfonso el Sabio -C:\Users\Govert\Desktop\Signatura comienzo 19.11.2019\sietepartidas24kb.txt 0.08630399236470776

22. Gonzalo de Ayora -C:\Users\Govert\Desktop\Signatura comienzo 19.11.2019\GonzaloAyoraA MiguelPerezAlmazan15kb.txt 0.08682598771284766

23. Hernán Núñez -C:\Users\Govert\Desktop\Signatura comienzo 19.11.2019\hernannuñez Trescientas21.txt 0.0892601379686172

24. Corónica Adramon -C:\Users\Govert\Desktop\Signatura comienzo 19.11.2019\adramonObra30kb.txt 0.08970820906146382

25. Juan de Capua -C:\Users\Govert\Desktop\Signatura comienzo 19.11.2019\engañosypeligrosObra25kb.txt 0.09008125740676731

26. Juan de Padilla -C:\Users\Govert\Desktop\Signatura comienzo 19.11.2019\retablo cartujo14kb.txt 0.09121665551458402

27. Juan de Flores -C:\Users\Govert\Desktop\Signatura comienzo 19.11.2019\triunfodeamorprologo4kb.txt 0.09433496797588037

28. Garci Rodríguez de Montalvo -C:\Users\Govert\Desktop\Signatura comienzo 19.11.2019\AmadisCuatro21kb.txt 0.09700066527912965

29. Gonzalo de Ayora -C:\Users\Govert\Desktop\Signatura comienzo 19.11.2019\GonzaloAyora79kb.txt 0.09786867633168228

30. Martin de Cordoba Jardin doncellas -C:\Users\Govert\Desktop\Signatura comienzo 19.11.2019\martindecordoba12kb.txt 0.09818062157787122

31. Jacobo de la Voragine -C:\Users\Govert\Desktop\Signatura comienzo 19.11.2019\flos sanctorum21kb.txt 0.09960449484370115

32. Vidal de Noya -C:\Users\Govert\Desktop\Signatura comienzo 19.11.2019\vidal de noyaJugurthaguerra28kb.txt 0.10064379825054182

33. Garci Rodríguez de Montalvo -C:\Users\Govert\Desktop\Signatura comienzo 19.11.2019\AmadisTres21kb.txt 0.10173217394170064

34. Boccaccio -C:\Users\Govert\Desktop\Signatura comienzo 19.11.2019\BoccaccioIlustresmujeresprologo9kb.txt 0.10283826725418543

35. Ysopo -C:\Users\Govert\Desktop\Signatura comienzo 19.11.2019\ysope primer libro1495.txt 0.10418791096189983

36. Gordonio Niños -C:\Users\Govert\Desktop\Signatura comienzo 19.11.2019\GordonioNiños32kb.txt 0.10877279923404759

37. Andrés de Li -C:\Users\Govert\Desktop\Signatura comienzo 19.11.2019\SumaDePaciencia1493Prologo6kb.txt 0.10915706745137221

37. Andrés de Li -C:\Users\Govert\Desktop\Signatura comienzo 19.11.2019\SumaDePaciencia1493Prologo6kb.txt 0.10915706745137221

39. Juan de Flores -C:\Users\Govert\Desktop\Signatura comienzo 19.11.2019\griselobra21kb.txt 0.11073555221066966

40. Gonzalo Fernández de Oviedo -C:\Users\Govert\Desktop\Signatura comienzo 19.11.2019\fernandezoviedobatalla90-130tiene34kb.txt 0.11113917671138296

41. Gonzalo Fernández de Oviedo -C:\Users\Govert\Desktop\Signatura comienzo 19.11.2019\fernandezOviedo-indias 21kb.txt 0.11123776639108462

42. Juan Paez de Castro -C:\Users\Govert\Desktop\Signatura comienzo 19.11.2019\juanpaezdecastroCartas23kb.txt 0.11142098538919243

43. Lucas Fernández -C:\Users\Govert\Desktop\Signatura comienzo 19.11.2019\lucasfernandez dereniego del amor21kb.txt 0.11424975496445544

44. Juan de Ávila - Oliveros -C:\Users\Govert\Desktop\Signatura comienzo 19.11.2019\oliveros de castilla obra21kb.txt 0.11546901645488017

45. Tercer Viaje de Colon -C:\Users\Govert\Desktop\Signatura comienzo 19.11.2019\TercerViajeColon24kb.txt 0.11570508361929221

46. Gil Vicente -C:\Users\Govert\Desktop\Signatura comienzo 19.11.2019\GilVicenteSibila31kb.txt 0.11584132969131

47. Juan del Encina -C:\Users\Govert\Desktop\Signatura comienzo 19.11.2019\Encina eglogasantes1509 num3-40kb.txt 0.11590274620980645

48. Thebayda -C:\Users\Govert\Desktop\Signatura comienzo 19.11.2019\thebaida incompleta21kb.txt 0.1159549091767007

49. Gonzalo Fernández de Oviedo -C:\Users\Govert\Desktop\Signatura comienzo 19.11.2019\FernandezOviedoClaribalte21kb.txt 0.11608590080224501

50. Martin de Cordoba Jardin doncellas -C:\Users\Govert\Desktop\Signatura comienzo 19.11.2019\martindecordobaprohemio2kb.txt 0.1163862392943753

51. Juan Ramírez de Lucena -C:\Users\Govert\Desktop\Signatura comienzo 19.11.2019\Ramirez Lucena exhortatoria.txt 0.11657722146908989

52. Juan Ramírez de Lucena -C:\Users\Govert\Desktop\Signatura comienzo 19.11.2019\RamirezLucena a Zapata.txt 0.11705040910134734

53. Garci Rodríguez de Montalvo -C:\Users\Govert\Desktop\Signatura comienzo 19.11.2019\AmadisUno21kb.txt 0.11731563056578109

54. Linda Melosina -C:\Users\Govert\Desktop\Signatura comienzo 19.11.2019\lindamelosina21kb.txt 0.1175202100222511

55. Alonso de Proaza -C:\Users\Govert\Desktop\Signatura comienzo 19.11.2019\alonsodeproazaProsa no Celestina-12kb.txt 0.1205114250024748

56. Diego de San Pedro -C:\Users\Govert\Desktop\Signatura comienzo 19.11.2019\arnalte incompleta21kb.txt 0.12140516631717024

57. Martín Martínez de Ampiés -C:\Users\Govert\Desktop\Signatura comienzo 19.11.2019\BreidenbachTierraSantaRomaTratado8kb.txt 0.12374617556828238

58. Balado Merlin anonimo -C:\Users\Govert\Desktop\Signatura comienzo 19.11.2019\baladroprologo1498-7kb.txt 0.1259390433769364

59. Gil Vicente -C:\Users\Govert\Desktop\Signatura comienzo 19.11.2019\GilVicenteComediaViudo20kb.txt 0.12641715281408983

60. Gonzalo García Santa Maria -C:\Users\Govert\Desktop\Signatura comienzo 19.11.2019\GarciaSantaMariaCoronicaAragonObra27kb.txt 0.12704270728000921

61. Gonzalo Fernández de Oviedo -C:\Users\Govert\Desktop\Signatura comienzo 19.11.2019\fernandezOviedo1532catálogo21kb.txt 0.12912383813725792

62. Tratado de Fisonomía -C:\Users\Govert\Desktop\Signatura comienzo 19.11.2019\tratadofisonomiaProemio8kb.txt 0.13130091796919863

63. Gil Vicente -C:\Users\Govert\Desktop\Signatura comienzo 19.11.2019\GilVicente Don Duardos65kb.txt 0.1327197113392421

64. Tratado de amores -C:\Users\Govert\Desktop\Signatura comienzo 19.11.2019\tratadodeamores15kb.txt 0.1353082541901378

65. Diego de San Pedro -C:\Users\Govert\Desktop\Signatura comienzo 19.11.2019\carceldeamor21kb.txt 0.1368176171633786

66. Gonzalo García Santa Maria -C:\Users\Govert\Desktop\Signatura comienzo 19.11.2019\evangeliosepistolas1485-64kb.txt 0.1382683859417927

67. Pedro Carrillo de Huete -C:\Users\Govert\Desktop\Signatura comienzo 19.11.2019\halconero1489year32kb.txt 0.1395456519292244

68. Lucena -C:\Users\Govert\Desktop\Signatura comienzo 19.11.2019\repeticionamores ajedrez4kb.txt 0.14167690916504272

69. Juan de Flores -C:\Users\Govert\Desktop\Signatura comienzo 19.11.2019\griselprologo2kb.txt 0.14364708773199564

70. Juan de Flores -C:\Users\Govert\Desktop\Signatura comienzo 19.11.2019\grimalteobra21kb.txt 0.1437112927362676

71. Infancia Salvatoris -C:\Users\Govert\Desktop\Signatura comienzo 19.11.2019\InfanciaSalvatoris36kb.txt 0.14400152360770502

72. Carta Hiseo respuesta Tristan -C:\Users\Govert\Desktop\Signatura comienzo 19.11.2019\respuestadetristan.txt 0.14426631097900044

73. Juan de Flores -C:\Users\Govert\Desktop\Signatura comienzo 19.11.2019\grimalte prologo3kb.txt 0.14440655066061403

74. Juan de Ávila - Oliveros -C:\Users\Govert\Desktop\Signatura comienzo 19.11.2019\olveros de castilla epílogo.txt 0.14442955287447057

75. Flor de virtudes -C:\Users\Govert\Desktop\Signatura comienzo 19.11.2019\flordevirtudesobra22kb.txt 0.15056642255990926

76. Tratado de Fisonomía -C:\Users\Govert\Desktop\Signatura comienzo 19.11.2019\tratadofisonomiaIntroduccion3kb.txt 0.15188541086339802

77. Tratado generación criatura -C:\Users\Govert\Desktop\Signatura comienzo 19.11.2019\TratadoGeneracionCriaturaObra24kb.txt 0.15195644442902523

78. Gil Vicente -C:\Users\Govert\Desktop\Signatura comienzo 19.11.2019\GilVicente AutoPastoril1502 16kb.txt 0.16125181093924712

79. Cronica Troyana -C:\Users\Govert\Desktop\Signatura comienzo 19.11.2019\cronica troyana obra21kb.txt 0.16380806534946657

80. Alonso de Cardona -C:\Users\Govert\Desktop\Signatura comienzo 19.11.2019\alonsodecardona22kb.txt 0.1703080135859173

81. Enrique fi de Oliva -C:\Users\Govert\Desktop\Signatura comienzo 19.11.2019\enrique fi de oliva21kb.txt 0.17708788210203252

82. Boccaccio -C:\Users\Govert\Desktop\Signatura comienzo 19.11.2019\BoccaccioCaydaPrincipe.txt 0.18162716581180138

83. Juan de Flores -C:\Users\Govert\Desktop\Signatura comienzo 19.11.2019\grisel introduccion2kb.txt 0.18297366145951577

84. Balado Merlin anonimo -C:\Users\Govert\Desktop\Signatura comienzo 19.11.2019\baladromerlin21kb.txt 0.18498894648039166

85. Juan de Ávila - Oliveros -C:\Users\Govert\Desktop\Signatura comienzo 19.11.2019\olveros de castilla prologo1498and1499.txt 0.1851333259000374

86. Juan de Ávila - Oliveros -C:\Users\Govert\Desktop\Signatura comienzo 19.11.2019\oliverosdecastilla introduccion.txt 0.18771109707633649

87. Libro hebreo oraciones -C:\Users\Govert\Desktop\Signatura comienzo 19.11.2019\siddurtefillot21kb.txt 0.1883875937377486

88. Tratado de Fisonomía -C:\Users\Govert\Desktop\Signatura comienzo 19.11.2019\tratadofisonomiaObra22kb.txt 0.19158120835056325

89. Andrés de Li -C:\Users\Govert\Desktop\Signatura comienzo 19.11.2019\SumadePaciencia32kb.txt 0.19254920485024996

90. Carta Hiseo respuesta Tristan -C:\Users\Govert\Desktop\Signatura comienzo 19.11.2019\cartahiseolabrunda.txt 0.19604431919548848

91. Fernando de Rojas -C:\Users\Govert\Desktop\Signatura comienzo 19.11.2019\fernando de rojas14kb test2.txt 0.2039558701037727

92. Nicolás Núñez -C:\Users\Govert\Desktop\Signatura comienzo 19.11.2019\NicolasNuñezTractado32kb.txt 0.20427603072702616

93. Nicolás Núñez -C:\Users\Govert\Desktop\Signatura comienzo 19.11.2019\NicolasNuñezTractadoprologo2kb.txt 0.23846959011875002

94. Compendio de Salud humana -C:\Users\Govert\Desktop\Signatura comienzo 19.11.2019\compendioSaludHumana25kb.txt 0.2858220040543913

95. Compendio de Salud humana -C:\Users\Govert\Desktop\Signatura comienzo 19.11.2019\CompendioSaludhumanaprologo13kb.txt 0.41389785707333404

15.5.4 1496 Cancionero Proem to Prince

EncinaCancioneroPrincipeProhemio29kb.txt   C:\Users\Govert\Desktop\Signatura comienzo 19.11.2019\EncinaCancioneroPrincipeProhemio29kb.txt
Canonicizers:
   Normalize Whitespace
EventDrivers:
   Character NGrams n : 4
      EventCullers:
         Most Common Events numevents : 50
Analysis:
   Nearest Neighbor Driver with metric Cosine Distance
1. Juan del Encina -C:\Users\Govert\Desktop\Signatura comienzo 19.11.2019\encina al principe 28kb.txt 5.472738787037912E-6
2. Alfonso el Sabio -C:\Users\Govert\Desktop\Signatura comienzo 19.11.2019\sietepartidas24kb.txt 0.016014145982558015
3. Alonso Fernández de Madrid -C:\Users\Govert\Desktop\Signatura comienzo 19.11.2019\fernandezdeMadridHernanTalavObra91kb.txt 0.018566170503227508
4. Prologos Fernández de Oviedo -C:\Users\Govert\Desktop\Signatura comienzo 19.11.2019\PrologosFernandezOviedo1-96kb.txt 0.018701251233357863
5. Garci Rodríguez de Montalvo -C:\Users\Govert\Desktop\Signatura comienzo 19.11.2019\AmadisDos21kb.txt 0.020647380640268054
6. Francisco López de Villalobos -C:\Users\Govert\Desktop\Signatura comienzo 19.11.2019\villaloboscostumbres humanas21kb.txt 0.021284521714314497
7. Gonzalo Fernández de Oviedo -C:\Users\Govert\Desktop\Signatura comienzo 19.11.2019\FernandezOviedoSumarioIndias27kb.txt 0.021833067676279128
8. Gonzalo Fernández de Oviedo -C:\Users\Govert\Desktop\Signatura comienzo 19.11.2019\fernandezoviedobatalla90-130tiene34kb.txt 0.02497162271512854
9. Lucena -C:\Users\Govert\Desktop\Signatura comienzo 19.11.2019\repamores mitad libro51kb.txt 0.0259379089192594
10. Juan de Flores -C:\Users\Govert\Desktop\Signatura comienzo 19.11.2019\griselobra21kb.txt 0.03221846129705064
11. Corónica Adramon -C:\Users\Govert\Desktop\Signatura comienzo 19.11.2019\adramonObra30kb.txt 0.03252946716403837
12. Gil Vicente -C:\Users\Govert\Desktop\Signatura comienzo 19.11.2019\GilVicenteCuatroTiempos21kb.txt 0.03335442367170538
13. Duobus amantibus -C:\Users\Govert\Desktop\Signatura comienzo 19.11.2019\piccolomini pp20 hasta30-21kb.txt 0.03402559427736618
14. Juan del Encina -C:\Users\Govert\Desktop\Signatura comienzo 19.11.2019\EncinaBubolicaReyesPrologo8kb.txt 0.034550123733309124
15. Gonzalo de Ayora -C:\Users\Govert\Desktop\Signatura comienzo 19.11.2019\gonzaloayoraAvila67kb.txt 0.03523892488536351
16. Cronica anónima Reyes Católicos -C:\Users\Govert\Desktop\Signatura comienzo 19.11.2019\cronicalucena21kb.txt 0.035933883939432976

17. Juan Ramírez de Lucena -C:\Users\Govert\Desktop\Signatura comienzo 19.11.2019\vita beata21kb.txt 0.03754792720137812

18. Linda Melosina -C:\Users\Govert\Desktop\Signatura comienzo 19.11.2019\lindamelosina21kb.txt 0.0377150262397411

19. Ysopo -C:\Users\Govert\Desktop\Signatura comienzo 19.11.2019\ysope primer libro1495.txt 0.03784446410419606

20. Hernando del Castillo -C:\Users\Govert\Desktop\Signatura comienzo 19.11.2019\hernando de castillo prologo6kb.txt 0.03919937475053048

21. Gil Vicente -C:\Users\Govert\Desktop\Signatura comienzo 19.11.2019\GilVicenteSibila31kb.txt 0.0394006920291351

22. Gonzalo Fernández de Oviedo -C:\Users\Govert\Desktop\Signatura comienzo 19.11.2019\FernandezOviedoClaribalte21kb.txt 0.0395251903450 1645

23. Gonzalo de Ayora -C:\Users\Govert\Desktop\Signatura comienzo 19.11.2019\GonzaloAyoraA MiguelPerezAlmazan15kb.txt 0.03958561043453401

24. Juan de Ávila - Oliveros -C:\Users\Govert\Desktop\Signatura comienzo 19.11.2019\oliveros de castilla obra21kb.txt 0.03986556189807

25. Garci Rodríguez de Montalvo -C:\Users\Govert\Desktop\Signatura comienzo 19.11.2019\AmadisTres21kb.txt 0.040322105457270774

26. Martin de Cordoba Jardin doncellas -C:\Users\Govert\Desktop\Signatura comienzo 19.11.2019\martindecordoba12kb.txt 0.04121529196076468

27. Juan Paez de Castro -C:\Users\Govert\Desktop\Signatura comienzo 19.11.2019\juanpaezdecastroCartas23kb.txt 0.041926497752134084

28. Garci Rodríguez de Montalvo -C:\Users\Govert\Desktop\Signatura comienzo 19.11.2019\amadisdegaula1496 prologo8kb.txt 0.04207204884050897

29. Garci Rodríguez de Montalvo -C:\Users\Govert\Desktop\Signatura comienzo 19.11.2019\AmadisUno21kb.txt 0.042646243024390906

30. Gonzalo de Ayora -C:\Users\Govert\Desktop\Signatura comienzo 19.11.2019\GonzaloAyora79kb.txt 0.04348140700677838

31. Juan Ramírez de Lucena -C:\Users\Govert\Desktop\Signatura comienzo 19.11.2019\Ramirez Lucena exhortatoria.txt 0.04408781297027975

32. Juan Ramírez de Lucena -C:\Users\Govert\Desktop\Signatura comienzo 19.11.2019\RamirezLucena a Zapata.txt 0.04443092723042197

33. Diego de San Pedro -C:\Users\Govert\Desktop\Signatura comienzo 19.11.2019\arnalte incompleta21kb.txt 0.04456218104945675

34. Thebayda -C:\Users\Govert\Desktop\Signatura comienzo 19.11.2019\thebaida incompleta21kb.txt 0.045790069634236374

35. Jacobo de la Voragine -C:\Users\Govert\Desktop\Signatura comienzo 19.11.2019\flos sanctorum21kb.txt 0.04616729001844233

36. Pedro de Portugal -C:\Users\Govert\Desktop\Signatura comienzo 19.11.2019\condestablePortugalSatira90kb.txt 0.046389769999693575

37. Boccaccio -C:\Users\Govert\Desktop\Signatura comienzo 19.11.2019\BoccaccioIlustresmujeresobra21kb.txt 0.04698932723582028

38. Garci Rodríguez de Montalvo -C:\Users\Govert\Desktop\Signatura comienzo 19.11.2019\AmadisCuatro21kb.txt 0.0481427059152 8569

39. Juan de Flores -C:\Users\Govert\Desktop\Signatura comienzo 19.11.2019\triunfodeamorprologo4kb.txt 0.04884509585943808

40. Balado Merlin anonimo -C:\Users\Govert\Desktop\Signatura comienzo 19.11.2019\baladroprologo1498-7kb.txt 0.04927050704910263

41. Juan de Capua -C:\Users\Govert\Desktop\Signatura comienzo 19.11.2019\engañosypeligrosObra25kb.txt 0.049318545664642555

42. Gil Vicente -C:\Users\Govert\Desktop\Signatura comienzo 19.11.2019\GilVicente Don Duardos65kb.txt 0.05119491257896858

43. Lucas Fernández -C:\Users\Govert\Desktop\Signatura comienzo 19.11.2019\lucasfernandez dereniego del amor21kb.txt 0.05227105607879423

44. Hernán Núñez -C:\Users\Govert\Desktop\Signatura comienzo 19.11.2019\hernannuñez Trescientas21.txt 0.0538884416945703

45. Juan del Encina -C:\Users\Govert\Desktop\Signatura comienzo 19.11.2019\Encina eglogasantes1509 num3-40kb.txt 0.0543921626955739

46. Diego de San Pedro -C:\Users\Govert\Desktop\Signatura comienzo 19.11.2019\carceldeamor21kb.txt 0.054883644090438

47. Juan del Encina -C:\Users\Govert\Desktop\Signatura comienzo 19.11.2019\EncinaCancioneroReyesProhemio7kb.txt 0.05704174682030083

48. Tercer Viaje de Colon -C:\Users\Govert\Desktop\Signatura comienzo 19.11.2019\TercerViajeColon24kb.txt 0.05705521370435951

49. Gonzalo Fernández de Oviedo -C:\Users\Govert\Desktop\Signatura comienzo 19.11.2019\fernandezOviedo-indias 21kb.txt 0.06113488995700056

50. Gil Vicente -C:\Users\Govert\Desktop\Signatura comienzo 19.11.2019\GilVicente AutoPastoril1502 16kb.txt 0.06124843667123425

51. Gonzalo García Santa Maria -C:\Users\Govert\Desktop\Signatura comienzo 19.11.2019\GarciaSantaMariaCoronicaAragonObra27kb.txt 0.06213845166925425

52. Tratado de amores -C:\Users\Govert\Desktop\Signatura comienzo 19.11.2019\tratadodeamores15kb.txt 0.0641187782873478

53. Juan de Flores -C:\Users\Govert\Desktop\Signatura comienzo 19.11.2019\triunfodeamor7kb.txt 0.06475213777356525

54. Flor de virtudes -C:\Users\Govert\Desktop\Signatura comienzo 19.11.2019\flordevirtudesobra22kb.txt 0.06561797094525335

55. Juan de Flores -C:\Users\Govert\Desktop\Signatura comienzo 19.11.2019\grimalteobra21kb.txt 0.07046264829951487

56. Gil Vicente -C:\Users\Govert\Desktop\Signatura comienzo 19.11.2019\GilVicenteComediaViudo20kb.txt 0.07130500314961663

57. Gonzalo Fernández de Oviedo -C:\Users\Govert\Desktop\Signatura comienzo 19.11.2019\fernandezOviedo1532catálogo21kb.txt 0.07276967626840203

58. Enrique fi de Oliva -C:\Users\Govert\Desktop\Signatura comienzo 19.11.2019\enrique fi de oliva21kb.txt 0.07335022629383481

59. Vidal de Noya -C:\Users\Govert\Desktop\Signatura comienzo 19.11.2019\vidal de noyaJugurthaguerra28kb.txt 0.07412387602093684

60. Tratado generación criatura -C:\Users\Govert\Desktop\Signatura comienzo 19.11.2019\TratadoGeneracionCriaturaObra24kb.txt 0.0747821738458525

61. Gonzalo García Santa Maria -C:\Users\Govert\Desktop\Signatura comienzo 19.11.2019\evangeliosepistolas1485-64kb.txt 0.07489286989069666

62. Carta Hiseo respuesta Tristan -C:\Users\Govert\Desktop\Signatura comienzo 19.11.2019\respuestadetristan.txt 0.0763080699307278

63. Boccaccio -C:\Users\Govert\Desktop\Signatura comienzo 19.11.2019\BoccaccioIlustresmujeresprologo9kb.txt 0.07780258944969742

64. Lucena -C:\Users\Govert\Desktop\Signatura comienzo 19.11.2019\repeticionamores ajedrez4kb.txt 0.08016869532552218

65. Alonso de Proaza -C:\Users\Govert\Desktop\Signatura comienzo 19.11.2019\alonsodeproazaProsa no Celestina-12kb.txt 0.08033348902008963

66. Cronica Troyana -C:\Users\Govert\Desktop\Signatura comienzo 19.11.2019\cronica troyana obra21kb.txt 0.08359474562069713

67. Juan de Flores -C:\Users\Govert\Desktop\Signatura comienzo 19.11.2019\griselprologo2kb.txt 0.08366863821588011

68. Boccaccio -C:\Users\Govert\Desktop\Signatura comienzo 19.11.2019\BoccaccioCaydaPrincipe.txt 0.08381057414519133

69. Juan Ramírez de Lucena -C:\Users\Govert\Desktop\Signatura comienzo 19.11.2019\RamirezLucena a galardones.txt 0.08621802124860

70. Gordonio Niños -C:\Users\Govert\Desktop\Signatura comienzo 19.11.2019\GordonioNiños32kb.txt 0.0871595082372596

71. Alonso de Cardona -C:\Users\Govert\Desktop\Signatura comienzo 19.11.2019\alonsodecardona22kb.txt 0.08769350104661833

72. Pedro Carrillo de Huete -C:\Users\Govert\Desktop\Signatura comienzo 19.11.2019\halconero1489year32kb.txt 0.08860980183378442

73. Juan de Ávila - Oliveros -C:\Users\Govert\Desktop\Signatura comienzo 19.11.2019\olveros de castilla epílogo.txt 0.09303431702572496

74. Tratado de Fisonomía -C.\Users\Govert\Desktop\Signatura comienzo 19.11.2019\tratadofisonomiaProemio8kb.txt 0.09384880759011105

75. Infancia Salvatoris -C:\Users\Govert\Desktop\Signatura comienzo 19.11.2019\InfanciaSalvatoris36kb.txt 0.09465888954917312

76. Martín Martínez de Ampiés -C:\Users\Govert\Desktop\Signatura comienzo 19.11.2019\BreidenbachTierraSantaRomaTratado8kb.txt 0.09903049088768556

77. Juan de Flores -C:\Users\Govert\Desktop\Signatura comienzo 19.11.2019\grimalte prologo3kb.txt 0.09981850424060013

78. Juan de Flores -C:\Users\Govert\Desktop\Signatura comienzo 19.11.2019\grisel introduccion2kb.txt 0.10337052068003483

79. Nicolás Núñez -C:\Users\Govert\Desktop\Signatura comienzo 19.11.2019\NicolasNuñezTractado32kb.txt 0.11010441060697207

80. Carta Hiseo respuesta Tristan -C:\Users\Govert\Desktop\Signatura comienzo 19.11.2019\cartahiseolabrunda.txt 0.11252199338949975

81. Andrés de Li -C:\Users\Govert\Desktop\Signatura comienzo 19.11.2019\SumaDePaciencia1493Prologo6kb.txt 0.11632064175352164

81. Andrés de Li -C:\Users\Govert\Desktop\Signatura comienzo 19.11.2019\SumaDePaciencia1493Prologo6kb.txt 0.11632064175352164

83. Juan de Padilla -C:\Users\Govert\Desktop\Signatura comienzo 19.11.2019\retablo cartujo14kb.txt 0.12896879497987424

84. Martin de Cordoba Jardin doncellas -C:\Users\Govert\Desktop\Signatura comienzo 19.11.2019\martindecordobaprohemio2kb.txt 0.13923519424190633

85. Nicolás Núñez -C:\Users\Govert\Desktop\Signatura comienzo 19.11.2019\NicolasNuñezTractadoprologo2kb.txt 0.14145532058569998

86. Balado Merlin anonimo -C:\Users\Govert\Desktop\Signatura comienzo 19.11.2019\baladromerlin21kb.txt 0.16032001320671885

87. Juan de Ávila - Oliveros -C:\Users\Govert\Desktop\Signatura comienzo 19.11.2019\oliverosdecastilla introduccion.txt 0.1647636263496799

88. Juan de Ávila - Oliveros -C:\Users\Govert\Desktop\Signatura comienzo 19.11.2019\olveros de castilla prologo1498and1499.txt 0.17031371908935533

89. Tratado de Fisonomía -C:\Users\Govert\Desktop\Signatura comienzo 19.11.2019\tratadofisonomiaObra22kb.txt 0.17944231151393053

90. Fernando de Rojas -C:\Users\Govert\Desktop\Signatura comienzo 19.11.2019\fernando de rojas14kb test2.txt 0.18659224244673056

91. Andrés de Li -C:\Users\Govert\Desktop\Signatura comienzo 19.11.2019\SumadePaciencia32kb.txt 0.19162957389423474

92. Tratado de Fisonomía -C:\Users\Govert\Desktop\Signatura comienzo 19.11.2019\tratadofisonomiaIntroduccion3kb.txt 0.1960175337496043

93. Libro hebreo oraciones -C:\Users\Govert\Desktop\Signatura comienzo 19.11.2019\siddurtefillot21kb.txt 0.19998039541413515

94. Compendio de Salud humana -C:\Users\Govert\Desktop\Signatura comienzo 19.11.2019\compendioSaludHumana25kb.txt 0.26865972407008776

95. Compendio de Salud humana -C:\Users\Govert\Desktop\Signatura comienzo 19.11.2019\CompendioSaludhumanaprologo13kb.txt 0.3640071918519032

15.5.5 1496 Cancionero Foreword to Alba

EncinaCancioneroAlbaPrologo6kb.txt C:\Users\Govert\Desktop\Signatura comienzo 19.11.2019\EncinaCancioneroAlbaPrologo6kb.txt
Canonicizers:
    Normalize Whitespace
EventDrivers:
    Character NGrams n : 4
        EventCullers:
            Most Common Events numevents : 50
Analysis:
    Nearest Neighbor Driver with metric Cosine Distance
1. Juan del Encina -C:\Users\Govert\Desktop\Signatura comienzo 19.11.2019\EncinaBubolicaReyesPrologo8kb.txt 0.03825453383434796

2. Garci Rodríguez de Montalvo -C:\Users\Govert\Desktop\Signatura comienzo 19.11.2019\AmadisDos21kb.txt 0.042621565899530145

3. Juan del Encina -C:\Users\Govert\Desktop\Signatura comienzo 19.11.2019\encina al principe 28kb.txt 0.04630777352145332

4. Gonzalo de Ayora -C:\Users\Govert\Desktop\Signatura comienzo 19.11.2019\gonzaloayoraAvila67kb.txt 0.048657448262476755

5. Duobus amantibus -C:\Users\Govert\Desktop\Signatura comienzo 19.11.2019\piccolomini pp20 hasta30-21kb.txt 0.05059975339584688

6. Alonso Fernández de Madrid -C:\Users\Govert\Desktop\Signatura comienzo 19.11.2019\fernandezdeMadridHernanTalavObra91kb.txt 0.051157854996124685

7. Prologos Fernández de Oviedo -C:\Users\Govert\Desktop\Signatura comienzo 19.11.2019\PrologosFernandezOviedo1-96kb.txt 0.051576970585464954

8. Pedro de Portugal -C:\Users\Govert\Desktop\Signatura comienzo 19.11.2019\condestablePortugalSatira90kb.txt 0.0518300813992304

9. Lucena -C:\Users\Govert\Desktop\Signatura comienzo 19.11.2019\repamores mitad libro51kb.txt 0.054214482121862195

10. Juan del Encina -C:\Users\Govert\Desktop\Signatura comienzo 19.11.2019\EncinaCancioneroReyesProhemio7kb.txt 0.05427460339792134

11. Gil Vicente -C:\Users\Govert\Desktop\Signatura comienzo 19.11.2019\GilVicenteCuatroTiempos21kb.txt 0.055026192496440585

12. Alfonso el Sabio -C:\Users\Govert\Desktop\Signatura comienzo 19.11.2019\sietepartidas24kb.txt 0.05543463623362521

13. Garci Rodríguez de Montalvo -C:\Users\Govert\Desktop\Signatura comienzo 19.11.2019\AmadisCuatro21kb.txt 0.05704859763158254

14. Boccaccio -C:\Users\Govert\Desktop\Signatura comienzo 19.11.2019\BoccaccioIlustresmujeresobra21kb.txt 0.0585410791672073

15. Cronica anónima Reyes Católicos -C:\Users\Govert\Desktop\Signatura comienzo 19.11.2019\cronicalucena21kb.txt 0.05917474707664738

16. Hernán Núñez -C:\Users\Govert\Desktop\Signatura comienzo 19.11.2019\hernannuñez Trescientas21.txt 0.06109814967557681

17. Francisco López de Villalobos -C:\Users\Govert\Desktop\Signatura comienzo 19.11.2019\villaloboscostumbres humanas21kb.txt 0.06129986117650632

18. Gonzalo Fernández de Oviedo -C:\Users\Govert\Desktop\Signatura comienzo 19.11.2019\fernandezOviedo-indias 21kb.txt 0.06275033567515587

19. Hernando del Castillo -C:\Users\Govert\Desktop\Signatura comienzo 19.11.2019\hernando de castillo prologo6kb.txt 0.06319707997020807

20. Gonzalo Fernández de Oviedo -C:\Users\Govert\Desktop\Signatura comienzo 19.11.2019\FernandezOviedoSumarioIndias27kb.txt 0.06683281438810329

21. Juan de Capua -C:\Users\Govert\Desktop\Signatura comienzo 19.11.2019\engañosypeligrosObra25kb.txt 0.06737146283981366

22. Lucas Fernández -C:\Users\Govert\Desktop\Signatura comienzo 19.11.2019\lucasfernandez dereniego del amor21kb.txt 0.06812619959293864

23. Garci Rodríguez de Montalvo -C:\Users\Govert\Desktop\Signatura comienzo 19.11.2019\AmadisUno21kb.txt 0.06958135180472724

24. Tercer Viaje de Colon -C:\Users\Govert\Desktop\Signatura comienzo 19.11.2019\TercerViajeColon24kb.txt 0.07253312317707594

25. Juan de Flores -C:\Users\Govert\Desktop\Signatura comienzo 19.11.2019\triunfodeamor7kb.txt 0.07399958069528434

26. Corónica Adramon -C:\Users\Govert\Desktop\Signatura comienzo 19.11.2019\adramonObra25kb.txt 0.0743790386089459

27. Gonzalo Fernández de Oviedo -C:\Users\Govert\Desktop\Signatura comienzo 19.11.2019\fernandezoviedobatalla90-130tiene34kb.txt 0.07460509927352321

28. Juan de Flores -C:\Users\Govert\Desktop\Signatura comienzo 19.11.2019\griselobra21kb.txt 0.07467250911379342

29. Gil Vicente -C:\Users\Govert\Desktop\Signatura comienzo 19.11.2019\GilVicenteSibila31kb.txt 0.0752755242060208

30. Gonzalo Fernández de Oviedo -C:\Users\Govert\Desktop\Signatura comienzo 19.11.2019\fernandezOviedo1532catálogo21kb.txt 0.07550784471417715

31. Gonzalo de Ayora -C:\Users\Govert\Desktop\Signatura comienzo 19.11.2019\GonzaloAyora79kb.txt 0.0757481317072447

32. Jacobo de la Voragine -C:\Users\Govert\Desktop\Signatura comienzo 19.11.2019\flos sanctorum21kb.txt 0.07618128804303048

33. Thebayda -C:\Users\Govert\Desktop\Signatura comienzo 19.11.2019\thebaida incompleta21kb.txt 0.07711440744800335

34. Juan Ramírez de Lucena -C:\Users\Govert\Desktop\Signatura comienzo 19.11.2019\vita beata21kb.txt 0.07717668635912522

35. Diego de San Pedro -C:\Users\Govert\Desktop\Signatura comienzo 19.11.2019\carceldeamor21kb.txt 0.07789115093171717

36. Linda Melosina -C:\Users\Govert\Desktop\Signatura comienzo 19.11.2019\lindamelosina21kb.txt 0.07795049864906822

37. Balado Merlin anonimo -C:\Users\Govert\Desktop\Signatura comienzo 19.11.2019\baladroprologo1498-7kb.txt 0.07877324090690918

38. Juan de Flores -C:\Users\Govert\Desktop\Signatura comienzo 19.11.2019\triunfodeamorprologo4kb.txt 0.08077905734458213

39. Gonzalo Fernández de Oviedo -C:\Users\Govert\Desktop\Signatura comienzo 19.11.2019\FernandezOviedoClaribalte21kb.txt 0.08207008972805419

40. Gil Vicente -C:\Users\Govert\Desktop\Signatura comienzo 19.11.2019\GilVicente Don Duardos65kb.txt 0.08377889723720466

41. Gil Vicente -C:\Users\Govert\Desktop\Signatura comienzo 19.11.2019\GilVicenteComediaViudo20kb.txt 0.08458930975686374

42. Diego de San Pedro -C:\Users\Govert\Desktop\Signatura comienzo 19.11.2019\arnalte incompleta21kb.txt 0.08460569432620091

43. Martin de Cordoba Jardin doncellas -C:\Users\Govert\Desktop\Signatura comienzo 19.11.2019\martindecordoba12kb.txt 0.08476454641892617

44. Juan de Ávila - Oliveros -C:\Users\Govert\Desktop\Signatura comienzo 19.11.2019\oliveros de castilla obra21kb.txt 0.08501654586915153

45. Gonzalo de Ayora -C:\Users\Govert\Desktop\Signatura comienzo 19.11.2019\GonzaloAyoraA MiguelPerezAlmazan15kb.txt 0.08558374327031348

46. Garci Rodríguez de Montalvo -C:\Users\Govert\Desktop\Signatura comienzo 19.11.2019\amadisdegaula1496 prologo8kb.txt 0.08605955481034488

47. Gordonio Niños -C:\Users\Govert\Desktop\Signatura comienzo 19.11.2019\GordonioNiños32kb.txt 0.08621843834281662

48. Garci Rodríguez de Montalvo -C:\Users\Govert\Desktop\Signatura comienzo 19.11.2019\AmadisTres21kb.txt 0.08705477583643983

49. Ysopo -C:\Users\Govert\Desktop\Signatura comienzo 19.11.2019\ysope primer libro1495.txt 0.08709441617892155

50. Boccaccio -C:\Users\Govert\Desktop\Signatura comienzo 19.11.2019\BoccaccioIlustresmujeresprologo9kb.txt 0.08757622747848204

51. Flor de virtudes -C:\Users\Govert\Desktop\Signatura comienzo 19.11.2019\flordevirtudesobra22kb.txt 0.08767397797152487

52. Juan del Encina -C:\Users\Govert\Desktop\Signatura comienzo 19.11.2019\Encina eglogasantes1509 num3-40kb.txt 0.09056408685892658

53. Juan Ramírez de Lucena -C:\Users\Govert\Desktop\Signatura comienzo 19.11.2019\Ramirez Lucena exhortatoria.txt 0.09284638240223564

54. Juan Ramírez de Lucena -C:\Users\Govert\Desktop\Signatura comienzo 19.11.2019\RamirezLucena a Zapata.txt 0.09315370593480676

55. Juan Paez de Castro -C:\Users\Govert\Desktop\Signatura comienzo 19.11.2019\juanpaezdecastroCartas23kb.txt 0.09655640431110202

56. Pedro Carrillo de Huete -C:\Users\Govert\Desktop\Signatura comienzo 19.11.2019\halconero1489year32kb.txt 0.09695069255017008

57. Tratado de amores -C:\Users\Govert\Desktop\Signatura comienzo 19.11.2019\tratadodeamores15kb.txt 0.09708420960621411

58. Juan de Flores -C:\Users\Govert\Desktop\Signatura comienzo 19.11.2019\grimalte prologo3kb.txt 0.09888990745693982

59. Tratado generación criatura -C:\Users\Govert\Desktop\Signatura comienzo 19.11.2019\TratadoGeneracionCriaturaObra24kb.txt 0.10106042342025001

60. Juan de Flores -C:\Users\Govert\Desktop\Signatura comienzo 19.11.2019\griselprologo2kb.txt 0.10133101037416259

61. Carta Hiseo respuesta Tristan -C:\Users\Govert\Desktop\Signatura comienzo 19.11.2019\respuestadetristan.txt 0.10181397267444858

62. Gonzalo García Santa Maria -C:\Users\Govert\Desktop\Signatura comienzo 19.11.2019\GarciaSantaMariaCoronicaAragonObra27kb.txt 0.10314630733936647

63. Lucena -C:\Users\Govert\Desktop\Signatura comienzo 19.11.2019\repeticionamores ajedrez4kb.txt 0.10390610956312474

64. Juan de Ávila - Oliveros -C:\Users\Govert\Desktop\Signatura comienzo 19.11.2019\olveros de castilla epílogo.txt 0.10435754132492137

65. Alonso de Cardona -C:\Users\Govert\Desktop\Signatura comienzo 19.11.2019\alonsodecardona22kb.txt 0.10729855187717974

66. Gil Vicente -C:\Users\Govert\Desktop\Signatura comienzo 19.11.2019\GilVicente AutoPastoril1502 16kb.txt 0.11035306298693803

67. Alonso de Proaza -C:\Users\Govert\Desktop\Signatura comienzo 19.11.2019\alonsodeproazaProsa no Celestina-12kb.txt 0.11228339914011776

68. Vidal de Noya -C:\Users\Govert\Desktop\Signatura comienzo 19.11.2019\vidal de noyaJugurthaguerra28kb.txt 0.11557047424354427

69. Juan Ramírez de Lucena -C:\Users\Govert\Desktop\Signatura comienzo 19.11.2019\RamirezLucena a galardones.txt 0.11559925866475529

70. Juan de Flores -C:\Users\Govert\Desktop\Signatura comienzo 19.11.2019\grimalteobra21kb.txt 0.12092829491654788

71. Juan de Padilla -C:\Users\Govert\Desktop\Signatura comienzo 19.11.2019\retablo cartujo14kb.txt 0.12171680196989565

72. Gonzalo García Santa Maria -C:\Users\Govert\Desktop\Signatura comienzo 19.11.2019\evangeliosepistolas1485-64kb.txt 0.12795124912098854

73. Martín Martínez de Ampiés -C:\Users\Govert\Desktop\Signatura comienzo 19.11.2019\BreidenbachTierraSantaRomaTratado8kb.txt 0.12892925711955827

74. Enrique fi de Oliva -C:\Users\Govert\Desktop\Signatura comienzo 19.11.2019\enrique fi de oliva21kb.txt 0.1299264944129218

75. Andrés de Li -C:\Users\Govert\Desktop\Signatura comienzo 19.11.2019\SumaDePaciencia1493Prologo6kb.txt 0.13074408393434922

75. Andrés de Li -C:\Users\Govert\Desktop\Signatura comienzo 19.11.2019\SumaDePaciencia1493Prologo6kb.txt 0.13074408393434922

77. Tratado de Fisonomía -C:\Users\Govert\Desktop\Signatura comienzo 19.11.2019\tratadofisonomiaProemio8kb.txt 0.13205485389469807

78. Cronica Troyana -C:\Users\Govert\Desktop\Signatura comienzo 19.11.2019\cronica troyana obra21kb.txt 0.13893107965117657

79. Carta Hiseo respuesta Tristan -C:\Users\Govert\Desktop\Signatura comienzo 19.11.2019\cartahiseolabrunda.txt 0.14141323006464368

80. Fernando de Rojas -C:\Users\Govert\Desktop\Signatura comienzo 19.11.2019\fernando de rojas14kb test2.txt 0.14348898341930116

81. Juan de Flores -C:\Users\Govert\Desktop\Signatura comienzo 19.11.2019\grisel introduccion2kb.txt 0.15015749519746402

82. Boccaccio -C:\Users\Govert\Desktop\Signatura comienzo 19.11.2019\BoccaccioCaydaPrincipe.txt 0.15216184712212788

83. Nicolás Núñez -C:\Users\Govert\Desktop\Signatura comienzo 19.11.2019\NicolasNuñezTractado32kb.txt 0.1524540022795775

84. Martin de Cordoba Jardin doncellas -C:\Users\Govert\Desktop\Signatura comienzo 19.11.2019\martindecordobaprohemio2kb.txt 0.1556819215612083

85. Infancia Salvatoris -C:\Users\Govert\Desktop\Signatura comienzo 19.11.2019\InfanciaSalvatoris36kb.txt 0.1586769580276446

86. Tratado de Fisonomía -C:\Users\Govert\Desktop\Signatura comienzo 19.11.2019\tratadofisonomiaIntroduccion3kb.txt 0.16536073076341584

87. Libro hebreo oraciones -C:\Users\Govert\Desktop\Signatura comienzo 19.11.2019\siddurtefillot21kb.txt 0.1705134682766839

88. Juan de Ávila - Oliveros -C:\Users\Govert\Desktop\Signatura comienzo 19.11.2019\oliverosdecastilla introduccion.txt 0.1709371388982206

89. Juan de Ávila - Oliveros -C:\Users\Govert\Desktop\Signatura comienzo 19.11.2019\olveros de castilla prologo1498and1499.txt 0.17863993332405248

90. Balado Merlin anonimo -C:\Users\Govert\Desktop\Signatura comienzo 19.11.2019\baladromerlin21kb.txt 0.1939606789928422

91. Tratado de Fisonomía -C:\Users\Govert\Desktop\Signatura comienzo 19.11.2019\tratadofisonomiaObra22kb.txt 0.19441923064143363
92. Andrés de Li -C:\Users\Govert\Desktop\Signatura comienzo 19.11.2019\SumadePaciencia32kb.txt 0.20643354215095655
93. Nicolás Núñez -C:\Users\Govert\Desktop\Signatura comienzo 19.11.2019\NicolasNuñezTractadoprologo2kb.txt 0.20788974553942596
94. Compendio de Salud humana -C:\Users\Govert\Desktop\Signatura comienzo 19.11.2019\compendioSaludHumana25kb.txt 0.25889719985744364
95. Compendio de Salud humana -C:\Users\Govert\Desktop\Signatura comienzo 19.11.2019\CompendioSaludhumanaprologo13kb.txt 0.35728302325554273

15.5.6 1496 Foreword to child of Alba

EncinaCancioneroAlbaHijoPrologo4kb.txt C:\Users\Govert\Desktop\Signatura comienzo 19.11.2019\EncinaCancioneroAlbaHijoPrologo4kb.txt
Canonicizers:
    Normalize Whitespace
EventDrivers:
    Character NGrams n : 4
        EventCullers:
            Most Common Events numevents : 50
Analysis:
    Nearest Neighbor Driver with metric Cosine Distance
1. Martín Martínez de Ampiés -C:\Users\Govert\Desktop\Signatura comienzo 19.11.2019\BreidenbachTierraSantaRomaTratado8kb.txt 0.06814730057006746
2. Pedro Carrillo de Huete -C:\Users\Govert\Desktop\Signatura comienzo 19.11.2019\halconero1489year32kb.txt 0.07765071624086495
3. Gonzalo de Ayora -C:\Users\Govert\Desktop\Signatura comienzo 19.11.2019\gonzaloayoraAvila67kb.txt 0.08378812660212476
4. Andrés de Li -C:\Users\Govert\Desktop\Signatura comienzo 19.11.2019\SumaDePaciencia1493Prologo6kb.txt 0.09072125978355006
4. Andrés de Li -C:\Users\Govert\Desktop\Signatura comienzo 19.11.2019\SumaDePaciencia1493Prologo6kb.txt 0.09072125978355006
6. Gonzalo Fernández de Oviedo -C:\Users\Govert\Desktop\Signatura comienzo 19.11.2019\fernandezOviedo-indias 21kb.txt 0.09131370465648814
7. Hernán Núñez -C:\Users\Govert\Desktop\Signatura comienzo 19.11.2019\hernannuñez Trescientas21.txt 0.09770740311445603
8. Gonzalo Fernández de Oviedo -C:\Users\Govert\Desktop\Signatura comienzo 19.11.2019\fernandezOviedo1532catálogo21kb.txt 0.10455937828466111
9. Cronica anónima Reyes Católicos -C:\Users\Govert\Desktop\Signatura comienzo 19.11.2019\cronicalucena21kb.txt 0.10498011112787531
10. Gonzalo García Santa Maria -C:\Users\Govert\Desktop\Signatura comienzo 19.11.2019\GarciaSantaMariaCoronicaAragonObra27kb.txt 0.10615700850483056

11. Alonso de Proaza -C:\Users\Govert\Desktop\Signatura comienzo 19.11.2019\alonsodeproazaProsa no Celestina-12kb.txt 0.10735363278288923

12. Boccaccio -C:\Users\Govert\Desktop\Signatura comienzo 19.11.2019\BoccaccioIlustresmujeresobra21kb.txt 0.10946282921113626

13. Juan del Encina -C:\Users\Govert\Desktop\Signatura comienzo 19.11.2019\EncinaBubolicaReyesPrologo8kb.txt 0.11231511949385797

14. Juan de Capua -C:\Users\Govert\Desktop\Signatura comienzo 19.11.2019\engañosypeligrosObra25kb.txt 0.11273626503305911

15. Lucas Fernández -C:\Users\Govert\Desktop\Signatura comienzo 19.11.2019\lucasfernandez dereniego del amor21kb.txt 0.11563909785538695

16. Lucena -C:\Users\Govert\Desktop\Signatura comienzo 19.11.2019\repeticionamores ajedrez4kb.txt 0.11711620182148319

17. Prologos Fernández de Oviedo -C:\Users\Govert\Desktop\Signatura comienzo 19.11.2019\PrologosFernandezOviedo1-96kb.txt 0.12029887706497422

18. Fernando de Rojas -C:\Users\Govert\Desktop\Signatura comienzo 19.11.2019\fernando de rojas14kb test2.txt 0.12055458637853744

19. Duobus amantibus -C:\Users\Govert\Desktop\Signatura comienzo 19.11.2019\piccolomini pp20 hasta30-21kb.txt 0.12107304247232942

20. Juan de Flores -C:\Users\Govert\Desktop\Signatura comienzo 19.11.2019\triunfodeamorprologo4kb.txt 0.12346320889875406

21. Boccaccio -C:\Users\Govert\Desktop\Signatura comienzo 19.11.2019\BoccaccioCaydaPrincipe.txt 0.12551388399565444

22. Juan de Ávila - Oliveros -C:\Users\Govert\Desktop\Signatura comienzo 19.11.2019\oliverosdecastilla introduccion.txt 0.1274597052274007

23. Juan de Ávila - Oliveros -C:\Users\Govert\Desktop\Signatura comienzo 19.11.2019\olveros de castilla prologo1498and1499.txt 0.13017944048313623

24. Juan del Encina -C:\Users\Govert\Desktop\Signatura comienzo 19.11.2019\encina al principe 28kb.txt 0.1315424489704895

25. Garci Rodríguez de Montalvo -C:\Users\Govert\Desktop\Signatura comienzo 19.11.2019\AmadisDos21kb.txt 0.1351330340900826

26. Juan de Ávila - Oliveros -C:\Users\Govert\Desktop\Signatura comienzo 19.11.2019\olveros de castilla epílogo.txt 0.13538047395600927

27. Jacobo de la Voragine -C:\Users\Govert\Desktop\Signatura comienzo 19.11.2019\flos sanctorum21kb.txt 0.1358716768937558

28. Libro hebreo oraciones -C:\Users\Govert\Desktop\Signatura comienzo 19.11.2019\siddurtefillot21kb.txt 0.13602160369126937

29. Andrés de Li -C:\Users\Govert\Desktop\Signatura comienzo 19.11.2019\SumadePaciencia32kb.txt 0.13659414056225694

30. Balado Merlin anonimo -C:\Users\Govert\Desktop\Signatura comienzo 19.11.2019\baladroprologo1498-7kb.txt 0.13659873636802933

31. Balado Merlin anonimo -C:\Users\Govert\Desktop\Signatura comienzo 19.11.2019\baladromerlin21kb.txt 0.13714899756382914

32. Pedro de Portugal -C:\Users\Govert\Desktop\Signatura comienzo 19.11.2019\condestablePortugalSatira90kb.txt 0.14073239085890343

33. Gonzalo García Santa Maria -C:\Users\Govert\Desktop\Signatura comienzo 19.11.2019\evangeliosepistolas1485-64kb.txt 0.14087581563925122

34. Alonso Fernández de Madrid -C:\Users\Govert\Desktop\Signatura comienzo 19.11.2019\fernandezdeMadridHernanTalavObra91kb.txt 0.1414963935265411

35. Vidal de Noya -C:\Users\Govert\Desktop\Signatura comienzo 19.11.2019\vidal de noyaJugurthaguerra28kb.txt 0.14235888732902025

36. Gonzalo Fernández de Oviedo -C:\Users\Govert\Desktop\Signatura comienzo 19.11.2019\FernandezOviedoSumarioIndias27kb.txt 0.14269492370568537

37. Juan de Flores -C:\Users\Govert\Desktop\Signatura comienzo 19.11.2019\triunfodeamor7kb.txt 0.14517225811489898

38. Juan del Encina -C:\Users\Govert\Desktop\Signatura comienzo 19.11.2019\EncinaCancioneroReyesProhemio7kb.txt 0.14750427678071976

39. Juan Ramírez de Lucena -C:\Users\Govert\Desktop\Signatura comienzo 19.11.2019\vita beata21kb.txt 0.14954810106388483

40. Gil Vicente -C:\Users\Govert\Desktop\Signatura comienzo 19.11.2019\GilVicenteCuatroTiempos21kb.txt 0.1509033261435314

41. Linda Melosina -C:\Users\Govert\Desktop\Signatura comienzo 19.11.2019\lindamelosina21kb.txt 0.15179246114679368

42. Gil Vicente -C:\Users\Govert\Desktop\Signatura comienzo 19.11.2019\GilVicenteComediaViudo20kb.txt 0.15870676422532992

43. Cronica Troyana -C:\Users\Govert\Desktop\Signatura comienzo 19.11.2019\cronica troyana obra21kb.txt 0.16038284360280308

44. Francisco López de Villalobos -C:\Users\Govert\Desktop\Signatura comienzo 19.11.2019\villaloboscostumbres humanas21kb.txt 0.1605710563321382

45. Gonzalo Fernández de Oviedo -C:\Users\Govert\Desktop\Signatura comienzo 19.11.2019\FernandezOviedoClaribalte21kb.txt 0.16094022455270718

46. Gonzalo Fernández de Oviedo -C:\Users\Govert\Desktop\Signatura comienzo 19.11.2019\fernandezoviedobatalla90-130tiene34kb.txt 0.16151546744252554

47. Diego de San Pedro -C:\Users\Govert\Desktop\Signatura comienzo 19.11.2019\arnalte incompleta21kb.txt 0.16191696354004226

48. Tratado de amores -C:\Users\Govert\Desktop\Signatura comienzo 19.11.2019\tratadodeamores15kb.txt 0.1622074491451545

49. Garci Rodríguez de Montalvo -C:\Users\Govert\Desktop\Signatura comienzo 19.11.2019\amadisdegaula1496 prologo8kb.txt 0.16247446302806035

50. Alfonso el Sabio -C:\Users\Govert\Desktop\Signatura comienzo 19.11.2019\sietepartidas24kb.txt 0.163136350624831

51. Diego de San Pedro -C:\Users\Govert\Desktop\Signatura comienzo 19.11.2019\carceldeamor21kb.txt 0.1659049308785019

52. Lucena -C:\Users\Govert\Desktop\Signatura comienzo 19.11.2019\repamores mitad libro51kb.txt 0.1664106000698662

53. Thebayda -C:\Users\Govert\Desktop\Signatura comienzo 19.11.2019\thebaida incompleta21kb.txt 0.16832118748514902

54. Garci Rodríguez de Montalvo -C:\Users\Govert\Desktop\Signatura comienzo 19.11.2019\AmadisUno21kb.txt 0.16926927805091052

340

55. Juan de Flores -C:\Users\Govert\Desktop\Signatura comienzo 19.11.2019\grimalte prologo3kb.txt 0.17002401238262999

56. Juan Paez de Castro -C:\Users\Govert\Desktop\Signatura comienzo 19.11.2019\juanpaezdecastroCartas23kb.txt 0.17043181374233674

57. Gordonio Niños -C:\Users\Govert\Desktop\Signatura comienzo 19.11.2019\GordonioNiños32kb.txt 0.17059607407490418

58. Garci Rodríguez de Montalvo -C:\Users\Govert\Desktop\Signatura comienzo 19.11.2019\AmadisCuatro21kb.txt 0.1706991568571783

59. Gonzalo de Ayora -C:\Users\Govert\Desktop\Signatura comienzo 19.11.2019\GonzaloAyora79kb.txt 0.17130797095620642

60. Juan de Ávila - Oliveros -C:\Users\Govert\Desktop\Signatura comienzo 19.11.2019\oliveros de castilla obra21kb.txt 0.1715299059651586

61. Flor de virtudes -C:\Users\Govert\Desktop\Signatura comienzo 19.11.2019\flordevirtudesobra22kb.txt 0.17180596627196643

62. Alonso de Cardona -C:\Users\Govert\Desktop\Signatura comienzo 19.11.2019\alonsodecardona22kb.txt 0.17198046316725335

63. Gonzalo de Ayora -C:\Users\Govert\Desktop\Signatura comienzo 19.11.2019\GonzaloAyoraA MiguelPerezAlmazan15kb.txt 0.17262960333677768

64. Juan Ramírez de Lucena -C:\Users\Govert\Desktop\Signatura comienzo 19.11.2019\Ramirez Lucena exhortatoria.txt 0.17497566948842702

65. Juan Ramírez de Lucena -C:\Users\Govert\Desktop\Signatura comienzo 19.11.2019\RamirezLucena a Zapata.txt 0.17539094855403936

66. Hernando del Castillo -C:\Users\Govert\Desktop\Signatura comienzo 19.11.2019\hernando de castillo prologo6kb.txt 0.17557298949320133

67. Juan Ramírez de Lucena -C:\Users\Govert\Desktop\Signatura comienzo 19.11.2019\RamirezLucena a galardones.txt 0.17574209689788856

68. Martin de Cordoba Jardin doncellas -C:\Users\Govert\Desktop\Signatura comienzo 19.11.2019\martindecordoba12kb.txt 0.17867959932089306

69. Gil Vicente -C:\Users\Govert\Desktop\Signatura comienzo 19.11.2019\GilVicenteSibila31kb.txt 0.17928643970370517

70. Tercer Viaje de Colon -C:\Users\Govert\Desktop\Signatura comienzo 19.11.2019\TercerViajeColon24kb.txt 0.18037138259235996

71. Juan de Flores -C:\Users\Govert\Desktop\Signatura comienzo 19.11.2019\griselobra21kb.txt 0.18096689446737224

72. Corónica Adramon -C:\Users\Govert\Desktop\Signatura comienzo 19.11.2019\adramonObra25kb.txt 0.18270143747824252

73. Boccaccio -C:\Users\Govert\Desktop\Signatura comienzo 19.11.2019\BoccaccioIlustresmujeresprologo9kb.txt 0.18467205670980602

74. Tratado generación criatura -C:\Users\Govert\Desktop\Signatura comienzo 19.11.2019\TratadoGeneracionCriaturaObra24kb.txt 0.18503633728114632

75. Juan de Flores -C:\Users\Govert\Desktop\Signatura comienzo 19.11.2019\griselprologo2kb.txt 0.1871615693657459

76. Tratado de Fisonomía -C:\Users\Govert\Desktop\Signatura comienzo 19.11.2019\tratadofisonomiaProemio8kb.txt 0.1874503886626816

77. Ysopo -C:\Users\Govert\Desktop\Signatura comienzo 19.11.2019\ysope primer libro1495.txt 0.1887479582027417

78. Juan de Padilla -C:\Users\Govert\Desktop\Signatura comienzo 19.11.2019\retablo cartujo14kb.txt 0.19036680998962396

79. Garci Rodríguez de Montalvo -C:\Users\Govert\Desktop\Signatura comienzo 19.11.2019\AmadisTres21kb.txt 0.1923096412005274

80. Juan de Flores -C:\Users\Govert\Desktop\Signatura comienzo 19.11.2019\grimalteobra21kb.txt 0.19232373699371674

81. Carta Hiseo respuesta Tristan -C:\Users\Govert\Desktop\Signatura comienzo 19.11.2019\respuestadetristan.txt 0.19302679831703573

82. Juan del Encina -C:\Users\Govert\Desktop\Signatura comienzo 19.11.2019\Encina eglogasantes1509 num3-40kb.txt 0.1960668974951022

83. Gil Vicente -C:\Users\Govert\Desktop\Signatura comienzo 19.11.2019\GilVicente Don Duardos65kb.txt 0.2059510590242034

84. Enrique fi de Oliva -C:\Users\Govert\Desktop\Signatura comienzo 19.11.2019\enrique fi de oliva21kb.txt 0.20675731451182422

85. Gil Vicente -C:\Users\Govert\Desktop\Signatura comienzo 19.11.2019\GilVicente AutoPastoril1502 16kb.txt 0.2104756816045643

86. Infancia Salvatoris -C:\Users\Govert\Desktop\Signatura comienzo 19.11.2019\InfanciaSalvatoris36kb.txt 0.2112247110466503

87. Juan de Flores -C:\Users\Govert\Desktop\Signatura comienzo 19.11.2019\grisel introduccion2kb.txt 0.2151266609286766

88. Compendio de Salud humana -C:\Users\Govert\Desktop\Signatura comienzo 19.11.2019\compendioSaludHumana25kb.txt 0.2412557945130427

89. Tratado de Fisonomía -C:\Users\Govert\Desktop\Signatura comienzo 19.11.2019\tratadofisonomiaIntroduccion3kb.txt 0.2441610623123449

90. Nicolás Núñez -C:\Users\Govert\Desktop\Signatura comienzo 19.11.2019\NicolasNuñezTractadoprologo2kb.txt 0.2484404502507751

91. Martin de Cordoba Jardin doncellas -C:\Users\Govert\Desktop\Signatura comienzo 19.11.2019\martindecordobaprohemio2kb.txt 0.2519027660814912

92. Tratado de Fisonomía -C:\Users\Govert\Desktop\Signatura comienzo 19.11.2019\tratadofisonomiaObra22kb.txt 0.2534053376267117

93. Nicolás Núñez -C:\Users\Govert\Desktop\Signatura comienzo 19.11.2019\NicolasNuñezTractado32kb.txt 0.2574766420338014

94. Carta Hiseo respuesta Tristan -C:\Users\Govert\Desktop\Signatura comienzo 19.11.2019\cartahiseolabrunda.txt 0.2679110310732201

95. Compendio de Salud humana -C:\Users\Govert\Desktop\Signatura comienzo 19.11.2019\CompendioSaludhumanaprologo13kb.txt 0.3414870410533286

15.6 Chapter 14

15.6.1 1511 Cancionero – Foreword

hernando de castillo prologo6kb.txt C:\Users\Govert\Desktop\Signatura comienzo 19.11.2019\hernando de castillo prologo6kb.txt
Canonicizers:
  Normalize Whitespace
EventDrivers:
  Character NGrams n : 4
    EventCullers:
      Most Common Events numevents : 50
Analysis:
  Nearest Neighbor Driver with metric Cosine Distance
1. Hernando del Castillo -C:\Users\Govert\Desktop\Signatura comienzo 19.11.2019\hernando de castillo prologo6kb.txt 0.0
2. Alfonso el Sabio -C:\Users\Govert\Desktop\Signatura comienzo 19.11.2019\sietepartidas24kb.txt 0.03157112966968001
3. Garci Rodríguez de Montalvo -C:\Users\Govert\Desktop\Signatura comienzo 19.11.2019\amadisdegaula1496 prologo8kb.txt 0.037923817286045325
4. Juan del Encina -C:\Users\Govert\Desktop\Signatura comienzo 19.11.2019\EncinaCancioneroPrincipeProhemio29kb.txt 0.0391993747505307
5. Francisco López de Villalobos -C:\Users\Govert\Desktop\Signatura comienzo 19.11.2019\villaloboscostumbres humanas21kb.txt 0.04337560698462262
6. Prologos Fernández de Oviedo -C:\Users\Govert\Desktop\Signatura comienzo 19.11.2019\PrologosFernandezOviedo2-93kb.txt 0.04631937740632275
7. Juan Ramírez de Lucena -C:\Users\Govert\Desktop\Signatura comienzo 19.11.2019\Ramirez Lucena exhortatoria.txt 0.050724135776652246
8. Gonzalo Fernández de Oviedo -C:\Users\Govert\Desktop\Signatura comienzo 19.11.2019\FernandezOviedoSumarioIndias27kb.txt 0.05092143291381157
9. Corónica Adramon -C:\Users\Govert\Desktop\Signatura comienzo 19.11.2019\adramonObra30kb.txt 0.05118516104848858
10. Juan Ramírez de Lucena -C:\Users\Govert\Desktop\Signatura comienzo 19.11.2019\RamirezLucena a Zapata.txt 0.05134226959874055
11. Garci Rodríguez de Montalvo -C:\Users\Govert\Desktop\Signatura comienzo 19.11.2019\AmadisDos21kb.txt 0.05334398163883547
12. Juan de Flores -C:\Users\Govert\Desktop\Signatura comienzo 19.11.2019\griselobra21kb.txt 0.05477428227308412
13. Boccaccio -C:\Users\Govert\Desktop\Signatura comienzo 19.11.2019\BoccaccioIlustresmujeresprologo9kb.txt 0.055046251579563665
14. Juan del Encina -C:\Users\Govert\Desktop\Signatura comienzo 19.11.2019\encina eglogas antes 1509-287kb.txt 0.05524363679984168

15. Pedro de Portugal -C:\Users\Govert\Desktop\Signatura comienzo 19.11.2019\condestablePortugalSatira90kb.txt 0.05822154733492724

16. Gil Vicente -C:\Users\Govert\Desktop\Signatura comienzo 19.11.2019\GilVicenteCuatroTiempos21kb.txt 0.05886973016761432

17. Lucena -C:\Users\Govert\Desktop\Signatura comienzo 19.11.2019\repamores mitad libro51kb.txt 0.05905045736021919

18. Juan del Encina -C:\Users\Govert\Desktop\Signatura comienzo 19.11.2019\EncinaBubolicaReyesPrologo8kb.txt 0.059906231129332355

19. Gonzalo de Ayora -C:\Users\Govert\Desktop\Signatura comienzo 19.11.2019\GonzaloAyoraA MiguelPerezAlmazan15kb.txt 0.06181551176826949

20. Juan del Encina -C:\Users\Govert\Desktop\Signatura comienzo 19.11.2019\encinacoplas1521.txt 0.061947951706078475

21. Cronica anónima Reyes Católicos -C:\Users\Govert\Desktop\Signatura comienzo 19.11.2019\cronicalucena21kb.txt 0.06265186146805046

22. Gonzalo Fernández de Oviedo -C:\Users\Govert\Desktop\Signatura comienzo 19.11.2019\FernandezOviedoClaribalte21kb.txt 0.06278035880420241

23. Juan del Encina -C:\Users\Govert\Desktop\Signatura comienzo 19.11.2019\encina1521-8kb.txt 0.06436838404774525

24. Linda Melosina -C:\Users\Govert\Desktop\Signatura comienzo 19.11.2019\lindamelosina21kb.txt 0.0648454659665686

25. Gonzalo de Ayora -C:\Users\Govert\Desktop\Signatura comienzo 19.11.2019\gonzaloayoraAvila67kb.txt 0.06592725744217864

26. Juan de Flores -C:\Users\Govert\Desktop\Signatura comienzo 19.11.2019\triunfodeamor7kb.txt 0.06789333355672222

27. Juan del Encina -C:\Users\Govert\Desktop\Signatura comienzo 19.11.2019\EncinaCancioneroAlbaPrologo6kb.txt 0.06818965131163468

28. Juan Paez de Castro -C:\Users\Govert\Desktop\Signatura comienzo 19.11.2019\juanpaezdecastroCartas23kb.txt 0.06916872286095355

29. Garci Rodríguez de Montalvo -C:\Users\Govert\Desktop\Signatura comienzo 19.11.2019\AmadisCuatro21kb.txt 0.06962114119182317

30. Balado Merlin anonimo -C:\Users\Govert\Desktop\Signatura comienzo 19.11.2019\baladroprologo1498-7kb.txt 0.06988283140619878

31. Juan de Flores -C:\Users\Govert\Desktop\Signatura comienzo 19.11.2019\triunfodeamorprologo4kb.txt 0.06999966234794008

32. Gonzalo de Ayora -C:\Users\Govert\Desktop\Signatura comienzo 19.11.2019\GonzaloAyora79kb.txt 0.07085023889353814

33. Juan del Encina -C:\Users\Govert\Desktop\Signatura comienzo 19.11.2019\EncinaCancioneroReyesProhemio7kb.txt 0.07111967041323741

34. Juan de Ávila - Oliveros -C:\Users\Govert\Desktop\Signatura comienzo 19.11.2019\oliveros de castilla obra21kb.txt 0.07255397949416009

35. Gonzalo Fernández de Oviedo -C:\Users\Govert\Desktop\Signatura comienzo 19.11.2019\fernandezoviedobatalla90-130tiene34kb.txt 0.07298748605079763

36. Jacobo de la Voragine -C:\Users\Govert\Desktop\Signatura comienzo 19.11.2019\flos sanctorum21kb.txt 0.07409624091697398

37. Martin de Cordoba Jardin doncellas -C:\Users\Govert\Desktop\Signatura comienzo 19.11.2019\martindecordoba12kb.txt 0.07426012485424471

38. Juan Ramírez de Lucena -C:\Users\Govert\Desktop\Signatura comienzo 19.11.2019\vita beata21kb.txt 0.07550989469052893

39. Diego de San Pedro -C:\Users\Govert\Desktop\Signatura comienzo 19.11.2019\carceldeamor21kb.txt 0.07609353528389695

40. Duobus amantibus -C:\Users\Govert\Desktop\Signatura comienzo 19.11.2019\piccolomini pp20 hasta30-21kb.txt 0.07668543478906953

41. Garci Rodríguez de Montalvo -C:\Users\Govert\Desktop\Signatura comienzo 19.11.2019\AmadisTres21kb.txt 0.07695135052058066

42. Juan del Encina -C:\Users\Govert\Desktop\Signatura comienzo 19.11.2019\EncinaBubolicaPrincipePrologo8kb.txt 0.07848273087397306

43. Garci Rodríguez de Montalvo -C:\Users\Govert\Desktop\Signatura comienzo 19.11.2019\AmadisUno21kb.txt 0.0795577448537198

44. Ysopo -C:\Users\Govert\Desktop\Signatura comienzo 19.11.2019\ysope primer libro1495.txt 0.08153177242163057

45. Tercer Viaje de Colon -C:\Users\Govert\Desktop\Signatura comienzo 19.11.2019\TercerViajeColon24kb.txt 0.0816740148314864

46. Juan de Flores -C:\Users\Govert\Desktop\Signatura comienzo 19.11.2019\grimalteobra21kb.txt 0.08239574473194178

47. Juan de Capua -C:\Users\Govert\Desktop\Signatura comienzo 19.11.2019\engañosypeligrosObra25kb.txt 0.08294606207773603

48. Gil Vicente -C:\Users\Govert\Desktop\Signatura comienzo 19.11.2019\GilVicenteSibila31kb.txt 0.08331108547366783

49. Boccaccio -C:\Users\Govert\Desktop\Signatura comienzo 19.11.2019\BoccaccioIlustresmujeresobra21kb.txt 0.08484716142151327

50. Thebayda -C:\Users\Govert\Desktop\Signatura comienzo 19.11.2019\thebaida incompleta21kb.txt 0.08864846002037152

51. Vidal de Noya -C:\Users\Govert\Desktop\Signatura comienzo 19.11.2019\vidal de noyaJugurthaguerra28kb.txt 0.09095093922610431

52. Diego de San Pedro -C:\Users\Govert\Desktop\Signatura comienzo 19.11.2019\arnalte incompleta21kb.txt 0.09165725820429138

53. Gil Vicente -C:\Users\Govert\Desktop\Signatura comienzo 19.11.2019\GilVicenteComediaViudo20kb.txt 0.0932071011762744

54. Juan de Flores -C:\Users\Govert\Desktop\Signatura comienzo 19.11.2019\grimalte prologo3kb.txt 0.0933408321325534

55. Tratado de amores -C:\Users\Govert\Desktop\Signatura comienzo 19.11.2019\tratadodeamores15kb.txt 0.09426607350928673

56. Gil Vicente -C:\Users\Govert\Desktop\Signatura comienzo 19.11.2019\GilVicente Don Duardos65kb.txt 0.09686661362263493

57. Juan Ramírez de Lucena -C:\Users\Govert\Desktop\Signatura comienzo 19.11.2019\RamirezLucena a galardones.txt 0.09713634255204084

58. Hernán Núñez -C:\Users\Govert\Desktop\Signatura comienzo 19.11.2019\hernannuñez Trescientas21.txt 0.09904116525077555

59. Gordonio Niños -C:\Users\Govert\Desktop\Signatura comienzo 19.11.2019\GordonioNiños32kb.txt 0.10246228116821765

60. Gonzalo Fernández de Oviedo -C:\Users\Govert\Desktop\Signatura comienzo 19.11.2019\fernandezOviedo-indias 21kb.txt 0.10635334770290816

61. Carta Hiseo respuesta Tristan -C:\Users\Govert\Desktop\Signatura comienzo 19.11.2019\respuestadetristan.txt 0.10797992462357697

62. Lucas Fernández -C:\Users\Govert\Desktop\Signatura comienzo 19.11.2019\lucasfernandez dereniego del amor21kb.txt 0.10994056695569665

63. Cronica Troyana -C:\Users\Govert\Desktop\Signatura comienzo 19.11.2019\cronica troyana obra21kb.txt 0.11027861470390776

64. Enrique fi de Oliva -C:\Users\Govert\Desktop\Signatura comienzo 19.11.2019\enrique fi de oliva21kb.txt 0.1108683533464837

65. Juan del Encina -C:\Users\Govert\Desktop\Signatura comienzo 19.11.2019\encinabubolicaArgumentos5kb.txt 0.11223206259991236

66. Juan de Flores -C:\Users\Govert\Desktop\Signatura comienzo 19.11.2019\griselprologo2kb.txt 0.11521214312960193

67. Boccaccio -C:\Users\Govert\Desktop\Signatura comienzo 19.11.2019\BoccaccioCaydaPrincipe.txt 0.11535119753569167

68. Gonzalo García Santa Maria -C:\Users\Govert\Desktop\Signatura comienzo 19.11.2019\GarciaSantaMariaCoronicaAragonObra27kb.txt 0.11576530218383696

69. Tratado generación criatura -C:\Users\Govert\Desktop\Signatura comienzo 19.11.2019\TratadoGeneracionCriaturaObra24kb.txt 0.11711873262551231

70. Juan de Ávila - Oliveros -C:\Users\Govert\Desktop\Signatura comienzo 19.11.2019\olveros de castilla epílogo.txt 0.11917173254225122

71. Tratado de Fisonomía -C:\Users\Govert\Desktop\Signatura comienzo 19.11.2019\tratadofisonomiaProemio8kb.txt 0.11974876825391167

72. Carta Hiseo respuesta Tristan -C:\Users\Govert\Desktop\Signatura comienzo 19.11.2019\cartahiseolabrunda.txt 0.12013576187844022

73. Flor de virtudes -C:\Users\Govert\Desktop\Signatura comienzo 19.11.2019\flordevirtudesobra22kb.txt 0.12164563403958617

74. Lucena -C:\Users\Govert\Desktop\Signatura comienzo 19.11.2019\repeticionamores ajedrez4kb.txt 0.12283084540082201

75. Juan de Padilla -C:\Users\Govert\Desktop\Signatura comienzo 19.11.2019\retablo cartujo14kb.txt 0.12389898432804947

76. Gil Vicente -C:\Users\Govert\Desktop\Signatura comienzo 19.11.2019\GilVicente AutoPastoril1502 16kb.txt 0.12530559991511225

77. Juan de Flores -C:\Users\Govert\Desktop\Signatura comienzo 19.11.2019\grisel introduccion2kb.txt 0.12598505000702886

78. Alonso de Proaza -C:\Users\Govert\Desktop\Signatura comienzo 19.11.2019\alonsodeproazaProsa no Celestina-12kb.txt 0.1282850009264439

79. Martin de Cordoba Jardin doncellas -C:\Users\Govert\Desktop\Signatura comienzo 19.11.2019\martindecordobaprohemio2kb.txt 0.12963580313363465

80. Alonso de Cardona -C:\Users\Govert\Desktop\Signatura comienzo 19.11.2019\alonsodecardona22kb.txt 0.1320768949491672

81. Gonzalo Fernández de Oviedo -C:\Users\Govert\Desktop\Signatura comienzo 19.11.2019\fernandezOviedo1532catálogo21kb.txt 0.13374067475454643

82. Gonzalo García Santa Maria -C:\Users\Govert\Desktop\Signatura comienzo 19.11.2019\evangeliosepistolas1485-64kb.txt 0.1379067540207145

83. Nicolás Núñez -C:\Users\Govert\Desktop\Signatura comienzo 19.11.2019\NicolasNuñezTractado32kb.txt 0.13833265216024193

84. Infancia Salvatoris -C:\Users\Govert\Desktop\Signatura comienzo 19.11.2019\InfanciaSalvatoris36kb.txt 0.14113237443917714

85. Juan de Ávila - Oliveros -C:\Users\Govert\Desktop\Signatura comienzo 19.11.2019\oliverosdecastilla introduccion.txt 0.14909673471041962

86. Juan de Ávila - Oliveros -C:\Users\Govert\Desktop\Signatura comienzo 19.11.2019\olveros de castilla prologo1498and1499.txt 0.15180391863493392

87. Andrés de Li -C:\Users\Govert\Desktop\Signatura comienzo 19.11.2019\SumaDePaciencia1493Prologo6kb.txt 0.15449396143558425

87. Andrés de Li -C:\Users\Govert\Desktop\Signatura comienzo 19.11.2019\SumaDePaciencia1493Prologo6kb.txt 0.15449396143558425

89. Pedro Carrillo de Huete -C:\Users\Govert\Desktop\Signatura comienzo 19.11.2019\halconero1489year32kb.txt 0.1564612974796581

90. Tratado de Fisonomía -C:\Users\Govert\Desktop\Signatura comienzo 19.11.2019\tratadofisonomiaIntroduccion3kb.txt 0.17163531297318957

91. Juan del Encina -C:\Users\Govert\Desktop\Signatura comienzo 19.11.2019\EncinaCancioneroAlbaHijoPrologo4kb.txt 0.1747214737568933

92. Balado Merlin anonimo -C:\Users\Govert\Desktop\Signatura comienzo 19.11.2019\baladromerlin21kb.txt 0.20865435826066636

93. Tratado de Fisonomía -C:\Users\Govert\Desktop\Signatura comienzo 19.11.2019\tratadofisonomiaObra22kb.txt 0.2261759227531338

94. Fernando de Rojas -C:\Users\Govert\Desktop\Signatura comienzo 19.11.2019\fernando de rojas14kb test2.txt 0.2379820680941498

95. Andrés de Li -C:\Users\Govert\Desktop\Signatura comienzo 19.11.2019\SumadePaciencia32kb.txt 0.2421216868508932

96. Libro hebreo oraciones -C:\Users\Govert\Desktop\Signatura comienzo 19.11.2019\siddurtefillot21kb.txt 0.2620472393300215

97. Compendio de Salud humana -C:\Users\Govert\Desktop\Signatura comienzo 19.11.2019\compendioSaludHumana25kb.txt 0.32697214396399277

98. Compendio de Salud humana -C:\Users\Govert\Desktop\Signatura comienzo 19.11.2019\CompendioSaludhumanaprologo13kb.txt 0.38641220191879544

15.6.2 1491 Siete Partidas

sietepartidas24kb.txt   C:\Users\Govert\Desktop\Signatura   comienzo 19.11.2019\sietepartidas24kb.txt

Canonicizers:
    Normalize Whitespace
EventDrivers:
    Character NGrams n : 4
        EventCullers:
            Most Common Events numevents : 50
Analysis:
    Nearest Neighbor Driver with metric Cosine Distance

1. Juan del Encina - Alonso el Sabio -C:\Users\Govert\Desktop\Signatura comienzo 19.11.2019\sietepartidas24kb.txt 0.0
2. Juan del Encina -C:\Users\Govert\Desktop\Signatura comienzo 19.11.2019\EncinaCancioneroPrincipeProhemio29kb.txt 0.016014145982558348
3. Francisco López de Villalobos -C:\Users\Govert\Desktop\Signatura comienzo 19.11.2019\villaloboscostumbres humanas21kb.txt 0.018415685477467303
4. Garci Rodríguez de Montalvo -C:\Users\Govert\Desktop\Signatura comienzo 19.11.2019\AmadisDos21kb.txt 0.02134868968703052
5. Prologos Fernández de Oviedo -C:\Users\Govert\Desktop\Signatura comienzo 19.11.2019\PrologosFernandezOviedo2-93kb.txt 0.0241672995301794
6. Gonzalo Fernández de Oviedo -C:\Users\Govert\Desktop\Signatura comienzo 19.11.2019\fernandezoviedobatalla90-130tiene34kb.txt 0.02595589806163434
7. Lucena -C:\Users\Govert\Desktop\Signatura comienzo 19.11.2019\repamores mitad libro51kb.txt 0.026526872321732675
8. Gonzalo Fernández de Oviedo -C:\Users\Govert\Desktop\Signatura comienzo 19.11.2019\FernandezOviedoSumarioIndias27kb.txt 0.02658687736979115
9. Corónica Adramon -C:\Users\Govert\Desktop\Signatura comienzo 19.11.2019\adramonObra30kb.txt 0.029025561703755365
10. Juan de Flores -C:\Users\Govert\Desktop\Signatura comienzo 19.11.2019\griselobra21kb.txt 0.03067675655349733
11. Juan del Encina -C:\Users\Govert\Desktop\Signatura comienzo 19.11.2019\encina eglogas antes 1509-287kb.txt 0.03105872172221602
12. Hernando del Castillo -C:\Users\Govert\Desktop\Signatura comienzo 19.11.2019\hernando de castillo prologo6kb.txt 0.03157112966968012
13. Ysopo -C:\Users\Govert\Desktop\Signatura comienzo 19.11.2019\ysope primer libro1495.txt 0.03252225031087108
14. Gonzalo Fernández de Oviedo -C:\Users\Govert\Desktop\Signatura comienzo 19.11.2019\FernandezOviedoClaribalte21kb.txt 0.03513854369196634
15. Juan de Ávila - Oliveros -C:\Users\Govert\Desktop\Signatura comienzo 19.11.2019\oliveros de castilla obra21kb.txt 0.035763088145661315
16. Cronica anónima Reyes Católicos -C:\Users\Govert\Desktop\Signatura comienzo 19.11.2019\cronicalucena21kb.txt 0.037192269533136146

17. Gil Vicente -C:\Users\Govert\Desktop\Signatura comienzo 19.11.2019\GilVicenteCuatroTiempos21kb.txt 0.03774106451703263

18. Garci Rodríguez de Montalvo -C:\Users\Govert\Desktop\Signatura comienzo 19.11.2019\AmadisUno21kb.txt 0.038200452828903275

19. Garci Rodríguez de Montalvo -C:\Users\Govert\Desktop\Signatura comienzo 19.11.2019\AmadisCuatro21kb.txt 0.03964879801959598

20. Juan Paez de Castro -C:\Users\Govert\Desktop\Signatura comienzo 19.11.2019\juanpaezdecastroCartas23kb.txt 0.039695832205907444

21. Martin de Cordoba Jardin doncellas -C:\Users\Govert\Desktop\Signatura comienzo 19.11.2019\martindecordoba12kb.txt 0.03995703460016731

22. Diego de San Pedro -C:\Users\Govert\Desktop\Signatura comienzo 19.11.2019\carceldeamor21kb.txt 0.04151294101429859

23. Juan del Encina - Linda Melosina -C:\Users\Govert\Desktop\Signatura comienzo 19.11.2019\lindamelosina21kb.txt 0.04195406892644893

24. Juan Ramírez de Lucena -C:\Users\Govert\Desktop\Signatura comienzo 19.11.2019\Ramirez Lucena exhortatoria.txt 0.042880638318402386

25. Garci Rodríguez de Montalvo -C:\Users\Govert\Desktop\Signatura comienzo 19.11.2019\amadisdegaula1496 prologo8kb.txt 0.042935553726720976

26. Gonzalo de Ayora -C:\Users\Govert\Desktop\Signatura comienzo 19.11.2019\GonzaloAyoraA MiguelPerezAlmazan15kb.txt 0.04299435734553214

27. Juan Ramírez de Lucena -C:\Users\Govert\Desktop\Signatura comienzo 19.11.2019\RamirezLucena a Zapata.txt 0.04330591987123822

28. Duobus amantibus -C:\Users\Govert\Desktop\Signatura comienzo 19.11.2019\piccolomini pp20 hasta30-21kb.txt 0.043456588325478385

29. Garci Rodríguez de Montalvo -C:\Users\Govert\Desktop\Signatura comienzo 19.11.2019\AmadisTres21kb.txt 0.04460558628705702

30. Gonzalo de Ayora -C:\Users\Govert\Desktop\Signatura comienzo 19.11.2019\GonzaloAyora79kb.txt 0.04481128322919525

31. Pedro de Portugal -C:\Users\Govert\Desktop\Signatura comienzo 19.11.2019\condestablePortugalSatira90kb.txt 0.04569748541760976

32. Jacobo de la Voragine -C:\Users\Govert\Desktop\Signatura comienzo 19.11.2019\flos sanctorum21kb.txt 0.04588080346526102

33. Gil Vicente -C:\Users\Govert\Desktop\Signatura comienzo 19.11.2019\GilVicenteSibila31kb.txt 0.046471305571480714

34. Diego de San Pedro -C:\Users\Govert\Desktop\Signatura comienzo 19.11.2019\arnalte incompleta21kb.txt 0.04658730050089921

35. Gonzalo de Ayora -C:\Users\Govert\Desktop\Signatura comienzo 19.11.2019\gonzaloayoraAvila67kb.txt 0.04705330787155415

36. Balado Merlin anonimo -C:\Users\Govert\Desktop\Signatura comienzo 19.11.2019\baladroprologo1498-7kb.txt 0.04720740437217952

37. Juan del Encina -C:\Users\Govert\Desktop\Signatura comienzo 19.11.2019\encina1521-8kb.txt 0.04898832059057712

38. Tercer Viaje de Colon -C:\Users\Govert\Desktop\Signatura comienzo 19.11.2019\TercerViajeColon24kb.txt 0.049042697750519504

39. Juan del Encina -C:\Users\Govert\Desktop\Signatura comienzo 19.11.2019\encinacoplas1521.txt 0.04912141875106257

40. Gil Vicente -C:\Users\Govert\Desktop\Signatura comienzo 19.11.2019\GilVicente Don Duardos65kb.txt 0.04935374060979447

41. Thebayda -C:\Users\Govert\Desktop\Signatura comienzo 19.11.2019\thebaida incompleta21kb.txt 0.050313311051982335

42. Juan de Capua -C:\Users\Govert\Desktop\Signatura comienzo 19.11.2019\engañosypeligrosObra25kb.txt 0.05500014684304977

43. Boccaccio -C:\Users\Govert\Desktop\Signatura comienzo 19.11.2019\BoccaccioIlustresmujeresobra21kb.txt 0.05598336381517233

44. Juan del Encina -C:\Users\Govert\Desktop\Signatura comienzo 19.11.2019\EncinaBubolicaReyesPrologo8kb.txt 0.057357207728396586

45. Juan de Flores -C:\Users\Govert\Desktop\Signatura comienzo 19.11.2019\triunfodeamor7kb.txt 0.059608116166250946

46. Gil Vicente -C:\Users\Govert\Desktop\Signatura comienzo 19.11.2019\GilVicente AutoPastoril1502 16kb.txt 0.06017432298933045

47. Enrique fi de Oliva -C:\Users\Govert\Desktop\Signatura comienzo 19.11.2019\enrique fi de oliva21kb.txt 0.06050749173043246

48. Flor de virtudes -C:\Users\Govert\Desktop\Signatura comienzo 19.11.2019\flordevirtudesobra22kb.txt 0.06136330618971886

49. Tratado generación criatura -C:\Users\Govert\Desktop\Signatura comienzo 19.11.2019\TratadoGeneracionCriaturaObra24kb.txt 0.06253225274060548

50. Juan de Flores -C:\Users\Govert\Desktop\Signatura comienzo 19.11.2019\triunfodeamorprologo4kb.txt 0.06389491745964582

51. Juan Ramírez de Lucena -C:\Users\Govert\Desktop\Signatura comienzo 19.11.2019\vita beata21kb.txt 0.06419565031116636

52. Juan de Flores -C:\Users\Govert\Desktop\Signatura comienzo 19.11.2019\grimalteobra21kb.txt 0.06430857372651977

53. Gonzalo García Santa Maria -C:\Users\Govert\Desktop\Signatura comienzo 19.11.2019\GarciaSantaMariaCoronicaAragonObra27kb.txt 0.06716290126924096

54. Lucas Fernández -C:\Users\Govert\Desktop\Signatura comienzo 19.11.2019\lucasfernandez dereniego del amor21kb.txt 0.06746260584375452

55. Cronica Troyana -C:\Users\Govert\Desktop\Signatura comienzo 19.11.2019\cronica troyana obra21kb.txt 0.06817272318566658

56. La Celestina -C:\Users\Govert\Desktop\Signatura comienzo 19.11.2019\CelestinaPrologo9kb.txt 0.0683035834218807

57. Hernán Núñez -C:\Users\Govert\Desktop\Signatura comienzo 19.11.2019\hernannuñez Trescientas21.txt 0.06833636754831318

58. Gil Vicente -C:\Users\Govert\Desktop\Signatura comienzo 19.11.2019\GilVicenteComediaViudo20kb.txt 0.06952839956631762

59. Tratado de amores -C:\Users\Govert\Desktop\Signatura comienzo 19.11.2019\tratadodeamores15kb.txt 0.07025887283971144

60. Juan del Encina -C:\Users\Govert\Desktop\Signatura comienzo 19.11.2019\EncinaCancioneroAlbaPrologo6kb.txt 0.07118461840996326

350

61. Gonzalo Fernández de Oviedo -C:\Users\Govert\Desktop\Signatura comienzo 19.11.2019\fernandezOviedo-indias 21kb.txt 0.07382207031520671

62. Vidal de Noya -C:\Users\Govert\Desktop\Signatura comienzo 19.11.2019\vidal de noyaJugurthaguerra28kb.txt 0.07396773760050823

63. Boccaccio -C:\Users\Govert\Desktop\Signatura comienzo 19.11.2019\BoccaccioIlustresmujeresprologo9kb.txt 0.07515158326230342

64. Carta Hiseo respuesta Tristan -C:\Users\Govert\Desktop\Signatura comienzo 19.11.2019\respuestadetristan.txt 0.07991212906579048

65. Gonzalo Fernández de Oviedo -C:\Users\Govert\Desktop\Signatura comienzo 19.11.2019\fernandezOviedo1532catálogo21kb.txt 0.08027381382510412

66. Gonzalo García Santa Maria -C:\Users\Govert\Desktop\Signatura comienzo 19.11.2019\evangeliosepistolas1485-64kb.txt 0.08099668441211005

67. Gordonio Niños -C:\Users\Govert\Desktop\Signatura comienzo 19.11.2019\GordonioNiños32kb.txt 0.08106367583411989

68. Juan del Encina -C:\Users\Govert\Desktop\Signatura comienzo 19.11.2019\EncinaBubolicaPrincipePrologo8kb.txt 0.08267010599369817

69. Juan de Flores -C:\Users\Govert\Desktop\Signatura comienzo 19.11.2019\grimalte prologo3kb.txt 0.08313962798081809

70. Juan de Ávila - Oliveros -C:\Users\Govert\Desktop\Signatura comienzo 19.11.2019\olveros de castilla epílogo.txt 0.08534325569282497

71. Boccaccio -C:\Users\Govert\Desktop\Signatura comienzo 19.11.2019\BoccaccioCaydaPrincipe.txt 0.0854920037659821

72. Juan del Encina -C:\Users\Govert\Desktop\Signatura comienzo 19.11.2019\EncinaCancioneroReyesProhemio7kb.txt 0.08630399236470776

73. Lucena -C:\Users\Govert\Desktop\Signatura comienzo 19.11.2019\repeticionamores ajedrez4kb.txt 0.08686209397498301

74. Tratado de Fisonomía -C:\Users\Govert\Desktop\Signatura comienzo 19.11.2019\tratadofisonomiaProemio8kb.txt 0.08840068840772675

75. Juan del Encina -C:\Users\Govert\Desktop\Signatura comienzo 19.11.2019\encinabubolicaArgumentos5kb.txt 0.08897874313738063

76. Infancia Salvatoris -C:\Users\Govert\Desktop\Signatura comienzo 19.11.2019\InfanciaSalvatoris36kb.txt 0.08952217472508428

77. Alonso de Cardona -C:\Users\Govert\Desktop\Signatura comienzo 19.11.2019\alonsodecardona22kb.txt 0.09079563869132434

78. Alonso de Proaza -C:\Users\Govert\Desktop\Signatura comienzo 19.11.2019\alonsodeproazaProsa no Celestina-12kb.txt 0.09394483522256325

79. Nicolás Núñez -C:\Users\Govert\Desktop\Signatura comienzo 19.11.2019\NicolasNuñezTractado32kb.txt 0.09685747735345629

80. Carta Hiseo respuesta Tristan -C:\Users\Govert\Desktop\Signatura comienzo 19.11.2019\cartahiseolabrunda.txt 0.10137361702764425

81. Juan de Flores -C:\Users\Govert\Desktop\Signatura comienzo 19.11.2019\griselprologo2kb.txt 0.10508461623738985

82. Juan Ramírez de Lucena -C:\Users\Govert\Desktop\Signatura comienzo 19.11.2019\RamirezLucena a galardones.txt 0.10572040739999711

83. Pedro Carrillo de Huete -C:\Users\Govert\Desktop\Signatura comienzo 19.11.2019\halconero1489year32kb.txt 0.10788957521468134

84. Juan de Flores -C:\Users\Govert\Desktop\Signatura comienzo 19.11.2019\grisel introduccion2kb.txt 0.118834201876857

85. Martin de Cordoba Jardin doncellas -C:\Users\Govert\Desktop\Signatura comienzo 19.11.2019\martindecordobaprohemio2kb.txt 0.13257421737616992

86. Juan de Padilla -C:\Users\Govert\Desktop\Signatura comienzo 19.11.2019\retablo cartujo14kb.txt 0.1330178172070745

87. Andrés de Li -C:\Users\Govert\Desktop\Signatura comienzo 19.11.2019\SumaDePaciencia1493Prologo6kb.txt 0.14282736856017708

87. Andrés de Li -C:\Users\Govert\Desktop\Signatura comienzo 19.11.2019\SumaDePaciencia1493Prologo6kb.txt 0.14282736856017708

89. Juan del Encina -C:\Users\Govert\Desktop\Signatura comienzo 19.11.2019\EncinaCancioneroAlbaHijoPrologo4kb.txt 0.16418066003079257

90. Juan de Ávila - Oliveros -C:\Users\Govert\Desktop\Signatura comienzo 19.11.2019\oliverosdecastilla introduccion.txt 0.17397444646189097

91. Juan de Ávila - Oliveros -C:\Users\Govert\Desktop\Signatura comienzo 19.11.2019\olveros de castilla prologo1498and1499.txt 0.17782617266200107

92. Balado Merlin anonimo -C:\Users\Govert\Desktop\Signatura comienzo 19.11.2019\baladromerlin21kb.txt 0.17993106175639006

93. Tratado de Fisonomía -C:\Users\Govert\Desktop\Signatura comienzo 19.11.2019\tratadofisonomiaObra22kb.txt 0.1910380715597686

94. Tratado de Fisonomía -C:\Users\Govert\Desktop\Signatura comienzo 19.11.2019\tratadofisonomiaIntroduccion3kb.txt 0.19500543376205182

95. Andrés de Li -C:\Users\Govert\Desktop\Signatura comienzo 19.11.2019\SumadePaciencia32kb.txt 0.20719993903173128

96. Fernando de Rojas -C:\Users\Govert\Desktop\Signatura comienzo 19.11.2019\fernando de rojas14kb test2.txt 0.2163303362672927

97. Libro hebreo oraciones -C:\Users\Govert\Desktop\Signatura comienzo 19.11.2019\siddurtefillot21kb.txt 0.23878164602424823

98. Compendio de Salud humana -C:\Users\Govert\Desktop\Signatura comienzo 19.11.2019\compendioSaludHumana25kb.txt 0.26038322320576124

99. Compendio de Salud humana -C:\Users\Govert\Desktop\Signatura comienzo 19.11.2019\CompendioSaludhumanaprologo13kb.txt 0.33644831589473445

15.6.3 1511 Renaldos de Montalvo, book I and II

renaldosdemontalbán20kb.txt   C:\Users\Govert\Desktop\Signatura   comienzo 19.11.2019\renaldosdemontalbán20kb.txt

Canonicizers:
  Normalize Whitespace
EventDrivers:
  Character NGrams n : 4
    EventCullers:
      Most Common Events numevents : 50
Analysis:
  Nearest Neighbor Driver with metric Cosine Distance

1. Juan de Ávila - Oliveros -C:\Users\Govert\Desktop\Signatura comienzo 19.11.2019\oliveros de castilla obra21kb.txt 0.030429557405228125

2. Juan del Encina - Linda Melosina -C:\Users\Govert\Desktop\Signatura comienzo 19.11.2019\lindamelosina21kb.txt 0.03233298923171157

3. Garci Rodríguez de Montalvo -C:\Users\Govert\Desktop\Signatura comienzo 19.11.2019\AmadisDos21kb.txt 0.038410912343821435

4. Gil Vicente -C:\Users\Govert\Desktop\Signatura comienzo 19.11.2019\GilVicenteSibila31kb.txt 0.04140472011400054

5. Gonzalo Fernández de Oviedo -C:\Users\Govert\Desktop\Signatura comienzo 19.11.2019\fernandezoviedobatalla90-130tiene34kb.txt 0.04149320209221263

6. Juan del Encina -C:\Users\Govert\Desktop\Signatura comienzo 19.11.2019\encina eglogas antes 1509-287kb.txt 0.042738597296233305

7. Juan de Flores -C:\Users\Govert\Desktop\Signatura comienzo 19.11.2019\grimalteobra21kb.txt 0.042891815928388866

8. Garci Rodríguez de Montalvo -C:\Users\Govert\Desktop\Signatura comienzo 19.11.2019\AmadisUno21kb.txt 0.04518680219328286

9. Prologos Fernández de Oviedo -C:\Users\Govert\Desktop\Signatura comienzo 19.11.2019\PrologosFernandezOviedo2-93kb.txt 0.04527169228341521

10. Garci Rodríguez de Montalvo -C:\Users\Govert\Desktop\Signatura comienzo 19.11.2019\AmadisTres21kb.txt 0.04572817347524738

11. Balado Merlin anonimo -C:\Users\Govert\Desktop\Signatura comienzo 19.11.2019\baladroprologo1498-7kb.txt 0.04580649674926196

12. Corónica Adramon -C:\Users\Govert\Desktop\Signatura comienzo 19.11.2019\adramonObra30kb.txt 0.04634446486218058

13. Gonzalo Fernández de Oviedo -C:\Users\Govert\Desktop\Signatura comienzo 19.11.2019\FernandezOviedoClaribalte21kb.txt 0.046407098371429645

14. Francisco López de Villalobos -C:\Users\Govert\Desktop\Signatura comienzo 19.11.2019\villaloboscostumbres humanas21kb.txt 0.04936647543614825

15. Gonzalo de Ayora -C:\Users\Govert\Desktop\Signatura comienzo 19.11.2019\GonzaloAyoraA MiguelPerezAlmazan15kb.txt 0.04956108324885078

16. Ysopo -C:\Users\Govert\Desktop\Signatura comienzo 19.11.2019\ysope primer libro1495.txt 0.050850662112349454

17. Gonzalo Fernández de Oviedo -C:\Users\Govert\Desktop\Signatura comienzo 19.11.2019\FernandezOviedoSumarioIndias27kb.txt 0.05171684817112676

18. Juan del Encina -C:\Users\Govert\Desktop\Signatura comienzo 19.11.2019\encinacoplas1521.txt 0.051846883452097536

19. Juan del Encina - Alonso el Sabio -C:\Users\Govert\Desktop\Signatura comienzo 19.11.2019\sietepartidas24kb.txt 0.05251071786276007

20. Jacobo de la Voragine -C:\Users\Govert\Desktop\Signatura comienzo 19.11.2019\flos sanctorum21kb.txt 0.05376389156682071

21. Juan del Encina -C:\Users\Govert\Desktop\Signatura comienzo 19.11.2019\EncinaCancioneroPrincipeProhemio29kb.txt 0.054022856643597184

22. Juan de Flores -C:\Users\Govert\Desktop\Signatura comienzo 19.11.2019\griselobra21kb.txt 0.05409940072398689

23. Juan del Encina -C:\Users\Govert\Desktop\Signatura comienzo 19.11.2019\encina1521-8kb.txt 0.054210465993147605

24. Gil Vicente -C:\Users\Govert\Desktop\Signatura comienzo 19.11.2019\GilVicente Don Duardos65kb.txt 0.05634378395426898

25. Juan Paez de Castro -C:\Users\Govert\Desktop\Signatura comienzo 19.11.2019\juanpaezdecastroCartas23kb.txt 0.05795114790389155

26. Enrique fi de Oliva -C:\Users\Govert\Desktop\Signatura comienzo 19.11.2019\enrique fi de oliva21kb.txt 0.05868441751135378

27. Lucena -C:\Users\Govert\Desktop\Signatura comienzo 19.11.2019\repamores mitad libro51kb.txt 0.060715805291687075

28. Gil Vicente -C:\Users\Govert\Desktop\Signatura comienzo 19.11.2019\GilVicente AutoPastoril1502 16kb.txt 0.06092123736005339

29. Diego de San Pedro -C:\Users\Govert\Desktop\Signatura comienzo 19.11.2019\carceldeamor21kb.txt 0.06132493605471545

30. Juan del Encina -C:\Users\Govert\Desktop\Signatura comienzo 19.11.2019\encinabubolIcaArgumentos5kb.txt 0.06273423710822901

31. Garci Rodríguez de Montalvo -C:\Users\Govert\Desktop\Signatura comienzo 19.11.2019\amadisdegaula1496 prologo8kb.txt 0.062778897550815

32. Juan Ramírez de Lucena -C:\Users\Govert\Desktop\Signatura comienzo 19.11.2019\RamirezLucena a Zapata.txt 0.06386536998660775

33. Juan Ramírez de Lucena -C:\Users\Govert\Desktop\Signatura comienzo 19.11.2019\Ramirez Lucena exhortatoria.txt 0.06393022534433157

34. Martin de Cordoba Jardin doncellas -C:\Users\Govert\Desktop\Signatura comienzo 19.11.2019\martindecordoba12kb.txt 0.0640390841572771

35. Gonzalo de Ayora -C:\Users\Govert\Desktop\Signatura comienzo 19.11.2019\GonzaloAyora79kb.txt 0.06568424770312897

36. Tratado de amores -C:\Users\Govert\Desktop\Signatura comienzo 19.11.2019\tratadodeamores15kb.txt 0.0660901423760078

37. Thebayda -C:\Users\Govert\Desktop\Signatura comienzo 19.11.2019\thebaida incompleta21kb.txt 0.06614954074178392

38. Gonzalo García Santa Maria -C:\Users\Govert\Desktop\Signatura comienzo 19.11.2019\GarciaSantaMariaCoronicaAragonObra27kb.txt 0.06695021083693076

39. Garci Rodríguez de Montalvo -C:\Users\Govert\Desktop\Signatura comienzo 19.11.2019\AmadisCuatro21kb.txt 0.06741811009553078

40. Pedro de Portugal -C:\Users\Govert\Desktop\Signatura comienzo 19.11.2019\condestablePortugalSatira90kb.txt 0.06785725892523964

41. Alonso de Cardona -C:\Users\Govert\Desktop\Signatura comienzo 19.11.2019\alonsodecardona22kb.txt 0.06786043481036574

42. Diego de San Pedro -C:\Users\Govert\Desktop\Signatura comienzo 19.11.2019\arnalte incompleta21kb.txt 0.07080414261533585

43. Nicolás Núñez -C:\Users\Govert\Desktop\Signatura comienzo 19.11.2019\NicolasNuñezTractado32kb.txt 0.07523640801282927

44. Infancia Salvatoris -C:\Users\Govert\Desktop\Signatura comienzo 19.11.2019\InfanciaSalvatoris36kb.txt 0.07571719383697717

45. Duobus amantibus -C:\Users\Govert\Desktop\Signatura comienzo 19.11.2019\piccolomini pp20 hasta30-21kb.txt 0.0778429494033801

46. Gil Vicente -C:\Users\Govert\Desktop\Signatura comienzo 19.11.2019\GilVicenteCuatroTiempos21kb.txt 0.0793614039780276

47. Carta Hiseo respuesta Tristan -C:\Users\Govert\Desktop\Signatura comienzo 19.11.2019\respuestadetristan.txt 0.08034097046995392

48. Vidal de Noya -C:\Users\Govert\Desktop\Signatura comienzo 19.11.2019\vidal de noyaJugurthaguerra28kb.txt 0.08042706471115857

49. Lucas Fernández -C:\Users\Govert\Desktop\Signatura comienzo 19.11.2019\lucasfernandez dereniego del amor21kb.txt 0.08228093573996953

50. Cronica Troyana -C:\Users\Govert\Desktop\Signatura comienzo 19.11.2019\cronica troyana obra21kb.txt 0.08313462470128563

51. Juan del Encina -C:\Users\Govert\Desktop\Signatura comienzo 19.11.2019\EncinaBubolicaReyesPrologo8kb.txt 0.08572720412696222

52. Hernando del Castillo -C:\Users\Govert\Desktop\Signatura comienzo 19.11.2019\hernando de castillo prologo6kb.txt 0.08618615504268134

53. Gil Vicente -C:\Users\Govert\Desktop\Signatura comienzo 19.11.2019\GilVicenteComediaViudo20kb.txt 0.08785484655827569

54. Carta Hiseo respuesta Tristan -C:\Users\Govert\Desktop\Signatura comienzo 19.11.2019\cartahiseolabrunda.txt 0.09060985736319649

55. Juan de Capua -C:\Users\Govert\Desktop\Signatura comienzo 19.11.2019\engañosypeligrosObra25kb.txt 0.09221413403974033

56. Juan Ramírez de Lucena -C:\Users\Govert\Desktop\Signatura comienzo 19.11.2019\vita beata21kb.txt 0.09413452880208517

57. Alonso de Proaza -C:\Users\Govert\Desktop\Signatura comienzo 19.11.2019\alonsodeproazaProsa no Celestina-12kb.txt 0.0941452151781621

58. Boccaccio -C:\Users\Govert\Desktop\Signatura comienzo 19.11.2019\BoccaccioCaydaPrincipe.txt 0.09550707968613448

59. Gonzalo de Ayora -C:\Users\Govert\Desktop\Signatura comienzo 19.11.2019\gonzaloayoraAvila67kb.txt 0.09586409341520497

60. Boccaccio -C:\Users\Govert\Desktop\Signatura comienzo 19.11.2019\BoccaccioIlustresmujeresobra21kb.txt 0.09676761704149117

61. Cronica anónima Reyes Católicos -C:\Users\Govert\Desktop\Signatura comienzo 19.11.2019\cronicalucena21kb.txt 0.09976072262621838

62. Tercer Viaje de Colon -C:\Users\Govert\Desktop\Signatura comienzo 19.11.2019\TercerViajeColon24kb.txt 0.10134981149948785

63. Flor de virtudes -C:\Users\Govert\Desktop\Signatura comienzo 19.11.2019\flordevirtudesobra22kb.txt 0.10195990269759925

64. Gonzalo Fernández de Oviedo -C:\Users\Govert\Desktop\Signatura comienzo 19.11.2019\fernandezOviedo1532catálogo21kb.txt 0.10464554311000573

65. Gonzalo García Santa Maria -C:\Users\Govert\Desktop\Signatura comienzo 19.11.2019\evangeliosepistolas1485-64kb.txt 0.10779166474377744

66. Lucena -C:\Users\Govert\Desktop\Signatura comienzo 19.11.2019\repeticionamores ajedrez4kb.txt 0.11080041052865086

67. Juan de Ávila - Oliveros -C:\Users\Govert\Desktop\Signatura comienzo 19.11.2019\olveros de castilla epílogo.txt 0.11151033558919021

68. Juan del Encina -C:\Users\Govert\Desktop\Signatura comienzo 19.11.2019\EncinaCancioneroAlbaPrologo6kb.txt 0.11336354902871149

69. Juan de Flores -C:\Users\Govert\Desktop\Signatura comienzo 19.11.2019\grisel introduccion2kb.txt 0.11566436994126594

70. Juan de Flores -C:\Users\Govert\Desktop\Signatura comienzo 19.11.2019\triunfodeamorprologo4kb.txt 0.11617066840542278

71. Hernán Núñez -C:\Users\Govert\Desktop\Signatura comienzo 19.11.2019\hernannuñez Trescientas21.txt 0.12104772875216385

72. La Celestina -C:\Users\Govert\Desktop\Signatura comienzo 19.11.2019\CelestinaPrologo9kb.txt 0.12168962295007113

73. Tratado generación criatura -C:\Users\Govert\Desktop\Signatura comienzo 19.11.2019\TratadoGeneracionCriaturaObra24kb.txt 0.12246776540854898

74. Juan de Flores -C:\Users\Govert\Desktop\Signatura comienzo 19.11.2019\grimalte prologo3kb.txt 0.12419684998019054

75. Pedro Carrillo de Huete -C:\Users\Govert\Desktop\Signatura comienzo 19.11.2019\halconero1489year32kb.txt 0.12493692344790552

76. Juan del Encina -C:\Users\Govert\Desktop\Signatura comienzo 19.11.2019\EncinaBubolicaPrincipePrologo8kb.txt 0.1258328340418705

77. Juan Ramírez de Lucena -C:\Users\Govert\Desktop\Signatura comienzo 19.11.2019\RamirezLucena a galardones.txt 0.12583685106033615

78. Juan de Flores -C:\Users\Govert\Desktop\Signatura comienzo 19.11.2019\triunfodeamor7kb.txt 0.12722464217368756

79. Juan de Flores -C:\Users\Govert\Desktop\Signatura comienzo 19.11.2019\griselprologo2kb.txt 0.1275573864187165

80. Gonzalo Fernández de Oviedo -C:\Users\Govert\Desktop\Signatura comienzo 19.11.2019\fernandezOviedo-indias 21kb.txt 0.12774066333820855

81. Juan del Encina -C:\Users\Govert\Desktop\Signatura comienzo 19.11.2019\EncinaCancioneroReyesProhemio7kb.txt 0.1327395212736382

82. Boccaccio -C:\Users\Govert\Desktop\Signatura comienzo 19.11.2019\BoccaccioIlustresmujeresprologo9kb.txt 0.13379844824956655

83. Andrés de Li -C:\Users\Govert\Desktop\Signatura comienzo 19.11.2019\SumaDePaciencia1493Prologo6kb.txt 0.15893795723818915

83. Andrés de Li -C:\Users\Govert\Desktop\Signatura comienzo 19.11.2019\SumaDePaciencia1493Prologo6kb.txt 0.15893795723818915

85. Gordonio Niños -C:\Users\Govert\Desktop\Signatura comienzo 19.11.2019\GordonioNiños32kb.txt 0.1655727601263941

86. Juan del Encina -C:\Users\Govert\Desktop\Signatura comienzo 19.11.2019\EncinaCancioneroAlbaHijoPrologo4kb.txt 0.17594615639883548

87. Tratado de Fisonomía -C:\Users\Govert\Desktop\Signatura comienzo 19.11.2019\tratadofisonomiaProemio8kb.txt 0.18127079593034834

88. Juan de Padilla -C:\Users\Govert\Desktop\Signatura comienzo 19.11.2019\retablo cartujo14kb.txt 0.18582137085384853

89. Martin de Cordoba Jardin doncellas -C:\Users\Govert\Desktop\Signatura comienzo 19.11.2019\martindecordobaprohemio2kb.txt 0.20008308754173476

90. Balado Merlin anonimo -C:\Users\Govert\Desktop\Signatura comienzo 19.11.2019\baladromerlin21kb.txt 0.21232663241845995

91. Juan de Ávila - Oliveros -C:\Users\Govert\Desktop\Signatura comienzo 19.11.2019\oliverosdecastilla introduccion.txt 0.22233859024369196

92. Juan de Ávila - Oliveros -C:\Users\Govert\Desktop\Signatura comienzo 19.11.2019\olveros de castilla prologo1498and1499.txt 0.23373416307363026

93. Fernando de Rojas -C:\Users\Govert\Desktop\Signatura comienzo 19.11.2019\fernando de rojas14kb test2.txt 0.2507229635734941

94. Andrés de Li -C:\Users\Govert\Desktop\Signatura comienzo 19.11.2019\SumadePaciencia32kb.txt 0.2718709754449333

95. Libro hebreo oraciones -C:\Users\Govert\Desktop\Signatura comienzo 19.11.2019\siddurtefillot21kb.txt 0.29072511566864834

96. Tratado de Fisonomía -C:\Users\Govert\Desktop\Signatura comienzo 19.11.2019\tratadofisonomiaObra22kb.txt 0.30235721915998814

97. Compendio de Salud humana -C:\Users\Govert\Desktop\Signatura comienzo 19.11.2019\compendioSaludHumana25kb.txt 0.3247978051044802

98. Tratado de Fisonomía -C:\Users\Govert\Desktop\Signatura comienzo 19.11.2019\tratadofisonomiaIntroduccion3kb.txt 0.32763207628721125

99. Compendio de Salud humana -C:\Users\Govert\Desktop\Signatura comienzo 19.11.2019\CompendioSaludhumanaprologo13kb.txt 0.43643762188429136

15.6.4 1498 Oliveros de Castilla Obra

oliveros de castilla obra21kb.txt C:\Users\Govert\Desktop\Signatura comienzo 19.11.2019\oliveros de castilla obra21kb.txt

Canonicizers:

    Normalize Whitespace

EventDrivers:

    Character NGrams n : 4

        EventCullers:

            Most Common Events numevents : 50

Analysis:

    Nearest Neighbor Driver with metric Cosine Distance

1. Juan de Ávila - Oliveros -C:\Users\Govert\Desktop\Signatura comienzo 19.11.2019\oliveros de castilla obra21kb.txt 0.0

2. Gonzalo Fernández de Oviedo -C:\Users\Govert\Desktop\Signatura comienzo 19.11.2019\fernandezoviedobatalla90-130tiene34kb.txt 0.024725622231715705

3. Prologos Fernández de Oviedo -C:\Users\Govert\Desktop\Signatura comienzo 19.11.2019\PrologosFernandezOviedo2-93kb.txt 0.02707523504881093

4. Garci Rodríguez de Montalvo -C:\Users\Govert\Desktop\Signatura comienzo 19.11.2019\AmadisDos21kb.txt 0.02948730061292637

5. Garci Rodríguez de Montalvo -C:\Users\Govert\Desktop\Signatura comienzo 19.11.2019\AmadisUno21kb.txt 0.029935607330028202

6. Gonzalo Fernández de Oviedo -C:\Users\Govert\Desktop\Signatura comienzo 19.11.2019\FernandezOviedoSumarioIndias27kb.txt 0.03126469213697891

7. Jacobo de la Voragine -C:\Users\Govert\Desktop\Signatura comienzo 19.11.2019\flos sanctorum21kb.txt 0.03450622310340645

8. Juan del Encina - Linda Melosina -C:\Users\Govert\Desktop\Signatura comienzo 19.11.2019\lindamelosina21kb.txt 0.03537372644927805

9. Ysopo -C:\Users\Govert\Desktop\Signatura comienzo 19.11.2019\ysope primer libro1495.txt 0.0356461905820713

10. Juan del Encina - Alonso el Sabio -C:\Users\Govert\Desktop\Signatura comienzo 19.11.2019\sietepartidas24kb.txt 0.035763088145661315

11. Lucena -C:\Users\Govert\Desktop\Signatura comienzo 19.11.2019\repamores mitad libro51kb.txt 0.03749810824701061

12. Diego de San Pedro -C:\Users\Govert\Desktop\Signatura comienzo 19.11.2019\arnalte incompleta21kb.txt 0.03857611316179266

13. Francisco López de Villalobos -C:\Users\Govert\Desktop\Signatura comienzo 19.11.2019\villaloboscostumbres humanas21kb.txt 0.0388464278962658

14. Gonzalo Fernández de Oviedo -C:\Users\Govert\Desktop\Signatura comienzo 19.11.2019\FernandezOviedoClaribalte21kb.txt 0.03952260572687594

15. Juan del Encina -C:\Users\Govert\Desktop\Signatura comienzo 19.11.2019\EncinaCancioneroPrincipeProhemio29kb.txt 0.03986556189806967

16. Juan del Encina -C:\Users\Govert\Desktop\Signatura comienzo 19.11.2019\encina eglogas antes 1509-287kb.txt 0.041182171664051914

17. Corónica Adramon -C:\Users\Govert\Desktop\Signatura comienzo 19.11.2019\adramonObra30kb.txt 0.04152143825162735

18. Martin de Cordoba Jardin doncellas -C:\Users\Govert\Desktop\Signatura comienzo 19.11.2019\martindecordoba12kb.txt 0.041542901002026844

19. Juan de Flores -C:\Users\Govert\Desktop\Signatura comienzo 19.11.2019\griselobra21kb.txt 0.04453956932565595

20. Pedro de Portugal -C:\Users\Govert\Desktop\Signatura comienzo 19.11.2019\condestablePortugalSatira90kb.txt 0.045641774148214354

21. Garci Rodríguez de Montalvo -C:\Users\Govert\Desktop\Signatura comienzo 19.11.2019\AmadisCuatro21kb.txt 0.048768885992929056

22. Garci Rodríguez de Montalvo -C:\Users\Govert\Desktop\Signatura comienzo 19.11.2019\AmadisTres21kb.txt 0.04921474338657128

23. Gil Vicente -C:\Users\Govert\Desktop\Signatura comienzo 19.11.2019\GilVicenteSibila31kb.txt 0.04931887127387302

24. Diego de San Pedro -C:\Users\Govert\Desktop\Signatura comienzo 19.11.2019\carceldeamor21kb.txt 0.051100903901044714

25. Balado Merlin anonimo -C:\Users\Govert\Desktop\Signatura comienzo 19.11.2019\baladroprologo1498-7kb.txt 0.051606548450417455

26. Juan Ramírez de Lucena -C:\Users\Govert\Desktop\Signatura comienzo 19.11.2019\Ramirez Lucena exhortatoria.txt 0.05165059756373569

27. Juan Ramírez de Lucena -C:\Users\Govert\Desktop\Signatura comienzo 19.11.2019\RamirezLucena a Zapata.txt 0.05183916048303039

28. Enrique fi de Oliva -C:\Users\Govert\Desktop\Signatura comienzo 19.11.2019\enrique fi de oliva21kb.txt 0.05344589722536608

29. Duobus amantibus -C:\Users\Govert\Desktop\Signatura comienzo 19.11.2019\piccolomini pp20 hasta30-21kb.txt 0.05372482796423983

30. Boccaccio -C:\Users\Govert\Desktop\Signatura comienzo 19.11.2019\BoccaccioIlustresmujeresobra21kb.txt 0.05769782589753725

31. Gonzalo de Ayora -C:\Users\Govert\Desktop\Signatura comienzo 19.11.2019\GonzaloAyoraA MiguelPerezAlmazan15kb.txt 0.05773664094605202

32. Juan de Flores -C:\Users\Govert\Desktop\Signatura comienzo 19.11.2019\grimalteobra21kb.txt 0.05814220414901328

33. Juan Paez de Castro -C:\Users\Govert\Desktop\Signatura comienzo 19.11.2019\juanpaezdecastroCartas23kb.txt 0.05880011054571399

34. Thebayda -C:\Users\Govert\Desktop\Signatura comienzo 19.11.2019\thebaida incompleta21kb.txt 0.05940085032096254

35. Gil Vicente -C:\Users\Govert\Desktop\Signatura comienzo 19.11.2019\GilVicenteCuatroTiempos21kb.txt 0.06132649495348108

36. Gonzalo García Santa Maria -C:\Users\Govert\Desktop\Signatura comienzo 19.11.2019\GarciaSantaMariaCoronicaAragonObra27kb.txt 0.06137157943358795

37. Juan del Encina -C:\Users\Govert\Desktop\Signatura comienzo 19.11.2019\encina1521-8kb.txt 0.06164724937992894

38. Gil Vicente -C:\Users\Govert\Desktop\Signatura comienzo 19.11.2019\GilVicente AutoPastoril1502 16kb.txt 0.06180543208577638

39. Gil Vicente -C:\Users\Govert\Desktop\Signatura comienzo 19.11.2019\GilVicente Don Duardos65kb.txt 0.062364289105562576

40. Gonzalo de Ayora -C:\Users\Govert\Desktop\Signatura comienzo 19.11.2019\GonzaloAyora79kb.txt 0.06261305734284117

41. Juan del Encina -C:\Users\Govert\Desktop\Signatura comienzo 19.11.2019\encinacoplas1521.txt 0.0648216688529315

42. Juan de Capua -C:\Users\Govert\Desktop\Signatura comienzo 19.11.2019\engañosypeligrosObra25kb.txt 0.06504675370637836

43. Tratado de amores -C:\Users\Govert\Desktop\Signatura comienzo 19.11.2019\tratadodeamores15kb.txt 0.0679233863543609

44. Garci Rodríguez de Montalvo -C:\Users\Govert\Desktop\Signatura comienzo 19.11.2019\amadisdegaula1496 prologo8kb.txt 0.06822386676252834

45. Cronica Troyana -C:\Users\Govert\Desktop\Signatura comienzo 19.11.2019\cronica troyana obra21kb.txt 0.06825577173978958

46. Cronica anónima Reyes Católicos -C:\Users\Govert\Desktop\Signatura comienzo 19.11.2019\cronicalucena21kb.txt 0.06989678672892108

47. Gonzalo de Ayora -C:\Users\Govert\Desktop\Signatura comienzo 19.11.2019\gonzaloayoraAvila67kb.txt 0.07023733422374911

48. Carta Hiseo respuesta Tristan -C:\Users\Govert\Desktop\Signatura comienzo 19.11.2019\respuestadetristan.txt 0.07030744091622232

49. Juan del Encina -C:\Users\Govert\Desktop\Signatura comienzo 19.11.2019\EncinaBubolicaReyesPrologo8kb.txt 0.07033254269138112

50. Juan del Encina -C:\Users\Govert\Desktop\Signatura comienzo 19.11.2019\encinabubolicaArgumentos5kb.txt 0.07145065535354678

51. Flor de virtudes -C:\Users\Govert\Desktop\Signatura comienzo 19.11.2019\flordevirtudesobra22kb.txt 0.07159843789402442

52. Hernando del Castillo -C:\Users\Govert\Desktop\Signatura comienzo 19.11.2019\hernando de castillo prologo6kb.txt 0.07255397949416009

53. Gonzalo Fernández de Oviedo -C:\Users\Govert\Desktop\Signatura comienzo 19.11.2019\fernandezOviedo1532catálogo21kb.txt 0.07343215588976215

54. Vidal de Noya -C:\Users\Govert\Desktop\Signatura comienzo 19.11.2019\vidal de noyaJugurthaguerra28kb.txt 0.07413360789939527

55. Tratado generación criatura -C:\Users\Govert\Desktop\Signatura comienzo 19.11.2019\TratadoGeneracionCriaturaObra24kb.txt 0.0743529841791295

56. Hernán Núñez -C:\Users\Govert\Desktop\Signatura comienzo 19.11.2019\hernannuñez Trescientas21.txt 0.07597633314909868

57. Infancia Salvatoris -C:\Users\Govert\Desktop\Signatura comienzo 19.11.2019\InfanciaSalvatoris36kb.txt 0.07649448976615136

58. Gil Vicente -C:\Users\Govert\Desktop\Signatura comienzo 19.11.2019\GilVicenteComediaViudo20kb.txt 0.07689019631861982

59. La Celestina -C:\Users\Govert\Desktop\Signatura comienzo 19.11.2019\CelestinaPrologo9kb.txt 0.07743136999185962

60. Juan Ramírez de Lucena -C:\Users\Govert\Desktop\Signatura comienzo 19.11.2019\vita beata21kb.txt 0.07861181231265801

61. Alonso de Cardona -C:\Users\Govert\Desktop\Signatura comienzo 19.11.2019\alonsodecardona22kb.txt 0.08270699289504402

62. Tercer Viaje de Colon -C:\Users\Govert\Desktop\Signatura comienzo 19.11.2019\TercerViajeColon24kb.txt 0.082951607993067

63. Nicolás Núñez -C:\Users\Govert\Desktop\Signatura comienzo 19.11.2019\NicolasNuñezTractado32kb.txt 0.08389790474330894

64. Juan de Ávila - Oliveros -C:\Users\Govert\Desktop\Signatura comienzo 19.11.2019\olveros de castilla cpílogo.txt 0.08514177216436969

65. Lucas Fernández -C:\Users\Govert\Desktop\Signatura comienzo 19.11.2019\lucasfernandez dereniego del amor21kb.txt 0.08859793584564302

66. Juan de Flores -C:\Users\Govert\Desktop\Signatura comienzo 19.11.2019\grimalte prologo3kb.txt 0.09275338494863439

67. Lucena -C:\Users\Govert\Desktop\Signatura comienzo 19.11.2019\repeticionamores ajedrez4kb.txt 0.0928306689398889

68. Gonzalo García Santa Maria -C:\Users\Govert\Desktop\Signatura comienzo 19.11.2019\evangeliosepistolas1485-64kb.txt 0.09395214500655646

69. Alonso de Proaza -C:\Users\Govert\Desktop\Signatura comienzo 19.11.2019\alonsodeproazaProsa no Celestina-12kb.txt 0.0942589437395176

70. Juan de Flores -C:\Users\Govert\Desktop\Signatura comienzo 19.11.2019\triunfodeamor7kb.txt 0.09473915372777264

71. Juan del Encina -C:\Users\Govert\Desktop\Signatura comienzo 19.11.2019\EncinaCancioneroAlbaPrologo6kb.txt 0.09553988519870316

72. Boccaccio -C:\Users\Govert\Desktop\Signatura comienzo 19.11.2019\BoccaccioCaydaPrincipe.txt 0.09710664631974919

73. Juan de Flores -C:\Users\Govert\Desktop\Signatura comienzo 19.11.2019\triunfodeamorprologo4kb.txt 0.0986885341069691

74. Gonzalo Fernández de Oviedo -C:\Users\Govert\Desktop\Signatura comienzo 19.11.2019\fernandezOviedo-indias 21kb.txt 0.09874078233755879

75. Juan del Encina -C:\Users\Govert\Desktop\Signatura comienzo 19.11.2019\EncinaBubolicaPrincipePrologo8kb.txt 0.09890946010943691

76. Pedro Carrillo de Huete -C:\Users\Govert\Desktop\Signatura comienzo 19.11.2019\halconero1489year32kb.txt 0.10118141553466808

77. Carta Hiseo respuesta Tristan -C:\Users\Govert\Desktop\Signatura comienzo 19.11.2019\cartahiseolabrunda.txt 0.10173516912031966

78. Boccaccio -C:\Users\Govert\Desktop\Signatura comienzo 19.11.2019\BoccaccioIlustresmujeresprologo9kb.txt 0.10875514197879099

79. Juan del Encina -C:\Users\Govert\Desktop\Signatura comienzo 19.11.2019\EncinaCancioneroReyesProhemio7kb.txt 0.11546901645488017

80. Juan Ramírez de Lucena -C:\Users\Govert\Desktop\Signatura comienzo 19.11.2019\RamirezLucena a galardones.txt 0.11566215909607913

81. Juan de Flores -C:\Users\Govert\Desktop\Signatura comienzo 19.11.2019\griselprologo2kb.txt 0.12057526947167363

82. Gordonio Niños -C:\Users\Govert\Desktop\Signatura comienzo 19.11.2019\GordonioNiños32kb.txt 0.1265114849620813

83. Juan de Flores -C:\Users\Govert\Desktop\Signatura comienzo 19.11.2019\grisel introduccion2kb.txt 0.1269616322730872

84. Tratado de Fisonomía -C:\Users\Govert\Desktop\Signatura comienzo 19.11.2019\tratadofisonomiaProemio8kb.txt 0.1316614564537808

85. Juan de Padilla -C:\Users\Govert\Desktop\Signatura comienzo 19.11.2019\retablo cartujo14kb.txt 0.1517137460330117

86. Martin de Cordoba Jardin doncellas -C:\Users\Govert\Desktop\Signatura comienzo 19.11.2019\martindecordobaprohemio2kb.txt 0.16193984857969324

87. Andrés de Li -C:\Users\Govert\Desktop\Signatura comienzo 19.11.2019\SumaDePaciencia1493Prologo6kb.txt 0.16286379017611696

87. Andrés de Li -C:\Users\Govert\Desktop\Signatura comienzo 19.11.2019\SumaDePaciencia1493Prologo6kb.txt 0.16286379017611696

89. Juan del Encina -C:\Users\Govert\Desktop\Signatura comienzo 19.11.2019\EncinaCancioneroAlbaHijoPrologo4kb.txt 0.17189401933869008

90. Balado Merlin anonimo -C:\Users\Govert\Desktop\Signatura comienzo 19.11.2019\baladromerlin21kb.txt 0.1848242035914216

91. Juan de Ávila - Oliveros -C:\Users\Govert\Desktop\Signatura comienzo 19.11.2019\oliverosdecastilla introduccion.txt 0.20238420030329185

92. Juan de Ávila - Oliveros -C:\Users\Govert\Desktop\Signatura comienzo 19.11.2019\olveros de castilla prologo1498and1499.txt 0.2113190368652531

93. Tratado de Fisonomía -C:\Users\Govert\Desktop\Signatura comienzo 19.11.2019\tratadofisonomiaObra22kb.txt 0.21636259500491672

94. Fernando de Rojas -C:\Users\Govert\Desktop\Signatura comienzo 19.11.2019\fernando de rojas14kb test2.txt 0.22402668723517605

95. Andrés de Li -C:\Users\Govert\Desktop\Signatura comienzo 19.11.2019\SumadePaciencia32kb.txt 0.24028148708455832

96. Tratado de Fisonomía -C:\Users\Govert\Desktop\Signatura comienzo 19.11.2019\tratadofisonomiaIntroduccion3kb.txt 0.24777597270197738

97. Libro hebreo oraciones -C:\Users\Govert\Desktop\Signatura comienzo 19.11.2019\siddurtefillot21kb.txt 0.2681789046828006

98. Compendio de Salud humana -C:\Users\Govert\Desktop\Signatura comienzo 19.11.2019\compendioSaludHumana25kb.txt 0.27947464065076844

99. Compendio de Salud humana -C:\Users\Govert\Desktop\Signatura comienzo 19.11.2019\CompendioSaludhumanaprologo13kb.txt 0.3718534517194133

15.6.5 1513 Trapesonda Third analysis

Trapesonda3 renaldosdeMontalban21kb.txt C:\Users\Govert\Desktop\Signatura comienzo 19.11.2019\Trapesonda3 renaldosdeMontalban21kb.txt

Canonicizers:
  Normalize Whitespace
EventDrivers:
  Character NGrams n : 4
    EventCullers:
      Most Common Events numevents : 50
Analysis:
  Nearest Neighbor Driver with metric Cosine Distance
1. Juan de Boscan -C:\Users\Govert\Desktop\Signatura comienzo 19.11.2019\BoscanElCortesano47kb.txt 0.031435875199722574
2. Prologos Fernández de Oviedo -C:\Users\Govert\Desktop\Signatura comienzo 19.11.2019\PrologosFernandezOviedo2-93kb.txt 0.03922272235011959
3. Feliciano de Silva -C:\Users\Govert\Desktop\Signatura comienzo 19.11.2019\Silva amadis de grecia20kb.txt 0.040828798431777225
4. Jerónimo Fernández -C:\Users\Govert\Desktop\Signatura comienzo 19.11.2019\jeronimofernandez3año1579-113kb.txt 0.041213841750175284
5. Juan del Encina -C:\Users\Govert\Desktop\Signatura comienzo 19.11.2019\encina eglogas antes 1509-287kb.txt 0.043085722161628426
6. Gil Vicente -C:\Users\Govert\Desktop\Signatura comienzo 19.11.2019\GilVicenteSibila31kb.txt 0.043094413187944824
7. Bernardo de Quirós -C:\Users\Govert\Desktop\Signatura comienzo 19.11.2019\VillalonViajeTurquiaVillalon109kb.txt 0.04384513377790766
8. Gonzalo García Santa Maria -C:\Users\Govert\Desktop\Signatura comienzo 19.11.2019\GarciaSantaMariaCoronicaAragonObra27kb.txt 0.04411727708511337
9. Sancho de Muñón -C:\Users\Govert\Desktop\Signatura comienzo 19.11.2019\Acevedo Celestina corto21kb.txt 0.04559358242716971
10. Francisco López de Villalobos -C:\Users\Govert\Desktop\Signatura comienzo 19.11.2019\VillalobosAnfitrionTextosProsa38kb.txt 0.04580435411648254
11. Francisco López de Villalobos -C:\Users\Govert\Desktop\Signatura comienzo 19.11.2019\villaloboscostumbres humanas21kb.txt 0.04647665159788372
12. Juan de Valdés -C:\Users\Govert\Desktop\Signatura comienzo 19.11.2019\ValdesJuanCartas1-3-completo114kb.txt 0.04657509767009471
13. Gonzalo Fernández de Oviedo -C:\Users\Govert\Desktop\Signatura comienzo 19.11.2019\FernandezOviedoClaribalte21kb.txt 0.04710821980038127
14. Francisco de Osuna -C:\Users\Govert\Desktop\Signatura comienzo 19.11.2019\OsunaTerceraParteAbecedario64kb.txt 0.04797472099433231
15. Juan de Timoneda -C:\Users\Govert\Desktop\Signatura comienzo 19.11.2019\TimonedaCaminantes21kb.txt 0.04812242872577832

16. Gonzalo Fernández de Oviedo -C:\Users\Govert\Desktop\Signatura comienzo 19.11.2019\fernandezoviedobatalla90-130tiene34kb.txt 0.04878841507510989

17. Jerónimo de Urrea -C:\Users\Govert\Desktop\Signatura comienzo 19.11.2019\UrreaJeronimoClarisel42kb.txt 0.048838326896332496

18. Cristóbal de Castellejo -C:\Users\Govert\Desktop\Signatura comienzo 19.11.2019\CristobalCastillejoDialogodeMujeres21kb.txt 0.048954312526905075

19. Gonzalo de Ayora -C:\Users\Govert\Desktop\Signatura comienzo 19.11.2019\GonzaloAyoraA MiguelPerezAlmazan15kb.txt 0.049581143308650266

20. Gonzalo Fernández de Oviedo -C:\Users\Govert\Desktop\Signatura comienzo 19.11.2019\FernandezOviedoSumarioIndias27kb.txt 0.05058332689349321

21. Lope de Rueda -C:\Users\Govert\Desktop\Signatura comienzo 19.11.2019\lopederuedaAceitunas42kb.txt 0.05086972874734064

22. Lope de Rueda -C:\Users\Govert\Desktop\Signatura comienzo 19.11.2019\LopedeRuedaEufemia37kb.txt 0.05137564696860564

23. Diego de San Pedro -C:\Users\Govert\Desktop\Signatura comienzo 19.11.2019\arnalte incompleta21kb.txt 0.05146035611797439

24. Juan de Flores -C:\Users\Govert\Desktop\Signatura comienzo 19.11.2019\griselobra21kb.txt 0.051477132961748384

25. Cristóbal de Castellejo -C:\Users\Govert\Desktop\Signatura comienzo 19.11.2019\CristobalCastillejoAulaCortesano21kb.txt 0.05289755122621098

26. Juan Paez de Castro -C:\Users\Govert\Desktop\Signatura comienzo 19.11.2019\juanpaezdecastroCartas23kb.txt 0.05334991115242216

27. Juan de Valdés -C:\Users\Govert\Desktop\Signatura comienzo 19.11.2019\ValdesJuan doctrinacristiana75kb.txt 0.053743634413636165

28. Jorge de Montemayor -C:\Users\Govert\Desktop\Signatura comienzo 19.11.2019\MontemayorDianaObra73kb.txt 0.05406489576959894

29. Diego de San Pedro -C:\Users\Govert\Desktop\Signatura comienzo 19.11.2019\carceldeamor21kb.txt 0.05446938840658054

30. Alonso de Cardona -C:\Users\Govert\Desktop\Signatura comienzo 19.11.2019\alonsodecardona22kb.txt 0.05493081614192796

31. Alfonso de Valdés -C:\Users\Govert\Desktop\Signatura comienzo 19.11.2019\valdesAlfonsoCartas34kb.txt 0.05515419281254974

32. Centurio 1507 -C:\Users\Govert\Desktop\Signatura comienzo 19.11.2019\Celestina viejos archivos\celestina cap15-19 Centurio.txt 0.05572945203087376

33. Gil Vicente -C:\Users\Govert\Desktop\Signatura comienzo 19.11.2019\GilVicente Don Duardos65kb.txt 0.05593523642725651

34. Lucena -C:\Users\Govert\Desktop\Signatura comienzo 19.11.2019\repamores mitad libro51kb.txt 0.05654601334248588

35. Juan de Flores -C:\Users\Govert\Desktop\Signatura comienzo 19.11.2019\grimalteobra21kb.txt 0.05698128831652283

36. Gil Vicente -C:\Users\Govert\Desktop\Signatura comienzo 19.11.2019\GilVicente AutoPastoril1502 16kb.txt 0.05746382237180281

37. Juan de Sedeño -C:\Users\Govert\Desktop\Signatura comienzo 19.11.2019\sedeñoAmores Buenaventurança26kb.txt 0.05806558644024984

38. Francisco López de Villalobos -C:\Users\Govert\Desktop\Signatura comienzo 19.11.2019\VillalobosTresGrandesObra35kb.txt 0.05843368134148952

39. Juan del Encina -C:\Users\Govert\Desktop\Signatura comienzo 19.11.2019\EncinaCancioneroPrincipeProhemio29kb.txt 0.05866260247297439

40. Juan de Sedeño -C:\Users\Govert\Desktop\Signatura comienzo 19.11.2019\sedeñocalisto111kb.txt 0.05877897322868697

41. Gáspar de Gómez -C:\Users\Govert\Desktop\Signatura comienzo 19.11.2019\gaspargomezdeToledoObra23kb.txt 0.05985874168844374

42. Cristóbal de Castellejo -C:\Users\Govert\Desktop\Signatura comienzo 19.11.2019\CristobalCastillejoDialogoSobreMujeres21kb.txt 0.061202757376969896

43. Baltasar del Rio -C:\Users\Govert\Desktop\Signatura comienzo 19.11.2019\baltasardelrio1504Tratado22kb.txt 0.0614677273808637

44. Francisco López de Villalobos -C:\Users\Govert\Desktop\Signatura comienzo 19.11.2019\VillalobosTresGrandesObra21kb.txt 0.06194400552526136

45. Francisco de Osuna -C:\Users\Govert\Desktop\Signatura comienzo 19.11.2019\OsunaTerceraParteAbecedarioPrologo13kb.txt 0.062106602642926334

46. Gonzalo de Ayora -C:\Users\Govert\Desktop\Signatura comienzo 19.11.2019\GonzaloAyora79kb.txt 0.0622027911346561

47. Alonso Núñez de Reinoso -C:\Users\Govert\Desktop\Signatura comienzo 19.11.2019\clareoyfloriseaCorto21kb.txt 0.06220448551278279

48. Alonso de Proaza -C:\Users\Govert\Desktop\Signatura comienzo 19.11.2019\alonsodeproazaProsa no Celestina-12kb.txt 0.06263442364256921

49. Juan Justaniano -C:\Users\Govert\Desktop\Signatura comienzo 19.11.2019\luisvives formacion21kb.txt 0.0631666661006598

50. Sebastián de Horozco -C:\Users\Govert\Desktop\Signatura comienzo 19.11.2019\HorozcoHistoriaEvangelica.txt 0.06423315759160086

51. Thebayda -C:\Users\Govert\Desktop\Signatura comienzo 19.11.2019\thebaida incompleta21kb.txt 0.06432708087642414

52. Ludovico Escriva -C:\Users\Govert\Desktop\Signatura comienzo 19.11.2019\EscrivaLudovico1537y21kb.txt 0.06536301338659878

53. Hernán Diaz -C:\Users\Govert\Desktop\Signatura comienzo 19.11.2019\peregrino obra135kb.txt 0.06635359128599205

54. Jerónimo de Urrea -C:\Users\Govert\Desktop\Signatura comienzo 19.11.2019\UrreaJeronimoOrlandoFuriosoTraduccion22kb.txt 0.06645113424572291

55. Sebastián de Horozco -C:\Users\Govert\Desktop\Signatura comienzo 19.11.2019\HorozcoRuth.txt 0.0667156320709561

56. Ramón de Petras -C:\Users\Govert\Desktop\Signatura comienzo 19.11.2019\traso auto11kb.txt 0.06702634733868318

57. Francisco Cervantes de Salazar -C:\Users\Govert\Desktop\Signatura comienzo 19.11.2019\CervantesSalazarCronicaNuevEspaña21kb.txt 0.07069305670409487

58. Gonzalo Fernández de Oviedo -C:\Users\Govert\Desktop\Signatura comienzo 19.11.2019\fernandezOviedo1532catálogo21kb.txt 0.07093268651817997

59. Sebastián de Horozco -C:\Users\Govert\Desktop\Signatura comienzo 19.11.2019\HorozcoEntremeses.txt 0.07214760865042835

60. Feliciano de Silva -C:\Users\Govert\Desktop\Signatura comienzo 19.11.2019\silva Celestina39kb.txt 0.07314060499980113

61. Hernán Pérez de Olivia -C:\Users\Govert\Desktop\Signatura comienzo 19.11.2019\perezolivaSalamanca Razonamiento24 kb.txt 0.07351968890771399

62. Juan Ramírez de Lucena -C:\Users\Govert\Desktop\Signatura comienzo 19.11.2019\Ramirez Lucena exhortatoria.txt 0.07362719414185426

63. Juan del Encina -C:\Users\Govert\Desktop\Signatura comienzo 19.11.2019\encina1521-8kb.txt 0.0736779215910841

64. Juan Ramírez de Lucena -C:\Users\Govert\Desktop\Signatura comienzo 19.11.2019\RamirezLucena a Zapata.txt 0.07386358033228191

65. Francisco Delicado -C:\Users\Govert\Desktop\Signatura comienzo 19.11.2019\lozanaepilogo5kb.txt 0.07602000103801809

66. Luis de Lucena -C:\Users\Govert\Desktop\Signatura comienzo 19.11.2019\LuisdeLucenaParteTestamento14kb.txt 0.07749816154421252

67. Jerónimo Fernández -C:\Users\Govert\Desktop\Signatura comienzo 19.11.2019\jeronimofernandezhector1547-5-17kb.txt 0.07831142481698017

68. Juan de Segura -C:\Users\Govert\Desktop\Signatura comienzo 19.11.2019\JuandeSeguraQuejayAvisoContraElAmor21kb.txt 0.07861035583099285

69. Gil Vicente -C:\Users\Govert\Desktop\Signatura comienzo 19.11.2019\GilVicenteComediaViudo20kb.txt 0.08061421765676136

70. Nicolás Núñez -C:\Users\Govert\Desktop\Signatura comienzo 19.11.2019\NicolasNuñezTractado32kb.txt 0.0813175783651593

71. Gil Vicente -C:\Users\Govert\Desktop\Signatura comienzo 19.11.2019\GilVicenteCuatroTiempos21kb.txt 0.08386880246875372

72. Lucena -C:\Users\Govert\Desktop\Signatura comienzo 19.11.2019\repeticionamores ajedrez4kb.txt 0.08477308464835331

73. Juan del Encina -C:\Users\Govert\Desktop\Signatura comienzo 19.11.2019\EncinaBubolicaReyesPrologo8kb.txt 0.08519297371954848

74. Francisco Delicado -C:\Users\Govert\Desktop\Signatura comienzo 19.11.2019\lozanaapologia6kb.txt 0.08561539290747922

75. Francisco Delicado -C:\Users\Govert\Desktop\Signatura comienzo 19.11.2019\lozano54kb.txt 0.08947508318132191

76. Hernán Pérez de Olivia -C:\Users\Govert\Desktop\Signatura comienzo 19.11.2019\perezolivaRioGuadalquivirRazonamiento23kb.txt 0.09052637437445266

77. Gonzalo de Ayora -C:\Users\Govert\Desktop\Signatura comienzo 19.11.2019\gonzaloayoraAvila67kb.txt 0.091915483891306

78. Juan del Encina -C:\Users\Govert\Desktop\Signatura comienzo 19.11.2019\EncinaCancioneroAlbaPrologo6kb.txt 0.09268226379441313

79. Francisco Delicado -C:\Users\Govert\Desktop\Signatura comienzo 19.11.2019\lozanaepistola3kb.txt 0.0940004463605143

80. La Celestina -C:\Users\Govert\Desktop\Signatura comienzo 19.11.2019\CelestinaComedia-1.txt 0.0952021990938341

81. Fray Antonio de Guevara -C:\Users\Govert\Desktop\Signatura comienzo 19.11.2019\guevaraEpistolasfamiliares21kb.txt 0.0952194109062432

82. Hernando del Castillo -C:\Users\Govert\Desktop\Signatura comienzo 19.11.2019\hernando de castillo prologo6kb.txt 0.09572373035905557

83. Hernando del Castillo -C:\Users\Govert\Desktop\Signatura comienzo 19.11.2019\hernando de castillo1527 prologo5kb.txt 0.10032935265353649

84. Juan de Sedeño -C:\Users\Govert\Desktop\Signatura comienzo 19.11.2019\sedeño summaPrologo y Epistola19kb.txt 0.10181861258863345

85. Francisco Delicado -C:\Users\Govert\Desktop\Signatura comienzo 19.11.2019\legno2 8kb.txt 0.10301400976928954

86. Lucas Fernández -C:\Users\Govert\Desktop\Signatura comienzo 19.11.2019\lucasfernandez dereniego del amor21kb.txt 0.10367175164536024

87. Hernán Núñez -C:\Users\Govert\Desktop\Signatura comienzo 19.11.2019\hernannuñez Trescientas21.txt 0.10492980113592698

88. La Celestina -C:\Users\Govert\Desktop\Signatura comienzo 19.11.2019\CelestinaPrologo9kb.txt 0.10722831495650953

89. Gonzalo Fernández de Oviedo -C:\Users\Govert\Desktop\Signatura comienzo 19.11.2019\fernandezOviedo-indias 21kb.txt 0.10735958523608014

90. Fray Antonio de Guevara -C:\Users\Govert\Desktop\Signatura comienzo 19.11.2019\GuevaraMarcoAurelioObra22kb.txt 0.10882010870099756

91. Juan Ramírez de Lucena -C:\Users\Govert\Desktop\Signatura comienzo 19.11.2019\vita beata21kb.txt 0.11400677237014711

92. Juan del Encina -C:\Users\Govert\Desktop\Signatura comienzo 19.11.2019\EncinaCancioneroReyesProhemio7kb.txt 0.11616665206943111

93. Juan de Sedeño -C:\Users\Govert\Desktop\Signatura comienzo 19.11.2019\sedeño summaEpistolaobra54kb.txt 0.11842714423881728

94. Bartolomé de las Casas -C:\Users\Govert\Desktop\Signatura comienzo 19.11.2019\BartolomeDeLasCasasBrevisimak34b.txt 0.11985137436297666

95. Juan del Encina -C:\Users\Govert\Desktop\Signatura comienzo 19.11.2019\EncinaBubolicaPrincipePrologo8kb.txt 0.12751331093187657

96. Diego Hurtado de Mendoza -C:\Users\Govert\Desktop\Signatura comienzo 19.11.2019\diegohurtadodemendoza granada47kb.txt 0.13472069669972653

97. Juan del Encina -C:\Users\Govert\Desktop\Signatura comienzo 19.11.2019\EncinaCancioneroAlbaHijoPrologo4kb.txt 0.1370085070779392

98. Juan Ramírez de Lucena -C:\Users\Govert\Desktop\Signatura comienzo 19.11.2019\RamirezLucena a galardones.txt 0.14175622955075795

99. Juan Manuel Calvete de Estrella -C:\Users\Govert\Desktop\Signatura comienzo 19.11.2019\CalveteEstrellaViajeDonFelipe53kb.txt 0.1491197701734882

100. Hernando del Castillo -C:\Users\Govert\Desktop\Signatura comienzo 19.11.2019\Hernando de CastilloSantoDomingoObra5kb.txt 0.15609545183029605

101. La Celestina -C:\Users\Govert\Desktop\Signatura comienzo 19.11.2019\carta celestina1501-3kb.txt 0.1576236183197789

102. Juan Agüero de Trasmiera -C:\Users\Govert\Desktop\Signatura comienzo 19.11.2019\trasmiera salamanca21kb.txt 0.16346649775578137

103. Hernando del Castillo -C:\Users\Govert\Desktop\Signatura comienzo 19.11.2019\Hernando de CastilloSantoDomingoLector9kb.txt 0.18145649419101406
104. Fernando de Rojas -C:\Users\Govert\Desktop\Signatura comienzo 19.11.2019\fernando de rojas14kb test2.txt 0.19841259562380598
105. La Celestina -C:\Users\Govert\Desktop\Signatura comienzo 19.11.2019\CelestinaMs1520TextoCorrecto27kb.txt 0.2294295410545324
106. manual de mujeres -C:\Users\Govert\Desktop\Signatura comienzo 19.11.2019\manualdemujeres21kb.txt 0.26060602873597716

15.6.6 1542 Baldo

baldo18kb renaldo4-1542.txt C:\Users\Govert\Desktop\Signatura comienzo 19.11.2019\baldo18kb renaldo4-1542.txt
Canonicizers:
    Normalize Whitespace
EventDrivers:
    Character NGrams n : 4
        EventCullers:
            Most Common Events numevents : 50
Analysis:
    Nearest Neighbor Driver with metric Cosine Distance
1. Prologos Fernández de Oviedo -C:\Users\Govert\Desktop\Signatura comienzo 19.11.2019\PrologosFernandezOviedo2-93kb.txt 0.017141884250976624
2. Jerónimo Fernández -C:\Users\Govert\Desktop\Signatura comienzo 19.11.2019\jeronimofernandez3año1579-113kb.txt 0.018362594644918295
3. Feliciano de Silva -C:\Users\Govert\Desktop\Signatura comienzo 19.11.2019\Silva amadis de grecia20kb.txt 0.018371985561303594
4. Jerónimo de Urrea -C:\Users\Govert\Desktop\Signatura comienzo 19.11.2019\UrreaJeronimoClarisel42kb.txt 0.022389069094083003
5. Francisco de Osuna -C:\Users\Govert\Desktop\Signatura comienzo 19.11.2019\OsunaTerceraParteAbecedario64kb.txt 0.02355008138808734
6. Bernardo de Quirós -C:\Users\Govert\Desktop\Signatura comienzo 19.11.2019\VillalonViajeTurquiaVillalon109kb.txt 0.025212004726651527
7. Juan del Encina -C:\Users\Govert\Desktop\Signatura comienzo 19.11.2019\EncinaCancioneroPrincipeProhemio29kb.txt 0.027397325088735047
8. Juan del Encina -C:\Users\Govert\Desktop\Signatura comienzo 19.11.2019\encina eglogas antes 1509-287kb.txt 0.028300891891123836
9. Diego de San Pedro -C:\Users\Govert\Desktop\Signatura comienzo 19.11.2019\arnalte incompleta21kb.txt 0.028942576020590915
10. Gonzalo Fernández de Oviedo -C:\Users\Govert\Desktop\Signatura comienzo 19.11.2019\FernandezOviedoSumarioIndias27kb.txt 0.029165557933001907
11. Francisco López de Villalobos -C:\Users\Govert\Desktop\Signatura comienzo 19.11.2019\villaloboscostumbres humanas21kb.txt 0.029402810966945525

12. Juan de Boscan -C:\Users\Govert\Desktop\Signatura comienzo 19.11.2019\BoscanElCortesano47kb.txt 0.029539978770839026

13. Lucena -C:\Users\Govert\Desktop\Signatura comienzo 19.11.2019\repamores mitad libro51kb.txt 0.030392412903629817

14. Juan de Flores -C:\Users\Govert\Desktop\Signatura comienzo 19.11.2019\griselobra21kb.txt 0.03188449199189647

15. Cristóbal de Castellejo -C:\Users\Govert\Desktop\Signatura comienzo 19.11.2019\CristobalCastellejoAulaCortesano21kb.txt 0.03204703883101079

16. Sancho de Muñón -C:\Users\Govert\Desktop\Signatura comienzo 19.11.2019\Acevedo Celestina corto21kb.txt 0.032418727897716715

17. Juan Paez de Castro -C:\Users\Govert\Desktop\Signatura comienzo 19.11.2019\juanpaezdecastroCartas23kb.txt 0.035417650324315986

18. Thebayda -C:\Users\Govert\Desktop\Signatura comienzo 19.11.2019\thebaida incompleta21kb.txt 0.03556102138626305

19. Alonso Núñez de Reinoso -C:\Users\Govert\Desktop\Signatura comienzo 19.11.2019\clareoyfloriseaCorto21kb.txt 0.0358032123204588

20. Francisco López de Villalobos -C:\Users\Govert\Desktop\Signatura comienzo 19.11.2019\VillalobosTresGrandesObra21kb.txt 0.03592062545731933

21. Gonzalo Fernández de Oviedo -C:\Users\Govert\Desktop\Signatura comienzo 19.11.2019\fernandezoviedobatalla90-130tiene34kb.txt 0.0362965828859787

22. Francisco López de Villalobos -C:\Users\Govert\Desktop\Signatura comienzo 19.11.2019\VillalobosTresGrandesObra35kb.txt 0.03717915696446972

23. Juan de Timoneda -C:\Users\Govert\Desktop\Signatura comienzo 19.11.2019\TimonedaCaminantes21kb.txt 0.03794575110948517

24. Baltasar del Rio -C:\Users\Govert\Desktop\Signatura comienzo 19.11.2019\baltasardelrio1504Tratado22kb.txt 0.03835838904390931

25. Diego de San Pedro -C:\Users\Govert\Desktop\Signatura comienzo 19.11.2019\carceldeamor21kb.txt 0.038536517332309894

26. Lope de Rueda -C:\Users\Govert\Desktop\Signatura comienzo 19.11.2019\lopederuedaAceitunas42kb.txt 0.038649097115401654

27. Gil Vicente -C:\Users\Govert\Desktop\Signatura comienzo 19.11.2019\GilVicenteSibila31kb.txt 0.03879404630586314

28. Ludovico Escriva -C:\Users\Govert\Desktop\Signatura comienzo 19.11.2019\EscrivaLudovico1537y21kb.txt 0.039029457931723965

29. Hernán Pérez de Olivia -C:\Users\Govert\Desktop\Signatura comienzo 19.11.2019\perezolivaSalamanca Razonamiento24 kb.txt 0.03921262696000816

30. Francisco de Osuna -C:\Users\Govert\Desktop\Signatura comienzo 19.11.2019\OsunaTerceraParteAbecedarioPrologo13kb.txt 0.03973776872801127

31. Gonzalo Fernández de Oviedo -C:\Users\Govert\Desktop\Signatura comienzo 19.11.2019\FernandezOviedoClaribalte21kb.txt 0.04000239277020501

32. Francisco López de Villalobos -C:\Users\Govert\Desktop\Signatura comienzo 19.11.2019\VillalobosAnfitrionTextosProsa38kb.txt 0.04023395999395307

33. Jorge de Montemayor -C:\Users\Govert\Desktop\Signatura comienzo 19.11.2019\MontemayorDianaObra73kb.txt 0.04074622929007987

34. Gonzalo de Ayora -C:\Users\Govert\Desktop\Signatura comienzo 19.11.2019\GonzaloAyoraA MiguelPerezAlmazan15kb.txt 0.04102695394011935

35. Lope de Rueda -C:\Users\Govert\Desktop\Signatura comienzo 19.11.2019\LopedeRuedaEufemia37kb.txt 0.04182999248175523

36. Hernán Pérez de Olivia -C:\Users\Govert\Desktop\Signatura comienzo 19.11.2019\perezolivaRioGuadalquivirRazonamiento23kb.txt 0.04350927592471043

37. Juan Justaniano -C:\Users\Govert\Desktop\Signatura comienzo 19.11.2019\luisvives formacion21kb.txt 0.044052392134783624

38. Gonzalo de Ayora -C:\Users\Govert\Desktop\Signatura comienzo 19.11.2019\GonzaloAyora79kb.txt 0.0441376572514931

39. Cristóbal de Castellejo -C:\Users\Govert\Desktop\Signatura comienzo 19.11.2019\CristobalCastillejoDialogodeMujeres21kb.txt 0.04628560231824019

40. Gonzalo de Ayora -C:\Users\Govert\Desktop\Signatura comienzo 19.11.2019\gonzaloayoraAvila67kb.txt 0.047413950589978215

41. Hernán Diaz -C:\Users\Govert\Desktop\Signatura comienzo 19.11.2019\peregrino obra135kb.txt 0.04757178688944341

42. Gil Vicente -C:\Users\Govert\Desktop\Signatura comienzo 19.11.2019\GilVicente Don Duardos65kb.txt 0.047773161442506984

43. Cristóbal de Castellejo -C:\Users\Govert\Desktop\Signatura comienzo 19.11.2019\CristobalCastillejoDialogoSobreMujeres21kb.txt 0.04798751920239852

44. Juan del Encina -C:\Users\Govert\Desktop\Signatura comienzo 19.11.2019\EncinaBubolicaReyesPrologo8kb.txt 0.04802136236880694

45. Alfonso de Valdés -C:\Users\Govert\Desktop\Signatura comienzo 19.11.2019\valdesAlfonsoCartas34kb.txt 0.048236632761134435

46. Juan Ramírez de Lucena -C:\Users\Govert\Desktop\Signatura comienzo 19.11.2019\Ramirez Lucena exhortatoria.txt 0.048852412494352127

47. Juan Ramírez de Lucena -C:\Users\Govert\Desktop\Signatura comienzo 19.11.2019\RamirezLucena a Zapata.txt 0.048866018644044495

48. Centurio 1507 -C:\Users\Govert\Desktop\Signatura comienzo 19.11.2019\Celestina viejos archivos\celestina cap15-19 Centurio.txt 0.05021957926873022

49. Luis de Lucena -C:\Users\Govert\Desktop\Signatura comienzo 19.11.2019\LuisdeLucenaParteTestamento14kb.txt 0.05115320306825888

50. Gil Vicente -C:\Users\Govert\Desktop\Signatura comienzo 19.11.2019\GilVicenteCuatroTiempos21kb.txt 0.0524334696441664

51. Juan de Valdés -C:\Users\Govert\Desktop\Signatura comienzo 19.11.2019\ValdesJuanCartas1-3-completo114kb.txt 0.05320705030448569

52. Sebastián de Horozco -C:\Users\Govert\Desktop\Signatura comienzo 19.11.2019\HorozcoEntremeses.txt 0.05407749561357955

53. Jerónimo Fernández -C:\Users\Govert\Desktop\Signatura comienzo 19.11.2019\jeronimofernandezhector1547-5-17kb.txt 0.05455890360262172

54. Ramón de Petras -C:\Users\Govert\Desktop\Signatura comienzo 19.11.2019\traso auto11kb.txt 0.05457183375136632

55. Francisco Delicado -C:\Users\Govert\Desktop\Signatura comienzo 19.11.2019\lozanaepilogo5kb.txt 0.05486902235151814

370

56. Gil Vicente -C:\Users\Govert\Desktop\Signatura comienzo 19.11.2019\GilVicente AutoPastoril1502 16kb.txt 0.055434609900292475

57. Juan Ramírez de Lucena -C:\Users\Govert\Desktop\Signatura comienzo 19.11.2019\vita beata21kb.txt 0.055731432993560315

58. Juan de Valdés -C:\Users\Govert\Desktop\Signatura comienzo 19.11.2019\ValdesJuan doctrinacristiana75kb.txt 0.05624470126377179

59. Juan de Flores -C:\Users\Govert\Desktop\Signatura comienzo 19.11.2019\grimalteobra21kb.txt 0.056448520559623794

60. Juan del Encina -C:\Users\Govert\Desktop\Signatura comienzo 19.11.2019\EncinaCancioneroAlbaPrologo6kb.txt 0.05757494655767981

61. Hernando del Castillo -C:\Users\Govert\Desktop\Signatura comienzo 19.11.2019\hernando de castillo prologo6kb.txt 0.057781625889474

62. Francisco Cervantes de Salazar -C:\Users\Govert\Desktop\Signatura comienzo 19.11.2019\CervantesSalazarCronicaNuevEspaña21kb.txt 0.05843346457331933

63. Jerónimo de Urrea -C:\Users\Govert\Desktop\Signatura comienzo 19.11.2019\UrreaJeronimoOrlandoFuriosoTraduccion22kb.txt 0.058625331139235626

64. Gil Vicente -C:\Users\Govert\Desktop\Signatura comienzo 19.11.2019\GilVicenteComediaViudo20kb.txt 0.058793738012932306

65. Juan de Sedeño -C:\Users\Govert\Desktop\Signatura comienzo 19.11.2019\sedeño summaPrologo y Epistola19kb.txt 0.058885789460768945

66. Juan del Encina -C:\Users\Govert\Desktop\Signatura comienzo 19.11.2019\encina1521-8kb.txt 0.06327899973270878

67. Juan de Sedeño -C:\Users\Govert\Desktop\Signatura comienzo 19.11.2019\sedeñoAmores Buenaventurança26kb.txt 0.0636215700754692

68. Hernán Núñez -C:\Users\Govert\Desktop\Signatura comienzo 19.11.2019\hernannuñez Trescientas21.txt 0.06381441827064016

69. Alonso de Proaza -C:\Users\Govert\Desktop\Signatura comienzo 19.11.2019\alonsodeproazaProsa no Celestina-12kb.txt 0.06421843733413779

70. Fray Antonio de Guevara -C:\Users\Govert\Desktop\Signatura comienzo 19.11.2019\GuevaraMarcoAurelioObra22kb.txt 0.06483672856669742

71. Fray Antonio de Guevara -C:\Users\Govert\Desktop\Signatura comienzo 19.11.2019\guevaraEpistolasfamiliares21kb.txt 0.06586986959836105

72. Juan de Sedeño -C:\Users\Govert\Desktop\Signatura comienzo 19.11.2019\sedeñocalisto111kb.txt 0.06616394420639149

73. Francisco Delicado -C:\Users\Govert\Desktop\Signatura comienzo 19.11.2019\lozano54kb.txt 0.06702532158302466

74. Francisco Delicado -C:\Users\Govert\Desktop\Signatura comienzo 19.11.2019\legno2 8kb.txt 0.06708446456647388

75. Gonzalo Fernández de Oviedo -C:\Users\Govert\Desktop\Signatura comienzo 19.11.2019\fernandezOviedo1532catálogo21kb.txt 0.06964565957229019

76. Gonzalo Fernández de Oviedo -C:\Users\Govert\Desktop\Signatura comienzo 19.11.2019\fernandezOviedo-indias 21kb.txt 0.07007541027965469

77. Sebastián de Horozco -C:\Users\Govert\Desktop\Signatura comienzo 19.11.2019\HorozcoHistoriaEvangelica.txt 0.07047703436094399

78. Juan del Encina -C:\Users\Govert\Desktop\Signatura comienzo 19.11.2019\EncinaBubolicaPrincipePrologo8kb.txt 0.07102355506003166

79. Lucas Fernández -C:\Users\Govert\Desktop\Signatura comienzo 19.11.2019\lucasfernandez dereniego del amor21kb.txt 0.07129148874488889

80. Juan del Encina -C:\Users\Govert\Desktop\Signatura comienzo 19.11.2019\EncinaCancioneroReyesProhemio7kb.txt 0.07159273579926684

81. Gáspar de Gómez -C:\Users\Govert\Desktop\Signatura comienzo 19.11.2019\gaspargomezdeToledoObra23kb.txt 0.07182509992827302

82. La Celestina -C:\Users\Govert\Desktop\Signatura comienzo 19.11.2019\CelestinaPrologo9kb.txt 0.07233978595783908

83. Alonso de Cardona -C:\Users\Govert\Desktop\Signatura comienzo 19.11.2019\alonsodecardona22kb.txt 0.0724215667670296

84. Diego Hurtado de Mendoza -C:\Users\Govert\Desktop\Signatura comienzo 19.11.2019\diegohurtadodemendoza granada47kb.txt 0.07359246257036511

85. Francisco Delicado -C:\Users\Govert\Desktop\Signatura comienzo 19.11.2019\lozanaapologia6kb.txt 0.07507040260287345

86. Sebastián de Horozco -C:\Users\Govert\Desktop\Signatura comienzo 19.11.2019\HorozcoRuth.txt 0.07568373828616837

87. Gonzalo García Santa Maria -C:\Users\Govert\Desktop\Signatura comienzo 19.11.2019\GarciaSantaMariaCoronicaAragonObra27kb.txt 0.07598004777880352

88. Bartolomé de las Casas -C:\Users\Govert\Desktop\Signatura comienzo 19.11.2019\BartolomeDeLasCasasBrevisimak34b.txt 0.07635897519275625

89. Juan de Sedeño -C:\Users\Govert\Desktop\Signatura comienzo 19.11.2019\sedeño summaEpistolaobra54kb.txt 0.0765564301079632

90. Feliciano de Silva -C:\Users\Govert\Desktop\Signatura comienzo 19.11.2019\silva Celestina39kb.txt 0.07796494765557271

91. La Celestina -C:\Users\Govert\Desktop\Signatura comienzo 19.11.2019\CelestinaComedia-1.txt 0.07854869248418106

92. Nicolás Núñez -C:\Users\Govert\Desktop\Signatura comienzo 19.11.2019\NicolasNuñezTractado32kb.txt 0.08550631451602375

93. Lucena -C:\Users\Govert\Desktop\Signatura comienzo 19.11.2019\repeticionamores ajedrez4kb.txt 0.0902139596735001

94. Hernando del Castillo -C:\Users\Govert\Desktop\Signatura comienzo 19.11.2019\Hernando de CastilloSantoDomingoObra5kb.txt 0.10552263335076772

95. Juan de Segura -C:\Users\Govert\Desktop\Signatura comienzo 19.11.2019\JuandeSeguraQuejayAvisoContraElAmor21kb.txt 0.10625198562167204

96. Juan Ramírez de Lucena -C:\Users\Govert\Desktop\Signatura comienzo 19.11.2019\RamirezLucena a galardones.txt 0.11130319625772167

97. La Celestina -C:\Users\Govert\Desktop\Signatura comienzo 19.11.2019\carta celestina1501-3kb.txt 0.11188788837572661

98. Francisco Delicado -C:\Users\Govert\Desktop\Signatura comienzo 19.11.2019\lozanaepistola3kb.txt 0.11692496576520328

99. Hernando del Castillo -C:\Users\Govert\Desktop\Signatura comienzo 19.11.2019\hernando de castillo1527 prologo5kb.txt 0.12415409092494756

100. Hernando del Castillo -C:\Users\Govert\Desktop\Signatura comienzo 19.11.2019\Hernando de CastilloSantoDomingoLector9kb.txt 0.13081925745013567

101. Juan del Encina -C:\Users\Govert\Desktop\Signatura comienzo 19.11.2019\EncinaCancioneroAlbaHijoPrologo4kb.txt 0.13502427948140927

102. Juan Agüero de Trasmiera -C:\Users\Govert\Desktop\Signatura comienzo 19.11.2019\trasmiera salamanca21kb.txt 0.13754604922034908

103. Juan Manuel Calvete de Estrella -C:\Users\Govert\Desktop\Signatura comienzo 19.11.2019\CalveteEstrellaViajeDonFelipe53kb.txt 0.15699891072140177

104. Fernando de Rojas -C:\Users\Govert\Desktop\Signatura comienzo 19.11.2019\fernando de rojas14kb test2.txt 0.18153765995543247

105. La Celestina -C:\Users\Govert\Desktop\Signatura comienzo 19.11.2019\CelestinaMs1520TextoCorrecto27kb.txt 0.19403955345103618

106. manual de mujeres -C:\Users\Govert\Desktop\Signatura comienzo 19.11.2019\manualdemujeres21kb.txt 0.2115723675761766

Books written by Govert Westerveld

Many of the books, written in English, Spanish and Dutch are in the National Library in The Hague (Koninklijke Bibliotheek at Den Haag).

Nº	Year	Title	ISBN
01	1990	Las Damas: ciencia sobre un tablero I	84-7665-697-1
	2014	Las Damas: ciencia sobre un tablero I. 132 pages. Lulu Editors.	None
02	1992	Damas españolas: 100 golpes de apertura coronando dama. 116 pages.	84-604-3888-0
	2014	Lulu Editors. Damas españolas: 100 golpes de apertura coronando dama. 116 pages. Lulu Editors.	None
03	1992	Damas españolas: 100 problemas propios con solamente peones.	84-604-3887-2
	2014	Damas españolas: 100 problemas propios con solamente peones. 108 pages. Lulu Editors.	None
04	1992	Las Damas: ciencia sobre un tablero, II	84-604-3886-4
	2014		None
		Las Damas: ciencia sobre un tablero, II. 124 pages. Lulu Editors.	
05	1992	Las Damas: ciencia sobre un tablero, III	84-604-4043-5
	2014		None
		Las Damas: ciencia sobre un tablero, III. 124 pages. Lulu Editors.	
06	1992	Libro llamado Ingenio...juego de marro de punta: hecho por Juan de Timoneda. (Now not edited).	84-604-4042-7
07	1993	Pedro Ruiz Montero: Libro del juego de las damas vulgarmente nombrado el marro.	84-604-5021-X
	2014	Pedro Ruiz Montero: Libro del juego de las damas vulgarmente nombrado el marro. 108 pages. Lulu Editors.	None

08	1997	De invloed van de Spaanse koningin Isabel la Católica op de nieuwe sterke dame in de oorsprong van het dam- en moderne schaakspel. Spaanse literatuur, jaren 1283-1700. In collaboration with Rob Jansen. 329 pages. (Now not edited)	84-605-6372-3
09	1997	Historia de Blanca, lugar más islamizado de la región murciana, año 711-1700. Foreword: Prof. Dr. Juan Torres Fontes, University of Murcia.	84-923151-0-5
	2014	900 pages. Historia de Blanca, lugar más islamizado de la región murciana, año	978-1-291-80895-7
	2014	711-1700. Volume I. 672 pages. Lulu Editors. Historia de Blanca, lugar más islamizado de la región murciana, año 711-1700. Volume I. 364 pages. Lulu Editors.	978-1-29-80974-9
10	2001	Blanca, "El Ricote" de Don Quijote: expulsión y regreso de los moriscos del último enclave islámico más grande de España, años 1613-1654. Foreword of Prof. Dr. Franciso Márquez Villanueva – University of	84-923151-1-3
	2014	Harvard – USA. 1004 pages. Blanca, "El Ricote" de Don Quijote: expulsión y regreso de los moriscos del último enclave islámico más	978-1-291-80122-4
	2014	grande de España, años 1613-1654. 552 pages. Lulu Editors. Blanca, "El Ricote" de Don Quijote: expulsión y regreso de los moriscos del último enclave islámico más grande de España, años 1613-1654. 568 pages. Lulu Editors.	978-1-291-80311-2
11	2004	Inspiraciones	Without publising
12	2004	La reina Isabel la Católica: su reflejo en la dama poderosa de Valencia, cuña del ajedrez moderno y origen del juego de damas. In collaboration with José Antonio Garzón Roger. Foreword: Dr. Ricardo Calvo. Generalidad Valeciana. Consellería de Cultura,	84-482-3718-8

		Educació i Esport. Secretaría Autonómica de Cultura. 426 pages.	
13	2006	Los tres autores de La Celestina. Volume I. Foreword: Prof. Ángel Alcalá – University of New York. 441	10:84-923151-4-8
	2009	pages. (bubok.com) Los tres autores de La Celestina. Volume I. 441 pages (bubok.com)	None
14	2007	Miguel de Cervantes Saavedra, Ana Felix y el morisco Ricote del Valle de Ricote en "Don Quijote II" del año 1615 (capítulos 54, 55, 63, 64 y 65. Dedicated to Prof.Francisco Márquez Villanueva of the University of	10:84-923151-5-6
	2014	Harvard. 384 pages. El Morisco Ricote del Valle de Ricote.	978-1-326-09629-8
	2014	Volume I. 306 pages. Lulu Editors El Morisco Ricote del Valle de Ricote. Volume II. 318 pages. Lulu Editors.	978-1-326-09679-3
15	2008	Damas Españolas: El contragolpe. 112 pages. Lulu Editors.	10:84-923151-9-2
16	2008	Biografía de Doña Blanca de Borbón (1336-1361). El pontificado y el pueblo en defensa de la reina de	10:84-923151-7-2
	2015	Castilla. 142 pages. Biografía de doña Blanca de Borbón (1336-1361). 306 pages. Lulu Editors	978-1-326-47703-5
17	2008	Biografía de Don Fadrique, Maestre de la Orden de Santiago (1342-1352). 122 pages. Biografía de Don Fadique, Maestre de la Orden de Santiago. 228 pages. Lulu Editors.	10:84-923151-6-4 978-1-326-47359-4
18	2008	Los tres autores de La Celestina. Volume II. 142 pages. (Now not	10:978-84-612-604-0-9
	2009	edited) Los tres autores de La Celestina. Volume II. 142 pages. Ebook (bubok.com)	None
19	2008	El reino de Murcia en tiempos del rey Don Pedro, el Cruel (1350-1369). 176	13:978-84-612-6037-9
	2015	pages	978-1-326-47531-4

		El reino de Murcia en el tiempo del rey Don Pedro I el Cruel (1350-1369). 336 pages. Lulu Editors	
20	2008 2015	Los comendadores del Valle de Ricote. Siglos XIII-XIV. Volume I. 178 pages Los Comendadores del Valle de Ricote. Siglox XIII-XIV. 316 pages. Lulu Editors.	13:978-84-612-6038-6 978-1-326-47485-0
21	2009 2015 2015	Doña Blanca y Don Fadrique (1333-1361) y el cambio de Negra (Murcia) a Blanca. 511 pages. De Negra a Blanca. Tomo I. 520 pages. De Negra a Blanca Tomo II. 608 pages Lulu Editors	13:978-84-612-6039-3 978-1-326-47805-6 978-1-326-47872-8
22	2009 2015	Los tres autores de La Celestina. Volume III. 351 pages. (Godofredo Valle de Ricote). Los tres autores de La Celestina. Volume III. 424 pages. (bubok.com)	13:978-84-613-2191-9 None
23	2009 2015	Los tres autores de La Celestina. Volume IV. 261 pages. (Godofredo Valle de Ricote). Tres autores de La Celestina. Volumen IV. 312 pages. Ebook (bubok.com)	13:978-84-613-2189-6 None
24	2010	El monumento del Morisco Ricote y Miguel de Cervantes Saavedra. 80 pages.	13:978-84-613-2549-8
25	2011 2012	Un ejemplo para España, José Manzano Aldeguer, alcalde de Beniel (Murcia), 1983-2001. 470 pages. Foreword: Ramón Luis Valcárcel Sisa. (Now not edited) Un ejemplo para España, José Manzano Aldeguer, alcalde de Beniel (Murcia), 1983-2001. 470 pages. Ebook (bubok.com)	978-84-614-9221-3 None
26	2012	The History of Checkers of William Shelley Branch. 182 pages. (Now not edited).	None
27	2013	Biografía de Juan Ramírez de Lucena. (Embajador de los Reyes Católicos y padre del ajedrecista Lucena). 240 pages. Lulu Editors.	978-1-291-66911-4

28	2016	El tratado contra la carta del Prothonotario de Lucena. 182 pages. (Now not edited)	None
29	2012	La obra de Lucena: "Repetición de amores". 83 pages. (Now not edited)	None
30	2012	El libro perdido de Lucena: "Tractado sobre la muerte de Don Diego de Azevedo". 217 pages. (bubok.com)	None
31	2012	De Vita Beata de Juan de Lucena. 86 pages. (Ebook – bubok.com)	None
32	2013	Biografía de Maurice Raichenbach, campeón mundial de las damas entre 1933-1938. Volume I. 357 pages. Lulu Editors.	978-1-291-68772-9
33	2013	Biografía de Maurice Raichenbach, campeón mundial de las damas entre 1933-1938. Volume II. 300 pages. Lulu Editors.	978-1-291-68769-9
34	2013	Biografía de Amadou Kandié, jugador fenomenal senegal´s de las Damas entre 1894-1895. 246 pages. Lulu Editors.	978-1-291-68450-6
35	2013	The History of Alquerque-12. Spain and France. Volume I. 388 pages. Lulu Editors	978-1-291-66267-2
36	2013	Het slechtse damboek ter wereld ooit geschreven. 454 pages. Lulu Editors.	978-1-291-68724-8
37	2013	Biografía de Woldouby. 239 pages. Lulu Editors.	978-1-291-68122-2
38	2013	Juan del Encina (alias Lucena), autor de Repetición de amores. 96 pages. Lulu Editors	978-1-291-63347-4
39	2013	Juan del Encina (alias Francisco Delicado). Retrato de la Lozana Andaluza. 352 pages. Lulu Editors.	978-1-291-63782-3
40	2013	Juan del Encina (alias Bartolomé Torres Naharro). Propalladia. 128 pages. Lulu Editors	978-1-291-63527-0
41	2013	Juan del Encina, autor de las comedias Thebayda, Ypolita y Serafina. 92 pages.	978-1-291-63719-9

		Lulu Editors	
42	2013	Juan del Encina, autor de la Carajicomedia. 128 pages. Lulu Editors	978-1-291-63377-1
43	2013	El Palmerín de Olivia y Juan del Encina. 104 pages. Lulu Editors	978-1-291-62963-7
44	2013	El Primaleón y Juan del Encina. 104 pages. Lulu Editors.	978-1-291-61480-7
45	2013	Hernando del Castillo seudónimo de Juan del Encina. 96 pages. Lulu Editors	978-1-291-63313-9
46	2013	Amadis de Gaula. Juan del Encina y Alonso de Cardona. 84 pages. Lulu Editors	978-1-291-63990-2
47	2013	Sergas de Esplandián y Juan del Encina. 82 pages. Lulu Editors	978-1-291-64130-1
48	2013	History of Checkers (Draughts). 180 pages. Lulu Editors.	978-1-291-66732-5
49	2013	Mis años jóvenes al lado de Ton Sijbrands and Harm Wiersma, futuros campeones mundiales. 84 pages. Lulu Editors.	978-1-291-68365-3
50	2013	De Spaanse oorsprong van het Dam- en moderne Schaakspel. Volume I. 382 pages. Lulu Editors.	978-1-291-66611-3
51	2013	Alonso de Cardona, el autor de la Questión de amor. 88 pages. Lulu Editors.	978-1-291-65625-1
52	2013	Alonso de Cardona. El autor de la Celestina de Palacio, Ms. 1520. 96 pages. Lulu Editors.	978-1-291-67505-4
53	2013	Biografía de Alonso de Cardona. 120 pages. Lulu Editors.	978-1-291-68494-0
54	2014	Tres autores de La Celestina: Alonso de Cardona, Juan del Encina y Alonso de Proaza. 168 pages. Lulu Editors.	978-1-291-86205-8
55	2014	Blanca, una página de su historia: Expulsión de los moriscos. (With Ángel Ríos Martínez). 280 pages. Lulu Editors.	None
56	2014	Ibn Sab'in of the Ricote Valley, the first and last Islamic place in Spain. 288 pages. Lulu Editors.	978-1-326-15044-0

57	2015	El complot para el golpe de Franco. 224 pages. Lulu Editors.	978-1-326-16812-4
58	2015	De uitdaging. Van damsport tot topproduct. Hoe de damsport mij hielp voedingsproducten van wereldklasse te creëren. 312 pages. Lulu Editors.	978-1-326-15470-7
59	2015	The History of Alquerque-12. Remaining countries. Volume II. 436 pages. Lulu Editors.	978-1-326-17935-9
60	2015	Your visit to Blanca, a village in the famous Ricote Valley. 252 pages. Lulu Editors.	978-1-326-23882-7
61	2015	The Birth of a new Bishop in Chess. 172 pages. Lulu Editors.	978-1-326-37044-2
62	2015	The Poem Scachs d'amor (1475). First Text of Modern Chess. 144 pages. Lulu Editors.	978-1-326-37491-4
63	2015	The Ambassador Juan Ramírez de Lucena, the father of the chessbook writer Lucena. 226 pages. Lulu Editors.	978-1-326-37728-1
64	2015	Nuestro ídolo en Holanda: El senegalés Baba Sy campeón mundial del juego de las damas (1963-1964). 272 pages. (bubok.com).	None
65	2015	Baba Sy, the World Champion of 1963-1964 of 10x10 Draughts. Volume I. 264 pages. Lulu Editors.	978-1-326-39729-6
66	2015	The Training of Isabella I of Castile as the Virgin Mary by Churchman Martin de Cordoba. 172 pages. Lulu Editors.	978-1-326-40364-5
67	2015	El Ingenio ó Juego de Marro, de Punta ó Damas de Antonio de Torquemada. 228 pages. Lulu Editors.	978-1-326-40451-2
68	2015	Baba Sy, the World Champion of 1963-1964 of 10x10 Draughts. Volume II. 204 pages. Lulu Editors.	978-1-326-43862-3
69	2016	The Origin of the Checker and Modern Chess Game. Volume I. 316 pages. Lulu Editors.	978-1-326-60212-3
70	2015	The Origin of the Checker and Modern Chess Game. Volume III. 312 pages. Lulu Editors.	978-1-326-60244-4

71	2015	Woldouby's Biography, Extraordinary Senegalese checkers player during his stay in France 1910-1911. 236 pages. Lulu Editors.	978-1-326-47291-7
72	2015	La Inquisión en el Valle de Ricote. (Blanca, 1562). 264 pages. Lulu Editors.	978-1-326-49126-0
73	2015	History of the Holy Week Traditions in the Ricote Valley. (With Ángel Ríos Martínez). 140 pages. Lulu Editors.	978-1-326-57094-1
74	2016	Revelaciones sobre Blanca. 632 pages. Lulu Editores.	978-1-326-59512-8
75	2016	Muslim history of the Región of Murcia (715-1080). Volume I. 308 pages. Lulu Editors.	978-1-326-79278-7
76	2016	Researches on the mysterious Aragonese author of La Celestina. 288 pages. Lulu Editors.	978-1-326-81331-4
77	2016	The life of Ludovico Vicentino degli Arrighi between 1504 and 1534. 264 pages. Lulu Editors	978-1-326-81393-2
78	2016	The life of Francisco Delicado in Rome: 1508-1527. 272 pages. Lulu Editors.	978-1-326-81436-6
79	2016	Following the Footsteps of Spanish Chess Master Lucena in Italy. 284 pages. Lulu Editors.	978-1-326-81682-7
80	2016	Historia de Granja de Rocamora: La Expulsión en 1609-1614. 124 pages. Lulu Editors.	978-1-326-85145-3
81	2013	De Spaanse oorsprong van het Dam- en Moderne Schaakspel. Deel II. 384 pages. Lulu Editors.	978-1-291-69195-5
82	2015	The Spanish Origin of the Checkers and Modern Chess Game. Volume III. 312 pages. Lulu Editores.	978-1-326-45243-8
83	2014	El juego de las Damas Universales (100 casillas). 100 golpes de al menos siete peones. 120 pages.	13-978-84-604-3888-0
84	2009	Siglo XVI, siglo de contrastes. (With Ángel Ríos Martínez). 153 pages. (bubok.com). Authors: Ángel Rios Martínez & Govert Westerveld	978-84-613-3868-9

85	2010	Blanca, una página de su historia: Último enclave morisco más grande de España. 146 pages. (bubok.com). Authors: Ángel Rios Martínez & Govert Westerveld	None
86	2017	Ibn Sab'in del Valle de Ricote; El último lugar islámico en España. 292 pages. Lulu Editors.	978-1-326-99819-6
87	2017	Blanca y sus hierbas medicinales de antaño. 120 pages. Lulu Editors.	978-0244-01462-9
88	2017	The Origin of the Checkers and Modern Chess Game. Volume II. 300 pages. Lulu Editors	978-0-244-04257-8
89	2017	Muslim History of the Region of Murcia (1080-1228). Volume II. 308 pages. Lulu Editors	978-0-244-64947-0
90	2018	History of Alquerque-12. Volume III. 516 pages. Lulu Editors.	978-0-244-07274-2
91	2015	La Celestina: Lucena y Juan del Encina. Volume I. 456 pages. Lulu Editores.	978-1-326-47888-9
92	2015	La Celestina: Lucena y Juan del Encina. Volume II. 232 pages. Lulu Editores	978-1-326-47949-7
93	2018	La Celestina: Lucena y Juan del Encina. Volume III. 520 pages. Lulu Editors.	978-0-244-65938-7
94	2018	La Celestina: Lucena y Juan del Encina. Volume IV. 248 pages. Lulu Editors.	978-0-244-36089-4
95	2018	La Celestina: Lucena y Juan del Encina. Volume V. (In press)	978-0-244-07274-2
96	2018	Draughts and La Celestina's creator Francesch Vicent (Lucena), author of: Peregrino y Ginebra, signed by Hernando Diaz. 412 pages. Lulu Editors.	978-0-244-05324-6
97	2018	Draughts and La Celestina's creator Francesch Vicent (Lucena) in Ferrara. 316 pages. Lulu Editors.	978-0-244-95324-9
98	2018	Propaladia Lucena	In Press
99	2018	Question de Amor Lucena	In Press
100	2018	My Young Years by the side of Harm Wiersma and Ton Sijbrands, Future	978-0-244-66661-3

		World Champions – 315 pages. Lulu Editors.	
101	2018	The Berber Hamlet Aldarache in the 11th-13th centuries. The origin of the Puerto de la Losilla, the Cabezo de la Cobertera and the village Negra (Blanca) in the Ricote Valley. 472 pages. Lulu Editors.	978-0-244-37324-5
102	2018	La gloriosa historia española del Juego de las Damas – Tomo I. 172 pages. Lulu Editors.	978-0-244-38353-4
103	2018	La gloriosa historia española del Juego de las Damas – Tomo II. 148 pages. Lulu Editors.	978-0-244-08237-6
104	2018	La gloriosa historia española del Juego de las Damas – Tomo III. 176 pages. Lulu Editors.	978-0-244-98564-6
105	2018	La fabricación artesanal de papel en Negra (Blanca) Murcia. (Siglo XIII)	In Press
106	2018	La aldea bereber Aldarache en los siglos XI-XIII. El origen del Puerto de la Losilla, el Cabezo de la Cobertera y el pueblo Negra (Blanca) en el Valle de Ricote.	In Press
107	2018	Analysis of the Comedy and Tragicomedy of Calisto and Melibea	978-0-244-41677-5
108	2018	Diego de San Pedro and Juan de Flores: the pseudonyms of Lucena, the son of doctor Juan Ramírez de Lucena. Lulu Editors. 428 pages. Lulu Editors.	978-0-244-72298-2
109	2018	Dismantling the anonymous authors of the books attributed to the brothers Alfonso and Juan de Valdés. 239 pages. KDP Amazon Editors.	978-1-790-96099 KDP Amazon
110	2018	Revelation of the true authors behind Villalon's books and manuscripts. 429 pages. KDP Amazon Editors.	978-1-791-30458-4 KDP Amazon
111	2018	Doubt about the authorship of the work Asno de oro published in Seville around 1513. 225 pages. KDP Amazon Editors.	978-1-792-03946-1 KDP Amazon
112	2018	Damas Españolas: Reglas y estrategia. Tomo I. 138 pages. KDP Amazon Editors.	978-1-792-11849-4 KDP Amazon

113	2019	*El Lazarillo,* initiated by Lucena and finished by Bernardo de Quirós. 282 pages. KDP Amazon Editors.	978-1-793-28591-1
114	2019	Damas Españolas: Direcciones para jugar bien. Tomo II. 150 pages. KDP Amazon Editors.	978-1-793-37764-7
115	2019	Damas Españolas: Principios elementales y Golpes. Tomo III. 142 Pages. KDP Amazon Editors	978-1-794-04933-8
116	2019	Damas Españolas: Concepto combinativo y Juego posicional. Tomo IV. 117 pages. KDP Amazon	978-1-794-40304-8 KDP Amazon
117	2019	Een zwarte bladzijde in de geschiedenis van Murcia. Wetenswaardigheden over de gehuchten en dorpen langs de vreemde route van de twee vermiste Nederlanders in de Spaanse deelstaat Murcia. 303 bladzijden. KDP Amazon Editors	978-1-796-41834-7 KDP Amazon
118	2019	Damas Españolas: La partida. Tomo V. 130 páginas. KDP Amazon	978-1-092-95834-9 KDP Amazon
119	2019	Damas Españolas: Los problemas. Tomo VI. 114 páginas. KDP Amazon	978-1-075-33238-8 KDP Amazon
120	2020	Tradiciones y costumbres holandesas. Vida familiar, social y comercial.	978-1-692-68394-8 KDP Amazon

www.ingramcontent.com/pod-product-compliance
Lightning Source LLC
Chambersburg PA
CBHW060323100426
42812CB00003B/862